THE CORNER

David Simon's *Homicide* won an Edgar Award and became the basis for the NBC award-winning drama. *The Corner: A Year in the Life of an Inner-City Neighbourhood* was made into an HBO mini-series. Simon is currently the executive producer and writer for HBO's Peabody Award-winning series *The Wire*. He lives in Baltimore.

Ed Burns was a teacher in the Baltimore public school system. Before that he served twenty years in the city police department. For much of that time, he worked as a detective in the homicide unit.

'Powerful and revealing . . . it shows us the plight of urban America honestly and without condescending to those trapped on its mean streets. I defy you to read about them and not be moved.'
WASHINGTON POST

'A brave, unblinkered and heartbreaking look at the residents of a few blocks of West Baltimore's ghetto . . . So far above most reporting on the underclass as to demand attention.'
NEW YORK TIMES BOOK REVIEW

'*The Corner* is an intimate, intense dispatch from the broken heart of urban America. It is impossible to read these pages and not feel stunned at the high price, in human potential, in thwarted aspirations, that simple survival on the streets of West Baltimore demands of its citizens. An important document, as devastating as it is lucid.'
RICHARD PRICE, author of CLOCKERS

THE CORNER

A YEAR IN THE LIFE OF AN INNER-CITY NEIGHBOURHOOD

David Simon
and
Ed Burns

CANONGATE

Edinburgh · London · New York · Melbourne

First published in Great Britain in 2009 by
Canongate Books Ltd, 14 High Street, Edinburgh EH1 1TE

Originally published in hardcover in 1997 and in paperback in 1998 by
Broadway Books, a division of Bantam Doubleday Dell Publishing Group Inc.,
1540 Broadway, New York, NY 10036

1

British Library Cataloguing-in-Publication Data
A catalogue record for this book is available on
request from the British Library

ISBN 978 1 84767 317 6

Designed by James Sinclair

Printed and bound in the UK by CPI Mackays, Chatham ME5 8TD

This book is printed on FSC certified paper

Mixed Sources
Product group from well-managed
forests and other controlled sources
www.fsc.org Cert no. TT-COC-002341
© 1996 Forest Stewardship Council
FSC

www.meetatthegate.com

For my parents,
Bernard & Dorothy Simon

For Anna Burns

"You can hold back from the suffering of the world. You have free permission to do so and it is in accordance with your nature. But perhaps this very holding back is the one suffering you could have avoided."

—Kafka

CONTENTS

MAP LEGEND

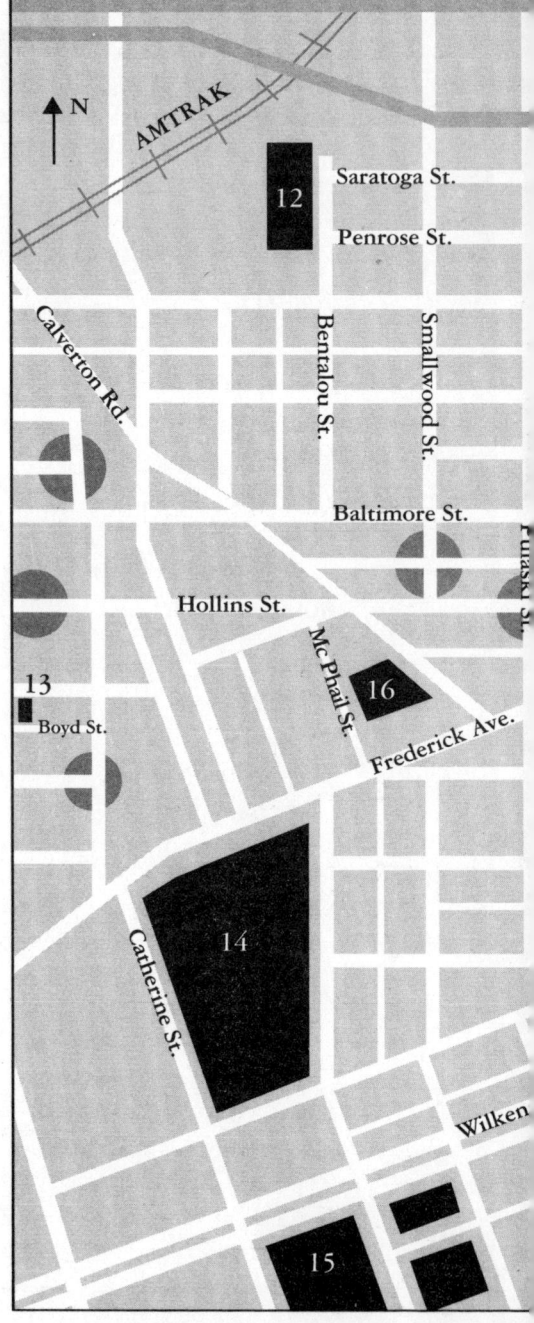

⬤ = Open-air drug markets in 1993
Numbers in italic type refer to inset

1. Martin Luther King Jr.
    Recreation Center
1a. MLK center playground
2. The Dew Drop Inn, 1625 Fayette
    Street (home to Fran, DeAndre,
    DeRodd in January 1993)
3. 1717 Fayette Street
    (vacant house, once home to Gary,
    Fran, and DeAndre)
4. 1806 Fayette Street
    (Ella Thompson's apartment)
5. 1827 Vine Street
    (the McCullough home)
6. 1825 Vine Street (Annie's house)
7. 1846 Fayette Street (Blue's house)
8. R.C.'s apartment building
9. St. James Methodist Church
10. St. Martin's Roman Catholic
    Church
11. Monroe and Fayette
    (Fat Curt's corner)
12. Bentalou Recreation Center
13. 2526 Boyd Street (new home for
    Fran, DeAndre, and DeRodd as
    of late September 1993)
14. Westside Shopping Center
15. United Iron & Metal Company
16. The scrap yard on McPhail Street
17. Bon Secours Hospital
18. Scoogie's house
19. Tyreeka's house in January 1993
    (the family's later move to Riggs
    Avenue puts them twenty blocks
    north by northwest, off the map)
20. Francis M. Woods Senior High
    School
21. Franklin Square Park
22. Union Square Park
23. Seapride Crabhouse (one of four
    in the Pratt and Monroe Street
    area, known as "Crab Alley")
24. Pops' shooting gallery
25. Brown's funeral establishment
26. Fairmount and Gilmore
    (DeAndre's winter corner)
27. McHenry and Gilmore
    (C.M.B.'s summer corner)
28. Mt. Clare Shopping Center

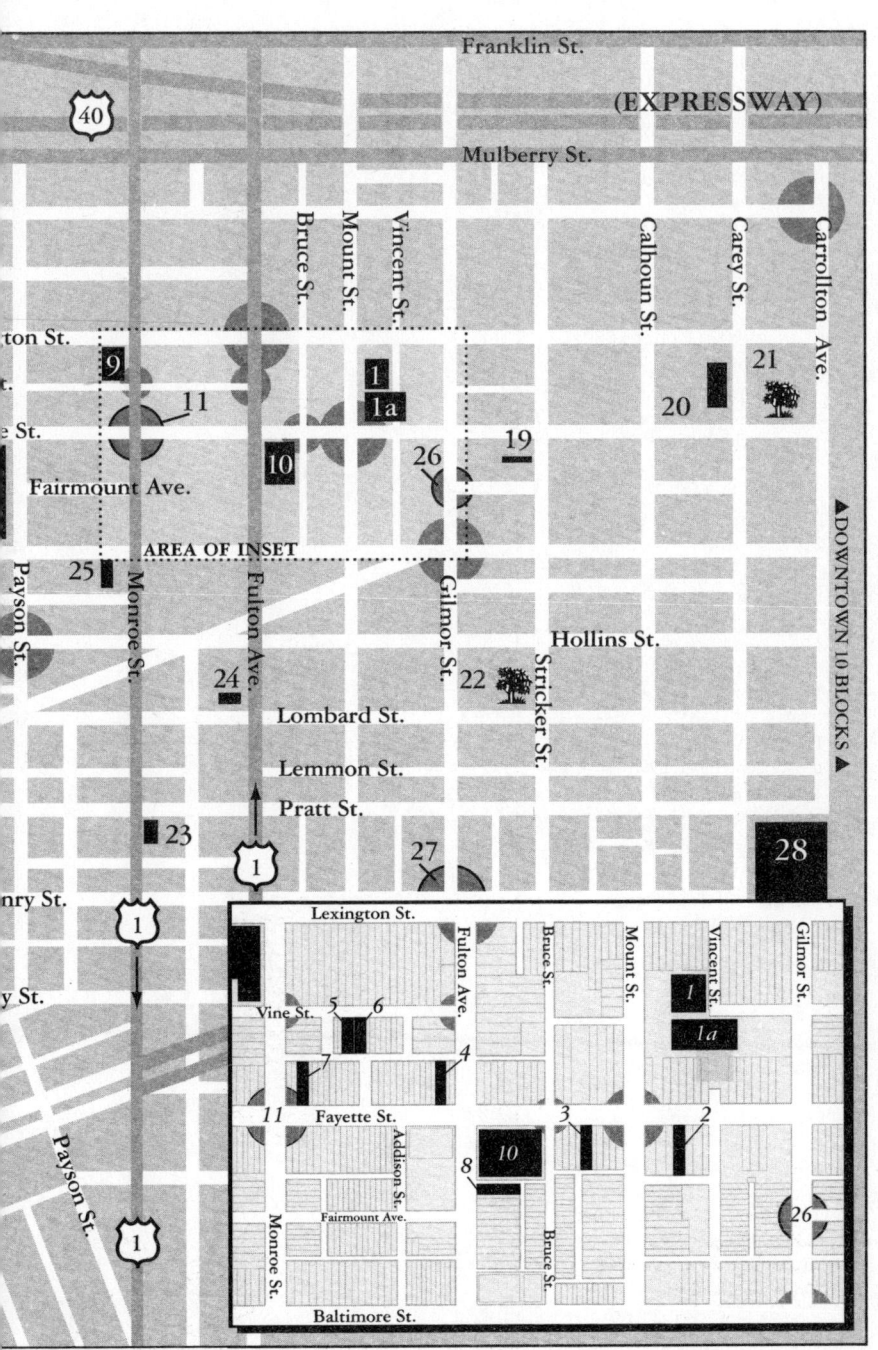

WINTER

ONE

Fat Curt is on the corner.

He leans hard into his aluminum hospital cane, bent to this ancient business of survival. His fattened, needle-scarred hands will never again see the deep bottom of a trouser pocket; his forearms are swollen leather; his bloated legs mass up from the concrete. But then obese limbs converge on a withered torso: At the heart of the man, Fat Curt is fat no more.

"Yo, Curt."

Turning slightly, Curt watches Junie glide over from the other side of Fayette, heading into Blue's for the evening's last shot. Curt stops, a few feet from Blue's door, and here's Mr. Blue himself, standing on the front steps of what was once his mother's pristine rowhome, scratching at the edges of his beard between arrivals, pocketing two bills from each, though it's two more if you need a fresh tool. No charge, of course, for share and share alike.

From down the hill near Gilmor comes a short string of gunshots— too even, too deliberate for firecrackers. Barely tensing, Blue allows Junie to edge past him on the marble steps. A regular: no charge for Junie.

"They shootin' already," says Blue.

Curt grunts. "Motherfuckers can't tell no time."

Blue smiles softly, then turns to follow Junie inside.

Fat Curt slips slowly toward Monroe, reddened eyes tracking a white boy who pulls to the curb in a battered pickup. But there's no play here; one of Gee Money's younger touts has already laid hands on the sale.

Curt works his way around the corner to Vine, passing Bryan, who nods acknowledgment. No sale here, either; not with Bryan Sampson out here working his own tired hustle, selling that baking soda. Curt shakes his head: Bryan looking to get his ass shot up again behind that Arm & Hammer shit.

From down the hill, from somewhere around Hollins and Payson

this time, comes more crackling syncopation—the beginning of the
deluge to come, though it isn't quite eleven yet. Curt shrugs it off and
shuffles back toward Fayette. Time enough left, he knows, to make a
little money.

"Wassup?"

Finally, a face he knows from down on Mount Street, a gaunt dark-
skinned fiend, scurrying up the hill in the hope of catching a better
product. Coming right at Curt.

"Wassup now?"

Curt growls assent. Shop's open.

"Somethin' good?"

Fat Curt, the oracle. Twenty-five years in service on these streets,
and everyone knows there's no better tout at the corner where Fayette
meets Monroe. Curtis Davis is the gravel-voiced purveyor of credible
information, a steadfast believer in quality control and consumer advocacy.
No bullshit, no burn bags, no watered-down B-and-Q garbage. Fat Curt,
a tout among touts.

"Might try 'round the way," he says, turning and gesturing with his
cane toward the entrance to Vine Street.

The fiend takes his hunger down the block as Curt gives a confirming
nod to the lookout at the mouth of the alley. Slowly, the aging tout
canes his way back to the corner, shuffling beneath the jaundiced glare
of sodium vapor. The city has put stage lighting out here; it's harsh and
direct, openly contemptuous of the scene itself. Fat Curt is forever exposed
in the ugly glow, but he can remember when dull blue light washed
more gently over these deeds, a time when the neighborhood was
permitted some small privacy. Now, at an hour to midnight, the corner
is visible at a full block's distance. Dope and coke. Coke and dope.
Twenty-four, seven: twenty-four hours a day, seven days a week.

More gunshots. Fulton and Lex by the sound of it. But Curt is still
on post, waiting for the next sale, when the Western uniforms roll up
for a last pass at the corner. The radio cars move slowly down Monroe,
but it's not a jump-out this time, just the ceremonial eyefuck and a sullen
showing of the colors.

From down near Hollins and Payson again comes a long, staccato
string. Ten or twelve in a row and nine millimeter by the report. But the
police ignore it, their faces instead scanning the foot traffic, their brake
lights showing red.

The lookouts raise up and go. The touts, customers, and runners stream away, evaporating like mist, moving down Fayette and into the back alleys. Fat Curt, too, turns from the police cruisers, stepping cane-to-foot-to-cane so slowly that any movement is more implied than real—just enough effort to suggest a polite, territorial retreat. From experience, Curt knows that it will be a short visit, that no right-minded police will be out on these streets fifteen minutes from now.

Over his shoulder, he watches as the brake lights go dark and the cruisers roll quietly through the traffic light, first one car, then its companion heading down Monroe. Curt, having covered barely half the distance to Lexington, turns back again. Shop is still open, but the salvos are now coming seconds apart, hitting all points on the compass. Six in a row echoing from over by the hospital; the snap of a .22 up on Lexington; the roar of what has to be a shotgun from somewhere down on Fairmount.

Time to go, thinks Curt. Time to go before they're digging some hopper's bullet from my lonesome black ass. He staggers around the corner and up the steps to Blue's house, rapping the front door with his cane. Blue cracks the door, then gives way; Curt slips inside. The corner watches its aging wise man; Fat Curt tells them it's time to go and the last soldiers take heed and drift in behind him. Eggy Daddy and Hungry, then Bryan and Bread and finally Curt's brother, Dennis, who's got a hospital cane all his own since he spiked himself in the neck and caught some spine. One by one they cross Blue's threshold and cluster together amid the cookers and candles and syringes, most of them waiting for Rita to make her rounds. Rita, the corner physician, works a rare magic, finding veins in cold, dying places where no living blood vessel has a right to be.

Outside, the streets are empty. No touts, no runners, no fiends. No police either, as Curt predicted. At a quarter to the hour, all the radio cars are in Western District holes, parked hood-to-trunk behind tall ware-houses and school buildings, or, better still, below something solid.

All across the west side, the distinct reports of individual shots now blend into cacophony. Down Fayette Street toward the harbor, and up Fulton toward the expressway, the bright orange-yellow of muzzle flashes speckles from front steps, windows, and rooftops. They look like fire-flies amid the crescendo, beautiful in their way. A window is shattered on Monroe Street. Another on Lexington. And a block north on Penrose, some fool without sense enough to come in from the rain suddenly winces, grabs his forearm, and races for the nearest doorway to examine the wound.

The hour approaches, and the great, layered dissonance grows even louder, the flashes of light racing up and down the streets as visible proof of this explosive percussion. It is a sound both strange and familiar: the signature sound of our time, the prideful, swelling cannonade of this failed century. Shanghai. Warsaw. Saigon. Beirut. Sarajevo. And now, in this peculiar moment of celebration, West Baltimore.

On Fulton Avenue, two teenaged girls stand in the vestibule of their rowhouse, ready for a run to a girlfriend's apartment on Lexington. They start down the steps, giggling, edging into the maelstrom, but they don't even make the curb when the next-door neighbor appears in his doorway, grinning drunkenly, gripping a .38 long barrel with both hands in a crude military stance, aiming up into the ether.

Six flashes light the street; the girls dive back to their front stoop. Still laughing, they peek across the marble steps as the reveler returns to his vestibule, reloads, then chimes out six more in perfect sequence. Like a statuette in some bastardized Swiss timepiece, the gunman drops his arm and slides backward through the door to reload again, and the girls, having timed the process, now risk the run up Fulton. They race up the block, consumed in adolescent laughter, holding their ears against the din.

The hour itself arrives with perfect vacancy—a rare midnight with no one soldiering on the Monroe Street corners or down Fayette. No touts, no slingers, no fiends on Mount Street. No crew manning the intersection of Baltimore and Gilmor. And certainly no stray citizens either—most taxpayers with sense fled this neighborhood years ago; the few that remain are now nestled inside hallways and interior rooms, as far from a stray bullet's reach as they can manage. Twenty blocks east, there are thousands milling around Inner Harbor promenades and down-town hotel lobbies, watching fireworks of a different kind in the night sky. But here, in West Baltimore, the celebration of sound and light requires an empty landscape.

The crescendo continues for ten full minutes before individual salvos can be distinguished from the din; another ten beyond that before the tempo slips noticeably; a full half hour before there are only odd, scattered reports from the belated few. Then, slowly, this world begins to stir. A Vine Street drunk drifts down the alley and makes for Lexington. A tout materializes on Mount, and a police radio car glides past the crumbling commercial strip on Baltimore Street. A fiend skates across Fayette and bangs on the door of Blue's house; Blue answers, collects two bills, and peers outside at the sudden calm as the man slips wordlessly past him.

A moment or two later, Fat Curt appears. Cane-to-foot-to-cane, he moves across Blue's vestibule and onto the front steps, pausing there to take stock. Head tipped to one side, bloodshot eyes scouring the corners from Monroe to Mount, Fat Curt is the oracle again, the keeper of this lost world's cumulative knowledge, the presignification of whatever still passes for truth out here. He stands on the threshold like a village shaman, reading the street for the pagan hordes clustered behind him in the shooting gallery, his antennae tuned to who knows what frequency. If the fat man sees his shadow, perhaps, they'll all stay inside and shoot dope for another half hour. If not, shop's open.

A semiauto's long crackle carries from somewhere down by the crab-houses, but Curt pays no mind. Too little, too late, and too far away; the flood has crested and gone. Once again, he hobbles to the corner of Fayette and Monroe, laying claim to the pavement.

Fat Curt is on the corner.

Gradually, the entire neighborhood seems to take the cue. By ones and twos, the shooting gallery gives up its wraiths; Junie and Pimp and Bread slide out onto the sidewalk and get back into their game. The touts reappear at the mouth of Vine Street. They're back in business on Mount Street, too, where Diamond in the Raw has the best package. And around the corner on Fulton, where the Spider Bag crew has set up shop. And down the bottom at Baltimore and Gilmor, where it's all Big Whites and Death Row and whatever else the New York Boys are using to market dope this week.

The fiends begin to drift back toward the corners. Rail-thin coke freaks and abscessed shooters press dirty singles and fives into waiting hands, then line up for the quick run down into the alley, where the slingers work ground stashes hidden in used tires, behind cinder blocks, or in the tall grass by the edge of a rear wall. Tattooed, toothless white boys, up from Pigtown in battered pickups and rusting Dodge Darts, idle nervously on Mount, watching for trouble through cracked rearview mirrors, hoping that whichever nigger took the twenty dollars is coming back with some product. Soon enough, all of them will be heading to some shithole rowhouse in absolute, dick-hard anticipation, battering their way past every remaining shard of their life to reach the room with the spikes and the pipes and the burnt-bottom bottle caps. They'll fumble with these things impatiently, kicking the old sofa's ass in a futile hunt for matches or jabbing themselves a dozen times in search of a vein. But at last they'll slam it home and wait for that better-than-sex feeling to crest. Then it's back again to the corner.

Fat Curt, up on post, watches them come. Year in and year out, he tells it true, steering them away from the trash, hooking them up to whatever will work. As always, he weds his timeworn credibility to some younger soldier's dope.

"Who got that Gold Star?"

"Come right here with it."

"Good as yesterday?"

"Man, that shit's a bomb."

"Awright then."

By one in the morning, this night is like any other, and Curtis Davis knows that it can never end, that money and desire will not be denied. He can tell this story going back a quarter century, back to when he stood on these same corners and the game was just beginning. He had some money in those days, and God knows he had the desire. He has stayed out here nearly every night since, until only his desire remains. He was out here yesterday and he's out here tonight, and come tomorrow, he'll be at Monroe and Fayette, watching the same scenes play.

No point in talking about changing, or stopping, or even slowing down. In his soldier's heart, Curt knows that everyone talks that shit and no one believes it a minute after they say it. Like Blue—running and gunning tonight, but telling himself he's going to quit come tomorrow. A resolution, says Blue. Naw, Curt tells himself, the shit is forever.

"Yo Curt."

"Hey, hey."

"Wassup, Mr. Curt?"

Curt smiles sadly, then growls out simple truth: "Oh, man, ain't nuthin' here but some of the same foolishness."

He touts for another hour at Fayette and Monroe, then drags himself back to Blue's for his last blast of the night, the syringe finding a way through one of the fat man's swollen limbs. When he leaves the shooting gallery, he's fortified with a good cap and carrying a small eighth of cheap rye in his hand—a rare liquid concession to this evening's traditions.

Cane-to-foot-to-cane he struggles up Monroe Street, heading nowhere in particular, wandering a bit beyond the usual boundaries of his shrunken world. Penrose Street. Saratoga. Curt limps on, nipping at the bottle and caning his way down the pavement until this short, spontaneous excursion toward the expressway overpass becomes a modest declaration of free will. Tonight in West Baltimore, for no reason whatever, Fat Curt is no longer on post. At last report, he's left the corner traveling due north. He's walking; goddamn if the fat man isn't taking a walk.

At Mulberry Street, a passing Western radio car slows at the sight. Maybe the cop is pausing to consider invoking the city liquor laws, which in this neighborhood would be a little like handing out littering citations in a hurricane. More likely, a veteran roller, familiar with Fayette and Monroe, is stunned to see one of that corner's fixtures several blocks north of where he should be. Either way, Curt senses the attention and tries to palm the bottle in his bloated hand. It's enough of a gesture to imply submission. The cop gives a little nod, then rolls away.

Walking on, Curt almost manages to smile.

Happy New Year.

Gary McCullough waits in front of the Korean joint, just off the Mount Street corner, shifting his weight from one foot to the other in the morning cold. One hand plays at a rubber band loose against the other wrist. He hums a Curtis Mayfield tune, the notes coming soft and barely discernible beneath the din of the nearby touts and slingers. Gary is in the background, just barely scenery. He is here, yet not here. He is good at waiting.

Tony Boice comes around the corner from Mount Street, back from the marketplace, smiling knowingly at Gary. Warmed to his soul, Gary grins beatifically at his running buddy. Hooked up: got that good thing from Family Affair. Yes, oh yes. The two men turn together, pushing back up Fayette, heads bowed into a rush of frigid January wind. Gary cups a hand to his mouth and coughs deeply.

"Dag."

"What?" says Tony Boice, looking around.

"Cold," says Gary.

"Oh yeah," agrees Tony. "Motherfuckin' hawk is out."

Gary looks furtively down Fayette, then across the street at the Death Row crew—all of them busy with business and paying no mind. They pass the trash of the vacant lot, back to where the New York Boy was lying dead a week earlier, the top of his head oozing away beneath a White Sox cap, a nine with a full clip useless in the waist of his sweats.

Gary edges past the spot and glances over despite himself; his eye finding the dull rust-red oval that still stains the weeds and dirt. Dag.

They move past the vacant lot and draw even with a redbrick rowhouse. Plywood greets them at the door of 1717 West Fayette, a street address that never fails to pull Gary back into his past.

"In here," he decides, bounding up the steps.

"Around back," says Tony, furtive.

"No, this'll work," Gary insists, suddenly impatient. He steps to the front door of the derelict house, glances once again down Fayette, then presses his weight against the plywood barrier, bending it enough to slide through. Tony follows and Gary shoves the plywood back into place. The two listen in the darkness for an extra moment, assuring themselves that the place is empty, though the piss-stench in the front hallway says it isn't always so.

"He was okay with that?" asks Gary.

Tony Boice grunts affirmatively. Negotiations went well enough: The corner boy gave him two Death Row bags for eighteen, which was all Tony carried. Short the two bills, Tony offered lamely to have a little more on the next go-round, and the younger dealer gave it up for the cash on hand, knowing anything else was money he would never see.

By fixed memory, Gary leads the way back through the darkened corridor, turning and reaching out for the rounded rail of the center stair. He holds it a moment, remembering the beautiful curve of the thing.

"Victorian," he says, savoring the word. "This is a Victorian design."

Tony says nothing.

"Look at that trim. That was original."

Tony stays silent as they climb the stairs.

"Know what that means, Mo?" Gary stops at the second-floor landing. "Money. There's big money in a house like this."

Two steps below him. Tony stares at some lead-painted piece of shit-brown wood, no doubt wondering how there can be a dollar left anywhere inside this rowhouse. They've been through the place two dozen times, liberating every last bit of copper pipe and aluminum window guard, cannibalizing the vessel of Gary McCullough's earlier life in their daily pursuit of the perfect blast. Whatever obvious money there was in this house had already been dragged ten blocks south to the scales of the United Iron and Metal Company, weighed up, paid out, and melted down. But Gary climbs to the third floor, his frozen breath clouding in front of him as he talks, rambling on about period restorations and licensed subcontractors and real estate values.

". . . I'm serious as a heart attack, Mo. There's money to be made if you know how to go. You just don't know . . ."

Tony grunts his way up the stairs.

". . . like with the market. Some of those technology stocks, like computer companies and all, man, I'm telling you. You can turn ten thousand dollars into ten times that inside of six months if you know what you're doing."

"Aw yeah," says Tony.

"No, really," says Gary, insistent.

"Yeah, no," says Tony blankly. "You right."

"Man, you just don't know."

And Gary McCullough, perhaps the only living person in a twenty-block radius who knows the difference between a price-earnings ratio and a short-term capital gain, shakes his head in sad frustration. The past is past, and Gary can't reconcile any part of it with the likes of Tony Boice, who is laboring only in this moment.

"You just don't know," he says again.

It wasn't so long ago that Gary had everything figured. He was a workaholic with two full-time jobs and his own home development company on the side. He held the deed on several properties on Vine Street. He drove a new Mercedes-Benz. Every workday, he scoped the inside columns of the *Daily Investor* for stock tips, parlaying a Charles Schwab brokerage account into $150,000 cash money. And Gary had a plan, too, for this three-story rowhouse, which had been purchased not merely as another investment, but as a centerpiece to the fine, righteous life he was busy constructing. He would renovate this place, make it beautiful again, make it his castle.

Tony slides past him on the landing, intent on nothing beyond the business at hand.

"Where at?" he asks.

"In back," says Gary, nodding to the rear bedroom.

Gary finds two bottle caps on the windowsill, but his partner takes care of everything else. Tony is a whirlwind of efficiency as the glassine bags are opened and the powdered heroin meted out. Water from the syringes, flame from a match, then the slow draw of liquid up into the plastic cylinders. Thirty on the hype, cocked and ready. No coke to go on top, but this is enough to get them out of the gate.

Tony pokes softly at the back of his arm, a red droplet collecting there to mark the landing zone. Gary uses his left forearm, choosing a midway point on a darker brown stretch of oft-used roadway. Tony slams everything home, indifferent to the notion of an overdose. Gary sees a puff of pink in the bottom of his spike, fires, then stops short at the halfway point, gauging the rush, waiting cautiously. A few moments more with the syringe resting gently between thumb and forefinger, and then the sprint to the finish.

"It's something," mutters Tony, vaguely disappointed, "but not like yesterday was."

"Yesterday was a bomb," Gary agrees.

Tony steps back into the sunlight, which is pouring through the rear window panes, measuring a patch of crosshatched warmth on the bedroom's stained carpet. Oblivious to the cold, Gary sits in the shade by the far wall, watching a universe of suspended dust float across the room in rays of light.

Tony nods.

"Better than you thought, Mo," laughs Gary.

"Gettin' there."

For a while they simply sit, letting the chemistry happen, warming themselves in the rush. Both of them at perfect ease, feeling nothing more of the freezing cold. Soon they are laughing together about the caper that got them here.

Caper. That is Gary's word for it, and it is Gary's mind-set, too. For him as for any dope fiend, the raw adventure of the thing always has to be acknowledged and on some level, enjoyed. In West Baltimore, you can be proud of a good caper; hell, a working, viable caper is to be celebrated. And though it might be lost to any prosecutor reading the Maryland Annotated Code, everyone living off a corner understands and accepts the distinction between a caper and a crime. Stick a gun in a man's face and take his wallet; that's a crime and, hey, you're a criminal. But steal the copper plumbing from a rowhouse under construction and sell it for scrap; that's a caper. Shoot a corner dealer in the knee and take his stash; you're a stickup boy and fair game for either the slingers or police. Watch the same dealer sling vials for two hours until he turns his back, and then sneak off with his ground stash; a caper, plain and simple. Breaking into a house where honest-to-God taxpayers are sleeping is definitely a crime. Breaking into parked cars and liberating cassette tape players is nothing more than caper. In Gary's mind, it isn't only the severity of the act that qualifies a crime, but the likelihood that any human being other than yourself might get hurt. In the life of Gary McCullough, this point is essential.

He will shoot dope, to be sure. And if there is no paycheck on the horizon, he will steal a bit to get the money for that dope. And then, if he has to—if there is no other sensible alternative—he will tell a lie or two about his stealing and his doping, though in actual practice, Gary is too honest a soul to carry a deceit past anyone in this neighborhood. But it ends with this: no crime, no cruelty, nothing beyond the simple caper. The sad and beautiful truth about Gary McCullough—a man born and raised in as brutal and unforgiving a ghetto as America ever managed to create—is that he can't bring himself to hurt anyone.

Like this morning, when the caper almost went bad in the basement of that rowhouse on Fairmount. Gary and Tony were down there in the dark, groping for the cold water cutoff even as a half-dozen crackheads were arguing over cocaine a floor above them. He and Tony were stumbling around, bumping into things until Gary found the valve and shut off the water. They cut out that good No. 1 copper as quietly as they could, while above them the voices rose and fell in profane cadence.

"My turn."

"Fuck it is. This mine."

"Man, that's my time. That ain't right."

"Bitch, everything I say, you hear backwards."

Tony began squeezing air through his lips, trying to suppress laughter. Gary struggled with it, too, until they couldn't so much as look at each other without losing control. Side by side in the dark, they were holding it together as best they could, wincing inside with each soft squeak as the pipe cutter did its work. Then, from above them, a loud, shrewish wail—a woman's voice.

"MAW-REECE . . . MAW-REECE!"

"What?"

Gary and Tony froze, scared and still at the woman's shout. Gary guessed that Tony was willing to fight if it came to it, but in his own heart, he was down for capers only. Gary would take all of an ass-whipping if Maurice brought his coked-up self downstairs.

Tony recovered first, giving the cutter another go, until one last stretch of copper came away from the plumbing with a dull thump.

"MAW-REECE!"

"What?"

"AIN'T NO WATER IN THE TAP."

"Say what?"

Then both of them were racing toward the back basement door, laughing through the adrenaline rush. Gary paused at the far wall only long enough to collect the rest of their copper haul. Somewhere above them, Maurice was still berating his woman for smoking up whatever money was supposed to pay the water bill. Out in the rear alley at the far end of the block, Tony began laughing freely.

"Dag," said Gary, his strongest expletive.

Smiling and shaking his head, he gripped some of the soon-to-be-melted copper in his outstretched hand like a royal scepter, holding it up in daylight for a proper examination.

"At least thirty."

"Yeah, thirty," Tony agreed.

Reality deferred. The joy of the caper allows that no matter what you snatch—copper pipe, tin roofing, aluminum screen doors—it's always, at first glance, worth more than it actually is. Gary and Tony, at that moment, held up the pipe length and figured thirty dollars easy. Enough for two good blasts of dope and then coke to go on top. The sweet anticipation made the ten blocks to United Iron and Metal feel like a stroll through the yard.

"Tally ho," said Gary, beaming.

But, of course, eighteen even was all they got at the United Iron scales—eighteen dollars that went directly to the young boy working the Death Row package. In return, two $10 glassine bags at a discount, all of it now in the pipeline.

Comfortable in his own patch of sunlight, Tony looks over at Gary and laughs softly.

"Got-damn," says Tony.

Gary laughs back.

"Got-damn if she wasn't right upstairs trying to turn the water on and we was down below."

"And you was makin' me laugh," says Gary.

"Man, I couldn't help it."

Each true caper brings its own rush, a childlike thrill that stays close to the heart of every addict, no matter how many years he's played the game. It's the same feeling any hot-blooded twelve-year-old gets when he walks from a five-and-dime without paying for a candy bar, or when he tosses a crabapple at a passing police cruiser, gets chased by the cop, and manages to escape. It's down there in every one of us—the unbridled joy that accompanies any unpunished sin, the self-satisfaction that often follows when you manage to get something for nothing.

"Man," says Gary, finally. "That was wild."

They laugh again, loudly at first, feeding on each other's good humor, then softly for a time. Then they fall silent as the heroin rides over them.

Gary pulls down his hoody to scratch the top of his head. With both legs stretched in front of him, he feels the edge of his receding hairline and frowns. Every day he's looking a little more like his father, which would be just fine if his father didn't have more than thirty years on him. Gary wonders for a moment whether it's heredity or drugging or both that is balding him out. Dope and coke have definitely changed him; this he knows. Every day, his skin seems to him a little darker and his eyes a bit more dusty, even when he isn't riding a blast. The smile stays the same, of course. You can pick Gary out of a crowd a block away if he has that wide-mouthed beam working. And save for the tracks on his arms, his body, too, is about the same as he remembers it—compact, proportioned, athletic. Then again, Gary has been hardcore drugging for only four years; he can look across the room into Tony's yellowed eyes and see the future. Tall and firm, Tony Boice is still a powerful man— Gary has seen him deliver an asskicking on more than one occasion—but now there is a little less flesh to the face, a little more shadow in the eyes. The more Gary looks at Tony, the more he is drawn to comparison. After all, both of them are wearing the same hooded sweatshirts and camouflage gear, looking like lost commandos on some doomed mission. It was Gary who had argued for the uniforms. We're out here chasing capers every day, he reasoned; if we're hardcore soldiering, we could do with some military styling.

But now, with the rush weakening, Gary takes a close look at Tony, then down at himself, then back at Tony. He feels a chill in the moment, as if something dread has slipped into this house. Gary tries to laugh again, but the noise gets caught in his throat. Instead, he's left wondering whether the virus has caught Tony and thinned him out. Nowadays, The Bug is all over Fayette Street.

"Wassup?" asks Tony, looking at him.

"Huh?"

"What you wonderin' at?"

Gary catches himself and straightens. He looks away from his partner, focusing for the first time on the empty room. "This was Andre's," he says finally. His son DeAndre's room. Third floor rear, with the blue carpet and the southern exposure.

Slowly, Gary rises from the floor, stretches, and steps over Tony to look out the back window. His breath clouds a cracked pane as he stares down at the mounds of trash in the backyard. Clothes, grocery wrappers, Clorox bottles, broken furniture. If Gary had his way that yard would be fully enclosed in cement and Plexiglas, a private refuge with a patio and small lap pool. For a moment in Gary's mind, it is just so: Fran and Gary and DeAndre together at poolside, living large, showing this tired old city a little something.

DeAndre. Where is he now? A block down on Fayette Street, maybe, in that shithole of a shooting gallery where his mother lays her head. Or more likely around the corner at Baltimore and Gilmor, slinging for one of the New Yorkers.

Gary silently curses himself for thinking these thoughts, for ruining his own hard-won high. Leaving Tony to nod, he steps from the window, looks around, and then walks back out into the hall. The staircase: so beautiful, his favorite part of the house. He wanders down to the second floor and the master bedroom, admiring the ornate trim along the top of the built-in armoire. All of it original. And the twelve-foot ceiling, too. Fran had loved the high ceilings most of all.

This used to be their bedroom, though it's hard to see that now. The only bed remaining is a solitary mattress on the floor, covered by dirty linens. Milk crates stand in for furniture. A battered pine bureau sits in the corner with every drawer broken. A dozen pornographic pictures are taped to the four walls—every breast and crotch highlighted by crude circles and triangles drawn in thick black marker.

The art gallery was DeAndre's contribution, still on display from the summer before, when Gary's son turned fifteen and began slinging heroin on Gilmor Street. When his mother found out, Fran got so angry she put him out of the house. DeAndre stayed here for a while, and Gary did, too, using this place as a hideaway during his heroin binges. That summer, father and son would sometimes pass each other in these empty halls, both of them unable to manage any real connection. DeAndre was furious at his father's descent, yet refused to part with any emotion. And Gary, though filled with real pride to see his firstborn becoming a manchild, could never risk words. Too much shame lurking there. Too much history.

Gary walks across the bedroom toward the front windows, trying to wrap his mind around some better thought. Two plastic milk crates filled with old record albums are stacked hard by one window—flotsam from that happier time. Gary leans forward, hands on both knees, scanning the remains of his collection. Marvin Gaye. Barry White. The Temptations. And, of course, Curtis Mayfield, who used to mean everything to Gary. Curtis, always speaking for sanity, warning that if there's hell below, we're all going to go. Gary pulls out an album, looks at it, then returns it carefully to the crate.

Ancient history here, too; vinyl sound-of-soul relics gathering dust in the age of hip-hop rhythm kings and gangsta posers. Gary has no ear for what the younguns call music nowadays.

He sings.

"If you had a choice of colors . . ."

A beautiful voice. A strong tenor for any church choir.

". . . which one would you choose, my brothers."

The sound echoes through the house. Gary hears Tony stirring a floor above him. Gary starts another couplet, but the moment is broken by a tumult below the front windows. The lyric is lost amid angry cursing.

"On the ground! On the ground, motherfucker!"

Gary creeps to the right window, peering around the edge of the dirty sheet that passes for a curtain.

"Get your hand out of your pocket. You hear me? Get your hand out of your pocket."

Plainclothesmen. Knockers. Six police jump out of two unmarked Chevrolets and shove two men to the sidewalk right below Gary's window.

"What?" asks Tony from the doorway.

"Shsshhhh," Gary hisses. "Poh-leece."

"Who is it?"

Gary shakes his head.

"Bob Brown?"

Bob Brown is the predominant constabulary scourge of every doper in the Franklin Square neighborhood—fiends in this part of town invoke the name as something distinct from the rest of the Baltimore Police Department. Whenever he makes an entrance, lookouts actually shout "Bob Brown," rather than the generic "Five-Oh" or "Time Out."

Gary shakes his head. Not Mr. Brown, not this time. "Knockers," he whispers. "I don't know none of 'em."

Tony steps softly toward the edge of the other window and looks down at the encounter. These police aren't regulars in the neighborhood, and the two on the ground aren't familiar faces either. Both are on their backs; one on the sidewalk, the other in the dirt where the pavement breaks at the base of a small tree. Both are pleading innocence. Three of the plain-clothesmen stand over them, shouting; a fourth stands in the street, eyefucking the crews on the Mount Street corners. The other two are waiting next to the unmarked Chevrolets, both cars idling in the fast lane of Fayette Street, the front and rear doors splayed open.

"Don't fucking lie to me!"

"No, we just . . ."

"Motherfucker, get your pants down."

Gary and Tony stand silently at the windows, watching the scene play out. A white police is doing the shouting; two black companions poke through jacket pockets. The young man in the dirt is still trying to argue the case, but his partner has already gone cold, his hardest game face now showing only hate. Slowly, still on their backs, the two lower their pants to their knees, their exposed legs shaking in the winter air. A police picks at the waistbands of their boxers, looking south. Dickie checks in ten-degree weather, but there's no dope down there in those Jockeys or anywhere else for that matter. On the sidewalk is the brown sandwich bag one man was carrying. A knocker picks it up, looks inside and then, satisfied, drops it back on the pavement.

The white police checks the sidewalk farther down Fayette Street, looking for loose paper or vials.

"I didn't see anything get thrown," a black police says. A subtle suggestion, perhaps; one cop trying to tell another that, hey, maybe he got this one wrong.

"Man, I swear we clean," says the man in the dirt.

"Shut up," says the white police.

But the sidewalk search yields nothing. After a moment or two more, with the wind whipping trash and dead leaves down Fayette Street, the young man in the dirt looks up at the black police and risks another plea.

"Man, can we put our pants on?"

The cop gives a quick, cursory nod and both men hoist themselves up on their elbows, undulating like crabs on the sidewalk as they work to dress themselves.

The white plainclothesman tires of the game. He walks back toward one of the idling Chevrolets, turning to shout a final line at the two men on the ground. Dope or no dope, there's always a moral to the story.

"Don't let me see your ass out here again."

Then they're gone, the Chevrolets roaring up Fayette Street toward some new encounter. With every tout and dealer watching from the Mount Street corners, the two young men slowly gather up their humiliation and step off.

Gary and Tony are still right above them in the window, bearing witness with no small amazement. Across the street, the Death Row and Diamond in the Raw crews immediately reopen the Mount Street shop.

"Man, I can't believe that," Gary says, shaking his head in disgust. "They were just coming out of the carryout. The one boy had a sandwich is all."

Tony snorts in agreement.

"I can't believe it," Gary says again. Twenty people standing out there at Mount and Fayette Streets—all of them selling or buying drugs, half of them dirty with the shit—and the knockers are jumping out and messing with two dopeless niggers and a meatball sub. Undressing them in the street, telling them they can't be out here, then driving off to do the same to someone else.

"Like they did to me last year," says Gary. "Knocked out my teeth over a corn chip. And then afterward telling me I can't stand on the street where I live."

Gary shakes his head slowly, but without any real sense of indignation. The shit just happens out here nowadays; it doesn't have to make sense. Out here, any fiend can tell you, the rule of thumb is that the less sense something makes, the more people run to it. The dealers, the touts, the users, the knockers—all of them are out here every day and every night, pretending to play this game like it can be won or lost, like the game has rules even. But it's somehow beyond all that; from the inside looking out, it's obvious to Gary that every last rule will be broken. His breath clouds a windowpane as he watches the Death Row tout begin taking new orders, sending two white boys around the corner toward the alley on Mount. Then Gary's eyes fix on a new sight.

"Dag," he says, and with good reason, for coming up the hill from Gilmor is the Gaunt One herself, the skin-and-bone harbinger of all that Gary loves and fears in this neighborhood.

"Ronnie," he says.

Veronica Boice, Tony's cousin and Gary's on-again-off-again girl, is walking up Fayette Street in a slow glide. Her eyes dart from corner to corner, her wide mouth curls at one end in bemused confidence. It's Ronnie on the prowl.

Feeling vulnerable, Gary steps back from the window and begins charting out a potential disaster, burning out his high in the process. A frantic computation clicks through his brain: Ronnie catches me and Tony up here; Ronnie figures we had a caper; Ronnie knows we did the blast without her; Ronnie makes me pay.

When the issue is thirty on the hype, hell hath no fury like Ronnie Boice. Like that time last year, when Gary cut Ronnie out of a blast and she actually called the police on him, made him take a domestic assault charge that was still hovering over him, floating around the city court system somewhere. Or the time before that, when Ronnie burned some Jamaicans for a stash and then put the thing on Gary, who was completely baffled when a six-pack of wild-eyed Jakes kicked in his door and demanded repayment. And Ronnie—all ninety pounds of her—managed to create such mayhem with only her mind and her mouth. On these corners, she was a force of nature, and Gary, though he had every reason to fear her, could never manage to get past his awe. Ronnie would burn him time and again; she would water his drugs and switch his syringe. She would tell him she loved him even as she was putting him in harm's way. Eventually, if he wasn't careful—and Gary wasn't careful—Ronnie would get him dead. But the woman could make money out of nothing. For that reason alone, Gary stayed with her.

But he does not want to see her now. Definitely not now.

Gary motions to Tony, and one behind the other, they lurch down the stairs to the first floor. In the hallway, Gary catching a glimpse of a luminous stretch of canvas on the wall. Commissioned by Gary and painted by his friend Blue, the work pictured an ancient rune that Gary had chosen from a cosmology book, a life-force symbol that he took as the logo for Lightlaw, his home development company. Another time, another life.

They pass through the wrecked kitchen, then down a half flight of stairs into a narrow corridor of unfinished basement. They make their way toward the rear, where a sliver of light is visible from the other side of a rotting wooden barrier. Tony opens the door and sunlight streams through the portal. Like true commandos in their camouflage gear, they stride out the door and through the trashed rear alley, hunching into the wind.

"Where you headed?" asks Gary.

"Up the way. You gonna see Ronnie?"

Gary nods. He'll run up to Fulton, then come back down Fayette and catch Ronnie from the other direction. Make it seem like he just rolled out of bed at his mother's house. Ask Ronnie if she's got her hooks into any kind of caper—something that'll get him over—all the while hoping she won't see the dust in his eyes.

"Well, okay, you'll see what's up," says Tony.

"Awright, Mo," says Gary. "I'll be back to you."

"Awright then."

Tony heads south toward Baltimore Street, and Gary turns right, taking the long way back onto Fayette. Ronnie is still downslope at Mount Street, still scoping the corners for opportunity. Finally she sees Gary, and lets go of a smile so knowing and lethal that even in ten degrees, Gary can feel a separate chill down his spine. She knows.

"Hey, love," she says, looking hard into his eyes.

"Hey," he says.

"How you doing?"

"Awright," Gary mumbles.

"How you feeling?"

"Okay."

"Mmm hmm," says Ronnie Boice.

She knows. Dag, she always knows.

DeAndre McCullough wakes to the morning cold fully dressed and still weary from the night before. Slowly, he rolls sideways on the narrow mattress, leaving a worn blanket in the center trough where the springs have all but collapsed. He lets one arm fall over the higher edge of the bed and slowly opens one eye. Below and to the right of him on the baseboard, he catches the brown sheen of a cockroach and reaches under the bed. He comes up with his one of his mother's shoes, firing it against the wall, missing by inches. The roach scurries off.

DeAndre closes his eyes, trying to regain sleep, but the noise from the old Zenith, which runs nonstop in this back bedroom, has grabbed his attention. He buries his face in the mattress, but he can't help listening.

"Boy," he mutters with contempt, sensing his younger brother at the foot of the bed. "You watch some stupid shit."

DeRodd shrugs. "It was on when I got up."

"That don't mean you got to watch it."

DeRodd says nothing. The dinosaur starts into his dinosaur song and DeAndre raises his head just high enough to glare at his brother.

"Barney ain't shit," he says finally.

"I'm not watching," DeRodd insists.

"Off-brand, purple-ass dinosaur," mutters DeAndre, swinging an open palm at the younger boy's head.

"Ow," says DeRodd softly.

DeAndre raises his legs slowly and drops first one, then the other over the edge of the mattress until he's finally sitting up, rubbing both eyes with his hands. He can remember staggering up here about two in the morning with a cheesesteak from Bill's; the wrapper is on the floor in front of him. He can remember that he had a good day down on Fairmount yesterday; money in his pocket and Boo owing him still more for the vials DeAndre fronted him. He can remember getting blunted up with Tae and Sean. In fact, he can remember pretty much everything; that business about weed making you forget things is all bullshit.

"Why ain't you in school?" DeAndre asks.

"Saturday."

DeAndre grunts. A good enough answer, but it's not in him to give any eight-year-old the last word.

"You should go anyway."

"Ain't no school on Saturday."

"You should go there and wait for Monday."

DeRodd pouts and DeAndre swings again with an open hand. This time the younger boy is ready and ducks away.

"Where Ma at?" asks DeAndre.

DeRodd shrugs.

Stretching slowly, DeAndre rises and catches a glimpse of himself in the mirror above the dresser. The forest of short dreds that top his head Bart Simpson-style is crushed to one side by the night's sleep; in profile, he looks like a coal black rooster. His hair is his most distinctive feature, a detail that declares him unique in a neighborhood where image is everything.

Otherwise, he is a study in urban conformity, and within minutes, he is primed and dressed to match the set: a black puff ski parka left open to flap in the breeze, a thick blue and white flannel shirt worn outside oversized jeans that ride low on the hips, the requisite high-top Nikes that go for upwards of $125 a pair.

Running down the steps from the second floor, he digs one hand into the front pocket of his denims, pulling out a tight roll of twenties, tens, and fives. He pauses in the empty vestibule to count it off; four hundred twenty-five and some change, and for once it's all there. Not like last weekend when he and the boys brought some girls to the vacant house up the block on Fayette. They smoked like ten bags of weed, and the next morning, DeAndre woke alone and hurting in his parents' old bedroom, his gallery of pinups mocking him from all sides. When he checked his pocket that morning, it wasn't seven hundred, but about three-forty on the roll. And DeAndre for the life of him couldn't remember where it went. Weed? Girls? Or maybe someone waited for him to fall out on the mattress and then dipped into the bank.

He had slept in today. By the time he gets down the block and around the corner, it's afternoon and the fiends—white boys coming north from Pigtown, those of his own hue rolling down the hill from Monroe Street—have collected into a loose, shifting crowd around the corner of Baltimore and Gilmor. Moving down the litter-blown block, he looks older than his fifteen years, outwardly confident in a way that teenagers seldom are. The wayward hairstyle is recognizable a block away, the clothes tailored to this season's G-thang look, but nothing carries enough flash to attract unnecessary attention. No gold on the neck or hands to catch the winter sun—nothing that glimmers enough to attract stickup boys or that a knocker might take for cheap probable cause. By and large, the McCullough boy is a study in a lower key.

Arriving at the alley entrance to Fairmount, he takes stock of his real estate. This is mine, he thinks, watching the touts work the crowd. I made it happen. Ain't no kid stuff, like that bullshit last summer when his crew tried their hand at slinging only to get plucked bad by the big boys.

For two years now, DeAndre and the others—Tae and R.C., Boo and Manny Man, Dinky and Brian and the rest—have been carrying themselves like a gang, calling themselves C.M.B. for Crenshaw Mafia Brothers, a name agreed upon after the fourth or fifth viewing of *Boyz in the Hood* at Harbor Park. So far, C.M.B. was something of a rump creation, sandwiched between the more established Edmondson Avenue Boys to the north and the Ramsay and Stricker crew down bottom. More lethal than all of them is the crew from the high-rise projects to the east. A five-tower nightmare at the western edge of the city's downtown, Lexington Terrace has so many buildings from which to draw members that the Terrace Boys are always deep. Still, the C.M.B. contingent had Fayette

Street to itself, and ever since they turned twelve and thirteen, the boys had been playing at gangster. Two years ago, that meant mostly street fights and dotting brick walls and asphalt with Crenshaw Mafia tags. Last summer, they stepped up a bit, stealing cars one after another for the joy of it or sneaking down to the Pulaski corners to try their hand at drug slinging. In any other world, it would be called criminal; on Fayette Street, it still amounted to casual misadventure. At Hollins and Pulaski, C.M.B.'s initial foray on a corner ended comically enough, when their supplier waited until the summer's last re-up, then disappeared on them with all their pooled profits.

Tae, R.C., and the others were still moaning about it, but DeAndre, at least, had been spared that disaster. Instead, he had spent the last half of the summer under the wing of a New Yorker, Bugsy by name, who saw promise in DeAndre and set him up with a sixty-forty split on packages of blue-topped coke vials. Working on consignment, DeAndre and a handful of others had gone big-time, opening up the old strip where the 1500 block of Fairmount Avenue runs into Gilmor.

Fairmount had been dead most of the last year, when Stashfinder and the other knockers hit it hard, chasing the action back up to Mount and Fayette, or down to the lower end by Baltimore and Stricker, leaving Fairmount to the ghosts. But it was still prime territory. Tiny Fairmount, a two-block alley street of rowhouses teeing into Gilmor, offered darkness and a warren run of side alleys and walkways. A tactical nightmare for the knockers, it was ideal terrain for a young dealer working a ground stash. Of course, it was also a nice setup for the stickup boys, so that the likes of Odell or Shorty Boyd could jump on a whole crew, lining them up and taking every damn thing. But DeAndre would carry that; getting jacked now and again was, after all, a part of the game.

Fairmount had been slow going at first. He had to get the word out, draw the fiends in to sample his product. He and his cousin's boyfriend, Corey, spent a lot of time out on the corner, working hard to get the shop up and running. The knockers had mostly moved on to other hot spots, but the stickup boys were a bitch, feeding in a frenzy once they discovered the new market. He got jacked once, and he lost a ground stash or two, but by and large, most of the profit was realized. In August, he got caught by a couple knockers with a handful of pills, but no matter—DeAndre played that, too, to his advantage, showing Bugsy the juvenile court papers and telling the dealer he got nailed with the whole bundle. Bugsy took it off the account; DeAndre then emptied the blue-tops into pinks and sold off pure profit behind his supplier's back.

Until his big setback, it was a fine summer. And when his number came up, it was the result of neither a Western District patrolman's vigilance, nor the business end of a stickup boy's nine millimeter. Ultimately, DeAndre McCullough fell at the hands of his own mother. Fran copped his stash.

There is precious little privacy on Fayette Street, which is a problem for a young corner boy looking to hide inventory. Try to be invisible around here, try to tiptoe into a vacant house, and someone is always watching, clocking your moves, hoping you slip. Leave a ground stash unattended and Little Kenny or Hungry or Charlene will be quick to carry it off. Trust a tout like Country or Tyrone and your package will be nothing but memory. Rent an apartment from one of the regular stash-house girls and you better pay someone to sit in there or the bitch will blow profit up her nose and lie about it later. For DeAndre, the possibilities are limited to a single option: his mother's room. It's not much, but Fran Boyd is lucky to have that: one rear bedroom at what the Fayette Street fiends like to call the Dew Drop Inn, the closest thing to a shooting gallery east of Blue's.

The three-story rowhouse in the 1600 block of West Fayette is the last stop for all the Boyds, save Fran's older brother, Scoogie, who got their grandmother's house up on Saratoga. For the two upper floors of 1625, Fran's sister, Bunchie, pays thirty-two dollars a month under a federal Section 8 housing reimbursement. She, in turn, pushes that weight off onto three siblings—Fran, Stevie, and Sherry—charging each fifty a month for a bedroom. For Fran and her two sons, home is the second-floor rear room, all eight-by-ten feet of it.

They share a cluttered cubicle coated with the acrid tang of Newports and crammed with a single bed, a battered dresser, two chairs that are oozing their stuffing and, of course, the sleepless television. The bed usually goes to DeRodd and DeAndre, with Fran making do on the old sofa in the front room. Some nights, though, the bed mattress is taken by Fran and DeRodd, with DeAndre in a bedroll on the floor. Other times, it's Fran on the bedroll, giving her sons the better chance at a night's sleep. On the worst of nights—weekends or check days, perhaps, when pipers and gunners are ranging ceaselessly through the second-floor apartment—it's all three of them together, fighting for a thin sliver of the single mattress as myriad forms of human dysfunction take place just outside the bedroom door.

Beyond the bare necessities, the back room features little else: an overstuffed closet; a makeshift nightstand on a milk crate, where Fran can chase her lines if the basement is otherwise occupied; a couple of Polaroid shots pinned to the walls, hinting at some better time; a funeral home pamphlet from the service for Fran's mother last year. This is the space that DeAndre can pretend to control, and it's therefore where his stash has to go.

Not that it had always been so. Early last fall, DeAndre thought he had it made when Fran, angry at his drug slinging, put him out of the Dew Drop. Summarily evicted from 1625, DeAndre went immediately up the block to 1717 Fayette, where his father was haunting what was left of the old house. Gary gave up the master bedroom and DeAndre suddenly found himself in a teenager's dream, a paradise of unencumbered real estate that he was quick to turn into his clubhouse, decorating the walls with raw centerfolds, smoking blunts and downing forties with the other C.M.B. boys, and generally doing as he damn well pleased at the ripened age of fifteen. Yeah boy.

There was a downside. The plumbing didn't exist and the electric was shut off, which made for some chilly nights. Not much in the way of furnishings either. And then there were the house guests, if you could call them that. For some months, Gary McCullough had been shuttling between 1717 Fayette and his mother's house on Vine, staying the cold nights in his mother's basement, but running the remnant of his former home as a kind of low-bottom rooming house. Trouble was, Gary, being a fiend, couldn't afford to offer any of the usual amenities, and his boarders, being fiends, couldn't afford to pay rent. Nor was anyone inclined to leave.

There was some young white girl from the county on the run for bad checks; with her was her dark-skinned boyfriend, who fed off her and occasionally touted for Diamond in the Raw. They shared the third floor with an older woman who haunted the Baltimore Street strip, trading her body for shot money. On the second floor was Arthur, a stone psycho whose room was closest to the front. Having supped heavily on the gore of Harbor Park slasher movies, DeAndre had no illusions about Crazy Arthur, not after he accidentally on purpose stuck his head into Arthur's room one morning to find a stained mattress, a green garbage bag leaking moldy clothes, and a forest of glass bottles in all shapes and sizes, hundreds of them, some capped and some open but all of them filled to the brim with piss. Before that day's night, DeAndre had rigged the connecting walkway with an assortment of boards, bits of fencing, strips of metal, and a tangle of rope—all of it woven into a kind of homemade tripwire to discourage Arthur from any midnight stroll toward the front bedroom.

Instead, the real peril at 1717 Fayette turned out to be his father. No matter how carefully DeAndre hid his stash, Gary found a way to the vials. His father didn't skim a whole lot at first, but it was enough eventually to cut through DeAndre's margins and enough finally to drive him back down the street to Fran and that godforsaken second-floor room.

Since moving back with his mother before Thanksgiving, DeAndre had been working Fairmount from package to package, more part-time than in the summer, but still enough to keep the roll fat. For a fifteen-year-old, the corner was not yet a job, and DeAndre, for all his pretense, could play at gangster for only as long as it took to get spending money. When he wanted to work, he and Corey would go to Bugsy or some other connect for a G-pack or a New York Quarter. Then they'd sell off. Then they'd play.

Short of the occasional juvenile charge or stickup, DeAndre had life pretty much the way he wanted it, provided there was a place on this earth where he could keep a stash. At the old house, it was his father helping himself to a few vials here, a few there. At the Dew Drop, it was cat-and-mouse with his mother. In December, when no one was around to watch, DeAndre did the only thing he could think to do: he hid the coke, the cash, and the .38 that Bugsy had given him for muscle in the closet, inside the sleeve of a leather jacket, which he then stuffed deep in a mass of balled-up laundry.

There wasn't any better choice. Uncle Stevie's room next door was more a shooting gallery than a bedroom, with Stevie, a certified welder, now torching nothing larger than a bottle cap. Same with upstairs, where Aunt Bunchie and Alfred and Aunt Sherry and her man, Kenny, were keeping house. Sherry might not be a worry; she was a drinker more than anything, but the other three were hardened players who wouldn't hesitate to move on him. As for the second-floor living room, that was also out of the question. Too much foot traffic and besides, little Ray Ray was now sleeping there, hitched to a cardiac monitor because Aunt Sherry's last baby was a crib death. You never knew when someone might come stumbling past to check on Ray Ray.

So it was the closet and hope for the best. But Fran was bolder than Gary, and it wasn't a week before DeAndre walked into the rear bedroom and sensed disaster the minute he caught sight of the leather jacket lying cold and lonely on the bed.

Damn. He raced out of the room, down the stairs and into the basement, where he found Fran and Bunchie. Two cats who had swallowed the canary.

"Where my stuff?"

Just seeing them sitting there together in the basement was answer enough.

"DeAndre, you got to be joking, leaving that shit in there. Suppose DeRodd found it." Fran played it easy, holding in her fangs.

"Where my stuff?" he persisted.

"Where you think?"

"I ain't joking. That's not my shit."

"I don't care. It's gone."

"Then you're gonna pay."

"You threatening me?" Her anger began to show.

DeAndre turned away. "That's all right. It ain't on me. It's Bugsy's shit."

He was determined not to let it drop. He knew his mother, and if he had any hope of using that room in the future he had to let her know how far he was willing to go.

"So what you saying? You gonna tell him?" she exploded. "You little shit. You gonna tell him? I'll tell him. Tell him about using a minor to sell drugs. Tell him about going to jail. DeAndre you must be joking."

"Yeah," he said, stalking out. "We'll see."

Two days later, Bugsy showed up on the front steps asking for Fran. Scared her, too, it seemed to DeAndre. Scared her enough to get the .38 back and keep her from his stash.

So now, with the turn of a new year, the stash problem seems settled and things seem to be working as if by plan. Half of the Fayette Street regulars are rolling down the hill to little old Fairmount, looking for blue tops, looking for DeAndre. The white boys, too, are scurrying across the DMZ from South Baltimore, ducking Bob Brown and his puppies, coming north for better vials. And young DeAndre McCullough is carrying it like he's King of the Strip.

"Got them Blues."

"Got the Ready Rock."

"Blues. Right here for them Blue Tops."

All along Fairmount and Gilmor, brand-name recognition rings in the night air. DeAndre's got a bomb and the fiends know it. He's moving two, sometimes three G-packs a night with the lion's share going to Bugsy, but still he's pulling in six, maybe seven or eight hundred on a good night, less the spillage and expenses. He was here yesterday. And the day before. And the day before that. And today he's back at it again, waiting on one of the Fairmount stoops for the next customer, taking stock of his position. He checks in with Boo, who's been working for him this last week, moving half a pack for DeAndre as a sixty-forty subcontractor.

"How many from what I gave you last night?"

Boo counts in his head.

"How many from the fifty?"

Boo is lost in the math. Twelve, he guesses.

"Twelve?"

"Um."

If you want a job done right, DeAndre thinks, you got to work alone. Oblivious to the bite of the winter wind, he settles in to mind shop, working through the afternoon and into the early dark. Eyes darting, he's alert to the flow of the street.

A minute or two more and his attention focuses on a shadow that jerks its way up Gilmor. A white boy, a reed-thin piper, creeping his way north. The stick man hesitates and half turns back to Baltimore Street, then turns once more toward Fairmount. DeAndre stands, revealing himself. Stepping off the stoop, he gives a slight wave before moving around the corner into the darkness of Fairmount Avenue. The piper locks onto the motion and stumbles forward on the new vector. DeAndre leads down Fairmount to the lip of a side alley, away from the crowd on Gilmor.

"What up," DeAndre asks, voice neutral.

No sales pitch. No need.

The stick man bends into DeAndre, a supplicant extending a small wad of bills. DeAndre takes the offering and steps into the middle of the street to catch a bit of the street lamp on Gilmor. Slowly he smooths the money and makes the count. Satisfied, he pockets it, and without a word, he's down the alley. The stick figure presses against a brick wall, seeking protection from the wind, no doubt worried that the black kid is gone with the dollars.

But DeAndre is straight up. He won't shake the vial or cut the product. He's not greedy that way. Wired and twitching, the stick man gets served and slips offstage quickly, bolting around the corner and southward. He's a charged particle loosed beyond the human condition, frenzied, spinning through the streets from one vial to the next. Those on the pipe are so coke-crazed, so hungry for that ready rock that even hardcore dope fiends are apt to show disgust. A man can carry an addiction to heroin, or at least he can pretend to carry it; cocaine always carries the man.

The sale registered, DeAndre returns to his stoop, waiting in the night's cold for the next customer and the next after that. He's a player here. On this small corner, at least, he's the shit.

When things are going bad, the question for DeAndre McCullough is always, where in hell is the money going to come from? But when things are going good, it's exactly the opposite: Where do the money go? Nike high-tops. Timberlands. Tommy Hilfigers and Filas. Weed from the E.A.B. crew up on Edmondson. Quarter-pounders and Happy Meals from McDonald's. Cheesesteaks from Bill's. Movies downtown at Harbor Park with one of the neighborhood girls. Video games on Baltimore Street. As fast as he makes his money, he spends it—and the more money he makes, the more shit he manages to buy. Like now, with so much cash coming at him from Fairmount Avenue, he can't even get mad on waking to find half his roll missing; he'd make that back again in an hour or two. Even DeAndre has to admit that it's too much wealth for any fifteen-year-old to handle. He's fucking up and can hardly bring himself to worry it.

And it's all so damn easy. He could walk off this corner now and have money enough to carry him through a week or two. Come back with another package and he'd be flush again in a day. With the right connect and a little bit of rep, there isn't anything so right as the corner. Time and again, he would finish a run with a nice, fat roll and tell himself that he was done, that he would go back to school and maybe get a straight job and be satisfied with a little less adventure, a little less pocket money. Then he would spend, and spend some more, until the only way he could right himself was to get back on Fairmount. Compared to that, the school-work meant nothing, and a minimum-wage job even less. Still, there was something inside that made DeAndre hold back, something that kept him from declaring once and for all that the corner would be his place in the world. In the back of his mind, he told himself that he hadn't yet made a choice. He was fifteen; a distribution charge still meant nothing worse than a juvenile petition. And he was smart—all his teachers said so—and still on the rollbook at Francis M. Woods. He could bear down, get some class time, maybe make the tenth grade with a social promotion. He could play at this corner, but step off when it was time. And DeAndre trusted himself; he would know when it was time.

The night before, in fact, the knockers rolled past on him on Fairmount. No big thing. It wasn't like he was dirty when they came through, but he got a good once-over from Collins. And he knew Collins wanted to beat on him; he would have beat on him that one time if Fran hadn't been around to stop it. The roll-past gave DeAndre something to think about, and he's thinking about it still. It isn't so much a question of fear; DeAndre is grown enough to take either a charge or a legal ass-whipping if need be. But still, last night seems like warning enough. He's poor no more; he's got all the Tims and Nikes and designer wear he needs. And Fairmount is up and running; it will be here for him whenever he's ready to move back into the mix. Now might be the time to step off, before Collins and the rest get their chance. Now might be the time to go see Miss Davis and make sure he's still on the class rolls.

Sitting on the stoop, DeAndre decides that this is his last night on Fairmount. He works his package down that evening, and the next morning, he does his laundry in the tub. Dressed in still damp clothes, he heads down Fayette Street past the Fairmount corner and two blocks farther to Francis M. Woods Senior High School, the only school in Baltimore that would consider for more than a second the idea of enrolling DeAndre McCullough. Chin to chest, eyes cast down, he is deep inside himself as he walks stiff-legged, driving his heels mechanically into the pavement.

He climbs the school steps like he belongs, trying several of the front doors. All locked. He rings the buzzer, content to wait. He's spent an inordinate amount of time on the wrong side of a locked school door, in most cases accompanied by his mother, waiting for the authorities to reach a decision, waiting to start again. Standing here today in the January cold, he stares indifferently into the lens of the security camera. Finally, he hears the buzz of the door release and snatches the handle.

Inside, he's greeted by Gould, the school security officer.

"Good to have you back, brother."

DeAndre smiles sheepishly, then enters the front office to wait for

Miss Davis. He's sure she will claim him, his confidence secured, at least for this moment, by his newfound resolve to attend class and do the work. For his part, he's willing to let bygones be bygones, and he's hoping the assistant principal sees it the same way.

Rose Davis has created a haven at Francis M. Woods for those rebellious, damaged spirits shipwrecked and abandoned by the rest of the city school system. She is everywhere at Francis Woods: a calming influence, encouraging and chiding, trying to get her charges to realize some of their potential, or at least some of their value, fighting what amounts to an endless rearguard action against the corner itself. She makes it her business to travel the local markets, where she sees many of her students and former students hanging. She's seen DeAndre on Fairmount; she knows what that's about.

He sits there in the office, wrapped in an unlikely innocence, waiting to be given yet another chance, accustomed to this moment of feigned redemption. DeAndre is forever in a school's administrative office, forever waiting to talk to an administrator. His academic standard is defined by a long streak of second-day suspensions, allowing him the opportunity to attend the first day of every semester, showing off new outfits and high-tops, fronting for the girls. Once all joy is squeezed from that first day, DeAndre follows up by quickly scuttling the academics with a disciplinary suspension of no less than two weeks, or with any luck at all, a month or more. His friends' school disciplinary sheets aren't shabby, but DeAndre always manages to go them one better. For all of them, school is something to endure until the age of fifteen and a half; the law says sixteen, but the children of Fayette Street have the juvenile court backlog figured into the equation. Within that framework, most learn to at least go through the motions. A few of the C.M.B. regulars—R.C., Dorian, or Brooks—don't bother showing up, preferring to take their chances with the juvenile system. But the rest manage, with some regularity, to take a seat in classrooms that seem to them entirely disconnected from the facts of their world.

For DeAndre, there is no common ground with anything resembling authority, and his juvenile sheet chronicles a constant struggle to stand true to himself regardless of the damage done. DeAndre McCullough doesn't bend and he doesn't forgive and he never forgets. In the classroom, he flies the flag of piracy and insolence. He is about struggle.

In nursery school, he had words with a little girl and ended up crowning her with a chair. That was the first suspension. In the second and fourth grades, he fought with his teachers, taking charges for assault and more suspensions. In the fifth grade, he was asked to leave three separate schools. In the seventh grade, he failed to embrace an antidrug presentation at the school and joined the select few who can claim a charge of punching an armed Baltimore City police officer during classroom hours.

It's not as if school officials weren't aware of the challenge. They caught on to DeAndre early and sent him, at age ten, to a big brother program, hoping a role model would have a positive influence. It didn't take, but still they moved him along. He's too smart to be held back, they would tell Fran, who learned to anticipate that on the second day of any given semester, she could expect an invitation to meet with some vice principal at some school somewhere in the city.

But things seemed to change last September, when DeAndre came to Francis Woods and the enlightened administration of Miss Rose Davis. Fresh from his wild summer on Fairmount, DeAndre arrived at school in high spirits, and come the second day of classes, he stayed put. He was there the third day, as well. And the fourth. His mother began to believe that her son had turned a corner.

What she didn't know about this sudden commitment to academics was its origin, which had to do with a hot weekend night that summer, when the boys of C.M.B. got deep and decided to take a walk into South Baltimore, down to Ramsay Street in search of a rumored house party. They found it, but they weren't exactly welcomed—at least not by the Stricker and Ramsay crew, who sensed a territorial violation. Eyes glaring, the two groups managed for a time to keep their distance, but when you're traveling with the likes of Boo and Dorian, trouble is assured. Words got tossed, then fists, until a full-blown brawl tumbled outside. C.M.B. held its own; DeAndre and R.C. were doing most of the damage until one of the Stricker and Ramsay boys—Sherman Smith, by name— tilted the table and came out with his iron. A couple of misspent shots and C.M.B. was on the run.

It wasn't anything special. They'd had their share of shooting and being shot at and were usually content to laugh it off in the safety of Tae's basement or the rec center playground, R.C. often taking the lead in editing the encounter: "Yo, we was fucking them up. Yo, did you see DeAndre hit that motherfucker? Yo, he dropped him."

That they got run off, that they were fighting tame when the other side had their guns out didn't matter. In R.C.'s version, victory would always be assured.

But on that occasion, R.C.'s revisionism wasn't enough for DeAndre, who crept back home to get his .380 semi, a weary thing that could have used a little more care. Creeping back down in the bottom that same night, DeAndre spotted Sherman near McHenry Street and let one fly, but missed. Sherman returned fire and a rolling gun battle ensued, at least until DeAndre's gun fell apart, the clip hitting the ground, the bullets spilling onto the pavement.

Aw shit. He tried frantically to stuff the bullets into the clip, but Sherman, sensing weakness, pressed the attack and sent DeAndre scurrying back up top. Safe on the other side of Baltimore Street, his body soaked in sweat, DeAndre vowed revenge. And true to that purpose, he spent the rest of the summer hunting Sherman from Westside to Mt. Claire, but the boy was nowhere to be found.

Until September, when on that first day of class, during the home room roll call, DeAndre caught the sound of two magic words: "Sherman Smith."

Yeah boy. Brightening, he scanned the room.

". . . Sherman Smith . . ."

No response. Marked absent.

DeAndre left school that day inspired. Of all the schools and of all the classes, fate chose to put Sherman in the same blessed room. All he had to do was wait him out, and for that, DeAndre was in school the next day and the day after that and for as long as it took, all the time praying that Sherman wasn't locked up, or doing so well on some corner that he wouldn't ever come to class. As the September days ran one to the next, his resolve never wavered. Every morning he was up and out, attending each of his first three classes, then maybe cutting out only when he was convinced Sherman was a no-show.

He even asked his mother to help him get up in the mornings. Fran responded initially with suspicion, but after a week or so, DeAndre could see she was impressed at his effort.

Two weeks into the semester, DeAndre was in a third-floor hallway when he focused on the vision that was Sherman, bending over to open a metal locker.

"Yeah boy!"

DeAndre dropped his binder and charged. Sherman had a second to straighten up before DeAndre crashed into him, sending both boys sprawling across the floor. DeAndre was on top quickly, raining fists as Sherman balled up like a possum.

Later in her office, Rose Davis let loose on both DeAndre and
Sherman, ordering them to come back the next day with a parent.
DeAndre left first and quickly found R.C., who was hanging on Fulton
Avenue with Dorian.

"Look at these," he declared, raising his swollen hands with pride.
"Fucked that boy up."

"DeAndre, you a crazy nigger, yo," R.C. assured him.

Then it was off to tell Fran, who listened to the whole story and gave
back only a cold look of disappointment. Watching her, DeAndre actually felt bad for the first time and found himself promising to continue
with school if Fran would go and talk with Miss Davis.

"Andre, you got to be joking," she told him.

But the next day, Fran went with her son to see Rose Davis, who
greeted Fran warmly and ushered her into her office. As long as DeAndre
could remember, Fran had always attended these meetings and, regardless of her own problems, had always managed to wear her concern into
the room.

"You can come in, too," added Rose, her eyebrows raised. DeAndre
had settled in on the couch in the outer office. "There are no secrets
here."

True to form, Rose had spent part of the previous day tapping into
her considerable sources, pinning down the details of the McCullough-
Smith feud. With the three of them seated in her office, she let a long
silence undermine DeAndre's confidence, staring at him until he dropped
his head and began to fidget. She related to Fran her son's history with
Sherman.

Damn, thought DeAndre. Who snitching?

"Well, DeAndre," Rose said, turning her attention to him, "your
attendance has certainly improved from last year."

He was out of his depth and he knew it, hiding behind a mumbled,
"Yes'm."

"So now that you've settled your little score, I guess we won't be
seeing very much of you around here anymore."

"No, I'm going to go," he insisted. "I'm going to go."

"Well, let's just write that down."

She handed him her little account book, the repository for so many
handwritten promises, all duly signed. Some were kept, most were
forgotten, but all were used to try to bind her students to her, to put it
on a personal level.

DeAndre had signed that promise, but as the fall days grew shorter, he felt the ache of his poverty, the desolation of the rear bedroom on Fayette Street and the lure of the nightly action. Slowly, inexorably, he slipped off to Fairmount Avenue.

Now he's back. And of course, Rose Davis will take him on the rolls, give him another chance, promise even to promote him if he can pull himself together. She sees no other choice. Like so many of her students, DeAndre is keeping a foot in both camps, straddling for a brief moment the two disparate worlds. If she can keep him coming to school four days out of five—three days a week, even—she might have a shot. If he stops entirely, then she has lost another one—a gifted one, in fact—to the corner.

The door to Rose Davis's office opens. She acknowledges DeAndre with a rueful nod.

"Hey," he says, breaking the ice.

"You can come in," she tells him.

DeAndre rises, glancing again at Rose as he steps past her in the office doorway. To his surprise, she is smiling.

Ella Thompson prepares herself slowly in the back bedroom of her apartment. Black dress, black hat, dress heels, gold earrings—she's getting better at this drill than any person ought to be. Last month, the service was at March's; today, the homecoming is at New Shiloh, and next week, it will be at Brown's on Baltimore Street for a neighbor's son. And Ella is always in the middle of it, measuring out a little more of herself for each eulogy, for each gospel hymn, as if sitting demurely in these pews and bearing witness to tragedy is some kind of career.

She pauses at the mirror with her makeup, listening for signs of life in the room across the hall. Nothing. Her youngest, Kiti, is pretending to be up and running when she knows he's still face down in his pillow.

"Kiti?"

Silence.

"Keee-Teee! Are you up?"

She begins moving toward his bedroom door, but the click-clack of her heels gives warning. Before she can knock, her son greets her, bleary-eyed, at the bedroom door.

"Ma, I'm up."

She smiles. "I'm serious now. You've got to get yourself dressed or we'll be late."

The seventeen-year-old nods, then pads to the bathroom. Ella goes back to the mirror, peering into the glass at a face that has somehow managed to keep a look far younger than forty-six years. Ella is very dark, with the deepest of brown eyes and perfectly straight, jet-black bangs that give her face a girlish quality. Even after five children, she has kept her figure, so that among the children of Fayette Street, the general consensus is that Miss Ella might be more than thirty, maybe even thirty-five if you count carefully.

On the other hand, such agelessness is wasted on Ella Thompson, who seems to concede nothing to her own vanity. She doesn't work at looking younger, at changing her appearance or at obscuring her status as a middle-aged grandmother. Instead, she works at nearly everything else, and somehow, in a rush of well-spent days and months and years, she has forgotten to age.

But on this morning, quite naturally, the mirror gives Ella back a hint of fear. Today is for Dana Lamm, but her son, Tito, is the young man most on her mind.

The two had been inseparable since childhood. It had been a three-some, really—Tito and Dana, and then Gordon—three fine boys who were always rambling in and out of her rowhouse apartment, sharing with her their earliest triumphs, seeking her comfort when they stumbled. Ella had nurtured her son and his friends alike, encouraged them as she did everyone, watched with a cautious joy as each turned away from the corner. She had seen all the possibilities in those three boys and she had fought for those possibilities, inoculating each with her own unlikely optimism, her unwavering Christian purposefulness. School, work, respect, love, responsibility—from most any other soul on Fayette Street, such things were easily marked down as platitude. But from Ella Thompson, these things were life itself. With God's own grace those three boys raised themselves up and got out. Her son to the navy, Gordon with him, and Dana to the marines.

Victories, she thinks, hunting down her black purse.

But then what is today? A victory emptied of itself, with Dana lost despite it all, dead from an electrocution at Camp LeJeune. A training accident. To survive a childhood in West Baltimore and then fall by random chance as a peacetime warrior—where in such an ending do you put your faith? Ella shakes her head. It makes no sense.

Worse still, Tito has disappeared. When Gordon called her with the news of Dana's death, her thoughts jumped to her oldest son. She phoned

Tito in California that night and listened as he poured out his grief, the hurt turned bitter because the navy had denied him permission to fly home for the funeral. His pain was fierce, and she let him rant and cry, absorbing as much of his suffering as she could. She consoled and counseled, finally eliciting from him a promise not to go absent without leave. But since then, it has been four days of silence.

Last night again, she had stayed up late trying to reach him, fretting away the three-hour time difference. Tito's roommate was solicitous, but had no answer: "Haven't seen him. Sorry, ma'am. I don't know where he is."

She knows her son. He is strong-willed. He would jeopardize everything to be with Dana today, and there is a part of her that wouldn't be surprised to see Tito at the church an hour from now.

She pulls back from the mirror, brushing a few specks of lint from the dark fabric. Inspection complete.

"Kiti?" she calls, sending her voice down the narrow hallway to his room.

"In a minute," he answers.

She waits for him in the living room, a cluttered but clean space at the front of the first-floor apartment. The walls are filled with pictures of family and friends, and she pauses at the door to seek out Tito's portrait, the one of him in uniform. She vivdly remembers the day the picture was taken. Dana was supposed to be in the portrait, too, but he couldn't find his dress pants, so he begged off while Tito and Gordon, decked in their military finery, went to the downtown studio. And next to that picture, the shot of Tito at his high school prom, and below that, a photo of her children—all of them—clustered together on a sofa. For a moment, Ella lets her eyes gaze on the face of her youngest, Andrea, who is about ten in the photograph. Then Ella quickly looks away, fighting down the wave of emotion that inevitably rolls over her when she thinks of Fatty Pooh.

Finally, Kiti joins her. She looks to him fondly as she adjusts his tie. She is a tall woman, but Kiti, a high school senior, towers over her as he submits to mothering.

"You look nice," she says.

He smiles awkwardly. They go out the apartment door and onto the steps, where Ella surveys the Fayette Street strip as she pulls the front door closed. No one is hanging here in front of 1806, though just down the hill, Bruce Street is bustling. A look out slouches along Fulton Avenue.

Two regulars glide past, heading down the hill from Monroe. "Morning," says the one closest.

"Good morning," she replies. Her tone is open, a careful effort to avoid judgment; it's Ella's way to exclude no one. "How are you today?" Both men offer affirmative grunts. Neither breaks stride as they sail on toward Bruce Street, wrapped in certainty and purpose. Kiti pockets his house key, ambles to the car, and at last they're off, only to be snagged a block away by the traffic light at Monroe. As the engine idles roughly in the January cold, Ella watches Smitty and Gale in front of the bar; Gale, holding her baby as she touts a package, oblivious to the winter wind. Curt appears in the crosswalk, lifting his cane in acknowledgment of Ella, and from the front steps of the shooting gallery, with his satchel at his feet, Blue waves with genuine pleasure. An artist by trade, Blue still keeps his paints, markers, and a book of poems in that satchel, carrying it with him everywhere for fear of losing it in the needle palace. And Ella is working on Blue, trying to recruit him for an art class at the rec. She tries again today.

Kiti rolls down the passenger window and Ella calls to her neighbor. "Hello, Mr. Blue. When you coming down?"

"Soon. Soon, Ella."

"We need you, Blue."

He flashes a self-deprecating smile, but only waves. No commitment this time; too much running and gunning. A shame, she thinks, watching the traffic up and down Blue's steps.

The light changes and she drives on. The world of Fayette and Monroe fades, to be replaced in its turn by an endless succession of drug corners as the car rolls north through the heart of West Baltimore. Fulton and Lexington, Fulton and Edmondson, Fulton and Lanvale—all of them the same.

"It doesn't make sense," she says, as much to herself as to Kiti. If Ella Thompson has a practiced mantra, this is it: It doesn't make sense. And to her, on the outside peering in, the corner world would never make sense. Strange, since she has spent so many years living at the edge of it. Stranger still, since she has seen it creep into her own life and destroy so much.

She was married a year and a half before she even had a clue. Allen was from a hardworking family, with steady work down at the General Refractors plant in Curtis Bay. It was a union job, decent money, and for a time, their life together seemed to promise a better future. Ella had been through one relationship already; her oldest child, Shulita, was by that man, and two more, Donilla and Tito, quickly followed from the marriage to Allen. At the least, a hardworking husband promised to take her away from the endless drudgery of packaging canned soups at the Gross & Blackwell Company, a merciless job for a twenty-five-year-old woman. For that alone, Allen was salvation of a kind, a knight in shining armor, and maybe that was why she was so slow to figure things out. They were always short of money as young couples with children are always short of money, so, naturally, she only noticed the backsliding when paid-for things started to disappear around the house. It was little things at first, food and small appliances, but eventually the big-ticket stuff too. Love kept her blind until the day she found his tools. With the spike out in the open, she swallowed her fear and tried confrontation, but that just made for another broken promise. What could she do? And where could she go? She was young then, with three children under the age of four, just frightened and foolish enough to try to ignore the drugging, and later, to ignore the beatings that came from guilty rage. She tried to wait him out, hoping against all logic that things would get better if she just loved him enough.

Her sister offered her refuge after one of those bad nights of abuse and tears. But even in that sanctuary, she couldn't see her way to a solution. I've made my bed hard, she told her sister, then went home to suffer some more. Eventually, and through no decision of her own, she caught a break: Allen fell for three years on a state drug charge. He took that gray corrections division bus to Hagerstown; Ella and her children used the pause to fashion their escape.

Taking Fulton across North Avenue, Ella and Kiti reach the top end of Monroe Street and the New Shiloh Baptist Church, a bastion of the older order in black Baltimore, a magnet that still draws together the fragments of broken neighborhoods in a genuine display of power and glory.

On this cold, cloudy Friday, the parking lot is filling fast; cars, trucks, and minivans line up behind the hearse and limousine already waiting at the entrance. The good people—the whole of black Baltimore that stands apart from the corner—have come together in grief and tribute for one of their own.

Ella and Kiti join the throng as it moves rapidly through the lobby, filling the amphitheater of pews that fan out from the pulpit. Ella and her son move down an aisle and find seats; immediately, Ella begins looking around, scanning the faces row by row.

"Thank God," she says finally.

Tito isn't here.

A few minutes before the choir breaks out with the opening hymn, Gordon finds her. They embrace and he guides Ella to a coterie of polished young soldiers, introducing her to his friends. She smiles on all of them, so crisp in starched dress uniforms. Strong, fine men, she tells herself. Like Dana. Like Tito. Serious young men, they extend polite handshakes and soft words.

The service begins. Ella steps back into the aisle, grasps Gordon's hand once again, then moves lightly to her own seat. Among the scores of churches that speckle black Baltimore from Hilton Parkway on the west side to Milton Avenue on the east—gothic piles and storefronts, old stone monoliths and rehabbed rowhouses—New Shiloh holds upper-rung status. On the west side, only Bethel A.M.E. and its legendary choir can argue greater standing in the community than New Shiloh. For Ella, who calls a more modest African Baptist church at Baltimore and Pulaski home, the vast auditorium and a full house of more than five hundred mourners gives weight and authority to Dana's homecoming. So, too, does the Reverend Harold Carter.

"I am sad this morning," he says, bearing down on the eulogy with a ringing tenor, "I am grieved, but I cannot, I will not be disappointed today."

It isn't the usual West Baltimore funeral oratory, the kind that gracefully forgives the frailty of the departed, that struggles to understand the will of God in a merciless world. Today, the Reverend Mr. Carter can offer words that are unlike so many others spoken from city pulpits. Today, he does not have to account for another young life squandered amid the drugs and the guns. Today, he is free to hail a right-living young man who transcended the corners to serve his country and, ultimately, to give his life not to a needle or handgun, but to the random chance of a loose electrical cable. In Baltimore, this is close enough to be called victory.

All of which is not lost on the reverend, who chooses this eulogy to draw the comparisons: Dana's short life, the lives of so many others expended on the city's streets. To the call-and-response of willing, waiting mourners, he hits every note:

". . . because for once I am not here to bury a young man who lost his way in drugs and violence . . ."

"YES, LAWD."

". . . and for once I do not have to help a young man's family and friends hold their heads high, for their heads are not bowed. There was no shame in the life of this fine young man."

"TELL IT. TELL IT."

The eulogy rolls outward in waves—cresting, ebbing, then cresting again until Harold Carter is at the crescendo, displaying for the faithful the talents that have accorded him the New Shiloh pulpit. Then, almost as a relief, the choir chimes in, followed by telegrams and messages of condolence and, finally, an accounting of an unfinished life, the obituary of Dana Lamm.

At the end of the service, Ella consults briefly with Kiti. They decide to ride with friends in the procession to the burial site at Arlington National Cemetery, south of Washington. Tito would have wanted that, and on this winter morning, his mother and brother are his loyal surrogates.

"Must be fifty cars," says Kiti, as the procession begins to roll south on Monroe Street, or old U.S. 1 as it appears on the road maps. Monroe snakes south through block after block of rowhouses until it crosses the west side expressway.

At the intersection with Fayette, Ella sees that the packages are now out. Curt is on post in front of the liquor store with a half-dozen others, and Blue is tending to shooting gallery business from his front steps. The funeral rolls past them, then down the hill into the edges of hill-billy Pigtown and across Wilkens Avenue, where Monroe Street wraps itself around Carroll Park and then glides past the vacant Montgomery Ward warehouse and up the hill to the interchange with the interstate. The rowhouses, the corners, the raw, rust-belt industry give way to the clean, bare woods of the Baltimore-Washington parkway.

The forty-mile trip to Arlington takes more than an hour, a journey that ends with a phalanx of soldiers, black and white, gathered for a time-honored ritual as only the military can provide. A bugler sounds tender notes. On the ridge above, a squad in dress blues snaps to a muffled command. Rifles fire a sharp retort, and the mourners jump and bristle uncomfortably, the sound itself measured differently in the world they know. Ella watches, awed, as the stretch of flag is held taut above the finished coffin, the warriors making crisp, triangular folds. Then, with the click of locking heels, the folded flag is delivered to the grieving mother.

On the way home, Kiti sleeps soundly, and Ella is alone to think on the hallowed perfection of Arlington and to enjoy the greenery that surrounds Interstate 95 between the cities. Then Baltimore rises up, the vista of the city's west side extending outward in a complex of broad horizontal lines, block after block of flat-roofed rowhouses, broken only by the occasional church spire.

Kiti wakes when Ella hits a red light at Carey Street.

"It's depressing," she says, confronted once again by the litter of men and women on the usual corners. "Even the air smells different."

When Kiti gives her a look, she laughs. "I'm serious . . . It's so depressing to come home. It's sad."

Kiti says nothing.

"What time is it?" she asks him.

"Two-thirty."

Ella rushes into the apartment for a quick change of clothes, with Kiti behind her, heading listlessly toward his bedroom. She won't worry about Kiti right now. He'll be in his room, maybe on the phone with one of his girlfriends. Kiti doesn't hang much, and for that, Ella is grateful.

Dressed in jeans, a sweatshirt, and a green hooded jacket, she leaves her car on Fayette, preferring to walk as a way of showing the flag. She moves at a brisk pace, looking neither right nor left, her visage set, her eyes cloaked. In this neighborhood, even Ella Thompson has a game face.

When she crosses Bruce, a tout steps up and announces his product without conviction. He can tell there's no sale here, but figures there's no harm trying.

A young slinger glares at the tout. "Not her, yo."

He apologizes and Ella pushes on toward Mount, where the market chatter increases in volume. A generation back and Mount Street was lucrative territory that competing crews might war over. Now, though, with so many crews working so many packages, territory has ceased to be an issue. In Baltimore, anyone can sell anywhere, so long as there are fiends willing to pay. Now, a drug corner is all about product and name recognition.

"Got orange tops."

"Big whites. Big white bags."

"Reds. Red tops. Reds make you sparkle. Red tops."

And, as always, "In the Hole."

Black Beauty, a dark-skinned tout known for her hard look, is busy touting today for that crew, which sells heroin under a brand name that has its origin in local geography. Perfectly isolated, the back alley that runs between Mount and Vincent on the south side of Fayette has long been known as the Hole. In service of that brand, Black Beauty walks a tight circle on Mount Street, barking in mindless repetition, like a mating bird left lonesome in spring.

"In the Hole. In the Hole. In the Hole."

Ella cuts diagonally across Mount and enters an alley that sits hard against the rubble of a collapsing rowhouse. She surveys an expanse of cracked, uneven blacktop, strewn with glass shards, corralled by the tatters of a chain-link fence. An old, twisted backboard with no rim, a swing set, monkey bars, and a sliding board with a mean metallic bite at the bottom are the archaeological remnants that suggest a playground.

On the northern edge of the lot squats a single-story, cinder-block building, its eyeless gray facade capped with a ribbon of dull red paint. Small and ugly and brooding, the thing was given life by an architect who might have learned his craft on the Maginot Line, so closely does it resemble a wartime bunker.

Ella catches sight of two adolescent figures leaning against one of the two concrete planter boxes that flank the metal grate. Manny Man and Tae are idling, waiting for the recreation center to open.

"Why aren't you two in school?"

"We got a half-day," Tae says easily.

The standard answer, delivered four times a week on the average. Ella gives them each a quick look, letting them feel her suspicion, but the boys stay passive. She mounts the steps, unbolts two heavy locks, and bends to pull up the metal grate. It squeaks protest and fights her all the way. She unlocks one of the two double doors and enters; the boys follow. Above the doorway, a bent square of tin proclaims, "The Martin Luther King Jr. Recreation Center."

Stepping into the darkness, Ella fiddles with her key ring as she rushes to open the small back office and turn off the alarm system. She returns to flip up the bank of light switches.

"Sign the book," she says as Tae bumps past Manny Man and claims the privilege of being the first to sign the composition notebook that serves as a roster for the flock of children who find their way here five days a week.

"I'm first," says Tae, admiring his signature, "Dontae," written in a neat, tight script on the first line.

"So what?" says Manny. "I been first before."

Tae thumbs through the notebook. "Look who's always first. R.C. Damn, that boy don't never go to school," he says.

Tae is deep into the notebook. He is a bantam-sized fifteen-year-old, with a wiry body of broad shoulders, long arms, and bowed legs. His hair is cut close and the skin of his face is pulled taut, giving him a pinched, sharp look. He flashes a wide grin.

"DeAndre, too. Them two boys be crazy," he says with relish.

Tae still plays the game, going to school, doing his homework, obeying his mother's curfew. He runs track and gets low-B grades and still has college or the military within his grasp. But today, he cut early to hook up with Manny Man and check the rumor that Miss Ella is thinking about a basketball team.

"When we gonna play?" asks Manny, trying to provoke her into a commitment.

"I don't know yet. I wish you worried me about school the way you do about basketball," she says.

"Miss Ella, we'd be good," Manny pleads.

"We'll see. Now don't be pushing me."

Ella retreats to her small back office, hoping for a moment or two to herself. She's torn about the basketball idea and would like to think it through. A fifteen-and-under team would be a big commitment for her and the rec, but she knows she needs something to occupy the older boys, who are getting too rough for the smaller children. Some days, it's all she can do to keep a semblance of order.

Outside, as if on cue, the larger room erupts in noise. There's wild pounding against the double metal doors and laughter from Tae and Manny Man.

"I SAID OPEN THE DAMN DOOR."

So much for a chance to think. Ella pushes her chair back, sighs, and goes out to open the door for Richard Carter.

"OPEN THE MOTHERFUCKING DOOR," shouts R.C., as Tae and Manny sit smirking, content to watch him through the wire-mesh windows as he pounds away in frustration. They, in turn, are safe behind the rule that only Ella or her part-time assistant at the rec, Marzell Myers, is permitted to open the door.

"R.C., please," says Ella, ending the standoff. "You don't have to curse."

"MISS ELLA," he wails, his voice raised, as usual, to the level of a shout. "THEY WON'T OPEN THE DOOR."

"R.C., you know the rules."

"YEAH, BUT MISS ELLA, THEY WAS LAUGHING," R.C. counters, his heavy face forming into its perpetual pout. The world has conspired against him; this is a belief so central to his being that it qualifies as religion.

"I know, R.C. Just calm down and sign the book."

"Yes'm," he says, still glaring hard at his tormentors. Walking past Ella, he lunges at Tae, grabbing the ledger from the smaller boy's hands. Manny Man jumps to Tae's defense, tossing a shot of his own in an effort to stir Ella's ire: "R.C. don't never be going to school."

But R.C. recovers instantly. "Ringing a bell don't do nothing for me," he announces with pride.

Good one. Tae slides off the counter to salute R.C.'s wit with a high five. Friendship restored, the two head for a row of tables where they can mess with a handful of battered board games, leaving Manny in the wake of Tae's change of loyalty. Then, faithful as a puppy, he picks himself up and follows.

The rec proper isn't much bigger than a good-sized classroom. Rows of tables and chairs on either side of a center aisle take up much of the space. To the right of the aisle, small cubby spaces designated "Library" and "Arts and Crafts" hug the wall. The four shelves of the library contain a perplexing assortment of hand-me-downs that, except in a rare case, sit untouched. The Arts and Crafts center, marked by a few pots of paint and glue, is a big hit with the younger kids.

To the left of the aisle stands a row of tall lockers, each emblazoned with a stern warning not to open them and remove the playthings, a right once again reserved for Miss Ella or Marzell. The lockers hold most of the remnants of games and toys that somehow have found their way to the rec. Candy Land, Connect Four, checkers, bits and pieces of Monopoly.

Stacked next to the lockers atop plastic milk crates are an ancient receiver, a speaker, a dusty turntable, an old TV, and a VCR. On the adjacent wall hangs a cheerful mural—the work of Neacey, Gandy, and some of the other older girls—depicting fairy-tale characters under the leafy arms of a tree.

Between the bathrooms on the back wall is a weight set, the lone bar resting in the metal arms of a vinyl bench. A metal stand adorned with a collage of African masks created by the younger children and a wall poster featuring coloring book representations of famous African-Americans add to the rear of the room.

All of this is spotlessly clean, lovingly maintained by Ella and Marzell, with some occasional help from the older girls. The tile floor is mopped daily, the tables cleaned, the chairs neatly aligned. The depressing weight of the dropped tile ceiling is lightened a bit by a long string of red and green crepe paper adorned with balloons, a leftover from the Christmas pageant. In all, the interior of the rec is festive enough, appealing to the little ones, who accept the illusion. The older kids need more, Ella knows, and so she worries.

A soft knocking catches her ear between R.C.'s raucous bellows, as he celebrates victory in a game of Connect Four. Ella checks the clock—half past three, not yet time for the little ones to be here—before getting up to again open the rec door. In totters six-year-old Dena Sparrow, barely able to move in a bundle of winter clothing but early as usual because her family lives just across the alley. Ella welcomes Dena, guides her over the threshold, and reaches back to close the door. It doesn't budge.

"DeAndre, let go of the door," she orders.

A solemn DeAndre McCullough enters, walking past Ella without so much as hello. Chin riveted to his chest, arms stiff at his sides, he moves with his practiced roughneck walk, a gait of locked knees and stiff spine. The cold day clings to his demeanor.

"Hello, DeAndre," says Ella.

"Huh."

"Hello, DeAndre," she tries again.

"I said hey," he mumbles, obviously irritated. He stops at the desk and signs the book, then sheds his coat, throwing it casually on the counter. Unencumbered, he stalks past the others without a glance of recognition. He unbuttons his flannel shirt and lets it fall in a heap. His T-shirt follows, the one with the cartoon of a hopper smoking a blunt. Bare-chested and muscled, he swings onto the bench and hefts the weight. He does bench presses mindlessly, with no program, tiring quickly.

"Twenty-five. Yeah boy," he says, sitting up.

He lifts the bar again and does ten long, slow arm curls. Finishing, he sets it on the floor. Turning to the others, he flexes his arms. "Steel," he says, banging his chest. "I'm a man."

The others ignore him, but little Dena, watching from a chair near Ella's office, makes her way slowly across the room. She smiles broadly, intrigued by the free weights and DeAndre both. The girl bends her little body over the bar and tries a lift. DeAndre stoops behind her and curls the weight up and over her head.

"Girl, you strong," he announces, helping her set the bar down. He lifts her in the air, and she beams a smile. He spins her around, his face alive with joy. "She stronger than you, R.C.," he laughs, as Dena hugs him.

Ella watches, pleased. For all his bluster, DeAndre is good with the little ones.

More roughnecks arrive. Huggie and the twins, Arnold and Ronald, bound through the doors, excitement glowing on their faces. "Got that cat," Arnold announces, proudly, piquing R.C.'s interest.

"Yeah. We got that cat been hitting our coop," Ronald boasts.

"What cat?"

"Cat been getting our birds," Ronald says. "Huggie killed it dead."

"Yeah, what you do?" R.C. asks.

"Caught that cat and threw it in with Shamrock's pit bull. Tore his ass up," Huggie says proudly.

"Shit, that ain't nothin'," R.C. says, punching a hole in their glee. "You shoulda got DeAndre."

"Oh, yeah?" Ronald says, a little hurt. "You should of heard that bitch scream."

"DEANDRE," R.C. roars, "DEANDRE, COME HERE. YO, TELL THEM WHAT YOU DO WHEN A CAT GOES AFTER YOUR BIRDS."

DeAndre puts Dena down and slowly joins the boys.

"Go on, tell them," R.C. urges.

DeAndre smiles. "This cat been around my coop, trying to get in. I saw him and went and got this pair of thick gloves, the kind my uncle uses with the crabs, real thick so you can't get scratched. Then I trapped that motherfucker. He tried to get me but he couldn't get through the gloves."

DeAndre has seated himself on a table. The other boys, R.C. included, are silent as DeAndre's enthusiasm for his tale catches hold of them.

"He was tough," DeAndre says. "I broke his legs, broke each one. Then I tied him up and hung him from this tree . . ."

His voice drops, drawing the others closer.

". . . got me some lighter fluid, squirted that sucker down, then hit him with a match. Fucked him all up."

"MAN, YOU A CRAZY FUCKER," R.C. shouts, while Tae and Manny bang the table in approval.

"Damn," Ronald says, admitting admiration.

Ella has stopped working with the little children. Frozen by DeAndre's account, she is slow to respond. "DeAndre," she asks finally, "why did you do that? That cat was only doing what it has to."

"Miss Ella, a cat gotta do what a cat gotta do and I gotta do what I gotta do," DeAndre answers, nonchalant. His response touches something deep within the other boys and they howl approval.

"You sick, boy," R.C. says, elated with it.

"Cat killed my birds," says DeAndre with finality. "Cat gotta pay."

Ella shakes her head. She has known DeAndre most of his life; she's seen him as a lovesick puppy, chasing her Pooh up and down Fayette Street, working through the agony of that first childhood crush. She's seen him running the streets, getting into more and more mayhem as he has grown. She knows DeAndre is clever and open and capable of wonderful moments, like before, when he had Dena Sparrow laughing with delight. She also knows he can, if the idea suits him, torture and burn a cat.

The phone rings and Ella steps back into her office. Good news, thank God. Tito is home in California, having gone no farther than a long, all-night drive down the coast. Ella gets the word from her daughter, hangs up and sighs, visibly relieved.

"Miss Ella?"

Little Stevie is at her office door.

"What, Stevie?"

"Can we take the football out on the playground?"

"If you bring it back."

He races off and Ella leaves the office to spend the rest of the afternoon with the younger children. The older boys soon depart, off on some business best discussed outside the rec. R.C.'s voice lingers, carrying from Mount Street.

Eventually, the darkness presses in and Ella checks the clock. It's half past six, time to send her charges home. As a last ritual, she gathers Tastykakes and potato chip bags—snacks that come to the rec center from Echo House, the neighborhood outreach center, and the St. Martin's parish soup kitchen—passing them out as the kids move back across the threshold, huddling on the blacktop around the dim light that escapes from the windows in the rec center's doors.

Inside, surrounded by the sudden silence, Ella lugs out the bucket and mop, and begins to clean. She returns the toys and games to the lockers, straightens the chairs, cleans the finger paint from one of the table tops. She looks around, satisfied at last. Then she turns out the light, locks the door, rolls down the grate, and steps into darkness. Some of the kids are playing on the sliding board, some follow her to Mount Street, where the constant drone becomes specific.

"Got them red tops."

"In the Hole."

"Death Row."

Ella watches two of the children cross Fayette Street amid a swarm of dealers scrambling to serve two white men in a pickup.

She draws her coat close and crosses Mount Street, moving once again through the corner crowd.

No sense at all.

Fran Boyd is up out of the basement early this morning, smoking the day's first Newport and watching from the top step, her usual perch, as Mount and Fayette begins to stir. Up at Mount, Buster and Country have dragged their tired carcasses to the corner and are waiting stoically for Scar to bring the package. A couple doors from Fran, Ronnie Hughes is out front as well, tinkering with the engine of his shit-brown Buick, trying to get it started on this late January morning. DeRodd's father, Michael Hearns, waits beside Ronnie wordlessly, his breath freezing above him in small soft clouds. The two are planning an expedition to a county mall, and Ronnie likes to get an early jump whenever possible. Better to get in and out before the security people are fully alert.

"Hey, Fran," Ronnie calls. An invitation.

She nods curtly, but says nothing. Sitting there in the cold, her narrow behind resting on an old sofa cushion, Fran is dressed more for fall than the deep of winter. Seemingly oblivious to the chill, she looks past Ronnie to scour the traffic around Fayette and Mount, searching for that first thin thread of a caper that can be parlayed into a vial or two of coke to go on top of the morning's blast of dope. As for a daytime boosting spree with Ronnie and Michael, she'll pass. For one thing, it hasn't been great with Michael lately; she can't remember what it was she saw in him. For another, things haven't been feeling right in the stores, what with Fran worrying about another charge and security always breathing down her neck. Instead, she settles down on the front steps of the Dew Drop, waiting for a better alternative. She sits and glares, her rock-solid, don't-tread-on-me visage offering nothing beyond raw calculation.

The front matters to Denise Francine Boyd, because the tough exterior is always an essential part of her game. Can't let anyone believe there are cracks in the facade, because facade is most of what she is about. The I-don't-give-a-shit stare, the implication of recklessness accord her a high berth in the pecking order. And like anyone else closing in on a second decade of addiction, she's also blessed with a mind that can find angles in a circle. Little Fran, all ninety-five pounds of her, is a coke-thinned wraith pushing the far side of her thirties, making it mostly on bark and only the rare bite. She has a face for the corner, armored by hard-boiled eyes that float in a sienna tea—a cold glare to deny even the suggestion of complex feelings. But behind the front is a woman with a battered, but still usable conscience—a caring soul that time and again proves itself a burdensome source of pain. Fran isn't like Bunchie, her sister; years of living together have convinced Fran that Bunchie could truly care less about anything but getting that blast. Same with Stevie. Same with Sherry, if you counted liquor.

There is Scoogie, of course, the oldest Boyd, living large a few blocks over in their grandmother's house. Scoogie has a job and a car and cable TV and air-conditioning and everything else that doesn't exist at the Dew Drop Inn. But there's distance between Fran and her brother; she can't lean on him, particularly with Scoogie insisting that he's clean now, that he hasn't been high in more than four years.

Fran doesn't believe it, and resents Scoogie for pretending to be better than she suspects he is. Still, Scoogie is living head-and-shoulders above the Dew Drop, and Fran is, therefore, by default, the closest thing to a moral force at the Fayette Street house. She's the one who ventures into the kitchen to make sandwiches for DeRodd and his nephew, Little Stevie, who makes sure the school clothes are there, who interrupts the party in the basement to go upstairs and check on Ray Ray and her heart monitor. If there's any weakness in Fran's game, in fact, it's in the vestiges of morality that her mother planted inside her, that special something the other children didn't seem to get. But that all belongs to the early years, before her father's anger managed to beat her mother down, before her mother found solace in the bottle and turned her back on Fran, before the Boyd children followed each other from malt liquor to cough syrup, weed to dope, dope to coke. So much pain, too much to think on right now.

Fran continues scanning the street, and finally, sees Tyrell post himself on the corner, hooking up with Buster and Country. Fran gives him a little wave from her doorway. He nods slightly.

Yes Lawd, she thinks, Tyrell's down for the usual. Scar will be along soon and, as Scar's lieutenant, Ty will then be in possession of the package, responsible for getting it out on the street, handling the money and the drugs while Scar sits back on rowhouse steps and eyes the action. Country and, if he's lucky, Buster, will do the touting for Scar's green tops. But it's Tyrell who will take most of the risk, and Fran knows that Tyrell is beginning to stumble, dipping into the product.

She saw him at it last month in the vestibule of her house; his body bent over, his nose dipping into his palm. Sensing her, he jerked himself erect and tried to play it off. Something in my eye, he muttered, and she just smiled.

Out here, necessity always gives birth to a caper and it wasn't long before Fran had Tyrell coming around the back of her house after Scar gave him the package, hooking up with Fran in the few minutes before he re-upped his workers. Just inside the basement door, she would shake the vials, skimming some of the coke off the top. Nobody was the wiser.

So now she waits, her eyes locked on the other half of her little conspiracy. In another minute or two, Scar turns onto Fayette Street from Gilmor and walks toward Mount. Dressed in army fatigues, a walking bill-board for his Green Tops, there isn't much flash to Scar— just a New York Boy, solitary and mysterious, a stranger to the neighborhood who showed up on the corner four or five years ago and began hustling. Nobody thought to challenge Scar because, in the end, nobody cared. His product is decent and that's what matters. Besides, rumor has the New Yorkers all wired up with heavy connections. Fuck with them, and they blow you up and move to some new corner. No one on Fayette was really all that interested in taking any chances until last year, when the Diamond in the Raw crew started stretching out, declaring that Baltimore was for Baltimore people alone. There were three or four bodies—a couple of New Yorkers and a couple locals—and Scar felt compelled to disappear for a time. But then some of the Diamond crowd got scooped up by the Feds and things cooled. Scar was soon back on post, still a stranger; no one knew his name, his family, or even where he laid his head.

Reputation and mystery aside, it is the lot of the New Yorkers—Scar, Primo, Gee Money, and the rest—to rely on the locals to sling and tout their product, and in West Baltimore, at least, good help is hard to find. Scar has a professional's sense of discipline; save for weed, he doesn't get high. Tyrell, however, is weak and Fran has found him.

Fifteen minutes later, she's up from the basement for the second time today, feeling very good indeed after reaping the benefits of her back-door confederacy. She's out on the stoop, watching Collins make a pass by the Mount Street touts in one of those new baby blue police cruisers, when Gary McCullough slips around the corner, his face aglow.

"Hey," says Gary.

"Hey," says Fran.

"Stevie upstairs?"

Fran nods and Gary starts past her. When they were together, Gary would talk forever about all this bullshit, rambling on about religion or politics or the stock market until Fran's head was pounding. Now, between them, most conversations have a utilitarian simplicity. Gary spoke to her when he had something, when he needed something, or worst of all, when he failed to get something. Lord, she couldn't stand to hear that man cry and whine.

"Want some?" he asks her on the way inside.

Fran shakes her head, thinking there ain't going to be anything to share if he's going to have Stevie cop for him. Gary was forever looking for someone else to go up to the corner on his behalf, thinking that a player with a harder look is less likely to get burned, when in fact it's always a crapshoot. And Stevie—Lord, Fran's brother might bring real dope back, but he had a dresser drawer upstairs with half a dozen syringes, each cocked and loaded with nothing stronger than tap water, each set to a different dosage—from twenty on the hype all the way to sixty. A mark like Gary would take his eyes off Stevie for half a second and the magic would never come.

Sure enough, he's downstairs on the steps ten minutes later, his ten dollars wasted and his face contorted in epic grief.

"Man," he says. "It was doo-doo."

Fran shakes her head.

"You just don't know," says Gary, wounded. "I mean, dag."

Fran snorts derisively. "Gary," she says. "You get watered-down so much you should have leaves and shit growing out your arms."

"What?"

"You a got-damn plant."

No sympathy shown. Fran is hard; she can play the corner, but Gary is another thing entirely. By Fran's reckoning, the longer he stays out here, the longer he takes abuse.

"This isn't your game," she tells him.

"Yeah," he says, bitterly. "All right."

"I'm serious. You not made for this."

"Yeah, right."

She shakes her head and Gary drifts up the block, muttering to himself. Fran watches him go, feeling an utter sense of loss. Gary has been out here for years now, but still, on some level, she cannot accept it. Though there is no love left, she still cares for him and it's hell to see him lost out here in a world for which he is totally unsuited. A part of Fran still wants to protect Gary, but the greater share of her knows there is no such thing as protection. For worse rather than better, Gary is in the mix.

His fall from grace had a slow inevitability, but there were moments when it seemed like a rush job because Gary never did anything half-heartedly. Fran actually cried the first time she saw him on the corner copping ready rock. People had been telling her for weeks that he was on the pipe, that he was up on Monroe Street every day, but she had never seen it and didn't believe it. Gary had for years been about nothing stronger than an occasional joint of weed; he had, for most of their time together, been down on Fran for her drugging. More than dope or coke, Gary was into his mysticism and cosmology, talking that high-on-life bullshit and working three jobs at once, bringing home so much money. When they were together, when DeAndre was little, Fran spent a lot of her time rushing around the county shopping malls trying to spend it, buying so many outfits and shoes, so much jewelry that she could never manage to wear it all. She just left most of it in the boxes or gave it away to friends. And DeAndre would be bouncing around the living room on Fayette Street with a $100 bill in his pocket—a child too young to even know what the cash was about. Gary would give him the money to show that he could, to make it clear to everyone that there was more than he needed.

Looking back, Fran sees that she never really appreciated what they had, that she never understood why Gary worked so hard at so many jobs. In fact, she had never really been in love with him. At best, she had loved the idea of Gary, the raw energy of this wide-eyed workaholic who couldn't stop spinning plans for them—plans that had started to take shape and very nearly became reality.

She met him sixteen years ago when he was working at the pharmacy at Lexington and Fulton, making legitimate money as a counterman and then dealing some weed on the side. Fran did what came naturally; she flirted and talked enough shit to mess his little mind. Soon enough, her weed was for free.

But the Boyds were street and Gary was, well, a McCullough. One of those churchgoing McCulloughs from Vine Street. From the first, Fran knew it was an unholy union. She saw how vulnerable he was, how little prepared he was for the real world of Fayette Street. Gary sold weed because he wanted quick money, but he was terrified of anything stronger; then he quit dealing altogether when his mother expressed her disapproval. Fran played at him for a while and Gary was enamored and willing. But he wasn't hard like the others. He didn't seem man enough to her.

They had sex exactly once before Gary went off to college in Ohio. Fran knew she was pregnant, but let him go anyway, figuring it was his due, reasoning that Gary had no real business in her world. Five months into the pregnancy, she sent a telegram to Youngstown—not to bring Gary McCullough back, but simply to let him know what he had a right to know.

To her amazement, the boy came back to West Baltimore.

And Fran Boyd had never in her life had that kind of loyalty. She had never had anyone tell her he loved her to a point where she actually started believing it. But she wasn't the right woman for Gary; she knew that much now. She wasn't ever going to be the stay-put type, the happy homemaker that he was looking for. From the moment they moved in together, Gary made it clear he wanted her to be like his mother, and Fran made it equally clear she wasn't Miss Roberta. She was the party girl and she'd been at the party ever since school days.

Gangsters and players and users peopled her world. Yet there she was playing house with Gary, a true believer, a man who embraced everything from Muslim theology to vegetarianism. He worshiped science, too, as if it was a religion, reading his high school physics text over and over, talking endlessly about the great day when he would go back to Ohio State and become an engineer.

But with DeAndre in a crib, the college plans were deferred. Still, Gary managed to manufacture a future far beyond anything Fran had ever allowed herself to imagine. The union job down at the Point became a supervisory position—$55,000 a year—and on top of that, Gary was moonlighting as a security guard out in Woodlawn. Fran had a good job downtown at the phone company and Gary was making even more money with his stocks and mutual funds. He bought the house at 1717 Fayette. He bought investment properties around the neighborhood and then he, Blue, and Blue's brother started Lightlaw, their development and drafting company. Gary bought Fran a Mercedes. Bought himself another. Bought all kinds of things for Fran and DeAndre and everyone else.

At first Fran loved it. She tried harder to love Gary, and for a time, all things seemed not only possible, but certain. But thinking back, Fran can remember a pivotal moment somewhere back in '80 or '81, a point at which she really had to decide. DeAndre was three or four, almost school age, and they were considering a house out over the city line in Catonsville, a suburban spread like those acquired by the older McCullough children, who were using new money and new opportunity to escape Fayette Street. Gary wanted that life, too; Fran balked. She couldn't see herself out there where Gary wanted her, tooling around some kitchen counter with an apron on. No parties, no drama, no corners—that wasn't her at all.

They stayed in the house on Fayette Street instead, and the neighborhood began to wear at them the way it wears at everyone. Soon, the weed and beer and pills were the sum of all days. She was twenty-four and living with Gary on the day she truly found her future—the day they buried her sister, Darlene. That, too, would have been '80 or '81 if she remembered right, and Fran was out-of-her-mind grieving at the wake when a family friend brought dope to her for the first time.

"Do a line of this," he told her.

Three years older than Fran, Darlene had died in a house fire at 1625 Fayette, burned over eighty percent of her body in the same back bedroom where Fran was now laying her head. On the day of the wake, she put her head down on that mirror, snorted all she could of that powder and came up forgetting that her sister was dead. The same friend came looking for Fran the next day, found her, and gave her the same. The day after that, he didn't come. The day after that, Fran went looking for the friend.

After a time, she got so she'd keep the shit right by her bed, do some of it the first thing every morning before getting dressed in her downtown clothes. She didn't even know she had a habit until the dose wasn't there one morning and she realized she was too hungry to go to work without it. Sick in the mornings and missing work, or happily indifferent and cursing her supervisors, Fran kept messing up until the phone company fired her; the union did precious little to prevent it.

When he couldn't find a future in Fran, Gary, too, began to lose himself on Fayette Street. At first he fought with her over the drugging. And when he laid hands on her, she moved out, telling herself that she wouldn't be beaten as her mother had been beaten. Gary wandered off in search of other women and new religions and a half-dozen other schemes—all of it delaying the inevitable crash. And when nothing else worked, Gary chose, consciously and deliberately, to lose himself in dope and coke. The jobs and the cars and the houses were stripped away and, in the end, he and Fran were both scraping bottom—separate, yet together—moving to the same tired rhythms.

The neighborhood blamed her for what had happened to Gary. Bullshit, she told herself. As if the two of them didn't make their own choices; as if she had some kind of power over Gary that he didn't have over himself; as if she didn't have enough problems of her own.

What she couldn't stand about Gary was the pity parties he would throw for himself, the crying and complaining about how he once had it all and how he had been betrayed. Like today, when he wanders off bitching and moaning at the injustice of it all, at having been watered down, as if anyone out here had any guarantee of fair treatment. Outwardly, at least, Fran would never let anyone see her show hurt that way. With no regrets, she ran her own games on people when she could, and she couldn't really blame anyone who managed to run a game on her. It pissed her off when Gary came to her with his wounds. She couldn't make it better for herself; how was she going to help Gary?

For another hour, she watches the ebb and flow on Mount and Fayette, watches as the touts sell out, then re-up, then sell out again, watches as the knockers roll up to the carryout, jack the corner boys against the wall and come up empty. Every day, the street parade passes in front of these steps and every day, rain or shine or snow, Fran is outside to watch it pass.

She misses precious little. Too many years on Fayette Street have provided her with an extra sense, a hunter's instinct that allows her to see things on the street that would be lost on an outsider. Without a scorecard, she knows at any given moment who is selling for whom, who is stealing from whom, who is about to get hurt, and who will do the hurting. Fran can spot confrontations and connections a block away; it's her stock-in-trade, an acquired gift that allows her an edge. Like now, when she glances two full blocks down Fayette Street and picks up the outline of a teenage boy—one in a group of four—crossing the asphalt with a stiff-legged gait.

DeAndre. With R.C. and Dorian and Boo, probably.

If he tries to tell her he was in school today, he's got a surprise coming,

she thinks. Expecting him to go straight to Fairmount, she's surprised
when he peels off from the group and heads her way.

"Why you not in school?"

"Half-day."

"Half-day? It's not even eleven."

"Half half-day," he assures her.

"Andre, you is a trip," she says, shaking her head. "All that work to
get back into Francis Woods, and here you at, running the streets."

"My teachers let me out," he insists.

"Please," says Fran.

He shrugs. Not every lie need be believed; some are spoken simply
as a formality.

"You got cigarettes?" she asks.

"Not for you."

"Lemme have one," she insists.

DeAndre ignores her and walks to the carryout. She smolders as
she watches him go. Goddamn if he doesn't think he's the little king of
everything. He goes out on the corner for a week or two, gets some
money in his pocket and thinks he's some kind of man. And it's worse,
she thinks, since he put Bugsy on me. DeAndre thought he'd backed her
down because of that shit. Fuck no, that wasn't the way it played at all.
Of course, he don't know that, the little shit.

Three weeks back, Bugsy had showed up at the front steps, asking for
Fran, asking for the sixty-five vials and two hundred in cash that she had
found in the closet. Like the other New Yorkers, Bugsy generally kept his
business to himself. But when there was a problem, he came right at you.

"Black says you took my stuff," said Bugsy, using DeAndre's favorite
street name. The dealer was softspoken and very calm, strangely so for
someone no older than twenty. Fran still couldn't believe her son—who
had put her in, and worse, she was unnerved by Bugsy's seeming reason-
ableness. If he had come on strong, Fran would have known how to deal
with that. But the quiet certainty in Bugsy's play was scary—not only
for Fran, but for her child. As pissed as she was at DeAndre, she had to
think about both ends. Bugsy could come back on him.

"He shouldn't've brought it in my house."

"That's between him and you. I want what's mine."

"Look," she said, quickly reasonable herself. "I can get you the gun
back, but I ain't got the money or the stuff. If you're going to hurt him,
I can pay you back, but I'm going to need some time."

Bugsy mulled it over for a moment. "Get me the gun. He'll pay me back the money. He only owes me sixty from the last one."

"Okay. I'll get the gun and give it to him."

"That'll work," he agreed, still very relaxed.

Things had evened out since then. Fran knew DeAndre believed she had learned her limit; Fran, however, was merely biding time. If her son brought more of his misadventure into her home, she would pluck him good. And while Fran knew she had provoked the crisis by stealing the stash, she told herself that she had, in the end, proved herself a mother by protecting DeAndre from the wrath of his supplier.

Not that he knew any of that, strutting around here like Big Daddy Kane. DeAndre wasn't humble by nature, and he was at his worst with a little money in his pocket. Yet even from inside the heroin fog, Fran knew she had pushed her son into open rebellion, that his time on the corner was as much about her drugging as it was it was about status or money.

The boy had lived in the equivalent of a shooting gallery for the last three years. He was old enough now to judge her and to act on that judgment. By degrees, he had rendered his verdict and established himself apart from her. And his new universe, Fairmount and Gilmor, offered a ready-made haven for a child in full rebellion. For a time, she had railed against it, trying at every turn to retain her authority, to demand that DeAndre do as she told him, not as she herself did. Last year, when he was slinging, she put him out of the house only to watch him set up his little clubroom up at 1717. Last month she tried to lay down some law and ended up breaking a broom handle over his head. DeAndre simply wrested the stump from her grip and backed her against the kitchen wall, menacing her, letting her know his strength before laughing loudly and stalking off.

In DeAndre's mind, Fran knows, there is the notion that at fifteen years, he's a man. Her son is by no means cutting the ties with her; they are still family, to be sure, but he is no longer letting her treat him as her child. The change infuriates Fran. And it pains her.

Because in ways that matter, Fran tells herself, she's been a real mother to DeAndre and DeRodd. True, the coke and dope haven't left much money for new high-tops or weekend movies or Sega Genesis games. Still, her habit has never clouded her love for her sons, and she knows they both feel it. The back bedroom isn't much, but her children have never been without a place to lay their heads. Nor has there been a day when they went hungry, or left the house without school clothes. Time and again, she feels, she has proven herself a mother to DeAndre by standing with him against the city bureaucracies. She's been there for the meetings with the vice principals and for the suspension hearings at the school headquarters on North Avenue. She's been there at the precincts to take custody of him after every arrest, or at the juvenile hearings at the courthouse downtown. She's been there with him at Bon Secours and University Hospital, there in the emergency room for the skinned knees and broken bones, the asthma attacks and kitchen burns. And she's always been there for him in the quiet moments, when he would lose his bluster and let his fears show, when he needed to be stroked and comforted.

She isn't consistent; she knows that. In calmer moments, Fran can readily admit to shortcomings, citing her failures as a parent with cold precision. But she will argue in the next breath—and argue with some validity—that her sons are better off than so many others who are running loose on Fayette Street, raising each other in packs on the corners, making up the rules as they stumble through the shards of broken childhood. Dink-Dink, for instance, who at thirteen is already a stone sociopath, out on the corners at all hours, shooting at grown men over drug debts, or disrespect, or simply for the sheer joy of pulling the trigger. Or Dink-Dink's running buddies, Fat Eric and Lamont— children crazed enough to fire pellet guns at passing police cars or to storm into the Korean carryout with their zippers open, waving their equipment at customers and the embarrassed counter girls. Or the twins—Arnold and Ronald, the oldest sons of Gary's girl, Ronnie—who left school at fourteen to run wild. Two years from now, they will be keeping house in an apartment on Fairmount, an address they'll acquire when the adult occupant is sent to jail. The twins will kick in a back window, then come and go as they please, their days occupied with the sale of drugs along Gilmor Street, their nights spent turning the apartment into an amusement park for the rest of the neighborhood kids. Fetid trash will be left where it's dropped; human feces in the corners, bullet holes in every kitchen appliance, chair, and wall. And all of it will go on with their mother in the apartment directly below, concerned with nothing beyond her high.

The Dink-Dinks and Fat Erics of the neighborhood were a year or two behind DeAndre and his contemporaries, but even among the Fayette Street regulars they are regarded as a wild, new breed: violent, unsocialized, devoid of responsibility, without connection to family or friends or even to themselves. And while Dink-Dink and his crew mark the first wave, the disaster is clearly accelerating. Younger packs are already making their mark in this neighborhood; Old Man and Chubb, for example, are already up on the corners at nine or ten years, running for the Mount Street dealers.

Fran has given DeAndre and DeRodd more than that. Even now, though lost in addiction, there are things that she won't do:

She won't put her kids out on the corner to work a package for her benefit; that DeAndre is on Fairmount is his own decision and against her will. She won't hold DeAndre's drugs, or hide his gun, or teach him what she knows about how to cut dope or stretch a package into better profit. She won't wink at his misadventures on the corner, allying herself with his cause for the sake of the dollars or vials that might come to her. She hates that he is already on the corner; she hates listening to the gunshots that echo from Fairmount and Gilmor at night, wondering if the ambo siren is for DeAndre or if the police wagon racing around the corner has been called for her son. She hates that he's already smoking those big Philly blunts, starting out with $10 bags of weed, the same way she did. She can't stop any of it, of course; she's compromised, a parent without proper standing. But neither will she give it the sanction so many others do.

Nor will her sons be seen eating at the soup kitchen at St. Martin's so that their mother can spend the food money on drugs. DeAndre will not suffer Easter without a new outfit and a new pair of Nike Airs; DeRodd won't mark his birthday without a cake, or Christmas without some kind of toy. These things matter to Fran, who can tell herself that she manages to keep just enough balance in a world that is tumbling all over the place. And by that thin standard, she's entirely correct: Where so many others have given up entirely, Fran Boyd is still a mother to her children.

Not that Andre acknowledges it. Now that he's out from under her wing, taking what she's given as his due, he demands more, and his manner turns sullen and pouting when more isn't forthcoming. I'm on my own out here, DeAndre likes to tell his friends. Nobody does nothing for me.

He just doesn't know. Fran is tempted to put him out again like she did last summer, or at least charge him some rent if he's not going to go to school. What she ought to do—what she would like to do—is whip his ass good. But those days are long gone.

So all right then, she tells him in an imagined rant, you're a big boy now. You're the man. You just go ahead and play it like that and the next time Collins gets out of a police car to kick your ass, you're on your own. And the next time they call me from the school about one of your fuck-ups, you're not going to have me down there lying for you. And the next time you're downtown for a juvenile hearing, you won't see me. Your ass'll get flat on that courthouse bench waiting for your mother to show.

Fran pumps herself full of indignation, squirming on that crushed couch cushion now, aching to pounce the next time he rolls past her steps. She's had her fill; her eyes flash anger as she looks up toward Mount Street and sees DeAndre stepping from the carryout. Look at him, she thinks, all wrapped up in himself, as if it's all about him. Fuck that.

Halfway down the block, DeAndre seems to sense her glare and quickly locks into it, goading her with a blank stare of his own as he moves toward her. He slows his pace, but his eyes never waver. Fran rises as DeAndre nears the foot of the stoop, his hands buried deep in his coat pockets. He barely breaks stride as one hand snakes out and tosses her a small paper bag, which she catches instinctively.

Smokes. She shakes her head. "Why you play me that way?"

DeAndre laughs, walking on toward Fairmount.

"Damn you, Dre," she shouts. "Get back here."

But DeAndre ignores her.

Shit, says Fran to herself, glumly peeling the cellophane from the pack. Why he got to be like that? Always setting her up just to knock her back down. Always letting her see the worst in him, and then, at the last possible moment, coming through with a little bit of heart.

Like this last Christmas Eve, when the money was gone and DeRodd had his Santa list of toys all written out. Fran felt like she had no choice and rode the bus out to Reisterstown Mall, then raced through the stores on a last-minute boosting spree. She was just starting to get it done, too, until she forgot to take the security tags from several items, setting off alarms as she left one store. One mall guard actually chased her into the parking lot and Fran just managed to get on a southbound M.T.A. Scared and breathing hard, she looked back over her shoulder and saw one of them jawing into his walkie-talkie. A few blocks farther, when a police cruiser pulled alongside the bus, Fran slipped out the rear doors, turned a corner, and got so damn lost in Northwest Baltimore that by the time she made her way home, the stores were closed.

Thinking on it now, she can remember climbing the steps to that back room in the worst kind of mood, kicking herself for letting it slide to the eleventh hour, dreading the look in DeRodd's eyes. She went drag-ass into the bedroom to find DeAndre on the bed watching television, a pile of shopping bags on the floor in front him.

"Wassup," he said.

It was all there—everything on DeRodd's wish list and more besides, all of it purchased with the cash from Fairmount Avenue. Fran was overwhelmed.

"Thought you might be havin' some trouble," her son said.

"I was."

And that time, DeAndre didn't play it for pride or advantage. He didn't shame her. If anything, he was a little embarrassed by it all. She reached across the bed, tugging on his shirt sleeve, pulling his head next to hers. No words, but a quick embrace. A connection.

Damned if that wasn't DeAndre, too. Hardheaded, arrogant, sullen —but at moments he could step outside of himself, drop the game face, and be capable of anything. Fran smiles at the memory; her boy is a trip.

She watches him turn the corner at Gilmor, pulling his denims back up over his ass and hunkering himself into his lock-legged strut. If I could get past this, she thinks, if I could get myself clean, there would still be time and I could make it right with him.

She's so wrapped in her thoughts that she's holding the cigarette pack in the open, tapping one out with half the corner watching. Damn.

"Can I get one?"

"Huh?" she says, slow to recover.

"A smoke?"

"Hmmm," she grunts, giving it up.

"Hey Fran . . ."

And another.

"Borrow one?"

And another still. This corner soaks up Newports like a dry sponge; she had to be a damn fool to be sitting out here with a whole pack in her hands.

"Yo, Fran . . ."

"Got-damn, Stevie, I done gave away half the pack."

Her brother shrugs, wounded.

"Here," says Fran, pulling out a last giveaway and putting the rest in her pocket. Stevie lights up off her own.

"Ronnie's back," he says.

That he is. Fran watches Ronnie Hughes and Michael Hearns roll up Fayette and park the Buick just across the street. Car doors swing open and the two men get out slowly, smiling, stretching like athletes on the sidewalk before walking back to the car trunk. Must be good, thinks Fran.

Ronnie opens up and the two men lift out the items on the very top of the pile—women's dresses and men's sportswear, the store tags flapping up in the winter wind. They're standing there in the middle of Fayette Street, holding the shit up in the air by the curl of the hangers, displaying it with pride for the crowd at Mount and Fayette. The day's catch.

"Ain't this a bitch," says Fran, smiling.

Michael walks toward her, his arm extended, his hand gripping an evening dress as if it's a five-pound bass. Fran notices the Macy's label. Not bad at all, she has to admit.

"Look at you," she says.

Michael grins. A breadwinner.

"We can sell this shit," she assures him.

Already, her mind is a step ahead. Where to sell it. What to ask. What to settle for and what to take for her cut. Out here on Fayette Street, the party never ends.

TWO

We can't stop it.

Not with all the lawyers, guns, and money in this world. Not with guilt or morality or righteous indignation. Not with crime summits, or task forces, or committees. Not with policy decisions made in places that can't be seen from the lost corner of Fayette and Monroe. No lasting victory in the war on drugs can be bought by doubling the number of beat cops or tripling the number of prison beds. No peace can come from kingpin statutes and civil forfeiture laws and warrantless searches and whatever the hell else is about to be tossed into next year's omnibus crime bill.

Down on Fayette Street, they know.

Today as on every other day, the shop will be open by midmorning and the touts will be on the corners, chirping out product names as if the stuff is street legal. The runners will bring a little more of the package down and the fiends will queue up to be served—a line of gaunt, passive supplicants stretching down the alley and around the block.

The corner is rooted in human desire—crude and certain and immediate. And the hard truth is that all the law enforcement in the world can't mess with desire. Down at Fayette and Monroe and every corner like it in Baltimore, the dealers and fiends have won because they are legion. They've won because the state of Maryland and the federal government have imprisoned thousands and arrested tens of thousands and put maybe a hundred thousand on the parole and probation rolls—and still it isn't close to enough. By raw demographics, the men and women of the corners can claim victory. In Baltimore alone—a city of fewer than seven hundred thousand souls, with some of the highest recorded rates of intravenous drug use in the nation—they are fifty, perhaps even sixty thousand strong—three of them for every available prison bed in the entire state of Maryland. The slingers are manning more than a hundred open-air corners, serving up product as fast as they can get it off a southbound Metroliner. And the fiends are chasing down that blast twenty-four, seven.

In neighborhoods where no other wealth exists, they have constructed an economic engine so powerful that they'll readily sacrifice everything to it. And make no mistake: that engine is humming. No slacking profit margins, no recessions, no bad quarterly reports, no layoffs, no naturalized unemployment rate. In the empty heart of our cities, the culture of drugs has created a wealth-generating structure so elemental and enduring that it can legitimately be called a social compact.

From the outside looking in, it's tempting to see this nightmare as a model of supply and demand run amok, as a lawlessness bred from an unenforceable prohibition. But the reckoning at Fayette and Monroe and other places like it has grown into something greater than the medical mechanics of addiction, greater even than the dollars and sense of economic theory.

Get it straight: they're not just out here to sling and shoot drugs. That's where it all began, to be sure, but thirty years has transformed the corner into something far more lethal and lasting than a simple marketplace. The men and women who live the corner life are redefining themselves at incredible cost, cultivating meaning in a world that has declared them irrelevant. At Monroe and Fayette, and in drug markets in cities across the nation, lives without any obvious justification are given definition through a simple, self-sustaining capitalism. The corner has a place for them, every last soul. Touts, runners, lookouts, mules, stickup boys, stash stealers, enforcers, fiends, burn artists, police snitches—all are necessary in the world of the corner. Each is to be used, abused, and ultimately devoured with unfailing precision. In this place only, they belong. In this place only, they know what they are, why they are, and what it is that they are supposed to do. Here, they almost matter.

On Fayette Street today, the corner world is what's left to serve up truth and power, money and meaning. It gives life and takes life. It measures all men as it mocks them. It feeds and devours the multitudes in the same instant. Amid nothing, the corner is everything.

We want it to be about nothing more complicated than cash money and human greed, when at bottom, it's about a reason to believe. We want to think that it's chemical, that it's all about the addictive mind, when instead it has become about validation, about lost souls assuring themselves that a daily relevance can be found at the fine point of a disposable syringe.

It's about the fiends, thousands of them, who want that good dope, need it the way other souls need to breathe air. Working men on their lunch hour come here, rubbing up against corner dwellers who haven't seen a job in ten years. White boys from county high schools, quietly praying they won't get burned for their allowance, stand next to welfare mothers who petition the same god on behalf of their check-day money. Up on Monroe Street, there's a ninety-one-year-old retiree in the line handing his cash to fourteen-year-old slingers. And down the hill on Mount, there's that prim little matron who shows up in her Sunday best—print dress, heels, white pillbox hat and veil—a churchgoing woman shuttling between choir and corner. And every other day on Mount or Gilmor Streets, the regulars get a glimpse of that tired little white girl from downtown, the one with the bloated hands who everyone says is some kind of lawyer. Black niggers, white niggers—you get down here at ground zero and, finally, the racial obsessions don't mean anything. With twenty on the hype hanging in the balance, there's only the perfect equality of need and desire. Here on Fayette Street, the fiends wait the wait, praying for the same righteous connect, taking a chance and carrying a little piece of the package away. Then they fire up and feel that wave roll and crest.

And it's about the slingers, the young crews working the packages, all of them willing to trade a morality that they've never seen or felt for a fleeting moment of material success. And, true, the money is its own argument—not punch-the-clock, sweep-the-floor, and wait-for-next-Friday money, but cash money, paid out instantly to the vacant-eyed kids serving the stuff. Still, they are working the package with the hidden knowledge that they will fall, that with rare exception, the money won't last and the ride will be over in six months, or four, or three. They all do it not so much for the cash—which they piss away anyhow—but for a brief sense of self. All of them are cloaked in the same gangster dream, all of them cursed by the lie that says they finally have a stake in something. By such standards, the corner proves itself every day. That it destroys whatever it touches hardly matters; for an instant in time, at least, those who serve the corners have standing and purpose.

This is an existential crisis rooted not only in race—which the corner has slowly transcended—but in the unresolved disaster of the American rust-belt, in the slow, seismic shift that is shutting down the assembly lines, devaluing physical labor, and undercutting the union pay scale. Down on the corner, some of the walking wounded used to make steel, but Sparrows Point isn't hiring the way it once did. And some used to load the container ships at Seagirt and Locust Point, but the port isn't what she used to be either. Others worked at Koppers, American Standard, or Armco, but those plants are gone now. All of which means precious little to anyone thriving in the postindustrial age. For those of us riding the wave, the world spins on an axis of technological prowess in an orbit of ever-expanding information. In that world, the men and women of the corner are almost incomprehensibly useless and have been so for more than a decade now.

How do we bridge the chasm? How do we begin to reconnect with those now lost to the corner world? As a beginning, at least, we need to shed our fixed perceptions and see it fresh, from the inside. We've got to begin to think as Gary McCullough thinks when he's flat broke and sick with desire, crawling through some vacant rowhouse in search of scrap metal. Or live, for a moment at least, as Fat Curt lives when he's staggering back and forth between corner and shooting gallery. Or feel as Hungry feels when he's out there on a Monroe Street stoop, watching and waiting and gathering himself up for the moment when he'll creep down the alley and, for the third time that week, grab up some New York Boy's ground stash, consigning himself to yet another bloody beating because stash-snatching is a caper he knows, and blood or no blood, Hungry will have his daily blast.

We need to start over, to admit that somehow the forces of history and race, economic theory and human weakness have conspired to create a new and peculiar universe in our largest cities. Our rules and imperatives don't work down here. We've got to leave behind the useless baggage of a society and culture that still maintains the luxury of reasonable judgments. Against all the sanction we can muster, this new world is surviving, expanding, consuming everything in its path. To insist that it should be otherwise on the merits of some external morality is to provoke a futile debate. In West Baltimore or East New York, in North Philly or South Chicago, they're not listening anymore, so how can our best arguments matter?

Consider the corner, for a moment, as something apart from a social disaster, as something that has instead become organic and central within our cities. In the natural world, much is often made of the watering hole, the oasis in a small stand of acacia trees to which creatures great and small come for sustenance. The life-giving elixir brings them all—predators and prey, the vast herds and the solitary wanderers, the long of tooth and those new to this vale. Brick and mortar, asphalt and angles—the corner is no less elemental to the inner cities of America. Day and night they come, lured by coke and dope, ignoring the risks and dangers as any animal in need of a life force must. Wildebeests and zebras, no; the predominant herds on this veld are the hollow-eyed gunners and pipers, driven to the water's edge by a thirst that cries out from every last cell, each doper or coke fiend reassured against risk by the anonymity of the crowd, by the comfort that greater numbers allow. There are the big cats, the dealers, who rule the turf on reputation and occasional savagery, and the jackals who follow them: burn artists and stash stealers roaming the fringe, feeding on the weak and inattentive. The hyenas, the stickup boys, are nocturnal outcasts whose only allegiance is to opportunity itself. Lumbering elephants? The police, perhaps, who are heard from a distance and arrive with bombast. They rule only where they stand.

Once, it was altogether different. Generations back, it was a hipster's game, a fringe hustle played out in basements and after-hours clubs. The dope peddlers were few—and anathema; the users cool and carried by bebop rhythms, their addiction more or less a function of social rebellion or alienation. And the numbers? If there were two thousand addicts in the Baltimore of 1958, then the city police department's three-officer narcotics squad had its hands full. But came the 1960s, and that early innocence was followed hard by the heroin wave that crested in every East Coast city.

In Baltimore, there were $1 capsules for sale in all the Pennsylvania Avenue nightspots, and a single dollar of that ancient shit would drop a dope fiend for the entire day. Demand moved beyond the musicians and beats, out into the back alleys, inching its way toward a handful of corners in the worst housing projects. East side, west side—the dealers, once defiantly anonymous, became success stories for an increasingly alienated ghetto world, bona fide gangster caricatures with territories and soldiers and reputations. Little Melvin, Big Lucille, Gangster Webster, Kid Henderson, Liddie Jones, Snyder Blanchard—these West Baltimore names still ring in the ears of the older players and fiends, names that produced organizations and inspired the next generation of street dealers.

Overnight, the money got serious. The users, an army unto themselves, were serviced daily in back alleys and housing project stairwells
by men who were, on some level, careerists, committed to distribution
networks that paid them, protected them, paid their bails, and took care
of their people when they went away to Hagerstown or Jessup. These
men were professional in outlook, lethal but not reckless, and by and
large, they lived with an acknowledged code, to wit:

They didn't use what they sold. They didn't serve children or use
children to serve, just as they wouldn't sell to wide-eyed virgins looking
to skin-pop for the first time. They carried the threat of violence like a
cloak, but in the end, they didn't shoot someone unless someone needed
to get shot. When a bullet was necessary, there were always pros available—Dennis Wise or Vernon Collins by name—men willing, in the
Pennsylvania Avenue gangster parlance, to get in close, take aim, and
hit the right nigger. What was bad for business was hunted with a
vengeance: stickup boys, if they survived, carried a bounty on their heads;
burn artists were driven deep into the shadows.

This earlier generation stayed serious, cautious. On a business level
at least, they understood responsibility and were therefore responsible
with the package. More often than not, the count was exactly right and
all the cash got turned over on time. They took precautions; they wouldn't
sell to just anyone who came past. They knew what a dope fiend looked
like. If they didn't know your name or face, they'd check your shoe
leather, your clothes, your build, the veins on your arms—all of it was
scrutinized because, in the end, it was pure humiliation for them to serve
a police. They were a fixture in the neighborhood, but they were discreet.
They took your money, but ten minutes might pass and they'd be half
a block away before some other drone handed you the glassine bag. They
could jail if they had to, but they tried their damnedest to stay out of
the cuffs. To them, a charge was something to be avoided at all costs,
and, by and large, when a charge came, they didn't snitch; they worked
the lawyers to limit the time.

By the mid-1970s, a succession of federal task forces had knocked
down most of the name dealers: Melvin was in Lewisburg; Liddie, in
Marion; Gangster Webster would soon fall to a fifty-year bit; Kid
Henderson was dead and Big Lucille Wescott, dying. But the seeds they
planted surpassed them and grew to maturity. Their children numbered
in the tens of thousands and were now down on the neighborhood
corners, no longer a mere irritant on the periphery, but out in the open

and in full opposition to the community. The organized drug rings shifted, merged, diverged, then shifted again. Still, on some basic level, the code was maintained—at least until the coke came.

Cocaine changed the world.

The heroin trade was limited to the hardcore, but the arrival of cheap, plentiful cocaine in the early and mid-1980s broke down all the barriers and let everyone play. Both are white powder, but each has a distinct, pharmacological flavor: Dope is the downer, the heavy; a couple of trips to the corner, a $20 investment and a fiend has enough in him to suffer the day. Coke is the rush to the wire, all of it gone in a flash and never enough to slake that thirst. With heroin, even the hungriest fiend can look to a limit; coke demands that every bill that can be begged or borrowed or stolen goes up to the corner. And unless a fiend is set on firing speed-balls, coke can go in clean—no need for any squeamishness about the syringe. A pipe and a nugget of ready rock does fine; even a quick snort is enough for the rush. In the beginning, they said it wasn't even addictive— not like dope anyway; they called it "girl" or "Jane" or "Missy" in feminine contrast to "boy" or "John" or "Mister" for king heroin.

But coke has a power all its own. When coke hit Baltimore in the mid-1980s, it went beyond the existing addict population, gathering a new market share, for the first time bringing the women to the corner in startling numbers. More white boys came for it, too, some of them from the hillbilly neighborhoods just down the hill, others from the farthest reaches of suburbia. And many of them kept coming back— four or five times an hour—feeding their frenzy until the money ran out. And where once the coke fiends began their tour with a snort, by the late eighties most of the trade was on the pipe, smoking up that boiled-down rock. Crack, they called it in New York. Ready rock, cried the Fayette Street touts. Got that ready.

By the turn of the decade, the survivors graduated to speedballs, mainlining the coke and dope together for the ultimate rush. The heroin was the base; it leveled you out and got you well. The coke went on top, for that extra boost that morphine always lacked. Baltimore stumbled and staggered through the decade-long cocaine epidemic, emerging in the mid-1990s as the city with the highest rate of intravenous drug use in the country, according to government estimates. And of the tens of thousands of hardcore users, the vast majority were using coke and dope simultaneously. Even those fearful of the needle could find snorting-heroin that was 60 percent pure, then top that off with a pipeful of ready.

Old-time dopers were disgusted. To them, heroin alone seemed a reasoned lifestyle choice when compared to the havoc that followed. Watching the pipers and speedballers get bum-rushed on the corners, they would shake their heads and mutter. Even to them, it was low-bottom addiction. Even to them, it was pathetic.

With heroin alone, the sources of supply seemed finite and organizational; access was limited to those with a genuine connection to the New York suppliers, who had, in turn, cultivated a connection to a small number of importers. The cocaine epidemic changed that as well, creating a freelance market with twenty-year-old wholesalers supplying seventeen-year-old dealers. Anyone could ride the Amtrak or the Greyhound to New York and come back with a package. By the late eighties, the professionals were effectively marginalized in Baltimore; cocaine and the open market made the concept of territory irrelevant to the city drug trade.

It didn't stop there either. Cocaine kicked the dealer's code in the ass, because as the organizations gave way, so did standards. On every corner, street dealers began using minors, first as lookouts and runners, then as street-level slingers. In the beginning, these were the toughest kids, the criminal prodigies born and bred in the most distressed families, welcomed by dealers who were contending with stiffened penalties for sale. It made sense to hire juveniles for the street work: Why risk a five-year bit when any fifteen-year-old with heart could sling vials, take a charge, then carry whatever weight a juvenile court master might put on him?

It was a reasonable strategy at first, but ten years down the road the internal logic was no longer valid—amid chronic prison overcrowding, few adults were getting time for street-level drug distribution in Baltimore; probation and pretrial time served was the order of the day. Yet the children stayed on the corners, not so much as camouflage, but because good help was hard to find.

The code had failed: the touts, the runners, even the street-level dealers were violating the cardinal rule and using their own product. And not just dope—which might have permitted some stability—but coke, or coke and dope together; the pipeheads graduated to heroin, the dope fiends speedballed. And somewhere in this wild cocktail party, the packages started coming up short, the money began disappearing, and the touts and lookouts were suddenly wandering off post. Down on Fayette Street, reliability was out the window and not even the threat of violence could stop Country from putting a quarter of Scar's package up his nose, or Eggy Daddy from claiming that he had to give sixty dollars of Gee Money's profit to some imaginary stickup boy. What was a slinger to do?

The children weren't exactly captains of industry either; they'd mess up in their own way, if you let them. But most weren't using anything harder than weed, and most were ready and willing to work conscientiously for a bit of pocket money. In contrast to the hardcore fiends, dealers came to see that you could extract some loyalty from adolescents, or intimidate them if necessary. The teenagers would, in turn, bring in younger kids to sling and run for them, until, at last, the day of the ten-year-old drug dealer was at hand.

The trend only accelerated as more young mothers went to the corner chasing coke, and single-parent families already under pressure began to implode. More than heroin ever did, cocaine battered at what had for generations been the rock-hard foundation for the urban black family. Heroin had been claiming its share of West Baltimore men for thirty years, but the cheap cocaine of the 1980s had turned the women out, bringing them to the corner in numbers previously unthinkable. Where once, on Fayette Street, there had been a network of single mothers who managed to get the essentials done, there was now raw anarchy in many homes. And where a discussion of single-parent households once seemed relevant to places like Fayette Street, now there loomed the new specter of children who were, in reality, parentless.

Unattended and undisciplined, these children were raising themselves in the street, free to begin their inexorable drift, drawn not only by quick money, but by the game of it. Thirteen-year-olds who had cut classes and played hoops and run the back alleys together now banded together as a crew, playing gangster, slinging vials, and ducking the police. In West Baltimore, the corner became the funhouse, offering camaraderie and standing and adventure. What, after all, could compete with the thrill of suddenly being The Man, of having your own bomb of a package on a corner, standing there under the sodium-vapor lights as grown men and women seek you out and commence to begging? This one wants a job as a tout; this one is short four bills and asking to slide; that one offers her body for three vials. And in the end, it wasn't just the valedictorians of Hickey School and Boys Village and every other state juvenile facility out there on the corner, it was all save the stoop kids— the well-parented few who weren't allowed beyond their front steps. All across the inner city—from Lafayette Courts to Sandtown to Cherry Hill—slinging drugs was the rite of passage.

When children became the labor force, the work itself became child-like, and the organizational structure that came with heroin's first wave was a historical footnote. In the 1990s, the drug corner is modeled on nothing more complicated than a fast-food emporium, an environment in which dealing drugs requires about as much talent and finesse as serving burgers. No discretion, no precautions; the modern corner has no need for the applied knowledge of previous generations.

Where once a competent street dealer would never be caught touching the dope, the more brainless of his descendants now routinely carries the shit in one pocket, money in the other. Wiser souls might work a ground stash—a small inventory of coke or dope hidden in the weeds or rubbish a few feet away—but ten minutes after selling out, they'll be out under a streetlight, counting their grip, manicuring the $10 and $5 bills into a clean roll and fairly begging for the attentions of a knocker or stickup artist. Close scrutiny of customers has become anachronism, too. The new school serves anyone—known fiends and strangers, ragged or well-heeled, white or black, young or old, in battered pickups or fresh-off-the-lot BMWs—with an indifference as careless as it is democratic.

The precision and subtlety of the game have been replaced by raw retailing—open-air bazaars with half a dozen crews out on post, barking the names of their product like Lexington Market grocers. Corners are crowded with competing crews, each pushing the claim that their own product is true and righteous. With heroin, labels are stamped right on the glassine packet: Killer Bee, Lethal Weapon, The Terminator, Diamond in the Raw, Tec Nine. Free testers are tossed out every morning as word-of-mouth advertising for the coming package, and the touts are constantly trumpeting blue-light specials: two for the price of one, or a free vial of coke with every dime of dope, or family-size packets offering much more blast for just a little more cash. Where only $10 vials of coke are being sold, a fresh crew can carve a niche with a $5 offering. And if one crew's product is too good to match straight up, a competing group might lace its package with a little strychnine—a bomb that might or might not drop a fiend dead, but definitely gets his attention either way.

Dealers and fiends alike go about this business with a herdlike trust in their own overwhelming numbers to protect them from the random drug arrest. Violence, too, is no longer the prerogative of the profes-sional but a function of impulse and emotion. The contract killers and the well-planned assassinations of earlier eras are mere myth on these corners. Now, the moment of truth generally comes down to some manchild with hurt feelings waving a .380 around and spraying bullets up and down the block. The accidental shooting of bystanders—a rare event in the organizational era—is now commonplace. As for snitching, that part of the code is also dead and buried. No organizational ethic makes sense when everyone is shorting and getting shorted by everyone else, when loyalty is absent even within a crew that grew up together. In the new order, anyone can and will say anything for even the smallest advantage.

When the arrests come, they are regarded as routine misadventures, small setbacks that in most cases mean little more than a few nights on a city jail tier, followed by an appointment with a state probation officer that is, more often than not, ignored. Worse still, the absence of a real deterrent has bred a stupidity in the new school that is, for lack of a better word, profound. Few seem to learn from the experience of getting caught; they take the same charge time and again, jacked up by the same police who use the same tricks to gather the same evidence from the same corners. At times, the younger ones senselessly provoke the charge through pride and bluster as no old-timer would; eyefuck for eyefuck, curse for curse, insult for insult, until Collins or Pitbull or Peanuthead is out of the cruiser and swinging the nightstick hard, enraged at being called a bitch by some seventeen-year-old hopper.

Once charged, there is no strategy or defense, nothing for the lawyers to work with, no attempt to limit time because, in most cases, there is no time. When someone does finally go away for a year or two on a fourth or fifth offense, well, it's all in the game. Prison itself is regarded with vague indifference: The operant corner logic is that the hardcore gangster stance is what matters, that if it's time to jail, then you jail. You carry it like it means nothing, telling yourself the old prison-tier lie that says you really only do two days—the day you go in and the day you come out.

Cocaine and the expanding marketplace have changed the landscape of the corner, forging a boomtown industry that has room not only for the professional criminals and the committed addicts who have lingered on the fringe of the neighborhood for so long, but for everyone and anyone. Men and women, parents and children, the fools and the clever ones, even the derelicts and outcasts who had no viable role when drug distribution was a structured enterprise—all are assimiliated into the corner world of the 1990s. At Fayette and Monroe and so many other corners in so many other cities, it's nothing more or less than the amateur hour.

And why not? Consider the food chain of the average drug corner, the ready fodder for all the ambo runs and police calls:

At the top are, of course, the dealers, ranging from disciplined New York Boys to fifteen-year-old locals who manage to parlay Nike and Nautica money into a package of their own. The stereotypes no longer apply; every now and then a showpiece with gold chains and an Armani shirt pops out of a Land Rover with custom rims, but for the most part, there's little flash to the drug slingers making real money.

There is no singular connection, no citywide cartel to enforce discipline and carve up territory. Looking up the skirt of the wholesale market from Fayette and Monroe, the drug sources are random and diffuse. A supplier could be a twenty-five-year-old Nigerian fresh from airport customs or a New Yorker in his thirties with a line back to his uncle in the Bronx, a seventeen-year-old junior at Southwestern who sat down next to the right kid in homeroom, or even a fifty-year-old veteran of the old westside heroin organizations, coming home from Lewisburg or Marion after doing ten of a twenty-five-year stint and hooking up with some younger heads for one last fling.

The product itself is, by and large, ready to sell. Gone are the days of uncut dope on the table and four or five gangsters battling the scale, trying to get the purity down and maximize profit. Gone are the cut-buddies, who could wield the playing cards and mannitol with skill to ensure a proper package. Much of what sells on a Baltimore corner is purchased as a prepackaged item with little assembly required. A G-pack of a hundred coke vials, sold on consignment, can make you one thousand dollars, with six hundred kicked back to the supplier. Do that a couple times, then ride the bus or the rails to New York, catch the IRT up to Morningside Heights or the Grand Concourse and lay down the grip; what comes back is precut product, with the equivalent number of vials all neatly wrapped. No math, no chemistry—a sixth-grader with patience and a dull blade can fill the vials and be on a corner inside of an hour. Do that two or three times, ride the rails with one thousand dollars or so and you can come back home with two full ounces. Turn that over and—even allowing for short counts and spillage and fuck-ups—you've got five or six thousand. Same game, different numbers with dope, but either way, you're a businessman. On most corners, if you can last two weeks without messing up, you're the reincarnation of Meyer Lansky. The bottom line is this: Anyone who can work the numbers, dodge the stickup boys, and muster enough patience to stand on a corner for six hours a day can call himself a drug dealer.

Serving the larger street dealers are a host of employees, a few working for profit, most for product, but all within a fragile hierarchy, a structure predicated on such short-supply qualities as trust and reliability. You get to be a runner because a dealer trusts you to handle the dope and coke directly, to bring it in small quantities from the stash to the corner all day long without succumbing to the obvious temptations. A runner who proves himself time and again, who won't cheat his boss by lightening the product, can step up. He might handle some of the money or, in the dealer's absence, supervise the street sales. He might just make lieutenant. On the other hand, a runner who fucks up is on his way to becoming a tout.

Touts, less trusted, are there to promote the product and bring in business. All are fiends: Some are ten- or twenty-year veterans of the corner, and consequently, only a rare few—Fat Curt for one—can be relied upon to handle product. Touting is day work, a meat-market selection, with the dealers hiring their help each morning and paying them for the most part in dope and coke. Touts serve as living billboards—walking, talking advertisements for the chemicals coursing through their bodies. A tout who staggers to his post and simply stands there—vacant-eyed, at a thirty-degree junkie lean, telling passersby that the Spider Bags are a bomb—is earning his keep. Rain or snow or gloom of night, he's out there on a double shift for three or four blasts a day and, if he's lucky, ten or twenty or thirty dollars in cash. No health benefits. No supplemental life. No pension. As much as any working man, the drug-corner tout is a soul in desperate need of a union.

Below the touts are the lookouts—the last hired and first fired of the corner world. Standing guard at the frontiers of the empire are the very young and the very damaged. For the children, it's a lark: trying their hands at the game for the first time, scooting around on bikes or riding the top of a mailbox. It beats the hell out of sixth-grade social studies and for a few hours' effort, you're up twenty or thirty dollars with very little risk. For the walking wounded, the low-bottom dope fiends who aren't allowed within a block of a stash, standing lookout is the last chance to get a free shot. They also serve who stand and wait, eternally on the spy for knockers, rollers, and, of course, the stickup crews. They spend hours chained to their post, watching the endless flow of traffic for the blue bubbles of the marked cars, or the small trunk antennas that are the tell-tale badge of an unmarked Cavalier. And God help the lookout who forgets to look both directions on one-way streets like Fulton or Fayette; most of the rollers will play the sneak and drive their cruisers the wrong way. Stray off post or take a nod and a lookout stands a good chance of seeing the business end of an employer's aluminum bat. And so all day, every day, they're raising up, sounding the alarm with a loud bark, or a whistle, or the standard shouts of "Five-Oh" or "Time Out" ringing from the four points of the compass, giving warning that Huffham or Pitbull is looking for an easy lock-up, or that a stickup artist like Odell is on safari with his four-four.

On the demand side of the market are, of course, the fiends, grazing around the oasis day and night, wandering from one crew to the next in search of the perfect blast. And they, too, must be serviced by a coterie of specialists.

The shooting galleries—vacant or near-vacant rowhouses, battered by the constant traffic, emptied of all valuables—are manned by a service industry all their own. The keepers of the inn guard the door, charging a buck or two for entry, maybe less if a fiend is willing to share some of the hype. For the price of admission, you get a patch of solid floor, a choice of bottle caps, a pint or so of communal water, and if you're lucky, a book of dry matches or a shared candle. You bring your own spike, but if you don't have one, there will likely be someone else at or near the gallery selling works for a couple bucks. Either that or you can walk the block or two to the established needle house—the home of some profit-minded diabetic—and get fixed for a dollar. At last, when you're equipped and ready but can't seem to find a vein, help is as near as the house doctor, the happy troglodyte wearing shoes decorated with candle-drippings, the healer who spends all night and day hunting wayward arteries for fiends lacking the skill or the patience or both.

But it doesn't end there. At the urban watering hole, the employment opportunities of sellers and users compete with those of the vanguard of raw capitalism, the true hucksters trying to sell steakless sizzle. Anyone can market dope and coke on the corner, but it takes a special breed to serve up nothing and call it something. Baking soda or bonita-and-quinine—B-and-Q—as dope, oregano as weed, battery acid as ready rock: Once chased from the corners by the organized drug trade, the burn artists have returned to a golden era. They stand where they want, sell what they want, and risk only the rage of their victims, or in a rare instance, the ire of a street dealer whose business or reputation suffers by proximity.

There are the other outcasts, too, those with no temperament for sales or service, just a willingness to risk all for a chance at the mother lode. The stash stealers, who will spend time watching the runners and touts, tracking them to the ground stash and then waiting for the ideal moment. Or the stickup boys, the crazed loners who gather information about this corner and that, tracing a product back until they're coming through the door of the stash house in an adrenaline rush, staking everything on the premise that no dealer will come back on them, that their ferocity will not be matched. A few of West Baltimore's stickup men have survived a decade or more, but most carry the doomed, thousand-yard-stare of shorttimers. Once, a stickup boy could go into battle relying at least on the organizational structure; they knew who they were going up against and the consequence of those actions. But today, when even fifteen-year-old hoppers have a loaded .380 hidden in the alley, the job is little better than a death wish.

Crowd them together—each pursuing his or her immediate ends—and what governs the corner no longer resembles either a corporate model or the orderly economics of the marketplace. It is, instead, the raw anarchy of the natural world. At the watering hole, the strong survive, the weak perish, and self-preservation and self-gratification dictate that any conceivable act of brutality or betrayal can and will occur. Social norms, morality, the values of the civilization that created the American cities—precious little of it remains at the oasis itself, where everyone must come to drink, regardless of the risk. Though it began as a criminal subterfuge and grew to become a neighborhood bazaar, the urban drug corner is now the social framework through which almost every soul in these battered communities must pass. Some, perhaps, will destroy themselves immediately, others will lose themselves in the mix, and a few stoics, astonishingly, will pass through the corner unscathed and uncorrupted. But pass through they must, because in places like Fayette Street, the corner *is* the neighborhood.

Yet there are still rules to this place—even anarchy creates its own axioms. The old code of the dealers is useless now; the new rules are different and have to be. Because, by necessity, any new logic must allow for a mother to stand on Monroe Street and tout Red Tops with her two-year-old in tow. It must allow for a fiend's theft of the television set from the recreation center, of chalices from the corner churches, of the rent money from his mother's bedroom. And the rules of the corner cannot stand if they prohibit a thirteen-year-old from holding up a single vial of coke and telling a playmate with brutal honesty that for one of these, your mother will step up and suck my dick.

Make no mistake: No one likes to play under the rules, no one on Fayette Street respects them or regards them as fair or worthy or in any way justified. Even the lowest needle freak knows guilt at the instant he's doing dirt, but knowing it changes nothing. The rules are not to be trifled with; they are not arbitrary, nor are they simply an afterthought or rationalization. The new postulates and proofs of the corner embrace the chaos, written as they are in an environment perfectly indifferent to anything beyond dope and coke. To exist in that environment—to seek or sell dope and coke—and at the same time to carry the burden of an outside morality is to invite abuse and failure. To ignore the rules, to try to live above them, is to walk blindly into the maw of the thing, risking destruction for something as ethereal and vague as human decency.

The rules of the game are a two-step program to nonrecovery, as valid a living credo as anything on those pamphlets that get tossed around at Narcotics Anonymous meetings. First among them is a basic declaration of intent as all-encompassing as the first commandmant to roll down the slopes of Sinai.

I. Get the blast.

Get it and live. For whomsoever believeth in good dope shall live forever, or if not forever, at least for that sugar-sweet moment when he chases down a vein, slams it home, and discovers that what they're saying about them Green Tops is true: The shit is right. And if the shit ain't right, if he cooks it up and guns it home and it's B-and-Q, or just enough to get him out of the gate, then the first rule still applies. Go back to the corner and get the blast. And then do it again. Because the next one, or the next one after, will be the true dose, the one to justify all faith. Ten or twenty or thirty years of addiction—it doesn't matter. Every fiend in the street is trying to re-create that first perfect shot of dope or coke, the one that told him this was what he wanted in life. The fiends are at it morning, noon, and night—none of them ever quite getting there, getting just close enough to feed the hunger. And if by some miracle one nails it, if he catches that perfect wave and experiences the chemical epiphany in the back bedroom of some rotting two-story pile, swaying and nodding and scratching to some angelic melody in the kingdom-to-come, if he can stumble back against the flaking plaster and paint, smile stupidly and, with utter reverence, proclaim the shit a bomb, then what? What price glory, save for another caper for another ten dollars and another trip back to the corner, hoping against hope that the vials are still packed, that whoever put that good dope on the street hasn't watered down the back end of the package.

If faith and spirituality and mysticism are the hallmarks of any great church, then addiction is close to qualifying as a religion for the American underclass. If it was anything less, if at Fayette and Monroe there was a single shard of unifying thought that could compete with the blast itself, then the first rule would be null and void. But no, the blast is all, and its omnipotence not only affirms the first rule, but requires the second:

II. Never say never.

On the corner, the survivors do what they've got to do and they live with it. When mere vice is sufficient to get the blast, it ends there. But eventually, it's sin that is required, and when sin falls short, absolute evil becomes the standard. Those who play the game and deny the progression, who insist that there are some moral limits that they will not violate, are forever surprising themselves. Never say never, cry the sages, because a true believer pays absolute homage to addiction, he turns to face it like a Muslim turns toward Mecca. The transformation is gradual but certain, and wrapped in a new vernacular of moral denial.

In the thought and speech of the corner, misdemeanors become not crimes, but capers. Those selling drugs are no longer peddling dope, but serving people; those buying the drugs are not addicts or junkies—perjorative terms of an earlier era—but dope fiends, a term that captures the hunger and devotion of the corner chase, rather than simple dependency. A player who undertakes an armed robbery, a street shooting, or a carjacking is no longer committing a felony, but simply doing a deed. A burn bag sold to a friend, a stash stolen from a first cousin's bedroom, is no longer a betrayal, but merely getting over. When you do these things, of course, you're simply playing the game; when these things are done to you, it's the work of a crudball, a cold motherfucker with no feelings or conscience. The term is never self-applied; corner logic doesn't work that way. One's own crudball adventures are not, of course, regarded as such; the most successful of them are recounted by the perpetrators in a bemused tone that suggests professional pride. The rest of the herd, too, can often manage a grudging respect for a player who breaks new ground in doing unto others, so that a crudball act that consistently yields a profit can easily rise in stature. It becomes, in corner parlance, a dope-fiend move.

It's almost better to be born into the world of the dope-fiend move, and stay there, than to arrive there as a matter of necessity, burdened by ethical baggage that serves no useful purpose. That can only make a player vulnerable. So it is with Gary McCullough, who can't easily justify anything worse than the penny-ante caper. And so it is with Fran Boyd, who has acquired an arsenal of fiendish moves only to be constrained by a lingering sense of obligation to her sons.

In the end, the corner best serves the hardcore, the junkyard dogs with neither the time nor inclination for pity. It's for Ronnie Boice, Gary's girl, who never misses her shot, though her children are running the streets; or Jon-Jon, training twelve-year-olds to sling his bags on Gilmor; or Bunchie, who can make the rent money disappear month after month, knowing that in the end, her brother Scoogie will shell out what's needed to prevent the eviction; or Dink-Dink, selling burn bags to fiends three times his age and almost hoping that they come back on him, figuring he'll go to his nine and catch himself a body.

By nature or by nurture, the mindset of the dope-fiend move, once acquired, becomes a lifelong companion. Once in the game, it's hard for a player to forget the lessons learned and operate in the legitimate world. The dope-fiend move becomes the immediate answer to all problems, the short-term response to life's long-term struggles. Off the corner and loosed upon the legitimate world, it's the lie on the housing application, the copied essay on the community college midterm, the petty theft from the register, and ultimately, the justification for returning to the world of the corner. It's a new way of thinking that can't be challenged with jobs or educational opportunities or drug treatment, because once you see the world as a dope fiend does, you can't see it any other way. A few years in the mix and the only voice in your head becomes the collective wail of the corner itself.

How could it be otherwise? Day after goddamn day, the corner proves itself and, by extension, every idiot on the corner is proven as well. Touts, runners, fiends—they're always where you expect them to be, stand-around-and-serve prophets of the new logic; they speak and you believe.

So when you go up to Fayette and Monroe and hear that your rap buddy just fell dead after slamming some Red Tops, you barely miss a beat. Fuck it, the prophet tells you, he didn't know how to shoot coke, not the way you do. Never mind that you were gunning with the dead man for a decade, never mind that you shared a hype with him a hundred times, never mind that he's pounded on your chest to bring you back more than once, he ain't shit now. Just another no-doping, skin-popping, scramble-shooting punk, says the corner. Nigger wasn't serious like you; couldn't handle the good shit. And you believe it; you want the Red Tops.

The corner prophet knows.

You go to court and the downtown judge gives you five years suspended, tells you you're on supervised probation. Fuck that, says the prophet. If you report and then mess up, they can find you; if you don't report, they ain't got no record of you. And you, of course, do like the prophet says, thinking you're getting over when you ain't. A month or two later, you take a charge and they drag your ass from city jail to the downtown courthouse. The same prune-faced judge looks down at you, talking about how you're in violation of probation, talking about how you're gonna eat the whole five years. And you do the bit, come back from Hagerstown, go back up to the same corner and find that motherfucker. Yo, what up?

And the prophet just looks at you like you're some kind of fool, talking about how you can get locked up for that shit, saying you should have reported.

And you don't miss a beat. You nod your head in agreement because, the man's a got-damn prophet; his shit has to be true. And when the next problem comes around, there you are again on the same corner, looking for more of the same.

"I'm saying, I can't get rid of this hole, man," you tell him, rolling up your sleeve to show a dime-sized crater. The prophet just shakes his head and a neophyte jumps into the lull, offering advice.

"Ain't no hole, man," says the newcomer. "That an abscess. You gotta get some ointment. Go to the emergency room, they got to give it to you. Clean it right up."

"Fuck that," you tell him. "I'm saying, you go there, you got to wait all day. Man, they don't got no time for no niggers. See, what I'm saying, I can't be doing that, man. I'm saying, this nigger got things to do."

And, of course, the prophet finally steps up.

"Shit, you want to clean it up or what?" he asks.

"Yeah, what I'm saying . . ."

"Get yourself some eggs, two should do it," the prophet says. "Boil 'em up in a pot 'til they hard. Then you gotta peel 'em real careful like. You want to get that thin skin, be under the shell? You know what I'm talking about, be under the shell?"

"Yeah, uh-huh."

"You got to peel that off and stick it over the holes. Wrap it up in some gauze. Word up: two weeks. It be like these."

The prophet shows you the back of his left hand. "Them the kind of scar you get."

You're not sure.

"Fuck it, I don't give a shit if your motherfucking arm falls off," says the prophet. "That's on you."

"No, I'm saying I ain't heard about doing that. That's all. I'm saying, it might work. You probably right."

Two weeks and a dozen eggs later you're pulling the gauze off your arm and, of course, the hole is now the size of a quarter. And when you go back to the corner prophet, he tells you he don't know shit about eggs. Potatoes, he tells you. Boiled potatoes are the cure. For a moment or two, you shake your head and curse the prophet, but two hours later you're pricing spuds at the Super Fresh, though in the end, you'll say to hell with it. No time for boiling shit up or waiting around emergency rooms. The corner knows; you're not about fixing the hole in your arm, you're about that blast.

So you learn: The prophet never lies; he can't be wrong. As it is for every other wandering animal, the watering hole is the only truth you can afford. It owns you, uses you, kicks your ass, robs your mind, and grinds your body down. But day after lonesome day, it gives you life.

For twenty on the hype, you believe.

Fat Curt lies still on a dirt-slicked mattress as the wind pushes through the cracks of the boarded-up windows, barely breaking stride before it rushes through the darkened rooms. All around him, the moans and coughs and curses of comrades scattered on makeshift bedrolls blend with groans from the boards and joists of Blue's old house.

Hard soldiering in a hard winter. Curt sheds the tatter of blankets and clothing that have covered him through a February night, throwaways and giveaways layered one atop another for enough warmth to keep the old heart pumping. Curt gropes for his cane, finding it at the edge of the mattress. He plants the rubber tip into the weathered floorboard and slowly shifts his weight forward. He grabs the middle of the cane with his left hand and, with a long grunt, pries himself up and out. Swollen hands grip the walking stick as he fights off a wave of vertigo; swollen feet pad between a sprawl of bodies in the front room.

"Hey Curt."

"Hey."

Pimp props himself against a bare wall.

"What time is it?"

Pimp asking the time, like he's got somewhere to be. Curt shakes his head: "Time to get on out there."

Curt stumbles down the narrow corridor and through a sea of trash in the stripped-bare kitchen, heading for the back door. He leans down on his cane to make an exit through the broken-out bottom panels, doing a sideways limbo to get to the morning sunlight in the back alley.

Hungry is out there already, his head bandaged from his latest misadventure with a New York dealer.

"He up here yet?"

Hungry shakes his head, a loose flap of white gauze fluttering in the wind. Not yet. Curt's up and out, but you can't punch the clock without a package.

He makes his way up the alley and out onto Monroe, but the early morning sun is lost in the shadow of the rowhouses on the east side of the street. So he canes his way down to Fayette Street, crossing over to the grocery and finding some pavement warmed by the day. The Korean is sweeping around the store entrance and Curt mumbles a greeting. The Korean nods, then waits, broom in hand, too polite to ask Curt to move. Curt senses this and returns the favor, stepping to the other side of the corner but still staying with the sun.

There he stands for the next hour or so, rooted on the corner that he has known his whole life, waiting for the rising tide of the day to pick him up and carry him along. Brothers-in-arms slide out of the alley, squinting in the sunlight, hunting up the morning's first Newport and telling the early-bird customers to hang in there, to go around the block once or twice more until things pick up.

Curt watches Eggy Daddy and Pimp drift up to the corner: Eggy, looking no worse for the wear, pretty good considering; Pimp, now stickthin from the Bug. Bryan follows them out of the alley carrying the piss bucket, dumping a night's fill into the gutter, then returning the metal pail to Blue's back door.

From the other direction, Bread saunters up smiling, looking a bit warmer than the rest. Bread still has a key to his mother's back door down the hill on Fayette, a warrior living all for the corner but keeping that one last connection to the world left behind, sleeping in his mother's basement when the winter chill is on. Still, Curt gives Bread some due as a soldier, because the man's been out here forever, as long as Curt even. He's forty-six and a legendary fixture, running and gunning dope at Monroe and Fayette since the corner lampposts were twigs.

"You look like a frog," he tells Curt.

"Yeah," Curt agrees. "Layin' down, the fluid come up and swell my face."

"Yeah, you swole all right."

"Makes my eyes pop out and shit," Curt grunts. "Like a got-damn bullfrog."

"Maybe I get Charlene to come past an' kiss you," says Bread, nodding at the tired form of Charlene Mack across the street. "You be a prince then."

"Sheeeet," says Curt, laughing aloud, a joyous rumble welling up in his dry throat and bursting out. Bread laughs, too, delighted to have put pleasure on his old friend's face. Making people smile is Bread's best game, really. He doesn't tout or sell much; nor is Bread one to go off the corner to boost or burglarize. Instead, he gets most of his dope because people like him, because he genuinely makes them want to share their blast.

"So what's up?"

"Either they late or I'm early."

There are enough of them now—prospective touts and lookouts—to open shop, as well as a handful of hungry fiends waiting listlessly at the entrance to Vine Street. Curt's brother, Dennis, is across the street by the liquor store, bumming a smoke from Scalio. And just down the block is Smitty, collecting aluminum cans in a plastic bag, singing in his pitch-perfect tenor.

One after the other, the dealers drift in—Gee, Shamrock, Dred, Nitty, Tiny—and assess the labor pool. They find their hires, set their wages, and ante up the day's first installment—the up-front blast to get the corner crew alive and working. Curt goes with Dred today; he'll do some touting, maybe even work from his own ground stash on Vine Street.

But later for that. Right now, it's back into Blue's, all of them moving down the alley like cattle, heading back into the vacant rowhouse where Rita is already up, candle burning bright, adding to the daylight that

streams from the gaps in the plywood boards. Strips of cloth are laid
out on a battered wooden table; bottle caps, matches, and fresh water
surrounded by dozens of dead-bent cigarette butts—a surgical amphitheater for the doctoring to come. And, of course, almost everyone but
Rita is impatient, some jostling for a better position in the queue. Curt
brings Bread along with him, and the two wait their turn quietly. Skinny
Pimp, too, doesn't bicker; he's in the corner on a dirty bedroll, feeling
a little too weak to stand around forever holding his place in line.

"Who next?"

"Naw . . . me."

But Rita imposes her calm on the group. She's the medicine woman,
the tribal herbalist, the mother hen that all of them come to see. In
every way that matters, she's a professional—with a few weeks of nursing
classes somewhere in her history—and she expects her clientele to act
accordingly.

"Hold your horses," she tells them.

Those willing and able to hit themselves go off to do just that. The
rest wait their turn at Rita's table in the front room: some because they're
not handy with a needle; others because their veins have retreated to
portions of their bodies that can be reached only by a second party;
others still because Rita is simply that good. From one end of the room
to the other, they gear up, prepping the flesh for the doctor's grand
rounds. This one rubs his neck to get the juices going; that one drops
his pants for a shot in the ass; the next soul ties up his arm and slaps
at cratered skin, searching for a passage home.

"What's working for you?" Rita asks, consulting with the patients as
every good doctor does, asking them how they're getting off lately and
where the blood still flows. She probes amid old graveyards of tracks
and scabs, feeling her way through the terrain like a dowser hunting
water. And then, at last, she's in and they're on, the pinkish cloud rising
into the syringe as bottom-line proof.

Rita Hale rarely blows a shot, rarely leaves the dope and coke in a
knotted, puffing lump under the skin, veinless and trapped—the wasted-
time-and-money mark of an amateur. Nor does she cheat—a fact that truly
marks her as special—because the search for an honest shooting gallery
doctor can be as exhausting as the quest for an honest auto mechanic. Her
line of work is crowded with those who can't resist taking advantage of
the helpless, but Rita will never pluck a patient. She's not about watering
them down, or switching bottle caps, or blowing B-and-Q in their veins.

There are shooting galleries in which the desperate and the naive are used and abused by the house staff. In such places, a newcomer asking for help getting on will get plenty of attention from a veteran. The old-timer will take the chump's tool and tell him to turn his head, the better to see that ripe vein bulging in his neck. And then, with a practiced motion too quick for the eye to follow, he's dropped the rube's hard-won dope in his pocket and come out with an empty breakaway. So the new-comer gets blasted with nothing more than the sting of cold air or maybe water. Rubbing a swollen bubble of skin, he'll start to bitch. But the old-timer will stand pat, shaking his head. Feel that bubble, he tells him. You feel that? That's your shit. Told you don't move, but you turned your head and see there, you blew your shot.

There's no such sleight-of-hand with Rita. She's not only good with a spike, she's willing to earn her keep. And why cheat? For plying her trade honestly, Rita gets more dope than God. Almost everyone who comes to Blue's ends up giving her a share of the hype, so that more than anyone in the neighborhood, Rita Hale lives the dope fiend's purest fantasy—thirty, sometimes forty shots a day—so many that she's reached that point where she no longer knows how it feels to want or need a blast. It's a symbiotic relationship: The patients bring whatever the doctor wants and the doctor is always in.

Medicinal work may have saved Rita from the daily travail of the corner world, but her ability to find a vein is a double-edged sword. She's become an essential service at Blue's, the only working appliance in the gutted rowhouse, and so, she's cursed with far too much coke and dope.

A few years back, Rita was among the most beautiful girls in the neighborhood; every man along Fayette Street remembers the curve of her figure, the symmetry of her face, the charm and humor that she brought to any conversation. Rita was something then, but for her the needle wasn't a part-time adventure. She didn't cast the straight world aside lightly; she hurled it down. Rita loved dope, and when she learned to doctor, there was nothing that could stop her. Within months, her hands and feet were as cruelly bloated as Fat Curt's, her skin, cratered and scabbed. But still she kept on until her left upper arm was little more than raw, rotting flesh, the stench strong enough to fill every room of the shooting gallery. A few of the fiends—Curt and Eggy, to name two— tried to warn her, to convince her to go to Bon Secours and give it a rest before she got gangrene. But the others, driven by self-interest, said nothing. Twenty-four, seven, they lined up at her table, though some offered pirated antibiotics and back-street remedies along with her share of the dope and coke.

Eventually, Rita couldn't leave the shooting gallery. With her body a caricature and her will destroyed, she became a prisoner. She was no fool: all the dope in the world couldn't kill Rita's wit and intelligence, and there was never a waking moment when she didn't face up to how far she had fallen. She was, in a word, ashamed—ashamed of the arm, of the smell, of the extremity of her condition. She wouldn't bear the looks of emergency room nurses or interns, or the counter help at the corner store, or the children playing on Vine Street. Even the most jaded police couldn't help but view her with amazement and revulsion; on the rare occasion when they raided the shooting gallery, they'd never include Rita in the lockups. They'd poke her into a back room with their nightsticks, cursing her for the stench, leaving her behind with the cookers and syringes.

Only Blue went beyond talk and acted to save her. It was his house, after all, and he felt some responsibility for the regulars. Time and again, he told Rita to get to the hospital and when every other approach failed, he actually put her out on the street, telling her not to come back until she got treatment. That was two weeks ago. Now, Blue is gone—he took a charge and was sent courtside to the jail on Eager Street—and Rita is back, no better than before.

One after another, they get the blast—the bystanders waiting patiently, focusing on Rita, watching the plunger fall, trying to gauge the rush. Whose dope is better? Who got shit? There's little time or inclination in the shooting gallery for small talk or theoretical debates, little energy wasted on human relations, on current events or communication for its own sake. When you speak, you speak about dope, or coke, or that motherfucker Bob Brown, or what's happening on what corner. Nothing else gets heard in this place, except from some rare bird like Gary McCullough, who gets his blast and then breaks etiquette by rambling on about Zen Buddhism. And fuck that shit, everyone else thinks: Shut up and shoot dope.

"What you get there?" Rita asks, ministering to Bread.

"Black-and-White," says Curt.

"That'll work, but Spider Bags better."

Curt grunts disdain. "S'all bullshit out there nowadays," he tells her. "Nothing but got-damn chemicals. Ain't been no real dope out here for ten years."

Curt has the same complaint every morning. Rita smiles and finishes with Bread, then it's Curt's turn. Just as she's finishing up, all hell breaks loose on the second floor—someone up there raising some kind of racket.

Curt goes to the bottom of the stairs and listens. No voices, just scraping and banging sounds from the back bedroom. The tout hesitates, torn between a residual loyalty to Blue and the need to get out on the corner and make a living. Another loud metallic clang seals his decision.

"Damn," he says, caning slowly up the battered stairs, stopping at the landing to catch his breath. "Got-damn."

The noise grows louder as he struggles up the last steps, reaching the second floor to see some fiend he half-recalls from somewhere down around Hollins and Payson, a dusty-looking motherfucker who's been coming to Blue's for the last few weeks. Curt tries for a name, but comes up empty.

"Ah . . . hey."

The fiend looks over, indifferent, then turns back to the business at hand. He rips another piece of aluminum guard from a rear window, stripping what's left of Blue's house for a few dollars at the United Iron scales.

"My man, I'm sayin', you know, it ain't like we ain't living here," Curt offers.

"This your house?"

"Naw, but, y'know . . ."

"Fuck you then," says the fiend.

"Man, leave it rest."

"What you gonna do?"

"I'm just sayin' give it a rest. You know the man ain't even home."

The fiend pauses at that, looking first at the haul of twisted metal on the floor, then back at what's left on the windows. Curt takes that as a truce of sorts, turns and canes his way back downstairs. It's time, after all, to punch that clock.

Curt goes back up to the corner to find Dred. He picks up his package, canes down through the alley, down past the litter-strewn lot where the alley tees into Vine Street. He crosses Vine and goes behind a vacant house, and—satisfied that no crudballs are watching—he hides the stash against the crumbling wall of a brick garage. Good enough, he thinks.

He heads back up Vine to Monroe, where all around him the regulars at Blue's are about the business, each one a small cog in a vast, indifferent machine. The fiends come in ones and twos, most on foot, a few pulling to the curb in cars and trucks; one white girl rides up to cop on a mountain bike. By a little after noon, Curt is halfway through his second bundle. He's lucky; he's selling Yellow Bag/Gold Star and it was good yesterday. Now fiends are coming out of the woodwork looking for more of the same, though if the product is anything like what Curt fired that morning, it's now merely adequate. That's the way it often is: A product gets a reputation at the beginning of its run, but by the end, the cut takes over and the quality drops precipitously. Still, today's business on the Yellow Bag circuit is brisk.

A wraith of a woman wearing a torn army jacket, her hair shoveled under a do-rag, makes the turn from Lexington and heads at Curt. She's yellow-eyed and listing hard to starboard, her feet swamped in heavy brown workboots at least a half-dozen sizes too large.

"What you got?"

"Yellows."

She cocks an eyebrow.

"It'll work," Curt tells her. He won't oversell. Curt tries to let a little truth into the game, especially with the fiends who are looking sick.

"Hmmm," she says, picking up on the equivocation. "Who got them Black-and-Whites?"

Curt sends her down toward Fayette, watching as she steers herself past the knots of touts and slingers clustered along the strip. She gets as far as the mouth of the alley in the rear of Fayette. Bryan is there, leaning against the bricks, holding up the back corner of the store, looking for all the world like he's gainfully employed. She stops and asks. Bryan starts nodding.

Aw shit, thinks Curt, a wrong turn for the little lady. Bryan has nothing at all to do with Black-and-Whites, and this poor girl thinks she's on the path. Bryan is selling his Arm & Hammer, or baby powder, or whatever else looks pretty and white inside a glassine bag. Boy ought to know better as many times as he's been shot up behind that lame-ass shit.

For the next couple of hours, Curt touts and slings and watches the intrigue play out around him. Variations on the same theme that always end the same way, with someone getting over and someone else getting mad. Curt is old enough and wise enough to manage a little distance, to keep his thing separate and distinct. No sense being a pawn in any game other than your own.

Curt sees the McCullough boy come around the corner from Fayette Street to join Kwame—his uncle, Gary's youngest brother—and Shamrock, Kwame's running buddy. DeAndre's been slinging a package with Sham and Kwame for a week now, working Fairmount early in the day and coming up the hill in the afternoons. Curt watches the boy make a few quick sales on Vine, the product coming right out of his pocket. Young people got no sense, thinks Curt, shaking his head at the sight.

The day grinds on. Curt sells, then gets his midday jolt at Blue's, then heads back out to the corner for more of the same. About three or so, the police roll through—not Bob Brown, but some of the downtown folk—riding up Lexington, then down Monroe, then screeching to a halt at the mouth of Vine Street. Curt turns politely toward Fayette Street and begins caning away at half-speed, giving the knockers their due though they're actually rousting some younger crew on Vine. Ten yards ahead of him, Curt sees DeAndre McCullough step quickly toward the liquor store. Just before turning the corner, he digs into his pocket and passes a plastic baggie to Tyrone, Ronnie Boice's brother. Tyrone stuffs the baggie down his dip and strolls across the street, DeAndre seeks the protection of the store, and Curt can't help but laugh.

The knockers, of course, don't come anywhere near DeAndre or Tyrone, choosing instead one of the young dealers they caught raising up on them as they turned into the block. They stay up at Vine, standing by their idling Cavalier, waiting for the wagon as the rest of the corner world drifts off, allowing them a respectful distance. Minutes later, DeAndre comes out of the liquor store, looks up and down the street, then around the corner on Fayette.

"Where Tyrone at?" he asks the wind.

Curt, within earshot, half-shrugs. Boy must be joking. Can't no one say where exactly Tyrone Boice might be, Curt muses, but wherever he is, your coke is right there with him and they getting along together just fine. DeAndre, wounded and bitter, waits a few minutes more, then stalks away.

Boy, you too young, Curt wants to tell him, too easy a mark. There was a time not long back when Curt or some other old-timer might've stepped up and said something, a time when a little wisdom might've mattered. Even on the corner, there was a day when people weren't afraid to talk to each other. Or to listen. Curt can remember how they once would've chased the McCullough boy's young ass home, told him not to be messing with things that weren't for him. And a burn artist like Bryan, too, would've heard a little something about right and wrong.

And back in the day, they might've actually listened, or if they didn't listen, at least they'd know the advice was from the heart. Like that day a few years back when Joe Laney, the lowest of the low-bottom, slash-stealing, game-running Fayette Street dope fiends shocked everyone and started chasing N.A. meetings. But even clean, Laney was coming up to Monroe and Fayette every day because, well, he had no other place to go. And Curt knew what had to be said.

He walked up and told him—one soldier to another—well now, seeing as you don't want anything up here, you shouldn't be hanging. And Joe heard this and knew it to be true, finding in Curt's words an absolution, a good-luck wish for a new life.

Nowadays, though, the right word to the wrong person would get your ass shot up. So Bryan burns the customers and DeAndre wanders up and down Monroe Street, and Curt, as he often does, sees the future before it happens but says nothing.

In the end, Fat Curt has become more of a spectator than a player at Monroe and Fayette—not only because the corner has changed, but because Curt has changed as well. He would never complain about it— "I like to shoot dope," he assures people—but somehow, Curt has outlived his time. All that running, all that gunning, and now, his body is giving out.

It's a cruel but routine fate for a man who has given his entire adult life to the streets of West Baltimore. He had chased heroin with complete abandon, asking for very little in return beyond a good day's blast, a few creature comforts, and—at least within the world of the corner itself— a degree of camaraderie and, yes, even dignity. At least in principle, the good day's blast is still out here, but Curt has been stripped bare of every last comfort until even walking is an exercise in agony. Worse still, there is no longer any joy for him in the everyday life on the corner: The friendships, connectedness, and shared humor that the old code had made possible have been supplanted by bickering and violence and desperation. Curt, who had lived by that code, couldn't settle comfortably into the new anarchy or find the human element that makes a hard life livable. To the older heads on the corner, he is still an oracle, but to the younger hoppers, Curt is merely one tout among many. If you were to tell them the whole story—the tale as every old head with a memory knows it—they'd have laughed at the idea. Curt? Fat Curt? The nigger on Monroe Street with them Popeye-looking hands?

But it's true. Curt had a run.

Go back twenty-five years when there was still a viable neighborhood around Monroe and Fayette and there was Fat Curt, out on the
edge of it, playing the gangster. He was a man of means, with money in
his pocket and a real future in the west side heroin trade. In his early
twenties, he fell into a comfortable niche under serious players like Teensy
and Ditty and a few of the other homegrown entrepreneurs who had
brought a wholesale heroin market to West Baltimore. Curt learned the
rules and kept enough of them so that, eventually, he was trusted to
make the trips to 116th Street and 8th Avenue—"Little Baltimore," they
called it, because that part of New York was home to many an exile from
the black neighborhoods of the harbor city.

Curt made the runs, sometimes by train, sometimes by bus, and once
in the city he'd go look up Sadie Briscoe, a Baltimore transplant who
made the rent by hooking up the out-of-town crowd with the New York
wholesalers. Curt would pass the money and pick up the package and
see it safely to a Baltimore stash house. He made many a trip, skirting
the newly forming interdiction squads, the stickup crews, and the burn
artists, getting that good New York City dope and getting high on the
excess. Back then, Curt had so much dope coming his way that for a
long time he had no sense that he had an addiction.

On what was then the neighborhood corner, Lexington and Fulton,
he was the show: He had a big de Ville, a car that kids like Gary
McCullough would wash and polish for a hefty tip; a heavy roll of
twenties, neatly manicured and passed freely for services rendered; and,
of course, the endless supply of shit that granted him admission to every
party. As time ticked on, others got greedy or sloppy or too notorious
for their own good. They fell to state or federal charges, but Curt held
fast to the middle rungs of the West Baltimore trade, never trying to
play the game for more than the good blast and a few dollars besides.
In part, his long run was a function of luck. But in part, Curt lasted
because he never lost touch with one of the great joys of the thing, the
cat-and-mouse adventure with the police, the running and dodging. Yet
because he stayed out of jail, he never got a serious break in the action—
a vacation from the needle that might have given his body a chance to
dry the cells and slow the swelling in every limb. That's the irony of a
drug arrest at the street-corner level: Locking up a hardcore fiend won't
close the shop or stop the product. It won't keep anyone from the game,
or pave the way toward rehabilitation unless a fiend genuinely wants to
quit fiending. The real tangible benefit from day-to-day police work in

the drug war is medicinal: A run-and-gun player gets hit with a charge and, like it or not, he gets a brief convalescence. He gets some food, some sleep, maybe even some antibiotics. He gives those tired old veins a respite. Then, when the whistle blows, he's charging out of the penalty box for more of the same.

And so, from the addiction itself he fell. Slowly at first, but relentlessly, he shed all of the big-score vestiges on the way down to Blue's. The Cadillac was ancient neighborhood lore; the trademark roll of twenties, just a gleam in the eye; and the dope was no longer the raw and wild New York quarter, but whatever stepped-on nonsense was out here on the corners. Rose, the girl of his youth, was out on Fayette Street, but making her own way; Curt Junior, now a teenager, was selling from the same corners as well. For a while, home for Fat Curt was nothing better than a third-floor walk-up, with the electricity pirated by extension cord from a back-alley utility pole. Finally, when rent on that shithole came due, home was Blue's.

Over time, it had reached the point where Curt couldn't take a charge if he tried. All day, every day he's selling or touting dope and coke and yet, somehow, his ubiquity at the crossroads of Monroe and Fayette has rendered him invisible. The police see him, of course; Curt is an epic sight. But as with Rita, the physical damage has kept him out of the police wagon for no better reason than that the street police are repulsed and frightened. They'd roll up on the corner, give the bloated tout a quick once-over, and then grab someone else. In the beginning, when Curt was thriving, there was no break because he was good or lucky or both. In the end, when Curt is slowly dying, there's no break because his body has been wrecked.

Like now. A couple of the knockers get bored waiting for the wagon and come down Monroe to clear the corner. Two plainclothesmen and a uniform move down the block in tandem, quickly overtaking Curt, but moving past him to tell Shamrock, Kwame, and a few more of the younger ones to get the fuck off the street. Curt stands unmolested in the same spot, unable to rate even a casual eyefuck.

For twenty minutes, the shop stays closed as cops and corner boys alike wait for the Western District wagon. When it arrives to cart the day's sacrifice to the district lockup, the rest of the herd watches placidly, insulated by their very numbers from worrying the thing too much.

The wagon finally rolls off down Monroe, turning the corner on Fayette, and Curt tries to pick up where he left off. But after roping in a quick sale, he's overcome with a strange uncertainty.

"Aw shit."

He hobbles up to Vine Street and looks down the alley at the row of vacant, battered brick. Third one down? Fourth one? Fifth? Who the hell can remember with all the shit going on?

"Oh Lord," says Curt, petitioning for divine intervention as he pokes his way down the lane. "Where mah dope? Lord, please help me find mah dope."

It's another hour before he manages to relocate his bundle where he left it, sell it off, and get back to Blue's for the midafternoon jumper. Curt's down in the front room, waiting for Rita to get herself off, when he hears the same damn racket above him. Up he goes to the second floor, his legs aching, his patience thinned. Sure enough, the same asshole is still at it.

"Well, got-damn . . ."

The fiend looks blankly at him.

"Just leave the shit be now."

"Fuck you, motherfucker."

Curt wonders why he cares, thinking to himself that there ain't much left to Blue's old house anyway, and what's left is going to get carted away by someone soon enough. Ever since Blue got locked up, Curt had been making a modest effort to hold the fort. But there was no telling when Blue might get home.

Two weeks ago—about an hour or so after Blue had told Rita to clean up and had put her out of the house—the police suddenly kicked in the front door and charged through the shooting gallery. This quite naturally scared the living shit out of all present, sending Blue himself out the second-floor rear window in a mad leap. It wasn't much of a raid, in fact. There was no warrant and the police who went charging through rooms with guns drawn weren't much interested in the handful of vials, syringes, and cookers scattered about. Instead, they were looking for an injured officer; someone, it seemed, had dialed 911 to report that a police was taking a beating inside the shooting gallery. The caller did not identify herself to the police dispatcher, but the gallery regulars figured Rita Hale, her feelings hurt by the eviction, to be the even-money bet.

As the police searched Blue's house that day, the hardcore soldiers—Curt and Eggy, Pimp and Dennis—sat silent, their hard-won highs ruined. Blue went rabbit because he thought he was supposed to go rabbit, because he was running a shooting gallery and the police were kicking through the door. The fall from the upstairs window didn't hurt a bit; getting grabbed and tossed around the back alley by a plainclothes detective who was responding to the officer-needs-assistance call—that was the problem. Convinced that there was no injured officer in the house, the raiding party managed to overlook the vials and syringes and leave everybody be—save for Blue and two or three others who had tried to run and had to be punished on principle. For Blue, the charge was burglary—to wit, breaking and entering into his own house.

So the lord of the manor is gone and Rita is back and now Curt is left to stare down a one-man demolition squad. There's a part of him almost ready to let it go, but something else keeps the confrontation going. For Curt, it goes back to the old code, back to the time when people talked to each other. Fuck it, he figures, it is Blue's house and Blue is a friend, and messing with the man's house when he's over at pretrial ain't right. He watches the fiend pull at the window-stripping and decides to give it one more try.

"I'm sayin' . . ."

But the fiend isn't listening anymore. Instead, he's crossing the room, picking up a long piece of jagged aluminum, and swinging hard.

The first blow tears Curt on the side of the face; he can feel the warm blood squirt from his cheek and neck. The second, he fends off, catching a deep cut in his left palm. The fiend brandishes the weapon again and Curt backs up into the front bedroom, assessing the damage.

The tout hears the enemy stalk down the stairs. Pausing for a moment to think it through, he drops his cane, grabs Blue's wooden chair, drags it over to the closet, and uses it to boost himself up through the trapdoor. In a Herculean effort, he struggles up into the attic's crawl space, managing somehow to push himself along to the trapdoor to the roof without getting wedged between the beams. He rests for a moment to steady a laboring pulse, then pops the roof cap and lifts himself onto the frozen black tar. A man on a mission, he ignores the wind's chilly breath on his sweating body, crawling to the edge of the roof. He peeps down on the Fayette Street sidewalk.

No fiend.

Curt takes a look across the roof and spots a loose brick near the chimney stack. He stretches for it and returns to position directly above the doorway. A couple minutes more and, blessed Jesus, the fiend not only steps onto the stoop but stands there. Curt leans over the edge, squares the target in the crosshairs, and it's bombs away.

The brick lands with a crack on the steps. A near miss.

Damn.

But the fiend continues to stand there, scoping the street. Somehow, the air raid didn't register. In fact, after a moment or two more, the man actually steps back inside Blue's.

Curt is flummoxed—how in hell did he miss?—but the initial failure does nothing to stay his anger. It's back down from the roof and into Blue's room, where Curt goes under the worn mattress for the old ax that Blue keeps.

Leaving his cane once again, steadied by his purpose, Curt hobbles out of the room, down the stairs, with a pause only at the bottom step, where the asshole obliges Curt yet again by walking past him down the narrow corridor. Curt rears back and comes down with a mighty chop. But no. The ax head flies toward the ceiling and nothing more lethal than the wooden handle glances off the fiend's shoulder.

"Huh," says the fiend, startled.

Curt stands there, looking at the wooden handle. The fiend is thinking, too, staring down at the loose blade on the floor. Suddenly, it clicks: "Man, shit."

Curt says nothing.

"I mean, I'm sayin' you all actin' crazy and shit."

Enough is enough, apparently. The fiend mumbles his way toward the door, talking about how all Curt had to do was say something, talking about it like Curt doesn't know how to act, pretending like there are still rules left in this game. He leaves Curt there at the bottom of the stairs, still holding the worthless toothpick of a handle, exhausted, bloodied, wondering how so many no-thinking people get to be so got-damned lucky.

To see it in retrospect, to look backward across thirty years on the Fayette Streets of this country is to contemplate disaster as a seamless chronology, as the inevitable consequence of forces stronger and more profound than the cities themselves.

Cursed as we are with a permanent urban underclass, an unremitting and increasingly futile drug war, and Third World conditions in the hearts of our cities, the American experiment seems, at the millennium, to have found a limit.

The poor will always be with us, declared the biblical sages, and this divided nation seems to go out of its way to prove the point. As America lurched away from the rubble of great societies and new deals, no less a populist than Ronald Reagan wryly declared that we fought a war against poverty and poverty won. Many of us heard him and smiled knowingly at what seemed to be unvarnished truth. For decades now, the ghettos have appeared to us as certain and fixed, their problems beyond the reach of programs or policies or good intentions.

Perhaps it was inevitable. Or perhaps there were a few moments early on, a lost opportunity or two in the generations before the inner city acquired its permanence. Perhaps there was another potential for the brown-stones of the South Bronx and the brick rowhouses of North Philadelphia, an alternative path for the broken streets of East St. Louis and West Baltimore. Concede for a moment that we might be jaded by decades of failure, that our vision is skewed by knowledge of the outcome. It might serve to just once see the thing as William McCullough—Gary's father and DeAndre's grandfather—saw it, walking Fayette Street with a full stride and twenty-eight years of life, standing on the painted stone steps of his Vine Street home and thinking it good.

His castle was a two-story Formstone rowhouse like twenty others in the 1800 block. But this one in particular—the worldly possession of W.M. and his bride—was the sum of all their struggles. Wedged between Lexington and Fayette, the alley street was barely wide enough for automobiles, but it was clean back then, the rowhouses tucked into small lots on the south side of the alley, the facing rear yards of the Lexington Street houses lush with summer gardens.

Vine Street was in its glory, a quiet haven in a neighborhood still racially mixed, still predominantly white, in fact. Working-class and middle-class white families lived mostly along the main streets; their black, working-class neighbors lived mostly behind them on alley streets named Vine and Fairmount and Lemmon. That was a time when the corner markets were mostly Jewish, free of bulletproof Plexiglas and willing to sell to local families on credit, a time when St. Martin's parish, once the largest in Baltimore, was still a thriving bastion of Roman Catholicism in the center of the neighborhood. That was before the Harbor Tunnel and I-95 replaced the long journey up Monroe Street and across North Avenue on old U.S. 1, a route from which a generation of interstate travelers might look out their car windows at the fresh Formstone, painted brick, and clean-scrubbed marble steps of Franklin Square and see the very essence of Baltimore's working-class rightness. That was the time of unlocked doors and open windows and sleeping

in Druid Hill Park on hot summer nights, a time when heroin was little
more than a whisper and violence rarely went beyond the occasional
domestic assault. By the calendar, that was 1955.

William McCullough had come to Baltimore fourteen years earlier,
a stowaway on the bus from Salisbury, North Carolina. As a small boy,
W.M. had picked cotton for pennies on the plantation of his birth,
the Cathcart farm just east of Winnsboro, South Carolina. He was the
great-grandson of slaves owned by the McCullough family, a West Irish
clan who had settled the land along the riverbank to the northeast of
Winnsboro; he was the grandson and son of sharecroppers who could
never quite make the land pay. The cotton fields were hard, tenant
farming harder. W.M. could remember the hardest Depression years in
Winnsboro, with his father struggling to squeeze money out of bad crop
settles and his mother and younger brother stalking through the woods,
looking for roots and nuts and anything else that might stave off hunger.
When Fred McCullough managed to land a job with the Southern
Railroad, it seemed to his older son that the very worst days were gone.

The family moved north to the rail hub at Salisbury, where at twelve,
W.M. began shining shoes and working in the kitchen of the Trailways
depot on Main Street. Week after week, he brought his pay back to the
wood-frame bungalow at the north end of town, where it was pooled
with what his father and brother managed to earn. When he was fourteen, he had the temerity to use a couple dollars from one week's pay
to purchase new overalls and a leather jacket. His father took a strap to
him and, no doubt about it, Fred McCullough could hit hard when he
was mad. It wasn't the first beating and unlikely to be the last, so W.M.
decided right then and there that he was gone. He said good-bye to his
brother, crawled out a side window, and jumped down into the weeds.
That night he slept inside a bathroom at the bus depot, and the next
morning, he convinced a northbound driver to take him to Baltimore.
He had an uncle up there making money. He would make money, too.

He had a strong back, enormous self-discipline, and an utter absence
of formal education. But he was unashamed of his limitations and
unafraid of hard work. He could read numbers, handle money, and work
harder than most anyone he knew. He believed these things were enough.

He landed at the bus station in downtown Baltimore with $1.40 in
his pocket, and the driver, doubtful of W.M.'s chances, told him that if
things didn't work out he should come back to the terminal the following
night, when the driver would be back through and could return him

south. But by then W.M. had a job working a grinding wheel at an iron foundry on South Charles Street. The plant produced wheels for railroad cars—the sheer weight of the things drove grown men to quit after less than a week—but W.M. lied himself up to eighteen years old to get hired. The company men had learned to trust in fresh black immigrants from the Carolinas and Virginia. Greenhorns just up from the cotton patch always work hard, the bosses believed, harder than the coloreds who had grown accustomed to city life. For his part, W.M. proved the rule; he was their John Henry, grinding and lifting and hauling deadweight for twelve years.

It was 1942 and William McCullough, at the age of fourteen, was a small but committed part of the largest ethnic migration in American history. It was larger than the flight of the starving Irish a century before, larger still than the succeeding waves of Eastern European and Italian immigrants who later crowded the halls of Ellis Island and Castle Garden. The black exodus from the rural South in this century would utterly transform the American cities of the East and Midwest. In the Mississippi Valley, the northward migration brought thousands of southern blacks to Memphis, Kansas City, St. Louis, and ultimately, to the terminus cities of Chicago and Detroit. In the East, the same phenomenon brought waves of migrants to Baltimore and Washington, Philadelphia and New York.

There was nothing surprising about this. Mechanization was changing the agrarian economy of the South, with the sharecropping and tenant farming that characterized so much of black rural life increasingly marginalized. By the early 1940s, even the farming of cotton—the most labor-intensive of Southern crops—was being transformed as mechanical cotton pickers were perfected and marketed. Once the South had staked both its society and economy on black labor; by World War II, the same labor force was expendable.

To the north, the smoking cities of the American industrial belt offered an alternative. Even in the Depression years, the pages of the black community newspaper in the McCullough hometown of Winnsboro were littered with notices of a generation drifting inexorably northward:

"We regret to report another departure for Baltimore . . ."

"Mr. Hill, a Winnsboro native and lifelong resident of the county, will leave to join relatives in Philadelphia."

"On Sunday last, a good-bye picnic was held for the Singletary family . . ."

"... the young gentleman will be departing our community next month with friends to pursue prospects in Washington ..."

Baltimore siphoned from the rural black population of both Carolinas and the Virginia tidewater. Southern whites—those with any sense of the future anyway—began to see the migration as beneficial, a pressure valve on their demographic time bomb. Though increasingly superfluous in the wake of mechanized agriculture, the black population had become a majority in many rural counties, a growing threat to the world of Jim Crow that might one day require a reckoning. Now, through migration, much of that reckoning would come in the North.

The Baltimore to which W.M. fled was America's most northern southern city, and it was here, as an adult, that he truly learned the ways of white folk. Every day, when he walked into a little luncheonette across from the foundry, the owner's trained parrot would stretch its wings and squawk, "Nigger in the house, nigger in the house." Of course, he couldn't sit at the counter, but he could carry his lunch out, so he didn't let it bother him. He couldn't go into the downtown hotels, or restaurants, or into most shops save for the basements of the Howard Street department stores, and he couldn't even think of using one of the changing rooms to try on clothes. But then again, he didn't have the money for downtown, so he didn't pay it any mind.

In the schools, theaters, ball yards, and swimming pools of Maryland's largest city, strict segregation had long been the rule. City politics, the police and fire departments, the patronage of civil service—all of it was lily white, just as strict housing patterns had limited the black belt to a handful of dense, crowded neighborhoods on the eastern and western edges of downtown. On the east side, Gay Street became the central boulevard for black Baltimoreans, and to the west, there was Pennsylvania Avenue— the Avenue as it came to be known, black Baltimore's Broadway, home to dozens of juke joints and the legendary Royal Theater. Beyond those core areas, in rowhouse neighborhoods like Franklin Square, black families were consigned to back alleys in a fashion that left them only half visible to neighboring whites. Little was heard from the colored folk in places like Vine Street and Lemmon Street alley, save for the occasional house-rent party or fish fry, or the righteous shout that went up from the backstreets whenever a radio announcer declared that Joe Louis had put another white man on his ass.

Until the great migration north, the Germans, Irish, and Lithuanians who made Franklin Square their home saw little possibility that anything would change. Until World War II, in fact, change on the city's west side came only gradually. Originally, the gentle slope to the immediate west of downtown had been farmland, the possession of a gentleman farmer who forfeited all when he went off to fight in a Confederate uniform. After the bloodletting at nearby Antietam in 1862 and Gettysburg the following year, the Union Army used the confiscated land for an encampment and field hospital. The ramshackle medical facility drew nuns and clergy and soon spawned a small Catholic parish that would, in time, grow into the gothic behemoth of St. Martin's, its stone bell tower ringed by gargoyles that, the locals now liked to say, were too damn scared to come down and take their chances on the street.

As the city stretched westward after the Civil War, the redbrick Federal-style rowhouses were filled by a proletarian class of Germans, with some Irish and Scots mixed in—an immigrant class that predated the war and found some contentment in looking down on later arrivals. The settlers were shopkeepers and small businessmen, factory workers and longshoremen, clerical workers and political ward heelers. Many of the westsiders worked at Baltimore & Ohio's huge roundhouse and rail yard off West Pratt Street, many others on the piers that lined the Upper Patapsco a mile or so to the east. H. L. Mencken, the sage writer of the city, had been born in the rowhouse at 1704 West Fayette, then proceeded to spend his writing years in a Hollins Street home on Union Square, just a few blocks to the southeast.

During the early years of the migration, the working-class and middle-class whites of Franklin Square had no great love for the blacks who began to crowd the west side alleys or the core of the black belt along Pennsylvania Avenue, but neither was there a great deal of overt racial conflict. Baltimore had settled into a practiced and—from the white viewpoint, at least—functional segregation. If more rural blacks chose to shake the Carolina clay from their boots and find Lemmon Alley, or Vine Street, or the battered rowhouse slum of the lower Avenue, it hardly required accommodation or even a serious reckoning from Baltimore's governing elite. The Mason-Dixon line was a good forty miles to the north; racial separation was the civic firmament.

It took World War II and the epic of industrial rearmament to destroy the illusion of equilibrium, if not Jim Crow itself. In Baltimore, as in every industrial city, the influx of migrant labor accelerated at astonishing rates as factories, steel mills, and shipyards began running two and then three shifts. Nor, by wartime, was the rural migration a singularly black phenomenon. From west of the Shenandoah came the Appalachian whites, weary of scrub farms and darkened coal mines in West and western Virginia, desperate in their pursuit of a factory wage in the nearest metropolis of the Eastern industrial belt. They settled into rental properties carved from the poorer housing stock in alleys and on side streets.

As much as or more than the Southern black migrants, the Appalachians battered communal sensibilities in Franklin Square and throughout the southwestern part of the city. Older German and Irish residents quickly came to regard the new arrivals as Huns and Visigoths; for some of the mountain folk, indoor plumbing was beyond aspiration, and trash removal consisted of tossing dinner scraps from the back kitchen window. Whereas white working-class discomfort with neighboring blacks was muted by the distance between boulevard and back alley, poor whites were unconstrained by racial geography. When a family of hard-living, hard-drinking ex-coal miners moved into a third-floor walk-up and began raising hell, the whole block knew it.

As the wartime boom continued, some of the poorer west side neighborhoods began to destabilize. Pigtown, a neighborhood surrounding the B & O roundhouse and terminus, was so named because of nearby slaughterhouses, but in time the name would be imbued with a cold sarcasm among older residents who watched the neighborhood sag under the weight of so many poor Appalachians. To the north and east, the colored enclave around Pennsylvania Avenue also began to sprawl, as the growing black population could no longer be easily contained in a handful of city blocks. By the end of the war, the lower end of the Avenue—"the Bottom" as it came to be known—was regarded as the worst and most crowded black slum on the west side.

It was to the Bottom that W.M. moved a few months after arriving in Baltimore. He had found his uncle that first day off the bus and he had stayed with him for a time, but the man was a drinker. For weeks, the older man pressed his nephew for liquor money, but rather than give up some pay, W.M. moved out, getting a room of his own in the 700 block of Saratoga Street. He was fifteen.

He worked and he saved. When his father finally learned his whereabouts and came north to bring him home, W.M. stood firm. He wouldn't go back; he was his own man now, surviving in a new world. The foundry was backbreaking work and there was precious little to come home to in the room on Saratoga Street, but in Baltimore, more things seemed possible than people ever dreamed about down in the country.

When he was sixteen and still grinding at the foundry, he met a thirteen-year-old girl, a quiet churchgoing thing named Roberta. The first and only woman in his life was a Baltimore native, living just off the Avenue with her family, who had come up from tidewater Virginia. Being underage, W.M. needed a guardian's signature to approve a marriage, so his uncle did the honors. When some of the neighborhood people went so far as to get in touch with his father, asking him to stop such a youthful union, they got a sharp response.

"He's a man," Fred McCullough told them. "If he's supporting himself, I can't stand here and tell him what to do."

They lived for some years with Miss Roberta's family, with W.M. sharing his pay and all the time looking for something better. Beyond his wife and in-laws, he had few friends as a matter of choice. He didn't drink and wouldn't carouse and managed to stay aloof from the high life along Pennsylvania Avenue. He simply didn't trust a good time, and more to the point, he didn't trust anyone who did. He'd seen too many country boys waste themselves and their pay in the jukes and bars, or down at the legendary Selene's, which would survive for more than a decade as the great temple of Avenue whoring and gambling. His young wife had religion, and W.M., though never enamored of preachers and collection plates, was more than willing to do his share as a family man.

After twelve years at the foundry he found a better-paying job at American Standard, where he would lift cast-iron bathtubs and toilets and carry them around the plant as if they were stage props. He was a legend at American Standard: He never shirked, never tried to look for an easy way. Not once did he call in sick; why lie around in bed when you could just as well work an illness out of you? He still couldn't read, but after a few years at American Standard, he could see ways to modify and improve the manufacturing process. Plant managers had him walk around with a herd of efficiency experts and engineers who were redesigning the assembly line. Production quickly doubled, though W.M. never got a dime for his ideas.

He was at American Standard about a year when, in 1955, they moved into the Vine Street house. Franklin Square was still majority white working-class; even on Vine Street, the McCulloughs were neighbors to a half-dozen white families. Black and white got along well enough— W.M. felt a camaraderie with all of his neighbors that seemed to him genuine. They worked hard; so did he. And when one family was in trouble, everyone else on the block was quick to pitch in. Newly integrated by the Supreme Court decisions, the schools around Franklin Square were still strong, still stable. The streets were clean, the corners clear. More often than not, when someone's kid was misbehaving, the child stood a good chance of taking one slap on the behind from a concerned neighbor, then a second when he got home.

For W.M. and Miss Roberta, this was the best time of their lives. The family was growing as McCullough families always had—Fred McCullough had stopped at thirteen children; W.M. would beat that mark by two. Kathy had come first in 1948, then Jay four years later, then William Junior a year after that. Joanne and Judy followed them and then in 1957 came Gary, the sixth child and third son.

Not surprisingly, the McCullough children reflected the values of the neighborhood and home that raised them. All were willing to work as hard as was necessary, to take care of business, to live for more than just today. Kathy would travel the globe as a field engineer with Westinghouse; Jay would hold a planning position with the city government; Joanne would make her mark as a program analyst with Bethlehem Steel, Judy as a computer programmer. The son born just behind Gary, Daniel, would join the U.S. Army, rising to staff sergeant and serving overseas.

Until the early 1960s, life was very much as it was supposed to be on Vine Street. The children were growing, reaching for a better life than their mother and father had ever envisioned; the neighborhood seemed safe and stable. For the McCulloughs, it seemed the immigrant experience was playing out as it had for all those who came before them, for the Irish and the Germans, the Jews and the Lithuanians. They were not a wealthy family, nor would they ever be, but all things being equal, they had what they needed and their children and their children's children would reap the just rewards of so much struggle.

But of course, things were not equal. For the cities, the black migration would prove to be the single greatest social and economic phenomenon of the century, yet it was an event that would never be addressed in any systematic way. In Baltimore as elsewhere in the mid- to late 1950s, the urban migration led to the construction of federally funded lowincome housing, sited and then utilized along distinct racial lines. With the majority of the high-rise and low-rise developments built in the core of the black belt, that area grew more crowded, more oppressive.

Realtors seized the day, busting block after block. In the neighborhoods just north of Franklin Square, frightened whites fled at the first sign of a black home owner; in the late fifties, stable communities such as Edmondson Village could go from white to black within a year.

Along Fayette Street, too, the whites ran—many heading west toward suburban Irvington and Catonsville, others south across Baltimore Street, which would remain a hard-and-fast racial boundary for another two decades. By the early 1960s, W.M. could count only a handful of white strays, older residents mostly. The Jewish families were still working the corner stores, but none lived above the shops anymore. They drove down from Park Heights in the morning, worked the counter, then drove back with the day's receipts.

Almost overnight, the sense of shared community that W.M. had discovered and prized in Franklin Square was dead and buried forever beneath a blizzard of real estate signs. He had been among the neighborhood's first black home buyers, the crest of the immigrant wave. What broke behind him was not only a deluge of black working-class families trying to buy their own homes, but the working poor, the sad fodder for carved-up rental units, many of which were rowhouses already battered by the earlier Appalachian migrants.

On the west side of Monroe Street, some of the white homeowners held for a time, selling off to individual black buyers at prices that accorded their tree-lined blocks the pride and stability that home ownership always brings. But from Monroe Street down the hill to Franklin Square itself, there was very little that the landlords and speculators didn't eventually claim. It only got worse when city planners rammed I-170 through West Baltimore, knocking down blocks of rowhomes just north of Franklin Square, forcing ever more poor refugees into the worst of the rental properties.

By the mid-1960s, the poor had come to Fayette Street and the problems of the poor became the problems of the neighborhood. Worst of all, the industrial and manufacturing economy that had originally propelled the migration began to disappear. Among the later migrants, particularly, unemployment was chronic as factories closed and the demand for unskilled labor collapsed. Nor were the schools what they had been; white refugees took the tax dollars with them, though until the end of the decade, an adequate public education could still be had at high schools like Frederick Douglass, Carver, and Mergenthaler.

In the McCullough family, the older children seemed for the most part immune. The neighborhood was changing, but they had all grown up on the values of their parents, on streets that were still generally benign. The corners weren't corners yet; the drug trade had not yet grown bold and vast. But the scent of the game was in the air and a few were learning where to go and who to find.

By 1966, Ricardo had been born, and Rodney, too. Kathy, now the oldest of nine, was already out of the house, attending college. Gary almost nine, was already showing the kind of utter earnestness that his father could recognize as a McCullough trait. That year, Gary got his first job as a stock boy at Nathan and Abe Lemler's pharmacy, grocery, and liquor store on Lexington Street, and the Lemlers imparted everything they knew about work and business to the child. Gary worked hard, stayed honest, and was, in turn, trusted by the family. He made twenty dollars a week.

To Gary, the Lemlers seemed to be good people—they extended credit and would fill prescriptions without charge if someone was sick and unable to pay—yet they were regarded as outsiders by the locals, who saw them as purely mercantile. Gary felt his loyalty stretched to the limit when some of the older heads would roll through the store—snatching liquor bottles and carrying them off—and the Lemlers would ask Gary to chase after them. Once, he had followed Fat Curt's brother, Dennis, who had lifted a bottle of rye whisky.

"Nigger," Dennis asked, when Gary caught up to him, "who the fuck you think you is?"

It was a question he never had to answer; the riots after the 1968 assassination of Martin Luther King Jr. decided the matter. From Fremont Avenue to Edmondson Village on the west side, the Lemlers and nearly every other Jewish shop owner were burned out, eventually to be replaced by Korean merchants who would neither extend credit nor hire children from the neighborhood.

The riots accelerated the decline along Fayette Street. At night, a quiet but persistent heroin trade opened up at Fulton and Lexington, the corner where the Lemler store used to be.

At 1827 Vine Street, William Junior—known to all as June Bey—was first to stumble, losing himself by the early 1970s in a heroin addiction that would consume the rest of his adult life. His mother and father tried to wait him out, tried to revive their hopes each of the two dozen times June Bey took himself off the street for drug treatment. He'd been to Kentucky for the detox program there; he'd been down to Carolina to stay with family. But nothing took, and when the appliances around the house began to disappear, W.M. finally put him out.

It was the first heartbreak. Miss Roberta took solace in religion and her other children, praying all the while that June Bey might still see himself in a new light. W.M. did what he had always done; he swallowed hard and went back to work.

In the mid-1970s, American Standard closed their Baltimore plant, and the company provided W.M. with a twenty-year pension that amounted to exactly thirty-seven dollars a month—an absurd sum that he often thought of questioning, though his inability to read discouraged him from seeking a detailed explanation. For a time, W.M. drove a truck interstate for Sky King, then worked for a limo service, and then, in 1980, he got a license from the public service commission and began driving for Royal Cab. Most weeks, he worked six days of double shift, rising early to catch the morning rush, then coming in for lunch and a nap, then back out until ten or eleven at night. He drove everywhere, worked every neighborhood, relying on his instincts to keep him alive in a line of work as lethal as any in Baltimore. After being robbed a half-dozen times, he started carrying a pistol under the driver's seat.

W.M. was never much on conversation; it was always Miss Roberta who provided the day-to-day childrearing, who would take hold of the minor problems and major disasters in their lives. But W.M. served as the moral example, as a standard for will and endurance against which his children took their measurement. Gary, more than most, stood in absolute awe, and his own double- and triple-shift life was a tribute to his father. He'd learned a lot about business from the Lemlers, and what he didn't know he set about learning in half a dozen jobs that took him through high school. He cooked crabs down at Seapride on Monroe Street, clerked at some of the shops on Baltimore Street, sold a bit of weed now and then, and still found time to run all kinds of errands for his mother and father.

He graduated with honors from Mergenthaler Vocational—"Mervo, where they teach you how to earn a living, but not how to live," Gary liked to say—then spent the half year at Ohio State before getting that telegram from a pregnant Fran Boyd. He came home—not only because it was the right thing to do, but because he was tired of school. College was all talk and theory; Gary wanted to be out there, working and earning and scheming.

His sister Joanne told him about an affirmative action program at

Bethlehem Steel. For years, the company had steadfastly refused to hire blacks for skilled positions and was now playing catch-up. Gary took the test and scored well, getting an apprentice job and becoming one of the first black craftsmen at Sparrows Point, eventually rising to supervisor. He took a night job as a guard out at the Social Security building in suburban Woodlawn. Then he started buying cheap, vacant rowhouse properties in the neighborhood, rehabbing some as rental units and setting up Lightlaw, which he registered at City Hall as a minority contractor. He worked every day of the year—Christmas, Easter, New Year's, his own birthday—sometimes for sixteen hours a day. When the money began rolling in, when there was more under the mattress than he could spend, he began soaking up the financial publications, trying, on his own, to decode the Babel of stock and fund listings. He got a brokerage account with Charles Schwab, began trading, feeling his way through some ventures. At one point, his income from investments alone reached more than two thousand dollars a month.

Gary McCullough was a whirlwind, a man of dreams and plans. Before long, he was the talk of the neighborhood. For W.M., his son seemed proof positive that whatever problems there were on Fayette Street, they weren't going to hold his family down. June Bey had fallen, but he could still be counted as the exception. Nothing out there made you take drugs, or hang on the corner, or laze around the house all day waiting on a welfare check. W.M. and Miss Roberta had proved the other way of living, the right way; now their children were proving it, too.

The oldest children—Kathy, Jay, and Joanne—were not so sanguine. Repeatedly, they urged their parents to move off Vine Street, to buy a house or take an apartment in the county. Since the 1970s, suburban flight had ceased to be a white prerogative in Baltimore; the black middle-class had been pushing westward since the late 1960s, a step or two ahead of the working poor that would follow them down Frederick Road to Irvington and Yale Heights, or out Edmondson and Liberty Heights Avenues to Edmondson Village and Forest Park. Now, western Baltimore County—Woodmoor, Woodlawn, parts of Randallstown and Arbutus— was home to the black taxpayer. Left behind were too many of the broken families, too many who had grown up without hope; too many migrants and sons of migrants who had come too late to the city, who had never caught hold of the union-scale wages that allowed one generation to climb out of poverty and carry the next on its back to the suburbs.

The irony was ripe: Segregation had leavened the ghettos by keeping

black professionals and middle-class families active in the life of city
neighborhoods; now they, too, were missing at the community meetings,
at PTA conferences, at recreation centers, at block parties. By the late 1970s,
many of black Baltimore's institutional treasures—Provident Hospital,
Douglass High School, even the grand boulevard of Pennsylvania Avenue—
were, to one degree or another, failing.

W.M. and Miss Roberta sensed this, of course, just as everyone else
in the city sensed it. They had seen their older children move to suburban
homes; now those same children were pleading for them to follow. But
the mortgage was paid on Vine Street and they wouldn't get much if they
sold out. There weren't any savings to talk about, though the children
offered to help pay for the move. Still, that wouldn't do; neither W.M.
nor his wife could stand for that kind of charity. Besides, it felt like
home. Miss Roberta had fed a family out of that small kitchen; W.M.
had stepped down the same stone steps for every working morning going
back twenty-five years. There were all of the usual ties to the neighborhood; Roberta McCullough never missed a church function at St. James
on Monroe Street. And there were still others like them, too—good
people who would stick it out with them if they stayed. Ella Thompson.
And Bertha Montgomery, across the alley. And Paul Booth around the
corner on Lexington.

They stayed, just as Gary stayed on Fayette Street when Fran convinced
him not to buy that house out in Catonsville. But there was an inertia
to their decision, an inability to see just how bad Franklin Square had
become, or how much worse it would get. Slowly, in ways that were
perceptible only over years, the Fayette Street corners grew more and
more treacherous. The New York Boys came. Then the cocaine vials, and,
finally, the pipers and the ready rock.

Among the younger McCullough children, Darren, Sean, and Chris
were all as hardworking and serious as their predecessors. But the corner
caught up with Judy's husband about 1984, driving him out of a happy
marriage and up onto the Monroe Street corners. It caught up to Ricardo,
too, when his friends lured him out of the house to run with the pack,
trying their hands as sneak thieves and stickup boys. It caught up to
Kwame, the youngest son, so angry at everyone and everything that W.M.
actually tried to talk to him, going out of character to make his boy see
that a man had to make peace with himself and the world. But Kwame
couldn't see it, couldn't feel it the way W.M. had. For a time, Darren got
him a job at the shoe store on Baltimore Street, where Darren had made

manager, but Kwame spent the rest of his time in the streets, working packages or sticking up younger dealers with Shamrock. The corner also caught up to Kenyetta, the youngest, who got involved with a boy who gave her a child and then took to shooting people before a state charge finally stuck and he rode the prison bus to Hagerstown. The baby, Shakima, toddled around Miss Roberta's kitchen every day while Kenyetta tried to finish school at Southwestern.

But the shocker was Gary. The third son, who had taken life by storm; the wide-eyed dreamer who had learned his father's lessons and taken them to a new level. When Gary began the fall into drugs in 1986, his parents were shaken to the core. Gary had made it in a way that W.M. understood; others among his children were equally successful, but their way had been paved by educational opportunities and career plans. All of them made W.M. proud, but Gary's victories resonated with his father because he had won them as W.M. had—by getting up early to chase a few dollars more.

There was no sense in it, nothing to W.M.'s eye to explain how his son could fall so far. Gary split with Fran for good in 1985 and four years after that, all of it—the craftsman's job at Beth Steel, the second job, the properties, the Mercedes-Benz, the bank accounts, the brokerage account—was gone. Gary had been hurt; W.M. knew that. He'd been hurt by Fran, by the women who followed Fran. Quite a few people in the neighborhood had taken advantage, too, stealing from Gary; his son was always a little too trusting that way. But nothing to W.M.'s way of thinking could take hold of someone with Gary's dreams and Gary's mind and transform that person into a drug addict.

In the end, it was Gary who let them know just how much worse it could get, who taught them to fear their neighborhood the way it ought to be feared, so that standing at the front door on a summer day, watching the dealers work a ground stash, Miss Roberta could turn to her husband and say, very gently, that maybe the children were right. Maybe they should have left.

There was no more to it than that. No anger, no recrimination, no polemics against the police or the government or the white man. That wasn't the McCullough way. If W.M. blamed anyone, he blamed the men and women in the street, the sons and the daughters who had lost their way, who didn't understand life the way he did. If it were up to me, he'd sometimes tell people, you wouldn't need prisons and you wouldn't need jails either. If he had possession over Judgment Day, that gas chamber

down on Eager Street wouldn't shut down until the corners were clear.
He could say things like that and mean them, feeling the vengeance warming
in his veins. And then he'd walk out to the cab for his afternoon tour and
see Gary coming from the alley tester line, or June Bey nodding at the pay
phone, or DeAndre, his grandson—and a bright boy, too—huddled at the
mouth of Vine Street with the other touts and lookouts. At such moments,
W.M.'s heart would break and all the anger would rush out.

He had lived the way a man was supposed to live. He had played by
the rules, working all his life, working still to make ends meet, though
he was now of an age when most men retire. He had never gone on
welfare, or sought a handout, or complained about what did or didn't
come his way. He had taken a good woman and kept his vows. He had
brought fifteen children into the world, loved them, given them food
and clothes and a home, and sent them to schools to learn things that
he never had a chance to know. He had not been as clever as other men,
perhaps, or as wise with his money and property. And he had never
really understood the forces arrayed against him. But then, none of that
can be claimed as part of our national premise, our enduring myth that
says America is the land of opportunity, the last best hope for all races
and religions, and that any man who stays true to himself and works
hard here can and will succeed.

For the last half-century in the city of Baltimore, William McCullough
has stayed true to himself and worked as hard as any man conceivably
can. At age sixty-five, he has the woman with whom he shared a lifetime,
Miss Roberta. He has many children and grandchildren, some of whom
make him proud, some of whom don't. He collects a $37-a-month
pension. Six days a week—some weeks, seven—he drives a cab.

And every night, he comes home to Vine Street.

The snake has found Gary McCullough curled on the bed, the soiled
sheets twisted around his legs. He's half-awake and half listening as the
clock radio sputters Sunday morning sermons in a dull, metallic whisper.

The snake speaks his name, and Gary, with a supreme effort, rolls
over and sits up at the edge of the sagging mattress, his feet touching a
linoleum floor wet from the Friday night rain that sent a flood rolling
down the back cellar steps of his parents' house on Vine. Hunching over
as a wave of nausea hits, he cups his pounding head. He longs to go
back to sleep, even that half-assed, no-resting heroin sleep that greets
him every night, but the snake has his attention.

He reaches up, stretching as he gropes for the bare lightbulb in the ceiling socket. He finds it, gives a twist, then falls back to the mattress, spent. The weak light pushes back a bit of the darkness behind the mounds of molding clothes that frame the thin room.

It's a grim, tight space at the bottom of the Vine Street rowhouse, sprinkled with flotsam and jetsam from Gary's wanderings, bits and pieces that could have had a purpose, that once sparked a righteous McCullough plan, but now lay discarded, gathering dust: a busted black-and-white TV, a car's rearview mirror, a set of keys, church fliers, a broken clock, a chipped porcelain statue of embracing lovers.

Within arm's length of the bed stands a broken dresser for life's few absolute necessities: bottle caps, matches, a jar of water, syringes. Behind the paraphernalia rests a box fan that makes do as a coat rack now, but come summer, it's all there is to push the stale air and help Gary breathe through his asthma attacks. At the head of the mattress is a homemade wooden stool that serves as Gary's library shelf. A well-thumbed Bible shares the perch with a high school physics book, a grade school civics text, Thoreau's *Walden*, and Elie Wiesel's *Night*—books rescued from trash piles or church basements, then read and reread by Gary with keen interest. The Bible is creased and marked at Psalm 38, a verse of shame and repentance that resonates in Gary's mind night after night.

> *For your arrows have pierced me and your hand has come down*
>   *upon me*
> *Because of your wrath, there is no health in my body*
> *My bones have no soundness because of my sin,*
> *My guilt has overwhelmed me like a burden too heavy to bear*
> *My wounds fester and are loathsome because of my sinful folly*
> *I am bowed down and brought very low*

True penitence from within the haze. Gary knows the words by rote, reading them over and over in the dim basement light. And in the margin of the psalm, he has inked a rough graffito plea: "God help me, please."

But not now. Not this morning.

The snake won't be placated with psalms or supplications. Gary scratches his cheek and looks above him to the narrow wall shelf that holds the the other religious artifact in his basement world, the Box of True Blasts. Shaped like a cigar box, but smaller, the balsa-wood container serves as repository and museum for the touchstones of Gary's life on the corner—a treasure chest of happy memories to be perused in the spirit of nostalgia. He takes down the box and dumps its contents on the bed: the glassine bags, marked and stamped with an array of designs, logos, and slogans; the plastic vials, in a variety of sizes, each with a different colored top. Each a memento, a remembrance of bombs past, each a keepsake from a successful crusade, from a moment when a fiend got within snatching distance of the holy grail.

The green vial on the top of the pile? He got that one last year at Mount and Fayette, from the New York Boy, Scar, back when Scar had something to sell. Drop a little of that coke in some dope and yes Lawd, you had a speedball that would sing. And the Family Affair bag from this fall. Dag, that was right. But the recollection makes him grimace. The box offers nothing for the here and now—only touchstones from days gone.

Gary leans forward, fumbling with the dresser's top drawer, pulling it toward him and rifling the contents for a Newport butt he left there last night. It's a new habit that Ronnie gave him back in November, so now, in the daily pursuit of dollars for dope, he has to husband a little bit more pocket change for smokes. More often than not, he's unable to afford a pack, so he buys singles from the Koreans for a quarter each. He lights up and pulls hard for the nicotine, getting off a good couple of puffs, then stubs the filter into the damp linoleum. He waits, checking himself, taking stock.

No good. No good at all.

He goes back to the dresser, this time for an empty glassine bag. He holds it to the light and gives a little tap, then another, staring hard. Against all visible evidence, he grabs a burnt-bottom bottle cap and taps lightly at the bag, coaxing out a few grains of residue. He takes a syringe and adds a few drops of water, then pulls it up without even bothering to wave a match under the bottle cap, hunts a vein and slams the shot. For a few seconds, he's hope defined: the junkie alchemist, trying desperately to turn lead into gold. But nothing, no rush.

Gary searches for his clothes. One pair of pants is balled up on the bed; a second pair lies on the floor along with his shoes, a flannel shirt, and a sweater. For a moment, he makes no move to retrieve them. Instead, he folds his hands and bows his shaved head, a monk sending a silent prayer to a silent god. Let this pass.

But the snake is on the move.

It's Gary's worst fear. That snake down there, sliding through his intestines, growing, gathering strength, pushing its way through the soft organs of his underbelly, into his stomach, the slow climb up his esophagus, and then into his throat, cutting off his air, strangling him on one end, breaking his bowels on the other. For many of the fiends, it isn't like that. For them, withdrawal is a few days of low-grade flu, a sickness to be dealt with like any other. You take some aspirin, you crawl into bed, and you stay there and get what sleep you can until you come out the other side. For them, it's mind over matter, withdrawal being more about soul than body.

But for Gary, there's no play in it; the thing is all physical. For him, the very idea of withdrawal is epic because the snake owns every cell, every vein, every organ. Like last month, when he let his mother send him down to North Carolina to stay with his younger brother, Dan. Willing and determined, Gary fortified himself with one last blast, then crawled into the back of his brother's van. And he tried. Lord, they don't know how he tried. But the nausea never seemed to stop, nor did the craving slacken. He wrestled the snake for a few days, then stole off to find a corner near his brother's house. And that was the thing, too: You can't run from it. The corner is everywhere.

Now, galvanized by fear, he dresses at flank speed, pulling on one pair of pants, then a second to brace him against the February cold. No socks in the basement, though, so the shoes get laced over bare feet, the leather edges digging into his ankles. He pauses for a moment, looking down, and almost manages a smile at the pointy-toed, two-tone dress shoes, burgundy and tan, bought on a lark for four bills in a second-hand shop because they reminded him of better days. He starts up the stairs, then stops, rubbing his head. Where's the hat? Can't go nowheres without the hat.

Dag.

He tears the bedding apart, finding it wedged between the mattress and the warped wall panel. A lucky California Angels cap that's seen him through it before. He wears it with the brim behind him, smoothing the band against his forehead. The backward angel, up and moving, ready to wade into the mix.

He navigates the narrow passage through the basement, then makes his way up the steep staircase, climbing over and around an avalanche of bundled clothing tossed down the steps. He emerges in the center of the rowhome's first floor, stepping into a dining room where the table has been pushed to the wall, then covered with clothing, papers, and a dozen other workaday things. In the McCullough home, the kitchen long ago gave the dining room a beating, forcing its furniture and formality against the far wall, giving the back of the first floor to Miss Roberta's cooking and the chipped Formica table from which her family feeds.

Gary pauses for a moment at the basement door, caught by the sunlight from the back kitchen window. He wipes at his eyes, trying to adjust to the sight of his mother, working the stove, fixing W.M.'s lunch.

"Uh, Ma, I . . . ah, I need . . ."

His voice is soft, fading beneath the talk-show chatter of daytime television. She shakes her head. She doesn't have it, she tells him, and Gary knows it's true. If she had twenty dollars, she would reluctantly give ten to him, despite herself, so as not to watch her child suffer. He nods, accepting, and she offers instead to cook him some breakfast. An egg-and-bacon sandwich.

Gary shakes his head. The nausea drives him out of the kitchen and through the front door. He's on Vine Street, the winter wind cutting through his sweater and savaging his bare ankles. Up on Monroe, there is a feeding frenzy as fiends flow from a tester line—freebies thrown to fiends as advertising for the day's package. Spider Bags, too—this was a double blow, as the bags with the black widow on them are a definite bomb.

Gary knows he's missed his chance, but he jogs up to the corner anyway, pushing into the wind, arriving in time to watch Tiny give out the last one and glide off. Gary stands there in the flow of just-served fiends, his hand out, his hunger on display. He tries a plea.

"Hey Janice."

He gives Janice his stepped-on puppy look, but she ignores him. She has her own need; they all do. Gary, though, takes the refusal to heart. When I had it, he tells himself, I shared it. I shared it with crudballs who won't give me the time of day now.

He's alone at the top of the alley, standing amid the wind-whipped trash. He feels the snake move, then makes up his mind and heads off to find Ronnie. She'll make him suffer, but she'll also get him out of the gate.

There is a part of Gary that hates himself for leaning into Ronnie's punches, for putting up with her games for the sake of a blast. She calls herself his girlfriend, tells him she loves him, but the truth is, there's no sexual charge in the relationship, nothing that anyone could mistake for affection. They had messed around a few times, for appearances' sake more than anything else, but Ronnie holds no real attraction for Gary, save for her ability to make it happen from nothing. Every day, Gary pisses and moans over her crudball moves, over the abuse he takes. Every day, he tells himself that it's all one way, that he has tried to end the relationship only to have her follow him around and pull him back. Every day, he tells himself that this is the last time, that after Ronnie gets him the blast he'll cut her loose for good.

But there is no getting around Veronica Boice. She is the neighborhood sorceress, a rare mixture of will and wisdom and evil. She's different from Gary, who can't wrestle with the snake without the fear rushing up and overwhelming him. Not Ronnie. She channels the pain into a demonic fury that seems likely to crush anyone standing between her and her shot. Gary saw it happen a few weeks back, when Ronnie took her ninety-pound frame up Fayette Street and stared down the New Yorkers.

"Gimme a blast," she told Gee. "Last one wadn't shit."

There she was in the middle of Fayette and Monroe, not a nickel to her name, a whippet of steel wire standing up to big, bad, bat-waving Gee, threatening: "Gimme a blast or I'll call the motherfucking poh-leece. You know I will."

The crowd took it in, amazed. Gee laughed, made a joke, tried to play it off in front of all the touts and customers. But he could see it; he could see the dusty bitch dropping dime over a single vial and he could see that the choice for him was between minor charity and felony murder.

Gee gave in, slipping her one just to see her gone. And Gary, watching all of this from the sidelines, was once again staggered by the kamikaze logic that Ronnie always brought to the game. Ronnie punking Gee in the middle of Monroe Street. Dag.

He warms now at the memory, at the thought of finding the girl. He cuts from Vine Street across the vacant lot and through the back alley behind his parents' house, then out onto Fayette Street through a second gap in the rowhouses, arriving at Ronnie's sister's house, where Ronnie's been spending the colder nights. Pulling one hand from inside the sweater cuff, he bangs twice on the door, then twice again.

One of the twins, sleepy, stumbles out of the front room, cracks the door, and stares mournfully out of the vestibule.

"She not here," he says, closing the door before Gary has a chance to react. His world is shrinking; the snake twists maliciously down in his bowels. He turns back toward Monroe, but Eggy Daddy and Fat Curt and the rest of the regulars are already on station, hustling the morning crowd. No work up there.

He heads down the hill. Fran might take care of him, for old time's sake. Or DeAndre. Yeah, Andre, who's got it going on down Fairmount. But at the Dew Drop Inn, only Bunchie is out on the stoop, looking none too good herself.

"Fran in bed," she says. "Andre gone to school."

School? DeAndre? Lord, please, what are the chances of that? Gary stumbles on, heading down Gilmor without any real plan, the snake now coiling and uncoiling in his throat. He goes around the block and turns toward Fayette, defeated, moving through the crowd at Mount Street, looking into the eyes of a half-dozen regulars who have already made their shot. By now, he's unable to gather his wits, to endure the snake long enough to manufacture a hustle.

"Hey, hey," a voice calls.

Gary looks up to see a face, vaguely familiar, smiling at him from the other side of Mount Street.

"What's up with you?"

Gary squints, trying to focus. Now he's got it. The guy from Stevie's room. The fiend who's been shuffling in and out of Dew Drop Inn for about a month now, firing with half a dozen others in Stevie Boyd's rogues' gallery. Doug, remembers Gary. Name is Douglas for sure.

Gary crosses the street.

"Nothin' yet," he tells Doug.

"Man," says Doug, taking stock, "you looking flat-out rough."

Gary nods agreement. "I feel bad. Can't get started."

"No, hey, I can hook you up with something," says Doug. "I got somethin' goin' on."

Gary takes this in. Doug is going to get him over. Doug, who hasn't done anything but use the same shooting gallery. Gary nods agreement, hopeful, but waiting for the shoe to drop.

"Found this spot," says Doug. "They practically asking you to take their shit. I'm serious. This one store out on Forty West been keeping me well all week."

Gary nods. He can do it. He can do anything if the snake goes back down into its hole. And Doug understands. He'll get Gary the jumper: twenty on the hype, free of charge, so long as they share the caper. To Gary's ears, it's burning bush time, with Yahweh himself shouting out to him from the unconsuming flames.

I'm up for it, Gary thinks. I'm up for anything.

An hour and a half later, he's stepping off the Route 40 bus out near Westview, walking around the county like a damn puppy at Doug's heels. He's out of his game now, stumbling through the shopping mall doors, still trying to fight the snake because Doug's twenty wasn't much.

"We go in separate-like," Doug tells him outside the J.C. Penney. "You follow me up the escalator where they got this shelf of irons. You the lookout, I scoop. Nothing to it, my man."

Gary just nods. Yeah. Lookout. Look out for what?

In they go and Gary looks around, trying to spot security guards from among the customers but not at all sure of what he's seeing. Doug's out in front, hellbent for the steam irons. Gary watches his partner sidle up to the display, watches as Doug comes out with a worn Penney's shopping bag. One, then two, three, four, five, six. Gary's on the other side of the aisle, fidgeting, looking around frantically for the handcuffs sure to come. But no, everyone on the floor is oblivious.

He follows Doug out the side entrance and into the parking lot, thinking, that they're both invisible. A couple of raggedy-ass, dope-eyed black men stumbling through a county shopping center, lifting appliances, and we're flat-out invisible. We just walk in and take what we want.

"See?" says Doug. "Nothin' to it."

A fine caper, and Gary is proud, the high of their success pushing the reptile deeper in his belly. At the bus stop, Doug intrudes on his reverie, wondering where they can off the merchandise. "Been dumpin' a lot of irons on Fayette," he says apologetically.

For that, Gary's got a plan of his own, a contribution to the cause greater than that of a mere lookout. With real delight, he tells Doug where the irons are going and who will be paying for them.

"Say what?"

Gary nods, smiling wickedly.

"The police gonna buy our irons," says Doug, doubtful.

"Yes indeed."

Which is pretty much what happens when the two of them get back to the city and find the right corner bar at Baltimore and Smallwood Streets, a place that Gary knows is a hangout for off-duty police. For good retail items, Gary has used the bar before, learning that the rollers, like everyone else, love a discount. Just like that, three of the irons are gone; ten dollars each and everyone's happy, no questions asked. Doug

is impressed, even more so after they walk back up the hill and Gary
goes salesman on the workers building the new wing at Bon Secours,
unloading two more irons on the hard hats.

Cash money. They head back for Mount and Fayette and Gary's mind
is spinning with the glory of the caper, oblivious to the cold, indifferent
even to the snake itself. It's all the better because he made it happen
without Ronnie. Now he's thinking that Ronnie isn't much, that he can
cut her loose. At Mount Street, they jump into the action like new shooters
at a crap table.

"Who got those Black-and-Whites?" Gary asks. Tallyho.

The next day, they're together again, county-bound, riding the MTA
out to the same stop, giddy at the possibilities. Doug talks like a broken
record, offering up the same plan. Gary shows no concern, because what
the hell, they're invisible. Same spot, same shelf—Doug hits the irons
while Gary stands around like some kind of referee. One, two, three,
four—then Doug stops, probably figuring there isn't much of a steam
iron display left. This time Gary is out the door first, crossing the
promenade, then turning to wait for his partner.

But no Doug.

Gary waits, then walks back to the entrance, close enough to catch
a glimpse of Doug being led off by two security guards. He feels his
stomach roll, his mind racing. Got to think. Got to think on this. The
guards walk Doug away, back to the security office, but no one comes
for Gary. He wanders down the promenade, retrieves a newspaper from
a trash can, then takes a seat on a bench, hiding behind the sports section
with no real plan. Panic steals his high.

Ten minutes later, Gary is still there when three security guards
suddenly appear, blocking him against the bench.

"Come with us."

"I wouldn't do . . . I wasn't with . . ."

Gary's protest is weak and he knows it; his ability to carry a lie is
the poorest part of his game. In the security office, he's reunited with
Doug, who gives him a guilty look. They're left to sit there in silence
while papers are shuffled and bodies move around them. Watching it all
from within the fog, Gary is dazzled by a voice, businesslike and droning,
then a hand extending papers. Gary, clueless, takes the pen and signs
away, then waits some more until the county police arrive and he's in
the back of a police wagon for the short run to the Wilkens lockup.
There, he sits in a common holding area, wondering when he might see

a court commissioner, and bargaining with the snake, trying to figure some way to make peace with the animal inside.

He's the very picture of abject poverty, at least until some tattooed white boy walks over, lifts his shirt, and tugs at an Ace bandage wrapped around his ribs. Three bags of dope fall to the ground and the white boy laughs at the expression on Gary's face.

He picks up one of the glassine bags and looks over in gratitude; the white boy seems Christlike, feeding the multitudes. No spike, so Gary breathes it deep into one nostril, then leans back to hear the white boy's laughter and feel the snake backing away.

A few minutes later, they give him his call. Gary handles the receiver gingerly, dreading the answer at the other end. He's causing pain they don't deserve, but he has to get out.

"Ma . . . yeah, Ma," he says. "I'm locked up . . . Out in the county, Ma. They got me locked up."

He winces visibly at his mother's voice, seeing her sagging down at the kitchen table, imagining the prayers running around her head. He tells the tale haltingly, painting himself a victim. Miss Roberta listens to a story that Gary hears as feeble even as he tells it. Finally, she cuts him off:

"Gary, what were you doing out there in the first place?"

He doesn't have an answer.

"Oh Gary."

She promises to call his brother Ricardo, who is now off the corner and doing all right for himself, making money down at the crabhouse and on a second job out at Social Security. Cardy might help, but beyond that she can't promise, telling Gary that money is tight, that she'll talk to his father when he gets home. Gary hears that and swallows hard.

"Ma, please," says Gary. He's begging finally, promising to change, get off the drugs, maybe get back his old job at the Point and do all the things he used to do. "Ma, I'm gonna make it up to you, I promise."

His mother reaches Ricardo, scrapes up the money and finds a bondsman, but Gary gets the bad news when he's pulled out of the bullpen in the afternoon: He can't be released by the county; he has a detainer from Baltimore city.

An old assault warrant, the turnkey explains. Gary tries to remember. Assault? Who? He didn't assault anyone. It doesn't register until he meets the city fugitive detective, thumbing his way through the paperwork.

"Says here, you hit, ah, Veronica Boice."

Ronnie's revenge. Her trumped-up humble of an assault charge from when Gary cut her out of a blast. Dag.

The next ride takes him downtown. It's Gary's first trip to the city jail, that tiered nightmare at the city detention center and state penitentiary complex on Eager Street. He's out of his depth and he knows it.

In the intake area, he unwinds slowly, his eyes trying to adjust. He's in a barred confine littered with maybe a dozen men—some white strays, but mostly black—being processed in and out of the facility. From behind a screen, a lieutenant pulls his paperwork, takes his thumbprint, and points him in the general direction of the bullpen. It's eighty bodies deep, a murmuring, stinking mob squeezed around a single metal toilet.

Gary struggles for space, eventually squeezing into a spot along one wall. He slumps down, tuning out the noise, eyes capturing a verse or two lifted from Isaiah, another fragment of raging prophesy about sin and redemption. He's barely digested that much when the guards send them out on the tier, into J-section, where a coterie of broke-down old-time hustlers share space with some of the younger souls. Gary draws an old white gunner from South Baltimore as a cellmate, a veteran who has been jailing for years, who knows to keep a low profile.

Soon enough, Gary knows it, too. He quickly gets a sense of the sharks, the kind you want to keep from, especially the crazed one in the cell directly across from him. Banging the bars, eyefucking anything that moves, the neighbor across the way spends the time talking to no one in particular, telling the world just how bad he is. Beyond him, though, J-section seems pretty tame.

Next morning, they let them out on the tier a half hour before breakfast for a chance to move around, maybe get to a telephone. Today, though, the sharks are making all the calls, so Gary heads off to the mess hall and a chance to look into that blue chain-linked sky along the way. Breakfast is two thick slices of bread, two packets of jelly, and a cold boiled egg. Gary throws it all together as a sandwich and forces it down. Then it's back down the funnel and back into that cell. Twice more like that and he can call it a day.

He's a novice here, jailing without a game face, genuinely incapable of the requisite brutality. No shank, no moves, no allies, no money, but he's making it, discovering that the words of Islam he learned in an earlier life can be a key. In the afternoon of that first day, he joins the little prayer group that nestles in one cell, hearing the words, talking the talk, giving it some meaning. The regulars are receptive; Gary is carving out a little niche, getting some breathing space and a chance at the phone. His mother promises that they'll have a paid bail on the city charge soon. And, most important, an old-timer in the section comes through with pills that manage to hold the snake at bay.

A day more and Gary's thinking he can be hard, like Gee or Drac or any of the corner gangsters. Hard like Ronnie, who can do a month in women's detention standing on her head. Gary is showing them all up in his mind, showing them he can do what he has to, thinking these thoughts until the white boy shows up, a kid, really, but shaded a little too far toward suburban, with wispy blond hair. Anyone with a soul has to wince when they drop the kid in with the madman across the way.

The kid sits at one edge of the metal bunk and looks across the aisle at Gary, who tries to give back a reassuring smile. Night comes on with the lights dimmed, the noise muted. Gary closes his eyes, but night never brings real silence to Eager Street. Screams, sobs, cursing, laughter punctuate the hours; in jail, you cry at night—at least you do if you're still capable of crying. After a time, Gary gives up trying to sleep and slides back against the wall, staring into the dimness. Passing time.

He catches a movement in the cell across the way. Gary thinks he sees the glint from a gold ring slicing through the air, smashing down into a sleeping form. He hears a whimper, then the ripping of fabric and flashes of white skin. And then, a shattering of sound, with the caged animal cursing over a piercing endless scream that banks off the bars and echoes down the tier. Something is tossed from the cell; Gary squints in the darkness until his eyes make out what looks like the bloody stub of a broken fluorescent tube.

The guards finally come and take the kid away. Gary closes his eyes, praying into that void, petitioning every power in the universe to take him home. No more dope, no more capers.

For all that night and the next, he's singing the redemption song, making plans for the better life to come, promising to wash the sin from his hands. He's still talking like that on the day after, when the bail money is right and he's gliding out from under the razor wire on Eager Street.

He's back on Vine the next day, breathing deeply, feeling good about himself, ignoring the chants of the touts, ennobled by the effort to make good on his oaths. I can do this, he tells himself. I can get it all back.

His father's cab comes in off Monroe, rolls down the slope and rides up over the curb to park in front of the neighbor's house. W.M. gets out, pausing a second from the effort.

Then he sees his son and lifts a huge hand to chest level for a small wave. Gary blinks, his eyes filling, and father and son search each other for a moment, but neither takes the moment any further. W.M. breaks the stare, then walks by in silence, wearily climbing the steps to the house. Gary watches him, loving him even from the depths of the abyss.

The front door slams and Gary is alone on the street, wondering whether the jailhouse pills got him through, whether the snake is dead or just waiting. He watches two women get served in front of a vacant garage and feels the vicarious pleasure of the transaction. He's still unwilling to go up to the corner, but equally unwilling to leave his front steps.

He sees her first up on Monroe Street, drifting back and forth at the mouth of the alley. Indifferent to her surroundings, the weather, her own physical being—a haunted creature, pinning him down with her eyes alone, drawing him wordlessly toward her. For a moment, he thinks to turn and run, to get into his mother's kitchen and ask for an egg sandwich. Instead, he walks up that hill pretending he'll do battle with her, scream at her, tell her how he suffered. But his voice isn't harsh enough for the task; the words come in sad appeal, not anger.

"Ronnie, why you do me like that?"

She snorts derisively, looking away.

"You had me locked up for nothin'."

She ignores him, watching a tout approach a customer near the pay phone.

"You put me in jail behind nothin' at all."

"Gary, you know there won't be no case when it comes to court."

He says nothing.

"You miss me, love? I got a welcome home gift."

Her hand comes out of a sweatshirt pocket, her fist balled.

Gary looks at the hand, then up into Ronnie's eyes. And it's over without a struggle.

"Careful," he says, "I don't want my mother to see."

Late the next morning, he's down in the basement, same as he ever was, waking slowly at the sound of his name. Ronnie lies on the edge of the mattress beside him.

"Gary . . . Gary . . . Gaaaarrry."

His mother is at the top of the landing yelling into the darkness, exasperated. "Gary!"

He finally stirs. "What time is it?"

"Gary, I need you to go to the store."

Ronnie giggles, and he shushes her down. He gets up and starts to dress, telling Ronnie to get out through the cellar door. She laughs again, then begins pulling herself together.

"Come over after," she tells him at the door. "I found some stuff in a garage we can take to the scales."

It's Gary who laughs this time. Ronnie doesn't know a damn thing about what sells and what doesn't at United Iron and Metal. It isn't her game and if that's all the plan she's got, then he's got to start worrying. The last speedball is already wearing thin.

Gary makes it upstairs to the dining room, into the light, looking worn and lost. His mother gives him one glance and knows, but says nothing because there's nothing left to say. She goes to the small break-front, rifling through a stack of chipped plates and saucers until she finds the $10 bill hidden there. She hands it to him, telling him to bring back five pounds of potatoes and two boxes of Hamburger Helper.

He stands there for a moment, staring at the bill, watching it burn his palm. The price of admission. Gary wonders whether his mother has lost her mind. She can see that he's ailing. She can't expect, and yet . . . He hesitates, his mind taking in the runoff from some rare reservoir of better nature. Something is going on here, something that suddenly seems more important than all the promises he gave no real thought to keeping.

He pockets the money, sensing that this, at least, is tangible, a real chance to go beyond the silence that stands between them, to justify both the loving mother and the dutiful son. This is a mission, a hero's journey.

"Be right back."

He's out the back door and into the alley, but it doesn't matter which way he goes. It's nearly noon and the shop is bustling from Monroe to Gilmor; he's surrounded. He's going to have to face it, wade through it, and emerge on the other side.

He heads up the alley toward Monroe Street, the shortest distance to the store. But walking past Blue's house, he sees Pimp ducking under the busted rear door, looking like he's flush. Gary wets his lips, pulls the Angel hat up, wipes at his brow. The snake hisses, cursing.

He makes it to Monroe, stepping out of the alley and into the beehive. Up the street, at Vine, it's all Spider Bags, and down on Fayette Street,

Death Row and the Pink Top vials are honey for another swarm of fiends. Gary watches with practiced eyes as those with short money look for hook-ups, as Fat Curt steers a couple of hungry souls down Vine Street, as Eggy Daddy sings the merits of the Pink Tops.

Gary rivets his eyes to the ground and pushes one foot, then the other down the pavement toward Pratt Street and the grocery. He's soon past the liquor store, across Fayette, and heading down the hill. So far so good.

"Gah-ray."

It's Junie talking. Gary makes the mistake of lifting his head. Dope and coke are flying everywhere: touts taking orders, dealers handing off, other bodies on urgent missions flashing past. It's in the air. He can smell it, taste it. And Junie's got that Mike Tyson. The shit's a bomb.

Gary's hand, the one with the death grip around Hamilton's throat, is coming alive, pulling itself out of his pocket, moving with a will all its own. I could tell her I got robbed. Or just not come home. Hang with Ronnie somewhere. Stay down on Fayette Street, give it a couple of days and she'd forget.

He looks at Junie's face. A mask, the eyes dead.

No. He jams the offending hand deep into his pocket.

"Ain't up," he says, then pushes past, crossing Baltimore Street, gaining speed, past Blue's son, Dontanyn, the last retailer in the line, before rolling downhill to the market.

Inside, he gathers the stuff, but dag, the prices are way high. He thinks about cutting the order. Maybe shave off a nickel. Tell her he got mixed up, or just drop the bag in the kitchen while she's upstairs sleeping. It would be nothing to keep five and find a hookup with some other short money. Get ten, maybe twenty on the hype. That'll work.

He's trapped in the aisle, holding one box of Hamburger Helper, then two, then one again. He looks at the label. The stuff ain't even good for you, too many chemicals. He stands there for a minute more, until the scales tip and he grabs both boxes and the taters, goes to the register and gives up a bill as crumpled as his spirit.

The way home is not the hero's journey. He climbs Monroe Street, package in hand. He drags his lonesome ass past the touts, feeling weak. The snake spits out its contempt.

"What took you so long?" asks his mother.

He mumbles half an answer.

"Want to eat?" she asks him, her voice now soft.

Gary looks at her, sees that she knows. Maybe she knew the whole time. He wants to say something, to bring it home, but the snake seizes the moment instead.

"No, Ma," he says, "I got to go out."

DeAndre McCullough leans against the oversized concrete flowerpots outside the rec center doors, his demeanor on chill, his face tucked down inside the hood of his sweatshirt. R.C. is perched next to him on the steps, lacing and relacing his new Jordans, listening with growing impatience as DeAndre tells the tale. Boo is against the other flowerpot, half listening, half waiting with a broken fragment of the playground's crumbling asphalt in his hand, watching for a rat to stick its head out of the discarded easy chair at the end of the alley.

"You was getting out the hack?"

"Right on Baltimore Street," says DeAndre.

"Sheeeeet," R.C. says. "We should call a meeting."

DeAndre nods agreement.

"We should send a message," adds R.C. "Go down there deep."

"You see who it was?" asks Boo.

DeAndre shrugs.

"But, yo, Black, you was comin' from the projects," insists R.C. "You was down the hill where they always be. That's why they took them shots at you."

DeAndre nods agreement. He likes it when anyone calls him Black. He fashioned the street name himself, figuring that any real gangster ought to be able to fashion his own corner legend, rather than leaving such important matters to random chance. His family used to call him Onion, because when he was little his head had that particular shape. DeAndre hated Onion.

"I'm saying we should go strong," adds R.C., warming to the idea. "Fuck them project niggers. They ain't all that."

It probably was the Lexington Terrace boys who took a shot at DeAndre on Baltimore Street, and by rights C.M.B. should mount up and march back down there in force. But DeAndre has other things crowding his mind; they all do since they started going off to sling drugs in ones and twos. Hard to raise a posse when the crew is scattered over a half-dozen corners.

"Must be them," says Boo, chiming in late. "Or maybe those niggers from Stricker and Ramsay."

"Boo, you stupid," says R.C. "They ain't gon' be up on Baltimore Street. And, yo, half of them is white anyway."

"So?" asks Boo, wounded. "Least I ain't stupid like you, R.C. Least I go to school."

"I go to school," R.C. says, then catches himself before the other two dissolve in laughter. "Well, I will go to school soon as my mother gets me into Francis M. Woods."

That's the current theory on Richard Carter's academic career. If he could only get out of Southwestern and into Francis Woods, then he'd turn it around, maybe get to the tenth grade before reaching the age of majority. It's a fine theory, and there are appreciable differences between the chaos of the Terrordome, as the local kids call Southwestern, and the controlled anarchy of Francis Woods. But the contrast is relevant only if a student were to attend more than, say, two or three days a semester. R.C. always hits a shopping mall for the back-to-school fashion sales, then shows up looking right for the first day of class. After that, it's back to the streets.

As for DeAndre, lately he's been living in both camps. Since Rose Davis put him back on the rolls last month, he's been making it down to Francis Woods for little more than half of his classes. He's also been slinging enough of his Blue Tops on Fairmount to keep money in his pocket. Not as much as he'd like, of course—Tyrone Boice plucked him good when he tried to bring his vials up to Monroe Street—but enough to get by.

"What you say?" DeAndre asks, changing the subject.

"Huh," says Boo.

"About the thing."

"Yeah," says Boo, throwing the asphalt chunk. Hitting the chair, missing the rat.

DeAndre waits for more of an answer. When none is forthcoming, he suppresses an almost overwhelming desire to smack Boo upside his head. He's been trying to give Boo a little piece of his package on consignment, bring on a subcontractor and make a little more than he could make on his own.

"I'm sayin' you'd get twenty-five," DeAndre tells him.

"Twenty-five dollar?"

R.C. laughs loudly from the steps. "Boo, goddamn!"

"No," says DeAndre. "That's the split."

"Oh yeah," says Boo, nodding until silence descends on them.

DeAndre looks over at Boo and waits. Boo is a loyal member of C.M.B., but sometimes talking to him is like banging your head on a wall. DeAndre's latest partner in the Blue Top venture on Fairmount was Corey, his cousin Nicky's boyfriend. And while Corey didn't mess up like so many others, he also wasn't spending as much time on the corner as DeAndre. So hiring Boo seemed to make sense, assuming simple math was at all within his grasp.

"How much I get?" Boo asks finally.

"DAMN, BOY," shouts R.C. "YOU IGNORANT AS SHIT."

"At least I ain't messin' up all the time like you do," says Boo, bitterly. "You always a fuck up."

Now DeAndre laughs. It was true enough: R.C. was always messing up the money; he couldn't sling drugs for two days without getting into some kind of hole.

"Fuck you, bitch," mutters R.C.

DeAndre breaks it down to Boo slowly: I give you forty, you sell out and one-fifty comes back to me and fifty you keep. You sell twice that, you make a hundred dollars. And the Blue Tops, DeAndre assures him, they are the bomb; he's selling out at five dollars a vial on Fairmount. If Boo wants to try them down at Ramsay and Stricker, they could go for dimes.

"Okay," says Boo.

They sit for a time on the two thin steps below the rec doors, glad for a February day with a little warmth. Distracted by a conversation that amounts to half war council, half marketing meeting, they hardly notice as bodies begin to drift in from Fayette Street, lining up meekly. In scarcely a minute, eighteen men and women are standing hard by the fence, on the edge of the playground, across the vacant lot from Mount Street. All in a row, all waiting patiently.

From here, too, they can see Collins come north up Vincent from Baltimore Street and park his radio car at the intersection with Fayette.

"Bitch always hanging 'round Malik's house," DeAndre says.

"Yo, that's cause Malik be snitching," says R.C. "Many times as he gets locked up and never goes to jail, I'm telling you that boy be snitching."

They watch a tall, lanky fiend walk up the middle of Fayette Street in front of Collins, pulling a new refrigerator balanced on a homemade wagon.

"Collins ain't shit," DeAndre declares. "Last summer, he pulled me up on Gilmor, sayin' he was gonna kick my ass. If my mother wasn't there, I'da fucked him up."

"Collins always be pickin' at us," R.C. complains. "Like we're the only ones doing shit."

"He ain't as bad as Bob Brown," says Boo.

"That's what I'm saying," says R.C. "They always be after us like we the gangsters."

"Bob Brown come 'round an tell me I can't even sit on my own steps," says DeAndre. "That shit ain't right."

Three teenagers—two males and a younger girl—come out of the side alley on Mount and head toward the line of waiting adults. The line seems to straighten in anticipation as one of the young men stands near the end of the line, his right hand tucked inside his jacket. The other escorts the girl to the front of the line, where she begins to hand each fiend a bag.

Testers.

From washing machines to widgets, every product needs marketing and promotion, and street drugs are no exception. In every open-air market in the city, samples are offered up early in the day to spread the word that so-and-so's shit is truly a bomb. And because a weak tester would be self-defeating, the free samples rarely disappoint. Word that a crew is putting out testers can come minutes or hours—and sometimes even a day or more—in advance of the actual event, and the possibility of free bag or vial can produce a lemming run through a back alley or vacant lot.

"Family Affair back slingin' like I don't know what," says R.C., watching the line dissolve.

Just around the corner from the tester hand-off, Collins still sits in his radio car, his view obstructed by the rowhouses on the north side of street. As the fiends skirt out of the alley in twos and threes, the patrolman seems to catch on. He pulls his cruiser into Fayette Street in a hurry, wheeling around the corner at Mount. Too late; the last of them is in full flight.

"Collins ain't shit," DeAndre says again, getting up to leave. R.C. stands up, too, stretching and yawning.

"Black," says R.C. "You gonna go to the dance?"

"When?"

"Valentine's. Miss Ella havin' a sock hop."

"What's that?"

"Like a dance."

"You going?"

"Oh yeah," says R.C., proud. "Me and Treecee. You gonna bring Reeka?"

Tyreeka Freamon has been DeAndre's girl since the summer. She hasn't been on Fayette Street long; until last year, she'd been living with her father in East Baltimore—her mother, too busy chasing vials to keep track of her, caught a drug charge that took her to women's prison in Jessup. Then, when Tyreeka couldn't get along with her father's new girl-friend, she landed at her grandmother's house on Stricker Street. DeAndre likes the newness of Tyreeka, the fact that there isn't a neighborhood history behind her; and he likes her show of independence, the way she doesn't always hang with the other girls on the fringe of C.M.B. That's partly because she's still going to school on the east side, partly because she likes to hang with the boys, which is good and bad for DeAndre— good because it made it easy to holler at her, bad because there are always others waiting to do the same.

She's young—thirteen last September—but she's not young. Every boy in the neighborhood has noticed the curves and the way Tyreeka moves. DeAndre knew Linwood had his eyes on her; so did Chris and Sean. In that crowd, DeAndre was hardly the best-looking suitor. Tyreeka, he knew, saw him as too dark-skinned at first, too ordinary looking back then, before he let his dreds grow out and found his look. But DeAndre got close to her first by playing that he was interested in her younger cousin, Tish, who had been nursing a child's crush on DeAndre.

"You know my cousin like you," Tyreeka told him.

"Yeah," he told her, "but I like you."

From then on, he was all over Stricker Street, spending near every dime he could scrape together by slinging at Hollins and Payson, or on Fulton, or on Fairmount. First, he bought her new Nikes; then it was trips to the movies at Harbor Park. By the time summer ended they'd seen every last thing that had come to the downtown theater complex—the good ones twice or three times. Whatever was left over went for shopping trips down at Mt. Clare or Westside, with DeAndre spending as much on his own clothes as he gave to Tyreeka. Then there was that video game down at Bill's, the one called Street Fighter; DeAndre had her learn enough to play him on it, and not a night went by that they didn't pour fifteen or twenty dollars in quarters into the slot. He was leaking money in those days, two hundred a week just to stay next to Tyreeka. Still, Linwood and Sean were losing their minds. Why, they asked Tyreeka, did you pick that ugly, black-ass nigger?

She knew where the money came from, of course. In the beginning, he actually brought her down to the corners to pass the time. She'd sit on the stoop; he'd serve a customer and then stop back to play around. But as things got more serious, he could see that it wasn't right. There is no respect in having your girl out on the corner with you.

The sex only started coming in the late fall, with DeAndre getting to her first in the back bedroom at the Dew Drop and later using his parent's old house up the block, where the pinup girls stared down on them as they went at it. Out in the street, he talked trash like everyone else did, telling himself and everyone else he was gonna bust the bitch. But he genuinely liked Tyreeka and so he tried to be good to her, it being her first time and all.

Now they're together, but DeAndre is still worrying. Tyreeka likes to fool with his friends, and when it comes to girls, he doesn't trust any of them. Linwood is still hungry for it. And Dewayne. And Tae is a creeper; he's been flirting with Tyreeka since the day she moved into the neighborhood. No, DeAndre definitely has to take her to Ella's dance, or she'll be there without him and that won't do.

"Ella say Kiti gonna be mixin'," says R.C.

"Yeah, I be there," DeAndre says, before turning his attention back to Boo. "You comin'?"

"Huh?"

"You comin' down?"

"Yeah."

And off he goes, a fifteen-year-old entrepreneur on his daily commute to the office. With Boo trailing, DeAndre walks past Stubby, who's back out slinging Pink Tops at Fayette and Vincent since Collins rolled out; on past Scar, who's selling green vials in front of the vacant house on the other side of the street; on past Drac, who's working out with Killer Bee along Gilmor; arriving at last at the Fairmount corners, the market niche that he has made his own. Fairmount and Gilmor, home of the Big Blue Top.

There, on his corner, DeAndre proceeds to have a day like no other, a sell-out-the-store bonanza that keeps him running into the late hours of night. He's got a bomb and his name is ringing. Customers are coming at him from Monroe Street, from Hollins and Payson, from down below Baltimore Street. He's out there when Boo sells off his allotment and settles up. He's out there still when Boo has gone home for the night. He's tired, working hard, and ultimately, getting a little bit lazy in the wee hours—all the more so after two Phillies blunts packed with that good Edmondson Avenue weed. By eleven or so, he's no longer ducking back into the labyrinth of alleys that run off the 1500 block of Fairmount. He's out in the open for most of the sales, carrying it with him, serving people right along Gilmor.

He's too busy to notice the unmarked Cavalier at the other end of Gilmor, too tired to bother sending the girl with the $10 bill back into the alley for her two vials, too ready to believe that he can go on like this forever, slinging on autopilot, making more money than even Tyreeka knows how to spend.

"FIVE-OH."

Aw shit. Coming up Gilmor. Two of 'em on a jump-out from a gray Chevy. And right when DeAndre was about to pass two vials to the girl. He drops them in the gutter and races into one of the side alleys. Behind him, he can hear the car doors slam and heavy footsteps. But fuck that, he knows Fairmount's alleys and he knows where he's going. He's also a fifteen-year-old running on adrenaline and $120 high-tops; not many rollers are going to stay with that, burdened as they are with utility belts, Kevlar vests, and hard-soled shoes.

The footsteps behind him fade, but as a precaution, DeAndre cuts through to Baltimore Street, then doubles back and waits a few more minutes before slipping back out onto Baltimore again. Then, finally, he saunters casually up to the corner, standing there for a moment, peering up Gilmor to Fairmount and the scene of the crime, so to speak. No cops, no crowds—just the regulars drifting back toward the corner.

Then from behind him, he hears the screech of radials. DeAndre turns and they're out of the car and on him—Huffham and some other roller that DeAndre doesn't recognize. This time he doesn't bother to run. He even manages a little smile, figuring he's gotten over.

"What's up?" he asks Huffham.

The cop is shaking his head, one meaty hand gripping DeAndre by the upper arm, lurching him into the liquor store window grate. It hurts like hell—especially when they yank his arms back and apply the cuffs.

"Why'd you run?" the other police asks.

"What?" says DeAndre.

Huffham shakes his head again, but DeAndre could care less. He beat them straight up, ran them into the dust in those back alleys. He could have stayed hid forever if he wanted; he only popped out on Baltimore Street because he knew they didn't have the coke. And now they're late; they're dragging his ass back up to Fairmount and the corner is cluttered with fiends and dealers. No way. They didn't have it and DeAndre knew they never would.

All the way up the block, he's holding down the smile, trying to manage a hard-as-nails gangster look for the sake of appearances. He sees Linwood in the crowd. Dink-Dink, too.

Huffham is still gripping his arm, moving him toward the curb in starts and jolts. The other cop is a few steps ahead, bending down. Aw shit.

"You want these back?"

Got-damn. Couldn't someone—anyone—out here have picked the shit up? Lord, please, I'm on a corner with every fiend in the neighborhood and not one of them sees fit to pick up two vials of coke lying in the gutter? He'd have gone on home if he thought the people at Fairmount and Gilmor were just going to leave Blue Tops lying all over the place.

He waits for the wagon. The corner—his corner—watches the dethronement with indifference. DeAndre shouts toward the closest recognizable face.

"Tell my mother I'm up the Western."

There's no comprehensive ass-kicking this time, though he did run from the police—a sin that often provokes a Western uniform to deliver some parting shots on principle. Perhaps it's because he's fifteen, perhaps because he didn't bolt a second time when they pulled up on Baltimore Street, and perhaps because Huffham and his partner are about police work by the rules. For whatever reason, DeAndre arrives at the station house unhurt.

Huffham is good about trying to reach Fran as well, but that's no surprise: the juvenile system is such a pain-in-the-ass complication for a working police that it's better by far to get a parent or guardian to come up to the station and sign for the kid. In fact, some police will actually lock a kid up, process him, and then drive the arrestee back home rather than suffer through the wait for a juvenile hearing officer. Worse, if the kid is committed to JSA custody, there's also that drive to Hickey or Waxter. So for the rest of the four-to-twelve shift, they're calling for Fran to come and get her son, trying to reach her by calling a neighbor who lets people from the Dew Drop use her phone. When that doesn't work, DeAndre gives Huffham the number at his grand-mother's house on Vine Street.

He's waiting and watching, listening to the cop try to explain the situation, probably talking to Miss Roberta, who's probably confused. No, she doesn't know where Fran is. Fran doesn't live here. Aw shit.

Nothing is working. Fran is out on her own adventure and the connections aren't getting made. At midnight, the shift changes and there's no alternative but to call for juvenile intake. DeAndre's still hoping that someone on Fairmount got the word to his mother, that Fran is on her way up to the Western now. But barring that, he's bound for Hickey.

It's nearly two in the morning by the time the intake officer has DeAndre McCullough properly processed as a delinquent child. She commits him to the Hickey School in Baltimore County, citing not only the lack of an available parent to take custody and the current offense of possession of cocaine with intent to distribute, but two other pending juvenile cases: another cocaine charge from September and a stolen car charge from August.

He's still waiting for the early-morning ride out to Hickey when word comes back that the training school is over capacity. New juvenile arrests are being sent fifty miles south of the city, to Boys Village in the lower reaches of Prince George's County. That's trouble. DeAndre was ready for Hickey; he'd heard about the place from half a dozen C.M.B. boys already. But Boys Village is way worse than Hickey, filled with D.C. niggers who like to beef with the Baltimore boys.

His sense of foreboding increases as he rides south, the amber glow of the city receding as he's hauled down Route 3 through miles of suburbs that give way to farms and woods and Lord knows what else. Highway signs point to places that DeAndre can only wonder about: Crofton, Bowie, Upper Marlboro. Watching the outline of an open-slat tobacco barn roll by under the moonlight, DeAndre wonders where in hell they're taking him. Klan country, probably.

On Fayette Street, the standing assumption is that any place in America without bricks and pavement and black people is, by definition, a playground for sheet-wearing, pickup-truck-wrecking, get-a-rope rednecks. It's a powerful and enduring myth to the young men and women of West Baltimore, a self-imposed construct of the corner mind:

They don't want us out there. They don't need us. Stray from the streets you know, you fall off the edge of the world.

Staring out the van window, DeAndre sees stars in the winter sky. Boys Village. Damn.

Might as well be the dark side of the moon.

THREE

R.C. is dying out there, his nostrils flaring, his breath coming in angry rasps. He muscles down to the low post, just outside the lane, one arm hard against his side, the elbow cocked. He's glaring at Brooks, who's looking like a lost ball in the tall grass of three-point land, dribbling, nervous after having been stripped the last two times down the court.

Brooks passes across the key to Tae, who fires the ball back and cuts, a step ahead of the Bentalou defender. Brooks, of course, doesn't see it. Nor does he see R.C. powering himself into position, using that elbow as a maul. A bounce pass and R.C. will be good for an eight-foot turnaround.

Brooks dribbles twice, then cocks the leather orb against one shoulder. R.C. can take it no longer. "Ball," he shouts. "Ball up."

Instead, Brooks lets go from thirty feet. The ball bricks with a brutal thud against the upper backboard. R.C. is wild-eyed; on the way back down court, he sidles over to Brooks and offers a quick shove.

"Fuck you, motherfucker," Brooks responds.

"You a fuckin' hawk," sneers R.C.

"So is you."

"Oh mah Gawd! You don't see me throwin' up shit like that."

"R.C., your shit is ass-ugly."

And so it goes. For exactly three minutes in the first quarter, the fledgling Martin Luther Kings had managed to stay with the B-squad of Bentalou's fourteen-and-under team. For a minute or so, in fact, they were actually leading by a bucket, courtesy of Linwood's penchant for grabbing offensive boards and then powering up.

Sitting courtside with a small coterie of teenaged girls and younger boys—a rooting gallery for the M.L.K. team—Ella Thompson and Marzell Myers are ecstatic. Win or lose, today marks the rec center's first foray into organized sports, and for a time at least, the boys seem to be holding together against a Bentalou squad culled from one of West Baltimore's most established recreation programs. Playing for Bentalou's teams marks a kid as possessing potential—if not as all-city, then at least as a coachable, teachable soul. Simply put, Herman Jones, who has run Bentalou for years, takes no shit; you obey the rules or you're gone, your place in the program taken by some other kid who knows how to behave. About half of the Martin Luther Kings had, at one time or another, wandered down the hill to try out for a Herman Jones team. None had lasted.

Six unanswered points and the early M.L.K. lead proves an illusion. R.C. and Brooks keep up their argument; Dewayne is stripped twice after trying to dribble into a crowded lane; Tae beats his man to the baseline, then wastes it on a 360-degree move that leaves him in no position to shoot. By contrast, the Bentalou squad runs a controlled offense, working the ball around a perimeter and down to the low post, where a six-foot-six prodigy unsettles the M.L.K. defense with a lazy, unstoppable turnaround move. Down by ten, Tae calls time.

"Take Brooks out," demands R.C.

"Fuck you, nigger," says Brooks.

"We gotta get our shit together," says Tae.

"You gotta pass the ball," R.C. pleads.

"I give it away and it don't come back," Tae counters.

On the other side of the court, the Bentalou team forms a tight circle and listens intently as Herman Jones critiques their performance, his voice never rising above monotone.

He is a coach, and in every fundamental way, his children are coached. By contrast, the M.L.K squad is under the direction of sixteen-year-old Dontae Bennett, who in his informal capacity as a leader of the Crenshaw Mafia Brothers has assumed control of the basketball team as well. Tae's responsibilities begin with the lineup, and end with making sure that everyone who made the trip from Fayette Street to the Bentalou gym gets some minutes. As for coaching or playmaking, there really isn't any point. The M.L.K. players run a street game: on offense, separate games of one-on-one in which each kid panders to the glory of the highlight film playing in his brain; on defense . . . well, Ella's boys don't exactly bother with defense.

Tae is the point guard. Linwood is low post. R.C. and Dewayne are the forwards. Brooks, the smallest kid in the gang, is the other starting guard. Boo, Brian, Manny Man, Dinky, and Randy are working off the bench. As for DeAndre, he's on the disabled list, trapped in a fifteen-and-under cottage on the Boys Village campus.

"What we gonna do?" asks Dewayne.

R.C. shows his frustration. "Man . . . What the fuck . . ."

"Shut up, R.C.," says Linwood. "Let Tae talk."

They all turn to Tae, who puts his head down and stares at the gym floor. The buzzer sounds and the Bentalou players drift back onto the floor.

"Shit," says Tae. "I dunno. Just go beat their ass."

When they meet again at the half, they're down eighteen.

"Damn," says Manny Man. "They fuckin' us up."

From the sidelines, Ella takes in the disaster with an optimist's detachment. True, they're losing, but then again, the Martin Luther King Jr. Recreation Center was without an athletic team a month ago. Now, in early February, she has ten of the corner's readiest recruits playing an exhibition game inside the house that Herman Jones built. It's a fine start, regardless of the score.

She needs a coach, of course. She'd had one for a week, a recovering addict known to all at Fayette and Monroe by the name of House, and Ella, on meeting him, understood just how right and perfect a street name could be. House was a six-foot-four, two-hundred-forty-pound brick structure topped with a wide smile and clean-shaven head. Legs like tree trunks, hands like shovels—when the man went out walking in West Baltimore, suburbanites in miles-away Catonsville got the urge to cross to the other side of the street. House was a presence.

Down at Francis M. Woods, Rose Davis offered Ella the school gymnasium three days a week, but only if she could assure adult supervision for the new rec team. A corner warrior come in from the cold, House seemed the ticket. He wasn't much of a coach, he told Ella, but he'd go down to the gym with the boys, keep them from foolishness.

A few weeks back, on the day of the first scheduled practice, House showed early and gave Ella some of his story, telling her about the years lost to dope and coke and about the Narcotics Anonymous creed that finally saved him. His heart damaged by recurrent endocarditis, his limbs and torso scarred from a half-dozen shootings and cuttings, House was proud and humble at the same moment. Two years clean, he assured Ella.

The boys drifted in—Tae and DeAndre, R.C. and Manny Man, Dewayne and Dinky, Brooks and Brian—and House took stock.

"This it?" he asked.

"This is the basketball team," said Ella, delighted.

R.C. grabbed a basketball from Brian's hands, then pantomimed a power move. "I'm nice," he assured the new coach. "What can I say? I have skills."

DeAndre snorted. Standing behind R.C., Tae reached in and stripped the ball free.

"Bitch!" shouted R.C.

"I got skills," mimicked Brian. "You got used, you mean."

R.C. jumped on Brian, who covered up, laughing, as R.C. wrestled him against the desk. "I mean, no, I mean you nice, R.C., you nice for real. Stop, boy."

House laughed nervously. Ella read his mind: "They just need some discipline," she told him. "You need to be firm."

He looked doubtful, but promised to meet them down at the gym in a few minutes. "I seen someone up on Mount Street I know," he explained. "Got to go see if I can talk sense to him."

On the way out, he stopped to watch some of his players bickering, trading insults and punches as they assembled for practice. "You know, I see a little of me in all of you," he told them. "You don't have to take the road I took."

House could see it wasn't going anywhere, but he couldn't help himself: "You won't find no self-esteem on the corner."

Silence.

"Anyone know what self-esteem is?"

More silence.

"No one hearin' me?"

R.C. gave back a bored, yawning stretch. "Feeling good about yourself," he said in a half-mumble. The rest of them stood there mute, staring down at their leather high-tops, unfazed, politely silent only because they wanted to play ball.

House headed off to Mount Street. Boo, last of the crew to post for this first practice, came running up a minute later. "Where the coach at?" he asked.

"Gone to get a blast," answered DeAndre dryly.

When the team showed up at the high school doors, ready to test the facilities, Rose Davis greeted them in the lobby. Seeing DeAndre in the pack, she singled him out.

"This one's mine," she said, giving him a quick hug.

DeAndre smiled, embarrassed by the attention. Rose led the way up the stairs, stepped inside to the electrical panel, then threw the bank of switches; one by one, the overhead lights began blinking on until, at last, the perfection of the place was revealed. Glass backboards, solid rims and nets, polished hardwood—the gym was crisp and clean, a sanctuary that received a long moment of genuine reverence from the crew.

"Gracious," said Tae, overcome.

"This shit is right," shouted R.C., racing across the floor to fire off an imaginary jumper. House walked in behind them, fresh from having taken his NA rap to the Mount Street users. With some confusion, the boys managed to form lines and run layup drills, but it fell apart quickly: Tae, with a 360-spin that couldn't find the backboard; R.C., with a double clutch that didn't reach to the rim. And with DeAndre's turn, the layups were abandoned entirely for three-pointers.

"We should play," said R.C., bored with the drill.

The pick-up game that followed—replete with traded insults and petty arguments—made the layup drill look professional. They weren't a team, they were a pack. They proved as much to House on the walk back to the rec, when Manny Man spotted a Lexington Terrace rival who had earlier banked Tae. This time, though, the Terrace Boy was alone and about four blocks west of where he should be.

They fanned out. Manny jumped the school's fence and moved on the kid from behind, while Tae, DeAndre, and R.C. headed directly toward the target.

At first the kid stayed put, oblivious. They were still about a hundred feet shy when something—some street-sharpened instinct—made him look up. He jump-started, bolting north toward the expressway, running in Timberlands that for some reason didn't slow him. The pack took off, baying like wolves, Manny Man getting the best angle as they raced up Stricker. At the end of the block, Manny was just behind, arm outstretched and closing, but the kid wouldn't break stride. He sprinted through Saratoga without looking; Manny pulled up to check the traffic.

"See the nigger run with them boots," said R.C., amazed. "Blew you away, Manny Man."

Manny defended himself: he got close. Tae agreed. The boy would've been caught if he hadn't risked getting run over.

"Fuck with one of us, you fuck with all of us," said DeAndre, offering up team spirit for the first and only time that afternoon. "One day, he won't be so lucky."

A week later, the new coach sent his regrets to Ella. She lost him not to the corner, but to a job on the night shift at University Hospital, where House joined the cleaning staff. Working full-time and still chasing his Narcotics Anonymous meetings, he couldn't hope to handle the weekday practices, nor could he post for evening games when he'd be on shift at the hospital.

Ella understood; a job was a rare thing indeed for someone who had spent years on the corner. She gave House her best wishes and proceeded to press the coaching job on any male acquaintance willing to listen. For a week, she seemed to have convinced Mr. Roland from over on Gilmor Street, and Mr. Roland knew the game well; he had coached rec teams in the past and for years had been a referee in the citywide Cloverdale tournament. Better still, the man had a fifteen-year-old son in the eighth grade at Harlem Park who had something of a jump shot.

"You're just what they need," Ella assured him.

He lasted exactly one afternoon, retiring in disgust after a Tuesday practice in which his son, playing a clean low-post, was savagely tripped, elbowed, and ultimately punched across the court by the entire C.M.B. crew. When Mr. Roland tried to put his players on the bleachers and deliver a lecture, he got back only insolence.

"You full of shit," Boo told him.

So in the end they were orphaned, freed from the burden of adult supervision to become the great uncoached horde of the west side rec leagues, fifteen- and sixteen-year-old Huns dragging their barbarian brand of roundball across the urban steppes and now, into the great cathedral at Bentalou. Their uniforms—basic unadorned black—said as much. Not black with white trim, or black and gold, but cotton shorts and tank tops marked only by a pair of two-inch-high, iron-on, already-starting-to-peel numerals.

The uniforms were Ella's personal contribution; with the rec budget tight, she went down to Mt. Clare with her own money, laying out more than two hundred dollars for ten sets of tank tops and trunks. For Ella, it was an enormous sum, but the uniforms gave permanence to the idea of a basketball team. The players gathered around her in the rec center office to get their mediums and extra larges, then rushed home to find a steam iron to attach the tiny numerals to the backs of the jerseys. The effect was immediate: They not only began wearing the uniforms to the weekday practices, but around the neighborhood as well, parading along Fayette with oversized jerseys over sweatshirts and flannels. Ella's uniforms became ritual objects, even among the vial-slinging caste.

"When you all play?" the older heads would ask.

"Ella got us a game with Bentalou."

"You playin' Bentalou?"

"We at Bentalou Friday next."

Even now, with the squad losing badly on the Bentalou court, there is something hard and prideful in the black uniforms, something akin to a pirate ship appearing off the starboard bow and running the Jolly Roger up the mizzen. As always, the Bentalou players are moving without the ball, passing, running piks and weaves and generally controlling the game in their satin-white jerseys, custom-lettered with red and blue trim. By contrast, the M.L.K. crew is running pickup ball and getting pounded. Yet the vacant black of their jerseys somehow speaks louder than their game. To the regulars in the Bentalou gym, Ella's team is an unknown quantity, anonymous and vaguely lethal. They also trail by twenty at the half.

"We were shit," mutters Dewayne, wounded by the score.

"You were shit," says Manny Man, correcting him. "I ain't played but a minute."

"You were shit for that minute," R.C. assures him.

"C'mon, Tae," pleads Manny Man, "put me in."

Tae figures there isn't anything wrong with the C.M.B. game that Manny can fix. He goes with the lineup that started the game. R.C. rolls his eyes at the mention of Brooks.

"Take Brooks out," he says bluntly. Brooks scowls, R.C. shoves him out of the team huddle, but Tae stays with his starters. The third quarter proves no different, with Bentalou substituting for their starters and still managing a twenty-six-point lead. On defense, R.C. holds his man to a single bucket and at the same time controls the boards; on offense, he's trapped and useless in the low post, forever dependent on an attack in which passing is anathema. In the last quarter, when Brooks launches another graceless, out-of-range jumper, R.C. finally explodes. Tae orders Brooks to the bench, and Brooks responds by ripping off his jersey and tossing it onto the court.

"Y'all can suck my dick."

Herman Jones, doubling as referee, calls the technical.

"Brooks," yells R.C. "Get off the damn court."

The smaller boy turns to confront his tormentor, his face bent into an ugly snarl, his eyes at the verge of tears. R.C. shoves him toward the bench.

"Motherfucker," shouts Brooks.

Double technical, and the Bentalou guard hits both foul shots to end the quarter. Brooks leaves the gym and the game lurches forward, with the team actually showing small flashes of poise at the end. Linwood, stoic amid the wreckage, has been cherry-picking on the offensive boards, putting up a quiet eighteen points from inside the paint. Tae manages to pick off two cross-court passes, turning them into layups. Even R.C. endures long enough to gather in a no-look dish-off from Dewayne and power up for a three-point play. In a last-minute flurry of competence, they lose by only fourteen.

R.C. keeps his own box score in his head, tallying it all up as if there's some posterity attached to a nonleague city rec game.

"I had seven," he calculates, sliding out of the gymnasium doors. "Four assists and ten rebounds. Three for five from the field and I hit my only foul shot."

For some, the game is nothing more than an evening's entertainment. But for Richard Carter, it's more than that; for him, basketball is life itself. And in her own corner of the gym, Ella, too, manages to see more in this event than a badly played basketball game.

Never mind the need for a coach. Never mind the score. Never mind that Brooks is scowling somewhere outside the Bentalou gym, gripping an empty soda bottle, hoping for the chance to toss it at R.C.'s head. All in all, she counts tonight a success. Her rec center now has a plan for the older boys.

For the younger children, too, she has made some progress in the last month, notably in the creation of an organized arts and crafts program with none other than George Epps at the helm.

Blue's involvement was a surprising turn of events, having as much to do with his state of mind as with Ella's constant appeals. At the end of January, Blue simply manifested himself on the rec center doorstep, looking sheepish and ill at ease, swaying a bit on the back of his heels, but not over-the-top blasted either.

Ella sensed the trepidation and hustled him inside quickly. She pulled out the finger paints and the construction paper and everything else in the arts and crafts corner. Blue scanned the inventory and Ella gave the idea her strongest sell, but she could tell he was still on the fence.

"They love this," she assured him. "They love art."

"Yeah, well, this is good. This is good," Blue offered. "You know, we'll see how it goes."

"You'll be great, Blue."

"I don't know, Ella. It's been, you know, it's been a while for me and . . . well, you know, there's the thing . . ."

But Ella wasn't hearing it. Blue had crossed the threshold; he was inside the rec center, the only place in the neighborhood where Ella's word is the last one. Slowly, methodically, she brought him around.

"Okay, Ella. We'll give it a try, you know, see how it goes. So, ah, when . . . when would be best to . . ."

Ella didn't hesitate: "Why not today."

"Today?"

Blue was caught. He came back that afternoon, scratching his beard nervously as Ella passed out drawing paper and crayons to the little ones.

"Today," she told them, "is going to be different because today we're going to have an art class with a real artist. Mr. Blue paints and draws and he lives in your neighborhood."

Blue edged forward, tentative.

"Okay. Okay then," he said, looking down at crayon works-in-progress. "That's very good. That's very nice."

He dropped his satchel, removed his Army coat, and managed one deep breath before launching himself. "Okay," he said again, sitting at the center table, using one of the small-kid chairs. "Okay, who knows what art is?"

Charday raised her hand. "A painting," she said.

"Uh huh. A painting is art."

"A drawing," said Umeka.

"Uh huh, right," said Blue. "But art can be a lot of things, can't it? It can be a sculpture, or a song, or a poem, or just about anything, really. Art can really be whatever you want it to be."

Ella heard it all from the back office, delighted. Awkward at first, Blue grew more comfortable with every sentence, though there was a vagueness hanging on him, a hesitance born of drug corner rhythms. Twice, Ella had to get up to quiet the older boys who were hanging in the front of the rec. But each time, as she turned back toward her office, she saw the faces of the littlest ones, captivated by the presence of George Epps.

"What's that?" asked Blue, looking over Michael's drawing.

"That's the Hulk," the boy told him. "He killing somebody."

"Huh," said Blue. "Well, that's art, too."

That was the beginning of professional art instruction at the rec center. The end came a week and a half later, when George Epps put Rita Hale out of the shooting gallery only to be arrested and charged with burglarizing his own house.

Still, Ella regarded that as only a modest setback. Blue would come home soon enough, she reasoned, and then his good work as an art teacher would surely resume. Until then, Marzell Myers would keep the weekly sessions going.

With the rec center, Ella had learned to measure progress in halfway-there increments, to look for partial victories in any battle. Stable volunteers, involved parents, a sufficient operating budget—these things were the suburban ideal, the raw materials for well-tended childhoods in places other than Fayette Street. For the Martin Luther King Jr. Recreation Center, there was no reservoir of commitment from the surrounding community, nothing save for the strays, like Blue or House, who might stumble off a corner and into the lives of Ella's children. And Ella, who knew this, learned to credit any stray willing to walk through the rec doors.

A few days after the Bentalou game, Ella is dessed in black yet again for a neighbor's son, a man dead from the virus after years on the corner. She leaves the services at Brown's on Baltimore Street in the company of two other men she has made part of her life. The first, Ike Motley, sings a hymn at many of the Fayette Street rites and Ella knows him well. Last month, Ike was singing for Linda Taylor, the next-door neighbor to the McCullough family on Vine Street, laid out at Brown's after a long fight with the Bug. Today, he sang for Edward Hicks, a casualty at forty-seven. Next week, he'll be back for some other corner soldier with whom he shared a childhood. Like Ella, Ike has become a fixture at funerals, his hymn a set piece in West Baltimore's accelerating cycle of grief.

"That was a beautiful song today," she tells him at the chapel door.

"Thank you, Ella," Ike says quietly, turning away on the steps of the funeral home. "You take care now."

"You, too."

Her second escort, a lanky, dark-skinned young man in a leather coat, nods an awkward good-bye to Ike, then follows Ella down Baltimore Street to Monroe.

"Still want me to come to that dance?" he asks.

"We'd love to have you, Ricky," she assures him. "We need some chaperones."

Ricky Cunningham is another man on the fence, caught halfway between community and corner. His sister, Gale, is on Monroe Street touting. He's living down near the projects, dabbling with it, disgusted at his inability to stop. A year ago, he had a good job cutting meat down at Lexington Market, but lost it after he took a charge behind this nonsense. For Ricky, Ella is the promise of new things; he looks at her and follows her from the funeral in a way reminiscent of adolescent love.

"I be there, Ella. Most definitely, I be there."

They turn the corner together and look up Monroe. Ricky seems to stiffen suddenly, unnerved by the site of clustered police cars blocking the intersection with Fayette Street.

"Somethin' up," he says.

A crowd is packed onto three corners; the fourth is empty, ribbon-wrapped in yellow police-line tape.

As the two make their way up from Baltimore Street, the scene slowly unfolds: the blood pool on the sidewalk near the liquor store; the detectives leaning against a radio car, arms crossed; the police lab technician, crouching low to the pavement, snapping off camera shoots. And the crowd—the complete inventory of the neighborhood corners from Monroe to Gilmor—all of them there to see the show. From teenaged slingers to dying touts, they mingle as if it were some hellish cocktail party.

In front of the the carryout at Fayette, Ricky pulls away from Ella and huddles for a moment with his sister and Smitty, her boyfriend.

"Bryan," he says, coming back to Ella.

She can't place the name.

"Tall Bryan," says Ricky, holding his hand a few inches above his own forehead. "Bryan who's always getting shot. He was burnin' people, stickin' people up and all . . ."

Ella shakes her head sadly at information for which she has no real use. "It makes no sense," she offers.

"You know, Bryan who . . ."

Ricky pauses, sees the vague expression on Ella's face, then shuts down, intuiting, perhaps, some unspoken mark against him for sharing in the corner's secrets. Bryan's name, why Bryan got shot—all of it is guilty knowledge of a kind, evidence that Ricky pretends to one world while living in another.

"Well," she says, "I guess I'll see you on Friday then."

Ricky nods, pausing halfway across the street. "Friday," he repeats, smiling. "I be there."

If not House, then Blue. If not Blue, then Ricky. If not Ricky, then maybe R.C.'s older brother, who made some noises the other day about maybe coaching basketball. Ella believes in her strays, waits on them. She watches Ricky drift away, then crosses to the other side of Fayette, where one of the detectives is shouting at June Bey McCullough for stumbling through the crime scene unawares.

Ella steps past the argument, stops at her apartment to change, and then heads down to the rec, where the business at hand is a Valentine's Day sock hop planned for Friday night. That leaves Ella with three days to transform her bunker of a rec center with red and white ballons, ribbons, hot dogs, punch, and candy. She's looking for a rare chemistry on Fayette Street, a magic that can beguile fifteen-year-old drug traffickers and fourteen-year-old mothers-to-be into accepting and enjoying an unlikely moment or two of shared innocence.

But come seven o'clock on Friday, only a few of the prepubescent girls show up to stand around the food tables while the chaperones— Ella, Marzell, and Joyce Smith of the Franklin Square neighborhood association—watch the door and wonder if the two-dollar admission fee might keep the older ones away. Ricky Cunningham, too, arrives to chaperone, then leaves for a time, his eyes showing a telltale glaze when he returns a half hour later. Ella senses this, but greets him warmly nonetheless.

"Oh Ricky," Ella teases. "You're in for it tonight."

Ricky struggles with a response.

"This is a rough crew we're dealing with," she says, laughing. "And we're going to have more than this. Otherwise the chaperones are going to outnumber the kids."

Ricky nods. He stations himself against the far wall, arms crossed, watching Ella watching the door.

Three of the older girls—Neacey, Gandy, and Shaneka—finally show up and follow Ella's rules for the dance, leaving their shoes at the door. They run through a few well-rehearsed dance routines, giggling at their mistakes and working out a handful of new steps. They laugh uproariously at every new move.

It's almost eight before most of the C.M.B. contingent wanders in. Tae, Manny Man, Dinky, Dorian, and Brian—but not R.C. and not

DeAndre, who, Ella has learned, will spend the weekend at Boys Village before getting a juvenile hearing. Each is reluctant to part with the price of admission, each argues about having to leave his high-tops at the door. DeAndre's girl, Tyreeka, starts to follow them inside, but when she hears about the socks-only rule, she runs home for a clean pair.

It's slow going at first, slow as any teenage dance always is—the boys looking uncomfortable in one corner of the room, the girls, across the floor, dancing with each other, glancing over their shoulders at every loud laugh or shout. Kiti has his sound system set up in the far corner and he stays shy and aloof behind the turntables, keeping the dance mix going. There are a few forays to the dance floor by a couple or two, but most end in childish laughter.

It's amazing really, considering the range of their sexual experience. Perhaps it's the colored balloons and candies, or perhaps it's Ella's presence that has the boys subdued, sitting in a row against the front wall, goofing with each other, Manny goading Tae to dance with Neacey or Shaneka. Suddenly, they're children again; nervous, excited, and only marginally competent to deal with the matter at hand. Somehow, the jaded sexuality has been dispensed with; the sordid histories forgotten. The adventures with that freak girl in Manny Man's apartment, the blow jobs from the hollow-eyed pipers down below McHenry Street—none of it stands with the fumbling modesty now on display.

At least until Tyreeka returns. Alone among the girls at the dance, Tyreeka has some mastery of her own bumps and curves, and she's quick to cross the no-man's land, hips and breasts moving suggestively inside tight denims and a clinging jersey. She beckons, then turns her back to Tae, grinding away just a few inches in front of him. Then, on down the line she goes: to Manny Man, then Dorian, then Dinky.

"Damn," says Manny.

Tae laughs nervously, pulling his wide-brimmed cap low over his eyes. He takes the challenge, edging out onto the dance floor as Tyreeka backs away. From the corner, Dinky shakes his head and smiles, obviously embarrassed. Tyreeka is DeAndre's girl and DeAndre, Dinky's second cousin, is locked up out in the county somewhere. Ever loyal, Dinky holds back.

But Tae doesn't seem to be worrying about DeAndre, who might stay locked up until spring for all anyone knows. Instead, he's right on Tyreeka, his hips grinding against her, his bandy legs moving forward in a jerking, syncopated motion. Manny Man and Brian are inspired; they issue cat calls and creep out to edge of the dance floor. Neacey and the other girls sense the moment and drift toward the center as well. The room is finally jumping.

Ella stands at the edge of the dance floor, pleasure and concern warring inside her as she watches the scene unfold. Her eyes scan the room, then fall on Kiti, who smiles back. Looking proud to have the party moving, her son keeps layering the mix on his turntables and laughing at the dance-floor antics. For a time, Ella watches him, his tall frame hovering from the equalizer to the turntables, then over to his crate of dance tracks, his head bobbing softly to the rhythms.

For Ella, just seeing her son this way is a blessing. Tonight, in the rec center bunker, the crepe-paper-and-balloon illusion does its number on Kiti, too, taking him beyond the usual precautions and calculations of Fayette Street. She knows how he hates the neighborhood; how he can't wait for graduation and a reprieve from the horror show that greets him every time he leaves their apartment. And she knows, too, how constricted he is, how he has held so much inside himself since they lost Andrea. She looks at him now and feels palpable relief. Tonight, at least, Kiti is out of that back bedroom, showing his stuff, feeling a little bit free.

Ella is watching her son so intently that she's caught by Joyce Smith, who creeps behind and pushes her onto the dance floor.

"C'mon," says Joyce. "We'll look foolish together."

Ella laughs off her embarrassment and begins to move.

"GO EL-LA, GO EL-LA, GO EL-LA."

Neacey and Gandy start the chant, but soon it's community property as all of the dancers cluster around the two women, who try a few old-school moves before they're overcome with self-conscious laughter.

Ella gets Marzell out on the floor and calls for Ricky to join them, but the young man is braced against the wall, trapped, a vague, uncomfortable expression on his face.

"Oh mah Gawd," laughs Marzell, dancing with Ella. "There you go now."

They are rescued only when Kiti changes up and slows the rhythm. Ella catches her breath and pushes her bangs up her forehead. She looks over to see Ricky Cunningham gone.

"Miss Ella, you was good," squeals Neacey.

"Miss Ella can move," Tae agrees.

Ella broods for a moment about Ricky, wondering if there was anything she might have said or done to keep him there. Then, shrugging it off, she gets back into the mix, showing off an old step or two, sidling up to Tae and bumping him with one hip as the girls dissolve in laughter. Tae buries his face in the brim of his cap and pivots away in modest retreat.

"I'm soooo old," she says, brushing her hair back and losing the rhythm. "I'm too old for your kind of music."

The dance floor once again belongs to Tae and Tyreeka, who resume their hormonal ballet in earnest. Joyce watches them grind around the room, then shakes her head softly.

"That one girl," she says finally. "How old is she?"

"Tyreeka is . . . thirteen," Ella tells her. "Or close to thirteen now."

Joyce rolls her eyes. "That girl is too bold for thirteen." When Kiti takes a break for hot dogs and punch, Tyreeka and Tae move to one corner of the rec. There she takes things a step further by sitting on his lap, making herself something of a centerpiece to the C.M.B. boys who settle with their food plates into the chairs on either side. The other girls hold warily to the opposite side of the room.

Dinky and Brian finish eating quickly, and with Kiti still giving it a rest, they fish a homemade mix tape from Dinky's winter coat and march over to the worn-down tape player that is among the rec center's most utilized assets. Brian slaps the cassette into place and punches play, then rushes to find the stop button when the music dissolves in a warped slur.

"Damn," he says, punching out the cassette.

"You gotta rewind it and put in the other side," says Dinky. "It fucks up like that on one side."

"Dinky."

"Oh, sorry, Miss Ella," he says, genuinely embarrassed. "I forgot where I was."

They rewind the cassette, turn it over, and punch the play button once again. A pulsing cacophony fills the rec center. The C.M.B. boys hoot and holler.

"That's the shit," yells Tae. "That's the shit."

This time, Ella doesn't even try to shout an admonition above the noise. The tape is the full dance mix of a local song that's all over the Baltimore stations this winter; a rollicking seven minutes of audio dissonance with lyrics that amount to a listing of bad-ass drug corners and housing projects, followed by a shouted one-line chorus.

"Here we go . . . Cherry Hill."

"GET YA GUNS OUT," shout the C.M.B. boys, delighted.

"La-fay-ette."

"GET YA GUNS OUT."

Tae lifts Tyreeka off his lap, then jumps up to dance. The good part is coming up.

"Mount . . . and Fayette," chants the rapper.

"GET YA GUNS OUT!"

The boys shout and stomp and fill their corner of the room with high-fives. Mount and Fayette, spoken like it was a place that mattered. Tae, Dinky, Manny Man, Dorian, Brian—they're all genuinely proud, so engrossed in the tape that they ignore the banging on the outer doors.

Marzell finally makes her way over from the food table and opens up to see R.C. out on the blacktop, one arm draped around his girl's shoulder.

"Tae in there?" he asks.

"Well, hello to you too, R.C."

"Um, hello, Miss Myers. Tae in there?"

She shouts for Tae, who saunters to the door, followed by Manny and Dorian. R.C. drops his arm around Treecee's waist and leans against her as Tae steps outside.

"W'sup," R.C. says.

Tae shrugs. "We dancin'."

"Who else in there?"

"Dinky, Brian, Reeka, Neacey and them girls, you know . . . um, Miss Ella and Kiti . . ."

"Man, shit sounds weak."

"Naw," says Tae. "We havin' fun."

R.C. looks at Treecee, who gives no sign either way.

"They give you food and shit," adds Tae.

R.C. relents and follows Treecee inside. Ella greets them at the door, explaining that their shoes have to come off. No tennis, just socks. R.C. is having none of it; he guides his girl back outside and follows her down the steps, shaking his head in disgust. Tae comes out after him.

"Man," says R.C., "fuck that no-shoes shit. I ain't about givin' up my Jordans."

"C'mon, R.C., it's fun."

"Naw, fuck that," he says, firm. "I know where we can get some good weed, get us blunted."

But tonight at least, Ella's got Tae. He turns back toward the dull orange glow filtering out of the rec center windows. R.C. and Treecee glide into the darkness.

"What's with R.C.?" asks Ella when Tae returns.

"He don't want to take his shoes off."

"'Cause his feet stink," says Brian.

"Brian," says Ella. "That isn't nice."

"It's true," says Dinky. "R.C. has some steady smellin' feets. He don't wear no socks is what it is."

The boys play their gangsta mix once more before Kiti comes back to his turntables. Again the party carries them together on the floor, culminating in a dance contest that delivers heart-shaped boxes of Valentine's candy to Shaneka and Tae. At eleven, the dance is over and those who paid their two dollars are reluctant to leave. Tonight, they've snatched a good and ordinary time from the streets of a sad and extra-ordinary place. Against long odds, the Valentine's dance is a victory for innocence that somehow survives Tyreeka's hip-shaking performance, and Dinky's profanity, and songs about drug corners and firearms.

"Good night," Ella tells her charges as they drift out the double doors into the dark. "Be careful, now. It's late."

She watches Tae walk Tyreeka down the alley to Fayette Street and wonders how that business will end. Tae has one arm around the girl's waist, but Tyreeka has her hands in her coat pocket, her body language noncommittal.

"Miss Ella," says Neacey, buttoning her winter coat in the doorway. "That was so much fun."

"I'm glad you liked it."

"Can we have another dance?"

"We'll have to see."

The young girl bounds down the steps, followed by Gandy, who catches up to whisper something in her friend's ear.

"Oh, Miss Ella, Miss Ella," says Neacey, reminded. "Wait."

Ella catches the center door just as it's closing. She peers out into the darkness, waiting with failing patience. Neacey is a favorite to Ella, a young girl groping through adolescence alone, ignored utterly by her mother, Ronnie Boice, and craving attention from all other quarters. Then again, the girl can talk you to death if you let her, and Ella will be here past midnight bagging paper plates and sweeping candy hearts off the floor.

"Neacey, what is it now?"

The two girls stifle a laugh, then steady themselves in the night air. Neacey whispers a one-two-three to time the thing.

"Thaaaaank you, Miss Ella."

Tyreeka Freamon is down on Fayette Street early, her best denims tight on her waist, her hair teased up and curled in the front and falling long and free on her shoulders. She's out on the sidewalk before the early package, before the touts and runners have cluttered the Mount Street corners. She's way too wired for the hour, primped and polished and bright-eyed. She walks the two wickedly cold blocks from her grandmother's house on Stricker Street against a blustery wind, arriving at the front door of the Dew Drop Inn well before nine, sliding out of the February air into the shelter of the rowhouse vestibule, then climbing the stairs to bang on the door of the second-floor apartment. She's hammering on it for two minutes before anything stirs.

"Who there?"

A male voice. Stevie probably.

"Reeka."

"Huh?"

"Reeka. Is Miss Fran up?"

"Hold on." Stevie sounds upset.

She waits out in the hallway for five minutes, watching her breath freeze in clouds outside the apartment door until the lock is unlatched and DeAndre's mother appears before her, the very picture of yellow-eyed, morning-after exhaustion.

"You early, girl," says Fran, stepping back.

"I didn't want you to go without me," Tyreeka explains.

Fran manages a half smile.

"Wait up front," says Fran, gesturing toward the front of the apartment, then padding back toward the bedroom. The arrangements call for the hack to show up sometime after nine, which in Fayette Standard Time means anywhere from ten to noon, but Tyreeka is taking no chances on getting left behind. She's been up since a little after seven, choosing her outfit and doing up her hair in the style that DeAndre likes best. She's saying something today and she wants to be sure the boy hears her.

The old console television in the front room is jabbering on from the night before, the screen muted by a green-yellow tint that suggests a dying picture tube. Tyreeka stares at the raving of a Sunday morning preacher and listens for the sound of movement in the house, but nothing. Not a sound from Stevie's room, and nothing at all from the others on the third floor. Ten long minutes pass before she hears another television come on in Fran's room, and another ten before she hears someone shuffle into the bathroom.

In the back, the television fare is cartoons. In the front room, Tyreeka is listening to the preacher talking about the Corinthians, talking about them like everyone knows their business. Tyreeka, listening, wonders where it is they fit in. She'd been to that church up on Edmondson Avenue as a little girl, sitting there in her Sunday clothes with her grandmother and sometimes even her mother, back before her mother fell. She'd heard enough in church to get the main parts of the story. She had the Jews and Romans and apostles down, but who the Corinthians were and what they were about, she couldn't say.

DeRodd slips out of Fran's room in his long underwear.

"You going to see my brother?"

Tyreeka nods.

"He locked up."

"Boy, you don't think I know that?"

"He in Boys Village."

Tyreeka ignores him. Sometimes she liked DeRodd, but sometimes he could wear on her with his little-boy nonsense. DeAndre would always tell her that DeRodd wasn't right for Fayette Street, that he belonged in the county somewheres. He'll never make it, DeAndre would say, he's always daydreaming and talking silly shit and if he don't toughen up soon the corners would chew his narrow ass up. Tyreeka figured it was true enough. Half the time, DeRodd was in another world.

"Where Boys Village at?" DeRodd asks.

"Prince George County."

"Where that?"

"In Maryland."

"Where at?"

She swings on DeRodd with an open palm, but he leans back from the blow and races behind the television set. He pokes his face up between the rabbit ears of the antenna, his tongue wriggling from his mouth in provocation.

"Boy, you stupid."

"You slow."

"I can catch your little ass."

"Can't."

"Catch it and whip it."

DeRodd smirks at the challenge. Again, he sticks out his tongue, this time accompanying the gesture with an insolent, two-handed wave, his thumbs wedged into his ears. Tyreeka exhales loudly and rolls her eyes. If she catches DeRodd, she'll have to torture him, and if she tortures him, she'll have to mess her hair. By such calculations are the lives of eight-year-old boys occasionally spared.

"Boy, don't trifle with me."

"Reeka scared . . ."

"DeRodd, shut up."

Fran finally emerges from the back room, her hair pulled back tight on her head, her eyes still struggling against the morning sunlight. She gives Tyreeka a grunt of recognition before flopping on the end of the couch and curling into a fetal position. She's ill this morning, and Tyreeka has spent enough time around Fran to know what that involves.

"You look tired, Miss Fran."

"Hmm."

"We leavin' soon?"

"'Bout ten."

DeRodd comes out from behind the television. "Ma," he says. "Can I go with you to see Andre?"

Tyreeka looks over with a silent plea, but Fran is way ahead of her on this one.

"No."

"I want . . ."

"I said no."

Slowly, Fran lifts her head off the worn sofa cushion and twists around to look out the window. Some of the Death Row crew are already at work on the other side of Mount Street.

"Miss Fran," asks Tyreeka. "Who was the Corinthians?"

Fran gives the girl a look.

"'Cause the television preacher was talkin' about them."

"Who?"

"The Corinthians."

Fran shakes her head, then pushes herself upright and wanders back into her room. When she returns, she's wearing her brown winter coat. "If the ride come," she tells Tyreeka, "tell 'im I be back in a few minutes."

She's gone for longer than that, but the neighborhood hack they've hired doesn't roll up until half past ten, and by that time, Fran is feeling a lot better about the day. In fact, she spends the first half hour on the road gently teasing Tyreeka.

"Your hair look nice," she tells her.

"You like it this way?"

"How long it take you to do that with the curls?"

"An hour about."

"Girl, when did you get up today?"

"Seven o'clock."

Fran shakes her head. "Reeka in love."

Tyreeka shoves Fran's shoulder gently, laughing with embarassment. Not love, she assures Fran. Like. She likes DeAndre. A lot. But nobody said nothing about loving nobody.

"Girl," says Fran, "there ain't no one alive gets up at seven o'clock to do their hair without being sure enough in love. My son done messed your little mind."

Tyreeka giggles at the truth, but holds to the denial for appearance's sake. "Ain't nothin' wrong with lookin' good," she insists. "I do my hair like this lots of mornings."

"Seven o'clock," Fran says, smirking. "Mmmm mmmm mmmm."

They ride south through the suburbs, then down Route 3 toward Prince George's, where farm fields and woods are punctuated by the occasional subdivision. In the back seat of a rusting Pontiac, Fran grows restive; she has never been comfortable outside the city. No black folk. No action. No corners. Once, when she was in a residential detox program out in Ellicott City, the rumor of a Klan sighting burned through an evening therapy session like wildfire. Scared them half to death.

But for Tyreeka, the trip to Boys Village is all grand adventure, one of the rare times she can remember going anywhere outside of East or West Baltimore. In Tyreeka Freamon, there is a rare optimism, a naive acquistiveness for things and facts and experiences that thus far has not been dulled by the realities of Fayette Street.

Her school grades are good; if she keeps at it, she'll be going to Carver next year, maybe get herself settled in one of the vocational programs. She likes school, or at least, she doesn't fight it the way so many others do. In class or on the street, she doesn't temper her curiosity, or front for the usual adolescent insecurities. If she doesn't know something— and there is a lot the Baltimore public schools have failed to teach her—she won't pretend otherwise. She'll ask whomever seems likely to know. Who was Babe Ruth? Was he black or white? Where's Pearl Harbor? Why is everyone always remembering it? Who's more important: the governor of Maryland or the mayor of Baltimore? How long would it take to drive to Florida? And when people buy a big, big house, do they have to pay all the money right away or can they pay a little bit at a time while they're living there?

These are queries external to the immediacies of the corner world; questions of a kind that the DeAndres and Taes of the neighborhood hesitate to ask, either from a fear of appearing ignorant or from a genuine indifference to the answers. Tyreeka may be unlearned—but raw, innocent hope has kept her mind open and willing.

"Yeah boy," DeAndre had declared, scanning her last report card. "My girl is smart. We gonna live in a big house when she gets to makin' money."

But DeAndre is smart, too. Everyone in the neighborhood knows him as one of the sharpest kids on the corner. Yet it always ends there on the corner; time and again, the boy has willed it so, shamelessly telling his school teachers that he won't do homework, that the quickest way to put a nigger to sleep is to put a book in his hands.

Somehow, Tyreeka still believes in a future more distant than the next G-pack, and given the first thirteen years of her life, even a shred of faith has to be seen as remarkable. Her mother had been failing her for years now, chasing that blast night after night, slipping out of her life by degrees until Tyreeka was in a new house with her father, his new girlfriend, and his girlfriend's children. They treated her bad, too; made her feel like she was in the way. After a few months she ran off to her grandmother's house—just up and left—an eleven-year-old moving her life crosstown on an M.T.A. bus. She made her grandma and aunt both promise not to send her back, and when her father came to get her, she stood up to him, too. You didn't treat me right, she told him. You let them mess with me and didn't take my side.

Her aunt was willing enough; her grandma, too. In time, Tyreeka settled in with her younger cousins. But there was no getting around the day-to-day absence of a mother and father, no solace for a young girl trying to learn life without the essential audience of her own parents. The report cards came home—passing grades every quarter— and Tyreeka would find herself showing them to people who couldn't conceal their indifference. Eventually, the graded essays and final exams were no longer given even a cursory display; the report cards were for

Tyreeka alone, to be dumped unceremoniously into the bottom dresser drawer.

On Stricker Street, her loneliness brought her off the stoop and into the street. Like any young girl, she wanted to be loved, or failing that, she wanted at least to be noticed. The neighborhood boys sensed as much; whatever instincts come naturally to the adolescent predator led them soon enough to the empty place in Tyreeka's world.

Tae was the first of the C.M.B. boys to chase her. In fact, she knew Tae before she knew DeAndre or Linwood or any of them. Last summer, she messed with Tae in a schoolgirl sort of way; heavy groping but not quite sex, because after all, she was twelve. She liked Dorian, too. And Dewayne. But most of all she liked hanging with boys, sharing the summer nights with them as they prowled the corners and pretended to be gangsters. She was both tomboy and flirt; sharing in their first awkward attempts at slinging vials and joining in for the occasional pack beatings unleashed on stray members of rival crews. She began skipping school—not enough to be held back, though her grades slipped—and spending a day or two a week holed up in some C.M.B. clubhouse, teasing and flirting and generally making herself the center of attention. The boys were fun that way; by comparison, the neighborhood girls her age were boring. That summer was the best time she could remember, but by the fall, when she was DeAndre's girl, it had come to an end. At first, he told her that he didn't want her talking to any boys other than C.M.B. boys. Later, when he began to sense the heat coming from Tae and Dewayne, DeAndre amended that: He didn't want to see her talking with boys, period. She liked that—his jealousy was a special brand of flattery—but at the same time, she missed running the streets. Now, with her boyfriend locked up, she was flirting again, not just with the C.M.B. regulars, but with some of the older boys down on Baltimore and Gilmor. DeAndre was her steady and she took that seriously enough, but there wasn't anything wrong with having fun. Like the dance: Tae made her feel good, but afterward, they had parted company on Fayette and she wandered down to Baltimore Street to play video games with some younger boys.

But today is special. She would be telling DeAndre something today just by showing up way out there in the country. That alone would let him know how she felt.

"What if they say it's family-only for visiting hours?" she asks Fran.

"Then you my daughter," says Fran.

Tyreeka smiles, vaguely proud at the suggestion.

At the security gate, they're told that someone will have to call ahead to have DeAndre brought to the administration building. They get out of the hack at the edge of the visitors' lot, where a staff member takes their information and wanders away, returning twenty minutes later for Fran and Fran alone.

"Only parents," he tells Fran. "No siblings."

Tyreeka is stricken.

"Where do they bring him to?" asks Fran.

"That building there," the staffer explains. "The van will bring them from the cottages and drop them off inside that gate at that door. You'll be in that room right there."

Fran turns back to Tyreeka. "You stand right here and watch that window."

"But can't I . . ."

"I make sure he see you."

Fran follows the staffer up to the visitors' center. Five minutes later, a security van clears the wire-mesh fence surrounding the building. Tyreeka squints her eyes in the midday sun, wishing she'd brought her eyeglasses, watching as a half-dozen young men—all but one of them black—tumble from the rear of the van and tramp up to the metal doors, the lot of them shackled together. All are wearing red-orange sweatsuits issued by juvenile services. All but one of the black kids have their heads covered by the hoods of the sweatshirts. The one who doesn't has what looks like dreds on top. She takes a guess.

"Andre! Over here, Andre!"

She's waving frantically, but the cold wind is coming down the hill, pushing her words back into her mouth. She wonders whether he's even among the group, or whether he's already inside.

Tyreeka watches as the van driver unshackles the boys and marches them through the metal doors single-file. When they're gone, she's left in the winter cold at the edge of the lot, waiting for a moment that won't come. She buries her neck in her shoulders and digs her hands down into her pants pockets, watching the corner windows of the visitors' center for any sign of movement. After ten minutes, the driver comes back out and the empty van pulls off.

The hack has the engine running and the heat on, but Tyreeka stands where Fran said to stand. Her teeth are chattering, her legs are bent slightly at the knees as she bounces on the balls of her feet to bring warmth. After twenty minutes, she thinks she can see a form at the corner window—a shoulder and an arm in the lower pane, and maybe a face just above it.

She waves, just in case, thinking that if it is DeAndre, and if he can see her now, he knows that she's standing by him. Seeing her, he has to know that it isn't just about all the money he fronted—all the movies and clothes and meals and video games—and that if she were like most of the girls around Fayette Street, she wouldn't be here now that he's locked up with nothing in his pockets but a toothbrush.

A gust of wind rolls down the hill and Tyreeka turns her back until it passes. When she turns again, the figure in the window is gone. Fran comes down the hill ten minutes late.

"He seen you," she tells Tyreeka.

"He did?"

"Mmm hmm. He seen you wave. You couldn't see him?"

"Not really."

They pile back into the car for the ride home. Fran runs through the conversation for Tyreeka's benefit. DeAndre doesn't like Boys Village a little bit.

"They got him in a cottage with a lot of D.C. boys," she explains. "And he sayin' the guards got no play in them."

More intimidating is the fact that the Village is the facility of last resort for the state JSA, and DeAndre is bunking with boys who've done shootings and murders, boys who'll be inside until their eighteenth birthday. He's holding his own, but it's not Hickey, where a West Baltimore kid can feel at home. At the Village, everyone gets pressed.

"He was telling me he seen this one boy, not more than ten years old, who's been trying to make a seven-year-old suck him off. Can you believe that? Ten years old." Fran snorts, half in wonder, half in disgust. "Andre wants me to bring his ass home," she adds, with a bemused smile. For the first time in a while, she has the upper hand with her son.

"When can he get out?"

"Soon as I hook it up so that he's staying somewhere with a phone. But I ought to leave his ass down here another week to teach him something."

The phone had been a problem from the beginning. A week ago, on the day after his arrest, a JSA van brought DeAndre back up to Baltimore for an initial hearing in the basement of the Mitchell Courthouse, a judicial backwater in which hundreds of teenagers stagnate on wooden benches, waiting for their cases to be shuffled in front of a half-dozen juvenile masters. DeAndre was in the juvenile bullpen for half the day, then waiting on the benches in the rear of a master's room for the rest of it. The routine calls for pretrial release to parental custody in most instances, but with DeAndre, there was that other cocaine possession charge and the stolen car case. So when his name was finally called, the master showed a little caution, agreeing to release young Mr. McCullough pending a hearing on the entire caseload, but only if he could be restricted to home monitoring.

No problem, Fran told the public defender. Deep down, she liked the idea of having DeAndre trapped in the house with one of those electronic bracelets around his ankle, unable to leave for fear that a check-in phone call would catch him sneaking down the block. DeAndre was hauled back to the bullpen for another hour and half while Fran filled out the forms, only to be informed at the end of the process that she had to have a working telephone.

"There isn't any phone at this address?" said the juvenile staffer, holding a hand to his forehead. "The monitoring system requires a phone."

"Uh umm."

"Can you get a phone at that address?"

"Not 'less you give me the money."

And so it was back down to the Village for another week, until Fran could arrange to have DeAndre stay with her aunt up above North Avenue. For some strange reason, the woman had a liking for the boy; and stranger still, DeAndre always behaved whenever he was up at her Etting Street rowhouse.

"They gonna let Andre stay on Etting?" asks Tyreeka.

"If I say so . . ."

Hearing the doubt in Fran's tone, Tyreeka pouts, but holds her tongue.

". . . but I feel like I ought to leave him be. I feel like I should tell them I can't control him no more."

Tyreeka stares sullenly out the window.

"He think he so much a man," says Fran. "He can just stay where he is until his hearing."

"That could be months," says Tyreeka.

Fran ignores her, rambling on instead about DeAndre having money still on the street. He had fronted Boo forty vials, for which Boo owed him two hundred dollars.

"He wants me to get his money for him," says Fran.

"From Boo?"

"Mmm hmm. He needs some things while he in there and I ain't got what to pay for it with," Fran explains. "He told me to get the two hundred that Boo owes him."

Wounded at the thought of spending spring and maybe even summer without DeAndre, Tyreeka says little else for the rest of the trip, but as it turns out, she has no need for worry.

In Fran's world, you stand with your children against the downtown agencies. DeAndre can't often be trusted, but the bureaucrats can't be trusted at all. Three days later, the paperwork is complete and DeAndre returns that morning to the same Baltimore courthouse and the same juvenile master, who informs him that his pretrial release will be violated if he fails to attend Francis M. Woods High School, or if he fails to remain inside his aunt's house after 3:30 P.M.

"You understand what you have to do?"

DeAndre nods.

"I didn't hear you."

"Yes, um . . . Yessir."

From the back bench, Fran allows herself a smirk at DeAndre, sitting there with his hands in his lap. No bluster. No defiance. She can't help savoring the moment. When they leave the courthouse, it's almost three; her son has only enough time to go by Fayette Street for some clothes before he has to be indoors on Etting Street.

"I got to get with Boo," he tells Fran.

"You ain't got time today."

"He got my money."

Fran shrugs. If Boo owes him money, she assures her son, then it's up to DeAndre to collect. When she tried to press Boo, he only gave her a few dollars, insisting he didn't owe any more than that.

"Me and him gonna talk," says DeAndre with some bitterness.

Fran shrugs again. "That's 'tween you two. But you best get your ass up to your aunt's house before you get violated."

DeAndre arrives at Etting Street before the first monitored call and stays indoors that evening. The next morning, he shows up at school on time, but slips out after his third period to run the streets. He checks Ramsay and Stricker, then all along McHenry, then at the basketball rim in the Lemmon Street alley. No sign of Boo. DeAndre is convinced: The nigger is ducking him.

He's up early the next morning, scouring the side streets from

McHenry to the expressway, trying to pick up the scent of lost money. The day is warmer than most, and DeAndre moves among clusters of kids walking with their schoolbooks, the older ones off to Southwestern or Francis Woods, the younger ones drifting north toward Harlem Park Middle School.

Out near the bus stop on Fayette, DeAndre strikes gold. He pulls up the hoody on his sweatshirt and begins racing down a side alley at a knot of kids on the corner.

R.C., Tyreeka, Manny Man, and Boo all turn to look at the figure running right at them, but with his hood up, DeAndre is almost on them before there's a glint of recognition.

"It's Andre," says Manny, finally.

"Hey, wassup?" says DeAndre, coming to a fast stop. Immediately, he's in Boo's face. "Where's my money?"

"I gave it to your mother," Boo insists. "I swear."

"I want my money," says DeAndre, giving off his best glare.

Boo looks around for help. Tyreeka shakes her head; she told Boo to hold the money for DeAndre, to keep Miss Fran from running any kind of game. Now Boo's got two choices: flat-out accuse DeAndre's mother of stealing from him, or pay the debt twice.

"I gave . . ."

DeAndre rears up with a quick combination, lefts and rights coming in practiced sequence. Boo collapses on the pavement, stunned by the punches. His anger quickly spent, DeAndre refrains from a full-tilt stomping.

Boo gets up slowly, embarrassed and hurt.

"Come on," DeAndre tells him, turning his head slightly and extending his chin. "Take a shot."

Boo looks at him strangely. He can't put it together fast enough and he's wary of a trap.

"I don't want to do that," says Boo.

Manny Man and R.C. are smiling now. Tyreeka, too. This is DeAndre on stage, at his corner best.

"Go 'head," he says, insistent. "I put your ass on the ground. I feel sorry for you. Take a shot."

Boo shrugs, then cranks up and launches a right hook. His blow lands solidly against DeAndre's left cheek, snapping it back for just a moment. Boo freezes in the follow-through, scared, still trying to see where this is going.

DeAndre doesn't even bother to feel his jaw. He laughs, and for a moment, Boo smiles back nervously.

"You sorry," DeAndre tells him.

R.C. and Manny Man fall out in a wild fit of laughter. Tyreeka is in love all over again.

"Boo, you a sorry nigger!" R.C. shouts, doubling over.

Boo smiles stupidly, hoping the beef is settled. But DeAndre is once again staring at him coldly, the laughter gone.

"Every time I see you," he assures him. "You gon' get beat until I get my money."

Boo seems convinced. The next day he finds DeAndre at the rec center and calls him outside. At the edge of the Vincent Street alley, he offers up thirty dollars.

"That's all I got right now."

DeAndre takes the money.

"I'll have some more later in the week."

DeAndre nods. In this world, thirty in the hand is worth twice that in money owed. And besides, DeAndre reasons, the threat of a daily ass-whipping can only carry so far with the likes of Boo, who gets points for being a C.M.B. member. That's the trouble with sub-contracting to friends: When the money or the package gets messed up, there's a limit to your response unless you genuinely want to do violence to the people you hang with. With a stranger, it might play differently.

Not only that, but there's now a small voice arguing for caution inside the head of DeAndre McCullough. It's not like him to listen, but Boys Village got his attention. If he wants to be on the street for his sixteenth summer, he's going to have to slow things down. The drug charge on Fairmount leaves him with three pending cases. True, the car case was bullshit; DeAndre wasn't even in the car when they gave him the charge. And true again, the first coke case was hovering at the edge of dismissal because the arresting officer, a white police named Weiner, got himself killed a few months back. But DeAndre figures he has to worry about general appearances. A juvenile master might see all the docket numbers, conclude he was a crime wave in the making, and bang him hard for the Fairmount arrest.

For the same reason, DeAndre has decided to take seriously the pretrial release conditions, showing up every day at school and then getting back uptown to his aunt's house by half past three. Fairmount

Avenue is still there for him, of course; he left that corner wide open and there is money to be made. But another charge now might cost him the summer.

For three weeks after his release from Boys Village, DeAndre is at the high school when the morning roll is taken. True, he often ducks out of the last class periods to run the streets a bit. True, he does a minimum of classwork and no homework at all. True, his class participation consists of putting his head on his desk and imitating a cadaver. Even so, three weeks of present-and-accounted-for is remarkable for DeAndre McCullough. Rose Davis is impressed and tells him so. A few months like this and DeAndre could make the tenth grade.

In the evenings, he has Tyreeka over to his aunt's house whenever possible. Other nights, he brings Tae or R.C. up to Etting Street to watch movies or play Nintendo. Beyond that, he's trapped inside with his young cousins, waiting for that juvenile hearing notice and figuring that if he can pretend to be a changed person for two months at most, he'll be back on the street.

Having dealt with Boo, there's just one other bit of unfinished business for DeAndre. He's heard the talk about Tyreeka and Tae. Tae, it turns out, wants to try for Tyreeka and, while sharing a hack up to Etting Street one day after school, he broaches the subject to DeAndre.

He likes Tyreeka, Tae admits, but he won't make a move unless DeAndre agrees. "So," he concludes, "what you think?"

DeAndre shrugs. He could say no, but that probably wouldn't stop Tae, especially with DeAndre stuck up on Etting Street every night. And, DeAndre reasons, if he says no and is ignored, he'll look vulnerable. On the other hand, it could be something of a test for Tyreeka. See how loyal his girl really is.

"I'm saying take your best shot," says DeAndre.

Tae nods and they shake on it.

"But do it now," DeAndre adds. "Because I'm gonna want her back by summer. The girl stood by me and shit. I mean, she stood with me when I was down and I'm gonna want her back."

Tae nods in agreement. Fair is fair.

"He's back," says Fat Curt, caning away.

"Damn," says Pimp. "I ain't even had the chance to get lonely for the man."

Curt laughs softly, and the two old friends beat feet toward the mouth of Vine Street. Grizzled and worn, Scalio is waiting there, a look of growing discomfort on his face.

"You seen him?" he asks Curt.

But there isn't a spare moment in which to answer. Just then, the man himself comes cruising around from Lexington, grimacing behind the wheel. Scalio sags at the sight.

"Shit," he says, falling in behind Curt and Pimp, "they gave him the wagon."

At Fayette and Monroe, there is no sight more unwelcome than that of Officer Robert Brown, back from his vacation, laying hands upon the sinners and working the silver bracelets hard. He leads this afternoon's blitzkrieg from the driver's seat of the Western District jail van. Bob Brown and his lockup-on-wheels.

"What day is it?" asks Bread.

"Today Tuesday," says Eggy Daddy.

"Zebra Day," says Bread, with finality.

The others nod in agreement. Zebra Day is the blanket corner explanation for anything involving drug enforcement in West Baltimore. If it carries cuffs and a nightstick and hits you hard, it's got something to do with Zebra Day.

"Where he at?"

"Gone down Fulton and round the block."

"Aw shit. Bob Brown comin' through."

The patrolman grabs a tout down at Gilmor, then wheels up to Lexington and rolls the wrong way around the corner at Fulton Avenue, coming up on the Spider Bag crew, where he grabs one of the lookouts. Then down to Fayette again and up the hill to Monroe, where he takes off a white boy trying to cop outside the grocery. Then down to Payson and back up Lexington to Monroe, where he grabs one of Gee's work-horses.

"Bob Brown collectin' bodies."

"Best move indoors."

Slowly, the corner crews drift off Monroe Street, moving through the back alley between Fayette and Vine, slipping through the minefield of trash and broken furniture until they're at the rear of 1825 Vine. They can't help but see Roberta McCullough framed in the rear kitchen window. Though most manage to avoid eye contact, some of the older heads try to be neighborly.

"G'mornin'," says Bread, waving.

And Miss Roberta, unsure, simply returns the wave.

That the shooting gallery has moved from Blue's to the rowhouse adjacent to the McCulloughs is no surprise; since Linda Taylor caught the Bug and died in January, ownership of 1825 had settled on Annie, her daughter. Already on probation from one drug charge, Annie was doing little more than waking up every morning and chasing the blast until she fell into bed at night.

And make no mistake: Rita and her patients caught a real break when Annie decided to open her house to them in the dead of winter. After all, there was no heat or running water in Blue's, and since Blue had been locked up, the fiends had stripped out all that was left of the furniture and most of the windows. By contrast, Annie would open the kitchen oven for warmth that could be felt throughout most of the first floor. And while Rita worked the candles and cookers at the kitchen table, the front room served as the lounge, with the regulars stacked up on what was left of an L-shaped sofa arrangement, all modular and maroon and looking like it belonged in the lobby of a Ramada Inn.

For the McCulloughs next door, the decline and fall of 1825 represented more than the daily irritation of nonstop drug traffic; that much was a given with crews already slinging at either end of Vine. For W.M. and Miss Roberta, a shooting gallery next door meant living with the possibility that they would wake up at three in the morning to the smell of smoke and find their Vine Street home and a half-dozen others ablaze. The McCulloughs could watch the foot traffic and imagine dozens of addicts stumbling in and out of that worn, wood-floor kitchen next door, dropping matches and knocking over candles. Any night now, Annie's crew might burn half the street out of doors.

The McCulloughs could call the police, of course; Miss Roberta had thought about that. But then again, she had seen how many times the police had run through Blue's and boarded up the place, only to have the fiends pull off the plywood and start over again. And what if Annie and her houseguests found out that the McCulloughs had called in on them, or even mistakenly believed that the McCulloughs had done so? If the police did come, it could mean more trouble than help. No, there was nothing to do but watch solemnly from the kitchen window, hoping against hope that Annie might pull herself together and tell the circus to move on.

Today inside 1825, the regulars warm themselves at the stove door and wait for Bob Brown to fish his limit. Bread, Fat Curt, Eggy Daddy,

Dennis, Rita, Shardene, Joyce and Charlene Mack, Chauncey from up the way, Pimp and Scalio—all of them lazing around the first floor, waiting on Mr. Brown.

"He comin' back down Vine," says Scalio, peering at the edge of the front shade.

Annie moves toward him, muttering nervously. "You should come back from the window," she warns. "He gonna see you signifyin.'"

"He ain't see shit," says Scalio, watching the wagon disappear at the east end of Vine. He moves to the door, cracking it enough to see Bob Brown's jail van turn north on Fulton. Heading back up to the Western, maybe. Going to the lockup with a wagonful.

"Motherfuckin' Bob Brown," says Charlene Mack.

"He too evil," agrees Bread.

Scalio goes outside, paces cautiously for a minute, then starts walking back up to Monroe. Down the block the Spider Bag crew is trying to set up their shop, the touts seemingly indifferent to the loss of their lookout. Pimp and Bread slip out the back door, then come back moments later with news.

"Death Row puttin' out testers."

In a heartbeat, the house is emptied of fiends, save for Rita, who stays in the kitchen, poking at the raw flesh of her left arm with a syringe. Two minutes more and a half-dozen of them are back, stumbling through the back door, winded from the run.

"You was quick," says Rita.

Bread snorts derisively. They didn't even get across Fulton before Bob Brown rolled down Lexington. And not just the wagon alone; Mr. Brown has a two-man car following him. The girl police, Jenerette, and that new white boy, the one with the marine cut.

"They just snatchin' niggers up," moans Annie.

"Zebra Day," says Eggy Daddy.

It's a timeworn phrase on these corners, dating back to the late 1970s, when some tactical wizard in the police department reckoned that the drug war could be won by alternating between East and West Baltimore and sweeping the corners clean at the rate of twice a week. Mondays and Wednesdays on the east side, Tuesdays and Thursdays on the west side, with Fridays off so the police could get a jump on their weekend—that was the Zebra schedule. On all other days of the week, the West Baltimore regulars might be subjected to ordinary law enforcement, but on Tuesdays and Thursdays, all bets were off and anything might happen. Knockers, rollers, wagon men, plainclothes jump-out squads—every spare soul in the police department seemed to be lighting on the corners. On Zebra Day, a routine eyefuck that might otherwise be ignored by a patrolman would buy a Western District holding cell, just as a routine insult would often result in a mighty ass-kicking. And on Tuesdays and Thursdays in West Baltimore, the Constitution and the Bill of Rights were largely without meaning. On Zebra Day, there was no such thing as probable cause; any police could go into your pockets by invoking the Zebra logic.

Of course, it was all myth. The years had passed and the corners had grown and the once-awesome spectacle of Zebra Day had become merely a trace memory, the Baltimore Police Department having moved on to new tactics and new slogans. These days the corner regulars invoked the voodoo incantation of Zebra Day more than the police ever had; even thirteen- and fourteen-year-olds—born after the advent of the original Zebra—were still citing it as explanation for whatever events happened to occur on those days. Like today, a Tuesday in March, when Bob Brown is pushing the jail wagon, harvesting the corners, moving the sullen herds to and fro like some saddle-assed West Texas cowpoke.

Must be Zebra.

Peeking out of Annie's front door, Eggy Daddy watches the top end of Vine for a few minutes more and, sure enough, the wagon makes the turn from Monroe, rumbling down the gentle slope of the alley street. Vine is empty now—Bob Brown has succeeded in momentarily chasing the crews indoors—but still the man is on an angry tear.

"He just all mean and miserable and a motherfucker," says Charlene Mack, ascending to alliteration. "One day, someone gonna hurt him."

Grunts of affirmation all around.

"Someone gon' put a bullet in his ass," says Eggy.

Someone, someday. Along Fayette Street, they've been saying such stuff about Bob Brown for twenty years, talking for two solid decades about a reckoning that never seems to come. Long after the rest of the police department has conceded the Fayette Street corridor to drug trafficking, Bob Brown is still decidedly undefeated. Long after every fiend in an eight-square-block grid wished him dead and gone, Bob Brown is still clinging to the real estate in eight-hour-shift installments. It's sad and comical, but in some way genuinely noble: Bob Brown, walking the beat or riding that wagon, trying to herd the pigeons, trying to rake all the dry, brittle leaves into a pile on a windy day.

On one level, they hate him for it. Hating Bob Brown is an obligatory act for every fiend in the neighborhood. But at the same time, the
souls on the corner allow a grudging respect for Mr. Brown and his
game. If nothing else, the man is consistent, a moral standard in a place
where it's increasingly hard to take measure of morality. He can be brutal,
but at the least he is consistently brutal, resorting to violence only when
there is some justification for it. And when Bob Brown turns a corner,
the odds are exactly the same for everyone. If he says get, you get or you
go to jail. If he wants to go into your pockets, you put your hands against
the liquor store wall and let him search, because there is no point in
running from Bob Brown. If you run today, you'll have to come back
to the same corner tomorrow, and then, as sure as night follows day,
there will come a reckoning. And if Bob Brown, while knocking you on
your ass, decides to call you a low-life motherfucking piece of shit, you
are—at that moment, at least—a low-life piece of shit. At street level,
there can be no arguing with the man.

Even those who want Bob Brown dead have to acknowledge that it
isn't racial. Oh yeah, Mr. Brown is big and white and nasty, and every
once in a while, on a day when he is truly pissed off, he might even let
go of an epithet. But the Fayette Street regulars have lived with Bob
Brown for years now; they've seen how much abuse he'll readily heap
on the white boys he catches creeping north out of Pigtown, venturing
across Baltimore Street for a chance to hook into a better product. In
their hearts, they know it isn't race; it's much more than skin-deep.

Bob Brown hates everybody, they are quick to assure you. And then,
later, they think on this and realize that not even a police as mean and
miserable as Mr. Brown can muster hate enough for everyone. Bob Brown
doesn't mess with the ladies up at St. Martin's, or Miss Roberta, or Miss
Bertha, or the people out at the bus stops going to work in the morning.
No, when pressed, they have to admit that Bob Brown is not quite so
unreasoning.

"He just death on drugs," says Gary McCullough, watching from the
steps in front of Annie's as Bob Brown and his full-up wagon bounce
around the corner and turn on Lexington.

"That's what it is," agrees Tony Boice. "He don't like dope fiends even
a little bit."

On the corners, they tell themselves that it's more than police work,
that it's something that happened to Bob Brown, or maybe to someone
in his family. His first wife got addicted and turned out by her supplier,

some claim. Not his wife, others argue, but a younger sister, who came up an overdose back in the seventies. The exact details have never been nailed down and, absent facts, such apocryphal stories become more melodramatic with each telling: Bob Brown grieving for lost loves and wasted relatives, swearing to make generations of Fayette Street fiends pay the price for some deep and painful family secrets. Out on the corner, only the worst kind of scenario could explain the angry timelessness of the Bob Brown Crusade.

The other police are different—more reviled, in some cases—but different nonetheless. Most no longer even pretend that they are trying to hold or reclaim their posts from the ceaseless drug trafficking. Instead, the best of them are content to harvest the comers for a quota of street-level arrests, a small sampling of lawlessness that will always prove as meaningless an act of enforcement as it is random. The worst of them have lost themselves in the siege mentality of the drug war, giving back to the corners the same hostility that greets them. Fayette Street for them is a place deserving of Old Testament justice: an eyefuck for an eyefuck, with handcuffs for minor insults and lead-filled nightsticks or slapjacks for any greater provocation. The new breed of police along Fayette Street—Pitbull and Shields, Peanuthead and Collins—has no feeling for the pavement on which they are warring, no sense of a communal past by which the present might be judged. For all of his bluster, Bob Brown carries that burden.

In that regard, Bob Brown is what every police official and neighborhood association claims as the solution to the trouble in their streets. He is every bit the old-time beat cop, the retrograde image of walk-the-footpost, know-the-people policing. Get the cops out of the radio cars, runs the latest theory, and you begin to get them back into the neighborhoods. Get them out walking their real estate, and they'll start to reconnect with the people, learn the neighborhood, prevent crime. Community-oriented policing has become the watchword of the nineties in law enforcement. Houston, New York, Washington, Detroit—everyone is nostalgic for foot patrols and grassroots policing and whatever the hell else kept the streets safe in 1950. That Bob Brown knows his post from one end to the other, that he can recite most of the players and their deeds by name, that he has fought for the same terrain for two decades—all of it seems the textbook model of what the visionaries in law enforcement are promoting. That there are already Bob Browns on the streets, that for all their will and desire and knowledge, they have lost their private wars in hardcore places like West Baltimore—that is somehow beside the point.

And lost it they have. On Fayette Street, Bob Brown has fought tenaciously, clearing corners, herding fiends, chasing slingers, and arresting hundreds every year. Yet he has watched helplessly as the rot from the vials and glassine bags rolls upslope from the housing projects and down across the west side expressway, reducing the working-class neighborhood where he began his career to little more than a collection of open-air drug markets and crumbling shooting galleries. He's witnessed a couple generations of young girls having their babies, then watched as those children were named and nicknamed, diapered and raised. And he's been there when those children began their inexorable drift away from the schoolyards and ball courts, when they started to play at the fringes of the corner. Unlike so many of the younger police, Bob Brown knew many of the fiends before they ever chased a blast, many of the slingers before they went to the corner with that first stepped-on, scrambled package. More than any other cop working Franklin Square, he can bring names and faces and family histories to the history of disaster, and now, with the neighborhood in chaos, he bears witness as the dope-and-coke tide crests the hill at Fayette and continues south across Baltimore Street, down into Pigtown and Carroll Park.

Down there, the hillbillies aren't proving to be any different; there are all-white and even some integrated crews selling coke all along McHenry Street, dope down at Ramsay and Stricker. The decay in West Baltimore is unremitting, epic; to police against it, you need either the quixotic rage of a crusader or sense enough to detach yourself from the totality of the nightmare, to hump your share of calls and make some cases and then grab that twenty-year pension.

The sad beauty of Bob Brown is that he shows no sense whatsoever. Against all evidence, he is still crusading, still defending a neighborhood at a time when the threat is from the neighborhood itself. For Mr. Brown, the question is the same on any day that he walks from the Western District roll-call room to a radio car: How do you make police work matter when more than half of Fayette Street, perhaps eighty percent of those between the ages of fifteen and thirty, is in some way involved in the use or sale of heroin and cocaine? To be sure, there are still citizens in Franklin Square: older men who still call 911 or 685-DRUG to provide information about the trafficking; women who let Bob Brown into their houses so he can peek from behind the drapes and watch slingers serving up in the alley. Still for every one of those embattled souls, two or three others are going to the corner.

Yet he endures. Like today, when he's dragging that jail wagon around the corners, filling it with a half-dozen of the prevailing herd—and all but one of them locked up as humbles, charged with failure to obey, or disorderly, or loitering in a city-designated drug-free zone ("where drugs are free," joke the sages and touts). The last of the unfortunates has gotten himself caught with a handful of vials, but no matter—all of them are going to disappear for a night, or a week, or a month at the most. And as Bob Brown finally tires of the chase and turns the wagon north on Fulton Avenue, heading toward the district lockup, the corners come alive again.

"Shop open," says Hungry, sliding out of Annie's.

The crews on Fayette and Vine Streets step gingerly back into the mix, one eye on the game, the other on the far corners, still nervous about seeing the motorized Mr. Brown making another pass. Back at Annie's, Rita takes a rest in a broken-backed kitchen chair while Annie peers out the front window, worried as always, thinking that it's her that they're looking for. Her and her house. Thinking that they're all out there—Bob Brown and Pitbull, Collins and Shields—wondering where the regulars from Blue's have gone. Wondering which door they'll have to kick in next to find the needle palace.

"I'm on probation already," she says sadly.

She nurses such fears alone. The rest of them are there with her, but thinking no thoughts about anything beyond shooting dope, shooting coke, and staying warm. They've found a home and they know that as long as Annie gets her share of the hype, they're going to be firing drugs and nodding off in a heated room with running water. With any luck at all, they'll be at Annie's until the March winds give way to April and true spring. By the standards of shooting-gallery life, the regulars from Blue's are fortunate indeed.

It seems that way for a week or more until a fresh crew of New Yorkers sets up shop at Lexington and Fulton and begins selling some Black Tops of coke that are an absolute bomb. Before long the morning tester lines are stretching across the vacant lot at the bottom of Vine Street and the alley itself is filled with drug traffic. Annie's refuge is suddenly in the center of the action, and the police seem to be snatching bodies off Vine Street on a daily basis. Sure enough, it isn't long before one of the white boys from McHenry Street gets spotted after hooking up with some Black

Tops on the vacant lot. The boy makes the mistake of trying to run with Pitbull chasing him; worse, he makes the mistake of trying to lose himself by running through the alley and up into Annie's kitchen door.

"Not in here, fool," yells Shardene.

But it's too late. Pitbull is right on the kid's heels, kicking through the warped wooden door and charging across the threshold with the back-up troops only a few seconds behind him. He grabs the white boy in the front room and slams him against the flaking plaster wall, punching him twice for luck. Out come the cuffs, with the white boy moaning and begging and Pitbull telling the kid to just shut the fuck up.

The other troops have everyone jacked against the wall, waiting, the room strangely silent in the wake of what amounts to a warrantless raid. On the kitchen table are Rita's candles, a plastic tub of dirty water, and a half-dozen syringes. Scattered around the room is a who's who of Fayette Street regulars, and when the rest of the occupants are ordered down from the second floor, it's a veritable convention.

"Look at this shit," says one of the younger police.

Leaning against the maroon sofa, Annie closes her eyes and waits for tears that won't come. She's lost her house, she figures. They'll bring the city work truck and board up the doors and windows, and she'll be out on the street with the rest of them. She might even take a charge, and that would mean a couple of years backing up on her, since she walked away from an Excel detox program, violating her last probation.

And yet, incredibly, after Pitbull drags the white boy out the front door, the other patrolmen follow him, leaving the fiends where they stand and the shooting gallery in place.

"They comin' back?" asks Hungry.

Annie stares through the front blind as the white boy is dragged to the wagon. Finally, she shrugs.

"Don' know."

"Well fuck it then."

The police stumble into a shooting gallery, the police leave the shooting gallery; the party goes on. It's a telling moment, a wake-up call for anyone along Fayette Street who still believes in an urban war on drugs. But no one in Annie's had any clue what to think until it happens again a week later, the cause on this second occasion being Bread, who'd been running and gunning at flank speed all month, chasing those Black Tops and slamming them home one after the next. They'd all been going at the coke heavy—Curt, Bread, Dennis, Rita, the whole crew—a celebration of sorts to mark the end of winter. They'd soldiered the hard months; now, there was a scent of easier times in the air, a hint of their just rewards for having struggled through so many twenty-degree mornings on the cold floor of Blue's empty vessel. But Bread had been twenty-four, seven on the strong coke, not even taking time out to crawl into his mother's basement door and sleep a morning or two away. When he did crash, it was on Annie's sofa or in one of the battered bedrooms upstairs. All of them were soldiers, but Bread had become the Viking.

So when he finally falls out, no one pays it much mind. He stays in the front room, slumped in a heap on the sofa, his winter coat under him, his breath coming in rasps and wheezes. He tosses fitfully for a few hours, then begins mumbling in a half-sleep, telling unnamed and unseen adversaries to go away and let him the fuck alone. Then his breathing becomes more erratic; Annie, watching from a chair in the other corner of the room, is unnerved to see her friend open his lids wide for a moment. The eyeballs have rolled up inside his head.

"Bread, wake up now."

"NNNAAAA."

"Bread . . . somethin' ain't right with Bread."

They get someone at the McCullough house to call 911, then open the front door and wait ten minutes for the ambulance, with Annie stroking Bread's hand and rubbing his head, telling him that help is on the way. But the paramedics can't stabilize him; they can't manage a steady pulse in a forty-six-year-old body that looks to be twice that old. They hit him with the Lidocaine and the steroids and whatever else they've got in the truck, but nothing seems to bring him up from the abyss. When two or three police come through to watch the paramedics, they again give the house a once-over, shaking their heads in disgust. Catching the scent of Rita's rotting arms, one of the young patrolmen actually orders her into the bathroom, using his nightstick to poke her across the threshold as if she's nothing more than viral.

"What did he have?" asks one of the paramedics.

"Huh?"

"What drugs did he use?"

There's only silence.

"I need to know what he had. If you care about this guy, tell me."

"Coke," says Annie. "Coke and dope both."

Once or twice, Bread seems to let out a moan, or maybe it's just an

explosion of air from his emptying lungs. When the ambo pulls off down
Vine Street, his eyes are fixed.

The funeral is scheduled for Saturday up at Morton's. Because it's
Bread, many of the fiends along Fayette Street make noises about going
up there, if not for the services, then at least for one of the viewings.

Bread had been one of the originals on these corners, one of those
rare few who had lasted long enough to make the consumption of drugs
seem something like a career. His standing was such that rumors about
his death swirl up and down Fayette Street, each a vain attempt to give
the event more meaning than it deserves. Some hear that he'd been given
a hot-shot by some New York Boys who wrongly thought he'd stolen a
stash. Others talk about how he'd been firing some of that China White,
the synthetic morphine substitute that killed about a dozen people in a
single week last summer. Still others are whispering that they'd heard
that Bread's friends—lifetime companions like Fat Curt and Eggy
Daddy—had panicked when they couldn't revive him and had simply
dumped the body in the back alley behind Annie's house. In the end,
the only rumor with any truth in it is the one that always follows a death
on the needle: When the fiends along Fayette Street hear that Bread had
succumbed to a blast of coke, they all, quite naturally, want to know
who is selling the shit. Bread is gone, they reason, and that's a shame.
But that doesn't mean the rest of us don't know how to handle the good
blast of coke that killed him. Come right here with that nasty shit.

Inside Annie's, among the people who knew Bread best, there is a
grief as sincere and heartfelt as for any taxpayer. Bread was of that earlier
epoch when the corner life had rules, when there were standards that
any self-respecting dope fiend had to consider. Bread had done twenty
years around Fayette and Monroe, and to anyone's best memory, he'd
never cheated his friends, or fallen to violence, or intentionally damaged
anyone other than himself. So Eggy Daddy promises he'll be at the funeral.
And Gary McCullough. And Annie, who cried the whole night through
when word came back from the hospital that Bread didn't make it, that
he had all but died right there on her sofa. And Fat Curt, too—he surely
wants to go up to Brown's for the homecoming, though he hasn't been
able to bring himself to so much as speak about his friend since the
ambo rolled away. For Bread, they all tell themselves, they'd surely step
out of their game for a day and pay the proper respects.

But at five o'clock on the morning of the funeral service, the snow
begins falling in thick, dry flakes all across Baltimore. By eight, there's

a foot of new whiteness on the ground and no sign of any break in the storm. On this day, the surprise blanketing—the only major storm of the year—transforms the corners of Fayette and Baltimore Streets, covering the trash and the discarded furniture, rendering uniform and pristine the usual scenery of broken rowhouses, corner stores, and vacant lots. The tester lines don't form up this morning; the package is late. Even the police radio cars are off the roads, waiting for the city plows to go to work.

The regulars inside Annie's figure that the service is canceled, or even if it isn't canceled, they reason that there is no way they're going to make it ten blocks north of the expressway in this kind of weather. More honestly, they look out the window and figure that it's a day to make money with the blizzard slowing the police cars to a crawl.

And so, the corner gives up its dead to an empty funeral parlor, with Bread Corbett laid out in a Sunday pinstripe for his mother and a handful of other family members. The preacher, who declares himself a recovering addict, offers no cheap platitudes; he goes directly at the tragedy, speaking bitterly of wasted years and misspent lives. The family that hears him already knows the story; the family that doesn't—the strange, extended clan in which Bread truly lived his life—is slogging through the snow on Vine Street, taking care of business. Only Joe Laney, sitting quietly in one of the back rows, is there at the end to say farewell. Joe had been on the corner with Fat Curt and Bread and the rest for years, only to pick himself up and walk away. He makes his way to Bread's mother with his regrets.

"He was a good friend," he tells her.

Two days later, spring is back in the air, the streets are covered in a dull, gray slush, and Annie's is still the shooting gallery. After leaving with the ambo crew, the police have not been back, and it has finally started to dawn on some of the regulars that it isn't about real estate anymore, that the police could care less. Up on the corner, Eggy Daddy is touting for the Gold Star crew, as is Hungry. Fat Curt is across the street in front of the grocery, his eyes yellow, his body bent against the warming breeze. He stands there, unmoving, with a thousand-yard stare on his face, one fat hand wrapped around a funeral parlor pamphlet, a token given him by Joe Laney. In loving memory of Robert E. Corbett reads the cover. The photograph is a high school graduation shot: Bread, circa 1965, in a dark sports coat and thin tie, deep brown eyes staring mournfully.

Curt pockets the pamphlet, but a few moments later, he takes it out and looks again at the photograph. This time, Bread. And before him it was Flubber. Cleaned himself up at the end and showed the courage to get up at those NA meetings and talk about having the Bug. First one to talk about it like that. And Joe Laney, now living a new life so that Curt only sees him when he rides by in that little car of his, heading up to his college classes. And House and Sonny Mays, both of them doing good, talking that NA twelve-step shit. And soon it will be Dennis, his own brother, dying by degrees, staggering around these corners as the virus chews him down to the bone. The fat man, ever more alone.

"Hey, Curt," asks Robin. "Who that?"

Curt looks again at the old photo.

"Bread."

"Got-damn. That Bread?"

"Back in the day."

He's still holding the funeral pamphlet, still looking at the ancient portrait through jaundiced eyes, when none other than Bob Brown turns the corner. Mr. Brown on the hunt.

Curt is slower than usual this time, distracted. He's barely able to plant his cane and take a step before the patrolman is on him. Bob Brown looks directly at Curt, then down at the pamphlet in his swollen hand. Wordlessly, he steps past the aging tout, concentrating instead on a coterie of teenagers hanging by the pay phone.

"Corner's mine," he tells them. "Move."

Curt wipes his eyes, then pockets the pamphlet. Slowly, he finds his step, but to no real purpose. The teenagers have moved off down Monroe Street, leaving two longtime veterans of Fayette Street alone for a moment on the corner.

"Hey," grunts Bob Brown.

Then he steps past Fat Curt again.

The paper bag does not exist for drugs. For want of that shining example of constabulary pragmatism, the disaster is compounded.

The origins of the bag are obscure, though by the early 1960s, this remarkable invention was a staple of ghetto diplomacy in all the major American cities. And for good reason, since by that time virtually every state assembly and city council had enacted statutes prohibiting the consumption of alcoholic beverages in public. They seemed good laws, reasoned attempts to prevent rummies and smokehounds from cluttering the streets, parks and sidewalks; codified weapons to prohibit unseemly displays of human degeneration. That these goals might have been accomplished in small-town America, or in the manicured suburbs, meant nothing, of course, in the core of any large city. There, on the corners of the poorest neighborhoods, dozens of men would live their lives at the lip of a bottle of 20/20 or T-Bird or Mickey's, public consumption law or no.

Long before the open-air drug market, the corner was still the assembly point, the clubhouse; those who spent their days there couldn't afford bar prices, but nonetheless preferred the corner ambiance to downing a bottle at home, particularly since home was more likely than not a third-floor walk-up with three screaming kids and a woman who hated you even when you weren't drinking. No, it was always the corner.

For the police working these ghetto posts, the public consumption law posed a dilemma: You could try to enforce it, in which case you'd never have time for any other kind of police work; or you could look the other way, in which case you'd be opening yourself to all kinds of disrespect from people who figure that if a cop is ignoring one illegal act, he'll probably care little about a half-dozen others.

But when the first wino dropped the first bottle of elderberry into the first paper bag—and a moment of quiet genius it was—the point was moot. The paper bag allowed the smokehounds to keep their smoke, just as it allowed the beat cop a modicum of respect. In time, the bag was institutionalized as a symbol; to drink without it was to insult the patrolman and risk arrest, just as it was a violation of the tacit agreement for a cop to ignore the bag and humble anyone employing it. In a sense, the paper bag allowed for some connection between the police and the corner herd; for the price of an occasional bottle, in fact, the smokehounds could often be relied upon to provide information about more serious matters. More important, the bag allowed the government to prioritize its resources, to ignore the inevitable petty vices of urban living and concentrate instead on the essentials. This is a truth once understood by any cop worth his pension—if you're policing an Amish town and the worst crime is spitting on the sidewalk, then enforce that law. But if you're policing Baltimore or a city like it, and the worst crimes are murder, rape, armed robbery and aggravated assault, then don't waste your time, men, and money throwing gin-breathed wrecks into a police wagon.

But with no equivalent to the bag in the war on drugs, there can be no equilibrium on the corners, no accommodation between the drug subculture and those policing it, no relativity in the contemplation of sins and vices. Without the paper bag, animosity and, ultimately, violence are the only possibilities between the police and the policed, because there is no purpose to diplomacy or proportion when war becomes total. Granted, a paper-bag solution wouldn't reduce the power of addiction, or steal any of the profit, or mitigate the disaster of a single life lost to narcotics; it is in no sense a cure for the drug epidemic. But there is still a priceless lesson in the idea, a valuable bit of beat-cop sensibility that could rescue both the patrolmen and their prey from their own worst excesses. No doubt some kind of war on drugs was a political inevitability, just as that war's failure to thwart human desire was inevitable as well. But we might have saved ourselves from the psychic costs of the drug war—the utter alienation of an underclass from its government, the wedding of that alienation to a ruthless economic engine, and finally, the birth of an outlaw philosophy as ugly and enraged as hate and despair can produce—if we had embraced the common sense that comes with the paper bag.

Instead, as the addict population grew, we could see no connection between the corner rummy and the corner dope fiend. One was deemed a harmless, self-destructive soul, while the other was declared a sworn enemy. That some of those chasing heroin are genuinely dangerous is beyond dispute; the first wave of the national drug epidemic helped to fatten all the crime stats in the late sixties and early seventies. But the other side of that statement—the assumption that many of those chasing a blast are more a threat to society than corner drunkards—has been neither considered, nor argued. Even today, with cocaine added into the mix, the corner is in large part home to a tired collection of bit players, struggling to make their shot within the confines of the drug culture itself. Touts, burn-artists, doctors, slingers, stash-stealers, stickup boys who never rob a citizen, who only hit dealers, metal harvesters, petty thieves who grab a few dollars by shoplifting or breaking into cars, fiends who spend only what comes by way of a government check—shake them all out and what's left to play the roles of predator and sociopath is maybe five percent of the population on any given drug corner.

Rather than target the truly dangerous, rather than concentrate on the murders, the shootings, the armed robberies, the burglaries, we have instead indulged all our furies. Rather than accept the personal decision to use drugs as a given—to seek out a paper-bag solution to the corner's growing numbers—we tried to live by mass arrest. And what has been lost in our abject failure to make any legal or moral distinction between a corner victim and a corner victimizer is any chance to change the drug culture itself, to modify the behavior of those chasing a blast, to wean the worst violence from the corner mind-set, to draw those who might have been willing to listen toward ideas like community, treatment, redemption.

Instead, we have swallowed some disastrous pretensions, allowing ourselves a naive sincerity that, even now, assumes the battle can be restricted to heroin and cocaine, limited to a self-contained cadre of lawbreakers—the quaint term "drug pusher" comes to mind—when all along the conflict was ripe to become a war against the underclass itself. We've trusted in the moral high ground: Just say no.

We threw a negative at them, though it's unclear what they're supposed to say yes to on Fayette Street. We've made war against drugs in a social and economic vacuum, until hopelessness and rage have the damned of our cities fighting for nothing more or less than human desire and profit, against which no one has ever developed a single viable weapons system.

Thirty years after its inception, the drug war in cities such as Baltimore has become an absurdist nightmare, a statistical charade with no other purpose than to placate a public that wants drug trafficking attacked and vanquished—but not, of course, at the price it would actually cost to accomplish such an incredible feat. In Maryland such cognitive dissonance translates to a state prison system that can manage a total of just over 20,000 prison beds for prisoners convicted of every act against the criminal code in Baltimore and twenty-three other counties. Yet in Baltimore alone there are between 15,000 and 20,000 arrests each year for drug violations, and in all of Maryland's jurisdictions, more than 35,000 are charged every year with drug sales or possession.

Build more prisons, you say? How many more? Five? Ten? Keep in mind that Maryland is no slacker when it comes to locking people up; the state ranks tenth nationally in its rate of incarceration. You could bankrupt the state government by doubling the existing prison space and still there wouldn't be enough space to house the estimated 50,000 heroin and cocaine users in Baltimore, not to mention the rest of Maryland. And that leaves no room for those priority cases who just happen to be convicted of murder or rape or armed robbery. Moreover, the construction of a prison is only the preamble; what inevitably follows is the financial drain of staffing the place, of feeding and clothing the prisoners, of maintaining security standards, of running a medical program that the U.S. Supreme Court says must correspond to outside community standards for health care. Soon enough, you're spending more to lock a man down than it would cost to enroll him at Harvard.

More prisons is the impulse answer, the quick-and-dirty response of so many hack politicians and talk-show hosts. It's what the Bush administration told state governments to do as early as 1989 and what the federal government itself has done amid the escalating drug war. Leading by example, the U.S. Bureau of Prisons has doubled its capacity in ten years in an effort to keep up with a federal inmate population that is rising at record rates—the logical result of the mandatory sentences and parole restrictions contained in all those omnibus crime bills.

Yet even with more than 100,000 souls in federal custody, the U.S. prison population is only a tenth of the total number of those incarcerated. State prisons and state budgets are responsible for the rest. In the drug war as in every other aspect of law enforcement, the federal courts handle only the tip of the iceberg—the major offenders, the headline cases, and the crimes that happen to occur in federal jurisdiction. And here's the rub: The U.S. government can happily build prisons into the next millennium because they don't need real money to do it. As with everything else in the federal budget, prison construction and operation can be undertaken simply by adding to the federal deficit. State governments, meanwhile, carry more than 90 percent of the burden of incarcerating people and they, of course, must spend real dollars and balance their budgets.

So what happens in places like West Baltimore? What becomes of all those bodies thrown into the police wagons, all those man-hours of police enforcement, all the dollars spent on court pay and overtime, all that work for the courthouse personnel, the pretrial investigators, the public defenders and prosecutors?

Not much. In a typical year, the Baltimore police department and the assisting federal agencies will lock up a greater percentage of the city's population for drugs than any other major urban area save Atlanta. The rate of arrest for drug charges in Baltimore will be nearly three times that of Los Angeles or Philadelphia, more than double that of Detroit or New York. In all, 18,000 or 19,000 arrests for the distribution or possession of drugs will be the usual result of a year's police work.

Yet just as typically, fewer than 1,000 of those drug defendants will be sentenced to state prisons and, of that number, less than half will be sentenced to more than a year. The rest of the city's drug docket will result in sentences of probation or dismissals. In short, for the vast majority of those arrested, the threat of incarceration is generally limited to a night or two in jail until a bail review hearing or, in the rare event that a money bond is set and a defendant is unable to pay, a month or two of pretrial detention.

It can't be otherwise, because whatever prison space is available is required for the thousands sentenced every year for violent crimes and other felonies. The state judges have known this for years. The lawyers know it as well. So do the police. And the learning curve reaches all the way down to the corner itself: As early as 1991, 61 percent of the felony cases brought into Baltimore Circuit Court were drug violations, and of those, 55 percent involved defendants with at least one prior conviction. Thirty-seven percent had two prior convictions; 24 percent had three.

Up at the Wabash Avenue district courthouse, where arrests from half of the city's police districts funnel into the judiciary, farcical scenes are played out on a daily basis. One morning after the next, the men and women of the corner flood the benches that line Courtroom 4, the Western District bench of Judge Gary Bass, a patient and beleaguered soul charged with making sense of this travesty.

One by one, the street-level drug cases—distribution, conspiracy to distribute, possession with intent to distribute, simple possession—creep off the docket and receive the only sanctions the state of Maryland can afford.

". . . one year probation, supervised."

". . . continuing your probation for a year, subject to random urinalysis to be performed by the Department of Parole and Probation . . ."

"Six months' unsupervised probation with the condition that you seek drug treatment."

". . . case placed on the inactive docket provided that you continue in your detox program . . ."

For Judge Bass, whose memory for faces is legendary, it's a recidivist hell. On occasion, a defendant who is charged with something more substantial than drug involvement and is unwilling to risk a circuit court trial will catch a year or three for a breaking and entering, or for a handgun. And, every now and then, there comes a drug slinger so arrogant or incompetent that he shows up in court loaded with prior convictions and pending cases. For him, there's a chance to slow down with a couple years at Hagerstown, which means parole in eight months or so.

At the federal courthouse, it's very different, of course, because the national government, with its freedom from fiscal constraint, has cranked up the war as loud as she'll go. The new mandatory sentencing guidelines can tag first-time drug offenders with five or ten years, just as the elimination of all parole assures that most of that time will be served. Yet by contrast to the state courts, the federal system is handling only a handful of prosecutions: those involving either major traffickers or minor players unlucky enough to get caught at the fringes of a major trafficker's organization. The variance between courthouses has produced an institutional schizophrenia in drug enforcement. Fiends and small-time slingers sometimes take three or four state charges, then get caught up in a case that goes federal. Suddenly, the man in the black robes is running wild, talking fifteen and no parole. Say what? Who changed the rules?

But federal sentencings are the odd, angry shot in this war. It's at the local level that the endgame has been reached: There are now a million Americans in prison and it still isn't enough to close the corners. Should we lock up a million more? Three million? The cost would be exorbitant. The death penalty for drug trafficking, then? The legal costs of killing a man by state decree are even higher than warehousing him for a couple of decades.

Meanwhile, out on Fayette Street, the absence of real deterrent has been factored into the psychological equation. As the cocaine epidemic has expanded the addict population, thousands more have flocked to the corners, and the drug slinging has become more brazen. There is still some cat-and-mouse with the police; no one wants to go to jail, even for an overnight humble, nor does anyone want to be among the unlucky handful who catch a three-year sentence from some dyspeptic judge. But in terms of real estate, the war is over; by the numbers, the drug trade has proven itself invincible.

In the drug enforcement establishment, the smarter players have caught the scent of defeat coming from places like Fayette Street and they've learned the vernacular of diminished expectation. No, we don't see any light at the end of the tunnel. No, we don't believe you can arrest your way out of the problem. The careerists in the Justice Department and the DEA, the top commanders in the nation's largest police departments—most have learned to embrace the comprehensive view. The prevailing wisdom has drug enforcement as only one facet, with drug treatment and education as equal partners in some kind of global strategy.

The smartest ones make it sound as if it's really a plan, ignoring the fact that all their enforcement is driving addicts toward a wealth of government-funded treatment slots that don't exist, and, let's face it, never will exist in sufficient numbers. As for education, what we have is media saturation; all those this-is-your-brain-on-drugs sound bites have reached and convinced those willing to be reached and convinced. The inner cities have heard the gospel and ignored it.

Still, give the drug warriors credit: They've learned to incorporate enough seeming perspective to justify their budgets and grab for more. And can you blame them? What commander ever admitted that a war was lost until the absolute end was upon him? The DEA, Customs, ATF, the joint regional task forces, the local narcotics squads—all of them are feeding voraciously at the wartime trough, their operating funds coming not only from budget line items, but from the shared revenue of seized assets. They're vested in this debacle. They're a growth industry.

Yet who can argue with a moral war? If you give up, they assure us, It will be worse. And in one sense, they're right: It will be worse in places where poverty is limited, where the demographics prohibit the growth of a ghetto underclass. Call off the drug war and it will be worse in Pittsburgh, or Kansas City, or Seattle. It will be worse in Nassau County, or Dearborn, or Orange County. In any place where the deterrent is still viable, where the lid is still being held down, a cessation of hostilities will result in greater damage.

But in West Baltimore and East St. Louis, in Washington Heights and in South Central Los Angeles—at the very frontiers of the American drug culture—it won't make any difference. War or no, 20,000 heroin addicts and another 30,000 pipers are going to go down to the corner in Baltimore tomorrow. Save for the twenty or forty that get tossed in a jail wagon, not one is going to miss his blast. Against that fact, the drug war stands as a useless and unnecessary brutalization, an unyielding policy that requires our government to occupy our ghettos in much the same way that others have occupied Belfast, or Soweto, or Gaza.

True, a policy of repression was never the intent. But greater ideals are soon enough lost to the troops on the ground. For them, there is only the absolute futility of trying to police a culture with an economy founded on lawbreaking, of pretending to protect neighborhoods that can barely be distinguished from the corners that are overwhelming them. By the standards of a national drug prohibition, half of Fayette Street's residents are deemed outlaws. As the radio cars roll past, they throw out their communal eyefuck, showing twenty-three-year-old patrolmen and twenty-six-year-old knockers what it's like to be despised, to be regarded as an absolute enemy. For the younger police—the ones who never knew the neighborhood when it was worth protecting, the ones for whom the fiends were always fiends—there is no harmony, no connection to the streets or the people who live there. They are not serving anyone; they are answering radio calls and running up the daily arrests, pulling down that court pay for jacking up one or two souls a day. They learn to throw the eyefuck back at the corner, to be cynical, brutal, and sometimes corrupt. They learn to hate.

Gone are the days in Baltimore when the police didn't get court pay for just any arrest, when they were judged instead by the greater standard of how they controlled their posts, when a beat cop culled information and tried to solve those genuine crimes that ought to be solved, when detectives still bothered to follow up on street robberies and assaults. Now, the worst of the Western District regulars have become brutal mercenaries, cementing their street-corner reps with crushed fingers and broken noses, harvesting the corners for arrests that serve no greater purpose than to guarantee hour after hour of paid court time at Wabash. And among this new breed of patrolmen are quite a few who are known by touts and dealers to be corrupt, who routinely keep some of what comes out of the pockets of arrestees. Win or lose, for them the war on drugs means pay day.

There's a racial irony at work, too. By the late seventies and early eighties, a predominantly white police department acquired enough racial consciousness to be wary of the most egregious acts of brutality. But on the Fayette Street corners today, it's a new generation of young black officers that is proving itself violently aggressive. A white patrolman in West Baltimore has to at least take into account the racial imagery, to acknowledge the fact that he is messing with black folk in a majority black city. Not so his black counterparts, for whom brutality complaints can be shrugged off—not only because the victim was a corner-dwelling fiend, but because the racial aspect is neutralized. Not surprisingly, some of the most feared and most despised Western District officers along Fayette Street—Shields, Pitbull, Peanuthead, Collins—are black. They seem to prove just how divisive and alienating the drug war has become, and how class-consciousness more than race has propelled the city's street police toward absolute contempt for the men and women of the corner.

Take, for example, the notable career of David Shields, a black officer who was allowed to run up four brutality complaints in little more than two years, yet stay on the street all of that time. A few months more and Shields claimed his first body—a twenty-one-year-old slinger from Monroe Street whom he chased into an alley and shot, the fatal bullet striking the victim from behind. And though the police review of the shooting cleared Shields, there wasn't a soul on Fayette Street who believed that the knife on the ground actually belonged to the slinger, or that the young man was dead for any other reason than that he had run from one of the Western's hardest and angriest soldiers. Finally, when one of the brutality complaints was sustained by an internal investigation and Shields was hit with a civil suit for brutality against a Fayette Street resident, the department moved him to desk duties. Shields may be the extreme in the Baltimore department, but many of those policing Fayette Street—black and white—routinely go out of their way to show contempt.

Take Pitbull Macer, who one day stood in the middle of Baltimore Street with his hand around Black Ronald's neck, choking the tired, yellow-eyed tout, demanding that he cough up drugs that, in this rare instance at least, Black Ronald did not have. And Pitbull, still unsatisfied, pulled out Ronald's wallet and let the contents—ID cards, telephone numbers, lotto tickets—tumble into the street as confetti, then drove away, leaving the man picking his papers out of the street in absolute humiliation.

Or Collins, perhaps, who one afternoon got out of his radio car, took off his gun belt, handed it to a fellow officer and offered to kick the shit out of fifteen-year-old DeAndre McCullough because the boy had taunted him with a hard look.

"You gonna beat a boy," Fran Boyd had yelled at him, shaming him back into the radio car, "and you a grown man."

Or a nameless Southern District patrolman, the one Ella Thompson saw on Baltimore Street, who grabbed a sixteen-year-old on a loitering charge at Baltimore and Gilmor, then punched him in the face as the boy stood cuffed against the radio car. "The boy said something to him," Ella recalled. "And he just knocked him down."

To watch this younger generation of police is to get no hint of the sadness involved, no suggestion that the men and women of the corner are tragic and pathetic and, on some basic level, as incapable as children. In Baltimore as in so many other cities, the great crusade is reduced to a dirty war, waged by young patrol officers and plainclothesmen already jaded beyond hope.

And yet the war grinds on. Not only because the police and prosecutors are vested in the disaster, but because the entire political apparatus is at the mercy of public expectation. In Baltimore, the mayor and council members and agency heads hear it at every community forum, every neighborhood association meeting from one end of the city to the other:

"I can't walk to the market anymore."

"They're out there on the corner twenty-four hours a day."

"I'm a prisoner in my own home."

Even along Fayette Street, where so many of the residing families are drug-involved, there is a vocal minority, a long-suffering network of old-timers still clinging to pristine rowhouses. They're the tired few who show up at the Franklin Square community meetings, who come out to the candidate forums, who are still willing to believe that government, if it truly cared, could end their nightmare. And they vote.

What is a police commander, a city councilman, even a mayor going to tell such people? The truth? That it can't be stopped, that the thing is beyond even the best of governments? Is an elected official going to stand up and declare that all the street sweeps, the herding of the corner pigeons, the thousands upon thousands of arrests have accomplished nothing in places like Fayette Street? Is he going to take the risk of admitting that for the sake of public appearances and a salve to our collective conscience, we are squandering finite resources on a policy that can never work?

The district commanders, the narcotics captains, the plainclothesmen—at every rank in the Baltimore Police Department, they still defend the prevailing logic, citing as evidence those beleaguered souls who show up at the community forums and demand action. These people are desperate, they tell you. They need help. We've got no choice but to chase the fiends, if only to give these people a break. So like clockwork, the government sweeps the corners and sends the bodies to Wabash. But in Baltimore, not only is the street-level drug arrest not a solution, it's actually part of the problem.

It's not only that the street-level drug arrests have clogged the courtrooms, devouring time and manpower and money. And it's not only that the government's inability to punish so many thousands of violators has stripped naked the drug prohibition and destroyed government's credibility for law enforcement. More than that, in cities like Baltimore, the drug war has become so untenable and impractical that it is slowly undermining the nature of police work itself.

Stupid criminals make for stupid police. This is a stationhouse credo, a valuable bit of precinct-level wisdom that the Baltimore department ignored as it committed itself to a street-level drug war. Because on Fayette Street and a hundred other corners like it, there is nothing for a patrolman or plainclothesman that is as easy, as guaranteed, and as profitable as a street-level drug arrest. With minimal probable cause, or none at all, any cop can ride into the circus tent, jack up a tout or runner, grab a vial or two, and be assured of making that good overtime pay up at Wabash. In Baltimore, a cop doesn't even need to come up with a vial. He can simply charge a suspect with loitering in a drug-free zone, a city statute of improbable constitutionality that has exempted a good third of the inner city from the usual constraints of probable cause. In Baltimore if a man is standing in the 1800 block of Fayette Street—even if he lives in the 1800 block of Fayette Street—he is fodder for a street arrest.

As a result, police work in inner city Baltimore has been reduced to fish-in-a-barrel tactics, with the result that a generation of young officers has failed to learn investigation or procedure. Why bother to master the intricacies of probable cause when an anti-loitering law allows you to go into anyone's pockets? Why become adept at covert surveillance when you can just go down to any corner, line them up against the liquor store, and search to your heart's content? Why learn how to use, and not be used by, informants when information is so unnecessary to a street-level arrest? Why learn how to write a proper search warrant when you can make your court pay on the street, without ever having to worry about whether you're kicking in the right door?

In district roll-call rooms across Baltimore, in drug unit offices, in radio cars parked hood-to-trunk on 7-Eleven parking lots, there are sergeants and lieutenants—veterans of a better time—who complain about troops who can't write a coherent police report, who don't understand how to investigate a simple complaint, who can't manage to testify in district court without perjuring themselves.

Not surprisingly, as street-level drug arrests began to rise with the cocaine epidemic of the late 1980s, all other indicators of quality police work—and of a city's livability—began to fall in Baltimore. The police department began using more and more of itself to chase addicts and touts through the revolving door at Wabash and the Eastside District Court, so there were fewer resources available to work shooting cases, or rapes, or burglaries.

For the first time in the modern history of the department, rates for felonies began falling below national averages. In one six-year span of time—1988 to 1993—the clearance rate for shootings fell from 60 to 47 percent, just as the solve rate for armed robbery fell below 20 percent for the first time ever. Arrests for rape declined by 10 percent, and the percentage of solved burglaries fell by a third. Alone among felonies, the arrest rate for murder remained constant in Baltimore, but only because the high-profile aspects of such crimes prevented department officials from gutting the homicide unit as every other investigative unit had been gutted. In a department where competent investigators were once legion, the headquarters building was threadbare; the coming genera-tion of police was out on the streets, running the corners, trying to placate community forums and neighborhood associations with an enforcement logic of sound and fury that signified nothing.

In those same years, the war on drugs failed to take back a single drug corner, yet the city's crime rate soared by more than 37 percent to all-time levels. In 1990, the city began suffering 300-plus murders a year—a rate unseen in Baltimore since the early 1970s, when baby-boom demographics and the lack of a comprehensive shock-trauma system could be blamed. Baltimore became the fourth most violent city in the nation, and its rate of cocaine and heroin use—as measured by emergency room statistics—was the worst in the United States. By 1996, the cumulative increase in the city's crime rate was approaching 45 percent.

In time, fewer and fewer of those living near the corners were fooled. On Fayette Street, those paying attention had lived with the drug war and the drug culture long enough to discern the range that separates sin and vice. To them, it said something that the kid who had shot three people this month was still on the street, or that the crew that had been breaking into area stores and churches was at it again, hitting the Apostolic Church on Baltimore Street just this week. It said some-thing that the stickup crews were working Fulton Avenue and Monroe Street with impunity, that no one bothered to even report armed robberies anymore because they knew there would be no follow-up investigation. And it said something, too, that the only police activity they did see all week was down at Mount and Fayette, where the Western

District day shift was, yet again, rounding up a handful of the usual
suspects.

Fran Boyd stretches her thin legs across the dashboard of her brother's
tired Pontiac, crossing her bare feet at the ankles and resting them just
above the steering wheel. She's slumped into the passenger seat, singing
background with the Staples in a wavering falsetto.
    "... I'll take you there ..."
But Fran's there already. She's been there and gone.
    "... I'll take you there ..."
She's got Scoogie's car radio cranked to WPGC out of Washington,
which is about how far you have to go to find old-school R&B on the
dial these days. If DeAndre were here, he'd try just about anything to
change the station. Find some gangsta rap, or some Boyz II Men at the
very least. For him, the Staple Singers are some kind of Grand Ole Opry
act, but for Fran, this stuff has all gone ripe in the hothouse of her own
nostalgia.
    Scoogie comes out of 1625 Fayette.
    "Damn, Fran," he says, watching her bop horizontally. "It must be a
bomb today."
    "Is it," she affirms, with her eyes closed.
    The Staples fade, the D.J. sputters for a moment, and the Commodores
arrive suddenly to fill the void. "*She's a brick ... hoowwwse.*"
    Fran grooves in her seat.
    "There it is," she laughs.
    Scoogie shakes his head, managing a distant smile. He's the straight
one—the only remaining member of the Boyd clan who can claim to
be drug-free and steady with a paycheck. He's working at Martin Marietta
out in Middle River and driving this battered aquamarine hulk from
one neighborhood mechanic to the next, trying to shove a few more
miles onto the odometer before the engine goes.
    That's the workaday world according to Scoogie; Fran carries her
own suspicions about her older brother, wondering why he's always broke
if he ain't on the pipe. And Scoogie is always down on Fayette Street
before work, always running in and out of the Dew Drop, always trying
to borrow ten dollars for this and that. Fran can't help showing her
cynicism when her brother starts talking that seven-years-clean business,
mumbling on about having left the corner life behind after all those
years of every kind of drug. She wants to believe that it isn't true, that

it's all some ridiculous charade of normalcy. Fran hates the implied accusation in her brother's talk, the suggestion that he's better than her, or Stevie, or Bunchie, or Sherry. He pisses her off, provoking her to sidelong looks and muttered sarcasm—just enough resistance to let Scoogie know she doesn't believe.

On the radio, the Commodores are giving it up to Rick James.

Scoogie leans against the front fender and begins rapping lightly on the metal with the fingers of one hand.

"You leavin' out?" Fran asks.

"Not right yet."

"Good," she says.

"You havin' a little dance party in there, huh?"

"Yes Lawd."

Fran is up on the mountaintop today, alone in the universe, looking down on Fayette Street from a great height and finding it tolerable.

She gets high every day, but she likes it especially on days like this— the first warm days that hint of spring, with no place to go and the radio blaring the right station. People that don't get high—not that she knows many—what in hell do they do on days like this? They have to be dead bored. How can you walk outside, greet a day like today, and not want to go all out, to ratchet that feeling inside your heart up to the highest level? She hates Fayette Street. There are times when she feels like she hates herself. But damned if she can't put all that shit aside by getting a blast.

"Scoo-gie," she says, accenting the last syllable. "You remember the Happy House." Even with her eyes closed, she can see him smile.

"Yeah," he says.

"That place was jumpin'."

Yes indeed. The Happy House on Bruce Street was where she learned to be a party girl. Weed and pills and acid. All of the Boyd children bouncing off walls in one communal chemical adventure, all of them bringing their paychecks home and throwing most of it into the party fund. On Bruce Street, Scoogie was dealing weed like mad until some gangsters kicked in the door and robbed the place, scaring the shit out of everyone. From middle school on, Fran had been chasing chemicals and the Happy House, ancestor to the Dew Drop Inn, took her from cough syrup to weed, wine to acid. Then came the dope, with that moment of instantaneous perfection at her sister's wake. And after the dope—Lord, please—when she got to smoking that rock a few years back, she went into a free fall, losing everything she ever had and waking up at the Dew Drop with the rest of the Boyds.

Still, for a while there, the Happy House was happy indeed. She conjures up another memory: all of them going downtown to see P-Funk, or was it War? One of them funk bands. And Scoogie fucked up on acid, wavering in the aisle, staggering down to the balcony railing and toppling over, pulled back by strangers at the last second.

"You remember that concert when you almost fell out the balcony? Down the Civic Center?"

"War," says Scoogie, remembering.

Fran is smiling now. "You was fucked-up."

"All a blur to me now. There's years back then that I can't get to," he says, and the past-tense tone of the remark ruins it for her. Scoogie, talking like it's all water under the bridge.

She turns the radio louder, trying to recoup her high, frustrated at the thought that no matter how good the dope is, it's always this way for her now. Time after time, she has to fight to stay on the mountaintop, to find these perfect idylls and keep hold of them. Because for Fran Boyd, the best part of the blast had always been the way it could take her outside of her life, to keep her from thinking about all the things that she really didn't want to think about.

Like family. Scoogie, for starters, with his job and his house and all, but always down on Fayette Street. Or Bunchie, running games with the rent money. Or Stevie, chasing that needle so bad that his hands are abscessed and open, waiting on that gangrene while Little Stevie, his nine-year-old son, sits at his feet, taking it all in, learning the corner to the point where he could tell his father when the tester lines are forming. Or Sherry, who can barely care for herself, much less an infant daughter— to the point that for a long while Ray Ray was using a cardboard box for a crib. And Fran, too, living the same nightmare right alongside them.

That's the worst of it, really—that she had for a time escaped, living large with Gary, bringing home the kind of money that made the rest of the family sick with envy. She had felt that. She knew that they wanted her to fall, that they were happier to see her children have less, to see her back in the common denominator of the Dew Drop. They are family, and on some level she is ready to love them some for that fact alone. But to Fran, her brothers and sisters are also hostile witnesses to her condition. Their faces float at the periphery of every good high, and if she acknowledges that, or thinks about it, the blast is wasted.

It's the same when she thinks about her mother, who left this world two years ago without ever coming to a reckoning with Fran. There would be no explanations for all of Daddy's beatings, or for her mother's unwillingness to shield herself or her children. Most of all, there would never be any reason for the distance between Fran's children and her mother. It seemed like she just singled out DeAndre and DeRodd as tar babies, offering them a peculiar coldness that left Fran hurt and confused. And then there was her father, who was little more than a silent and brutal force when they were all young, though now he could be found around the corner on Baltimore Street, hanging with the old-timers, lost in his own alcoholic haze. It's strange and depressing, this feeling of being surrounded by family but in every way alone.

Still sitting in Scoogie's car, Fran curses herself for thinking these thoughts, then curses the radio jock for talking too much and not playing music. First, she lost everything to her high, and now, goddammit, she's finding it harder and harder to keep the high itself. The Dew Drop Inn, the Fayette Street corners, the entire neighborhood—all of it has become an emotional minefield for her. Step off the marked path for a moment and you get blown apart by a memory. Like Gary, up the block, looking so damn bad, growing thin on that needle. Or DeRodd's father, Michael, hanging with the regulars on Mount and looking even worse. Or even the room where she is staying—the same room in which her sister was killed in the fire, the haunted box where Fran can't lay for a minute without thinking of Darlene dying in the hospital burn unit. For Fran, all of Fayette Street is filled with ghosts; some truly dead, others giving it their best. It's getting so she can't think a serious thought anymore without provoking her own anger or collapsing into depression, but still she can't stop herself from thinking. Not even today, when Diamond in the Raw is a bomb.

Fran opens her eyes and watches Scoogie glide around the corner with Stevie. Going to get served, probably. Scoogie, though, will swear it's only for Karen, the love of his life, a girl as hopelessly addicted as any of them. Fran gives up on WPGC, twisting the knob until she gets one of the hip-hop stations. Some crazy shit about girls wearin' their Daisy Dukes, a dance number for the warmer weather to come. She listens to the rap from the distance of a generation, then mutters an obscenity and twists the knob back again.

James Brown. She leans back in her seat.

"Huh," she says in poor imitation of the hardest working man in show business. "Huh. Gut God."

"Get it, Fran."

She opens her eyes to see DeAndre, leaning into the passenger window, vaguely amused at his mother's performance. Fran is almost glad to see him.

"Huh," says Fran, again. "You know that's like the whole message from James Brown. All he say is shit like that—get down, gut God—and he write it down like it's a real song."

DeAndre smiles. "Nigga can dance, though."

"Yeah, but he don't say shit."

DeAndre nods agreement, laughing, clearly happy to have caught his mother's better mood.

"Yo, Ma."

"Hmm."

"You comin' to court with me tomorrow."

It's more statement than question, and therefore irritating to Fran.

"Yeah."

"Tomorrow."

"Hmmm."

"Eight-thirty."

She closes her eyes. Now it's DeAndre messing with her high.

"And I don't wanna be late . . ."

"Goddammit, Andre. I said I be there." She's shouting now.

DeAndre straightens out of the car window, hurt. Fran looks over to yell some more but stops at the sight of a single piece of white paper, folded over once in her son's hand.

"That your court paper?"

DeAndre shakes his head.

She reaches for it and he drops it on the driver's seat with an air of indifference. She unfolds it and finds a Franklin Square job-bank form, carefully filled out, with DeAndre's name and address in big, block letters. Under job experience, DeAndre claims to be a volunteer at the Martin Luther King rec. He comes around to the passenger window while she reads.

"Ella say she gonna try and find me work."

Fran nods, feeling surprised and a little shamed. Since coming home from Boys Village last month, DeAndre has stayed away from the corner. He's gone to school. He's gone to basketball practice with that new rec team. And after that, he's spent every night at her aunt's on Etting Street, waiting for the home-monitoring call from his pretrial officer. She knows

he's off the corner, the proof being that there's no money in his pocket
and Easter is coming up. DeAndre's been talking about needing a new
Easter outfit, some Fila or Nike sweats, maybe. Talking now about finding
himself a job. Through February and into March, DeAndre has been at
his best; that much she had to admit.

"Which courthouse?" she asks, her anger almost gone.

"The big one downtown on Calvert Street. Eight-thirty in the morning
is when we got to . . ."

"I ain't deaf."

DeAndre wanders off, but he's done his damage. Fran is all the way
down from the summit, and not even the radio's offer of some sexual
healing from Marvin Gaye can bring her back. She's out of the car and
back into the mix before Scoogie comes back around and drives the
Pontiac away to work.

That night, she parties in the basement until well after midnight, but
never gets to the heights. In the morning, DeAndre has to peel her from
the sofa in the front room of the apartment, then keep her going through
the motions until they roll through the doors of the downtown courthouse, their progress slowed by the line at the metal detector.

"Dre," she asks him, "you got your toothbrush?"

Corner wisdom tells even the youngest kids to go to court with a
clean toothbrush, because you might not come home and something
better than a common toothbrush is hard to come by at Hickey or the
Village. DeAndre shakes his head, playing it off. Still, Fran can tell that
no matter how hard he fronts, his stomach is churning. He's facing a
juvenile master for the first time.

"You might gonna need it."

"Then I deal with that too."

"Oh, you big-time now," says Fran, smirking. "You a man."

"I can jail."

Fran's door-knocker earrings make the metal detector bleat angrily.
DeAndre slips through unmolested and waits, uncomfortable, while his
mother drops her adornments in the sheriff deputy's wicker basket and
walks through again, this time passing muster.

"We in Master Sampson," says DeAndre as she joins him.

They find the master's chambers, but a matronly clerk, who barely
looks up when the door opens, tells DeAndre to go to the other end of
the courthouse and find his name on the docket sheets. He does so, then
walks all the way back down the corridor.

"My name is up there for Master Sampson."

The woman nods.

"What do I do?"

"Go back there and wait for your name to be called."

"Damn," says Fran, looking at the early morning congestion on the juvenile floor. "Look at what you got me into."

They find a bench and sit. DeAndre grunts, then buries his chin on his chest. Fran unzips the front of her sweatshirt, leans her head against her son's shoulder and tries to sleep amid the comings and goings, her siesta interrupted by the calls of the juvenile division lawyers.

"Wagstaff . . . Antoine Wagstaff."

"Emmanuel Barnes. Is Emmanuel Barnes here?"

"Carter, Jerome . . . I need the mother of Jerome Carter."

"Last call . . . Antoine Wagstaff."

Fran yawns, stretches, then opens her eyes long enough to absorb the scene. There are a dozen wooden benches in the juvenile docket room, but those are jammed with waiting bodies and the overflow is out on a dozen other hallway pews, a sullen congregation extending in both directions around the rectangular courthouse hallway. Mothers and sons, all but a handful of them black, all waiting out their morning on the government clock, empty and listless, using up as little of their energy as can be managed under the circumstances. There is no shame to these crowded benches anymore, no sense of regret for choices made or roads not taken. For these families, time spent on the juvenile pews is as assured as time spent on those warped plastic chairs up at the social service field office on Ashburton, or in that modular waiting room at the school disciplinary office on North Avenue, or maybe on those chrome-legged boxes down at the University Hospital clinic.

The sons stare vacantly, or clown with kids they haven't seen since middle school, or maybe even throw out an eyefuck or two for the benefit of some member of a rival crew. The mothers wait with that as-long-as-it-takes look stenciled to their faces, knowing nothing about the process save for its eventual outcome. Today the government has a lease-hold on their lives, but they sense that after all is said and done, tomorrow will be just about the same. Arrests and summonses, juvenile intake workers and lawyers, probation officers and masters—a fine facsimile of the grown-up pretense of crime and punishment. Fran listens to the mother next to her on the bench, a woman not much older than herself complaining about a daughter who won't be disciplined, who beats on her when she tries. "I'm frightened," the woman admits, her daughter now down the hall and out of earshot. "I'm frightened of these childrens today."

"These younger ones jus' don' care," agrees another.

"They can take my child from me, I wouldn't have no problem," the woman says. "I can't control her no ways."

Three hours creep by on these benches before the word comes down that the masters have broken for lunch. Fran goes outside and brings back Newports and barbecued potato chips. It's an hour beyond that before DeAndre hears his name.

"Are you the mother?" a pretrial worker asks Fran.

"Hmm," says Fran.

"Come with me."

They're taken to a side office, where DeAndre is interviewed briefly about the charges. Stolen auto. Cocaine possesion with intent. And cocaine with intent a second time.

"Wasn't me in the car," he mumbles.

The pretrial worker makes a brief note and asks about the drug charges. DeAndre shrugs, then mutters something about the police finding the vials in the street and giving them to him.

"Why you?"

DeAndre shrugs.

"The police on the one charge got shot," says Fran, interjecting. The pretrial worker looks at her curiously until Fran explains that the arresting officer got killed in a shooting a month or so later.

"That charge dead," says DeAndre confidently.

The worker asks a few more questions, then sends them back to the benches. Twenty minutes later, they're called down to Master Sampson's chambers, a generous term for his shrunken imitation of a courtroom. Mother and son are directed to a pair of side benches, where they watch two other teenaged boys have their turn. The prosecutors are both young women, white and professional; the public defender is older, white, and rumpled, his glasses low on his nose, his white hair matted back into a comical cowlick. The juvenile master is a black man, middle-aged, well-dressed, and imperious. The foursome, joined by a clerk, spend ten minutes speaking in case numbers and shuffling files back and forth across two tables wedged hard against the slight rise of the bench.

Finally they locate a file and bend to the business at hand: a thirteen-year-old boy caught with a hundred bags. And caught isn't the word for it. The kid got turned in by his own mother, who's right there on the bench next to Fran.

DeAndre rolls his eyes at the statement of charges.

"Damn," whispers Fran.

"A hundert bags," says DeAndre softly. "He goin' away."

Instead the master remands the boy to his mother's custody, placing him on indefinite supervised probation. The case is resolved in minutes, without even a nod toward moral discussion or remonstrance. DeAndre is incredulous.

"Nigga got to be snitchin'," he tells Fran. "That much dope and he gets probation. Puh-leeze."

The next kid is called to the bench, represented this time by a different public defender, and Andre and Fran both lean forward, genuinely curious as the prosecutor begins reading a statement of charges. Cocaine this time. But DeAndre doesn't get a chance to see how it plays out.

"Mr. McCullough."

DeAndre looks up to see the rumpled defender gesturing toward the hallway. The old man stops in the doorway, and then, almost as an afterthought, gestures to Fran as well.

"You, too, mother. You should hear this too."

Without a moment of confrontation for DeAndre McCullough, a deal has been brokered on the three separate charges. The two drug violations—of which DeAndre is decidedly guilty—will be dropped. The stolen car charge will stand. As a first conviction, he'll get a year's probation, with the vague and implausible requirement that he make some restitution to the woman whose car was taken and damaged.

"Is that okay with you?"

DeAndre looks at Fran, barely able to stifle a smile.

"Mother?"

Fran nods, but a moment later, she's thinking twice about the terms of the deal. She's wondering whether the deal will keep him monitored, or whether the probation will be unsupervised. She wants to say something, maybe talk to the lawyer privately, without DeAndre hearing what she has to say. But the lawyer is back inside the master's chambers and Fran says nothing else. A minute or two more and the clerk chants her son's name, followed by a string of juvenile case numbers. The prosecutor acknowledges the dismissal of the two drug cases, then reads a brief statement of facts regarding the car theft. The statement has DeAndre being arrested in the stolen auto, although in fact, he was locked up days later.

DeAndre looks over at Fran, then at his lawyer, confused.

"I . . ."

The public defender leans over.

"I wasn't in the car."

Now it's the lawyer who's confused. The juvenile master, too, seems to sense the young man's trepidation. He questions DeAndre carefully about the plea agreement. Are you pleading guilty because you are guilty? The rush of activity in the chamber seems to lapse for a moment as DeAndre struggles with it.

"Um."

"Because by pleading guilty . . ."

DeAndre was in the car. He knew it was stolen. But the statement of facts is wrong and DeAndre is vaguely upset that he's caught on a lie. The first coke charge? Guilty as sin, but it's being dismissed because the police got killed. The second charge on Fairmount? Guilty again, but that case is being dropped without any argument at all. And then this car charge, where the evidence is exaggerated and guilt is a prearranged deal.

"You are giving up your rights . . ."

As the master drones on about the rights forfeited under a plea agreement, DeAndre looks at his mother. This is his first encounter with the judicial system, and he is being taught luck-of-the-draw, nothing more.

"Yes," says Andre, interrupting.

"Yes, what?" asks the master.

"Yes. I'm guilty."

With that minor obstacle removed, there is only the race to finish. Master Sampson gives him a year's supervised probation, then peers out over top of his glasses, managing a few moments of righteous intimidation.

". . . and I don't want to see you in here again or you will be dealing with all of these charges."

DeAndre nods.

"Do you understand me?"

A weak mumble.

"What was that?"

"Yes, sir."

"All right then."

From the side bench, Fran stands up suddenly, half raising her hand to get the master's attention.

"Yes, ma'am."

"Is this probation . . . Can you make it part of his probation that he has to go to school?"

DeAndre gives his mother a withering look. Fran, too, seems unsure where to go with this. The code of parenting on Fayette Street says that you stand with your children against any and all interventions; that, at least, is the standard Fran has always known. But just a moment ago, there was that mother who turned in her kid and a hundred bags.

"He's not going to school?" asks the master.

"He has been lately, with the probation and all, he was easier to deal with and . . ."

"Are you saying that you've been having problems controlling him? Are there problems at home?"

DeAndre stares sullenly at his mother. Fran is caught. She wants him to get the deal; she doesn't want him back at Boys Village. But she'd also like some leverage, and now, with the master leaning on her, she can't think of any way to ask for one thing without risking the other.

"No," she says, "no trouble."

"I can't make him go to school," the master says. "But he knows what it is he's supposed to be doing."

Fran sits back down and waits for the clerk to complete the paperwork. Supervised probation it will be, meaning a trip to see a juvenile P.O. once a week, coupled with an occasional home visit. By the time they leave, DeAndre is so delighted to be back on Fayette Street that he's even forgiven his mother's betrayal.

"That wasn't nuthin'," he tells her.

"That's what you say now," Fran snaps back. "But you was a scared little boy in front of that judge."

"I was," DeAndre admits, laughing. "He made me nervous. I ain't about to come back in his court."

In the weeks afterward, DeAndre seems to hold to that thought. His attendance at school becomes a little more sporadic now that his probation officer isn't counting, but he's staying off the corner. Fran can tell because he keeps crying the blues about his damn Easter outfit. Without cash money, he's leaning hard on Fran, and in a strange way, that gives her some pride.

It's the old DeAndre talking, she tells herself. My child, my son. And while she can always go boosting in the malls to get him some Easter clothes, she understands that to keep things right with DeAndre she'll

need more than that. If she could detox, she would be there for him,
although the thought itself is intimidating. Fran hasn't been clean and
sober for a good fifteen years and now, she's got nothing to speak of—
just some old furniture piled up in the basement of the Dew Drop
and $180 a month on check day. She's got a medical assistance card,
which grants no coverage for drug detox, so that means a long wait for
a government-money rehab bed. She's got some boosting charges coming
up in the city and two counties, any one of which might land her in
jail. And she has that second-floor bedroom, where nothing that she
ever acquires or accumulates will be safe from anyone else. That much
is evident two days after DeAndre comes home from court, when
Fran makes the mistake of buying more than a day's portion of tuna
fish, bread, and mayo at the Korean grocery. She uses about half to
make sandwiches for DeRodd and DeAndre, then puts the rest in the
refrigerator for the next day. But there are no next days on Fayette Street.
By morning, every last crumb is gone.

This, she tells herself, is no way to live. Even heroin no longer suffices
to obscure the daily insult that her life has become. Day after day, she
talks to herself about changing, and then, at the very thought of what
such a thing would require, she talks herself right back onto the corner.

On the first day of April, she's out on the stoop, same as she ever
was, watching the check-day traffic at Mount and Fayette. After a time,
Mike Ellerbee cruises up. This is the same Little Mike who was a regular
gangster on these corners, slinging coke and shooting people when
needed. Little Mike, who shot Joe Laney in the back that one time, who
would've killed Joe if he hadn't run out of bullets, who shot that other
stickup boy not even a year back, and, by Fran's reckoning, should still
be locked up behind that charge.

"Hey, Fran."

"How you?"

"I'm goin' to sea."

Fran looks at him as if he'd declared himself an astronaut. Mike has
supervised probation and ten years suspended hanging over him from
the last shooting; he's not going anywhere.

"You goin' where?"

"I'm gonna get on a ship. Soon as I get my Z-card."

"Huh?"

"My Z-card and a physical. I get that from the Coast Guard and I'll
be gone. Ricky and Bug helped me get in the union."

R.C.'s older stepbrothers, now more off the corners than on, were members of the seafarer's local. And the first part of Mike's story, when he tells it, rings true to Fran. He explains that despite his criminal record, Ricky and Bug paid the right people to get him into the union. For Mike, this is a last chance. If he stays on Fayette Street, he'll surely sling drugs, and he'll just as surely end up shooting the next fiend who tries to rob him. Mike has too much heart not to shoot. That or he'll take a drug charge; either way, he'll go back to Judge Johnson at Circuit Court to get banged with the whole ten years.

As to the rest of story, though, Fran is skeptical.

"You gonna be able to get on a ship when you on probation?"

"I'm gonna talk with the judge."

Fran nods, not buying it. No way, she thinks. No one here gets out alive.

"So you gonna be a sailor?"

Mike smiles broadly.

"You ever been on a ship before?"

"No. But they gonna teach me."

"Hmm."

Later that same day, she's down in the basement of the Dew Drop, her face hovering over lines on a mirror. But this time it isn't Bunchie down there with her, it's Gary, who has brought some vials for old time's sake.

"You know Mike?" she says abruptly.

Gary nods.

"He gonna go to sea."

"Who?"

"Little Mike. Mike Ellerbee. He goin' to sail the seas."

She smirks as she says it, wanting not to believe. But Gary is rubbing his chin, accepting it on its face the way Gary does everything. It's another one of the things she hates about Gary—his way of taking everything from the Koran to the *Wall Street Journal* as absolute gospel.

"He say he goin' to join the union."

"I thought he was in jail," says Gary.

"He got probation for shooting that boy."

"Dag."

A silence comes over them and for once even Gary has trouble filling it. He looks around the Dew Drop basement at the last relics of their dream home: the glass dining room set, some end tables, two dressers, an old mattress and box spring, even some battered stereo components.

Fran watches Gary as he silently calculates the value of each item in Baltimore Street secondhand-store dollars, but she knows it's an abstract exercise. He can't steal from her.

"You still got our things."

"Ain't too much left," she says, her eyes following his to the front of the room. Gary says nothing.

"We had it, didn't we," she laughs. "We were a team."

Gary looks at her, his eyes welling as Fran begins scratching at the scab.

"It don't make sense," she says, "the way they're all so glad to see us fall. My whole damn family is glad for it."

Gary nods, picking up on it. Even before he fell, when he still had most of his money, Gary told her that he was tired of being used by people, tired of them resenting his success even when he was willing to share it with them. If I fell, he had told her then, they'd like me. If I fell, I'd be just like them.

"I thought this is what they wanted," Gary says, sounding the same note. It's a pity party for the two of them; Fran usually can't stand that, but now it's exactly what she wants to hear.

"It's like what I do don't matter," she says bitterly. "When they needed something, they came to me. I kept the family together, but Scoogie gets the house, the money, everything. It don't make no sense. It's like everybody's glad we're down."

"That's what I'm sayin'."

"And the thing is, I know we can get back up. You know we got to. Because, I'm sayin' just look at us, look where we at with this shit."

"I'm gonna stop," says Gary, inspired.

"And DeAndre, he's actually tryin' now."

Gary looks surprised, but Fran nods him down. "He's off the corner and looking for a job. Gary, I'm tellin' you. He even going to school."

"Dag."

"Your son is growin' up."

"I know it."

"If he's gonna try, then we gotta try."

Gary is suddenly elated. He's the fallen angel, stumbling on a new religion. Fran watches as he gets up to walk the basement floor, poking at the stored furnishings of his own dead dreams, talking about how they can both detox together, maybe get a place of their own if Gary can find some kind of work.

"Be a family," says Gary.

One hopeful speech and Gary is ripe for a renewal of vows. Fran wants nothing of the kind; but still, it's a kick for her to see Gary so fired up.

"You gonna see," says Gary. "I'm gonna get right."

"You gotta find a program," Fran tells him.

"I can do it myself," he assures her.

She shrugs. For her, it's a program or nothing: "I might go down to BRC," she says. "They got a thirty-day program. See if I can hook up with that."

And then, because the dope is there, she does the last line.

SPRING

FOUR

Gary McCullough moves through the back alley in his camouflage gear and jump boots, a commando once again on a quest. He's a step or two in front of his usual consort, carrying the wheeled dolly, stepping heavily in the alley off Fayette, every other footfall bringing a plastic crackle from the pavement beneath him.

"Gracious," says Tony Boice.

Gary laughs softly.

"Like a got-damn graveyard," Tony mutters.

Gary snorts an affirmation. The Addison Street alley got a good cleaning from a city crew just after Christmas, but now, in early April, it's all junk and trash and stench—a dumping ground like any other ghetto back-street, save for the shimmering layer of empty vials and disposable syringes that seems to cover everything. Addison is sited halfway between two major drug markets, and you can't walk a couple steps without hearing a half-dozen fallen soldiers crunching underfoot.

"Dag," says Gary, scanning the ground.

Tony steps out of the mouth of the alley onto Baltimore Street, but Gary is still lost in the glassine backwash. He leans over, both hands on his knees, then reaches down for a solitary vial, a Black Top still harboring a white sediment along the bottom.

"Tallyho."

He puts the dolly against the wall for a moment, then holds the vial up to sunlight. Half a blast in there, right as rain. He pockets the find, grabs the dolly, then jogs out into the street to catch up with Tony. The two drift toward Fulton.

"Third floor?" asks Gary.

"No, second floor."

"Mmmm."

"Stereo, TV, refrigerator, and all that good stuff."

Ronnie had set it up. Ever since they'd started shooting their dope
down with Pops on Fulton Avenue, she'd been marking the walk-up
apartment across the street. A working man's place, or something close
to a working man anyway. Ronnie had the tenant leaving his apartment
empty and inviting every morning. As for the rest of the three-story
rowhouse, she figured it to be mostly vacant.

Ronnie was good at spotting a jackpot, and she was even better when
it came to planning the caper. Today, with this Fulton Avenue apartment, Gary expects nothing less from his girl than a smooth operation,
especially with Tony Boice as his comrade-in-arms. With Tony, Gary
knows what to expect; he can rely on him in ways that he can't with all
the others who run capers with him. Stepping around the corner onto
Fulton, Gary actually starts to strut beside his partner, thinking that
today, at least, the snake will have no say. Hey, you can forget the walk-
up. They're so good, they might just go downtown and knock off the
Federal Reserve.

A block from the house, they slip off Fulton and into the back alley
behind a mostly vacant stretch of three-story rowhouses. Gary ditches
the dolly in an overgrown locust bush. From here on, it's commando
mode, with the hoods pulled up over their heads and their jump boots
stepping softly amid the trash and rubble. They roll back out of the alley
and their conversation falls to a whisper.

"Which house?"

"Third, no fourth, in."

They slip inside like they belong. They march right up the steps and
pause for just a moment at the apartment door, listening for a sign of
life anywhere in the building. Nothing. A perfect quiet. Tony rears back,
lifting his boot, knee hugging his chest.

High as you can, Gary tells him. Got to get the lock.

Tony grunts, then kicks up like a wild mule, his boot leaving a perfect
imprint of grey dust on the painted door.

The second kick cracks the hinge. The third knocks down the door
and they're inside another man's living room. Gary roams off into the
apartment to take stock.

It's the perfect mission, all form and function as they wrap the small
television, the clock radio, and a few small kitchen appliances in Hefty
bags and drag them out the apartment door and down the stairs. Then
Gary goes back outside for the dolly, and in a minute or so, they've
emptied the refrigerator. Lifting it up and out of the kitchen, they roll

it toward the apartment door. They've got the monster halfway across the threshold when Gary notices a third-floor tenant smirking at him from the landing. His heart in his throat, Gary looks back at the man, then over at Tony, who's still inside the apartment.

"Hey," says Gary to the tenant, his voice friendly enough.

The man shakes his head.

Gary waits for Tony to poke his head around the door frame, and for a few seconds, the three of them are standing there with the game clock running, staring at each other stupidly. Again, Gary tries to break the ice.

"Hey, well . . . I'm sayin' . . ."

"You hook me up," says the man, interrupting, "and I won't say nuthin' 'bout it."

Without so much as a sales pitch, they're all back in business for the price of a single blast. Gary and Tony are laughing about this new twist all the way to Baltimore Street, rolling the refrigerator with the Hefty bags wedged inside, shepherding their haul through the midday traffic, gliding past the knowing smiles of a few players hanging in front of the grocery at Mount and Baltimore.

A police cruiser passes them on Baltimore, turning at Gilmor, but the two barely tense. Time has taught them that once on the street, they are invisible. The refrigerator, the dolly, the two fiends lugging it toward a cash sale—all of it is unseen by a police department that has neither the will nor the temperament to investigate property crimes. Here, too, the drug war has upended the priorities. Why stop two fiends and ask a few questions about the refrigerator? Why take the time to ask to see a receipt? Why bother to listen to their bull-shit about moving their grandmother's refrigerator, full up as it is with smaller appliances, to their uncle's house? Why bother to call back to the Western desk to find out if anyone has reported a burglary in the area? Why suffer through anything that resembles police work when you can make your stat simply by rolling up on a corner and going into a tout's pockets?

At first, it seemed incredible to Gary that he could drag large, stolen appliances from one end of the neighborhood to the other without going directly to jail, but over time, he had learned to gauge the priorities of the rollers working Fayette Street. Most of the police were about the drugs; they lived off the corner arrest, and for Gary and Tony, there would always be more risk when they went down Vine Street to cop than when they broke into someone's home. The important thing right now was not to look furtive or nervous. Just keep pushing this big white mountain down the street like it's no one's business.

On Baltimore Street, they get sixty-five dollars.

Walking back up the hill, Gary cuts through Vincent, hoping to meet up with one of the touts selling the Death Row package. An alley street between Mount and Gilmor, Vincent Street just north of Baltimore is a bombed-out string of vacant Formstone rowhouses, home now to an occasional shooting gallery or a corner crew using the rubble to work a package. Death Row was here yesterday, with lookouts at both ends of the block and a stash in one of the rotting basements, but there's no sign of them today.

"The mentality," says Gary.

"Huh?"

"I'm sayin', you know, it was his neighbor and all."

Tony laughs.

"No, really. You think on it and you see, the mentality out here is just amazing."

"All in the game," says Tony, unperturbed.

"Yeah, but when it's your neighbor . . ."

Gary can't let it go, this idea that some moral thresholds still exist, that one had been crossed by the third-floor tenant in the Fulton Avenue house. They were out here thieving, true, but it wasn't from their neighbor. Gary couldn't imagine ever being so trifling and low as to betray a next-door neighbor for the price of a blast.

". . . I'm sayin' it wadn't right."

"Hmm," says Tony.

"I'm sayin' he shouldn't get a blast for doin' that kind of dirt. He shouldn't prosper from that."

"No, indeed."

"An' you know that he don't even know us from Adam."

Gary clucks softly, shaking his head, muttering on about the sad mentality of some people, about the general lack of righteousness in the world. Coming out the alley at Fayette Street, he spots something in a fresh pile of debris on the vacant lot, something half covered by a soiled mattress.

"Praise be," he says, off on a new vector.

Tony waits at the edge of the lot, impatient to find Ronnie and get a little something in his veins. But Gary is rooting through the trash heap, liberating a few scraps of green aluminum and a heavy, grooved slate of steel alloy.

"Gary, c'mon."

"No, hey, Tony . . ."

He gestures until his partner finally joins him. Gary points out the remains of some kind of table saw or band saw, battered beyond repair but worth a buck or two nonetheless at the United Iron scales.

"Gary, we done for the day."

"Tomorrow," says Gary. "You got to always think about tomorrow bein' there. We can sell this."

"Man, later for it."

But Gary is now rambling on about the ant and the grasshopper, about the smart squirrel storing up his acorns for winter. He looks around for a stash hole, deciding finally on one of the abandoned houses.

"You'll see," says Gary. "That's twenty, right from jump."

It's an argument that Tony can't dispute though he shows his impatience, suffering and pouting as he helps Gary drag the metal remnants back down the alley.

They resume their victory march up the strip, locating Ronnie on the sofa in the front room of her sister's place, just a few doors up from Ella Thompson's apartment. Ronnie, in turn, locates a half-dozen Spider Bags and some Pink Tops, and they adjourn happily to the second floor of Gary's empty dream palace at 1717 Fayette. There, they break out the spikes and bottle caps, bending themselves to the business at hand.

That night, Gary doesn't go home. And late the next morning, with a sour taste in his mouth, he's thankful indeed to dig into his sweatshirt pocket and find that half-blast of dope, the one he rescued from the glassine graveyard. He's thankful, too, to be down on Wilkens Avenue an hour later, waiting at the scales with the broken pieces of an industrial saw.

"What you got?" asks a toothless alcoholic, a regular who's waiting in line with a half-dozen rain gutters.

"Saw," says Gary.

"Say what?"

Gary lifts the steel tabletop.

"Heavy?" asks the smokehound.

"Twenty dollars easy."

The alcoholic grunts affirmation. His gutters are aluminum and dirty aluminum at that. He's hoping for five dollars. Gary looks up and down the line and sees that the morning winner is some fiend who usually combs the area down around Westside, over by Catherine Street. The man is fat and happy with a shopping cart full of copper plumbing pipe. He's likely to clear forty dollars.

Behold, the ants. Alone and apart, they seem of little consequence, ripe for casual derision if not outright comedy. But by the dozens and hundreds, even the smallest insects can move mountains. The United Iron and Metal Company pays cash, no questions asked, as the wealth of the neighborhoods surrounding it—copper piping, aluminum roof flashing, cast-iron tubs, steel boilerplates—is carried off and melted down.

When Gary began living for the caper, there were only a happy handful who knew the metal game, a small number of pioneers who were guiding their shopping carts through the urban wastes, prying loose a few unguarded items for the dollars to get them through the days. Now, they are legion, stumbling over each other in a desperate fight to get there first and grab the most. During the day, they break into houses or salvage from vacant properties. At night, they devour any job site they can find, prying the plumbing and appliances from half-finished rowhouse renovations, then coming back a week later to do it again—so often that most city contractors have to make do with plastic piping in place of the standard copper plumbing. The ants have been up to Lexington Street, carting off their share of the construction materials left on-site for the rehab project there. And to Bon Secours, too, where the hospital is trying to renovate itself and add a new wing. One night, someone actually made one of those mini-bulldozers disappear. Another night, two of the portable toilets. Down at Lexington Terrace, the high-rises have been stripped of hundreds of aluminum alloy window casing assemblies—each set purchased by the city housing authority for hundreds of dollars, each offered up at the United Iron scales for thirty or forty. Uptown in Harlem Park, the good Baptists woke up one day to find it raining in the house of the Lord. And why not? The roof flashing was quality copper—a haul that probably brought some insect seventy-five dollars. Down in Union Square, someone was picking up cast-iron manhole covers. Over in the Westside parking lot, another genius managed to fell a free-standing streetlight and walk off with eighty dollars in aluminum.

The entrepreneur in Gary can't help wonder about where it all goes. He knows the value of the metals, the copper and clean aluminum, the stainless steel and chrome. He knows that he and every other fiend are getting a dime on the dollar, probably less, at the company scales. United Iron and Metal is a Baltimore institution; it's been down here on Wilkens Avenue since the big war, when rationing and rearmament made scrap metal a real commodity. But this is no longer wartime, and the men and women at the scales are not homefront patriots, planting victory gardens and cleaning out their basements and garages for the boys overseas. The people running the scales have to know the origin of all the rainspouts and plumbing and car bumpers; of course they know—that's why they pay cash, no questions asked. But Gary often tries to imagine the people at the top of the pyramid. He has never seen the United Iron owners, nor does he know their names, but he once heard that one of them lived in a huge mansion up in North Baltimore, way up near the county line. Waiting his turn at the scale, Gary tries to conjure a vision of the Metal King, tries to create a mind's-eye image of his palace. The business sense buried deep in Gary's soul has to smile at it: all of us ants working for the king, all of this damage being done so that the Metal King can live large. Whoever he is and wherever he lives, the King is a bold one, worthy of admiration.

Gary reaches the scales still dreaming of mansions. Just before him, the rain gutters bring the smokehound two bills. The toothless wreck curses mildly and staggers off. Gary grins like a salesman for the white boy handling the intake, then holds up the grooved tabletop of the saw, talking up the weight of the thing.

"Stainless steel," he says proudly.

Thirty pounds of it, in fact. The table and the smaller pieces bring a payday of $11.25. Not bad. Not bad at all for the day's first adventure.

Gary begins walking back up the United Iron driveway, feeling pretty good about his place in the great urban food chain and taking pride in his growing ability to spot salable metal even when it's buried beneath a rotting mattress. He knows this game well; better than Ronnie, better even than Tony.

He's not yet through the company's chain-link gates when the site of the Engineer humbles him. The train today is four shopping carts, each one tied to the next with plastic cords and strips of cloth. The Engineer is at the throttle, guiding the loaded freight down the driveway; his brakeman, a younger apprentice, is back with the caboose, guarding the rear carts against poachers.

Gary stops to watch, his capacity for admiration battling a more basic envy. Sewer grates, old batteries, copper pipes, rain gutters, steel-tire belts—the Engineer has tapped into the mother lode, the carts rattling behind him as he makes his way to toward the scales. He's Chisolm stomping proudly into Abilene with two hundred head of prime beef. Or maybe Cortez at the helm of his galleon fleet, returning from the New World with all that Inca treasure. Gary pulls down his hood and breaks into a wide smile as the train rolls past toward the scales.

"Hey, Mo," yells Gary, "you wearin' this city out."

His grand total of $11.25 now seems a little less grand. Still, Gary manages to fight down his jealousy. The Engineer has been around for years, graduating from one grocery cart to two, then three, and then finally the full complement. The man had to be in his fifties; Gary reckoned that he'd been harvesting for at least a decade, maybe more. So the Engineer might be grand master of the metal game, but he'd spent years acquiring that genius. Ten more years of this and Gary would surely be pulling his own Stainless Steel Special into the depot. Pulling his hood back up, Gary laughs again and then scuttles across Wilkens Avenue, warm at the memory of a similar moment.

A year ago, back when he had first started doing capers with Tony Boice, there wasn't a dope fiend on Fayette Street who hadn't heard about the treasure that was said to be ready and waiting in the basement of the vacant St. Martin's school building, a redbrick hulk at the southwest corner of Fulton and Fayette. Those privileged enough to glimpse the central steam line spoke of it with a reverence usually reserved for the Hope Diamond and the Star of India. Pure copper, 7 feet high, maybe 24 inches around—the pipe meant at least $150 cash for whomever had the poise and courage to get it down to the scales. A few had tried, breaking into the school building and struggling with crude tools to rip the prize from its moorings. But the pipe was rock solid in the old boiler, and even if you did get it free, you still had to find a way to get it out of the basement. So imagine the look on the faces of a dozen fiends when the ninja team of Boice and McCullough came across Wilkens Avenue, marching in military cadence, the Great Tube of St. Martin's resting on their shoulders in all its phallic splendor. And never mind that the chiseler running the scales cheated them out of their rightful due, paying out a measly eighty dollars; the truth was in the black-hearted envy on the face of every other soul in the line. Walking up Fulton, Gary lets himself relive the moment in full, telling himself that even the

Engineer—had he been there—would have been obliged to bless their successful crusade.

These were, of course, the musings of Gary McCullough, drug addict, for whom the glory of the caper was unquestioned. He had been hard-core living like this—harvesting metal and small appliances, chasing penny-ante scores from one day to the next—for a couple years. Now and again, though, the heroin mists would lift and Gary would find himself consumed by a very Christian guilt.

Like with the St. Martin's boiler. Gary knew what that meant: thousands of dollars, maybe ten thousand dollars of damage to a building that was vacant but nonetheless valuable. In fact, the old school was on the short list of sites for a neighborhood job-skills center that had been in the planning stages for years. Or worse still, these burglaries—where Gary and Tony were scooping up the few possessions acquired by people living from one check day to the next, some of them as desperate as Gary ever was. It was physical; it was addiction, true. But the call of the snake wasn't always loud enough to shout down the wrong of it. At times like that, he would then swear renewed allegiance to every last moral particle; he would promise to get involved in something worthwhile and charitable; or even—and here was Gary's daily resolution—promise to go through detox, to get clean, to reclaim the worthy life that had once been his. But these moments would pass, the needful cells would begin to cry out, and then the thrill of a new caper would take hold.

That the thrill was very much manufactured—a product of the need—was slowly becoming clear, even to Gary. The commando garb, the plotting, the furtiveness with which he and Tony ran their adventures—how much of it was really necessary? Like yesterday, with the Fulton Avenue burglary, where all the planning and subterfuge still left them in that hall-way, staring at a smirking neighbor. All that effort not to get caught, and then, when they did get caught, it hardly mattered. All that cloak-and-dagger and a half hour later they're walking a refriger-ator down Baltimore Street in broad daylight. All the hunting and gath-ering and harvesting of metal—most of it stolen outright—and then, down at the scales, it's not fenced, but sold off as a legal transaction. There were times when Gary had to admit that the capers were some-thing less than capers, that crime in West Baltimore had somehow ceased to be crime.

That the world was no longer paying much attention to right and wrong on Fayette Street was a fresh and unnerving thought for Gary, one that was just beginning to compete with the sheer adventure of his addiction. Four years of firing dope and he still could manage some misplaced pride in the daily struggle, in the full-time job that fiending is. He knew that people—straight people—didn't think of it that way; he hadn't seen it until he had lived it. But he knew hard labor better than most people, having lived one previous life as a workaholic, as a get-up-every-morning taxpayer with a mortgage and car payments and pension plans. He knew work. And against that, he could say that being a dope fiend is the hardest job there is.

Every day you start with nothing, and every day you come up with what you need to survive. And day after goddamn day, you swallow the pain and self-loathing, go out into the street and get what has to be got. Who else but a dope fiend can go to sleep at night with not a dime to his name, with not a friend in the world, and actually think up a way, come morning, to acquire the day's first ten? It's twenty-four, seven out here—always hustling, always looking for an edge, always trying to stay one step ahead of a hundred other fiends, all of them running around the same track. And it isn't just crimes and capers. You have to take opportunity—any opportunity—where you find it, keeping your eyes to the ground, picking up whatever might bring a dollar. It could be broken metal for the scales, or secondhand furniture for the pawn shop, or coke-filled vials dropped by some slinger running from the police. You have to know about an odd job or two that might get you an honest dollar when time is tight and capers are hard to come by. You have to have the heart to press your friends, your family for a few bills now and then, taking the attendant shame as interest on the loan. And there are moments in every day when some personal charm is required, some honest-to-god salesmanship in the American tradition.

Like the morning after the trip to the scales, when Gary and Tony are once again garbed in commando gear, walking the neighborhood, looking for a freshly vacant house, hoping for some copper pipe or window casings. But the metal game, which once seemed to Gary an inexhaustible source of cash, is becoming problematic as more and more fiends have stripped the neighborhood bare.

They've been down as far as Pratt Street and back with nothing to show, and now, with Gary singing gospel tunes in the warmth of late morning, they're drifting up Fulton. Tony wants to risk another daytime burglary.

". . . down on Fairmount, where they're fixing those apartments . . ."

"That's Stephen's Square apartments."

"The ones getting fixed up with new kitchens and all. You can creep on in there when the crew breaks for lunch . . ."

Gary nods, but he's distracted by something up at Baltimore Street. Tony follows his partner's line of sight to a cardboard crate, its top splayed open, lying on its side in the westbound lane. Gary jogs ahead to stake his claim, the law of the streets being comparable to the law of the seas.

"Bread rolls," says Tony, coming up after him.

"They bagels," says Gary, adding sagely: "Fresh-baked bagels, lox, and cream cheese—for Jews, that be soul food."

"Like to have fell from a truck," Tony concludes.

Gary takes a quick count. Fourteen dozen, each sealed in plastic, save for one bag at the top that has been torn open and reduced by a bagel or three.

"Birds got to that one," says Tony.

The sea gulls, apparently. A swirl of the scavenging birds is hovering above, waiting their turn. But the gulls lose out; Gary and Tony are now in the baked goods business.

"Fresh bagels," shouts Gary. "One dollar a dozen. Got the good bagels here. Bagel a day keeps the doctor ay-way."

He sells one dozen to a passing motorist. Another to someone coming out of the grocery down on Mount Street. After fifteen minutes, they've managed three dollars.

"It's a start," says Tony, hopeful.

They turn back down toward Mount and Fayette, seven dollars light for their morning jumper, still hoping to find the threads of a good caper. Halfway up the block, Gary sees the familiar outline of his son lumbering toward him, gripping a new basketball rim, the netting already attached.

"Hey," says Gary.

"W'sup."

"You know, just the same ol' thing."

DeAndre keeps his eyes on the pavement. Gary, too. Tony lingers at the edge of the conversation, then moves up the street to talk product with the Death Row touts.

"Where your ma at?" Gary asks.

DeAndre shrugs. "Aroun' somewheres."

Gary looks down at the orange rim.

"What's that about?"

"Belongs to the rec center. Ella got a new rim, but no one can figure out how to get it up on the backboard 'cause the backboard ain't straight on."

Gary nods thoughtfully. "You probably need washers."

DeAndre cocks his head sideways.

"Metal washers," says Gary, curling his finger to his thumb. "You know, to make the bolts tight."

DeAndre nods, not really understanding. The father asks to see the rim and the son obliges, then strolls off into the Korean carryout as Gary begins a scientific examination.

"These bolts he got ain't gonna make it," he says to no one in particular. "You need the longest bolts you can find."

When DeAndre comes out of the store, chewing on a bag of cheese puffs, his father is heading for the rec center blacktop. Just up the block, Tony eventually gives up hope, slipping into the street parade on his own. Gary spends ten minutes inspecting the holes on the sagging metal backboard.

"We need some hardware."

DeAndre nods, taken aback by the "we."

Ella springs for a few dollars and they make their way down to a hardware store at Pulaski and McHenry. DeAndre carries the rim so they can measure the bolts.

"So how's your girl?" Gary ventures, leaving the store.

"Reeka?" asks DeAndre. "Reeka not my girl." Gary looks over at him, surprised. He saw the two of them coming out of the Dew Drop Inn yesterday afternoon. "I mean, she's one of my girls, but I'm saying, it's springtime."

Gary laughs, shaking his head.

"Yes indeed," says DeAndre. "All these girls got so phat and fine over the winter, you know. I'm sayin' they don't even know it yet, but I'm gonna mess with every last one of 'em."

Ah, youth. Gary sighs loudly, glad for the chance at any kind of connection with his son. DeAndre, too, is allowing himself to feel it a bit, following Gary back up Fulton and talking up all his prospective conquests. Anything to let his father know he's done some growing.

Back on the rec playground, R.C. and Manny Man wait patiently as DeAndre and his father get a wrench from Ella and go to work. The rim eventually goes up, tight enough with the washers, but with an ugly forward list. There's no getting around the tilt of that backboard. R.C. inaugurates the court with a power drive from the rec center doors, double-pump faking with the right hand, then reversing to the left.

"R.C. use that move to death." says DeAndre.

"It work though," R.C. counters.

Standing near the top of the key, Gary asks for the ball and Manny Man gives it up, strangely polite. Gary grips the orb tightly, then backspins it off the blacktop in front of him so that it bounces into his hands. DeAndre is half-watching from beneath the basket, showing a vague embarrassment.

"You play, Mr. McCullough?"

"Well," says Gary, "back in the day."

"He ain't got nuthin'," says DeAndre.

Gary smiles, then cocks and shoots, catching only the front edge of the rim on a near airball. His son grabs the rebound and clucks derisively.

"One more," says Gary.

DeAndre fires him the ball. Gary backspins twice, cocks and puts a gentle fifteen-footer to bed. All net, my brothers. R.C. and Manny Man hoot and holler, giving the man his due.

"He got a little somethin'," says DeAndre, with sudden pride. "But not with me on the case."

"Oh, ho," says Gary, laughing. "Gracious."

DeAndre hikes his too-large denims back up over his rump and squares off against his father at the key. Gary lowers one shoulder, guarding the ball with his body, then dribbles awkwardly toward the baseline, struggling in a pair of worn dress shoes, unable to negotiate the ball against DeAndre's manic defense. In obvious desperation, he lets go with an off-balance hook that goes harmlessly off the back of the rim.

"Can't bring no old-school shot to me," says DeAndre proudly. "Ball up."

R.C. tosses the ball to DeAndre, who can't wait to give his father a lesson. But Gary is gazing across the blacktop and the vacant lot to Mount Street. Not Tony this time, but the Gaunt One, has his attention. Ronnie is waving her arm, giving him the come-right-now. DeAndre melts into the scenery.

"I'll be back 'round," says Gary, pulling up his hood.

He catches up to Ronnie in front of the carryout.

"Charlene been put out," she tells him. "Her shit is just sittin' on the street."

"Huh," says Gary.

"Best money is the sofa," says Ronnie. "Cushions don't match, but the wood is like new. Still, you got to get it down Baltimore Street."

No problem with that. Gary looks around for Tony, but his partner is long gone, bounding off on another adventure. He walks up Fayette toward Monroe, where he finds Scalio lounging on the sofa in question, sitting out there like Fayette Street is the den of his summer cottage, a lit Newport burning down between his fingers. The sofa is halfway into the street.

Scalio sees Ronnie coming and lifts the cigarette to his lips. He leans his head back to expel the smoke upward as traffic in the slow lane struggles to move around him.

"I gave him two smokes to guard the couch for me," Ronnie explains.

Scalio crosses his legs at the ankles and stretches his arms upward. "Only in the ghetto," he says dryly. "Only in America, in the ghetto, can life be so fine."

A Federal Express truck blares its horn directly behind him, but the old fiend remains theatrically indifferent. Gary has to smile at the performance.

"See here," says Scalio, waxing philosophical. "This . . . this is why they hate us . . ."

Gary laughs and Ronnie smirks. Scalio takes one last, luxurious drag off the Newport as the cars back up behind him. Gary can see the tortured faces of the motorists as they squeeze past the unlikely obstacle. White faces, black faces—all of them with that working-folk impatience, all of them wanting to ram their cars into this absurd tableau and none of them with heart enough to do it.

"Goddam niggers lazin' 'round in the street," says Scalio, getting up slowly. "Yes, Lawd, this is why they hate us."

The sofa brings twenty-five down on Baltimore Street. Gary and Ronnie adjourn to Pops' shooting gallery on Fulton, a third-floor walk-up where the ancient, rasping pincushion that is Pops welcomes all visitors for twenty on the hype. Gary is generally unwilling to use Annie's, it being next to his parents' house.

"You feelin' it?" Gary asks after they leave.

"Hmmm," says Ronnie, nodding.

"Mine's doo-doo," he tells her.

Maybe the Spider Bag package is weak today, or maybe Ronnie watered him. He tried to pay close attention when she was cooking; he didn't see her make any kind of switch. But Pops kept making conversation, and Ronnie is so damn quick.

"Man," says Gary, frustrated. "I don't feel too much."

He leaves Ronnie and heads back up the hill, hoping for a loan from his mother, something to get him out of the gate until he can hook back up with Tony. He finds her in the basement at St. James, working in the kitchen with the other ladies, mixing up potato salad for some church outing.

"Ma . . ."

But she's shaking her head before he can get the words out. Maybe when Cardy gets paid down at the crabhouse, she tells him. She might be able to spare something then.

Gary nods and from somewhere deep down, the snake gives a quiet little hiss. He's drifting out of the kitchen, into the adjacent meeting room and toward the side door of the church, nodding politely to one of the elderly church deacons, who at that moment is talking to some other folks and pulling papers out of his back pants pocket. Gary watches as two bills—a five and a one—come up after the papers and float silently to the linoleum floor. The deacon is oblivious.

Gary doesn't hesitate.

"Ho," he says, reaching down, "you dropped your money."

"Oh . . . I . . . goodness," says the old man. "I . . . thanks, son, thank you for it."

Gary goes out the church door onto Monroe Street, wondering where Tony might be hiding himself.

The choir is fine and full on this April afternoon, the layered voices soaring up from the altar and rattling through the old stone sanctuary on Baltimore Street. One soloist, then another, takes a turn at the hymns, their voices breaking to perfection on the blue notes, those flatted thirds and sevenths that eluded the colder construct of the European mind. It's the choir director herself who takes the microphone and struggles to the spiraled peak of the last crescendo, her voice trembling, her body racked by the drama of it all. She breaks completely after three wild choruses, her eyes fixed and glazed, her hand gripping the corner of the piano as she is helped slowly to a seat by the nearest singers. Her immediate reward is a church full of rapture, a fevered jumble of foot-stomping, hand-clapping, arm-waving humanity. The choir director's collapse is every bit an act of timed stagecraft that succeeds in bringing the congregation to full boil. The other singers, sensate to the moment, wail harder at the chorus, carrying it through.

". . . *something about King Jesus . . .*"

Ella Thompson jumps to her feet.

"*. . . makes me feel . . .*"

Arms above her head.

"*. . . so . . . so good . . .*"

From the twelfth pew back, Ella smiles broadly, applauding, her own voice sharing the last chorus with the whole of the congregation. This is her church, her choir, her spring concert, with every last grace note played to perfection.

She leaves the church with some reluctance, chatting with fellow parishioners on the steps and edging slowly into the sunlight on Baltimore Street. There were only a smattering of men in the pews for today's concert; women, most of them older than Ella, constituted the greater share of those gathered for the good news. And, Ella knew, much of the flock was now driving into the city from suburban enclaves, from Woodlawn and Woodmoor and Catonsville, where the black middle-class had established itself. Loyalty still lured them downtown to the city churches, but for how much longer was anyone's guess. There were some strong black congregations out in the county now, and even the leaders of black Baltimore's bedrock institutions had to worry that Sunday morning commuters comprised more and more of the faithful.

Still, the church as an ideal had endured for Ella. She counted it as one of the certainties in her world, a place of sanctuary in which she could risk a little physical and emotional release. More and more, her life was lived in transit between her church, her apartment, her rec center—these were Ella Thompson's safehouses, outposts where the spirit could be restored and core values affirmed. In the space between these places, there was precious little to inspire a woman's hope. She didn't walk the four blocks to her church, she drove the Oldsmobile; not so much out of any physical fear, but because driving would at least spare her the sadness of Monroe and Fayette.

So now, leaving the church concert, she walks down the hill to find her Cutlass where she left it on Smallwood Street, hard against the curb, where a tout from one of the Hollins Street crews raises his brow and extends the usual invitation. She's a few blocks away from Fayette Street; the crews on this side of Monroe haven't yet marked her as an unlikely sale. Ella ignores him, averting her eyes.

The tout holds his ground, waiting, as Ella fumbles with her car keys at the door of the Olds.

"Wassup?"

She gives a small shake of her head. She's wearing church clothes, for God's sake, but the tout is blank-faced and patient. She closes the door, turns over the engine, signals, and edges away, turning east on Baltimore and rolling back onto streets where she is known.

Moment by moment, the city is becoming a machine of small insults and petty failures that can wear down even the strongest soul. Here and now, it's the Smallwood Street tout stealing a little of her church-bought strength. The following day, it's the sight of R.C. and Manny Man, pummeling some younger boy on Fulton Avenue. Ella's in her car again, coming back from the market on Pratt Street, driving up Fulton at just the right moment to catch a glimpse of Manny grabbing the smaller kid from behind, clamping down on his arms, holding him tight for R.C.'s assault.

"R.C!" Ella shouts, rolling down the passenger window.

"Yes'm," says R.C., looking up after landing a gut punch.

"R.C., you let him be!"

R.C. smiles broadly and raises both arms in a gesture of surrender. He walks toward Ella's car and Manny Man follows behind. Free and clear, the younger kid begins scuttling sideways down the sidewalk, slowly at first, then into a full, loping gait.

"R.C., why are you hittin' that boy?"

"He my cousin," he assures her, leaning into the passenger door window.

"But why . . ."

"We just playing, Miss Ella."

Ella frowns, thinking to herself that the cousin in question is not hanging around for more fun. For his part, R.C. is on to new business and so, after a moment or two more, is Ella.

Parking on Mount Street, she once again does battle with the rec center's security grate, unlocks the doors, hits the lights, and walks directly to her office in the rear. She unfastens a third padlock on the door, slips inside, pushes aside a stack of boxes, and turns yet another key to deactivate the night alarm. She drops her purse on the desk, pulls off her jacket, and then, with the silence of the empty center weighing on her, she turns on the television.

It's a soap opera. No matter which one.

She listens only for the comfort of the noise, for the sound of other human voices filling the void. With the television on, Ella can work.

She begins with the chore of emptying two tall columns of stacked food cartons, restocking the office cupboards. Lorna Doones on the middle shelf, along with the miniature cinnamon rolls; salted pretzels on the bottom, with the copying paper, and the small bags of barbecue potato chips wherever there's room. Ella pulls all of it from the cartons, crowding the shelves with a fresh bounty of small bribes, tossing the emptied boxes out into the hallway. Children who manage a full day without doing damage to the rec center, each other, or themselves are rewarded for their restraint. They hover around the front desk, arms outstretched, the thank-you-Miss-Ellas echoing in waves as they grab their prizes and race away.

Having shelved the groceries, she turns her attention to the paper pile on her desk. There is a written reminder that she'll need to collect birth certificates for the basketball players if her team is to compete in a summer league. Then there are plans for a Boy Scout troop, as well as an aerobics class in the evenings to bring some of the neighborhood women down to the center. And she needs to talk with the Franklin Square board members about that rehab project underway on Lexington Street. Is there a chance—any chance at all—that some of her older kids can get summer jobs with the project?

In Ella Thompson's mind it's all connected. Not just the plans and potential of the rec center, but everything in the neighborhood. She is an inveterate joiner whose name never fails to appear on the legal-pad sign-up sheets passed around at every Tuesday night gathering. It begins with the Franklin Square board meetings, of course; the community association pays her $16,000 salary and governs her center. But it continues with church-group meetings, Jobs for Peace planning sessions, the neighborhood SHARE network, the Bon Secours home hospice program, and the Western police district's citizen's police academy. Ella doesn't speak a political language, nor does she measure her involvement by tactics and strategy. The inner politics of the organizations, the group dynamics and interpersonal agendas—all of that means little to her. She goes to the board meetings, listens carefully and agrees with anything said on the community's behalf. And if anyone asks for her help, she grants it without regard to the fact that she has already volunteered for a half-dozen other neighborhood initiatives. There is no priority or method to her across-the-board commitment, just the idea that there is a critical mass, that if she joins and serves and works hard enough, Fayette Street will surely get better.

In the face of all evidence, she is still compelled to commit herself to the idea of a community that no longer exists, that hasn't existed since she was a little girl. Ella isn't foolish; she knows the corner well enough. But to calculate the odds as they ought to be calculated is to entertain a judgment that cannot be tolerated.

Pooh made it so.

Five years ago, when the homicide detectives stood at her door with their softest look, Ella had, in one sense, been ready for the news. She'd seen the television. She knew what all those police cars and television cameras were doing in the alley behind Baltimore Street. The whole neighborhood knew.

But in the larger sense, she wasn't at all ready, just as no mother is ever ready to let go of a child. Fatty Pooh was thirteen; Ella had worried for her no less than anyone would worry about a daughter at the near edge of adolescence, and by November 1988, life on Fayette Street had already become a struggle. Mount Street was quiet back then, but Fulton and Lexington was an open-air market. So was Monroe Street. But to Ella, the drug trafficking and the corners and the mayhem had seemed a solvable problem, something for the community, police, and city officials to grapple with. Nothing in the streets seemed so sinister that it could reach out beyond those willingly on the corners; nothing out there seemed lethal enough to reach into Ella's home and claim one of her own.

She was wrong. Four days after the police came to her door, she buried Pooh. Weeks later she went to the arraignment, and months later, the court trial. And months after that, she went back for the sentencing hearing. Then, with nothing left to be said or done, Ella gave herself over to grief, until she found that she could not be alone in a quiet room. A friend, a radio, a television—anything. The memory of her daughter Andrea makes silence lethal; it demands that a soap opera be heard, if not seen, or that a radio stay cranked to a dance station. It is Fatty Pooh, thirteen forever, who requires Ella's almost manic involvement in new groups and causes, just as it was Pooh who brought Ella to this tiny building three years ago. Sitting now at her desk and looking around at

the wonderful, comforting clutter of the office, Ella can see the image
and ideal of her daughter in every last bit of it, in everything that she
had managed to gather or acquire or accomplish here. To her, this
safehouse matters more than all the others.

When Ella began here, only a few kids were actually coming regularly.
The center's director, a full-time veteran of the city's parks and recreation department, tried to make a go of it, but by then the rec was little
more than a shell. Community involvement was nonexistent. In fact,
when Ella herself showed up at the door of the bunker three years ago,
the director was taken aback.

"I'm Ella Thompson," she said. She wasn't yet sure if this was what
she wanted, but she felt a need to do something.

"Can I help you?"

"I'd like to volunteer."

"Excuse me," said the director. "What did you say?"

It took a year or so for the director to move on to greener pastures,
another year after that for the Franklin Square board to realize what they
had in Ella, their up-from-the-neighborhood temporary replacement. She
was no professional bureaucrat, nor did she have tenure with the city
recreation department or any experience remotely connected to running
a rec facility. That alone gave pause to some on the board, but in the end,
Ella's unbounded love for the center and its children could not be ignored.
Just before Christmas, Frank Long, Joyce Smith, and the other board
officers finally decided to make it official, and now, her formal approval
as center director was an item on the next board meeting's agenda, listed
under new business. So the center was hers, and Ella, true to form, couldn't
help looking at the cracked cinder blocks and yellowed linoleum and
seeing possibilities that would elude anyone else.

She saw the potential even though there was precious little beyond
the structure itself to lure the children, or to keep them coming. The
roof leaked, the furnace was questionable, and the operating money
required for basketballs and Wiffle-ball bats, finger paints and field trips
would always be limited. The rec center wasn't part of the city budget;
the city had, in fact, closed the center when federal funding dried up
more than a decade ago. Now the money comes from the Franklin Square
association, which relies on a single $38,000 city block-grant for all of
its needs. As for staff, Ella is—with the exception of Marzell Myers—
essentially alone. Few parents stop in and see what their kids are doing
in the gray bunker; fewer still are willing to volunteer their time. And

Ella, who can't bring herself to say no to any possibility, senses the weight that comes with every new face at the door.

For now, though, she clears her mind of larger issues and gets to the routine business of cleaning the center. As the soap operas churn in the background, she tackles the empty food cartons first, breaking them apart and stuffing them into the big plastic garbage cans. As she works, her thoughts run through the list of chores: The bathrooms could use a cleaning, and out on the playground, there is that broken bottle below the slide to pick up. Also, the toys and games ought to be out on the tables, a task that takes more and more time as the game boxes break apart and the pieces get loose and roll around the lockers.

Finishing with the cartons, Ella walks back into her office and checks the clock, measuring out a couple of hours in her head. If she hurries, there will be time left to run back up to Fayette Street and hand out some of the flyers promoting the community conference later this month. She'd promised Joyce she would get those out, but so far she's covered only her own side of the 1800 block.

Distracted, Ella doesn't hear the knocking until someone is fairly hurling himself against the metal doors.

"Coming," she yells.

She cracks the door and looks down at DeAndre. The boy is buried beneath his black hoody, hands in his pocket, a cold look drawn over his face.

"I have a lot to do," she tells him. "Why aren't you in school?"

He shrugs and she braces for the usual excuse. Half-day. Or quarter-day even. Or Tuesdays and Thursdays off. The children of Fayette Street have manufactured flextime school schedules in their minds, as if it's reasonable that the ninth grade actually meets for four hours every other week.

"Why didn't you go to school?" she asks again.

He looks up at her, a picture of adolescent righteousness, then shakes his head softly. "Couldn't go."

"Why not?"

"My clothes were still wet."

A ridiculous argument for any other kid in any other neighborhood, but Ella figures that for DeAndre McCullough, it's probably true. He's been wearing the same denims and flannel shirt for weeks now; if he starts the laundry too late at night, he spends the next morning watching television in his underwear waiting for his school clothes to dry.

"Can I come in?"

Ella steps aside and the boy follows her into the dry air of the rec. He lumbers over to the weight bench as she begins setting up the game tables for the little children. Minutes later, she's interrupted by more knocking on the metal door.

"MISS ELLA . . ."

Ella starts at the shout and looks through the wire-mesh window. R.C. is twisting his head this way and that, trying to scan every corner of the center. DeAndre gets up from the weight bench, walks within R.C.'s sight and smiles smugly.

"MISS ELLA."

Ella Thompson goes past DeAndre and cracks the door. "R.C.," she tells him, "you know the rec isn't open yet."

"HE IN THERE, MISS ELLA," R.C. shouts. "DEANDRE IN THERE."

"Quiet, R.C.," Ella says, "Why didn't you go to school?"

"I did," R.C. insists. "I got out early cause it's a half-day."

DeAndre breaks out laughing. "Yeah, R.C. That'll work."

Even Ella smiles. Reluctantly, she agrees to let him inside; to favor DeAndre on even the smallest point would leave R.C. with a mortal wound. "But you have to settle down," she tells him. "I'm serious, I have things to do today."

"I'm always good," says R.C.

Ella gives him a quick look and R.C. immediately begins backing up on himself: "Well, I try anyway. I try and there's some people don't never even do that."

"Who you talkin' 'bout?" asks DeAndre.

"You, nigger."

"Fuck you, bitch."

Ella shuts them down quickly, berating both for their profanity, eliciting mumbled apologies. She leaves them to a game of Connect Four and heads to the girls' bathroom with the bucket and mop. She's at it for almost an hour, cleaning floors and fixtures, listening out of one ear as DeAndre takes three games out of four and R.C. loudly declares him a cheater. The two grow bored and begin moving around the rec, dribbling and passing the rec center basketball and talking up Ella's new team.

"Miss Ella, we gonna get new uniforms for a summer league?"

"We'll see," says Ella.

"They should be black."

"Like your ass," says DeAndre.

"Like your face, bitch."

"You a whore, R.C."

"Nigga please."

The bickering continues, until both boys are restless enough to make a food run. When they leave, Ella can only marvel at the quiet, save for the droning television. It's past three. She hasn't time to deal with the community meeting flyers. Instead, she uses her last minutes alone to call Myrtle Summers at Echo House, the community outreach center. Myrtle wears two hats in the neighborhood hierarchy, working as an Echo House administrator and serving on the Franklin Square board. Ella asks about the possibility of renovating the rec's playground; there's a rumor that there's city money available to repave the blacktop and replace equipment. Myrtle's heard the same rumor and manages to feed Ella's optimism.

"Should I call Joyce or Frank?" Ella asks.

No, she's told, just wait. Someone from rec and parks will be coming by to assess the playground.

"Good. That's great."

As Ella gets off the phone, the children begin arriving. Soon enough, twelve names are etched into the attendance book. They're mostly first, second, and third graders, but a few are much younger, trailing along behind their older school-age siblings, all obedient to the rec center procedures—shedding jackets at the front desk, struggling to put them on hangers, happy and without complaint. A second wave, middle-schoolers, piles up around the desk. They follow the same script, but more aggressively. For two months now, they've seen the older boys basking in the glory of the fledgling basketball squad, and they've heard talk that Ella is considering the team for a summer league. So they have a case of their own.

"We gonna have a team, too, Miss Ella?" asks Little Stevie.

"I don't know yet. We'll see how the older boys work out."

"Then we ain't gonna play," says Daymo, shaking his head and walking toward a table.

"We don't get shit," says Stevie, bitter.

Ella ignores him, leading the younger children through a cut-and-paste adventure in African mask-making. In just a few minutes, she has to put Old Man out for pasting up a smaller boy's face. A few minutes more and she threatens Stevie and Michael with the same for tussling in the boys' bathroom.

The daily routine requires Ella to be all things to all manner of children, from wide-eyed first-graders to the almost-growns of C.M.B. For each age-group, the rec is a different kind of refuge, and the challenge is to somehow offer enough attention to each group in three-hour installments inside a single room.

A child of any age has to go to great lengths to be barred permanently from the rec center. Proof of this can be found on the metal lockers across from Ella's office, where a carefully painted portrait of a smiling teddy bear, garbed in a police uniform, still hangs unmolested more than a year after its creation. The art, proudly signed, is by Dink-Dink. And never mind that thirteen-year-old Dink-Dink is out there now at Baltimore and Gilmor running wild. Never mind that a week ago, Tyreeka Freamon was sitting on her front stoop on Stricker Street when crazy Dink-Dink came down the block carrying his nine, ordering everyone inside. Never mind that with the street free and clear, Dink-Dink shot a grown man in the leg over a drug debt, then walked away calmly, leaving the victim for the ambo. If Dink-Dink showed himself today at the rec doors, Ella would extend a welcome, show the boy to the arts-and-crafts corner and clear another place in the metal-locker gallery.

For Ella, no defeat can be fully acknowledged. Every day, her rec center is filled not only with children still oblivious to the corner, but with those who are already in the game. This makes for a considerable amount of mayhem.

Daymo, T.J., Chubb, Michael, and DeAndre's brother and cousin, DeRodd and Little Stevie—this is the Fayette Street of the future, and they've already been tutored by their elders. "Crimping 'em up" is a local expression for the process by which older kids toughen the younger ones, steeling them for the reality of Fayette Street with a thousand petty insults and savageries.

Childhood in West Baltimore comes replete with the usual cruelties and aggressions. But along Fayette Street, these small moments grow large, never tempered by that generosity of spirit that follows from a secure sense of self. Brothers and sisters trade insults ruthlessly; best friends bicker constantly over nothing; lovers betray each other with casual disregard, then bury all guilt and complicity in the coarse vocabulary of rage and abuse.

Inside the rec, Ella bears witness to the petty warfare of everyday life, the cold glint in the eyes of young children who have been properly crimped by those older and bigger. They've been taught that kindness is weakness, that compassion is a thing to be suppressed. It's vocational training of a kind: These are lessons of and about the corner.

Around here, those who suffer through childhood with dirty clothes or unchanged underwear are nothing more than a source of comedy, just as those who struggle with enormous gaps in comprehension— "The building with the plus sign on top," says Arnold, pointing to St. Martin's, "that's where we eat"—are a target for unremitting scorn. Around here, those too dark-skinned and those too light, those fat, or ugly, or awkward are never allowed to forget the liability. Just ask the chubby, moon-faced kid who came to last year's overnight party at the rec, only to wake at four in the morning to the smell of his own burning flesh and the howls of Dink-Dink and Eric, laughing with delight at just how much fun a burning book of matches can be. Around here, the tyranny of the grade-school pecking order has been institutionalized as sport. Just shout "Snatchpops" to any kid over the age of six who happens to be sucking down food or drink between Stricker and Monroe and watch him flinch. Snatchpops is a game that has endured for a couple generations on Fayette Street, a game in which the sole rule is this: At the sound of the word "snatchpops," any kid can justifiably take the potato chips, Sno-Kone, or Big Mac from another's hand and eat it with impunity. It's might makes right, legitimized.

Today it's Chubb, throwing an empty liquor bottle over the heads of two girls on the rec playground. Tomorrow it will be Little Stevie shouting snatchpops and grabbing at Daymo's fruit drink, spilling it all over the rec floor. Yesterday it was open warfare between Umeka and T.J. as Marzell Myers tried bravely to lead a dozen children through the environmental apocalypse that is finger painting.

"T.J. put paint on my face," complained Umeka.

"You lyin'," said T.J.

"You got green on your hands and there's green on my face."

"So?"

Marzell stared them both into silence, then walked to the bathroom sink just in time to miss T.J. planting a green thumbprint on Umeka's forehead.

"Bitch," cried Umeka spontaneously. She raised a hand to wipe at the paint, but T.J. was already on his feet, the open palm of his hand slapping her hard in the face, leaving Umeka with wet eyes and a trickle of blood from the corner of her mouth. The two stood facing each other:

Umeka, showing her best scowl, her hands balled in rage, unwilling to cry aloud or back away, but unwilling to risk a move against the stronger boy; T.J. standing opposite with a slight smile, waiting for her move, then tiring of the game and stalking away.

"What happened?" asked Marzell, returning.

And Umeka, properly crimped, said nothing.

That such things happen in better places is true enough. Children are, at odd moments, brutish and violent; the phenomenon isn't particular to Fayette Street. But here, there is so little in the way of countervailing argument—so little adult supervision, so little parental attention being paid, so little reward in the streets for charity and humility and compassion—that by grade school, the children of Franklin Square are too crimped, too broken to do much more than run with the pack that raised them. By then, an enormous amount of human potential has already disappeared.

And Ella has them three hours a day. Between three and six on weekdays, she can reward the good and punish the bad and try to make some kind of argument against the constant, grinding process that turns children into victims and victimizers. Against all the immediate evidence, she believes in those three hours.

Today, apart from Old Man and his paste and that ugly bit with Chubb and the liquor bottle, it's a good session that ends with the Lorna Doones and pork rings issued one-to-a-customer, and Ella slumping, exhausted, at her desk. Still unsorted, the mail in front of her is mostly junk, much of it shopping circulars that catch Ella's attention only when the Caldor or Woolworth ads feature children's toys and games. She will now and then clip out an item or two, stuffing them into the top drawer of her desk in preparation for that come-and-get-it day when the Franklin Square budget is fat enough to replenish the rec's toy chest.

Today's catch of circulars is halfway to the plastic waste can when she spots a gray-white envelope jutting from beneath a newsprint shopper:

Miss Ella Thompson
Martin Luther King Recreation Center
100 Vincent Street
Baltimore, Maryland

Not an exact address, but close enough. The ink is smudged and Ella can't really make out the letter's return address, but from experience she knows this envelope's point of origin. Jail mail, definitely, but the legible part of the return address is only a few digits of an inmate number and a portion of the Eager Street address. She doesn't know anyone down there, though her mind goes immediately to George Epps. But Blue is home now; Ella saw him on Monroe Street just this Saturday last and told him she wanted him back for art class. No, not Blue.

She looks again at her name on the envelope, and with some hesitation, finally opens it, half-convinced that the letter is intended for someone else. A name—Ricky Cunningham—is neatly printed on top. Ricky. She had wondered what happened to him after he ducked out of the Valentine's dance, particularly since his promise to help out at the rec had seemed so direct and sincere.

The handwriting is tidy and compressed, the letter itself beginning with an apology.

"Ella, I know how much you counted on me to help with the basketball team . . ."

Halfway down the page, the letter turns a corner.

"It means so much to me to come around the center and be with you. You make me feel wanted again. You don't know how much it hurts not seeing you . . ."

Ella is puzzled. Ricky had been to the center only a couple of times. How could that be so important to him? And why is he writing to her?

". . . every day, I think about you . . ."

Ella reads on, and to her surprise, the letter becomes florid and romantic. She's been remote from this kind of love for a while now, cautious around suitors and unwilling to risk whatever normalcy she's managed to establish in her life. With her history, that much could be expected: Along Fayette Street, the stronger women, the survivors, inevitably come to realize that most of the men in their world aren't very good at making life easier. Still, she's floored by the idea of Ricky Cunningham cultivating a schoolboy crush from some jail tier.

The letter wanders to-and-fro, waxing on in its love and admiration for Ella and all she stands for, and then, on its final page, culminating in a plea for her to be there in court at sentencing. The crime itself is a small absurdity: Ricky was caught in a Rite-Aid, stealing a jar of vitamins. The store security guard was a girl he went to school with, and he figured that would count for something. Now, for about eight dollars worth of iron, calcium, and vitamin C, he's been over at Eager Street for almost a month.

"I know it was wrong," he writes. "Wrong and stupid."

Ella folds the letter and walks back to her desk, trying to figure how this, too, has been added to her collective burden. She meets a young man in the neighborhood, hoping that he might be of some help to the rec center, and a couple of months after that, he's hoping, instead, for some help from her. The wearied portion of Ella's soul tells her to put the letter back into its envelope and bury it somewhere. But the rest of that soul is too earnest, too Christian for such a careless gesture.

Three weeks later, she is perched on one of the back benches in a chamber of the Wabash Avenue district courthouse. She seems to be the lone taxpayer in that courtroom, the last true citizen amid the regular human barnacles on the benches. Bail reviews. A plea. Another plea. This case postponed, that one dismissed, the next one sent up to the circuit court for a jury trial. Bailiffs and lawyers, police and defendants— all of them moving through a brutish ballet, all of them stepping with the cold certainty of veterans.

She sits there, listening with half an ear to the play-by-play between the judge and the lawyers, watching with a vague but genuine regret as the docket is sorted and shifted. Petty things: drugs, thefts, violations of probation, more drugs. And then, finally, Ricky comes into the room from the side door, handcuffed, with an aging jail guard behind him. For a moment, the defendant's attention is drawn to the judge and the lawyers, to the case numbers being read and the manila folders being passed. Then, as if sensing her, he turns around to scan the benches. Ella gives a little wave.

He sees it and breaks into a wide beam, then waves at her with manacled hands. The case—the schoolmate, the vitamins, the statement of charges, ridiculous in its simplicity—is read into the record by a young prosecutor. Then, the public defender begins to take up the outlines of an already agreed-upon plea.

But Ricky is hardly attending to this. He's turning constantly to meet Ella's eyes, his contortions distracting the proceedings.

"Thank you," he says in a stage whisper.

Ella nods, feeling awkward.

She is on that bench because of someone in need, nothing more than that. But of course there's no way to say any of this to Ricky, who can only mouth a few more thank-yous before being escorted through the side door. Ella goes back to her car and drives home; Ricky goes back to the jail van and heads downtown to finish a thirty-day bit.

Still, she is glad she went. Ricky is trying, and he'll keep trying when he comes home; that, she tells herself, is what that letter was all about.

Her small part in the matter leaves her hopeful, filled once again with the conviction that what everyone does in this world will ultimately matter.

That same afternoon, before going down to the rec, she sits out on her front steps with a glass of tea, making the most of a beautiful spring day. And most of the time on the steps is just that—absolutely beautiful—with the sun warming the pavement, and the schoolchildren drifting slowly into the block, coming up the street from Steuart Hill Elementary after a halfday session.

This, too, is a small victory for Ella. Last summer, the overflow from the Family Affair and Diamond in the Raw crews found its way up Fayette Street, with touts and lookouts settling on the Fulton corners. Ella and a handful of neighbors spent weeks trying to push the crews back down the hill, calling the police on them so often that the Western District officers and Fayette Street slingers were, for once, in absolute agreement: The Thompson woman was a damned nuisance.

Now, with the vials trading hands a good half-block away, Ella watches the glint of the chrome as the cars roll past on Fulton, then hears the music-box jingle of the ice cream truck all the way at the top of the block.

"Hey, Miss Ella."

"Hi, Dion."

"Rec open today?"

"Three o'clock."

She's watching the neighborhood as Baltimore people have always watched the neighborhood, living life at the front steps of a rowhouse. And today, at least, it's soothing the way it used to be, so right and fine that she can't yet bring herself to go back inside and ready herself for the rec. Sipping her tea, she watches a young white girl, freckled and athletic, weaving up and down the 1700 block on her ten-speed. The girl just seems to be riding aimlessly, cruising the neighborhood with no set purpose, just out to soak up that good sunshine.

A few minutes later, Kiti comes in from Francis Woods, then goes right back out again looking for Preston and the rest of his crew. Then Ella's grandchild, Tianna, pops out of the apartment, asking for help with a broken toy. When Ella looks up again, the Death Row touts and runners are chasing the white girl up Fayette, gaining as she struggles with the gears of her bike.

They catch her at Fulton, just in from the corner. They yank at the handlebars and knock her to the ground. Two of the younger ones kick and grab at her until she rolls over and they can snatch at the edges of a glassine sandwich bag beneath her sweatshirt. The girl is bloody and crying, but the attack continues as she tries to cover the bag. Ella watches it all from her steps with a feeling of utter helplessness. The touts finally liberate the baggie and its load of vials, carrying the stolen-for-a-moment ground stash back where it belongs. One of the young runners takes the ten-speed, declaring the bike as punitive damages. Business slowly returns to normal for the Fayette Street crews, though the white girl sits on a curb, crying and nursing her wounds.

Ella calls the police. After a long wait, a radio car pulls to the curb at Fulton and two officers pick up the white girl. Ella follows the petty drama to its conclusion, then files the episode with a hundred others in the far reaches of her mind. As the radio car rolls off, she also takes leave, going inside her apartment to heat up a macaroni-and-cheese lunch for her granddaughter. Tianna has been staying with Ella on weekdays while her mother, Donilla, works. The four-year-old is a joy and great company for Ella in the mornings. But at odd moments, she is reminded that Fayette Street is no place for any child.

"What are they doing outside?" Tianna asks.

"Who?"

"The police and the lady."

"Nothing," Ella tells her.

But how much can you ignore? Three days after the white girl is beaten for stealing a stash, the Martin Luther King Jr. Rec Center is itself burglarized. Suddenly, the menace is not just in the street among the corner players, but within the safehouses where Ella lives and breathes. And from what she gathers, the thieves knew their way around the cinderblock building, creeping into the back alley between the rear walls of the rec and one of the vacant Lexington Street houses. Once there, they knocked a plywood board from the outside of one of the small, high windows that had long ago been nailed and mortared shut, then kicked through the old brick, jumped down into the small library area, and grabbed the television and the VCR.

Ella herself discovers the mess late the following morning, after pulling up the grate to begin her day. The police are called for no apparent purpose other than the creation of a police report. This time, the responding officer happens to be named Huffham. Ella greets him at the door, talks it through for him, then volunteers to share her desk as he goes to work on his incident report. When his writing hand tires, Huffham pauses to take in the clutter of the rec office.

"That list," he says at one point, looking at a phone list for the rec center basketball team. "What's that about?"

"That's our team," says Ella, with some pride. "That's going to be the basketball team for the older boys."

"DeAndre McCullough," says the officer, reading from the list. "Him I know."

Ella looks up sadly. Huffham goes on, a bit embarrassed, perhaps, for Ella's sake. "I, ah, I locked him up a few months back," says Huffham, trying for a tone of casual conversation. "Got him for distribution down on Fairmount."

Ella says nothing.

"DeAndre's a smart kid," Huffham adds.

Ella nods politely.

"I'm serious," Huffham says, finishing up the report. "He's a very smart kid."

"Yes," says Ella. "He is."

"Well," adds Huffham, gathering up the paperwork. "I hope you get a chance to straighten him out."

Later that day, Myrtle Summers sends over a workman to board up the gaping hole in the alley wall, but the theft of the television and tape player isn't so easily repaired. The rec has a high insurance deductible and no rainy-day money to make good the loss, and so the Friday night movies—featuring rentals from the Route 40 Blockbuster—come to an abrupt end. The older boys are dismayed and there is some early talk about tracking down the culprits and exacting retribution. Word from the corners is that Dink-Dink, Eric, and Lamont might have had something to do with the theft, that they were seen down on Baltimore Street trying to sell a television.

"That shit ain't right," Tae declares.

But in the end, nothing much comes of it. The boys vent their indignation and move on to new business, uneasy about the notion of playing detective and confronting Dink-Dink or anyone else with C.M.B. credentials. The police don't call back. The Baltimore Street pawnshops ask no questions. About the burglary of its recreation center, the neighborhood speaks only in silences.

*   *   *

Fat Curt and Hungry stumble up Vine from Fulton Avenue, both acknowledging June Bey McCullough with a quick nod.

"Wassup, wassup," shouts June Bey.

Hungry smiles. Curt looks over at June Bey and wonders the same thing. June Bey is standing amid a huge pile of fetid trash, broken bricks, and shattered furniture, sorting it as if it was somehow important to know the contents of the pile. Just in front of June Bey, in one of the open garages across from the McCullough home, is more of the same. It seems as if trash has been accumulating in the Vine Street garages since before the Earth cooled.

"Man," says Curt, "what the hell you lookin' for?"

June Bey laughs.

"You lose your stash again?"

June Bey shakes his head. "Cleaning," he says.

The tout ponders this for a moment, reasons quite correctly that there isn't a dollar's profit in cleaning a vacant garage on Vine Street, and wanders up to Blue's, shaking his head. Hungry follows him as he slips through the broken back door. June Bey watches them go, and, sensing that they are flush and ready to load up, he feels his lips go dry.

"Ol' man river," sings June Bey, trying hard for a stereotype. He slogs into the trashed garage, pulling out pieces of a broken oven and tossing them into the pile. Then he pulls off his knitted cap, wipes his head and saunters a few steps down Vine, telling himself that the job is more than half finished. He starts toward the far corner, wondering if Curt and Hungry know something he doesn't, if maybe there's a tester line down on Fulton.

"June Bey!"

His mother's voice. June Bey turns abruptly on his heels and winces, one swollen hand raised in a gesture of mollification. He tries to smile back through the window, his eyes glancing off Roberta McCullough's fretful face.

"William," she says, cracking the storm door and resorting to formalities. "Where you goin'?"

"Nowhere."

"You know that you not close to done yet."

"Yes'm," says June Bey. "But I will be. I will be done, on earth as I am in heaven."

He's responsible not only for the small patch of pavement behind the McCullough rowhouse, but the garages on the north side of Vine to boot. He's doing his mother's bidding today: removing the dump piles, bagging the trash, sweeping the dog and rat droppings out from the corners of the empty garages. Alas for June Bey McCullough, a prodigal son suddenly in his mother's eye; it's spring, and along Fayette Street, that means spring cleaning.

In these fine late-April days, it's not just June Bey, but the whole neighborhood that is engaged in a ritual echoing from some earlier epoch, some time and place in which seasonal renewal was still a possibility. Now, with the sun warm on the Formstone and asphalt, the men and women along Fayette Street—even some of those long narcotized— are feeling the gentle sway. The days of communal litter marches and clean-block campaigns may be a generation gone, but the trace memory is still there in the season's warm breezes.

Around the corner, Blue is out on the front steps of his broken home, going through the only possessions that still have any meaning for him. With almost reverential care, he opens up his satchel and art supply box, then begins sorting his brushes, pencils, and drawing pads, taking inventory and preparing for the season to come.

The jail time cleared his head enough to allow him to hear a voice inside screaming to put a stop to all this nonsense. And Blue was able to abide that voice, for a short time at least. A month earlier, he had come home to his brother's house on the other side of the boulevard, where his brother had a working phone and the pretrial division was therefore able to place him on home monitor. But his brother had limited patience and soon enough, with no other location at which he might be detained, Blue was returned to the city jail. A week or so back, when the jail finally kicked him loose, they forgot to take the home-monitoring bracelet from his wrist. Now, he's back in the mix, still wearing his state-supplied jewelry as if it can pass as a corner fashion.

For Blue, it's back to square one, though the better half of his nature uses the early part of this day to take stock of his art supplies and talk to himself about scrounging up some sign-painting business, maybe even opening up a shop of his own in one of the vacant storefronts down on Pratt Street. Change is in the breeze, and Blue, though the same as he ever was, still feels the need to clean house.

"Hey," says Eggy Daddy, cruising up with Scalio.

"Mmm hmm," offers Blue, replacing the satchel's contents.

"Where you goin' at?"

"Down Pratt Street," says Blue, flush with purpose.

"Not now you ain't. We're sick."

Blue smiles. After the usual suspects began tearing down Annie's house, she made the supreme effort of forcing the shooting gallery to move once again, and so, Blue came home from courtside to a crowded house. Today, though, Rita isn't around, having come out of her lair to hunt down some antibiotics for her arms.

"Awright," he tells the two. "Go on inside and I'll be with you."

He picks up the satchel and follows, then returns to the steps a few minutes later, once again prepared for the sortie to the Pratt Street shops. "Hey, what can I say?" he tells no one in particular. "I'm a doctor."

Blue starts again across Fayette, but this time it's Fat Curt and Hungry coming at him, with Curt holding a bottle of wine. An hour earlier, three white boys had pulled up in a Ford Escort, made the connect with Curt, and had given him eight dollars for the trouble. It was enough for a Spider Bag, so Blue goes back inside his house and hits them with it, and only then does he make his way out the door and down the hill to the commercial strip with the satchel of new business slung heavy across his shoulder, thinking to himself that beginnings are always harder than they seem.

Another seasonal cleaning is taking place a block down Fayette Street, this one courtesy of the Franklin Square civic leadership. Down near the Mount Street corners, an old fiend named Gene lays claim to the most broke-down needle palace and it's his misfortune to be at 1702 Fayette, directly across the street from the Echo House community center. By virtue of that geography, Gene is about to be seasonally adjusted, though he doesn't know it yet. Across the street, out in front of Echo House, Joyce Smith and Myrtle Summers are standing with a young attorney from a legal aid group, taking stock of the wreckage at 1702 and wondering whether it might be possible to have the place condemned.

As officers of the Franklin Square board, Joyce and Myrtle are what remains of bedrock in the Fayette Street community; they are therefore more inspired than the average resident when it comes to the spring rites. Myrtle, for one, has been keeping an eye on Gene's battered shooting gallery for months now and she's been talking to people about the public nuisance statute, a relatively new section of civil code that allows the city to take control of properties that have become the source of chronic criminal problems. If Joyce and Myrtle can get the Western District commanders to raid 1702 Fayette, they'll surely come up with some drugs. And if they do that much, then the city might be able to take the rowhouse and put it to some better use. Myrtle is thinking about a men's shelter.

Around the corner from Gene's, Ella has shut down the rec center on this Friday afternoon so she can haul every stick of furniture to one side of the bunker and scrub and polish the walls and floors to a more perfect gloss.

She's got Marzell and Neacey helping her, with Neacey employed for the cost of lunch at McDonald's.

"Can Tosha get lunch, too?" asks Neacey.

"Is Tosha working with us?" asks Ella.

"No. She up at her mother's house."

Ella gives Neacey a look.

"Miss Ella, I was just askin' is all."

To the north on Lexington Street, the urban renewal project is now in full swing, with yet another nonprofit developer using government money to rehab a few dozen vacant rowhouses, proving once again that while no social problem can be solved, there is always money enough to gild a ghetto. Few along Fayette Street will be able to afford the rehabbed houses. Those with money enough for the mortgages will be from outside the neighborhood, and, naturally, when many of them get a look at the mayhem of the corners, they'll decide to own a home elsewhere. But it's spring, and the contractors are as busy dreaming of rebirth as everyone else in the neighborhood.

Farther down Lexington, Rose Davis and the rest of the faculty at Francis Woods are doing some housekeeping of their own, dusting off the attendance rolls and discovering just how many dozens of their charges have effectively ceased to be students. The warning letters are about to begin rolling out: DeAndre will get a couple from his math and science teachers; R.C. will hit for the cycle, getting you're-going-to-fail notices in all four of his core courses, with every teacher unable to evaluate his work because, well, they don't quite know who or where Richard Carter is or when he might actually appear in a classroom.

On the other side of Fayette Street, Fran Boyd feels enough spring in her blood to spend a day primping and dressing in one of her old downtown business suits, readying herself for a grandmother's funeral she has determined not to miss. She's had her hair done and now looks like a creature visiting from another world entirely. All the regulars at the Dew Drop Inn notice, a few actually going out of their way to say something kind. Scoogie comes around with his car to pick her up for the church services, leaving the rest of the Boyd family behind to contemplate their own inertia.

"I don't do funerals," Bunchie declares.

"Fran looked good though," says Sherry.

Although the Boyd clan is hard into the game by late afternoon, there are other signs of spring at the Dew Drop. DeAndre shows up with a dog, a small pit bull purchased from a litter for a few dollars. He ties the animal to a chain-link fence in the rear alley and begins feeding it lovingly, then washes it, then feeds it again. A boy and his dog on a warm afternoon.

"He loves me," DeAndre says.

"He don't know you," his neighbor Malik assures him.

"Yes he do," says DeAndre. "He knows me 'cause I feed him."

Later that day at the Dew Drop, Skip makes an appearance fresh from the Mount Street tester line, grandly attired in a grey tweed sports coat and pleated slacks, his shoes spit-shined, his freshly manicured hands gripping a crushed leather briefcase, an afternoon newspaper tucked under one arm. Skip, who's been living in a vacant house on Fulton Avenue, now looks as if he's just stepped out of the Legg Mason Tower downtown.

"What's up?" asks Stevie, impressed.

"Job interview," says Skip casually.

"Huh?"

"Only chumps go out and soldier in the warm weather," explains Skip, who nearly froze to death on Fulton in the winter months. "Time for me to put this ridiculousness behind me and do something new."

Stevie can only wonder at such a notion. Skip, like Gary McCullough, is the rarest breed out here, the thinking man's dope fiend. His last full-time position was as an executive assistant to a vice president at the Urban League—a nice gig until the boss came in after lunch one afternoon and found him drooling on his desk in a twenty-on-the-hype nod. But it's the season of new beginnings, and more than anyone out here, Skip can walk the walk and talk the talk. He'll need a new résumé, he tells Stevie as they go upstairs to fire, but that can wait. Tester first, then the vitae.

Of course, a week or two from now DeAndre's dog will be stolen off the fence, just as Skip will be back down at Westside Shopping Center wearing his am-homeless-please-help cardboard sign, just as Blue will put his brushes and pencils away and go back to hardcore doping. The

Vine Street garages will soon be a littered dumping ground again, just as Rose Davis will take back half the discards in her usual charitable fashion, just as Ella will stare at the rec center floor and wonder when she last scrubbed up the scuff marks and finger paint. And up at Gene's, the police will, eventually, kick down the door at the behest of the neighborhood association, raid one shooting gallery among dozens, and—by some perverse cosmic anomaly—come up absolutely empty. Not a spike. Not a bag. Not a vial. The police will shrug it off and move to new business, though Fayette Street fiends, in their awe and wonder, will rechristen the proprietor as Clean Gene, the man with the only shotless shooting gallery in West Baltimore.

But all of that is in the future. Now, with April ripe, the seasonal themes of rebirth and repair are marked on Fayette Street by one small epiphany after another, each more absurd and useless than the next. And layered atop all of it is the police department's own spring cleaning of the corners from Monroe to Mount, an effort that has no more lasting effect than any of the others. But for now, at least, the Fayette Street crews are chased and herded daily by every roller, knocker, and jumpout squad that the department can spare.

This, too, is at the behest of Myrtle Summers and Joyce Smith, who for the last month or two have made a habit of visiting the Western District and registering their displeasure. As president of the neighborhood group, Joyce made one appointment with the Western's major, and when he failed to post and sent only his community relations sergeant, she made another. And another. Finally, faced with a persistence that any government minion can recognize, the Western commander fully acknowledged the ladies from Fayette Street as the squeaking wheels they were. Lubrication came in the form of the ubiquitous Bob Brown, other uniformed officers, the Western's drug enforcement unit, and even some manpower from the Violent Crimes Task Force downtown.

As June Bey clears the garage, and Ella mops down her rec-center floor, the Baltimore Police Department does similar duty at Fayette and Mount, pushing the drug traffic down to Gilmor or up to Monroe for a time, making it possible for Myrtle, at least, to go from the front door of Echo House to St. Martin's without being proferred a vial or two. After so many police sweeps, it's understood by all concerned that the crews will open shop a block or two away, just as it's understood that the police sweeps must come to an end with the dealers returning to the usual terrain.

Still, it's spring and the Western commanders observe the seasonal rite by putting two additional foot patrolmen at Fayette and Monroe during the day shift, pushing the drugs off Vine and around the block onto Fulton. Bob Brown, Jenerette, and a handful of others take up the slack at the other end of the strip, sweeping the Mount Street corners for easy arrests. The crews migrate down the street and around the block to Baltimore and Gilmor, and the change in territory pushes competing products into proximity with each other, changing the distribution patterns. For years now, territory has been a dead concept in Baltimore's drug markets; anyone with a good product can set up shop, hire local fiends for touts, and share the same real estate as half a dozen other crews. But pressed by the police, the sprawl of the neighborhood drug bazaar is quickly compressed, so that more and more players—touts, slingers, stickup boys, burn artists—are hustling in a smaller space. There is a crossing of the corners' electrical currents: Dealers are more volatile than usual, the fiends, more desperate and nervous.

Violence picks up.

A tout for the Spider Bag crew is shot in the ass on Fulton in an argument over product. A few days later, a stickup boy wounds an older dealer on Baltimore Street. At Fayette and Mount, Eddie Bland, a steady presence on that corner, gets in an argument with a competing slinger and is cut in the head. A New York Boy messes up a package and is bludgeoned with baseball bats in the middle of Monroe Street. Over at Lexington and Fulton, Hungry tries to run his usual game with a ground stash but gets caught halfway down the block by Dred and his boys. They beat the man so badly an ambulance is required for the three-block trip to Bon Secours.

Gary McCullough sees him the following afternoon outside the grocery on Monroe Street, his face torn and scratched, his head wrapped in gauze.

"How you feelin?" Gary asks him.

"Makin' it," Hungry assures him.

Down on Mount, the Western troops do a warrant at the Schofield house, locking up Buster and half a dozen juveniles on drug conspiracy charges. At the other end, on Monroe Street, some plainclothesmen with the Violent Crimes Task Force downtown hit the corner house at Fairmount with another paper, grabbing six or seven more. A week later, some of the uniforms jump out on the Dew Drop Inn, rushing the first floor and coming up empty, missing Little Roy's stash downstairs in the basement.

The police are hard at it for a good two weeks, creating all kinds of disarray and paranoia. Fat Curt is up on the second floor of Blue's one afternoon when he hears a banging on the front door and a shout of panic from the floor below. He knows what's up right away. Knockers. A raid.

"They comin' in?" yells a voice from the back of the house. To Curt, it sounds more like a statement than a question. He hears another loud noise and a shout in the back alley. Blue and Hungry and Rita and everyone else are heading out the rear, probably. Fat Curt is all alone to face the police and take the charge. Got-damn.

He picks himself up out of a broken-backed chair. Maybe it's the coke rushing around in his head, or maybe it's the old thrill of the chase, but either way, Curt feels the adrenaline as if it were just another blast. He forgets that his limbs are bloated and scarred, that he's forty-six and looks to have twenty more years than that. He forgets that it's all pavement out there, that the drop from the second floor window is a good twelve feet. He forgets that the risk isn't at all worth it, that it's only a shooting gallery and the charge wouldn't go beyond possession or paraphernalia or maybe public nuisance. For one irredeemable moment, Fat Curt forgets everything and is transported back twenty years, back to a time when his game was complete, when he could do whatever had to be done. He goes rabbit.

He reaches the window and throws his cane out. Then he climbs up on the sill and jumps, landing sideways on his right ankle. He hears an ugly little pop.

"Ah shit. Got-damn."

It hurts like hell; the pain down there is pounding past the dope, kicking the shit out of the coke. Whatever else he's done, Curt has ruined his high.

"Curt, man, you hurt?"

Hungry and Scalio have come around to the rear yard to assess the damage and commiserate.

"Oh, man," Curt moans, "mah foot. Damn."

The ambo takes him to Bon Secours, where the X-rays tell the tale. Broken ankle.

"What did you do?" an intern asks him.

"Jumped out a window."

"Why?"

Damned if I know, thinks Curt. All that commotion and the police weren't even coming in the door; just one police up on the corner, jacking someone up against the liquor store. It was that good coke that had them all paranoid.

"Why'd you go out a window?" asks the intern.

Curt manages a small smile. "I got rabbit in my blood."

They kill the pain, reset the bone, and bind him up in a plaster cast. The hospital springs for a pair of wooden crutches, knowing full well that this is all money that Bon Secours will never see. Curt has been living beyond the safety net for years now. No welfare check. No Medicaid. No SSI. No state disability grant.

"How long am I wearing this?" Curt asks, looking over the plaster. "I'm sayin' when do I need to come back."

Two months, at least, he's told. The intern warns him to keep the ankle elevated, to stay off his feet as much as possible during the day. "You got to give it a chance to heal."

Curt grunts a vague affirmation, gathers up the crutches, and limps slowly out of the emergency doors, heading back down Fayette toward Monroe Street. Stay off his feet? Two months? Who keeps the calendar in the life of Curtis Davis? What tout ever made money by staying off his feet?

The next night, he's back out there on his corner, hooking up customers left and right, guiding them in like some sleepless air-traffic controller.

"Yo Curt."

"Hey."

"How's the leg?"

"Ankle busted."

"Aw man."

"Yeah, well, I'll deal with it."

Now Curt's more of a physical wreck than ever. He can barely move, his game down to small, exhausting struggles to get from the pay phone to the curb. A walk across Monroe Street to a white boy's car window becomes a forced march; a trip around the corner to visit a Vine Street ground stash is a Russian novel.

The corner gives no quarter to Curt, and none, of course, is ever asked. The shooting gallery regulars sympathize to a point: Fat Curt is a fixture in their lives, a flesh-and-blood touchstone loved in the same peculiar way that Bread was. But there isn't much they can do besides help him up the steps into the needle palace, or spare him a few extra steps toward a stash of vials. Wounded or not, the rule of thumb is the same for cornermen and commandos: You keep up with the mission or you get left behind. And Fat Curt is a soldier.

Still, it's painful to watch, this slow, steady collapse of a street icon. To anyone who has lived off the Fayette Street corners, Curt is one of the few constants, a pole star by which a thousand other fiends can compass their position in life. He was supposed to last forever out here— hell, by corner standards, he has already managed that. But first he was leaning on that cane. And now it's the crutches. To see him out in front of the liquor store—his shoulders hunched down, his yellow eyes bobbing to and fro, his mouth twisted in a grimace of permanent physical struggle—to see him broken down like this is to invite embarrassment, even sadness.

At Fayette and Monroe, there is now that awkward acknowledgment that comes when any aging athlete, his skills gone, his body wrecked, tries against all odds to make it to the end of one last, humiliating season.

"Curt."

"Hey, girlfriend."

"You look tired."

"I am, dear."

"How's the leg."

"Hurts."

Two weeks after his disastrous leap, Curt is out on Monroe Street one night, watching the aftermath of a street shooting. Nothing special, just a bit of gunplay between some Jamaicans and a boy who had run off with some of their product. The boy is down at University, bloodied but stable; the Jakes are gone, melting into the city's warm darkness. That leaves only a few shell casings and some bloodstains near the phone booth between Vine and Lexington. Still, the usual crowd is spread around the perimeter, signifying from behind the yellow police tape, their faces rendered strangely mechanical by the blue strobe lights of the idling radio cars. Two downtown detectives work the scene, then settle back to light smokes, waiting for the crime lab technician to finish taking the photos.

"Jesus Christ," says a Western uniform.

"What?"

"Look at that motherfucker's hands."

"Where?"

"The guy on crutches. Look at them hands."

The uniformed officers begin laughing. The detectives saunter across the street for a better look.

"Hey, pal . . . yeah, you . . . c'mere."

Fat Curt tenses.

"Hey, get this pretty motherfucker's picture," says the uniform, gesturing to the lab tech. "I swear this guy looks like Popeye."

Curt turns slowly, his face contorted in hurt and rage.

"No shit," says a detective. "It's Popeye the Sailor Man."

The cops are all laughing now, talking about Curt's hands and feet. They've never seen anything like it. One of them actually asks the medical miracle to shine a smile for the camera.

"Hey, Mr. Popeye, you must be one spinach-eating sonofabitch," laughs a sergeant. "Goddam if those ain't the fattest mitts I ever seen."

The lab tech slides around to the other side of a radio car and takes aim with the camera.

"Say cheese," she says.

The flash catches Fat Curt as he tries to limp offstage, his mouth muttering obscenities, his eyes low and glazed.

DeAndre spots her at the counter of the Baltimore carryout, and she is looking so special and so fine on a late-April afternoon that he's compelled to step away from the rest of his crew and offer up his very best line, the one that always seems to work.

"Can I buy that for you?"

The girl looks over at DeAndre and catches the mischief in his dark brown eyes, partly obscured by the dreds tumbling down his forehead. He gives up a quick smile, half embarrassed and half bold.

"Say what?"

He gestures at her sandwich, wrapped and waiting on the carryout counter. "Can I pay for that?"

She laughs. DeAndre pulls out his roll.

"Go 'head," she says.

The other boys in the carryout are holding back their laughter, waiting for this girl to take DeAndre's money and then put him in his place. He peels a five off and slides it into the Plexiglas turnstile. She gathers up her lunch and he gathers in the change; they leave together and the smirking stops.

Her name is Tracey and she's nineteen, so much older than DeAndre that as he leaves the carryout, he suffers a sudden lapse in confidence. He has the sneaking suspicion that a girl who looks this good, who fills out her clothes with full-grown curves and carries herself so well around boys has no reason to be playing with his almost-sixteen-year-old self. He's out of his league on this one.

Still, it's spring. You can't lose what you never had, he tells himself; you cannot win if you do not play.

Within days, it's not just sex. It's melodrama.

"I'm sayin' it ain't like with Reeka," DeAndre tells his mother. "Reeka just a girl. She too young an' triflin'. Tracey is all woman."

Fran rolls her eyes.

"I'm serious," says DeAndre. "She's a grown woman."

"And you a man," adds Fran, deadpan.

"Man enough."

"Please."

DeAndre is following this older girl around like a puppy, going to her apartment on Pratt Street, messing with her when she lets him, trying to figure out what else to do with her when she won't. He spends his money on her—and little enough it is since he's been on probation and off the corners.

Cash-and-carry has always been the rule of thumb for the boys along Fayette Street; the girls, in turn, measure sincerity and commitment by the dollar. Yo, yo, got hotel money—that was the battle cry of last summer's radio dance mix in West Baltimore. Now, DeAndre wears the T-shirt of the moment, declaiming that "I can't stand a beggin' ass bitch," to which the feminine fashion retort is, "I can't stand a broke-ass man." On Fayette Street, the children chase each other with leering cynicism, and even for the youngest boys, the pursuit of sex is but another attempt at material acquisition.

With Tracey, however, it's different. Not since their initial encounter has DeAndre's new girlfriend displayed a trace of a mercenary streak. She doesn't seem to rate him on how much he spends on clothes, or clubs, or weed, or movies. She's finishing high school and on her way to Coppin State college, so Tracey is a long step removed from the corner game and unimpressed with DeAndre's gangsta pose. There is nothing available in his world that she covets, no monetary standard by which she makes affection available: On the weekend after they meet, she actually goes out and buys him flowers.

All of which leaves DeAndre dazed and confused. Tracey is an alien presence in his universe; after little more than a week, in fact, he doesn't know what to do with her. Since losing his virginity to an older cousin at the age of eleven, DeAndre has come to regard sex as, at best, an exercise in amiable barter and, at worst, an act of raw prostitution.

With Tracey, though, the sex comes too willingly, without any of the struggle that a boy from Fayette Street understands. For DeAndre, the chase is as much a part of the adventure as the sex itself and, in this case, the girl is setting the pace. But even more confusing are the silences before and after, the fact that he doesn't have anything to say to this older girl who knows so much more than he does. She's getting ready for Coppin, working and making the rent on her own apartment; he's learning fractions and percentages by vialing up cocaine and living in the back bedroom of a shooting gallery. In the end, Tracey unnerves DeAndre by giving him a quick glimpse of the world apart from the corner, a world with which he simply cannot connect. After a few go-rounds at her place, he doesn't call and neither does she. When they come upon each other on Baltimore Street a week or so after the calls stop, they pass without so much as a nod.

And when his mother brings up the new romance a day after that encounter, DeAndre plays it off with a grunt.

"I thought you was in love," says Fran.

"Man, that thing dead," he explains. "Once you get with a girl, it just ain't the same."

Fran looks at him sideways.

"I'm sayin' it just wasn't the way I thought it would be," he continues. "You know there wasn't anything we could talk about. She goin' to college and all."

"So?"

"So, I ain't about that," says DeAndre. "Besides, I got my eye on some other things. R.C.'s girlfriend cousin been trying to holler at me and, Ma, I swear, she phat as I don't know what."

"What about Reeka?" asks Fran.

"What about her?"

"'Dre, that girl is in love."

"Ma, I can't talk to Reeka. She too young."

Fran shakes her head, vaguely disgusted. Day after day, Tyreeka is on her son like white on rice. She's seen them together down on McHenry Street, hanging with the C.M.B. crew; Tyreeka with her arms around

SPRING   255

DeAndre's neck, or sitting in his lap, both of them cutting classes and running the streets together—an act of minor consequence for DeAndre, but a major transgression for Tyreeka. Not to mention all the hours that the young lovers have spent in Fran's cramped bedroom at the Dew Drop, with her son locking the door from the inside and turning the television loud. And now, DeAndre is sitting here, blandly declaring that Tyreeka ain't it, that summer is coming and he has to look elsewhere.

"Well then tell the girl," says Fran.

"What?"

"Tell her you tired of her and let her get on past you."

DeAndre shakes his head.

"Can't do without the sex," says DeAndre, boastful.

Fran looks hard at him.

"What?" asks DeAndre, giggling.

"That's cold as shit," says Fran. "That girl thinks you for her and you just thinking about sex."

DeAndre shrugs it off, complaining that he isn't the only one cheating, that he'd heard that Tyreeka had gone off with Tae and other boys when he was locked up.

"Everyone think Reeka so innocent," he mutters.

There's a part of him that believes this argument and another part of him that doesn't. Tae was a creeper to be sure, and he had thrown everything he had at Tyreeka after DeAndre had so casually granted him permission. The girl swears up and down that she and Tae were just friends, that they just liked to hang together; for his part, Tae isn't saying. DeAndre has no proof, but he doesn't like the way they look and act together. His suspicion is circular: Not trusting himself, he won't trust Tyreeka either, which makes him inclined to further justify his own meandering affections. But the truth is that DeAndre's infidelities have little to do with Tyreeka or anyone else; it is simply a matter of hormones, a kid-in-the-candy-store mentality that is in every way about adolescence.

DeAndre will be sixteen come summer and if he has his way, no single girl will be allowed to lay claim to that. He aims to spend the hot months with Tyreeka on one arm and as many other girls as he can find on the other, figuring that Tyreeka, in her devotion, won't notice or, at worst, will notice but somehow let it slide.

But Tyreeka isn't making it quite so easy. By April, with DeAndre free of his home-monitor and the court-imposed exile on Etting Street, she has already heard the rumblings about Tracey from her girlfriends. DeAndre soon realizes that the grapevine between Tyreeka, Dena, and Treecee, R.C.'s girl—along with a half-dozen others between Fayette and McHenry streets—is sure enough keeping Bell Atlantic in business.

And Tyreeka isn't one to sit at home and pout either; she'll stroll down Baltimore Street unannounced, looking for the C.M.B. crew, talking about how she's just out for this reason or that when in truth she's trying to find and confront her man.

So the summer will be complicated; DeAndre could see that much already. He buries whatever guilt he feels about his wanderng attentions beneath an avalanche of small criticisms: Tyreeka wasn't looking her best for him anymore. She didn't do her hair, she didn't dress right. Yesterday she was out on Fayette Street walking around with her heels pushing down the backs of her shoes, looking like some old housewife on laundry day. And she talks about stupid shit, young-ass stuff that DeAndre can't have anything to do with. Most of all, by the end of April, DeAndre can see that Tyreeka is putting on weight, and not just a few pounds either. DeAndre finally has to ask the girl what's up, but Tyreeka just shrugs it off.

"You pregnant?" DeAndre asks her.

"No," she tells him.

"Cause if you is, I know it ain't mine."

He tells her that to see if she'll argue, to try to get her to admit she'd been with Tae or Dewayne or one of the others. But Tyreeka just glares at him, then tells him flat out that she isn't pregnant, but that if she was, there couldn't be but one father.

One early May morning, they are lying in Fran's room, DeAndre with one hand on her stomach, feeling the roundness.

"Reeka, you sure you ain't pregnant?"

"I just need to diet is all."

He doesn't ask about her period, about how many months late she is or whether she feels any sickness or any other sign. For all his worldly experience, DeAndre's sexual education is lacking when it comes to the female side of the equation. He knows of no connection between menstruation and pregnancy, nor is he particularly knowledgeable about the finer points of female sexual response. He knows what he likes and to some extent, he knows how to get what he likes; if God is in the details, then DeAndre's view of the sexual world is decidedly agnostic. Tyreeka ends the brief discussion by simply saying that her aunt is going to get her a clinic appointment. DeAndre takes her at her word and feels free to pursue whatever new business he can find.

At bottom, there is no great fear in either child's heart of an unwanted pregnancy, for the basic reason that a baby is in no way unwanted. Fran had given her son condoms on several occasions and had routinely left extras on the bedroom dresser. But DeAndre doesn't like sex in a rain-coat, nor does he particularly believe in any of the consequences. Half the neighborhood had the Bug, yet DeAndre can't help but associate the disease with the needle since virtually all of the people falling out and dying were long-time shooters. As for baby-making—that would be almost welcomed as the final proof of manhood. A fatalistic streak in DeAndre and the rest of his crew holds that they'll soon enough be dead or in prison. Against that notion, the production of a child, a male child in particular, would guarantee some tangible evidence of a brief existence.

So DeAndre left the condoms on the dresser, and Tyreeka, too, does nothing to avoid parenthood. The idea of having her own baby, of caring for a being that would love and depend on her without equivocation, is appealing enough. That she is still thirteen, that she has nothing but a child's love to provide any new life—these things are put aside by the self-meaning that procreation surely promises. Tyreeka, too, is looking for some kind of validation.

And DeAndre knows Tyreeka thinks this way. He can sense how needy she is, how she wants to believe that if she gets pregnant, he'll stay with her—that the child will bring them closer together and keep his eyes off the other girls. If that's what she believes, so be it; he'll deal with those expectations down the road. But for now, he's determined to have his fun with Tyreeka and other girls as well.

All through April, Tyreeka gets the bad news about DeAndre from her girlfriends, and all that month, she responds by seeking the boy out and time and again venting her anger and hostility, going out of her way to demonstrate just how betrayed she feels. But to DeAndre, this is only confirmation that the girl is taken with him, that she'll be there whenever he gets done messing with the rest.

Tyreeka knows that holding on to DeAndre will be difficult. If she's honest with herself, she'll have to regard as unlikely the possibility of a long-term relationship with any man; her world experience doesn't include more than one or two situations in which a child is being raised by two parents. But she loves DeAndre the way any girl loves a boy for the first time, and as it is with such things, her feelings could provoke the most absurd kind of optimism. A baby will straighten him out, she tells herself, maybe make him find a job and bring home some straight-world money. They could get an apartment and live together; DeAndre going to work and Reeka staying in school. Not right away maybe, but soon enough.

These are inner thoughts, of course. Outwardly, Tyreeka continues to deny the possibility of pregnancy to everyone who asks. As for the clinic appointment, Tyreeka changes the date regularly, advancing it from one week to the next, explaining that her aunt can't take off from work, or that the clinic is closed, or that she needed to be in school on the day of the appointment.

"When Reeka goin' to the clinic?" Fran asks at one point.

"Ma," says DeAndre. "I don't know what that girl has in her mind. She half-crazy and shit."

Meanwhile, DeAndre is now haunting the lower strip along Pratt and McHenry Streets almost every night as the weather warms. He's chasing after Treecee's cousin, as well as another girl he met at a house party over on Pulaski Street. And then, when he finds the time, he's back up on Fayette with Tyreeka.

She hears about some of it from Treecee and the other neighborhood girls, but DeAndre only gets mad and denies everything when confronted.

For a time, she tries to strike back by flirting with the other boys in DeAndre's crew. It's Tae, mostly, though she also lets Dewayne know he can holler at her. On one occasion, when Ella's basketball team takes a trip across town to a tournament at the Flag House projects, Tyreeka engineers it so that she rides not with DeAndre in Ella's Oldsmobile, but on Dewayne's lap in the backseat of Marzell Myers' car. By the time they reach the east side, she has her head nestled on his shoulder and her arms around his neck.

She likes both Dewayne and Tae, but more than that, she wants a little of her goings-on to get back to DeAndre, to let him think on the fact that you reap what you sow. But even this doesn't work the way it should. Soon after her flirtation in the car with Dewayne, DeAndre tells the rest of the Crenshaw Mafia Brothers that regardless of how many other girls he chases, Tyreeka is once and forever his property, that she is proscribed to them under pain of a full-blooded beat-down. Tae shrugs indifferently and moves on to other neighborhood girls, mostly because he'd rather preserve the friendship with DeAndre. And Dewayne, though obviously interested, is frightened away, much to Tyreeka's contempt.

"I don't know what it is," she tells Treecee glumly after her flirtations come to little. "Them boys is afraid of Andre. None of 'em got too much heart."

But facts are facts. Only Dinky—DeAndre's cousin and closest companion—hits as hard or fights as savagely as DeAndre. And though by summer, Dinky will go so far as to walk Tyreeka home a couple nights, he'll eventually talk himself out of things, telling her it wouldn't be right messing with his cousin's girlfriend.

Last summer was the best of her life. Last summer all the boys wanted her, fought for her. All she wants now is to get back to those first weeks when DeAndre was all about her, when he would take her places and talk to her and say things to make her feel special. Now, even when they are together, he time and again proves himself incapable of full-grown love. All he offers her is his basic presence, his casual lust, and odd moments of random cruelty.

Once, before the juvenile master ended DeAndre's home detention, Tyreeka found herself with DeAndre and R.C. riding in a hack up to Etting Street. DeAndre wanted her to spend the night, then go home the next morning before school. And Tyreeka was willing enough until the hack crossed the expressway on Gilmor Street and stopped at Mulberry, where R.C. spotted an older girl trussed tightly in a halter and shorts, grinding her well-contoured self down the sidewalk.

"AW, THERE IT IS," shouted R.C., leaning out the front passenger window. "GOT-DAMN, GIRL!"

And DeAndre didn't hesitate before taking up the braying.

"Yo, girl, where you goin' at? Hey . . . where you headin' with all dat. I know you know I need a number from you."

"Gracious," growled R.C. as the hack rolled on.

"She made me say, 'Ooooooouuccchhh,'" moaned DeAndre.

"Fuck you both," said Tyreeka bitterly, her eyes tearing as she pulled herself to the far edge of the rear seat. "You all common as shit."

DeAndre laughed.

"You make me sick," she wailed, punching him hard in the shoulder.

"I can't help it if the girl looked phat."

"You don't have to say something."

"You don't have to hear it."

"Fuck you, Andre."

When they got to Etting Street, DeAndre slid from the rear seat, waiting with the open door in hand for just half a moment.

"You comin'?" he mumbled.

"Fuck you, DeAndre," rasped Tyreeka, arms crossed and eyes streaked.

"Suit yourself," he said, shutting the car door.

She knows she can no longer press him for money or clothes or movies, the way she did when they first started going together. She knows that DeAndre is off the corner now; she wants him to see she won't be greedy like the other girls, that she can stay loyal to him even after the money runs out. She makes no demands whatsoever, save for Andre's attentions.

But DeAndre's eye continues to wander.

"I asked Andre why he don't just break up with you," Dena tells her at one point, after DeAndre takes up with a McHenry Street girl named Shanelle. "He just say you young and he don't want to hurt your feelings."

"My feelings been hurt," Tyreeka says. "DeAndre don't care about no one's feelings but his own."

At least she doesn't hear his boasting oratory, when he declares her nothing more than a handy sex object. Nor does she pick up news about the girls unknown to Dena and Treecee, or about the C.M.B. boys now and then pooling a few dollars for one of the crack-saturated whores down on Addison Street. Five dollar blow jobs or free for a vial, though any man with more than a passing knowledge of the viral universe wouldn't dare venture to Addison Street equipped with the penis of his worst enemy.

"You can't get AIDS from a blow job," DeAndre assures his mates after one such sortie. "And even if you can, ain't nobody likes sucking on rubber."

"How would you know, bitch?"

"Fuck you, R.C."

The worst manages to elude Tyreeka. But by May, she knows enough. If she doesn't know every detail and can't prove every allegation, she knows that at thirteen years of age, she is as alone as she ever was.

And, she knows, she is pregnant.

For two months now, she has been lying to DeAndre. In March, she missed her period. In April, again. And the clinic appointment—the one that she kept putting off in all her conversations with DeAndre—that had come and gone. The doctors had told her and her aunt everything that Tyreeka already knew.

But save for her aunt, she trusts no one with the truth. Certainly not DeAndre, who has proven so unworthy of trust. She worries that he'll force her to go to University for an abortion, or that he might tell others who would force her to go. She worries, too, about what her father might say when he finds out. She even worries about Miss Fran, thinking that DeAndre's mother might try to take the child away. And above all, Tyreeka wants this baby.

Once, in late May, she comes close to telling DeAndre.

"I might be pregnant," she admits as they watch television in the back of the Dew Drop one night.

"Huh," says Andre.

"I don't think I am though."

And DeAndre simply takes her word for it, telling his mother that Tyreeka is probably just talking about the possibility to keep him obligated. Then, for appearance's sake, he declares that if it is true, he'll buy into a package and go out on a corner and raise the money necessary for an abortion, that he has no intention of being tied down by Tyreeka or any other girl.

Fran can't stand his attitude. True, she'd made no pretense of trying to keep DeAndre from doing the dirty, and in practice, there aren't many mothers living amid the easy temptations of Fayette Street who have figured out how to prevent such a thing. But Fran did at least raise her son to show more caring than he is managing for Tyreeka Freamon. Hearing her son talking like a dog, she first tries to work on DeAndre's conscience, urging him to either commit himself to Tyreeka or let her go. When that proves futile, she goes out of her way to befriend Tyreeka, to play a maternal role with this child who is alone and raising herself.

Tyreeka responds immediately, confiding her love and fealty to DeAndre, complaining that her loyalty is being repaid with growing distance and a spate of hurtful insults. Fran listens sympathetically, then tells the girl that chasing DeAndre will only make him more bold.

"You not gonna keep him with a baby," Fran warns.

"I know," says Tyreeka, tearful, but Fran can see that she doesn't know, that she believes it's in her power to bend a fifteen-year-old corner boy to the role of husband and father.

"I'm sayin' Andre is gonna do what he gonna do."

"I know."

"Reeka," Fran asks finally. "Is you pregnant?"

Tyreeka shakes her head, still trying to front, still worried that someone will get between her and her child. "Don't think so," she says finally.

"When you last have your period?"

"Um, last month . . . no, February."

Fran shakes her head sadly but holds her tongue, asking only whether the girl is going to go to the clinic.

"My aunt gonna take me," Tyreeka lies. "I got a clinic appointment next Wednesday."

"Well," says Fran quietly. "You gonna know then."

It isn't about the welfare check. It never was.

It isn't about sexual permissiveness, or personal morality, or failures in parenting, or lack of family planning. All of these are inherent in the disaster, but the purposefulness with which babies make babies in places · like West Baltimore goes far beyond accident and chance, circumstance and misunderstanding. It's about more than the sexual drives of adolescents, too, though that might be hard to believe in a country where sex alone is enough of an argument to make anyone do just about anything.

In Baltimore, a city with one of the highest teen pregnancy rates in the nation, the epidemic is, at its root, about human expectation, or more precisely, the absence of expectation. On Fayette Street, the babies are born simply because they can be born, because life in this place cannot and will not be lived in the future tense. Given that fact, there is no reason to wait. The babies speak to these child-mothers and child-fathers, justify them, touch their hearts in a way that nothing else in their lives ever will. The government, the schools, the social workers, the public-service announcements wedged in between every black-family-in-the-burbs sitcom—all wail out the same righteous warning: Wait, don't make the mistake, don't squander every opportunity in life by having a child too young. But the children of Fayette Street look around them and wonder where an opportunity might actually be found. The platitude is precisely that, and no one is fooled.

From the moment that the children down here have any awareness at all, they are shaped by a process that demands that they shed all hope, that they cast off all but street-level ambition, learning to think and feel and breathe in ways that allow only for day-to-day survival. These children are not entirely unloved, or entirely unattended—even most of those growing up in the worst rowhouse hovels manage to reach adolescence in one piece, clothed and physically healthy. Fathering might be a lost concept, but on a rudimentary level, most of the mothers still manage some nurturing even in shooting galleries and crack dens. The love is there, but it makes itself felt only at odd moments, as an afterthought to the greater game of the corner.

True parenthood is more than love or intent or a set of learned skills; it's all of that—practiced relentlessly. On Fayette Street, the men and women of the corner know what to do and sometimes, when the blast is there, they actually do it. But the game itself is relentless; when the blast is late, there's no time for love's expression.

Constancy becomes a luxury, so that a regular player at Fayette and Mount can love his son with the intensity of any father, yet when confronted by a choice between a tester line and a trip to the Bon Secours E.R. with a hurt child—well, there is no choice. Both his son's arms are fractured from a bicycle fall, but Daddy ain't trying to hear about medical emergencies. Damn if he ain't a medical emergency all to himself. So the scene is that of a grown man backpedaling from his son toward the touts, mumbling a last-minute suggestion that some ointment might do the trick.

Day after day, the small promises that knit families together are frayed and unraveled: meals that aren't prepared; weekend trips that never manage to find the right weekend; school clothes that aren't there in time for September. Ultimately, the quiet moments that a parent and child ought always to have, the confidences and affection shared around a breakfast table, or at a bedside, or out on the rowhouse steps—these, too, become casualties of the corner. In time, it becomes clear to the children of Fayette Street that their look, their smile, even their unqualified love will never be enough to bring them what they need. Their cues go unnoticed by men and women obsessed.

So expectations change; tactics, too. The children learn that if they want to get fed, they better nag or whine: Ma, I'm hungry. Can I hold a piece of that there? Can I? Ma? In time, the begging becomes confrontational, demanding: I'm telling you. I can't go to school 'cause I ain't gonna wear these rags no more. Ma, you said you was gonna take me shopping at Westside. When you gonna take me shopping like you was sayin'?

The most important relationship in their lives is disappointing them, failing them, redefining them as less than they ought to be. This is the lesson that most carry from childhood: Even the most intimate relationship is essentially a construct of struggle and barter. Love is something to be spoken of, but rarely demonstrated.

Yet for the corner world, the lesson makes absolute sense. Children grow up in the Fayette Street rowhouses learning the manner by which human beings get and take what they need from one another. By adolescence, they understand that no one survives by carrying long-term expectations into any relationship, by giving of themselves, by risking anything valuable for the sake of that relationship. They watch their mothers scratch and claw their way through a string of failing, semi-hostile couplings—each running its predictable course, each fueled by genuine need and desire, yet built from such thin emotional material that it is less an act of human commitment than an exercise in planned obsolescence. They see their fathers—if, indeed, they see their fathers—hovering at the fringes, drifting in and out of the family as bit players, unable to provide and unwilling to commit. More likely than not, the men are on another path, caught up in new girlfriends, new addresses, new ambitions—all of it as fleeting and temporal as what came before.

With such grounding, the children venture into the streets, clumping into grade-school packs—boys with boys, girls with girls—and their play becomes savage as they crimp each other, honing the skills essential to the neighborhood. Their size, their shape, the quirks of their personalities—as with children anywhere, these things give them their early status, their reputation in the clique. But on Fayette Street, status exists only as it relates to the corner: This one can punch hardest, that one can shout loudest. This one can scheme and creep, that one is crazy and capable of anything. They each make their first pass at the game, and after an ugly failure or two, even the weakest manages to find a niche because that's the timeless truth of the corner: It's there for all of them, waiting and ready.

When the blood begins to warm, their status in the game is all that will matter, and what works on the corner will work with the girls. Sexual tribute will be paid to the hardest, the most daring, the craziest—but primarily to the teenaged slinger who at that moment carries the manicured bankroll.

For the corner boys and corner girls both, money becomes the centerpiece of a mating dance as ritualized as anything the middle-class mind might conjure. It begins with teenaged banter within the pack, with fourteen- and fifteen-year-old boys matching their wit and words with girls a year or two younger. The banter becomes flirtatious, and the flirtation ultimately produces the first, small transaction.

"Buy you a soda?"

If she's willing, it won't end with an Orange Slice. In the Victorian ideal, such conventions as love, fidelity, and personal commitment are the price to be paid, but those conventions can't and don't exist on Fayette Street. Instead, every embrace, every grope, every tryst is preceded and secured by a material exchange. For the girls, the process isn't remotely connected to prostitution. It is, instead, about validation, about being able to have your personal worth displayed and proven with measurable evidence. It makes no difference that a young girl from Fayette and Fulton might genuinely like a boy who hangs at Baltimore and Gilmor. The geography of such a courtship demands that both play out their roles, that the boy give up some bills for his girl's movie tickets and cheesesteaks and Nikes and jewelry, just as it demands that that girl part with her affections, measure for measure. Anything less from either party would constitute profound disrespect, so that in the eyes of the entire pack, the boy might easily be savaged as small-time and off-brand and the girl, if she tolerated such and still gave herself, might simply be branded a freak.

So the ritual brings the children of Fayette Street together, but they arrive burdened with the common awareness that nothing that passes between them can possibly last. They couple with little expectation that the relationship will succeed—if, indeed, any sexual relationship between fifteen- and fourteen-year-olds ever could—because no relationship they've ever known has ever succeeded. They find each other, copulate, and disengage; then they deconstruct the personal connections and move on. Anything beyond that would require real personal risk, a giving of the self that has nothing to do with the original terms of the transaction and can be justified only by a belief in tomorrow. To reveal one's self to another is to lay bare weaknesses and vulnerabilites, and to do so on Fayette Street is to violate the rules of the corner.

For their parents—or, more likely, for their parents' parents—legitimate birth and the nuclear family was at least a goal toward which you could strive. By contrast, this generation and much of the one before it have discarded even the pretense of that structure; whatever guilt haunted their fathers and grandfathers no longer nags at these young minds. On Fayette Street, the children have simply discarded the entire premise.

Shorn of all deeper meanings, what remains for this generation are the essentials: sex and babies. And because sex and babies, rather than fidelity and commitment, are the known terminus of any relationship, maturity has become utterly irrelevant. If validation requires only sexual capacity, then the mothers-to-be waiting on the plastic chairs at the obstetrics clinics at University Hospital and Johns Hopkins can be sixteen. Or fourteen. Or twelve.

Accident is not at all the word for it.

Most of these babies are very much wanted by the mothers and fathers alike. What better legacy for a sixteen-year-old slinger who expects to be dead or in prison by age twenty? What greater personal justification for a teenaged girl thirsting for the unequivocal love of another being? To outsiders, the babies are mistakes to be calculated in terms of social cost, as ward-of-the-state harbingers of yet another generation destined to spin through the cycle of poverty. But to the children suckled on the nihilism of the corner, such an outcome isn't the sum of all fears. Poverty and failure is what they know; it's what they accept for themselves every day and, by extension, what they accept for their children as well. For the child-fathers, the future is guns and vials and broken pavement; for the child-mothers, it is life as a twenty-two-year-old welfare mother, barefoot on the rowhouse steps, with the toddlers stumbling around her. And what, other than six years, is the substantive difference between a sixteen-year-old and a twenty-two-year-old welfare mother?

That the government pays something is helpful, of course. But the truth is that the government pays the mothers of Fayette Street only $234 a month and maybe $40 more for each new addition. Add food stamps and free formula from the WIC program and it's enough to put Gerbers and Pampers in the grocery bag, but hardly enough to justify all the birthing. At this level, the conservative impulse to snatch at the purse seems beside the point: It's not the lure of check-day that provokes these children to make children; something stronger than a couple hundred dollars is at issue, something that goes to the heart of the matter. Check or no check, the babies will come.

That we, as outsiders, know better is hardly the point. That we see lives stunted and consigned to poverty doesn't matter because in the minds of these children, their lives were already consigned there. That we know the young fathers will give up and wander off means little, because on some level, the girls themselves know this too. They know from the get-go that the relationship is emotionally finite and they quickly reap what they can in status, gratification, and babies, then let the boys wander. On Fayette Street, it's never about relationships, or boyfriends, or marriage, or living happily ever after.

Down here, a child is answer enough.

Once again, we know only what it is that works in our world, and so we talk welfare reform, devising middle-class solutions for a middle-class society. But, as they have with drugs and the drug trade itself, the men and women of the corner have judged our moral code useless under the circumstances. And they are right. As every fiend on Fayette Street knows that his place is at the point of a needle, so, too, does every teenager find some meaning in the obstetrics ward at University or the birthing rooms at Sinai. There, a girl acquires some womanhood; she is, for one dependent soul at least, the center of the universe. The father, a morbid and fatalistic boy, gives the infant his name and measures his doomed self to be one shade less mortal. If it didn't do this much for them—if it was just about condoms, or abortion-on-demand, or abstinence and shame—then there might be a social strategy with some chance of success. Instead, these children have concluded that bringing about life—any life whatsoever—is a legitimate, plausible ambition in a world where plausible ambitions are hard to come by. This they can do.

To ask more from life on Fayette Street, to expect more from boyfriends, or wives, or parents—even to believe in more for one's child—is to struggle against absurd odds, to ignore the living example of nearly everyone who came before you and who surrounds you now. Worse than that, to want more is to step beyond your own awareness—and that of everyone else on the pavement as well—about what's possible. To do anything more than dream is to invite a crushing emotional defeat.

On Fayette Street, to struggle against the weight of circumstance—to try, in any sense—is not regarded as an act of strength. It is, instead, a public demonstration of vulnerability. Caring, expecting, hoping—these things bring only pain and contempt. Some carry that weight from one blast to the next, wrapping the pain around a syringe, transforming it from a thinking, emotional beast into something purely physical. For the fiends, the blast is the psychic safety net, the daily willingness to part with hope, ambition, and love. And for the yonger ones, for those not yet on the needle or the pipe, expectation is readily sacrificed for the leavings of the here and now; girls, props, weed, new Jordans, crew clothes, a little pocket money. Only for a rare few along Fayette Street— the churchgoers and the do-gooders, the home owners, the addicts who survived to reach recovery—does the hard business of living in the future go on. Is it the wise ones or the fools who shut down, who learn to avoid the uncommon thought, to break faith with possibility itself and take pleasure where they can?

Save for that rare handful, the children of Fayette Street employ their sexuality in a stripped-down facsimile of life. The boys limit themselves to the ambition of making it through the day without getting locked up, or stuck up, or shot down. They hope to be around long enough to see a son born, or maybe a daughter. Maybe scrape together the roll for a bassinet or a high chair, or failing that, a bag of Pampers once a week. The girls break it down to the singular, forlorn hope that the father-to-be will go to the clinic, maybe even show up at the hospital for the birth and then keep coming around for a while afterward. Maybe he'll cover the cost of a crib or a stroller. And when the inevitable occurs, when he's moved on to some new girl, the best that can be expected is some kind of vague alliance, some small connection to the life he created.

If things work out, he'll show up once in a while to drag his son to the movies or down to Carroll Park for an afternoon. He'll drift at the fringes, putting a $5 or a $10 bill into the kitty, just as she'll feel the same cool allegiance now and then when he comes up short. They'll manage that much, and because they're from Fayette Street, they'll count themselves lucky, knowing on some level that they have no right to ask more.

The end result of these adolescent pairings may seem predictable enough, but there is still something remarkable in the degree to which the participants embrace their roles. Knowing on one level that the relationship itself has no future, boys and girls along Fayette Street nonetheless take every opportunity to play at something greater, pretending to ideals and responsibilities that will ultimately be discarded. Catch up with any fifteen-year-old girl who is four months into a pregnancy, and you're likely to hear about how the baby won't change anything, how she plans to be a good and loving mother, how she still plans to finish high school and maybe go to college. Catch up to the sixteen-year-old father and you're likely to hear that it's time for him to grow up, to get a straight job somewhere and be a provider for his child. On one level, the boys and girls know how hollow these intentions are. They are painfully aware of how little is possible for them and their baby, but something deeper—some trace of an external standard, perhaps—still requires them to pretend.

In the weakest couplings, there is no time to play house. But in any relationship longer than a month or two, there can be seen all the requisite stages of serial monogamy, delivered in the most rapid-fire sequence imaginable. Infatuation, intimacy, a period of shared commitment and then disillusion and withdrawal—such is the stuff of months, years, even lifetimes in places other than West Baltimore. On Fayette Street, though, all of the relationships are subject to unrelenting pressure and all are expected to fail momentarily. As a result, the boys and girls have learned to couple and procreate, betray each other and depart with remarkable haste. They squeeze what validation, what drama they can from the coupling. But when the child is born, it proves to be an uneven exchange.

A corner boy hovers for a moment or two, then passes out Phillie blunts to his friends and declares his offspring right and fine. Then he goes back to the corner.

But the girl—she'll be home in bed, the baby beside her, and she'll take that phone call from a girlfriend, the one who says he was down there not half an hour ago and went off with some new girl from around the way. She'll play it off, saying that he can do what he wants, that they haven't been together for weeks now. Then she'll get off the phone, go back to bed, and feel the sting.

Next time, she tells herself, she won't be so weak and stupid. Next time, it's going to cost more than some Harbor Park movie tickets and a trip to Mondawmin. More than some diapers and an off-brand stroller that lost a wheel after a week or two. Next time, she'll keep her feelings out of it and just play him the way he's playing her. It's a small comfort that does nothing to take her any distance from the crying baby, the room, the rowhouse, the neighborhood. She lies there on the worn mattress of her childhood bed, loving her child but half-wishing for a moment that it had never happened or, maybe, that it had happened with some other boy.

For the girls—but never for the boys—life actually changes when the child arrives. They learn some, they grow some. Most will go back to the corners, leaving the infant to be raised by grandmothers and great-grandmothers. But some will come to understand that it's not about a newborn's unequivocal love, but about a mother offering the same night and day, day and night.

For those girls, this is the moment of reckoning: The boy is gone. The child is here. And finally, with the end of childhood and all the work and worry in the world staring her hard in the face, it might seem possible for a fifteen- or sixteen-year-old parent to see the bargain for what it is, straight, without fantasy or pretense. It might seem the perfect moment to wish for other outcomes, other choices.

But no, this is happening on Fayette Street.

The young mother lies in her bed, her baby asleep at her side, her hopes and fears proscribed by the world she knows, her future limited to questions about where the next bag of disposable diapers will be coming from.

This, for her, is as good as it gets.

FIVE

Fran Boyd is out on her usual perch, chin in hands, her face rough and her body slack from another night in the basement. It's still early in the morning, way before the tester lines, and Fran is surprised to see Mike Ellerbee rolling past.

"Hey, stranger," she calls out.

Mike looks up and smiles, changing direction to cross Mount on the diagonal.

"Hey, Fran."

"Hey yo'self. Why you out early?"

Mike steps to the front of Dew Drop and smiles again. "Jus' breakfast and all. Got to get downtown today."

"Downtown? For what?"

"See the judge about my case."

Fran nods. Court explains why most everyone she knows ever rises before midmorning. "You got court today? For what?"

Mike shakes his head and sits next to her. "Got my appointment to talk with Judge Johnson about my probation. You know, getting my probation changed so I can leave out."

Fran remembers. Little Mike thinks he gonna sail away.

"You still going to sea?" she asks with a half-smirk.

But Mike doesn't catch her tone; he nods with absolute confidence, and tells her about the ship that Ricky Sanford will soon have for him. Got his union papers in, got his physical, got things settled with Ducey, his girl.

"Got my Z-card last week."

"What?"

Mike can't help his pride. He stands up and reaches into the back pocket of his denims, pulling out a laminated Coast Guard identification. Fran takes it and falls silent for a moment.

"All I need is for the judge to let me be unsupervised."

Fran hands back the card, more impressed than a moment before. Still, she can't imagine unsupervised probation for a corner soldier convicted of nearly killing someone.

"You think he gonna let you go?"

"Got to," says Mike, sitting down again and looking up toward Bruce Street, where the first few fiends are settling on the corners. "I need to get up from here."

"Me too," says Fran, rubbing her eyes.

"I'm serious," says Mike. "I can't be down here. There ain't a damn thing left for me here but jail or worse."

Fran grunts affirmation.

"Ducey say she gonna stop gettin' high. But she might say so 'cause she don't want me to go."

"How long they keep you on the boat?"

"Four months," he says, getting up from the stoop. "Five months. Sometimes for more than that. I don't care how long so long as I'm gone from here."

Fran hears him and thinks it a little ridiculous, as if getting out was just something you decide to do when you've had enough of Fayette Street. She has known Mike Ellerbee for years, watched him work the corners, counted him as no different than anyone else in the game. And now, quietly, the man is acting as if he's actually found the exit.

It can't be that simple; Fran knows this world well enough to see that Mike is asking too much. His suspended sentence for shooting a stickup boy was lucky enough—though Judge Kenneth Johnson was noted for leaving ten or fifteen years hanging over a defendant, then waiting for the inevitable violation of probation and banging the man with every last year. But to ask for unsupervised probation on top of that goes too far.

Besides, Mike is the same as her—he likes the coke and the corners and the party. He hasn't done much right to deserve any second chances. But if he can talk this way, then maybe she's entitled to the same kind of words. Either that, or she has to let the other side of her have the last say and come down on Little Mike Ellerbee for talking bullshit, pretending to a plan, thinking that he's better than the rest, that he can make a move that no one ever makes. But shit on that, she tells herself; if Mike says he's making the move, give him room.

"Well good luck with it," Fran says. "What you gonna tell the judge?" Mike shrugs. "Tell him I got a job, you know. Tell him to let me go."

Fran looks up the street. The corner is coming to life.

"Yeah," says Mike, smiling. "Well, I'll holler at ya."

He gets up and walks down to Gilmor Street, leaving Fran feeling strangely optimistic. It's time, she tells herself, trying to believe. It's been time for a long time. And if I don't drag my ass away from here, nobody's gonna do it for me. If I wait for anyone else to put a stop to this nonsense, I'll be on these steps forever. Her whole family is lost in this shit. Most all of her friends. Neighbors. Gary, too. Only Mike seems to be trying to make any kind of move. Mike and DeAndre.

Whether it's because he's intimidated by his juvenile probation or because he's genuinely tired of the corners, DeAndre is preparing for summer as if he has a plan of his own. Before his court hearing, he went to Ella asking for a job or help in finding one. Ella couldn't afford to hire him at the rec center, but she had a sister who ran some hospice houses around the city. The sister had a man doing maintenance for her and the man was looking for some help. It sounded like a start and DeAndre took the number, hooking up with the man and working a day or two, getting paid with a $40 check, which he traded to his uncle Scoogie, for cash. But the job wasn't steady work, and to make matters worse, the check bounced on his uncle, so that Ella had to work back through her sister to get DeAndre paid right.

Normally, this would have been enough of a setback to send DeAndre back to the corners, but to Fran's surprise, he kept on with his hunt, asking Gary's younger brother Ricardo if there was work down at Seapride. The crabhouse at Pratt and Monroe Streets had over the years given work to three or four of the McCullough men and Cardy had been sorting Chesapeake Bay blue shells there for years. Cardy went to bat for his nephew and DeAndre got hired a week later, just as the crab season was beginning to pick up.

Fran saw him leave the house for work three days in a row, carrying an extra pair of sweats and the thick crabbing gloves, stoic in his newfound role of working man. Having celebrated his sixteenth birthday the week before, he had finally straightened out, she told herself. And it wasn't just the search for honest work that impressed Fran; the end of the school year is only a month away, but DeAndre is still making a class or two at Francis Woods, trying to convince Rose Davis not to drop him from the ninth grade, maybe even give him some credit for work-study if he could hold on to the Seapride job.

A week ago, Fran made sure to walk down to Pratt Street on a lark, a proud mother, hoping for a glimpse of her son in his latest incarnation. Maybe that and a half-dozen crabs.

What she got instead appalled her. Walking up to the carryout counter, Fran's eyes met those of her wearied son, who was drenched in sweat from the steam of the crab pots, nauseous from the fumes, and generally fixing to die right there amid the hardshell crawlers.

"'Dre," she shouted. "C'mere."

DeAndre ignored her, pushing an empty pot through the steam, heading for the sorting room. But Fran kept at him until he finally came to the counter, where she could look him over and see just how bad it was.

"What the hell is wrong with you, boy?" she said. "You sick as a dog."

DeAndre shrugged. "Gotta work."

"You crazy. You ain't gotta make yourself sick."

"It's a job."

A woman yelled at him from the register, saying she needed more number twos, and DeAndre turned away, half stumbling back toward the sorters. His face and hands were bloated, his breath came in long wheezes. And the sweats—bad for anyone working in the hundred-degree heat of the steamers—were worse for a boy made sick by the very smell.

His allergy. Fran hadn't given much thought to it when he took the job, figuring that as long as he didn't swallow any seafood it wouldn't matter. But just breathing the crab smell was breaking him down. The crabhouse wasn't for DeAndre. Fran told him so that night, though he went back to work the next day, unwilling to give it up.

Only when the crabhouse manager ordered him to clean the crab pots did he finally balk. The pots gave off a thick iodine smell when you hosed them; you were breathing in the worst of the fumes. DeAndre told Miss Mary about his seafood allergy; how he would bloat up if he swallowed even a morsel of crab, how he could barely breathe from the smell. Mary told him to sweep the floor instead, and DeAndre, looking down at the water and spice and crab mess on the floor, took this as some kind of punishment, as make-work for having complained about the pots. Why him? Why not one of the other workers?

He asked Miss Mary those questions and the next day, he wasn't scheduled to work. Nor was he scheduled the day after. By the weekend, he learned from his uncle Cardy that he no longer had his job.

And yet he wasn't giving up, telling Fran that he had a line on something at the McDonald's over on the east side, the one up at North Avenue and Harford Road. The manager there was saying he needed to bring a birth certificate and social security card. He needed them by next Monday.

DeAndre is trying. And Little Mike is trying. And Fran is still out here on the steps, looking for the usual thing. She would get high today. And tomorrow. And the next day, too, though she couldn't help but feel guilty about it if people around her insisted on making a move. They were ruining her high.

So it is that two days later, Fran Boyd goes out of the Dew Drop on a late morning, runs a game on Buster to get right, and then feels good enough to walk down to Poppleton Street and stand under a canvas canopy, staring up at the reconditioned frontage of an old city school building. From a distance, the Baltimore Recovery Center looked like a small apartment house, but the double glass doors are government-issue, and the small lobby, with its lone metal desk perched precariously on a narrow landing between two stairwells, dispels any notion of hospitality. This is a way station for people's lives, nothing more or less.

"Can I speak to Antoinette?"

"Do you have an appointment?" asks the young man on the desk.

"I need to speak with her," says Fran.

Antoinette is little more than a name to Fran; a friend of a friend who is now one of the intake people at the center. The man picks up the phone and punches a few numbers, then waits for a moment or two before speaking softly into the receiver, turning to the side to shield his conversation. After a time, he turns, holding the mouthpiece and raising an eyebrow.

"Your name?"

"Fran."

"Fran . . . ?"

"Boyd. Denise Francine Boyd."

He hangs up and points to the only other seat in the lobby, a bench wedged against the opposite wall.

"She's with somebody now," the young man tells Fran. "She says she'll come down but you'll have to wait."

Now it's all about waiting. Five minutes in the lobby for Antoinette to come down the stairs and look at the desk man. A moment or two more for the desk man to point her to Fran, a minute or two for Fran to tell her story in a couple of sentences, and then a few more minutes for Antoinette to explain the process and the waiting list and the scarcity of state-funded beds.

". . . usually about six or eight weeks for one of the state beds to come open . . ."

Fran takes this in with some irritation. She's being played like a charity case. If she had any medical insurance beyond state assistance, BRC would probably take her today. The insurance carriers are paying up to ten thousand dollars for twenty-eight-day residential rehab. The state-funded slots, however, are few and far between.

Still, this is Fran Boyd's plan—linear and fixed in the same way that every dope fiend's plan ever is. I'll do A and B and then get someone's permission to do C so that I'll qualify for D. If at any point something doesn't come through, the whole enterprise comes crashing down and the fiend goes back to the nearest corner. If the judge doesn't let Mike off probation, he's off the ship and back to shooting people. If DeAndre doesn't get hired at the McDonald's, he'll be back with the rest of his crew, slinging down on Fairmount. And if Fran doesn't get into BRC, she'll stay on the stoop of the Dew Drop. There is a learned helplessness to these first, small steps—a single-minded dependence on someone else's favors. Never mind that there are other detox programs, other jobs, other alternatives. In the beginning, it's more than enough for any fiend to make that first call or go a half-dozen blocks out of the way to ask the first question. If that doesn't yield an encouraging response, all the more reason to surrender. If the response offers some vague opportunity, some distant prospect of change, then that's fine too. A six- to eight-week waiting list means six to eight weeks of getting high without guilt, of telling yourself that you're just waiting until the bed comes open.

For Fran, the minimum requirement is that she call down to BRC on Tuesdays—every Tuesday—to inquire about her status on the waiting list and to let the staff know she's still serious about the program.

"I call you?" she asks Antoinette.

"No, just leave a message at the desk. I'll get it."

Fran leaves with a manufactured hope, something to get her through the rest of spring and the coming summer, something she can use to assure herself and anyone else that she's trying, that she has a plan. DeAndre hears about her foray down to the detox facility and tells her to go for it, assuring his mother that he'll take care of DeRodd if she has to go away. Scoogie also offers to help, and Fran begins taking their encouragement to heart. It *is* a plan; she can do this. Get some money together so she can pay Bunchie a month's rent up front and leave something for DeAndre to live on. Now might even be the time to go up to Rosemont and get her older son put back on her social services check; he's been off since she put him out of the house last summer and Fran, lost in the inertia of addiction, had yet to deal with the paperwork involved in getting DeAndre back on her case file. More immediately, she needs to get DeAndre that birth certificate and see if he can hook up at Mickey D's. Then go inside and get clean, and maybe hold on to enough cash so she can get a place of her own and get the hell out of the Dew Drop. That she'll have to do, because there's no staying clean if she's down on Fayette Street with the rest of them. This, she tells herself, can work.

The first Tuesday she makes the call down to BRC.

Two days later, she arranges a ride up to the Bureau of Vital Statistics office in Northwest, where she waits out the bureaucracy to get a copy of DeAndre's birth record. And she feels good when she hands it to him the next day; she's getting it done, showing her son and herself that she can provide.

But the weekend comes, and weekends are always rough on Fayette Street. Fran gets up on Monday feeling like death itself, her eyes bloody and stinging from the night before. She gets a wet towel and goes back to bed until ten. Still, when she does get up, she gets herself right and makes the trip up to Rosemont, to take care of business that she hasn't dealt with in almost a year. It's been that long since she put Andre out of the house and lost sixty a month on her check; it's time now to get all of that back.

Six hours later, Fran Boyd drags herself up the stairs at 1625 Fayette, too tired for life. She's had a day of genuine striving, of venturing beyond the corner and dealing with the plan, of putting the blast second.

"Hey, Fran," says Stevie, watching her slope into the living room.

Fran grunts softly to her brother, then pitches forward into the frayed cushions of the sofa. She pries her running shoes off and props her feet on the arm of the couch.

"Where you been at?"

"Lord," says Fran. "You know what it is I don't understand?"

"Hmm," says Stevie.

"People who have days like I just had and then don't get high. I swear I cannot understand that. People actually go through this shit and not get high."

Stevie laughs.

"I went up to Rosemont to see about my check," she explains, rolling over on her stomach, feeling the scratch of the ruined fabric on her cheek. "I'm waiting there on those damn plastic chairs for hours."

Stevie clucks softly.

"Four hours so that the woman can tell me that they can't do nuthin' 'cause my worker is off today. Sayin' she'll call me back and shit. I'm sayin' look, Andre is my child and he back livin' with me and been livin' with me for months . . ."

She sinks her head into the cushion, tired of her own tale.

"Yeah," her brother drawls, "you know I got to get up Rosemont and ask about that check for Little Stevie."

"You want my knife?" asks Fran.

Stevie laughs. It's a standard joke around Fayette Street: The straight line says you're going up Rosemont; the punch line always comes when someone offers a blade. Whatever humor can be gleaned from this comes at the expense of Crazy Arnold, who left Fayette Street the summer before last, walked the half-mile north to the city social services office at Rosemont, argued briefly about his food stamp application, then stuck an eight-inch kitchen knife into a twenty-nine-year-old caseworker. On Fayette Street, the murder tested essential loyalties. Arnold Bates was a stone mental case, living in his mother's backyard and wheeling his push-cart around the neighborhood in search of enough aluminum cans to pay for his coke and phencyclidine. But when it came to food stamps, or AFDC, or dealing with the general indifference of the city welfare bureaucracy, the people of Fayette Street had experienced enough of Rosemont to give the benefit of the doubt to whichever poor bastard might be trying for a check. Fran had heard that Crazy Arnold's case-worker had run him around, asking for more and more documentation to accompany his food stamp application, until one fine day, Arnold gave her all the proof anyone ever needs. In real terms, it was shocking and sad—the DSS employee who got killed was hardly the worst case-worker at the Rosemont office—but in the abstract, the slaying connected a lot of West Baltimore welfare recipients to Crazy Arnold Bates, that most unconnected of souls. Arnold was living proof of that thought in the back of every Rosemont client's mind—the ugly notion that you can carve your way through a caseworker faster than you can hack past the paperwork.

"Where Bunchie at?" asks Fran, sitting up slowly.

"Downstairs."

Fran drags herself off the sofa, then stalks downstairs in search of a blast, which to her mind at least, she has earned. She's been trying—not every day, not all of the time, but enough that her brothers and sisters are starting to look at her differently. Only trouble is, she's tired. More tired than she's ever been.

She goes down to the basement where she finds Bunchie well into the game. Fran gets her share, emerging on the front steps a moment or two later, carrying the worn print cushion atop which she has marked countless hours of the street parade. She drops it on the top step and sits.

"Hey, Fran."

"Hey, you."

And so it continues, with the touts chanting their products and the buyers sliding up and the time-out calls when the occasional police cruiser lumbers past. The next morning, Fran forgets to call down to BRC, but she manages to do so on Thursday, two days late. The next week, she doesn't phone at all.

The plan is on hold, the corner world having reclaimed her attentions entirely. Until the next weekend, when she's on her way down to Kevin's store and she runs into someone who lets go with the news that Little Mike has actually left.

"Say what?"

"He gone."

"Gone?"

"He went to somewheres to get on a boat."

The idea of it pulls Fran up short. Mike gone.

He convinced the judge to let him be, then packed his bags and took himself a new life. Standing there in Kevin's, waiting for change to come

back to her through the Plexiglas, Fran can almost feel the universe slipping out of gear.

That afternoon, Fran asks around and hears that Mike took a plane
to New York and then another plane to Europe somewhere and then got
on a boat in Poland. She's amazed; all that talk wasn't just talk. Mike's
plan was really a plan. And the thing is, Fran thinks, Little Mike just did
it. He went from one step to the next like the end result was assured. To
Fran, it seems so perfectly simple: a plan that was straight and true, a
bullet-path from one world to the next.

"Mike a sailor," says Fran, finally. "Damn."

But nothing on Fayette Street is ever straight or true. The truth that
never made it to Fran's ears was that Mike Ellerbee's plan was always—
even down to its last moments—a wisp of a thing, frail enough to fall
apart at any one of a hundred moments. On the night before he left,
Mike was down at Fulton and Vine, hanging with some of his boys, when
one of the dealers rolled up and berated everyone for standing around
bullshitting on company time.

The dealer stepped out of his raggedy Lincoln and walked across the
street, shouting to touts and lookouts that they were bitches, that they
were supposed to be about his business.

"I know you not talkin' to me," Mike said.

Suddenly it was the old Mike, the one who would never be trifled
with, who couldn't stand on a corner and let a slur like that go past
him. The dealer walked back to his car trunk, popped it open and
pulled out a statement-maker. Sawed-off, taped, and ugly. Thirty-
aught.

"I'm sayin' bitches."

And bitches it was, with no one speaking a word until the dealer put
the shotgun back, slammed the trunk shut, and walked into the liquor
store. Then the boys looked at Mike.

"Ain't got my gun," he told them lamely.

But Anthony pulled up his shirt to show a .380. Still, Mike wouldn't
budge. For six months, he had written letters and turned in paperwork
and taken physicals so that tomorrow he would be leaving the country
for something new. He was backing up ten years for the last shooting;
throwing down now might mean all that time and more. He tried to
say some of that to his friends.

"I shoot his ass for you," offered Anthony, sympathetic.

Mike was on the edge.

"He ain't shit," Anthony prodded. "He can't talk to people like that."

"Naw, man," said Mike finally. "Jus' let it be."

The dealer walked back out to his car, turning to say he'd be coming back through and wanted to see what he was supposed to see on this corner. Mike swallowed that too—swallowed it for all of twenty minutes, which was about as long as it took for the scales to tip.

"I be back," he told the others.

He went home and got the big gun, the four-four. Then he walked back down to the mouth of the Vine Street alley where he waited in deadly earnest for the dealer to return. But the man did not come back, and the next afternoon, Mike Ellerbee was in a window seat, looking down at the Atlantic.

That was the real story. That was the plan—thin, precarious, and in the end, more a twist of fate than anything else. But coming back from Kevin's grocery, Fran can only see the Disney version, the one that says you succeed by simply wanting, by putting one foot in front of the other and waiting for the good things to happen.

"You got a quarter?" she asks Stevie.

"Naw."

"Kenny, lemme hold a quarter."

He gives her a dime, and Ronnie Hughes kicks in a nickel.

"Bunchie," she says. "I need a dime. Gotta make a call."

"Gimme the rock."

R.C. powers up over top of Manny Man to snag the rebound. He wheels left, then cuts back under the basket, emerging in front of Dewayne for a reverse, no-look layup. Dewayne hacks him good, but the shot goes in.

"Thirty-five," says R.C.

"You got thirty," DeAndre counters.

R.C. struts to the foul line, takes the ball and cocks his head sideways, a look of disgust on his face.

"You had twenty-five and that shit you threw up makes thirty," DeAndre insists.

R.C. shakes his head, chews his lower lip, dribbles twice, and lofts a perfect free throw. "There, bitch. Forty."

"You the bitch."

"Gimme the rock."

DeAndre fires it at him. Hard.

"Forty-five," he says, after dropping another from the line. "Or forty, it don't make no never mind."

This is where R.C. thrives, where he is at ease with himself and his place. He's got the best game on this court and he knows it. Tae is quick but thoughtless with the ball, DeAndre can't dribble, Brooks is too small, and Manny Man—he's best off with a football. On this court and for these few hours of so-called practice, R.C. sets a standard. More important, there is a purpose to his time on the court, a reason for being that transcends every other questionable moment. Here, it's win or lose.

He sinks another from the line. "What's the score. You tell me."

"Fuck you," says DeAndre.

And another. "Fifty."

Fifty is the name of the game being played as they wait for enough bodies to run full. They're up to six—R.C., DeAndre, Manny Man, Tae, Dewayne, and Brooks—when the interlopers slip through the gym doors.

Mike from Payson Street. Truck. Twin. These are the boys from Hilltop, the neighborhood due west of Monroe and the Fayette Street strip, the crest of the hill that slopes gently upward from Martin Luther King Boulevard and the city's downtown. Hilltop marks the frontier of blight in this quadrant of the city, its rental rowhouses only a little more livable than those down the hill. There's no reliable drug corner in the neighborhood proper; the Hilltop fiends have to cross Monroe Street, or go south below Baltimore Street to get full service. The violence, too, is still for the most part down the hill, between Monroe and Mount. Beyond Hilltop, there is the slope back down to Warwick Avenue, with its greenery and open porches and well-kept rowhomes. This is for the most part a neighborhood of home owners—black working-class, with a few middle-class families in the mix—holding fast to a small island in a roiling sea. In these few blocks, the grass is lush and freshly cut on postage-stamp lawns; the gardens, newly planted and cheerful. On this side of the hill, the residents are tightly knit and very conscious of the long odds against them. They are, quite simply, what Hilltop was ten years ago and what Fayette Street was twenty years back.

Some natural enmity exists between the C.M.B. boys and the Hilltop crew, with the Fayette Street contingent counting itself superior for living at the heart of the disaster. They don't live near a corner; they live on it. They don't hear the nightly echo of gunfire from down the hill; they see the muzzle flashes. More to the point, they know they aren't living in a neighborhood going to hell; no, they were born into a place that had already arrived there. It was their home that was the stuff of song this year. Mount and Fayette: Get ya guns out.

But in fairness, Hilltop has been in decline long enough that it can't really be counted as a world apart. When its children walk into the gym, they carry enough attitude to get over. Mike surely knows the game; Truck, too. Only last summer, R.C. tangled with Mike and his brother, beefing with them after C.M.B. moved over to work a package at Hollins and Payson, a corner that was more Hilltop than anything else.

And now, on a warm afternoon in May, Mike and Truck and Twin have crossed Monroe Street. They strip off sweats, lace new high-tops, and stretch against the bleachers in the Francis Woods gym—all of them carrying it like they could go either way. Fuck it, their faces say, we can run a game or we can beef. Your choice, motherfucker.

"Big Truck," says Tae without rancor, watching the largest of the three lurch onto the court. Truck was named right.

"Hey," says Truck.

The others follow Tae's lead. The game of fifty continues, with Truck and Tank, and finally Mike crowding under the basket with the rest, waiting for rebounds. The hatchet seems to be buried, at least until R.C. goes to the top of the key, where he ices his victory.

"What can I say," he says, half-shrugging. "I got skills."

A few seconds later, he brings down a rebound only to have Mike skirt behind him and strip the ball cleanly. R.C. glares over his shoulder as Mike spins into the corner for a long baseline jumper. Nothing but net.

DeAndre taps the ball back for the courtesy, but R.C. is there to intercept it. He dribbles off in the other direction, leaving Mike waiting in the corner.

"Ball up," says Mike.

"Man, fuck you," replies R.C.

And it begins—a fight that has something to do with whatever happened on that corner last summer, but much more to do with whatever status derives from this rec center team. Until today, R.C.'s standing on this court was unquestioned, but Mike is a good shooting guard and both Truck and Twin are six inches taller than anyone else. For R.C., their presence marks something of a challenge. What results is not so much a physical confrontation as a symphony of threat and counterthreat, an airing of grievances too ancient and petty to require open warfare, but sufficient to fill the gym with ripe insults. Whore. Bitch. Punk-ass mother-fucker. The usual verbiage boils down to Mike and R.C. leaning hard into each others' shoulders: R.C. showing his fiercest mien, eyes bulging, nostrils flaring, fists clenched; Mike, a half-foot shorter and maybe thirty pounds lighter, gives no ground, staring back with cold contempt.

R.C. rolls away from Mike's shoulder, then shoves the Hilltop boy backward. That brings up Truck into R.C.'s face, fists cocked at his sides. R.C. takes a half-step backward, but ends the retreat when Tae and DeAndre pull up next to him. DeAndre steps between Truck and R.C.; Tae pulls R.C. away.

"You down the hill now, motherfucker," says R.C., yelling past Tae's shoulder.

"Bitch," says Mike. "I ain't afraid a yo' punk ass."

"You ought to be after how I kicked your ass last time."

Mike's eyes go wide. "You kicked my ass?"

R.C. nods knowingly. "Sure as shit."

"You kicked my ass?"

"You heard me."

"Man, I kicked your weak ass up and down the street."

By now it's clear that this is going nowhere, that these two aren't quite ready to ratchet up. Truck, DeAndre, Tae—the rest of the troops drift back under the basket, waiting for rebounds, certain that while this afternoon might still promise a good hoop game, a good fight is out of the question.

To hear it with the logic of the external world, the threats and counter-threats sound like a prelude to war. But on Fayette Street, this is business as usual. It's gut-level knowledge for all them: Two boys get to beefing, throwing words, posturing, talking about how they're gonna come back with their Tec-Nine, and everyone else stands around for a minute or two trying to gauge whether the wait is worth the show. The bluster and brinksmanship is constant, but ninety-nine times out of a hundred, the thing ends with traded insults and maybe an unkept promise to come back with a gun or an older brother or the rest of whatever corner crew is involved. The hundredth time someone comes back in the worst way, but that's what the corner is about. And when the worst finally happens, of course, a homicide detective is left standing over the corpse, trash talking with his partner about the stupidity of the victim, about how the shooter promised to come back with a gun and the victim didn't do shit but wait for him. But the cop doesn't understand: In his world, the threat of a gun would be an epic event, something to bring the adrenaline to a boil. In West Baltimore, a suggestion of violence is the standard terminus to any dispute lasting more than four minutes. People live—and, on occasion, die—trying to sort the genuine threat from the usual rank corner talk.

"Don't make me come back down here with my MAC-10," says Mike, playing out the string.

"Man, sheeeet," replies R.C. "Go get your gun, motherfucker. Go get what you need and stop talkin' bullshit."

"Blow yo' ass up."

"Sheeeet."

And so it goes. R.C. delivers his last few insults from the bleachers, where he relaces his new Nikes; Mike is talking about murder even as he's fighting for a rebound at the far basket.

Dinky arrives to make ten.

"Let's run," says Tae.

"Choose up," says DeAndre.

"Tae and Dewayne. Choose."

They go to full court, two pickup teams with the C.M.B. and Hilltop contingents mixed. They run wild, with long alley-oop passes, cherry picking, and absolutely nothing resembling defense. But the new blood shows itself in odd moments of grandeur: Mike penetrates the lane time and again, only to dish off at the last second. Twin dominates the offensive boards. Truck muscles down low, using his size. The general level of play is still sloppy, but occasionally something happens on the court to show all of them that, taken as a whole, they're a better team.

Something else becomes painfully obvious. The marginal C.M.B. players—Manny Man, Brooks, Dinky, even DeAndre—are no longer as vital with the Hilltop boys on the court. DeAndre still has his shot, but with both Mike and Tae running point, his weak ballhandling is a liability. Brooks can't penetrate or connect with anyone's passing game. Dinky has his moments—he moves constantly without the ball, crashing the boards, stealing rebounds from taller players—but he can't finish; his shot is rushed and awkward. Manny Man is barely there.

On the other hand, the challenge brings R.C. to a new level. Mike can see the court the way R.C. sees it; the two of them, playing together in the last of three games, manage to get it done. With Mike regulating the offense, R.C. is rewarded for his rebounding, his defense, his movement without the ball.

Once, after fighting Truck successfully for an offensive rebound, R.C. turns under the larger boy, double-pumps, then dishes the ball to Mike, who cuts the lane for a layup. Two plays later, Mike drives to the hoop, drawing Truck and DeAndre, before tapping the ball back out to R.C. at the key. R.C. pumps, then shoots a no-look pass back to Mike, who's behind the basket. Mike fools what's left of the defense, then fires it back to a charging R.C. for an elegant finger roll.

Backpedaling downcourt on defense, R.C. wordlessly extends his hand to take five from the kid who was going to go home for his MAC-10.

"Good pass," says Mike.

Like R.C., Tae and Dewayne can keep pace with the Hilltop talent, but it's R.C. alone who manages to grow as a player, to fully integrate himself as part of a team. He's throwing his body, blocking out, setting piks, diving for loose balls—and sometimes congratulating others when they manage to do the same. At the end of practice, R.C. steps off the court in a rare humor, relaxed, even a little expansive.

He walks up Fayette with the rest of them, laughing at Tae's jokes, his loudspeaker of a voice modulated to a conversational tone. For R.C., basketball is the only affirmative act in his life. When practice goes well, he can live with himself. When it goes poorly, he can't live with anyone.

More than anyone in this crew, Richard Carter carries with him a mantle of fatalism of a kind rarely seen even along Fayette Street. In his every act, there is a show of insecurity, a complete unwillingness to accept for a moment the possibility that his fifteen-year-old life might be worth something, that existence itself isn't a game rigged to ensure his failure.

He has been loud ever since he could talk, literally shouting for attention as the youngest of five children. Before R.C. was born, his mother had fled to Baltimore from Vineland, New Jersey—a last-ditch effort to end a violent relationship with the father of R.C.'s older brothers —settling eventually into a third-floor apartment on Fulton Avenue. The building was a housing project subsidized by the archdiocese, and the Carter apartment was, by neighborhood standards, well-furnished. But R.C.'s mother, who worked hard at a Pimlico dry cleaner and was churchgoing, wasn't often around during the day. Carrie Carter was, ultimately, less of an influence on the youngest child than R.C.'s father, whom she had met and married shortly after coming to Baltimore.

Richard Junior lived to be in Richard Senior's eye, waiting for those moments in the day when he could turn his father's head with something new. He would sit on the living room sofa every evening, waiting for his father to come through the door. And in those early days, R.C.'s father was a thing to behold, strutting around in a full-length leather coat with a matching brim, cutting quite an image along Fayette Street. DeAndre could remember thinking that his friend's father was just about the slickest thing he'd seen, a sportsman with so much more style than anyone else on the corners. And for a long time, R.C.'s father was indeed a cut above the usual streetcorner slinger. He had connections; he was buying wholesale, dealing with Jamaicans and Dominicans and the other New Yorkers who were true players in the local trade.

The family was perfectly divided: a mother, slaving away with the starch and steam press up on Reisterstown Road; a father, trying to stretch a gangster hustle into real money. Two of R.C.'s older brothers, Ricky and Bug, took their father's package—and later their own product—down to the corners, and were repeatedly wounded by gunfire. Nor did it end there: R.C.'s oldest sister, Darlene, had been the beauty of the family, but she was now in a shooting gallery on Mount Street, chasing what her brothers were selling.

A third brother, David, fell all the way, losing himself in a heroin addiction that eventually wrecked both his body and his mind. Four years ago, on a warm October night, a pair of Western District police caught up to him in the middle of Franklin Street, near the McDonald's, where the twenty-six-year-old was wandering in traffic, rambling incoherently. At one point, David jumped on the hood of a police cruiser; bystanders would later tell the Carter family that this single act resulted in a severe beatdown. Pounded by the arresting officers and tossed in the rear of a wagon, he was delivered still breathing to the Western lockup and deposited in a holding cell. A few hours later, the turnkeys realized they had a problem and rushed him down to the Bon Secours emergency room, where he slipped in and out of consciousness. Transferred to a better intensive-care unit at University Hospital, he died days later nonetheless.

The autopsy was just ambiguous enough to take the police department off the hook. Citing as much physical damage from drug use as from the beating on Franklin Street, officials ruled the case a natural death. No one in authority ever contacted the Carters with an explanation, and when Carrie Carter went downtown to talk to someone in charge, she was shunted in and out of offices until a deputy commissioner told her simply that her son had died from drugs. But in the neighborhood, the death of David Sanford became local lore, a touchstone to be cited whenever the standing of law officers was at issue. On Fayette Street, no one—from older heads to gangsters to small children—ever spoke of the incident without acknowledging that the police had come across an addict in delirium, and with absolute impunity, had beaten the man to death.

Of all the siblings, David had been closest to eleven-year-old Richard Junior. From Carrie Carter's point of view, David's death seemed to bring R.C. to a new level of frustration, to make him shout louder or rant longer in his struggle to be acknowledged. Though he was in many ways her brightest child, school had always been a problem with R.C., who had, from an early age, abandoned all initiative when it came to his own education. She had approached city school officials a dozen different ways, looking for the key to open her angry child's mind; no one, it seemed, could touch R.C.'s basic insecurities. He was alive only on a ball court or in the streets, where he survived as much as a braggart as a fighter, a loud and profane voice constantly assuring the world of his talent and worth. He was one of the best athletes in the group, and he could carry himself in a fight, especially when he was younger and his thick, athletic frame was daunting to everyone in the neighborhood save DeAndre. But whereas DeAndre had sense enough not to talk up his game, R.C.'s wounded ego couldn't contain itself. He abhorred silence, yet all of his protestations and declarations accomplished little. It was as if all the self-praise seeped out a hole in the bottom of his soul.

When his father—the patriarch behind the family disaster—began hardcore drugging, things only got worse. For the last two years, Richard Senior had moved through life as an empty shell of himself, the tailored suits and full-length leathers giving way to the ordinariness of common addiction. By then he had little time for his youngest son. He had run the gangster hustle down to its last threads, messing up deals and packages as only a fiend can. Then, just before last Christmas, he crossed some Jamaicans and it was over. They found his body in the wilds of West Baltimore's Leakin Park. He had been badly bludgeoned, his sweatshirt pulled up over his head to prevent him from fighting back, his head and torso black-and-blue from the blows. The murder was never solved; in fact, it wasn't seriously investigated. Saddled with the possibility of an unsolvable drug slaying, city detectives convinced the medical examiner to list the case as pending, on the apparent presumption that the victim had wandered into the woods, pulled his sweatshirt above his head and then beaten himself into the ground. Again, as with David Sanford, the fact that there was heroin in the dead man's system was explanation enough.

That was five months ago. Now R.C. is in freefall; he no longer even bothers to maintain any pretense. Charged with truancy from the previous semester at Southwestern, he began the new semester promising a juvenile hearing officer he wouldn't miss a day if his transfer to Francis M. Woods was approved. With only a month to go, he has amassed a near-perfect attendance record—he has not been seen at school save for the first two days of the spring semester. He makes no show of looking for a job, nor does he have need of one. His mother has been giving him a portion of his father's social security death benefit, enabling R.C. to indulge in consumption that outpaces that of his contemporaries. For the poorest of the C.M.B. crew, Nike and Reebok, Timberland, and Tommy Hilfiger are components of a basic philosophy of life. To Tae or DeAndre, the worst insult is to have anything attached to you—your jacket, your high-tops, your girl, your hair—labeled as off-brand. But R.C. is a step beyond. In his bedroom, there are close to thirty-five pairs of brand-name athletic shoes, some rarely worn, others still in the original boxes. And yet the mall purchases, too, leak uselessly from that hole inside him.

In the end, it's a matter of degree: All of them—DeAndre, Tae, Manny Man, Brooks, Dinky—are slipping slowly into the corner world. But most are at the same time clinging to the last leavings of childhood, still making the effort in their minds to assemble the fragments of school, family, and hope into vague, improbable futures. But R.C. can no longer manage even a show of reluctance about the corner. He doesn't fight it; he seems to be going there deliberately.

For R.C., basketball is the only thing in his life that hasn't imploded, that can be trusted to remain a constant. On the court, he is gifted. Too short to dominate, but capable of playing within himself as the others are not, he has strong moves, good court vision, a physical game, and—most important—he understands instinctively what a basketball team is supposed to do with or without the ball. That he is playing with so many who don't is enormously frustrating. Still, the rec center team is precious to him.

The contradiction here makes R.C.'s effort in the Francis Woods gym seem transcendent: As the rest of his life settles inexorably onto the corner, a place where only the most self-centered and temporary passions are gratified, R.C. nonetheless takes the time three days a week to dedicate himself to the communal requirements of team basketball. He rebounds without reward; passes the ball without hope that it will come back; takes only those shots that offer a high percentage. The Hilltop boys notice, of course, but for the others—DeAndre, Tae, and the rest—their time on the court is mere play.

To R.C., the rest of the crew are profaning his god. Beneath the generalized fantasy that every city kid carries in his head, R.C. knows his athletic career will end with playground ball. He will never play for a school varsity squad because he can never find a school. But still, he can't give up on the idea of himself as a ballplayer. Nor can he indulge himself on the court as he does at every other point in life. Such is the power and mystique of this sport that for a few hours a day, it can socialize the likes of Richard Carter. Not that he can carry lessons about teamwork, selflessness, discipline, and hard work back into the street; they exist only within the baselines. R.C. will never follow through with an academic effort, or training regimen, or diet. For him, only the act of stepping onto the hardwood matters, and on those frequent occasions when the others show that it matters not at all, R.C. can be provoked to rage.

Arriving early during the next week's afternoon practices, he gives himself over to the pickup games with absolute abandon. It's R.C. on the boards, R.C. leading the break, R.C. diving into the bleachers for loose balls.

The Hilltop boys play well with him, but those in his own crew can't keep up. With Brooks and Boo, DeAndre and Manny Man, R.C. shows less patience and more fury. Soon, he's alienated everyone save for the newcomers.

On Tuesday, he jumps on Dewayne for dribbling too much. On

Wednesday, he rants because DeAndre wouldn't play defense and because Brian is easily stripped of the ball. On Thursday, the target is again the impish Brooks, who answers by clenching his fists and putting his scowling face directly below R.C.'s chin, daring the bigger boy to hit him, then threatening to run home for his gun when R.C. does precisely that.

"Man, let Brooks be," says Tae, tired of the bickering.

"He greedy," R.C. insists. "He always goin' hawk."

He's right: Brooks has trouble giving up the ball. But it's equally true that brutalizing your fellow players every day won't do much to instill a team concept. With Brooks gone for the last hour of the Thursday practice, R.C. settles into his game and the boys are soon running a quickbreak offense at flank speed. They end on a beautiful double-clutch, no-look pass from Tae to R.C., who goes past Twin and underneath the rim for a backhanded layup.

"We gonna beat Bentalou next time out," says Boo, confident.

But any sense of team can't survive the walk up Fayette later that same afternoon. The talk then is all about what happened the week prior, when Boo, R.C., Brian, Tae, and a few others went a few blocks to the southeast to check out the video games at Mt. Clare Junction. Boo had words down there with one of the white boys from Stricker and Ramsay, who asked him if he wanted to step outside.

Boo thought it was an invitation to a one-on-one, but when he started out the door of the shopping pavillion, he realized that the entire Stricker and Ramsay crew—white boys, black boys, even some of the adults—was following him. The C.M.B. contingent was badly outnumbered, with no other option but to throw a few quick punches and run like hell across Baltimore Street. Now, thinking on it, Boo wants to go back.

"I ain't tryin' to hear that," says Brian. "Some of those white boys down there hit like niggers."

"Sheeeet," says Tae. "We was outnumbered. We need to go back with all our peoples."

"DeAndre wasn't there," says Dinky.

"DeAndre always ready for a fight," says Boo, with admiration. "He was the only one that stayed when we got to fighting with the police down at Mt. Clare."

It was true. Last summer C.M.B. had tangled with the Stricker and Ramsay boys down at the shopping center. When the police showed,

they took the side of the white boys and started chasing down the C.M.B.
crew. DeAndre jumped on one Southern District police, just as the cop
was trying to handcuff R.C.

"Andre crazy as shit," agrees Tae.

"What the fuck you talkin' 'bout?" R.C. asks bitterly. "I stayed and
fought that time. I was there."

Boo shakes his head. "It was just me and Andre."

"And me," says R.C. as they cross Fayette near Gilmor.

"You wasn't around."

"Okay," says R.C. He pivots abruptly, cocking his right arm and firing
a sucker punch into Boo's jaw. Boo crumples into the fender of a parked
car.

The rest of the team laughs uproariously.

Gary McCullough nods, flustered, looking out at the Wabash Avenue
courtroom for some better truth, or some better way of telling it.
From the middle of the third bench, his mother covers her frown with
both hands, terrified at the image of her son's life hanging in the
balance. Gary catches her eye and tries to smile, then loses his train
of thought.

"It's like . . . judge, please, this is just crazy."

Judge Bass, sensing the panic, tries to put the defendant at ease. "Take
your time, Mr. McCullough, I'm listening to you. I just need you to speak
louder."

"Okay."

"Go ahead."

"All right."

Where to begin? What to say? What to leave unsaid? So much to
worry about now that all that foolishness with Ronnie is getting its day
in court. Gary has taken a charge behind this nonsense; he's seen the
bullpen on Eager Street because of it. And now, when he should be
speaking up for himself and putting it all to rest, he's a stammering
wreck. It's hell getting the God's honest truth out of your mouth when
the damn thing is wrapped up in lies.

"We had an argument . . . ," says Gary.

True enough.

". . . about some money."

Lie.

"An' Ronnie, I mean, Veronica began yelling."

True again.

"So I asked her to leave . . ."

Still true.

". . . but she kept cussin' me and telling me she wasn't going to go without the, ah, the, um . . . the money."

The lie again.

"Mr. McCullough, you'll have to speak up."

"Um . . ."

"You'll have to talk louder so I can hear you."

Gary nods, agreeable. "She just wouldn't leave," he tells Judge Bass, "so I finally shoved her a little, toward the door, like. I didn't hit her, I just pushed her to get her out of the house."

Truth, or close enough to it.

"And she threw a brick at me . . ."

Truth.

"A brick?" asks Judge Bass.

"And a knife," adds Gary.

Lie. A home run swing from Gary McCullough.

"She threw a knife at you?"

"I was standing in the doorway."

"What kind of knife?"

"Kitchen kind. Had a big blade and all."

The judge can't let that one go. He's looking up at the acoustic-tile ceiling, giving words to the thought running through the heads of everyone else in the courtroom.

"Where did she get the knife?"

Gary shrugs, wondering what that has to do with anything. He's sweating profusely, a prisoner inside his gray pinstripe church suit.

"I mean," says the judge. "Did she have the knife on her or did she go and get the knife from somewhere? She didn't just find it lying in the street, did she?"

Gary shrugs again, then scratches his ear, thinking about it. To look at him, to catch even a glimpse of the sincerity in his face, you'd think there might actually have been a knife involved. Who's to say? With Gary McCullough, a man far too honest about most things, the occasional lie always takes on a life of its own. Today, on a bright May morning, eight months after the fact, he truly believes Ronnie tossed a knife at him. If she had a knife, she surely would have.

Judge Bass raises an eyebrow, then glances over at the assistant state's

attorney, who lets the judge continue the redirect. "Do you know where
the knife came from?" the judge asks Gary.

"From Ronnie's hand. She threw it."

Laughter breaks from the clustered humanity on the court benches.
Even Judge Bass has to smile.

"But you don't know where she got it."

"Uh-uh."

"Okay, go on."

Go on, Mr. McCullough. Tell the tale as best you can. But leave out
the part about the vials of heroin, the part where you wouldn't share a
blast with Ronnie and she started to raise hell, calling you all kinds of
names. By all means, mention the brick—the kitchen knife, even—but
leave out the part where you ran out of the house afterward to confront
her, grabbing her neck, and then shoving her down the sidewalk. Tell it
in small pieces, as if it's a broken puzzle. Tell it the way you think they
might want to hear it.

"I didn't hit her," Gary says.

That this case is now being played out in court is, in itself, an incredible thing. That it couldn't be stetted or nol-prossed or reduced to
some unsupervised probation is testament only to the current political
imperatives. Gary and Ronnie both had come to court today certain that
they could make the thing go away; Ronnie would decline to testify and
the prosecutors would shrug and toss the casefile into a tall stack of
district court dismissals.

But no. It wasn't just the usual Western District prosecutor in court
today, but an assistant state's attorney from downtown somewhere.
And this case could not be dismissed as everyone desired because of
its status as a domestic violence complaint. In the eyes of the government, Ronnie Boice is no longer the quick-thinking, game-running,
syringe-switching wonder of Fayette Street. Consciousness has been
sufficiently raised so that now, by a policy new to the prosecutor's
office, all domestic assault cases are fully pursued—even when a wife
or girlfriend has attempted to back away from her original statement. For today at least, Ronnie Boice will be representing battered
womanhood.

It's a noble effort by the state's attorney's office, a worthy strategy in
those cases in which abused women are too frightened or intimidated
to testify against their assailants. In the present case, however, the new
policy is a source of unintentional hilarity.

Ronnie never had any intention of pursuing the case; she just wanted Gary to know that what was his—coke, dope, or both—was hers as well. But now she'll have to testify or risk being charged with obstructing justice. And if she tells the truth on the stand—tells them that it was a shoving match over a blast—well, that will mean a charge of false statement or perjury for her original complaint. When Gary declined a plea offer of six months in jail followed by spousal abuse counseling, the court trial was the only option left.

"Why would Miss Boice make a complaint against you if you didn't hit her?" asks the prosecutor, picking up the redirect.

"I don't know," says Gary, looking genuinely hurt.

"But you're saying she made all this up?"

"Yes."

"Why would she do that?"

Gary's mouth gapes open, then shuts. He wants to say it. He has to fight himself not to say it: Why do you think, fool? She wanted my blast. She wanted my blast and I said no and so she called the police. If Gary told them that, if he let it fall from his lips in the Western District court, everything would make sense. And neither the judge nor the prosecutor would bother to bring any charge from the admission of drug use, not in Baltimore, anyway. But Gary can't see that; he keeps his secret.

Ronnie, too. Just before Gary took the witness stand in his own defense, Ronnie gave her own grudging testimony. Questioned by the prosecutor, she made no mention of the blast, choosing instead to pretend that the argument was about Gary giving his attentions to some other girl. In sharp contrast to Gary's later panic, his girl managed to thread the needle masterfully. Droll from the witness stand, her eyes bouncing between Gary at the defense table and his mother three rows back, she destroyed the case without directly contradicting her original complaint. No, she did not throw a brick. No, there was no knife. Yes, Gary did shove her, and later, on the sidewalk, he slapped her. But yeah, well, she did push him, too. In fact, she might have pushed him first, now that she thinks on it.

"Mutual combat," said Judge Bass, looking at the state's attorney in bland resignation. Once Ronnie left the witness stand, it only remained for Gary to make some kind of denial and now, testifying in his own defense, he manages that much.

"Your honor. I didn't hit her. I swear."

Not guilty. The Western District prosecutor nods agreeably, then tosses the file into the discard pile. The domestic violence specialist from downtown looks crestfallen.

Out in the courthouse hallway, the victory celebration is brief and ugly. Gary walks out with his mother on his arm; Ronnie, right behind him, with her own mother, who apparently didn't want to miss her daughter's big day in court.

"Well," ventures Roberta McCullough, "at least that's over."

"Over and done with," agrees Miss Sarah.

"But I don't think our childrens should be together," Miss Roberta says, eyeing Ronnie fretfully. "They're just not good for each other. They don't do each other any good."

Ronnie's mother bristles. "What the hell you mean by that?"

Hands braced against her hips, she stares down at the smaller woman with contempt. Gary is behind his mother, looking at Ronnie in horror. Ronnie is smiling.

"I just mean . . ."

"They'se grown-up children," shouts Miss Sarah, performing for the entire building. "You can't tell them what to do, you ol' bitch cow."

Roberta McCullough's small frame seems to warp from the verbal assault, her eyes falling to the floor. Shaking, she holds one hand to her heart; Gary takes the other and tries to lead her to the stairs.

"Who the hell you think you is?" shouts Ronnie's mother. "Tell my daughter what she can and can't do. You can go an' fuck yo'self, you ol' cow."

From the top of the stairs, Gary helps his stricken mother to the rail, then looks back over his shoulder to see Ronnie and her mother following. Miss Sarah keeps bellowing insults; Ronnie is behind her, smiling so wickedly that Gary realizes that this is part of the price, that Ronnie—having known that his mother would be there for him—had contrived to bring her own mother to the show.

"You think you so high and mighty," yells Miss Sarah. "Your son ain't no better than my daughter."

The words echo down the stairs. Without turning, Miss Roberta falls back on the grace that she knows: "I'll pray for you," she tells her adversary. "That's all I can do."

"Don't need your got-damn prayers, bitch."

They leave the courthouse separately: Gary, consoling his mother, promising to have nothing more to do with Ronnie or her family; Ronnie, heading to Lafayette Market with the matriarch of the Boice clan, the two of them reliving the hallway battle in all its detail.

The episode is enough to keep Gary from Ronnie all that night and the next day. He runs the streets telling himself that nothing—no caper, no blast, no game—will be enough to subject his mother to anything like that again. And it is true that Gary loathes nothing so much as the idea that his life is bringing grief to his mother.

Besides, Gary has his own caper nowadays, and it's one that puts Ronnie completely on the outside. The new game is all Gary. He had seen it first—envisioning it in all its promise—and he had marshaled the necessary manpower and resources to put the plan into effect. The less Ronnie knew about it, the better, since this new deal could keep the vials coming for as long as there were autmobiles on the streets of Baltimore.

Amazing that he hadn't thought of before, really, but then again, the copper piping and aluminum gutters had been so plentiful for so long. Only after an army of fiends had stripped the neighborhood rowhouses bare was there incentive enough for Gary to sit down and think with the same patience and clarity that he used to reserve for picking stocks and mutual funds. At last it came to him, the physical equation slapping him cold in the face as he sat on a Fayette Street stoop and watched the traffic roll past. Anyone watching might have actually seen the lightbulb above his head.

Cars = Metal.
Metal = Money.
Cars = Money.

Elsewhere, great minds might be bent to the task of explaining the habits of quarks and quasars, or reconciling quantum physics with a unified field theory, but in West Baltimore, the mind of Gary McCullough had discovered movable metal, and in doing so had punched a hole in the known limits of the dope-fiend universe.

He started by hooking up with Will and Will's rusting blue pickup. Will was a fiend from the McHenry Street strip who had nothing to compare with Gary's vision and ambition, but was nonetheless in possession of the essential tools—notably his truck and a tow bar. Then, with Will on board, Gary put some feelers out in the neighborhood, offering a select service for a fee.

"For a couple hundred dollars," he would promise, "I can make your car disappear."

True, any fourteen-year-old could strip the ignition and drive the car away, but what then? Invariably, the damn thing turns up with no gas and a wrecked transmission on the other end of town, then gets towed by police down to the Pulaski Highway lot. You're notified and the insurance company won't total your loss, leaving you to cover the deductible and the towing and storage fees. Where was the victory in that?

No, Gary was offering the total package. He would not steal your car and dump it where it could be found. He would not leave you in fear of a comeuppence at the city impound lot. For a couple hundred bucks—more, if you bargained badly—Gary would make anything with wheels disappear for good and for certain. And while many people in the neighborhood were happily wedded to their vehicles, at least a handful of others were not.

From Catherine Street down to Gilmor and from Pratt to the expressway, cars and trucks and vans—most of them broke-down cripples—began to vanish, disappearing like socks in a laundromat dryer. Police reports were taken, vehicle numbers checked and added to the hot sheet, but all in vain. Because down on Wilkens Avenue, down at the scales, two characters in a blue Ford pickup were rolling into the United Iron and Metal driveway, towing yet another vehicle behind them. In addition to whatever fee they could collect from the individual owner, there was the cash to be paid by the scrap yard: forty to fifty for most cars; seventy or so for a van. And all that United Iron and Metal ever asked for in the way of proof of ownership was a signed note saying, yes, my name is Gary McCullough and for the fourth time in two weeks, I would very much like to have one of my autos—say, my '85 Cutlass—driven into the compactor and crushed into a metal briquette.

Simple, profitable, and relatively risk-free—this caper had an elemental beauty and, on occasion, when money was short, Will could persuade Gary that it was permissible to disappear an automobile chosen at random and for which their services had not been contracted. Later on, these excesses would make Gary feel genuine remorse at the thought of schoolteachers and factory workers going out in the morning to stare at empty asphalt. But presumably everyone was happily insured with low deductibles; in Gary's needle-fevered mind,

everything worked out in the end. And surely, it seemed, the supply
of movable metal was endless. Until such time as humanity learned
to liberate itself from the chains of internal combustion, Gary would
have the snake on the run.

For a week or two after the domestic assault trial, as Gary and Will
and some of Will's other running buddies chew their way through the
west side automotive stock, the dollars roll in. Time and again, the blue
pickup crawls up the driveway on Wilkens, trailing some derelict or
not-so-derelict ride behind. The crew unhitches the captive, bargains
with the scrap workers, and splits the proceeds—even shares all around.
Then the pickup bounces back down the driveway and rattles through
the West Baltimore Streets in search of a victory blast. More often than
not, the pickup rolls to Fayette and Mount with Will and his buddies
in the cab negotiating with the touts. And Gary—the idea man, the
mastermind—is usually watching from the back bed, leaning over the
cab roof like a submarine captain atop the conning tower, his proud
countenance surrounded by all of Will's tools and shovels and brooms
lodged upside-down in the truck's rear side braces. Those, too, are an
unintended approximation of naval panache; the brooms ride high in
the braces the way they do when a sub comes into port from a successful
tour. Broom up means a clean sweep—all torpedoes fired, all targets
destroyed. In West Baltimore this spring, it means pretty much the same
thing.

For Gary, however, the glory road reaches its end on a warm May
afternoon, when he sees Will and the rest of the crew towing an old
Chevy van across Baltimore Street. Gary waves. Will seems to see him
from the cab, but the blue pickup keeps on going.

The following day, when Gary goes down to Will's girlfriend's house
to see what's what, his fears are confirmed. The idea man has deep
thoughts, but Will has the truck.

"They cut me out. They stole my caper out from under me,"
Gary moans to anyone who will listen. "There isn't any morality to
people."

For the rest of that week, he fights an urge to call the police and give
them the story and the tag numbers on the blue pickup, but if Will's
loyalty can't be relied upon on the street, it probably isn't worth much
in handcuffs either. Will might speak up; everyone, himself included,
might take a charge.

Dispossesed of his best caper to date, Gary slowly drifts back to the usual, hooking up with Tony and Ronnie to run some cheap metal, then hanging along the fringe while Ronnie takes up touting a package for the New York crew on Monroe Street, though in truth she's palming as much as she's selling. Once again, Gary is a supplicant.

A few days after his girl finally gets fired by the New Yorkers, Gary manages to locate a pair of old water heaters in a rowhouse basement, pry them up and out, and drag them down to Wilkens. The take is twenty-three dollars and Ronnie is able to kick in another three. That's enough for a one-and-one each. Within minutes, the two of them are hooked up with speedballs and headed down to Pops', where Gary has been firing for the last two months.

Even to Gary, the needle party at Pops' is an end-of-the-line affair, with the lowest kind of addicts stumbling up to the third-floor apartment on South Fulton, then wallowing there amid the broken furniture and rotting mattresses. The shooting galleries closer to Fayette are all a bit more professional in outlook; Pops never cleans house or hurries anyone out, nor is he all that particular about what goes on in the two small rooms of his establishment.

Bounding up the stairs behind Ronnie, Gary finds the apartment door ajar. He knocks once for the sake of politeness, then steps across the threshold. The old man is on the sofa, a breakaway syringe stuck behind his ear like a pencil.

"Hey, Pops."

"Hey now," Pops mumbles, toothless. "What you bring with you."

Gary smiles warmly, pulling out one cap of dope and a vial of coke. On the other side of the room is a skinny, dark-skinned girl that Gary can't name, though he's seen her before. A red-headed white girl, Vera, has the stool by the bathroom. Another white girl is asleep on a mattress in the corner, her arms wrapped around some young black kid's bare torso. The mattresses are for the freaks, a handful of whom arrive at Pops in the morning, then whore themselves through the day, giving up their bodies for twenty or thirty on the hype, grinding it out in the center room in plain view of everyone else. Dope doesn't do that to girls; coke is required to create two-dollar prostitutes. The result is that most of West Baltimore's professional streetwalkers have been driven out of business. Who's going to pay twenty dollars when every coke-addled freak between McHenry and Fayette will give it up for half a cap?

Gary moves to a Formica table, borrowing a bottle cap from the dark-skinned black girl. Ronnie leans against the wall and watches as Gary heats up the cap and vial, mixing it with someone else's water and dipping his own syringe first. Ronnie gets hers next, and then comes Pops, who pulls the spike from behind his ear and hands it over. Gary gives the old man a light touch of what's left in the bottle cap.

Gary pauses for a moment, and then, with the cap in his hand, digs down in his pocket, coming back out with a second bottle cap and some fresh matches. Ronnie gives a half smile at the switch, watching as Gary puts the cap back on the table.

The dark-skinned girl passes her syringe and gets only water for her trouble. Pops got a little something for playing host, but there's no free ride for the rest of them. Vera gets watered. So does Jerome, another stray who comes in from the hallway at the last minute, nodding and scratching, already blasted from something good.

Pops and the black girl hit themselves, but Vera begins bleating in adenoidal fury that someone has to help her find a line. She pokes herself in the forearm a few times, but listlessly, without real hope of finding a vein.

"Can you hit me?" she asks Jerome. "You gotta hit me."

But Jerome is nodding, falling asleep against the wall for minutes at a time, then lurching upright and waving his water-filled spike around in the air as if conducting some hellish symphony.

"Wasn't much," says the black girl, disappointed.

"Hey, Gary," says Vera. "Can you lend me five dollars? I got this guy who's supposed to bring me twenty worth of coke in about an hour, but if you can lend me five now . . ."

"Dope fiends!" shouts Jerome, coming to.

". . . then when he comes back, I'll give you half the coke. You got five?"

Gary hits himself with the real thing. Ronnie, too. The whore on the mattress grunts, coughs, then goes back to sleep. Vera finally gets some blood in her needle, but pulls up too quickly, slipping off the line. Pops puts the syringe back above his ear.

"Dope fiends!" shouts Jerome again, waving his spike.

Ronnie pulls out her speedball and repeats the share-and-share alike process. But this time, even Pops gets watered.

"Wasn't much," says Jerome.

"Enough to get you out the gate," says Gary.

Jerome blinks at him, still floating on his morning blast.

"You already out the gate," adds Gary, reassessing.

"East side dope," explains Jerome, proudly. "East side dope is the best dope. I'm an east side boy."

Gary pockets the coke cap, empty now save for some residual essence that he'll save for later. Still trying to hit herself, Vera again begs someone, anyone, to give up five now for twenty dollars of cocaine that is never going to arrive.

"He said he was comin' back."

Gary zips up his army jacket, turns to Ronnie, and gives a small nod of affirmation, as if to say, I can play, I can water with the best of them. Ronnie turns toward the door with a vague smirk and Gary follows her down to South Fulton.

Out on the street, large, fat drops of rain begin slapping hard at them, slowly at first, then gradually accelerating until Gary surrenders and ducks into a vestibule. Ronnie follows and the two of them ride their high, waiting for the downpour to slow.

"Something I'm . . ."

"Huh?"

"I got something that I can't remember," says Gary.

"You just high."

"No, it was . . ."

Gary stares up Fulton, his pupils wide, trying with all his might to bring something to mind. The rain slows, they walk on, and by the time he reaches Vine Street, it comes.

"Oh man. What day is it?"

Ronnie shrugs.

"Tuesday," says Gary, answering himself. He counts forward on both hands, coming first to ten, then counting again and coming to eleven.

"Eleven days. I'm still okay."

"For what?"

"My county case. I got a notice that I have to go ten days in advance of court to talk with the public defender."

"Where do you got to go?"

"Towson."

Ronnie shakes her head, then pronounces Gary doomed. Baltimore County is another planet when it comes to court cases and jail time, especially for black folk from the city. Without a lawyer for his shoplifting case, Gary will be at the mercy of the beast.

"You best get up there today."

They get a hack and ride all the way up York Road to the county seat. Ronnie waits in the car while Gary goes inside, and after much confusion and a few wrong turns, he finds the office of the public defender. The white secretary in the outer lobby is surly and officious. Gary can sense the contempt that greets him as he shows her the court summons.

"You're too late."

"Ten days," he says, pointing to the summons.

"Ten working days."

"Huh?"

"Weekends don't count."

Gary is stunned. "What can I do?"

The woman shrugs, but Gary doesn't leave. Eventually his presence wears at her. She tells him to have a seat and wait for one of the investigators to interview him. He waits three-quarters of an hour to tell a staffer that he didn't take anything from the store, that his codefendant did all the scooping and the guards locked him up while he was reading a newspaper in the middle of the mall.

"What can I do?"

"Tell the judge you came up here and talked with us and then ask for a postponement."

"I can get it postponed?"

"You might. You might not."

Gary leaves and the rain again begins to fall hard. When he returns to Ronnie and the hack, he's soaked. All the way back into the city, Gary is beside himself with the thought of having no lawyer in a county full of angry white folk. The county judges don't play, he knows.

The hack pulls up on Vine Street in front of the McCullough house, where Gary takes off his wet windbreaker and goes inside to borrow ten from his mother—money she said she would have in the afternoon. He's in there for six or seven minutes, just long enough for Ronnie to show why she was born for the corner life, and why Gary McCullough, for all his trying, will never be able to keep up.

Looking over her shoulder, she picks up the wet windbreaker and slips her hand first into one pocket, then the next, finally locating the bottle cap. She gets out her matches and her spike, warms the crystallized remnant to a damp sludge, draws up, then fires it home.

She puts the cap back, just before Gary comes down the steps, grabs his jacket and pays the hack.

"Where you headin' now?" she asks.

"Got to run an errand for my mother."

"Okay, then," she says, getting out of the car.

Gary is already headed back inside, half up the steps, when Ronnie delivers the parting shot. "Gary," she says, catching up to him. "Can I have what's left in that cap?"

Instinctively, Gary reaches down into his jacket pocket and, to his relief, feels the thing. He shakes his head: "I saved that for later. That's from my shot."

"You ain't gonna even share it?" asks Ronnie, her face approximating that of a genuine victim. Gary turns away, looking down Vine Street, trying to think of something to say.

"All that I do for you and you so selfish," she says bitterly. "As much as I love you and worry about you and you just as hard and as cruel as can be."

"Ronnie . . . damn."

"You selfish. But that don't even matter to me because as hard as you are, I love you anyway. I love you and it doesn't matter how bad you treat me," adds Ronnie. She's pushing every button, storing up the emotional capital, carving out another pound of flesh for the absolute joy of it.

"It's mine," Gary says finally, as firm and as fierce as he can manage. "I saved it for later and it's mine."

"Okay, Gary, all right then," she says, sighing and turning toward Monroe Street. "You win again."

His hand is up. In the air.

Donna Thompson can't immediately fathom it—this vision of the McCullough boy looking blankly at her from the other end of the classroom, arm raised, palm open. Patient.

She asked for a volunteer, figuring that she might rope an actual high school student into a little bit of extracurricular oratory. Instead, and through no fault of her own, she gets DeAndre.

For a moment or two, she stares at the upraised hand, then elsewhere around the room, then back at the hand. DeAndre looks back at her with no hint of malevolence, but still, she's cautious, suspecting that this unlikely act of classroom participation is a setup. She figures DeAndre is looking for a chance to clown. Or raise hell. Or ask a question completely off point. Or, at best, respond to her sincere call for extra effort by asking, in the blandest of tones, if he can use the bathroom or sharpen his pencil.

She's given her query the proper wait-time, hoping for some other hands to shoot up. But now the empty pause is washing back on her, with DeAndre alone and waiting. She breathes deeply and then does what a Baltimore city school teacher has to do every day. She gives the kid the benefit of the doubt.

"DeAndre."

"I'll do it."

Heads turn, but the silence holds. No one is quite sure where this is going, and Donna Thompson is working hard to suppress that part of her ready to assume the worst.

"Have you read the speech before?"

"I heard it."

"You know it's for today's assembly?"

DeAndre nods. He's serious. Lord, he's serious. She arms him with a Xeroxed copy of Martin Luther King Jr.'s finest words and he begins to absorb them, his head lowered in quiet concentration. The rest of the kids are watching DeAndre expectantly, waiting on the mayhem that is sure to follow, figuring there must be a joke in here somewhere. But he ignores them, his lips moving silently through sentences that seem ancient and familiar.

And Donna Thompson can only wonder at the chain of absurdity that has brought them to this point. DeAndre has been deadweight in her class since September, his sole achievement being that he has been present for nearly as many days as not.

He's smart. She knows that. All his teachers know it; they lament him in the faculty room and the front office. The elusive Mr. McCullough floats in and out of their classes, never settling into a functional rhythm, never completing anything he begins or showing signs of real commitment. Yet they are given occasional glimpses of ability and wit, of the mind that denies them any connection.

In January he actually had a notebook. Blue denim, with a plastic pocket and a couple of No. 2 pencils. For a while, he filled it with copied questions and rote answers—the usual ditto-sheet fodder that the city teachers threw his way.

"Four resources of Africa: gold, silver, diamonds, oil."

"Define the following terms: tariffs, interpret, census."

"Who was Crispus Attucks?"

"Madame C. J. Walker invented the hot comb. She developed an entire line of beauty supplies. She was the first black millionaire."

But the notebook was long gone, left behind on the bleachers in the Francis M. Woods gym, unmissed and unmourned by a young man for whom the ditto sheets and blackboard questions had no meaning. Africa was somewhere else. Crispus Attucks was dead. No one he knew was clocking a roll by slinging hot combs.

Academically, what remained for DeAndre was the symbolic gesture of walking through the school doors, and then—by dint of some modest improvements in classroom demeanor—not being tossed back out by the school security guards on a regular basis. For him, school had for years been nothing more or less than a social event, a guaranteed happening in a life of daily sameness. His boys were all at school; the girls, too. You went because shit happened there and nothing much was going on anywhere else. For some kids, like R.C., television and basketball were enough. If it was a choice between school or television, R.C. would be back in the house after his mother went to work, lost in the animated bliss of X-Men or G.I. Joe or Spiderman until the soaps came on and it was time to grab some buckets. But for DeAndre, that didn't get it.

Rose Davis had let him back into the school on his promise that he would come to class. She, in turn, had promised that if he would show a glimmer of interest, or just sit quietly and go through the motions, he would be eligible for a social promotion to the tenth grade at the end of the year. Rose had faithfully recorded the agreement in her blue contract book, and DeAndre's signature had been affixed with an earnest and appreciative smile.

Social promotion was, of course, the endgame for all concerned. Everything else had failed: Braced with multiculturalism and a hands-on, child-centered approach, the curriculum had nonetheless lost all connection to DeAndre's world. He held suspect the interest or praise of caring teachers, knowing their values would never sustain him on Fayette Street. The promise of taking any other road, of securing some better life through the prospects of a high school diploma—this meant nothing to him. The negotiations had dwindled to a last, lonely ploy, one premised on unsubtle bribery.

All of which made DeAndre McCullough's single act of participation all the more extraordinary. Between his pursuit of a working wage and his indifference to academics, he hadn't managed enough class attendance this spring to remotely justify even a social promotion to the tenth grade. As for actual effort, his standard had been set since January, when he announced to every one of his teachers that they needed to get one thing straight: He would not do homework. Moreover, he had it in his mind already that if Rose Davis did not find it in herself to promote him simply because he was on the planet breathing air, he would not be back in September. Yet for reasons he himself didn't understand, DeAndre had volunteered to culminate his academic wanderings by learning the great words of a great man and speaking them in front of a school assembly.

As he walks with his English teacher to the school gym that afternoon, DeAndre McCullough is, even by his own reckoning, holding to the tail of a long string of improbabilities. What, he asks himself, am I doing here?

For one thing, he had to get up out of bed this morning, scratch together some clean clothes and begin walking east. Not south, toward the Ramsay Street playground and a day of pickup basketball. Not north to Edmondson and Mount for some of that good E.A.B. weed. Not west toward R.C.'s apartment. No, it was east toward the high school.

He had to bypass Gilmor Street and the chance to hook up with one of the crews selling there. He had to step past Tyreeka's aunt's house and the chance to convince the girl to skip the bus to Carver and spend the day running the street. He had to get to Calhoun Street and turn—not right toward Baltimore Street and the men selling the weed out of the auto garage, but left toward the school doors. He had to open those doors, then try not to provoke Gould, the school security officer, when Gould greeted him in the lobby.

"Good to see you, son."

"Yeah."

Then he had to dodge Rose Davis, who had tracked so many of his absences that she was likely to pull him into the office for another conference. He had to get through the hallways and past the bathrooms and out of the stairwells—all of which offered opportunities for companionship, disturbance, and adventure. He had to survive his first class, no easy feat when Mr. James is droning on about electrons and neutrons, and a couple of the McHenry Street boys are clowning in the back, throwing dice against the wall. Then he had to pass up a dozen other chances at escape—as a hundred other students were discharged into the common hallway—and step into his English class.

From there, some divine intervention was necessary. The kid who
had agreed to give the speech had to be absent, so that Miss Thompson,
in desperation, would have to appeal at the last minute to the rest of the
class. And her class, united in its detachment, would have to leave her
hanging there, waiting, until salvation was possible only from the unlike-
liest source. Then finally, he had to raise his hand.

In the gym, DeAndre can sense the palpable buzz of incredulity as
he's introduced.

He coughs once and offers a quick, furtive smile. Then he begins.

"'I have a dream . . .'"

He takes in curious looks from the faculty and suppressed laughter
from some of his boys in the bleachers.

"'I say to you today, my friends . . . that in spite of the difficulties
and frustrations of the moment . . . I still have a dream . . .'"

And he's good. So good, in fact, that the same teachers who custom-
arily mark Mr. McCullough's report card with a circled Comment
Number Five—"conduct interferes with learning"—are now looking at
each other from the edges of the gymnasium, their eyebrows up, traces
of a smile playing on one or two of the more generous faces. Rose Davis
nods knowingly, as if this outcome were certain and assured.

After the assembly, Donna Thompson is genuinely proud, telling
DeAndre that he was wonderful, encouraging him to take it further and
represent the school in the citywide oratory contest. He'll have two weeks
to memorize and practice, with Mrs. Thompson as his coach. And
DeAndre, caught in the elation of the moment, actually agrees.

He goes back up Fayette Street on that wet, clouded afternoon in
May with a tale of bona fide achievement, but precious few people with
whom he can share it. Brian and R.C. are over at the rec, hanging under
the shade tree by the monkey bars, but giving up a school story to either
of those two is impossible. Ella is inside, and though she'd be okay,
she's busy with the little kids when DeAndre pokes his head inside the
doors.

He veers off and crosses Fayette, heading toward home. Uncle
Stevie is halfway to the corner, doing a full twenty-five-degree list on
a windless day—the fiend's lean. Shit must be a bomb today, thinks
DeAndre.

He takes the stairs two at a time, landing loudly in the hallway of
the second-floor apartment.

"Ma."

Bunchie creeps around the corner from the kitchen, unnerved by the boisterous entrance. DeAndre sounds a little too much like a drug raid.

"Where's my ma at?"

"She downstairs."

He bounds back down the stairwell, then pauses in the vestibule, one hand on the knob of the basement door, wondering again just what he's expecting out of this. Below him, he can hear the noise of the television: Fran and Bunchie and the rest of them had dragged a set down to the bottom of the house to keep them company while they're getting high. In the bedroom, in the living room, in Stevie's lair, in the basement—the televisions play constantly at the Dew Drop, so that lives in this house can best be measured not by ordinary hours and minutes, but by what show is droning in the background. If Family Affair had testers out yesterday during "All My Children," then you best get your ass down to Mount Street when the same soap kicks up tomorrow. If you heard the gunshots in the middle of the local news, then the New York Boy got shot sometime after eleven, unless you were tuned to the Fox affiliate, in which case, he hit the pavement an hour earlier.

DeAndre opens the door and the TV noise gets louder. "Ma," he calls from the top, giving her a heads-up.

"What?"

"You alone?"

"Huh."

"You by yourself?"

"Yeah."

He moves slowly down the plank stairs, giving her the courtesy of a few extra seconds. When he arrives at the bottom of the stairs, Fran is sitting in the small square of sunlight from the rear door and the mirror is mostly clean.

"What's goin' on?"

"Nuthin'."

"Where your brother at? He at the rec?"

DeAndre shrugs, then turns away, shuffling awkwardly. He walks in a tight circle, looking down, then back at his mother, then off toward the other end of the basement.

"What's up?"

He shrugs again.

"Dre," she asks, her voice rising. "Why you come down here?"

He feels trapped. "You got a fug?"

She shakes her head. DeAndre stays put.

"What is it?"

DeAndre looks down, embarrassed, as if he's carrying the worst kind of news. His voice falls to a lost mumble.

"I gave a speech."

"Say what?"

"In school."

"A speech," Fran says.

DeAndre nods, smiling.

"You gave a speech? Why you ain't tell me?"

"The boy that was supposed to give it didn't show up. An' no one else was gonna step up so I jus' did it."

Fran is smiling now.

"I did it in the gym in front of the whole school. Miss Thompson says she wants me to do it downtown. They got a citywide contest."

"What'd you say?"

"I said okay."

"Huh?"

"I said I'd do it."

"No, I'm sayin' what'd you say in the speech."

DeAndre is fighting to keep his cool, play it off. He pulls a folded sheet of paper from his pants pocket, then hands it to his mother. Fran reads.

"This from Martin Luther King," she says, recognizing the words. DeAndre grunts agreement.

"Andre, you is a trip."

He looks at her curiously.

"I mean I'm proud of you."

He grunts again, embarrassed.

"When you go downtown?"

"Couple weeks."

"Well, I wanna see that."

"I dunno. They sayin' I got to wear a suit."

"Your father has a suit. Ask your father."

DeAndre walks over and begins picking at the chicken wire of the storage pen. He says nothing for a moment or two.

Fran prods him gently. "You gonna do it, ain't you?"

"I might."

"Well, you tell me when so I can be there."

"Hmm," he says.

"Andre, I'm serious. I want to go."

He shrugs and she insists. He leaves the basement with a grudging promise to let her know. He leaves without the printed copy of the speech.

Two weeks later, in the waning days of the school year, he wakes up late, washes, grabs the suit that Rose Davis let him borrow, and then rummages through the bedroom dresser and a dozen jacket and pants pockets, finding only a third of the necessary words. Half-dressed, he goes to the apartment door and shouts down the steps to Fran, who is on the stoop.

"Ma," he yells, almost belligerent. "Where my speech at?"

Fran shouts back from the front steps, telling him to look on the dresser top.

"I got that," yells DeAndre, bringing his mother up the front stairs. "Where the rest of it?"

"The rest of what?"

"There was more pages."

"That's all you showed me."

"Yeah, right."

Fran explodes, telling him she has no use for his school papers and no reason to lie about their whereabouts. "Why you want 'em anyway?" she yells from the stoop.

DeAndre mumbles a profanity.

"What?"

"Practice," he says, rooting through the dresser for a few more minutes. Slinging the suit over his shoulder, he cracks the bedroom door, then walks to the front stairs, waiting there until his mother leaves the stoop and descends to the basement. When she does, he slides quietly down the stairs. All the way down Fayette Street, he's telling himself that he can't give his speech, that he's missing the rest of the pages, that even if he had those pages, and even if he'd practiced, and even if this country-ass suit actually fit him, he still wouldn't tell his mother. She'd only try and tear him down like she always did, complain because he hadn't practiced or done more with it. She's always downing me that way, he tells himself, talking about what he should be doin' and how he should be livin' when she ain't doin' shit her own self.

He marches down to the high school in a foul mood, fully aggrieved

and convinced that he's justifiably done for the year, that it's just a matter
of telling Rose Davis that he can't wear a geechy suit and that his ma
threw his speech out. Either that, or just tell her, fuck it, I got other shit
to do.

On the front steps of the school, he runs across Randy, a C.M.B.
hanger-on, who's talking about going up to the Boys' Club to lift weights,
or maybe going downtown.

"Wait up," DeAndre assures him. "I be right back out."

But once inside, the gravitational field shifts. He's confronted in the
front hallway by Rose Davis, who catches a glimpse of him through the
outer office door and follows him down the corridor before he can think
of anything to say.

"DeAndre!"

"Huh."

"Where are you going?" she asks, guiding him gently with one hand
to his shoulder. "Mrs. Thompson is waiting upstairs."

"I don't think this fits," he says, holding the suit out by the hanger
ring, hoping she'll take it back.

"You tried it on, didn't you."

DeAndre shakes his head.

"Well, go up and see Mrs. Thompson," she says, steering him toward
the stairwell. "I'm sure it'll be fine."

He climbs the stairs with a tightness in his stomach, trying to muster
some anger at his predicament, telling himself that even if he was going
to give the speech, he looks all right now. Fuck this, he thinks. No need
to wear no white man's suit.

"We have to hurry," Donna Thompson tells him. "You're late."

He's a trapped animal. "Man, look at this geechy-looking thing," he
says. "I ain't wearing this outside."

"DeAndre, just try it on."

He looks at her, then down at the jacket.

"Go on."

He begins unbuttoning his shirt and the English teacher, taking her
cue, heads for the door. DeAndre plays the moment.

"All man," he declares, pounding his bare chest.

Donna Thompson ignores him.

He emerges five minutes later to find his English teacher and Rose
Davis waiting for him in the hallway. Shirt, slacks, jacket, belt, and shoes—
everything's a fit, though the shirt collar is a little tight. He carries the

necktie—striped, subdued, very Republican—in his hand, unable to negotiate any kind of knot.

"That fits nice," says Donna Thompson.

"Mr. James," says Rose Davis, calling to a teacher at the other end of the hall. "Could you come here and help this fine-looking young man with his tie?"

DeAndre laughs. Smiling broadly, Mr. James battles the necktie to a full Windsor while DeAndre finds more to complain about: "You chokin' me to death. I don't see how people wear clothes like this."

"But you look so fine, DeAndre," says Rose Davis.

"Mmmm hmmm," says Donna Thompson.

The two women begin to lead the way to the stairwell. It seems there's no going back on the bargain, though DeAndre is still looking for an out.

"I don't have my speech," he tells them. "My ma lost it."

The English teacher returns to her classroom for a fresh copy, and, minutes later, they're out the door. At least Randy is no longer waiting for him; that much is a relief to DeAndre, who feels shame at allowing himself to be displayed this way. Mrs. Thompson drives east across town, heading for a middle school at the other end of North Avenue. By the time DeAndre gets out of the car, the necktie is sagging and the shirt-tail hangs free—he is rebelling as best he can.

His teacher pauses to straighten him.

"I look geechy," DeAndre insists.

At the front doors of the middle school, two elderly women come out just as this unlikely apparition—this dredlocked, gold-toothed scholar, his street presence at odds with the corporate uniform—is on the way in.

"Young man, don't you look nice."

"Yes, he certainly does."

Suddenly, his head comes up in a broad smile. He loses all of his corner chill and actually struts through the front hall. The women at the registration table add to the accolades—even more so as it becomes clear that DeAndre is a participant in the dramatic reading competition, one of the few boys, in fact, to be included.

The attention has an effect. After registering, DeAndre squares his shoulders in a Cagney-like contortion, then glides into the auditorium as if his entrance is victory itself. Donna Thompson, however, is showing enough fear and trepidation for both of them.

"DeAndre stepped in when the young man who was supposed to read was absent," she explains to the registrar, fearing the worst for her charge. "He hasn't practiced as much as . . ."

Her voice trails off and the other women nod sympathetically.

Inside the auditorium, DeAndre is escorted to the stage; he's there in the nick of time, with only a minute before his group is scheduled. He's seated at the back of the stage in the center chair of three, with a girl on either side. The judges are in the front row facing the stage. Donna Thompson slips quietly into the last row. She drops her purse, crosses her legs and bows her head, one hand over her eyes in what seems to be a prolonged moment of prayer.

DeAndre is oblivious. All he knows at this point is that he's dressed to kill and they've dropped him between two sweet young schoolgirls, both of them nervous and earnest. The girls are sweating the contest; their worthy adversary judges their legs.

The white girl from Southeast is called first. She launches into Eliza Doolittle's vengeful rant from *My Fair Lady*. Just you wait 'enry 'iggins, she promises in a flawless Cockney, her face ripe with wounded pride.

She finishes with a righteous flourish, nods respectfully to the judges, and returns to her seat. DeAndre watches with a vague interest that grows deeper when the taller black girl rises to begin her own presentation.

"'. . . and I'm proud he was brave and helped save somebody else 'fore he got killed. But I can't help thinkin' Willie died fightin' in the wrong place . . .'"

The black girl is regal in her delivery of the soliloquy from *A Medal for Willie*, the William Branch play. Transformed into a middle-aged mother, she musters every ounce of dignity to deny those who had the audacity to misuse her son. The girl's voice is full and sonorous, flooding the auditorium with a mother's pain.

"'So you can take this medal back on up to Washington and tell 'em I don't want it. Take it back. Pin it on your own shirt. Give it to the ones who keeps this big lie goin' . . .'"

She sits, and the judges call for DeAndre McCullough from Francis M. Woods Senior High School. There is no show of panic, no sense that he's out of his league, that he's just witnessed two very polished presentations—each performed from memory, each with the flourishes of real stagecraft. He stands, walks almost casually to the podium, and goes into his jacket pocket for three sheets of paper that he slowly unfolds and arranges in front of him.

"'I say to you today, my friends . . .'"

His voice is firm, with some of the Southern Baptist texture required. He doesn't falter or stutter, but neither does he dare to lift his eyes from the paper and risk losing his place.

"'. . . that one day on the red hills of Georgia, the sons of former slaves and the sons of former slaveholders . . .'"

He is reading and reading well, and the absence of whatever dramatic emphasis is required for King's extraordinary dream is, for Donna Thompson, of secondary consequence. No, DeAndre will not win points from any judges today, but neither will he be embarrassed. For whatever reason, he raised his hand. And today he showed up, wore the suit, went through with it, so that for at least this moment, he has stepped from the shadows of the corner. In the back of the auditorium, Donna Thompson is caught up in the emotion of this small triumph. She visibly gives way to her own relief, opening her eyes and staring up at the ceiling with an expression of pure thankfulness.

"'I have a dream today . . .'"

DeAndre begins to sense the end, to realize that after a few paragraphs more, escape is certain. The dramatic flourishes are fewer; the words roll past in a rush, and perhaps intentionally, DeAndre inserts his own first-person ad lib at the very end.

"'. . . free at last, free at last, thank God almighty I'm free at last.'"

Free is free. DeAndre lumbers away from the lectern without acknowledging the judges. He leaves the pieces of his speech behind and makes his way up the aisle. Donna Thompson is there to embrace him.

He's been to the mountaintop, and only when he swims through the sea of congratulations in the outer lobby and emerges from the school building is the dream once again deferred. Out in the parking lot, DeAndre yanks the tie from his neck and strips himself of the jacket and dress shirt. He pulls the slacks off over his shoes, leaving only his knee-length shorts and a tank top.

He balls up the dress clothes, tossing them into the car trunk. He's quickly back in character, regaling Donna Thompson with a detailed assessment of the two contestants who preceded him: "Yeah boy, they was both fine as I don't know what. I be awright with either one an' better with both."

It's almost enough to make her believe that he couldn't care less, that the journey was lost on him. But as they get in the car, he stops her in an altogether different voice.

"You know," he says quietly. "I can win this next year if I want to."

You want to set a standard, to show them that you care. You have expectations. On this, the first day of a new school year, you're out to let them know that what happens in this room truly matters.

There are thirty-five names on the roll, but only twenty-six faces— black and brown, a stray white or two—stare back at you with some tentative interest. Thirty-five to a class is the standard for the city school system; it's what Baltimore can afford. So for the teachers, the no-shows and occasionals are almost a blessing. Twenty-six souls—and twenty-five of them are actually awake and alert on this first day of a fresh year. You can work with this.

You might want to tell them the rules. Or a little about yourself. Talk to them about teaching, or learning, or what they can expect if they're willing to work. You might start with a story, something with the right lesson attached.

"Once upon a time . . ."

Story time always works, even here in a high school. Right away, you've got their attention.

". . . we're talking a long time ago and we're talking insects. You know, your basic insect community . . ."

Some nervous laughter. You're playing them now and they're a bit off guard.

". . . and you know, most insects are hard workers. It's not that they are all about work, but work comes first. Work first—and then play. So in this community, we're talking ants and grasshoppers and one grasshopper in particular . . ."

The short kid in the second row pipes up: "I know this one. I like this one."

You're off. You're teaching.

". . . and the grasshopper comes around to the ants' house and tries to get them to go party. But they're about business. It's not that they're rude and brush him off. In fact, one tells him that when they're finished, they'll hook up with him . . ."

You've got them. They're buying it.

". . . so when the winter comes, our man is caught short. At first, all the other insects are willing to carry him, but this is a long winter and the stash gets low . . ."

"They gonna burn 'im," says a boy in the back.

". . . so one day, while the grasshopper's away, the wise old beetle calls a community meeting. And it's decided that they can no longer take care of the grasshopper. So when our man shows up and makes his play, he's told that's all there is and there ain't no more."

The moral is right there, waiting for them. But you play the thing out to the very end, taking your lazy grasshopper from door to door across Insectville, and finally dragging him out into the deep snow of a bleak, unforgiving winter.

"And," you say, savoring the lesson, "you know what happens to a hungry grasshopper in the dead of winter, don't you?"

A hand goes up, and you nod your head.

"He goes down the welfare building and gets his food stamps."

You look down at the wiseass in question, but what stares back at you from the middle of the end row is a neatly dressed, well-mannered girl who's not even trying to be funny. She has answered in absolute earnest and her answer is, in every sense, accepted and understood by the rest of the class.

You've crossed the chasm. You're a city teacher.

As such, you're beginning to realize not only that Aesop won't play in Baltimore, but that for the children of Fayette Street, the idea of educa-tion—the formal education of a classroom, at least—has no meaning. To those who argue that the urban school systems of this nation are underfunded, or understaffed, or poorly managed—and in Baltimore, at least, these are fair accusations, every one—there is this equal and opposing truth: The schools cannot save us.

The debate over tax bases and class size, efficacy and alternative curricula matters only for that finite portion of children ready and able to learn, to set genuine goals, to adapt their lives to the external standards of the culture. For these children, the key is a functional family and their place in that family. For them, some semblance of victory was assured before they ever walked into the classroom.

True, a better school might cultivate a few more minds, salvaging more of the marginal students in an environment that rewards skilled teaching and assures consistent discipline. It's always good to be better. But it's also true that in cities like Baltimore, the thing is now beyond the fine tuning of school superintendents and educational experts. Take the entire Phillips Exeter Academy, drop it into West Baltimore, and fill its ivy-covered campus with DeAndre McCulloughs, Richard Carters, and four hundred of their running buddies, and see just how little can be had for a dollar's worth of education.

As it is with our laws and our legal deterrents, our educational theories no longer matter within the all-consuming universe of the corner. We want the drugs to disappear because they are illegal or, more basically, because they are bad for people. But the drugs will not disappear in a culture where everything else—jobs, money, hope, meaning—has already vanished. With the same naïveté, we want the children to learn because learning is worthy, and right, and the last, best hope for their own future. It was the way out for us, and our parents, and the legacy that our grandparents worked to ensure. The public schools that launched the immigrant masses out of the pushcart ghettos and into manicured suburbs hold a place of honor in the American mythology.

But Fayette Street is no place for myth. Those that escaped from the heart of West Baltimore did so in a different time and a different way, with union-scale factory jobs or government work in a nation-state that seemed to have some use for them. But the factories are closed now, and the government isn't hiring, and the jobs today are all about doing something with a computer somewhere out in the county. For that kind of work, a City of Baltimore diploma and 750 on the college boards can't matter. Down on Fayette Street, they know how many finished products of the city school system are standing with them at the next register over in the Kentucky Fried. Or in the intake area of the Rosemont social service offices. Or, after a time, in the vacant lot off Vine Street, waiting patiently for the New York Boys to bring out the morning testers.

It's too simple to mistake this for cynicism; it is, in fact, certainty. Knowledge of the eventual outcome isn't limited to those already lost to the corner, or to those about to arrive there. It's there in the eyes of third-graders who have already segregated the world of education, pushing the classroom to the fringes of their lives.

By middle school, they're spouting future-tense fantasies in the same sing-song cadence used to offer remorse to a juvenile master or probation agent. Gonna stay in school. Get educated. Be a doctor. A lawyer. A pediatric neurosurgeon. Either that, or a cosmetologist. But take a closer look and you see a child with only the weakest grasp of literacy and basic arithmetic. Algebra, biology, composition—what does any of it mean to the corner, to the only working economic engine in their lives, to the place where most of them will eventually be consigned?

Even the socializing effect of an alternative curriculum—the kinds of skills designed by desperate educators to get these kids to the most basic level of employment—has no real application on Fayette Street. Job interview techniques, cooperative learning, managing emotions, interpersonal discipline—stuff like that will get you hurt at Fayette and Monroe, where the rules of the corner demand not social skills, but unhesitating ruthlessness.

At this age, these children are not yet aware that they are horribly alone, that the rest of America—its dreams, myths, standards—has walked away from West Baltimore. They don't fully sense that this country has reshaped itself as distinct and apart from the core of its cities, that it no longer even pretends to have a use for an underclass that once might have served it with raw labor, filling its rural spaces or crowding its sweatshops. These children don't know the whole truth, and yet by middle school, the compartmentalization that has allowed them to straddle both worlds is beginning to crumble. By middle school, the more savvy are already asking themselves and each other whether knowing the names of four African rivers will help them spot a drug corner stickup a minute before it happens. Or whether awareness of the Pythagorean theorem will allow them to squeeze ten more vials from an eight ball. Everything taught in the classroom becomes strangely dissonant; the contradictions between general knowledge and the rules of the corner are there and inexplicable.

And if, God forbid, you are a child with a genuine and innocent interest in something other than the business of the street, you'll be battered down. For the sake of their math book, how many twelve-year-olds are ready to endure the certainty of ostracism? Caught in the crossfire, they burrow in, play dumb, watch from the sidelines as the streetwise kids wreak havoc time and again, only to suffer precious little consequence. Eventually even the most timid realize that there isn't much bite behind all those rules.

The teachers learn as well. They recognize the ones who care—the kids who are still walking the fine line—but understand that they have to survive. Call on the same child repeatedly for right answers and, eventually, he'll shut down. Point out the high test score, and the unlucky achiever will be made vulnerable to the group. It's peer pressure, same as it is anywhere, but in urban Baltimore, it's compounded by the weight of numbers. In the classrooms at Harlem Park, or Lombard or any other inner-city middle school, it's not one or two roughnecks who refuse to buy into the educational experience. Here, in the toughest schools, that alienation can consume half a class or more.

By eighth grade at the latest, the choice has been made, with children opting out of the classroom in every way save for their physical presence. Creativity ceases, and what classwork remains is so disjointed and distant that it can be ignored in its entirety. By the end of middle school, a child is filling a desk in the Baltimore school system as little more than a social experience. He's there for banter and play. She's there for girlfriends and lunch.

This is a school system that dares not speak to the heart of the problem—the fact that its children now come from a world apart. But walk with a Baltimore teacher into a ninth-grade class and see the future:

It comes in the shape of Anthony, a child so beaten down by circumstance that in this class of kids going nowhere, he occupies the bottom rung. For him, there is no one at home who can manage the slightest recognition or interest. He's easy to spot; his filthy shirt and denims are the only set of clothes in his possession. There's always a fight when someone has to sit next to Anthony.

Or Marie, who sits nearest the door and at thirteen is going on thirty, now that her body has filled out and caught the interest of a twenty-four-year-old drug slinger. She can't be bothered with a notebook, spending her class time with pocket mirrors and jewelry and nail polish, preening for the other girls. Most days, her boyfriend sits outside the school at two-thirty, idling a glittering Acura, waiting to collect his girl. By next year, she'll be a transfer to the system's special school for young mothers.

Or Neal, a lumbering bear with the dead eyes of a battlefield casualty. Twice wounded in shootouts, he sits in the back of the class, content to do or say nothing the entire year. But he rules the hallways, with a group of lesser gangsters drawn to him because of the way he carries himself and the impressive rep of his older brothers' drug crew.

Or Michelle, a small, wiry fourteen-year-old in the middle row, her face a profusion of scars and scratches, reminders of her tooth-and-nail struggle for a small niche in this world. She's been living at her boyfriend's mother's house for the past two months. Her own mother is on lockup at women's detention.

Or the amazing Michael, a spinning whirlwind of disruption, unable to remain in his assigned seat for more than an instant. He's rushing about the classroom, coins clasped in his hand, offering lunch tickets, candy, and comic books for sale to any and all takers. Evasive to authority, he'll keep moving until he's cornered. He's living with his mother. His father gets supervised visits, and the written notes in the file hint at abuse.

Or Durrell, who comes to school from a homeless shelter. Or Clyde, a special education student with borderline retardation, who needs special attention and is, instead, doomed to this class. Or Tonya, who responds to any confrontation by fighting savagely and, by the end of the year, will be expelled for carrying a lock-blade. Or C.J., who will disappear in midyear never to return, amid news reports that have him fatally shooting an older boy in an argument over drugs and being sentenced as a juvenile to Boys Village until his eighteenth birthday.

And what remains for the teacher? What training, what lesson plan, what act of educational artistry will be sufficient to the reality? In Baltimore, as in every other beleaguered city system, the administrators and bureaucrats have for decades wrapped the failure in the latest educational trends, programs, and jargon, as if changes in approach or technique could ever matter. Back-to-basics, alternative schools, privatization, magnet schools, teaching the whole child—all of it is offered up as slogans in place of meaningful endeavor, as if the Titanic could have reached the New York harbor narrows with a more seaworthy set of deck chairs.

Ignore the hyperbole and slogans. Regardless of how many times an urban school system reconstitutes itself, the choice that remains for teachers at Harlem Park, or Lombard, or Hamilton middle schools is no choice at all.

They work in classrooms in which creativity and intelligence have been almost willfully extracted, a room of silences and by-rote drills and copied information. For many teachers in the city system, there is still the willingness to fight the inertia, to use their talents to battle back into the heads of children who have shut down, who cannot find it in themselves to bridge the chasm between their own lives and a world of learning. Sometimes, despite the long odds, these teachers actually succeed.

But for many others, a separate peace has been made with the forces arrayed against them. In too many city classrooms, in too many city schools, there is a readiness to participate in the charade, to pretend that dittoed handouts and assignments merely copied from the board constitute an educational experience. Similarly, there is a willingness to pretend that the relative few who make it to a high school commencement in Baltimore have actually received the equivalent of a high school education. These are the teachers and administrators who have given up on a system that cannot salvage its standards.

As with the drug war, the struggle to save the Baltimore school system has always been framed in incremental terms: With a little more money, with a teacher's union that is a little less obstinate, with more responsive administrators, the children will be saved. But the truth is that these things don't add up when the weight of numbers prevents anyone from accurately assessing and rewarding real achievement, or responding in earnest to disruptive behavior, or even making a legitimate effort to find out why so many desks are empty every day. In Baltimore, three social workers and four case managers are responsible for tracking two thousand chronic truants—children who have missed anywhere from a month to an entire year of their education. Facing this strange new generation of corner children, too many teachers will not extend themselves for a system that pays them thousands less than their counterparts in suburbia, arms them with torn, broken-back textbooks and ancient filmstrips, and then deposits them in a classroom environment so chaotic that no fewer than an average of one hundred and fifty teachers and thirty school police officers are assaulted each year. Those that can get out, will— either to the safe haven of a county school system or to another profession entirely. Those trapped by the inertia of years, by a vested pay scale, or by their own rank incompetence will remain. These teachers are not likely ever to rediscover a belief in their purpose, their students, or for that matter, in whatever acronym or slogan or program is now being touted as salvation by the superintendent's staff. Some of them were once good teachers; others never had a clue. But all of them are now looking only for survival, ready and willing to penetrate a young mind so long as classroom decorum can be maintained. It's perversely fair: By middle school, the students are pretending to learn; their teachers, pretending to teach.

And come the end of every academic year, the deceit culminates in a process that is known, in Baltimore at least, as the social promotion. When all else has failed, when the relationship between the child and the school is in tatters, it's time for the last, desperate act.

Social promotion—elevation based on age or behavior, rather than academic achievement—is anathema to many teachers and even some school administrators. They regard it as a turning away from the old standards, which hold that each academic year should build on a progression of skills, that it isn't in a child's best interest to be moved up until those skills are firmly in place. But all that presumes a functional society, one in which the occasional child with the most earnest intentions will for some reason struggle with the work. It presumes a failure rate proportionate and manageable, housed within the larger set of well-tended, well-taught school children. But in end-of-the-century Baltimore, the swelling horde of disconnected kids has forced a whole new logic on an educational structure that has neither the time nor the resources to respond.

To the individual child, a social promotion is a devaluation, a dumbing-down of the system's already fragile standards. Collectively, however, it seems to offer a solution to the backlog of repeaters, the hulking sixteen-year-olds clustered at the rear of every eighth-grade class. Without social promotion, the older kids are retained to terrorize the younger ones, or pass down their legacy of mayhem, or openly battle teachers for control of the class, or—at best—sit sullenly, embittered, no more willing or able to learn than they were the year before.

It's a Hobson's choice: The studies note that kids left behind will drop out sooner, but passing them without basic skills can hardly be considered a guarantee of success. Worse still, the social promotions send a message to the borderline students—the ones who just might, with the effort of a good teacher, be induced to continue working. For them, there seems to be no discernible difference in outcome. If they pay attention and do their work, they will see the ninth grade come September. So, too, will everyone else.

There can be no right decision here, nothing that can later be justified to anyone who actually cares why Johnny can't read—not that there's much hue and cry from any quarter. It's left to you and the other teachers to sit in that staff room on a late spring day as the vice principal rolls down the list. There's nothing in writing, nothing for the record, but everyone in the room knows what's feasible and what isn't. Three percent can fail, maybe 6 or 8 percent if you want to push it. But the system can't sustain itself on a 25 or 40 or 60 percent failure rate. So you sit there with your colleagues, roll book in front of you, and you begin, alphabetically as always.

"Abbott."

"He's okay . . . pass."

"Adams, Monique."

"I saw some improvement at the end of the year."

"Well, not in my class."

"You can fail her there, but I've got to pass her."

"Me too."

"Addams, Robert."

"Lord, one more year and I can adopt him."

"Hey," someone jokes, "third time's the charm."

"No way. I'm tired of him tossing books out the windows."

"Well Herbert Thomas sets his on fire and we passed him."

"Please. I can't deal with Robert."

"Okay, pass."

You sit there for two and a half hours, making judgments off the top of your head, all the while sensing the absurdity of the thing. You remember a test you gave back in March on Greek mythology—a unit that they invariably enjoy. That was the test where you offered a full review the day before, giving them the answers to every question, making a game of it and letting them team up to work on the material. Eighty-five percent of your students failed that exam; the highest score was an eighty-six. Hell, you were even offering a ten-point bonus just for reading the test directions.

"Please put your name and class number at the top of the sheet," you typed on the ditto sheet. "Then number the paper in the left-hand column from one to twenty-five. After answering the questions, on the back of the paper, for ten bonus points, draw a smiley face."

From twenty-two students, you got six grinning circles.

Now, you all sit here going through the motions, pretending that there is a difference between the kids you send to the tenth grade and those left behind. The no-shows are easy enough—if they didn't exist in your class, they can't exist now—but virtually everyone else is an open question.

Failing grades in the core classes? That alone could disqualify more than half of the eighth grade. Achievement, or the lack of it, is not enough of a filter. You factor in class absences, disruptive behavior, and indifference; still, the number of those actually deserving promotion is appallingly low. But next year, there will be another swarm of eighth-graders. And they can't be taught if a third of last year's class is hulking in the back of the room.

"Gregg."

"His stepfather got him working."

"Pass."

What is left at the end of such an exercise is a school system playing with numbers in the same way that the police department must, a bureaucracy still seeking some proportional response to a problem of complete disproportion. Just as Baltimore's police commissioner will seize the rostrum to proclaim 18,000 street-level drug arrests a victory, so does the school superintendent cull his files for anything that smells like hope or success. Reading and math scores are up a couple percentage points; never mind that Baltimore is trailing the rest of the state by 60 percent. The senior graduation rate is up in the mid-nineties; never mind that by the twelfth grade, 70 percent of the students have already been lost to attrition.

Yet these children, like children everywhere, have facile minds. You can hear it in their ease of language, in their rapid-fire mimicry of adult convention. You can see the innate intelligence on those rare occasions when a bit of information touches a nerve, provoking them with a challenge that they can understand and accept as relevant to their world. These children can, when it serves them, unravel a moral dilemma with subtle precision. They can respond to a classroom injustice with the most carefully formed arguments, or produce the solutions to the most intricate engineering and historical conundrums.

Ask Michelle whether Egypt or England are countries or continents and she has no interest and no clue. But ask how the Pharoah's architects managed to get the crypt inside the finished tomb, or how the ancients got the rocks to stand at Stonehenge, and invariably, she'll give you a working hypothesis. And Michelle's effort will readily provoke a vigorous class-room discussion, as kids previously dead to the process suddenly pour themselves into heated debate. Just don't ask for anything in writing, or expect the effort to sustain itself for longer than fifteen minutes or show itself in any review quiz a few days later. To see these students come alive, to sense the eagerness buried inside them, is to understand just how far the elemental human urge to learn has been subverted, how something natural to childhood has been brutally limited to a handful of raw lessons suitable to the corner.

Eventually, somewhere short of the sixteenth birthday, most of these children stop going through the motions. At some point in the ninth grade, the social promotions cease and some facsimile of actual schoolwork is required. But by then they're close enough to the age when they will no longer be a problem to the school system. The severance, when it comes, is rarely planned; it simply happens. One day, a kid starts out for Southwestern or Francis Woods but end ups down at the Carroll Park courts, or over at some girl's house, or out on the corner where his crew is hanging. He doesn't go back the next day. Or Friday either. A couple months drift away and he's dropped from the rolls; the academic exercise ends without so much as a word spoken.

For the children of Fayette Street, the result is never in doubt. One after another, the boys and their girlfriends follow each other down to Mount Street, or Fairmount, or Monroe, until the entire C.M.B. contingent reaches that station in life for which they were always intended. They arrive on the corners utterly intact, hardened to the business at hand and ready to deal with failure on a grand scale. All those Head Start programs, all those grade-school lectures about civics and drugs and violence, all the alternative curricula and vocational education and Afrocentric esteem-building—in the end, none of it sticks. None of it even counts for baggage as they journey to their place on the factory floor.

DeAndre pretends to school, but his efforts seem almost valid when compared to the rest of the crew. Dorian and Brooks, for example, jumped out of the system two years ago, wandering away from Harlem Park by the seventh grade, removing themselves so early that the truancy people were actually able to catch on and lock them up before they could got close to sixteen. That meant some time in group homes, but little improvement in school attendance. Dinky, DeAndre's cousin, felt the same but managed to wait a little longer to make his move. The truancy workers never laid a glove on Dinky.

This spring, it's Brian who escapes the eighth grade, walking away from middle school to work his uncle's package on Lemmon Street, then getting locked up with so many vials that schoolwork becomes the least of his problems. R.C. plays the system as best he can by missing virtually all of his ninth-grade year at Southwestern, then landing at Francis Woods and doing the same thing with a second set of teachers and administrators.

Then there is Tae, the leader of the pack and the only one of them to demonstrate any academic promise at all. Never having been held back a grade, Tae is finishing the tenth grade at Carver with a high-C average and standing on the track team. He's getting past algebra and talking scholarship, telling himself and anyone else who would listen that school isn't a problem. And Tae can talk that way without it bouncing back; he's a cofounder of C.M.B. and his corner status is such that any academic inclinations are unlikely to be criticized. In time, Tae will make it all the way to his senior year. In fact, he'll get all the way to the second semester of the twelfth grade before simply giving up and going down to McHenry and Gilmor full-time.

By then, the slow grinding will be done. The school system will have taken its shots, tallied its misses, and closed its files, relinquishing any further claim.

The corners will have them all.

SUMMER

SUMMER

SIX

"Oh mah Gawd," drawls DeAndre as the opposition enters the gym. "It's the old school."

Kiti laughs as he holds the gym door open for Preston. Shamrock and Jamie are already inside, lacing up on the bleachers.

"Who you callin' old?" grins Shamrock.

"Yes, Lawd," DeAndre adds. "They think they still got a game."

"You ain't never had a game," Preston assures him.

From the second row of the bleachers, Ella Thompson laughs. "Come on now, Preston," she says, feigning offense. "I don't want to hear you talking about my players that way."

Preston sees Ella and mumbles his apology.

"If it's your team, Miss Ella, then I respects that," Preston says. "But otherwise, I have to say, they don't look like too much."

Ella laughs again.

Preston; Shamrock; Jamie; DeAndre's uncle, Kwame—Ella has the older heads off the corners and in the gym for this one day in June. These are the eighteen- and nineteen- and twenty-year-olds, the Fayette Street crew just senior to C.M.B.; these boys are also the closest friends of her youngest son.

Kiti seems happy to be out of his room, joining up with his old crew to give his mother's rec center team a run. Ella watches him walk into the gym and senses the release in the moment. The past is present; the gym is sanctuary. As with the Valentine's Day dance, on this afternoon, Kiti gets to snatch at some freedom.

The bleachers are filled with younger kids from the rec center, neighborhood girls, even a few of the older street dealers. The game itself seems casual enough, but Ella had been trying to put it together since early spring. It took weeks for Ella and Kiti to pry Shamrock away from his daily regime of slinging and stickups and to bring Kwame,

Preston, and Jamie in from Fulton Avenue, where she could see them every day, drinking forties outside the liquor store, standing there amid the touts and runners and the 40-Dawg graffiti on the store wall. Today, all of them would relive just a bit of their childhood and give Miss Ella and her sixteen-and-under squad whatever remained of their court game.

Officially, this is the follow-up to the Martin Luther Kings' loss to Bentalou, an upstart challenge by the new breed along Fayette Street. Their elders used to own the neighborhood ball courts but now, with the obvious exception of Kiti, they are serving the corners full-time. Yet Ella has known these young men all their lives; she sees them not as they are, but as they want to be seen. When she asks them for a game—asks them two or three times until finally, they realize that she isn't just making conversation—they drop the package and the blunt and the forty of St. Ides and walk the five blocks down Fayette Street and strip down to their shorts.

"You all think you ready?" asks Shamrock.

"Born ready," answers DeAndre.

Ella laughs again. A ten-year-old is designated as the bank, then loaded down with gold chains, beepers, watches, wads of cash and spare change. Ella sees all this and pays no mind; nor does she worry that Kiti seems entirely at ease with Preston and Shamrock and the rest of his old crew. How could it be otherwise? This was his crowd until Preston and the rest went down to the corner; if not for Ella, Kiti would be with them in all things. She knows this. He knows this. His friends know it, too.

Tae captains the rec team, choosing his starters—Truck, Twin, and Mike of the Hilltop crew; R.C. and himself to represent C.M.B.—and calling for a two-three zone. Shamrock offers to let the younger team have the first possession, but Tae demurs. Our court, he tells him. Your ball out.

"Ol' heads," shouts DeAndre from the bench, as Preston brings the ball up. "Ol' heads gonna get tired."

The older boys work the ball well, giving it up, looking to penetrate by getting one pass ahead. There is less ego to their game, more of the distance required to play as a team. They work Kiti to a ten-foot turnaround that goes in and out.

Truck is quick off the rebound, with an outlet to R.C., who fires the ball crosscourt to Tae for a finger roll; even Shamrock has to smile.

DeAndre and R.C. declare immediate victory, assuring the old school that their time has passed.

Preston misses from the baseline, but Shamrock gets behind the defense for a tap-in. Tie score.

"Cheap," yells DeAndre. "Cheap bucket."

R.C. responds with a long jumper from the corner, then Tae steals a pass and dishes out to Twin. Suddenly, it's 6–2, and it's all the success the rec team can stand. Shamrock slows the game down to work the ball, running the offense with deliberate calm. Twice back and forth, and it's tied. Then it's 10–6, favor the old school. Then 14–8, 20–10 and—as Tae begins subbing his players, bringing DeAndre, Manny Man, and Dinky onto the court—the score bottoms out at 32–14, enough of a margin to make it apparent that any changing of the guard on Fayette Street will have to be rescheduled.

R.C. stalks off the court after a twenty-minute run, sitting with his head in his hands as he tries to catch his wind. He watches things go from bad to worse, growing visibly angry, at one point kicking the wooden bleachers for emphasis when DeAndre loses the ball off his own foot.

He subs himself back in, crashing the boards wildly, trying to force the game to another conclusion. He's going over people for rebounds, diving for loose balls, but no matter. The older crew wins by almost thirty.

Afterward R.C. is on the front steps of the school with the rest of the team, muttering to himself bitterly. Kiti comes through the doors, stepping past R.C., walking out into the sunlit afternoon.

"G'game," says Tae, slapping his hand.

"Yeah," says DeAndre. "You guys still got a little somethin'."

Kiti laughs, but glides slowly past them, down to the curb where Preston and Shamrock are leaning on a parked car, Preston trying to spin a worn leather ball on his finger.

"What can I say," Shamrock tells the rec team. "You young'uns talkin' shit. We had to set you down."

Laughing, Preston throws him five, then adds, "We nice. Boys tried to step up but they just not ready."

"Please," says DeAndre, smiling.

R.C. takes it hard. He gets up from the steps and walks back inside the school lobby in obvious disgust. The others give the old school its due.

Shamrock and Preston linger by the curb for a while, talking softly with Kiti. For Kiti, this is a rare chance to reconnect, but it doesn't come easy. Shamrock is steady slinging, and when that doesn't pay the bills, he's up for robbing dealers and stash houses, taking other people's drugs and money at the point of a gun. By next year, he'll be over in pretrial detention, charged with shooting a man to death on South Gilmor Street. When he hasn't been slinging and getting high on his own product, Kwame has been at Shamrock's side for a few of those robberies. And Preston and Jamie are together as well, working a package that Jamie brings down direct from his relatives in the Bronx. That leaves Kiti in a strange sort of purgatory. He likes his boys, he wants to be tight with them; but now, hanging can't be a casual act.

"We gonna go up the way," says Preston, gesturing toward Fayette Street. "Run by the store."

"Naw," Kiti replies. "Gonna walk with my ma."

So they clasp hands and roll out, leaving Kiti in self-enforced solitude outside the high school. He waits on Ella, who is moving slowly, surrounded as she is by a crowd of the younger rec kids. She's at the school doors, shouting for this one to come along and for that one to stop ringing the buzzer—but it's all good-natured chiding rather than real discipline. Kiti has to smile; he was raised by this woman and still he can't imagine where all the patience comes from. Ella is beaming at him as she comes down the steps, delighted at how the day turned out.

"My boys say they want a rematch," she tells her son.

Kiti laughs.

"They do. You tell Preston and them to come back down."

"Okay."

He falls in beside her, matching her step for step up the hill, shortening his stride to her pace. The younger children dart and shriek, racing around them like charged particles.

"Did you call Tito?" she asks.

"I'm gonna call tonight."

"Tonight," she says, affirming.

"Yeah."

Ella is of two minds about her youngest son's latest plan. Kiti's idea is to graduate this month from Francis Woods, work the summer for spending cash, then go to California to stay with Tito, his older brother, who has been discharged and has found work with the phone company. On the one hand, Ella knows that her youngest son hates Fayette Street, not so much out of fear anymore, but more from a sense of what it will do to him if he stays. His room and his music, his part-time job down at the tape and record store off Howard Street—Ella understands that these are not enough. For years now, ever since Pooh's death, in fact, Kiti has been on her to leave, to move to some other neighborhood where the choices don't seem so ugly and obvious.

She had thought about moving, even looked at the newspaper ads a few times, but there was only so much time in a day. Besides, she had raised her family out of 1806 Fayette; she felt connected with this neighborhood more than other, better places. To leave her apartment and her street and come to work at the rec center from outside the neighborhood seemed to Ella wrong.

Kiti would have his freedom soon enough. Tito was all for his brother coming out to Long Beach, where the want ads were full of jobs, where Kiti could work and maybe take some community college courses at the same time. Ella was tremendously proud of her youngest son, especially because Kiti had suffered Fayette Street at its worst. And yet, he found a way to endure.

The proof was there for Ella in late May, when she walked down to the Francis M. Woods gym for a ceremony honoring those scheduled to be graduated from the school. Kiti and forty-six others wore the black and gold class colors, each taking a turn at the rostrum to receive honor roll awards and outstanding student awards and most improved awards, followed by citations for carpentry, food service, child care, and video production—the vocational elements in the Francis M. Woods curriculum. By the end, there wasn't a young man or woman without at least one certificate of merit to go with the diploma. For Ella, as for the others in the audience, there was a sense not only of pride, but of relief at having seen a child through to this day. To reach their senior commencement, the forty-seven in the Francis Woods gymasium that day had traveled further in their education than the majority of those attending Baltimore public schools. Yet for most of the graduates, their formal education ended that day; high school fundamentals and participation in a vocational program might or might not get them a restaurant job or an apprenticeship at a downtown hotel.

Here again, Ella managed more hope than most. Kiti had been fascinated by his video production classes at Francis Woods; if he could find some broadcasting courses and stay with them, he might be on his way to something. In fact, this was part of the current California plan:

Kiti was going out west to enjoy life, maybe to get a job for some spending money and see that part of the world. But college was there for him, too, if he wanted it.

Ella would miss him terribly. She sometimes worried that California was too far, that she wouldn't be there for him if things went wrong. But watching him lope beside her now, she realized just how much he had grown this year. He seemed always to have towered over her, but now his face was that of a young man, his eyes showing new certainty and purpose. Even his bearing was different—the way he walked, or stood, or sat. Kiti had always been quiet; now, he was quietly in control.

"So what do you think?" she asks him.

"About what?"

"About my team."

Kiti laughs and shakes his head.

"That bad?" Ella asks.

"They all right," Kiti offers charitably. "They got a little something goin' on."

They pause at Gilmor. Ella looks down to the Baltimore Street corner and sees Linwood at the pay phone, working out with the B & G crew. She watches him take ten from a walk-up sale and point the customer down Fairmount toward the stash. The same Linwood who went to Francis Woods with Kiti, who played that first game at Bentalou with her team.

She sees Linwood and says nothing.

Kiti, too, catches sight of the sale. "You comin' home soon?" he asks his mother.

Ella sighs. She's got a long list of things to do at the rec. Summer camp starts next week. "I'll be home for dinner," she tells him. "You fix something if you get hungry before then."

They part and she watches him walk up Fayette Street, his hands loose and his arms swaying at his side. A couple of times he raises a hand in greeting but doesn't stop to talk. Once he crosses Bruce Street, Ella turns and walks up Gilmor toward the rec center. When she arrives, some of the younger crowd are ready and waiting.

"Miss Ella?"

"What Stevie?"

"You gonna open the rec?"

She shakes her head, sending Little Stevie, DeRodd, and a half-dozen other small fry into a state of indignation. They waited through the older boys' basketball game. They waited for her to make her slow stroll up from the high school. And now, for all that, they're not going to get anything whatsoever.

"Stevie, the rec is closed."

"The rec been closed," pouts DeRodd.

"We're getting ready for summer camp. You all know that. We close every year to get ready for camp."

"When camp?"

Ella rolls her eyes. "You got the flyers, you're signed up. You know when camp begins."

"When camp?"

"Next Monday," she says.

"Oh."

Inside the rec, silence is golden. Little Stevie Boyd soon thinks of another gambit and begins rapping on the doors, but Ella ignores him long enough for the voices outside to fall away. She's left with her preparations for the neighborhood summer camp, which this year promises to be more extensive and more complicated than ever before. The summer program involves not only the recreation center, but Echo House and St. Martin's Church as well; activities will be scheduled at all three locations and children will be shuttled along Fayette Street from one place to another. They'll be using the basement at St. Martin's, which doubles as the local soup kitchen, and they're hoping to use the church's auditorium at other times to introduce and educational component to the camp routine. They'll also be using the swimming pool in the basement of Francis M. Woods, which means coordinating with Rose Davis, as well as the Calhoun Street Boys' Club, which runs a camp of its own and will be sharing time at the pool. There will be some trips, too—day adventures to local parks and picnic grounds. And there's the training of the counselors—teenagers hired through the city summer jobs program and screened by Echo House—as well as new inventory for the daily snacks, new art supplies for the crafts classes, and a smattering of secondhand sports equipment for the blacktop outside. For Ella, summer camp is the most frantic time, with children around her the whole day long, rather than at three-hour, after-school intervals.

All the planning and preparation takes time and gives Ella little pleasure; she would much prefer to be with the children. Still, she tells herself, she needs to get through this stuff—and the logistics of the daily passage of campers along Fayette Street requires particular care. With the doors to the St. Martin's auditorium above Bruce Street, Echo House near the Mount Street intersection, and the rec center below that, the transfer of the children will involve a walking tour of the entire Fayette and Mount drug market. Every day promises to be a new adventure in civil liability, and Ella knows that some groundwork for dealing with the corner needs to be laid. She resolves to deal with it tomorrow.

She turns her attention to the camp sign-up sheet, double-checking the $5-a-camper donations to see who still owes what. But before she can get halfway down the first page, there comes a hammering on the rec doors too loud to be the likes of Little Stevie. Ella walks to the front to see a familiar face on the other side of the wire-mesh window.

"Miss Ella. Miss El-la."

R.C. has his face hard against the window, his hands cupped to his temples as a shield to the glare.

"Miss Ella."

"R.C., you know I'm closed up," she says, with the door half open. It's not just R.C., but a whole committee on her doorstep. Tae, Manny Man, Dinky—the basketball squad, come to bargain.

"Miss Ella," says R.C. "Can we get in a summer league?"

"I'm talking to Miss Summers about that. I'm talking to her about getting you all signed up for Cloverdale."

Tae fairly leaps off the steps, arms in the air, bouncing around until he can slap five with Dinky and Manny Man. Cloverdale is one of the best summer basketball leagues in the city, a six-week competition in July and August that brings teams from all over to an outdoor court near Druid Hill Park.

"We gonna kick ass," shouts Tae. "Yeah boy."

Ella tries to slow the celebration, explaining that she's been talking to Myrtle for a while about the possibility, that there is a $50 filing fee for each Cloverdale team and that a whole bunch of raffle tickets will have to be sold to pay for the league jerseys.

"I'm not making promises," she insists.

But R.C. is already across the blacktop, taking an imaginary turn-around below the imaginary rim of the rusting outdoor backboard. Seeing the boys react, Ella goes back to her office with one more item to add to her list. Sometime after she deals with the people at Fayette and Mount tomorrow, she needs to stop by Echo House and get a $50 commitment from Myrtle.

The following morning, she gets up when her daughter, Donnie, drops off four-year-old Tianna and heads to work. Ella makes her grand-daughter a stack of pancakes, then pads around the apartment until late morning, watching the clock, telling herself that today's chore is one she wants to deal with only once. Ten-thirty is too early; eleven is still before the worst of it. At half past eleven, she's ready to head down to Echo House, knowing that by the time she finishes talking with Myrtle Summers, the Mount Street corners will be ripe. Noon—that's when she'll be shepherding summer campers to lunch at St. Martin's.

At quarter past twelve, wearing a T-shirt and denims, Ella Thompson is standing amid the comings and goings of Mount Street. They're moving Red Tops, Pinks, and In the Hole today; she's looking for a break in the sales clamor to make her point. She stands silently, her face blank and calm, eyeing first one tout then another, her presence alone calling for attention. Within moments, the pitch has dropped, though the movement of fiends—foot traffic, autos, the occasional truck—doesn't abate. It's as good an opportunity as she's going to get.

She steps to the curb and raises her right hand.

"You know," Ella begins, adjusting her voice, "camp for the little kids starts Monday morning, next Monday . . ."

Buster and Stevie Boyd, Black Donnie and Eddie Bland stop their chattering and turn to listen. Their interest spreads to the others. Soon almost everyone on the corner is actively listening to the rec center lady, and those too caught up in the game to hear her out are at least unwilling to compete with her openly.

". . . I'm saying, the campers and the counselors will be walking past here starting Monday. One time in the early morning and then again about this time of the day when they go to lunch at the church, then back from lunch when they go to the pool."

Her voice is steady and unemotional; Ella is not naive enough to deliver anything resembling either a plea or a sermon. Instead, she dispenses simple information, believing that these men and women remain a part of her community, that they will take to heart what she has to say and then do what should be done.

". . . so when they come through, I would appreciate it if you could let them walk past together and stay as a group, and if you would keep the noise down so they can hear the counselors."

Some heads actually nod.

"Starting Monday," she reminds them with a smile. "Thank you."

Ella leaves the corner as casually as she arrived; for her, there is no absolute evil, save for maybe the vials themselves. Of course, the vials didn't break into the rec and steal the television. Nor was it the vials that chased and beat the white girl, then took her bike. And all the dope and coke in the world can't be blamed for what happened to Pooh. Those sins were peopled, though Ella clings to the opposite view. To her, the worst that can be said is that the men and women on Mount Street are wasting themselves, and in doing so, they are serving this neighborhood poorly. But Ella won't go beyond that; on faith alone, she grants them a perspective they may or may not have. She believes that if she's about the business of helping their children, if she's direct and honest and willing to make her case on the most basic level, they'll surely give her what she needs.

And come the following Monday, her judgment seems sound enough, as the counselors lead a string of campers across Mount and Fayette on the first day of camp. At that moment, at least, there is a tentative truce in the daily conflict between corner and community.

"Time out," yells one of the lookouts, seeing the six-year-olds leading the way out of St. Martin's and down the sidewalk past Echo House, on their way to the Francis Woods pool. The birdcall hawking of the touts dies away; the slingers take a step or two down Mount.

It's not a complete concession by any means—the corner world is too far gone to get everything right on the first day. As the children saunter hand-in-hand across Mount, Buster is still at the pay phone, arguing with one of his runners. Down the block, Alfred keeps working that ground stash, unwilling to give a white boy chance enough to walk past him and cop from someone else.

But Ella Thompson has not been disrespected. By right or by conscience, her children are taken into account; even in its desperation, the corner manages that much. By the second Monday, with camp in full swing, she can watch as the children file out the church doors and tramp down the sidewalk, knowing that what awaits them down at the corner is nothing worse than an awkward pause in the action. Every now and then, she hears someone trying to keep it in check:

"Chill for a minute."

"Man, let the little ones go past."

"Shorty comin'."

This tells Ella something, perhaps the wrong thing. She ventures down to the corner, gets what is due to her, and walks away believing that these people can be reached, that they want the same things as anyone else, and that they are on some fundamental level, in control of their lives. If these things are true—and she wants them to be true—then everything she does here has purpose. If they are not true, then she has no business on Fayette Street. She chooses to believe.

A week or so later, before escorting her campers down from the church one hot July afternoon, she heads from St. Martin's up the block to her apartment for a toy that Tianna has been asking for all day. Rushing up her front steps, she waves to Smitty and Gale, both of them sitting on the stoop of the vacant rowhouse just up from Ella's apartment. The three-story derelict is home to Smitty, Gale, and Gale's baby—a nuclear family nested on the corner—and Ella is accustomed to seeing them on the front steps, waiting for redemption or a cool breeze from the harbor, neither of which seems particularly likely. On this day, they're looking rough: Gale has her head in her hands and the baby on her lap; Smitty is looking blandly up the street, his eyes a watery yellow. Both nod at her casually, but Ella insists on a more genuine connection.

"Hello, Smitty."

"Hey, Miss Ella."

"Gale, how are you today? How's the baby?"

"Not so good today," she tells Ella. "My brother got killed yesterday and I just got told."

"Your brother?"

"Ricky. You know Ricky."

Ricky Cunningham. The young man who wanted to volunteer at the rec center. He had come to the Valentine's Dance, then fallen in love with Ella, then disappeared only to write from the city jail, asking Ella Thompson to be there for his court date. Shoplifting. Vitamins. The Rite-Aid security guard. The whole sad story rushes up at once.

"He was killed? Gale, I'm so sorry."

"He got shot," she tells Ella. "Down the projects. My family tryin' to find money to bury him."

"Why? Why did . . . ? It doesn't make sense."

"Mistaken identity," explains Gale, without really explaining. "You don't know about services yet?"

"Nuh uh," says Gale.

"Well, please let me know. I know he was a good person."

Ella leaves them there on the steps, promising to ask around the neighborhood about contributions for funeral expenses. Only later does a little more detail come her way. Ricky had done his thirty days for the vitamins, then left from the detention center with the idea that he would stay away from the vials, maybe do something good with his life. He had even called Ella at the rec center once to say he'd be coming past, to thank her again for coming to court for him, and to assure her that he still wanted to volunteer at the center.

But a few nights back, Ricky had been down by the Murphy Homes high-rises, walking through, when he was spotted and taken for his brother, who had supposedly done some stickups in the projects. There was no debate, no parley, just two to the back, plain and simple.

But if there is a lesson here, it won't take with Ella.

The random dispatch of Ricky Cunningham, who walks by the wrong corner at the wrong moment, will not add up for her the way it would for anyone beyond the frontier of West Baltimore. She will not connect what happened to Ricky with her own proximity to the disaster, to the presence of her family there, to the cold fact that her daily routine now requires her to walk into hell itself and rely on the cooperation of street dealers and drug addicts.

And for what is she fighting in this place? For a future? She's already raised one group up, watched them go from the sliding board to foursquare, from rec center dances to basketball games. She's been at it long enough to see all of her fifteen- and sixteen-year-olds—Tae and Brooks, Dinky and DeAndre, R.C. and Brian—go down to the corner and betray everything that the rec center means to her.

Yet even with the ending all but certain, she still loves them. She can look at them and see qualities worth celebrating. To her DeAndre and R.C. and Tae are not drug dealers; they are her children, her ball team, their lives still in the balance, their possibilities still before them. And Smitty and Gale aren't beleaguered addicts; they're neighbors. And Ricky Cunningham wasn't creeping past the high-rises, where he went to cop vials night after night; he was a bystander caught up in someone else's evil.

A half hour after talking with Smitty and Gale, she's back down the street, delivering the wayward toy to Tianna and leading the campers hand-in-hand across the battleground of Mount Street, taking perhaps too much satisfaction in the quiet decorum that once again greets her. It's a small moment, but small moments are the only kind Ella Thompson can acquire. She manages to string together three or four or five such moments and call it hope.

That afternoon she stays on the wooden bleachers at poolside in the basement of Francis Woods High School, gathering strength from the sight of her children squealing and splashing in the shallow end. She stays for the whole pool period, soaking up her share of the watery mayhem, laughing and racing down the tile floor when a few of the bold ones try to sneak up to the near edge of the pool and wet her down. And when the older boys finish their pickup game in the gym upstairs, when they come down the stairwell wasted and sweating, she turns her mercies to them.

"Miss Ella," asks Tae. "Can we swim today? We hot."

"The pool is only for the summer camp, Dontae."

"But we hot as I don't know what."

It's enough for Ella to sense another small moment. She goes to the pool manager and the lifeguard and uses up a favor. Two minutes later, the basketball team is racing out of the locker room—most with their gym shorts for bathing trunks, all with a look of salvation on their faces as they tumble into the deep end of the pool. She watches her boys dog-paddle about, clinging to the edge—most of them swimmers only in the most liberal sense. Tae dunks Dinky; Dinky splashes Brooks; Brooks threatens to go home and get a gun on anyone who puts his head under water.

"How's the pool, Dontae?" Ella asks from the bleachers.

Dewayne pulls him off the wall before he can answer. His smile disappears beneath the waves in a look of panic. Ella laughs at the spectacle.

"Miss Ella," says Tae when he regains the edge of the pool. "Miss Ella, you awright."

DeAndre leaves the Dew Drop early this morning. The air is still cool, but the summer heat is lurking, waiting its chance. He's halfway to Gilmor before his mother pokes her head out of the vestibule, shouting him back.

"An-dre."

He mugs impatience.

"Dre. C'mere."

Showing all kinds of irritation, he slogs back up the block. Fran meets him almost at the alley.

"Gimme some sugar."

The street is empty, thank God. Just the Korean sweeping up outside the store on Mount.

"C'mon, Andre. I might not be comin' home."

He finally cracks his smile, folding his arm around Fran's thin shoulders. The embrace is genuine, and when she kisses his cheek, he barely starts.

"You embarrassed?" she asks.

"Ma," he laughs awkwardly, "we out in the damn street."

At odd moments, life on Fayette Street isn't any different than life anywhere else; here, too, a grown-up boy doesn't want to be seen in his mother's arms.

"Good luck," he tells her.

"You too."

They are on different missions today: DeAndre is heading east to the McDonald's at Harford and North, where he has every reason to believe that a job is waiting for him; his mother is heading up to Wabash to deal with the first of three boosting charges from last year. She's got one case in the city, another out in Catonsville and a third floating around in the Anne Arundel County computer somewhere. The last hasn't popped up as a court date yet and Fran is beginning to believe that it won't, that the security officers at Harundale are satisfied to simply bar her from the mall.

Making his way east on Fayette Street, DeAndre mulls the probabilities in his mind. His mother is scared of court—this he knows. For all her time drugging and boosting, she's yet to be convicted of anything, so the idea of even an overnight stay at women's detention appalls her. But it might come to that. And if Fran gets locked up at court today, he'll be the man of the house. He'll have to take care of DeRodd. He'll have to get his mother's check money come the first of the month. He'll be out here on his own.

The idea is unnerving and at the same time exhilarating. First thing, he'll clean up their bedroom. Then, he'll make DeRodd act right. And before Fran comes home, he'll have the job at Mickey Dee's and take a driving test and buy a car and stay up all night running the streets with his boys. He'll bring girls up to the bedroom every damn night, smoking Phillie blunts until his eyeballs look like cherries in buttermilk. Yeah boy.

On the other hand, he realizes, if his mother has to jail, she'll miss her chance at detox. Her number will come up on the BRC waiting list and she'll be over on Eager Street somewhere, or trapped inside the Dew Drop, wearing one of those monitoring rings around her ankle. This alone ruins the fantasy for DeAndre. His mother was trying, or at least thinking of trying, and despite himself DeAndre has been allowing himself to hope.

"Ma," he told her at one point, "you lookin' better."

"What you mean?"

"You lookin' better is all. You doin' better."

He could see it. She was slowing down a bit, making enough time in her day to call the detox center, talking about the future as if she had a plan. DeAndre loved his mother; he could never deny that. But he had grown up inside the Dew Drop, and his familiarity with the crudball move gave him a wholesale contempt for her ways. DeAndre offered his mother only as much hope as he dared, bracing himself all the while for the inevitable disappointment. Apart from a few generous moments, he kept a safe distance. He knew he had to get out of 1625 West Fayette, and lately he had been telling himself that if Fran didn't make a move soon, he would have to find his own exit.

It was strange, but he blamed his father less. Part of what centered his scorn on Fran was the familiarity, the day-in-day-out sight of Fran's drugging. The other part came from knowing that it was his mother who fell first. He'd heard the neighborhood talk that said Fran had broken Gary's will, that she had turned a good man out. DeAndre believed that his father was a victim, that he had been, and still could be, the solution.

A week earlier, in a quiet moment after his mother had just emerged from the basement, he ventured to suggest as much, assuring Fran that if she went through detox, she could get back together with Gary and things would be as they once were. Fran looked for a minute as though she wanted to slap him.

"Dre," she said slowly. "You out yo' damn mind."

"Ma, we'd be a family."

"Andre, your father as much a dope fiend as I am."

He stalked out of the bedroom, but not before letting go with both barrels. He couldn't help himself; he felt the need to defend his father.

"You always downin' him," he yelled at her. "He'd still be on top now if you hadn't drug him down."

At that, Fran was beyond hitting him. She sat there seething. If he thought Gary was the solution, she told him, then he could go live with Gary. In Miss Roberta's basement on Vine Street. Watch Gary chase the needle. Learn just how much better his father was.

"Everyone out here doing what they do by hisself and for hisself," she told DeAndre, her voice low and hard. "Your father don't need my help to get high. He doin' all right on his own."

"You brought him down."

"Shut up, Andre."

And he did, for a time. But a few days later, hope again slipped into the fringes of their conversation. He saw Fran go across the street to the neighbor to make another call down to BRC; when she came back, she asked DeAndre if he could take care of DeRodd, if he would be there to help when she went into rehab.

"Yeah, you know that," he told her.

"Scoogie'll help," she offered.

"I got it covered."

He acted like it was no big thing: If she did what she had to do, then he'd surely do the same. When she mentioned that the McDonald's job would give him more money to care for himself and his brother, DeAndre readily agreed with that as well. She'd gotten hold of his birth certificate and social security card; now, he knew, it was up to him to get hold of the job.

That meant the long hike today, down Fayette and across downtown and up past Old Town to Harford and North, where an eastside McDonald's franchise was still hiring summer help. DeAndre had called over the week before and talked to a lady manager. She said to come Monday, talk to her, and fill out an application.

DeAndre didn't mind the idea of slinging fast food. Fact is, he'd been raised on McDonald's No. 2 Happy Meals. And he figured that McDonald's had to be easier than Seapride; he was almost grateful when Miss Mary stopped giving him hours at the crabhouse—the smell alone was enough to shut his lungs down. No, Mickey Dee's would be good for a couple months. It wasn't close to the kind of money he could make on a corner, but they didn't lock you up, stick you up, or shoot you down for slinging burgers. Not all the time anyway.

As for the distance, he'd have to learn the bus lines, figure out where to transfer downtown. He wouldn't be clocking enough cash behind burgers and fries to pay for hack rides every day. There were McDonald's outlets a lot closer—Franklin Street, Washington Boulevard—but they weren't hiring any more summer help. So it was East Baltimore or nothing.

Today, though, he doesn't mind the walk. He spends the time thinking about things, and he's comfortably past Lexington Terrace and all the way downtown before the heat of the summer day begins rising up from the asphalt and concrete. It takes another forty minutes to reach Broadway and North, where the lunch rush is in full swing.

"You in line?"

"Naw," says DeAndre, stepping aside.

He stands there for a few minutes watching the bustle around the counter, looking at the teenagers in their uniforms, watching them work the registers and chase down orders. After a long interval, he steps slowly forward.

"May I take your order, please."

"I'm lookin' for the manager."

"She's not in right now," says the girl at the register.

DeAndre's voice begins to rise. "She told me to come in Monday to fill out my application and get my uniform."

The girl raises a finger and turns, walking around the burger-laden stainless steel counter behind her. She reemerges a minute later with an older, dark-skinned man.

"Can I help you, son?"

"I was supposed to come by today and put in my application. Start working here. I called last week . . ."

"The manager isn't in now, but I can take your application and then you'll have to come back to be interviewed."

DeAndre detects a lilt in the assistant manager's voice. Gay as I don't know what, he tells himself. When the man comes back with the application form, he makes the mistake of giving the boy a once over. It's scrutiny connected with the hiring process, but DeAndre takes it the wrong way.

"What? What you lookin' at?"

The man smiles. "You might have to cut your hair."

"Naw," says DeAndre. "That won't do."

The man shrugs, telling him the manager will decide. He guides DeAndre to a table, giving him a pen and the application form.

"You'll need a birth certificate and social security card for the interview."

"Got it," says DeAndre diffidently.

The man gives him a last glance and DeAndre gives him a look back. It happens all the time—not only with white people, but with black folk in any station of life above Fayette Street. With his dreds and gold front, his baggy denims and don't-fake-the-funk-on-a-nasty-dunk T-shirt, DeAndre shows street without so much as trying. He dresses and looks and walks the same way every kid he knows does; it plays on the corner, but nowhere else. Others might find it in themselves to bow to authority, to accept the bargain and conform, but by and large, those people have a basic allegiance to the predominant culture, and DeAndre McCullough knows no such allegiance. The world can make no legitimate demands because the world hasn't done shit for him these sixteen years; he lives on Fayette Street.

"I ain't gettin' my dreds cut," he tells the cashier, handing back the finished application.

She shrugs. He orders a large Coke and leaves.

Back across town that same afternoon, he checks in at the Dew Drop long enough to learn that his mother threw the possibility of detox at the prosecutor and managed a one-time postponement up at Wabash. Fran is perched in front of the second-floor television, watching and not watching black-and-white cartoon images racing past.

"You get that job?"

"Manager wasn't in. She said come by and she not even there. But, you know, I filled out an application."

"When you supposed to hear?"

"Call back tomorrow. They sayin' I have to cut my dreds."

"You need to get them nappy things cut."

"I look right," he insists, twirling a dred with one hand. "And that ain't even the point. I ain't gonna change who I am for no one. Nigger think he better than I am 'cause of how he look and talk. That's how they all is. They get a little something and they get to forgettin' where they come from. Man, to hell with that. I don't need the job that bad."

"Yeah you do," says Fran.

"Not enough to have some gay-ass manager lookin' at me that way, actin' like he so much better. I know his faggy ass as black as mine."

The argument usually resonates with Fran; she lives on Fayette Street, too, so she's both heard and invoked the appeal to true blackness on more occasions than can be counted. A couple years ago, when Gary's sister offered to let DeAndre stay at her house out in the county, to go to school there and stay off the corners, DeAndre had to lean hard on this egalitarian ideal. At first willing enough to leave Fayette Street behind, DeAndre returned from Woodlawn a few weeks later, complaining about people who were as black as he was looking down at him because they had a little money, talking about how you can take a nigger out of the ghetto but you can't get the ghetto out of the nigger. Naw, he told everyone who would listen, fuck that and fuck them.

"You know what I'm sayin', Ma?"

She tells him she knows. But then again, she adds, there were the days when she was working down at the phone company and the white women there would always be laughing at stupid shit. Laughing about what just wasn't funny. And she'd laugh, too. Act like it was the funniest thing ever, because those white women ran the place. And then they'd walk away and the black workers would all be rolling their eyes, shaking their heads and laughing for real.

"Dre, I'm sayin' you got to play along a little bit."

"Naw. You don't want me as I am, then I'm gone."

Fran tries again, telling him about how there isn't a job out there that doesn't make you do something you don't want to do. She tells him that growing up is dealing with that and getting past it—all of which would be a fairly good lesson if it weren't for the fact that Fran lost the phone job for cussing a supervisor. Still, she goes all out to remind him that he needs a job, that he's not in school and that Tyreeka—for all her insistence that she isn't pregnant—has admitted to Fran that she's missed her clinic appointment twice. Tyreeka is looking heavier by the day.

"You just lookin' for an excuse to go back to the corner," she tells him.

DeAndre shakes his head. "Naw, I'm not about that."

"Then go back an' get the job."

"I said I was gonna call," he says, his voice rising.

But he doesn't pick up the phone the next day. The day after that, he calls but the manager isn't in. The next day, he forgets. Three long days after he was first supposed to call the McDonald's across town, DeAndre finally reaches the manager, who tells him that he still has to come back for the interview. Yes, she's still got an opening. Yes, she knows he came by and filled out the application form. But she needs to speak with him before she can tell him he has a job. She tells DeAndre to come Monday.

But Monday, he's sick as a dog, laid up with some kind of stomach bug. DeAndre calls that afternoon and leaves a message with some other girl, saying if he feels right, he'll be there tomorrow.

On Tuesday, he gets up late, still queasy, but manages to get dressed and borrow enough money for a hack. He gets across town to the McDonald's by midafternoon, walks up to the same girl as before, and asks again for the manager. This time, she's there; she comes to the counter and gives DeAndre much the same look as he got from the assistant manager.

"You were supposed to come in yesterday."

"I was sick. I called and talked to someone."

The manager frowns. "Well, I can't do applications today. I have to be somewhere else in fifteen minutes. You'll have to come back tomorrow. One o'clock."

DeAndre nods and backs away from the counter, listless in his movements. "You . . . um . . . you think I can get my uniform and start work tomorrow?" he finally offers.

At last, the manager seems to sense more fear than menace from this manchild. Suddenly charitable, she tries to put him at ease. "First we have to have the interview, then we'll talk about when you start. Understand?"

DeAndre nods.

"And, young man," she says, half smiling, "we're going to have to talk about that hairstyle."

DeAndre manages to nod at that as well.

The following day, he's late getting across town, arriving at the restaurant a little after two-thirty. Though a delay of an hour and a half is fairly punctual by corner standards, DeAndre understands that he's already testing the manager's patience. Still, he can't bring himself to conjure an excuse or—even less likely—an apology. He saunters to the counter wearing baggy shorts and a tank top, his Nikes unlaced, as if to declare that it makes no difference, that the world can take him or leave him.

But inside, he's churning. Inside, he knows that today he will be judged. In a moment or two, the manager will stare him down and size him up and render a verdict as to whether he's worthy enough to flip burgers and salt fries. For all the street-corner arrogance that DeAndre McCullough can project, the fear inside him is much the same as for any adolescent. In a moment or two, he'll be made to answer questions, to state his needs, to ask someone from the external world for a chance.

He waits like a condemned man, staring down at his warped reflection in the silver sheen of the counter, waiting for the girl at the register to finish serving a customer. He looks past her, counting heads in the kitchen area, strangely gratified to see that the manager isn't around.

"Can I help you?"

"Manager here?" His voice is a mumble.

The cashier points out into the restaurant area, where the woman is seated at a table, paperwork spread before her. A young girl is sitting opposite, hands in her lap, ankles crossed. The girl is talking; the manager is nodding her head.

DeAndre takes a few steps toward the woman, catching her eye. She looks from the young girl to check her watch.

"You're late," she says.

DeAndre nods.

"Well, you'll have to wait until I'm finished here."

He backs away, finding himself against the condiment counter. Breathing deep, he scans the ebb and flow of walk-in business, watching the manager out of the corner of his eye. The girl says something and the manager smiles. DeAndre paces a bit, until after a few minutes, the crowd thins, leaving him nearly alone in front of the counter. He feels foolish and exposed; the fear he's been holding down breaks free.

"Can I take your order?" asks an employee.

It's a heavyset boy this time, working the middle register.

"Yeah," says DeAndre, stepping forward. "Double cheese. Small fry. Medium Coke."

"Is that here or to go?"

"To go."

And when the food slides across the counter, he does.

"Let's go," says Tony.

"Awright then," Gary agrees.

Lump just nods.

As with all great journeys, it begins with a simple willingness, with an abiding faith in the unknown. Treasure and glory are not for the faint of heart; a crusade requires good knights of the realm. With his California Angels brim pushed low and a satchel of metaling tools gripped in his hand, Gary McCullough is on the road to Jerusalem. He and his two confederates are going to take off the Baker Street scrap yard.

It means traveling beyond the pale of the Fayette Street fiend, north beyond the expressway, beyond Edmondson Avenue and Lafayette, extending their hustle. It means doing deeds in Rosemont, the largest stable enclave of homes in the Western District and a neighborhood with no strong drug corners closer than its edges. The residents there are mostly home owners, more likely than not to mark the comings and goings of strangers or to call the police on a guess. The police, too, are more likely to come when called.

For Gary and Tony and Lump, lumbering down Lexington, trailing two empty shopping carts, the very idea is fat with risk. But the bottom end of the west side—the area closest to United Iron and Metal and the other area scrap yards—has by now been picked clean of copper and aluminum; too many scavengers working too many days have reduced the metal game south of the expressway to short-money scraps. For want of more valuable stuff, many harvesters are now tearing radiators and cast-iron sinks out of vacant houses, trying to make four or five dollars on bulk weight alone. Above the expressway and Edmondson is still virgin territory, though, and Tony Boice's brother had told him of an unwatched and seemingly unmanned scrap yard, a Sutter's Mill of old aluminum, copper, and cast iron that backed up against the railbed near the Baker Street underpass. Tony had been there once, creeping out with $30 worth of clean aluminum siding. If they could find it again, plunder it, and make their way back south, they would surely arrive at the scales on McPhail Street or down at United Iron with so much good weight that not even the Engineer, with his train of carts, could deny them their due. And if they did it once, they could always go back and do it again.

Gary's head spins with possibilities as the trio turns up Warwick and waits for the light at Franklin. They cross quickly—Gary and Lump each with a cart, Tony in front like an Indian scout—and continue north on Bentalou. After Edmondson, they're beyond the most blighted blocks, easing into a neighborhood of colored window awnings and plastic porch furniture. They rattle past the bus shelter, nodding generously to the older women who wait with shopping bags for downtown routes.

Near Winchester Street, Gary pulls up his cart, takes off his hat, and wipes his forehead. He's breathing hard, his asthma choking him in the heat of late June. He leans on the handle of the cart, looking over at the garden work adorning a half-dozen of the Bentalou rowhouses.

"That's nice," he says to no one in particular.

"Huh?" says Lump.

Gary points to a rose-covered trellis. "It's beautiful. The way they got the roses fixed up."

Lump says nothing and looks up the block at Tony, who has stopped short of the corner. Gary steps away from the cart to get a closer look.

"C'mon," Lump says, "we almost there."

Gary nods vaguely, still taken by the roses. Finally, he turns away, wiping the sweat from his face and returning the Angels cap to his head.

"Okay, Boss."

They power up the rest of the hill, past Carver High, turning at Baker

Street, where gravity takes over and the carts run gently down the slope. An old woman watches them pass from her front porch. Gary nods and smiles, trying hard to make the shopping-cart caravan seem like normal business.

Tony points to a patch of scrubs and trash, just off the sidewalk beneath the railroad overpass. "Carts stay here," he says.

They shove the metal carts deep into undergrowth, then scramble up the dirt path to the top of the railbed. From there, it's a couple hundred yards, maybe more, down the Conrail tracks, and then another forty feet through brush and vines and thorns. They're pushing through a jungle in ninety-degree heat, with insects jumping all over them. Gary looks down at his hand in time to see a tick crawling for the soft skin between his thumb and index finger.

"Dag," he says, flicking the bug away.

"This is fucked up," says Lump.

"You gotta pay to play," Tony assures them.

"We gonna carry all of it back through this?" asks Gary. He feels something on the back of his neck and gives an involuntary shiver. "We workin' for real."

"We soldiers," Tony assures him.

"We Vikings," says Gary, laughing.

They reach the back fence of the lot and find the hole from the last time Tony made the run. One by one, they crawl through and emerge in a metal harvester's heaven. Stacks and stacks of old batteries, aluminum siding, aluminum trim, storm doors—and no one guarding any of it, not even the proverbial junkyard dog. Gary walks around the scrap piles like an art collector at the Louvre, admiring this, coveting that.

"Ho, it's the Big Rock Candy Mountain," he says.

"I told you it was right," says Tony, proud.

Lord. If they could levitate this yard and deliver it whole to United Iron or to the scales on McPhail Street, they'd be instantly rich. More than rich, they'd be dead from more dope and coke than any fiend needs.

"Get them batteries first," says Tony.

George on McPhail Street pays a dollar apiece for old car batteries, so with each of them carrying three stacked batteries on their sortie from the yard, they've quickly liberated the rough equivalent of a blast. After that first run, they decide to divide the labor: Tony and Gary will bring the weight out of the yard and then haul it down the railbed to the overpass. Once they've had their fill, they'll roll the batteries down the dirt slope to Lump waiting on the sidewalk below. Lump will load the carts.

It's hellacious work, with the midday sun beating down and the heat radiating up from the gray-blue stone and creosote ties of the railbed. Gary and Tony trudge back and forth, carrying the batteries two-to-a-trip, ankles twisting as the railbed stones slip beneath their jump boots. In the yard, there's the vague fear of being watched, and in the jungle, there's the insect swirl—gnats, mosquitoes, and who knows what else buzzing around their eyes and ears, drawn by the sweat. But the stack of batteries that takes shape atop the overpass is gratifying. Twenty, then twenty-six, then thirty-two batteries—followed by some long pieces of aluminum trim.

"Enough for this run," says Tony.

With his breath coming in wheezes, Gary agrees, though there is a part of him that wants to keep going back. Get more while the getting is good.

"Heads up."

They begin rolling the car batteries down the dirt slope one at a time, giving Lump a chance to weight them evenly on each cart. But thirst and heat make for impatience, and after a dozen or so batteries, Tony gives the battery pile a kick, sending four or five down at once.

"Ho now," says Lump.

One battery catches a corner and goes bounding left, glancing off the overpass abutment and landing hard on the sidewalk below. Up top, Gary and Tony wince at the shriek that follows.

"Uh oh," says Gary.

All is silence, save for the sound of Lump trying to force some kind of mumbled apology out of his mouth. Tony steps back, but Gary goes down the slope far enough to see a well-dressed woman with two young ones in tow.

"People walk here," says the woman, outraged.

By the look of things, the wayward battery had just missed landing on someone's head. Gary looks at Lump, who looks back blankly. It's up to Gary to put things right before the woman goes off to hail a police; he pulls the brim from his head and ventures halfway down the slope.

"Ma'am, I'm sorry about that. I really am very, very sorry. It just got away from us and we weren't expecting . . ."

"Be more careful," she says, still frightened. "You could kill someone."

"You're right. You're right. We'll be careful."

She shakes her head, disgusted, then grabs both of her charges by the hands to walk them to the opposite side of the street.

"Man," says Gary. "You shoulda said they was coming."

"Crept up on me," Lump says, shrugging. "Didn't see'm."

In fear that the police will soon be arriving, they roll the rest of the batteries at full speed. Lump has most of the batteries in one cart; the rest are paired with the aluminum to fill the other.

"We outta here," says Tony, following Gary down the slope.

But Lump has paused just long enough to feel something on his leg. And Gary, too, has a feeling on his neck.

"Tony, check this out."

Gary bows his head for an inspection. Tony pulls off one tick, then another. He looks over at Lump, who has his pants leg rolled up.

"You got 'em too?"

"They got us, you mean."

Suddenly the caper is on hold, with the three of them pulling off shirts and socks and shoes. Gary finds a tick on the back of his leg, pries it loose and crushes it between his nails. "Parasites," he says, "livin' off someone else's blood."

Minutes pass before they're dressed again and ready for the road home. The first cart proves so heavy that Baker Street might as well be Everest. It takes all three of them to bring that weight up the short hill to Bentalou; Lump waits there with it while Gary and Tony return for the second cart.

Before long, they're a wagon train again, rolling southbound, with Gary and Tony struggling to keep the heavy cart away from parked cars and other obstacles. Soon they're crossing Lafayette, then Edmondson, then Franklin Street over by the McDonald's.

"Thirsty," says Lump.

"Let's get down to the bar," Tony tells him.

But on Warwick Avenue, where the road slopes and turns, they lose control of the heaviest cart, watching helplessly as it careens into the fender of a Mercedes-Benz parked outside a body shop. Metal hits metal like a thunderclap and two batteries bounce off the top and into the street.

"Dag," says Gary, looking around.

"More work for the body and fender man," says Tony.

They put their weight to the front of the cart, prying it loose from the Mercedes, setting it back on course. "Jus' keep it down the middle,

Mo," says Gary, assuming the role of riverboat pilot. "Steady as she goes."

They're off again, impelled by the promise of a cold forty from the bar at Warwick and Baltimore. They each ante up change and Gary goes inside, leaving the other two guarding the weight. Minutes later, they're sitting on the curb, the carts drawn up close, when a police cruiser idles down Baltimore.

"He pullin' up."

"Shit." The cruiser slows in front of them. Gary stands. It's a white patrolman unknown to the trio.

"What's in the bag?" asks the cop.

"Beer," says Gary. No point lying. The paper bag is wordlessly invoked.

"Pour it out."

Tony looks at Lump, who looks over at the haul of stolen metal. They're two blocks from the McPhail Street scales.

"Pour it out," says the cop, louder.

Gary nods affirmatively, reaching toward Lump for the bag. Even as he turns it upside down, the cruiser pulls off, allowing him to salvage some of the brew.

"Dag," says Gary.

They mount up and cover the last length of trail, pulling up at George's yard just before a truckload of cast-iron radiators arrives.

"We first," says Gary, proudly.

They get $42.65 in batteries and other weight, take their pay at the cashier's window and march back up the hill to Monroe Street. The touts see all that green and welcome them home in the traditional way, with one-and-one.

A speedball later, the trio is ready to part ways. Tony wonders whether they should leave the empty carts in the alley or keep them for tomorrow.

"Tomorrow?" asks Lump.

Tony nods.

"Yeah, we can hit that spot again tomorrow," says Gary.

"That'll do," says Lump.

"What's tomorrow?"

"Thursday ain't it?"

Gary's face clouds. He's got court tomorrow out in the county. His trial date on last winter's boosting charge from the J.C. Penney store.

"I'm messed up for tomorrow. I think I got court."

Tony nods. "It'll keep," he tells Gary.

There's nothing worse than a trial date to take a hustler away from his game, and Gary's scheduled rendezvous with the sentinels of suburban justice begins to wear at his disposition. That night he's careful to iron his church suit, thinking to himself that come tomorrow, he will be at the mercy of Leave It To Beaverland.

That's what Gary calls it. Several of the new judges at the western county courthouses are themselves black, but Gary can't help thinking of the other side of the city line as the kinescope stomping ground of Eddie Haskell, Wally, and the Beaver. All the desperation and foolishness that counted for something in a city courtroom only serve to make you a nigger in Catonsville or Owings Mills or Towson. That's how Gary had felt at the public defender's office—when the receptionist sneered at him, telling him he needed ten working days, and where they shrugged and told him to try to get a postponement. That's how he had felt earlier in the year at the mall security office, too, with all of those rent-a-cops gathered around, laughing at his story, making him sign their forms. And that's how he feels the morning after the great Baker Street caper, when he suits up and catches a hack out to the Catonsville District Court, a flat, brown slab of modernity hard by the University of Maryland satellite campus.

From a distance, Gary looks serious, studious even, in his pinstripes and black loafers. But up close—at, say, the distance between a judge's bench and a trial table—there are the telltales: the pinkish abscess on the back of one hand, the jaundiced eyes, the stubble left behind by a quick and indifferent razor.

"I need a lawyer," Gary pleads to the lady prosecutor in Courtroom Two.

"Talk to the public defender. She's over there."

"I need a lawyer," he tells the public defender, who is seated on a back bench, clutching two dozen case files.

"What's your name?"

"Gary Castro McCullough."

She checks the folders. "I don't have a McCullough here."

"I went to your office and they said to ask to get the case postponed. They said if I did that . . ."

"Then you should ask for that," she tells him. "But if I don't have the file, I can't do anything for you."

Gary gives her the lost-dog look, and even in the county, a public defender proves susceptible; she agrees to help him go before the bench and ask for a delay. A half hour later, Gary flashes the same puppy face at a black man in black robes, as reassuring a judicial image as might be conjured.

No, the P.D. explains, Mr. McCullough did not seek counsel ten working days prior to trial. No, she is not authorized to represent him. But he believes himself to be innocent of the charge of theft under three hundred dollars and wishes to go to trial if he can retain a public defender in advance of a new trial date.

"I'll grant a postponement," says the judge, barely looking up. Gary hears that much and begins nodding gratefully. "He can either go to trial today, or he can seek a jury trial and go to trial tomorrow in Towson. Mr. McCullough?"

The public defender turns toward Gary, her eyebrows raised. Gary is being asked to make a choice here, though it's hard for him to think of it as such. The judge explains again: He can plead guilty, or he can plead not guilty and have his trial right now. Or, if he wants a postponement, he can request a jury trial and have exactly one day before his case will be heard at the Towson Circuit Court.

"With a lawyer?" asks Gary, considering the third option.

"Mr. McCullough, you had ample time to go to the public defender's office and obtain counsel. I am not going to grant a postponement because you were late doing what you were supposed to do."

Gary's mouth opens, but nothing suitable emerges. He wants to tell some truth here, to explain that he's a dope fiend, that it's a near miracle that he managed to pry himself loose from Fayette Street long enough to get to the public defender's office in the first place. He wants the judge to know that he thought ten days meant ten days, weekends included. He wants to say that he was only the lookout, that he got scared and left, that he didn't really boost anything.

"Do you want to go to trial today, or try for another judge tomorrow?" the public defender asks. "The judge tomorrow might grant a postponement for you to get a lawyer. I don't know."

"Tomorrow," says Gary.

But tomorrow is even worse. At the Towson Circuit Court, Gary lands on the docket of a white judge, a county archetype with horn-rimmed glasses, Vitalis-slick hair, and a double chin. Before the court session, when Gary tries to seek a postponement, the circuit court prosecutor is contemptuous; he catches the scent of malt liquor on Gary's breath and berates him for coming to court drunk. Again, Gary wants to impart

some truth, to tell the man that he's not drunk, that he only downed a
bottle of Mickey's to keep the snake away, to get him through the morning
without a blast. But Gary says nothing and the prosecutor uses the silence
for a parting shot: "I'm not giving out postponements. This'll teach you
to come out to the county and steal."

Dag. Out here, they call it stealing. Out here, the petty capers once
again turn into crimes. Gary stumbles away to wait for his case to be
called. He watches a drug sentencing where the defendant gets eighteen
months.

"Gary Castro McCullough."

He takes a court trial, hoping that if he doesn't waste time filling the
jury box, the judge will be appeased. The store security guards testify
and Gary, alone at the trial table, is conscious enough to catch some of
their equivocation. They've got Gary as the lookout, though his selec-
tive memory is assuring him that he left before the boosting started.
They've got him signing the form voluntarily, but in fact, they threatened him, told him they'd have him charged with God knows what if
he didn't sign. They brought the statement the defendant signed with
them, but no, the security officer who took that statement is not here
to testify. They say they caught him on videotape, but no, they did not
bring the videotape to court.

Even a half-assed trial lawyer could have some fun ripping the case
apart. Defending himself, however, Gary offers precious little in the way
of a cross-examination, then takes the stand to mumble a generalized
protestation of innocence.

"You were in the mall when the guards found you?" asks the judge.
"What were you doing there?"

"Reading a newspaper," says Gary.

"But why were you there?"

Gary shrugs. "I was jus' readin'."

Guilty as charged. One year's supervised probation.

Not bad at all, considering the surroundings. Any other ghetto stray
would leave well enough alone, catch the bus back down York Road, and
keep on it until the greenery became concrete. But coming out of the
courtroom, Gary finds enough of his voice to ask the prosecutor about
an appeal. The man hears that and actually stops to give the convicted
man a once-over.

"Appeal?"

"I want to appeal."

No one from the city ever bothers to appeal a charge that ends in probation. Anyone lucky enough to leave the courtroom without silver bracelets is usually content with that much. But Gary is offended; he didn't take anything from that store.

"Talk to the public defender."

He takes an extra hour to go back to the P.D.'s office to file the necessary paperwork, telling himself that with a lawyer he can get out from under the weekly meetings with a state probation agent. By the time he finishes that chore, the snake is up and crawling; he has to get home.

An hour and a half later on Fayette Street, he's barely holding it together, looking for Tony, but knowing that even if he finds his partner, he won't be able to make the long run up to Baker Street in his current condition. He's got to get right first, and that means Ronnie.

He had managed to steer clear of the Gaunt One for a couple weeks now. The metal game was always something he could do without involving Veronica Boice; as long as he had a line on something good—copper and aluminum, especially—he didn't have to get near her web. Now, though, he needs her.

"Where Ronnie at?" he asks Pimp, who pops out of Annie's back door just as Gary is leaving his mother's kitchen.

"Ronnie Boice? She up on the corner."

"Huh?"

"Where you been, chief? Ronnie workin' out for Gee Money."

Gary can't believe his luck. He jogs up Vine Street, peers down the sidewalk to Fayette, and sure enough, his girl is standing in front of the liquor store, serving a white fiend.

The snake got no bite today.

"Hey," says Gary, sidling up.

"Hey yo'self."

How she got the gig is anyone's guess. Gary figures Gee must have been hard up for help this week to let Ronnie hold vials for him. Her count is never right; she always manages to lose as much as she sells. Now, like the spider to a fly, she welcomes him. Sure, she'll get him over with a vial or two; that's the price of admission for Gary, who'll be a good accomplice for the capers to come. Working alone, Ronnie will palm a few and make some of Gee's profit disappear; working with someone trustworthy, she can switch vials and sell B & Q and create untold confusion. With Gary at her beck and call, she can run two dozen hustles.

They're set. Or at least Gary thinks so until he comes back from his mother's basement an hour later to see the police wagon up at Fayette and Monroe, its back doors wice open against oncoming traffic. Ronnie is in bracelets, still managing a smirk as the wagon man pats her down. Gary's salvation is on her way down to women's detention.

"What happened?" he asks Fat Curt, who's been watching the proceedings.

"She sittin' on it like a mother hen," Curt explains. "Shit don' need to be kept warm. She thinkin' she got her ass on an egg or some shit."

Sure enough, the Western knockers rolled up and got her with twenty vials right under her ass. She tried to get up from the grocery steps and walk away, leaving the baggie behind, but by then it was way late. The lesson for Gary is immediate and obvious: Stick to what you know. Boosting was not his hustle and now he's on probation for it. Slinging is not Ronnie's hustle and now she's caught a charge. Aluminum, copper, light steel—these things are bread and butter to him, and Baker Street is still up there, waiting for him.

Gary cuts through the vacant lot to the back alley and Vine Street, where his brother is sweating in the afternoon sun, slinging for the New Yorkers. June Bey is tiring, wishing he could shift the load and have a few minutes to himself in the basement. He offers his brother a half share, but Gary has seen enough slinging. It's the right decision, too, because by early evening, Charlene Mack will have run off with June Bey's ground stash, prompting a beat-down from Dred's people. And that beating is followed by another the next morning, when June Bey gets a morning jumper from the Spider Bag crew that leaves him too high to work. Ronnie, June Bey, Charlene Mack, and Hungry, too, who is once again wanted for making off with a New York Boy's stash—all of them are running a game, all of them messing up. It's enough to make Gary sympathize with the dealers.

With Ronnie gone, Gary figures it's Baker Street or bust. He spends the earlier part of the next morning looking halfheartedly for Tony, all the while pondering the ethics of a fresh plan taking shape in his head. The moral dilemma is that the new plan doesn't call for Tony's muscle, but for Will's old pickup truck instead. When Gary comes up empty at a couple of Tony's haunts and starts feeling the snake, his decision is made. He heads down Baltimore Street for Pigtown and the alley rowhouse where Will's white girlfriend lives.

True, he's been angry at Will ever since being cut from his own carcrushing caper, but now that's neither here nor there. Will has a truck and Baker Street is too long a haul without one.

"I got the spot and you got the ride," he tells Will.

With that they're off, Gary riding shotgun with Will's girl in the old blue tank and Will's brother consigned to the truck bed. Gary is once again the favored passenger, the idea man granted renewed standing for having a handle on the caper. "Turn here," says Gary, as the pickup nears Baker. "And then park on the side there."

The caper is everything that Gary claimed it would be: hard work, yes, but not as hard as when the aluminum and copper and brass have to be pulled from rowhouse walls, and certainly not as risky as stealing an automobile from in front of someone's home. Within a half hour, they've got a $200 load of assorted metal in the pickup bed. And this time, Gary came prepared: long-sleeves, gloves, a hooded sweatshirt. No ticks.

Will jams the truck into gear and they slowly three-point their way around until the blue beast is facing the hill.

"Tallyho," says Gary.

"We gonna get paid," Will says, delighted.

But the old truck is loaded and wheezing, barely managing the grade up to Bentalou. Will downshifts, and for a second the truck almost seems to be going backward until finally, there's just enough engine to get them up and over. They pause at the crest and check for traffic, turning ever so slowly as a shiny black four-by-four with tinted glass and Halogens races around them and then squeals to a halt, blocking Bentalou. Out steps a white man. A big white man with a beet-red face. A big white man with a big brown baseball bat.

"Oh," says Gary.

"I'll kill all of you right here, right now," yells the man with the bat. "Get the fuck out!"

They tumble from Will's truck, begging, pleading, trying like hell to explain the unexplainable.

"What's up, boss?" says Will, arms raised in surrender.

"On your knees," growls the white man. "Now."

Three of them are down on the asphalt, making their peace with God. Gary comes out of the passenger door and starts walking sideways, hoping to make the sidewalk and slip down Bentalou as if he's some kind of bystander.

"Get the fuck over here!"

"I . . . I just got a lift from them. I'm . . ."

The white man cocks the bat and takes a step toward Gary, who goes down on his knees with the rest of his crew, everyone begging and praying as the traffic rolls around them. They're on a West Baltimore street, a moment or two from violent death and no one—but no one— is going to come to their defense. Never mind that it's three black men and a white girl held hostage in the street by a red-faced 'billy. Never mind that this is the heart of black Baltimore, that they're on their knees in the very shadow of the George Washington Carver Vocational High School. Never mind that Mr. Carver served a grateful nation by finding ten thousand things to do with a peanut. Never mind that it's four against one or that two dozen black citizens are examining this Deep South diorama through rowhouse doorways and automobile windows. All of that doesn't seem to mean much to the white man with the bat; he's right at home here in the southbound lane of Bentalou Street, yelling and screaming and strenuously asserting his right to take batting practice on behalf of his stolen property.

"Please," says Will, palms up in supplication.

The girl is crying.

"We'll put it back," says Gary.

"Goddam right you will."

"Yessir."

"I should kill you right now."

"Yessir. Please."

The short ride to the front gate of the scrap yard is a journey of a thousand miles. Gary and the others lug all the metal back inside the fence, trying in absolute earnestness to remember the original resting place of each item. At the end, the hillbilly puts them on their knees one last time, swearing to them that if they ever so much as dream about his metal again, they should wake up and apologize.

"Yessir. You right, sir."

On the way home, Will's brother is back at shotgun, with Gary riding alone in the empty pickup bed, the hot summer wind rushing past him as they rumble down Bentalou. Gary's heart is still racing, his stomach churning. He could have died back there—he could have actually died like a dog in the street, and no one would have said or done anything to stop it. Catching his breath, Gary feels some gratitude for the mercies shown, for the terrifying white colossus who, by God's sweet grace, decided to spare them all.

Near Winchester Street he glimpses the ruby glory of that rose-covered trellis again. But this time it brings no joy.

Dag, he tells himself. I need a job.

On Fayette Street, movement itself tells a story.

Fat Curt, for one, can tell from a man's walk whether he's flush, or illing, or carrying a semiauto down in the dip of his sweats. Having lived a life in the corner game, Curtis Davis sees all of it with precision, so that no one moves from here to there without the old tout divining the actual purpose.

When Curt sees Scalio do his slow, listing two-step across Monroe Street, he knows that there is no destination, that he's on his corner until the end of the business day. A police giving him a quick glance might actually be fooled by the illusion of forward progress, but come back in an hour and Scalio will be where you left him.

Or consider Eggy Daddy, a man on a mission, his thinned-out frame motivating away from the corner traffic in a brisk pimp roll; the sight tells Curt that Eggy's taking a little personal time for his medication. Or Chauncey, coming down Vine Street for the morning testers, giving it a half-strut, half-trot—Curt sees that and knows Chauncey got the word late, that the boy's giving it just enough to get his tired carcass to end of the line.

There's the sudden bolt of Stink from one side of the street to the other, followed by the slow creep into a gap between rowhouses. See something like that and you don't think police—only amateurs run from a police when they're dirty and Stink is no amateur. Fat Curt's better guess is that Odell or some other stickup boy will be coming around the corner next.

There's also the running glide, the silk-smoooth movement of Hungry, darting out from the Vine Street garages, then hugging the front of the rowhouses all the way down to Fulton. It's speed enough to guarantee escape, but not so much as to attract the attention of everyone on the street. Curt gets sight of the sideways glide and knows that Hungry has possession of someone else's vials.

Finally, there is the forty-meter dash, the out-and-out, headlong, I-don't-care-who-sees-me rush for glory or safety or revenge. Get a glimpse of a man running with that kind of heat and you know that he's going to vault any fence or crash any door to get there first.

So when Curt spots one of the Mount Street hangers-on, Wayne by name, cutting the corner onto Fulton, his neck craning around in terror, he understands and looks toward Mount. Sure enough, a New York dealer clears the corner, sprinting on the balls of his feet, slicing across Fayette. The dealer is closing the distance, gripping an aluminum bat in his hand as if it were a relay baton. The race soon has the attention of the entire strip, with touts and slingers from Mount to Monroe momentarily distracted. Time out for a street beating.

"They done talkin'," says Fat Curt dryly.

On Fulton, Wayne stumbles briefly as he goes from the sidewalk to the street, then rights himself before taking the front steps of his rowhouse in a single leap. He grabs the door handle and flings himself inside, slamming it shut just as the New Yorker clears the corner and races across Fulton.

"Motherfucker!"

The New Yorker slams the bat against the wood once or twice for emphasis, demanding that Wayne open the door and take a rightful whipping.

"Get the fuck out here, bitch!"

Wayne is unconvinced and stays put.

The dealer slams the bat against the door one last time, then turns away from the house just as Officer Robert Brown of the Western District rolls up in a radio car. Mr. Brown was down on Baltimore Street where, from a block's distance, he caught a glimpse of the New Yorker shifting to overdrive. He, too, can mark the movement of this world. And though the running dealer was all he could glimpse from Baltimore Street, he knew, instinctively, that around the corner somewhere, ahead of the New Yorker, was another man, sprinting for his life.

Having chased Wayne into his hole, the dealer heads back across Fulton, the bat cradled on his shoulder like an Englishman's umbrella. Bob Brown pulls to the curb, steps from the car, and with the indifference of a grade-school playground monitor, takes hold of the weapon. In a wordless exchange, the New York dealer gives it up without breaking stride.

"Mr. Brown got hisself a new bat," says Fat Curt, hauling his cast-heavy leg up Blue's steps.

"What happened?" asks Blue.

Curt snorts. "Some foolishness."

Blue is preoccupied, working with reds and blues and blacks on a lunch special sign for a Belair Road carryout, the only straight work for his talents in the last couple months. He'd come home from the city jail in April with all kinds of promises and plans, even spent a few days trying to fashion some of them into a better day. But down on Baltimore Street, there wasn't much work left for him. Where once he used to take orders for signage from all the local groceries and shops, now most of the window boards are mass-produced and cheap. And with so many of the corner stores run by Koreans, he can't even begin to make personal connections.

What's left for him is running the needle palace, or what was left of it after he came home from courtside. Curt's efforts notwithstanding, the fiends had carried anything worth selling out of the house. Now, when Blue charges two dollars a head to sit and fire a shot, what he delivers is four walls, a jar of water, and Rita Hale.

Meanwhile, Blue is back to hardcore drugging. He had slowed himself on New Year's as a resolution to himself, but by the time they locked him up in February, he was steady firing again. He'd come home from jail clean, having dried himself out in the infirmary. But that, too, didn't last and now Blue is the same as ever, though perhaps a little more convinced that he'll never find strength enough to deal with his hunger.

Worse, Ella keeps pressing for him to teach the art classes. Blue doesn't have the heart to tell her no, to explain that he's now too desperate to play at doing right, that he has to deal with himself first before he can worry about anything else. Ella believes in him, and he's grateful for that. But Ella and her art class will have to wait.

Instead, Blue's most creative act since coming home has been adding another page or two of verse to the composition book he carried in his satchel. Blue's poetry is heavy and remorseless, a running argument between himself and his addiction, and a week ago, during a late-night lull at the shooting gallery, he had turned inward long enough to put some more of the pain into words:

> Insanity is alive and well, taking on all new comers
> Fragile minds are overcome and subdued,
> And placed in a prison where
> the bars are invisible . . .

He meant every word. And the next morning, he thought about his life long enough to take another walk around the city, looking to see if anyone needed anything they owned drawn or painted. The best he can do is this bit of signage from the carryout at Belair and North.

"Lookin' good," says Curt, watching the paint go on.

"Yeah, well," says Blue, "it's my thing."

Pimp comes down from the corner, shaking his head, his lips curled into the strangest of smiles. Among the shooting gallery regulars, Pimp still carries some of his old legend. He used to be among the best of the old-style boosters, so quick with his hands that he could go into a downtown jewelry store and come out with a whole tray of rings. He could play the part, too: Put Pimp in a tailored suit, arm him with a Michigan roll faced with a $100 note, and he was good enough to go on the road, taking off jewelers up and down the coast. Now, though, there is nothing of the old game left. Pimp is ragged, thinned to nothing, his repertoire down to the usual corner tricks.

"This stuff is too crazy, too crazy," he says, by way of beginning. "You hear about what happened down on Mount Street?"

"Huh," says Curt.

"One of them Ay-rabbers from up on Bruce Street went down there to cop. Put his rig right there at the curb, you know, got the bag on the horse's face . . ."

Curt is interested. He used to A-rab on a produce cart.

". . . so he's down there dealin' with things and the horse takes a piss all over a ground stash."

Curt and Blue both laugh.

"Red Tops had a stash right at the curb. Horse pissed on it so they beat the poor man's ass right off the corner, like he had something to do with it. And when they get done beatin' on him, damned if they don't have at the horse."

Fat Curt gives him a disbelieving look.

"Why beat the horse?" says Pimp. "Horse don't know."

Blue shakes his head.

"Summer," says Curt. "People doin' all kind of stupid shit."

That they are. Summer brings the corner stew to a boil and the city medic units earn their keep. In mid-July, after the tenth consecutive ninety-degree day, bad counts and missing dollars bring a high-caliber argument; stolen stashes and burn bags are repaid at the bent edge of a kitchen knife. Summer is what makes a corner a corner—the drug-market regulars bemoan the coming violence in one breath, then lapse into prideful boasting the next.

"Mount and Fayette," says Eggy, watching the ambos roll up on a double shooting. "Only serious niggers need apply."

Last year in June, the Fayette Street strip tallied four murders and a half-dozen shootings. Half of the fatalities were on the home team, the other half New Yorkers—casualties brought on as the immigrants from the Grand Concourse and Flatbush struggled to establish themselves in this section of the city. Fayette was living up to its reputation; from Monroe down to Gilmor, the days and nights rang with gunfire, until the New York Boys had their share and everyone else had grown accustomed to their product.

This year, it's mostly East Baltimore that's burning. Every summer night, it seems, another body or two falls somewhere on the other side of the city. Over there, the Eastern uniforms are running from one call to the next, chalking this one and rolling that one. Their commanders are beside themselves, their careers suddenly at risk from the worst bloodletting ever seen on Gay Street, or East Madison, or Ashland Avenue. The municipal government of Baltimore is still pretending to some kind of control, but the truth is that the city fathers have lost possession over whole sectors of the east side.

Why there? Why not. The violence roams and fluctuates with its own rhythms, so that the scene of last year's holocaust—though still a twenty-four-hour drug market—is now marked by nothing worse than an occasional assault. Under the weight of sporadic police pressure, or competition among crews, or some other nomadic impulse, the corners themselves shift location, then shift back again. Overnight, the fiends and slingers sense a difference; they wander down Fayette, or over to Baltimore, or up to Lexington for a time. Equilibrium is restored—or not. Sometimes the smallest change in the weather can make the pavement run red. Sometimes a loose bullet catches flesh, sometimes the lock-blade gets an artery. But there's no real science to it: Put a tame corner under a microscope and you find dope and coke, fiends and dealers, stickup boys and burn artists, lookouts and touts. Put a hot corner under the scope and you find pretty much the same thing.

So far this year, the beatings, cuttings, and shootings on Fayette Street haven't amounted to more than the usual. It's enough to keep the ambos and trauma units in business, but nothing so lethal as to impress the regulars. But now, in the fetid days of midsummer, with the heat rising in waves from the black asphalt, the Fayette strip steps up to its reputation.

A stickup boy is shot down in daylight at the mouth of the Vine Street alley. An argument over a short package leaves a Mount Street dealer cut in the side of the head and a tout on the run. A white boy is robbed and shot crossing Baltimore Street. On Saratoga, the police are called to a rowhouse and find the bodies of two women shot to death. The house has been ransacked; word on the corners is that a package of raw coke was taken.

And then, just before it ebbs, the bloodletting reaches out and touches Hungry. Not that anyone is surprised when one of the neighborhood's most committed short-count artists and stash stealers suddenly has his number come up. Hungry's time had been borrowed for a good while, and maybe that's what makes his last go-round seem so tragic and absurd. A young slinger, Smiley by name, had been off Fayette and Monroe for a while now, plying the bottom end, competing with Dewayne and Boo and the other young boys, working vials along the lower McHenry Street strip. But come the heat of July, he finds himself back up top, paired with one of the New York Boys and a particularly weak package of heroin. He stands by the carryout, scouring the morning regulars on a day when good help is hard to find.

And Hungry gets his package.

To sell, of course—not to keep. But the distinction is lost on Hungry, who must be astounded that anyone on Fayette Street is still naive enough to give him a starter kit. No slinking, no ground-stash stealing, no palming a few vials and hoping against hope that the short-count doesn't get noticed—just a few nods of agreement and he's got the whole world in his hands.

Smiley heads off while Hungry takes the consignment into Blue's house. There, with Rita's help, it begins to go the way of all contraband— at least until Hungry notices that for all of this free dope, he's not getting off. The package isn't much.

Disappointed, he reasons that he might as well actually sell some off and take what profit he can. But up on Monroe Street, Smiley's garbage isn't moving. Word is already out that what Hungry has been given just ain't what it claims to be. And when Smiley comes back, with the New Yorker behind him, he isn't trying to hear any of it. The two come at Hungry hard—not once, not twice, but enough times that Hungry gets the whole you-gonna-die-if-I-ain't-paid-tommorow lecture. When he hears any part of it, Hungry winces, because Hungry is always short, always beholden, always waiting for the inevitable. He knows the beating;

he lives with the beating. It's the established rate of exchange. In Hungry's mind, it completes the transaction and settles all debts.

So when Smiley throws out his threats and walks away, Hungry doesn't quite take it in. He's still standing there the following afternoon, up against the metal grate of the carryout, when the dealer returns to make his final pass with a lock-blade.

Once in and once out. Hungry greets the knife with open arms and a vague expression of surprise. Then he walks a step and a half, his legs heading in the general direction of the Bon Secours E.R., where the day crew keeps his usual gurney ready. Then he drops.

Everyone on the corner sees it, watching as Smiley stalks away and Hungry tries to pick himself up off the curb. He grabs hold of a small tree, trying for purchase, then slips down and lies still. The crowd melts off. The ambulance arrives. The yellow crime scene tape goes up.

Inside the shooting gallery that day, no one says much; when Hungry is the subject, what's left to say? The most that anyone can manage is a few harsh words for the young hopper with the knife. What was the nigger thinking, anyway? You give a package to Hungry, you might as well toss it in a storm drain. And then to settle up with the man at the point of a blade—that was out of all the understood proportions. Hungry steals your shit, or comes up short you beat him down: fair is fair. But it wasn't personal. Hungry took everyone's shit; Hungry was always short. To cut him down on a crowded corner for $100 or $150 in lost product made about as much sense as sucker-punching that A-rabber's horse for pissing.

Fat Curt was just down the street and missed the murder. Pimp saw it though. So did Scalio. And Blue. And Robin Neverdon, a coke fiend from the other side of Fayette. And although it takes the detectives a good while to shake the tree—a cornerful of eyeball witnesses does not, in this neck of the woods, necessarily equate with a solved case—eventually there comes a knock on the front door of the shooting gallery, the one that says the world is suddenly paying attention to the people inside Blue's rowhouse.

"Poh-leece. Homicide."

Fat Curt's brother, Dennis, cracks the door, gets a look at two white men in suits and backs into the hallway.

"Where's Blue?" asks a detective.

Dennis mumbles something, the air wheezing through the hole in his neck. The trache is still there more than a year after the last emergency room visit.

"Where's Blue at?"

The suits press the issue, moving down the hallway, deeper into the catacomb. In the front room, Fat Curt is propped on a wooden chair, one swollen hand wrapped around a bent screwdriver that he's using to claw at his cast. He's gnawing at it like an animal caught in a trap.

"Cast got wet," he tells them.

Wrapped in deadweight, his leg has been hurting for weeks now. Worse, the summer heat has made the constricting plaster unbearable. Curt figures he'll doctor himself.

"You Blue?"

Curt shrugs. "Don't know the man."

The detectives move back into the kitchen and a shorter fiend slips down the stairs, turns into the hallway and makes for the door.

"Hey," says one suit, "you right there. Are you Blue?"

"Naw," Blue replies before leaving. "He gone."

For a veteran detective, the usual process would be to gather the nearest and dearest together and plead on the dead man's behalf—a standardized speech angled at family and friendship, loyalty and common decency. But after wandering the first floor of Blue's for a few minutes, it's clear to the police that none of that counts for much here. They go the other route.

"If we don't find Blue, everyone's getting locked up."

That cuts it. Dennis goes down the hall to the front door and yells for Blue to come home. When George Epps finally makes his way back, he's greeted by two very impatient police investigators.

"Why'd you say you weren't Blue?" the red-haired one asks.

Blue flashes a mock-innocent smile. "Man," he tells them, "you know how that is."

They know. They put him in the back of a Chevy Cavalier and ride him downtown, where they get confirmation on the story of Hungry and Smiley and the lost package. They grab Robin from across the street and Robin gives up much the same tale. A third witness cinches it and the radio cars roll up on Vine Street a few days later, slowing in front of the rowhouse where Smiley lays his head.

The murder and subsequent arrest is barely noted on the corner, spoken of only at odd points and in the most abstract terms. In the shooting gallery, Hungry is not mourned as a lost soul so much as he is missed for continuity's sake. At the least, death interferes with the illusion; it always ruins the high. When Bread fell out and died, the rest of them had to acknowledge their own certain terminus. Dennis, who has the Bug, can imagine himself collapsing on the couch at Annie's and being hauled off by the ambo. And Pimp, rail-thin with the same virus, can imagine his own people paying to have him laid out at Brown's, then buried without a headstone down at Mt. Zion. And Bryan, who survived the bullets this winter but now has to get his AZT at the University clinic and deal with the night sweats and nausea—he gets a glimpse of just how short his run might be. Hungry is gone. No one musters much grief for that fact alone; it's the absence of Hungry that bothers them. Here again is proof that not a motherfucker among them is getting out alive.

The summer slowly claims its casualties. Soon Bryan disappears, on the run again after sticking up Eggy Daddy for some of Gee Money's vials and cash. A desperate act, true, but Bryan can't think of what else to do when Gee doesn't pay him promptly at the end of a shift. Then Pimp goes down, coughing and rasping, with double pneumonia. And then, finally, it's Fat Curt's turn.

He soldiers until he can soldier no more, until the hot July day when he falls to the pavement at the crossroads that claimed him years before. He's had the wet cast off his leg for a couple weeks—long enough to prove that the doctors were right, that the ankle wasn't going to set right if he didn't stay off his feet. Without the cast, Curt is soon hobbling around with his foot twisted to one side, his metal cane getting him where he needs to be, his face etched with constant pain.

"Got to get it looked at," he tells anyone who asks. "Got to get some doctorin' on it."

But he never does. Despite weeks of agony, it isn't the ankle that brings him back to Bon Secours. It's Fat Curt lying on the corner of Monroe and Fayette, talking out of his head, delirious, his eyes buried beneath a yellow glaze.

"Curt . . . Curt."

"He ain't makin' sense."

"Somebody got to call nine-one-one."

On the last day of July, Curt is rushed into the E.R. at Bon Secours, stabilized, then sent up to the second floor and a semiprivate room. When he wakes up, he's on an intravenous feed, sick as a dog, his warped frame wrapped in a hospital robe. Before long, the young interns are crowded around his bed, pausing in their routine to take in the enormity of the damage.

"Treat me like a freak," he says after they leave.

The nurses are warmer to him, but even they test his patience with continual questions about his medical history—as if Bon Secours didn't already know everything there was to know about him from springtime, when he broke the ankle.

"I ain't sayin'," Curt tells one nurse who queries him.

"Why not? This is to help the doctors."

"'Cause I can't remember what I told you the last time and I don't want to get caught lyin'," Curt explains. "Keep askin' me the same damn questions an' I can't recall my answers."

Even the nurse laughs.

He's there for two weeks, and after the first two days or so, he's clean. For Curt, the snake has never been the problem. He likes shooting dope; it's his life. But if the dope isn't there, he'll get a little bit sick, deal with that, and then come up smiling. For two days, he looks like hell itself and then, slowly, some other being emerges from within, someone never seen at the corner of Monroe and Fayette.

"What's for lunch today, darlin'."

The nurses are all darlings. The other patients are good peoples. The sound of summer rain at his hospital window reminds him of better times. Even the hospital food is tolerable.

"Rather have some of that pork from Bittman's," he tells visitors. "Pork sandwich, fries, greens, and a Coke."

The dope goes away, but the dope fiend's sweet tooth doesn't. Stink shows up one day to catch Curt up on the corner news; Curt leans on him for a couple sodas from across the street. Rose and Curt Junior come by with drugstore candy and, for an afternoon, Curt's broken family is gathered together once again at his bedside, eating sweets and watching daytime television. Most of all, Curt dreams about getting uptown to that snowball stand at Laurens and Monroe, getting some coin together, and making summer official.

"Get me some pineapple flavor," he says. "Ain't nothin' better than the pineapple."

After long years of chemical torpor, the sudden liberation of body and mind is exhilarating to Curt and everyone who comes near him. His memory is clear and firm; long-lost stories pour from him, stories to pass the hospital hours. He's talking about the drug runs to New York and the adventures in that city, telling tales out of school about Little Melvin and Liddie and Junior Bunk and two dozen other long-gone players from his youth.

"Dead and gone. All my friends is dead and gone," he says, reflectively. "Outlived most of 'em. Just lost Bread to this foolishness not long ago. He was a good friend."

Curt is sad, of course; too much has been wasted to get beyond sadness. But now there is something more than sadness to him, something given full flower in the stable confines of a hospital bed. Now, with the corner at bay, all the normal needs and desires of life come rushing up at him. He wants the kid in the next bed over, the one recovering from a gunshot wound, to be comfortable and comforted. He wants the charge nurse to like him a little bit. He wants another soda. He wants something tastier than that nasty green Jell-O for dessert. Within a week, his wants grow into long-term aspirations. He wants to get an apartment. He wants to do something for Rose and for his teenaged son, who have been on their own for so long. He wants someone to take a picture of his legs and put it on a T-shirt, give it away at all the schools and let the children see what the needle does. He wants a little government money on check day—enough to pay the rent and buy groceries. And on several early mornings that other part of him is very much alive and then he wants the big-legged nurse on the night shift, the fine-looking one who's been kind enough to flirt.

Fat Curt is off the corner. And he is alive.

Physically, of course, he's falling apart: hepatitis, jaundice, his liver holding on by a thread, the enzyme counts hovering at levels that can be attained only through years of pharmaceutical riot. The lymphedema in all four limbs is now likely past the point of return; if Curt stops firing dope tomorrow, the hands and legs will still stay fat. The ankle is irrevocably disfigured. Fusing it might have some beneficial effect, but nothing can ever make it right. The healed abscesses are permanent scars; the open ones promise only sepsis.

"You keep shooting drugs," the social worker tells him, "and you'll be dead within months. Your liver has about given up."

Curt can only smile at the thought. "My liver got every right to give up. I know it. You ain't got to tell me that."

"I'm serious, Curtis. You'll die."

"I hear you. I know it."

Her name is Kathy. She leaves her name and number on Curt's chart, telling him that she'll help, that if he wants to do something different, she'll work with him on some kind of plan. "But," she adds, "I've been doing this a long time and I've had a lot of experience. I know that if you don't want to change yourself, then you're only wasting my time. And I'm not going to let you waste my time, you understand?"

Curt nods.

"Around here," says Kathy, "I'm known as the bitch."

"You the bitch, huh?" says Curt, now laughing. "I best watch out for myself then."

"You better watch out if you're wasting my time," she says. "You say you want to change, but I can't do this for you."

"I know," says Curt. "It's all about me."

"That's right."

"I got to want to change."

"Right."

The room goes silent. The social worker waits for the next logical assertion, but it never comes. "Curtis," she says, finally. "Do you want to change?"

"I need a break," he says grudgingly.

It's as close as he dares come. Still, Kathy offers to get him started. If he promises to attend the group sessions at Tuerk House every day, she can get him on the waiting list for the twenty-eight-day program there. She'll also help him fill out the applications for state social services, medical assistance, and federal disability through Social Security.

"What I need is a place of my own," says Curt.

"Well, that's something we can work on. But you've got to show me that you're serious. Are you going to go to these meetings and get yourself into Tuerk House?"

"Yeah. I'm tired. I'm tired of bein' tired."

He's discharged a week later, sent back out into the street with what's left of his liver and the same wreck of an ankle as before. For now, he'll stay with a sister up on Ellamont Avenue, using her rowhouse for his address on all the applications to be filled out at Rosemont and the Social Security branch office on Frederick Avenue. The caseworkers are not hopeful. Maryland is cutting back public assistance for adult males, and, as for federal disability benefits, it's a dead certainty that any applicant will be turned down for SSI benefits on the first attempt unless he's stone blind or quadriplegic.

So Curt stays on Ellamont, waiting for a check that may never come, rising late each morning to fight his sweatpants over the top of his bloated legs, then struggling to get his foot inside a pair of running shoes three sizes too large. Most days, Curt makes the noon meetings at Tuerk

House, the detox facility across the street from the Rosemont social services office, where he sits in a room with two dozen other wounded souls, most of them names and faces he knows from a life on the corner. They charge two bills for the Tuerk House meetings; two dollars to tell your true story and hear other people do the same. The reasoning is that after all these years of scratching out blast money, only a no-hustling dope fiend can't come up with two bills. Either that, or a dope fiend who isn't serious about changing, and therefore has no need for meetings. But if you pay your money and catch enough sessions, the social worker makes a call and you're off the waiting list. Then comes four weeks inside—enough time for some people to call themselves clean.

With every meeting, Fat Curt learns more of the cadence of a new language. And after three weeks in the back of the Tuerk House meeting room, he finds it in himself to stand and be heard.

"Name's Curt," he tells them. "I'm a drug addict."

"What's all the damn commotion?"

Fran Boyd is on the steps, joining the rest of the neighborhood, peering up Fayette Street at a cluster of police cars, their blue strobes flashing.

"Turtle, what happened?"

Little Stevie looks up at his aunt in absolute earnest, delivering what he knows in the most ordinary tone an eight-year-old can manage.

"Mr. Eddie shot somebody."

Fran glances back up the street then turns to her nephew, who looks back at her with complete dispassion. Stevie might as well have told her it was going to rain.

"Get in the house," she yells at him.

"Yes'm," says Stevie, stung by her harshness.

As another day begins on Fayette Street, Fran Boyd is still here in body, if not spirit. She's still scoping the terrain, still taking the shit as it comes. In her heart, though, Fran has taken the first few small steps on that long road to somewhere else. As the usual summer mayhem swirls around her doorstep, she finds it harder to manage the mind-set that sees everything as the stuff of low comedy or high drama. Increasingly, what she manages amounts to disgust, a lingering emotion she can't shake even in her sessions in the basement—sessions over which she's made an honest effort to gain some control.

She's still in the mix, of course—until the people from BRC call, Fran has got to negotiate her world—but lately, Fran has been talking about the corner more as a thing despised than as a thing mastered. She was good at the game, better than most, but the hot months bring a crazed senselessness. It makes even the best and most devoted players uneasy; it makes anyone thinking about change think a little harder. Today's distraction is a shooting. The day before, it was a police sweep. Tomorrow there will be something else. Now, since seriously beginning to contemplate her own escape, Fran sees less sense to this life than ever before. Day after day, she sits on her steps and watches the big-tent circus, still alert for her angles, but now she does so with a heightened awareness of the horror.

A week ago she saw a Mount Street regular named Clyde, home from the charge he took over the winter, arriving at his corner just in time to get snagged with some vials, tossed in the Western District wagon, and returned to the detention center.

"He came to visit for just a little while," Fran deadpanned. "Now he gone back home."

After that she witnessed R.C.'s sister Darlene go after another girl on Mount Street with a baseball bat and felt only broken nostalgia: "You know I used to baby-sit for her and Ricky and Bug. She was sweet back then. She crazy now."

More recently Fran was out on the steps when Stashfinder, one of the Western District's finest, came charging up Fayette to grab some pink-top vials off the vacant lot and give them to her brother, Stevie.

"What you doin', officer? They ain't mine," Stevie Boyd implored as they cuffed him up. "I swear to you, they ain't mine."

And they weren't. In point of fact, Stevie was touting heroin, not coke on this particular day. He was on the way out of the house wearing a green brim and black sweatshirt when the police snatched him. Alfred, Bunchie's better half, who was selling the Pink Tops, was also wearing a green cap and black hoody, but he had stepped back inside the Dew Drop to take a leak. It was a rare miss for Stashfinder—Sgt. Timothy Devine, by name—a veteran who had worked the bottom end of the Western District for years.

Devine had earned his nickname from the locals by doing police work the old-fashioned way. Stashfinder wouldn't simply throw probable cause to the wind, rolling up on a corner and diving into everyone's pockets. He'd get out of his car and creep. He'd watch a corner for hours from inside a vacant rowhouse, or from a rooftop, using a blanket that he kept in his cruiser trunk. He'd wait awhile, letting all the pieces come together. Ninety-nine times out of a hundred, when he did come down on the corner, he'd walk straight to the ground stash, pick it up, and bring it back to the right slinger. If he'd seen the money go from the tout to dealer, he'd follow that too, so that a supplier took his rightful charge.

Normally the idea of her brother wrongly arrested for someone else's package, and by Stashfinder especially, would send Fran—or anyone else at Mount and Fayette—into paroxysms of rage. The idea that the police were lying, that they always lie, was a recurring theme. And while much exaggeration went into this, there was enough that was true. A day in Western District courtroom saw enough perjury to make any lawyer think twice about asking anyone in a police uniform to take the oath. Street-level police work on many Baltimore corners had come to mean jacking everyone up, finding a stash, and then deciding at random who would eat the charge. This would infuriate the corner veterans, who liked to insist that there were standards. Of course they were all guilty in the larger scheme of things, but that was never the point. The touts and fiends weren't asking for some overall judgment; they simply wanted the police to play the cards dealt. But Fran had now lost her sense of outrage, so that after Little Roy, Stevie's supplier, put up the money to bail her brother out, she shrugged and chalked up the whole mess to raw chance.

"They locked up Stevie for Alfred's shit," Fran told people. "But you know Stevie got no right to complain. They might like to come back around five minutes later and lock his triflin' ass up for something else."

It was that old proverb: Beat your child once a day; if you don't know what for, he does. It was also, in the psychology of the corner, absolute apostasy. Get it straight, Fran: Police lie, and the corner can't be wrong.

She is slipping, and those around her begin to take notice of this at odd moments. On the day after Little Stevie sees Mr. Eddie throw a cap into some unlucky opponent, Gary arrives on the steps of the Dew Drop with a Double Shield tester, looking to fire up in the midst of a terrifying asthma attack. Out of nowhere, Fran ambushes him with an anti-drug lecture:

". . . and you standin' there, barely able to get your breath, thinkin' that shit gonna make you better. Gary, you killin' yo'self with that shit."

Fran Boyd as Nancy Reagan.

"Dag," Gary wheezes.

"I'm serious, Gary. You gonna die behind that shit."

Gary shuffles around for a moment, looking for an out. "So," he says, feeling deep in his pocket, "you sayin' you don't want to go down to the basement then."

"Sheeet," says Fran, following him inside. "I ain't the one coughin.'"

She still had to get over every day, but now, in her mind she was rebelling. Now, Fran would witness a beating and wonder aloud: Why they got to beat a man for being short on the count when he's always short on the count? They know he's a dope fiend. They know what's going to happen when they give him the vials. Now, Fran would hear about a shooting and ask what shooting people had to do with selling drugs. Everything else in this world gets sold without store clerks and customers getting killed behind it. Why couldn't the people at Mount and Fayette get their shit together?

And at the end of the month, when Bunchie had gone through her own check money and whatever rent her siblings have paid and is still unable to come up with the $30 rent on the Section 8 apartment, Fran expresses amazement. Is her sister that trifling? How could she go through every last dollar? How could she spend it all and not even be able to make the Dew Drop's paltry rent?

"I mean, she got to know that the end of the month is coming. And she talkin' about she can't even come up with thirty dollars?" Fran would wail. "What little shit we got left gonna be in the street . . . I got to get up from here."

This was the reconstituted Fran talking, the newly baptized soul who has been making those calls down to the detox unit, the one who now believes she could fall no farther. Bunchie hasn't changed; she is a fiend in good standing, and her job is to get the blast. It's Fran who is forgetting Rule One.

The following week Fran manages to get Antoinette from BRC on the phone. For her trouble, she learns that her name is nearing the top of the waiting list.

"I'm sure we probably gonna have a bed for you next week."

Fran can't believe it when she hears it.

"Next week?"

"Next week."

She hangs up the phone elated. One week.

Now she has a lot to get done. First, she'll have to scratch together enough money so DeAndre and DeRodd can make it to the end of the month. Then, she'll have to give her Independence Card to DeAndre and show him how to use the card in an automated bank machine. In

Maryland the social service agencies had gone to the equivalent of ATM cards rather than mailed monthly checks, thereby liberating recipients from the usury of check-cashing outlets and rampant check theft. The irony in the name of the new mechanism notwithstanding, Independence Cards have been designed to carry the economy of West Baltimore into the millennium.

She'll need some things for herself as well. Bath stuff and some new tennis shoes and slippers and some fresh clothes and assorted other sundries. She is cleaning up here, starting fresh. She might wear the same rags going into detox, but she plans on coming out brand spanking new. Normally, this would require a boosting run to a county mall, but Fran has sworn off her discount shopping sprees for months now—not only in deference to all the upcoming trial dates she's collected, but for fear that the next arrest will mean jail time, costing her this chance at drug rehab. Her last boosting venture had been at Easter, when she had worked the department stores long enough to acquire a new set of sweats for DeAndre's holiday promenade down to the Inner Harbor.

Now she'll have to shop from register to register, like a chump. That means more money, and that, in turn, means reaching out to anyone and everyone for whatever she can get. Suddenly, Fran's best dope-fiend move is to claim her place as an ex-dope-fiend-to-be. For the next full week, she plays her new status for all it's worth, leaning on her brother Scoogie for cash and a commitment to watch out for her children while she's detoxing. And Scoogie—he can't possibly say no, not after insisting that he's been clean for years. With his sister finally making the move, Scoogie will have to pay.

She also works Gary for the promise of a little money for his son. Michael, DeRodd's father, gets a call as well. And Karen, Scoogie's love and Fran's best friend from the good old days, offers to take DeRodd if necessary. Fran works anyone at all sympathetic to her new found cause. It's loaned money, she tells those willing to front a few bills; when she's back on her feet, the cash will come back. Even if few seem to believe her, Fran hears her own charity pitch and begins to believe it herself.

One day she actually goes to Bunchie and asks for a pass on next month's rent, but Bunchie stays firm. Her older sister seems a little put out by Fran's change of heart; in fact, her family—with the possible exception of Scoogie—is decidedly unenthusiastic about the whole endeavor. Stevie and Sherry are able to mouth the called-for platitudes, but Fran can see something else in their tired eyes. They don't want her to go. If she gets out, it will be, to them, a judgment.

As for Bunchie, she doesn't believe it for a second.

"You think you goin' next week, huh?" she asks Fran.

"Tuesday," Fran says. "BRC has intake on Tuesdays."

"Well, we all could use a break."

A break. The word meant exactly that—a pause in the action, a temporary respite from the ordinary grind. Bunchie doesn't need to quit snorting heroin and smoking coke altogether; she just needs a break. The same for everyone: Fiends don't need to give up the needle forever, they just need some time off for good behavior. Fran had been in treatment years before so she knows from experience what the word means and what it doesn't mean. She remembers being out at Oakview with the rest of them, talking the talk, telling stories and hearing the stories told. She can recall how many people came into detox with only the merest pretense of changing, when the real agenda was getting a brief vacation, a chance for the body to regain some strength before the next deluge. She had thought that way herself.

This time would be different, though. She's thirty-six years old; she's had her fun, and finally, she's ready. This is bottom. She can feel it.

On Saturday, when Gary comes down Fayette to the Dew Drop to share his morning blast with Fran, he hears the big news and is immediately suspicious—especially when he gets hold of the dollars-and-cents angle to Fran's sudden renewal. Yeah, he'll try to help DeAndre out a little bit, he says vaguely. Naw, he doesn't have ten dollars that Fran can hold right now. Later, when he goes upstairs and sees Fran packing her belongings in a green plastic garbage sack, he comes around.

"You really gonna do it," Gary says softly.

"Got to," she tells him. "You should go down there, too."

"I'm gonna," he insists. "You'll see. I'm gonna get past this for real. You gonna see."

She hears him and shakes her head dismissively. Dope fiends are always going to get past it. Twenty times in a bad day they're talking that shit to someone, usually to themselves. Miss a vein, you gonna quit. Shoot baking soda, you done. Get yourself stuck up, or fall out from an overdose, or have your money walk away—all are reasons to declare that you've had enough, that you're ready to get your name on a waiting list somewhere. Only it doesn't happen that way—the corner never gives anyone enough reason. It comes from within, or it doesn't come at all.

"Gary, you talkin' out your ass."

He gets mad, but Fran is feeling too different these days to care. And she isn't about to let Gary McCullough off with a mere lecture.

"You workin' now, right?"

"Down the crabhouse. Cardy got me some days."

She just looks at him. Too late. Gary sees the trap. True, after the Baker Street junkyard debacle, he'd found steady work at Seapride. And true, the crabhouse has for a couple weeks now been paying him six an hour, six shifts a week. But these are hand-to-spike dollars for Gary's habit, not for Fran's redemption.

"Lemme hold ten," she says.

Gary starts shaking his head, backing up, telling her that he doesn't get paid until whenever, that it's got to last him until God knows when.

"C'mon, Gary, I'm tryin' to do something here. I got to look out for Andre while I'm gone."

Gary has one hand to his forehead, trying to think of words that won't come fast enough.

"Gary, for your son."

"I'll get with Andre and help him out."

"Gary, c'mon."

"I will."

"Gary."

He looks up at her, angry and defeated. She has his number and he knows it. She's always had his number.

"Fran," he says, with a nod to the blast shared. "I just treated you and you askin' for more. I ain't got it."

"Lemme hold five then."

Gary takes the deal. Five dollars is the price for walking away from the Dew Drop Inn with some small piece of conscience intact. But he leaves feeling scammed, unable to find the words to wish her good luck or bon voyage or break a leg. He's halfway down the steps before Fran makes him come back.

"Where you goin' at?"

"What do you mean?" asks Gary.

"I be gone a long while," she says. "Don't I get a hug?"

Yes she does; she always does. They embrace at the top of the stairs and Gary can't keep the smile from his face.

"Why you mess with me so bad?" he asks her.

Fran laughs. Finally, she lets him go, promising that she'll keep one eye on the men's dorm and see if there's a bed for him. If not, she'll get him on the waiting list.

"You gonna look in on Andre, right?"

Gary says he will.

"Okay then."

For a few minutes, at least, she's alone. Spreading the bills out on the worn bedsheet, she calculates the necessities. This much for food money. That much to get some lotion and towels. This much she has to give Bunchie.

She's got sixty left. Party time.

And why should anyone be suprised at the notion? If she didn't have a problem in the first place, she wouldn't need detox. So the least she can do—the least anyone could expect her to do—is to step off Fayette Street in as fine a fashion as possible. For most of the city's drug rehab facilities, the pre-intake party is not a possibility; lacking medical staffing, they aren't willing to take people wet and then detox them. At Tuerk House or Francis Scott Key, you have to dry yourself out before going inside. But BRC has a medical unit and a doctor on call; they take fiends as any self-respecting fiend would want to be taken.

Come that first Tuesday in August, the sixty dollars is a memory and Fran is out on the steps, her bloodied eyes squinting in the morning sun. Her joints ache and her head is on fire. She presses a damp washrag to her eyes as she sits there, showing no more life than the green plastic sack at her side. She waits for the hack, thinking to herself that she's had her fun, that she feels so bad that even her morning snort can't set her right. She's wrecked. It is, in short, a beautiful day to detox.

"Ma."

"What?"

DeAndre pads down the steps wearing gym shorts. He rubs his eyes and peers out at the morning.

"When you leavin' out?"

"In a couple. Your brother up?"

"He still 'sleep."

He sits beside her on the steps, watching the street stir. There's nothing said—DeAndre isn't like that—but Fran can tell he's with her, that after all this time, he's still willing to believe.

"You got what you need?" he asks, gesturing at the bag.

"Yeah, mostly. You gonna visit?"

"I be by."

She puts an arm around his shoulder. He lets it stay.

"Well, you take care of DeRodd. You can take him to Karen's if you need to. You gonna go back to the McDonald's?"

DeAndre shrugs. "Man, to hell with that. I might make an appointment to go back and beat that faggy manager's ass."

Fran grimaces and DeAndre picks up on it. He tells her that he'll keep trying, that he plans to take a walk down to Mt. Clare and Westside and see if any stores are hiring.

Stevie comes down the stairs and gives her a hug. So does Sherry. Eventually, Fran hears that her youngest is up and she goes back upstairs to cuddle DeRodd a bit.

"You gonna come past and see me, right?"

"Yeah."

DeRodd doesn't have a clue, thank God. His mother's going away for a while for some kind of program, and he'll be staying with DeAndre or his uncle. Karen is the backup plan.

"You don't go runnin' off. You stay around here or up on Saratoga. You hear me?"

DeRodd pouts and nods.

She goes back downstairs where the hack is idling. She takes some last good-byes from Black Donnie, Alfred, and Ronnie Hughes, then she rolls out. On Mount Street, even Drac waves at her—a good-luck gesture to one of his more durable customers. They're turning down Baltimore Street when Fran sees her father on the stoop across from the supermarket, the paper bag in his hand. She waves but he doesn't see. At Gilmor, she sees Bunchie on the corner. She doesn't wave.

"I'm gone," she says, more to herself than anyone, as if she needs convincing.

Down at BRC, she nods to the receptionist, gives him her name, and slumps into the same chair where she waited for Antoinette on the last goround. She leaves her bag on her lap; biting her nails, she waits quietly.

"You have an appointment?" the man asks.

"I'm checkin' in. My bed came up."

The man nods, then pages Antoinette. Fran reaches into the sack for the wet rag, which she uses to daub her eyes again. The receptionist looks at her, then looks away quickly, but Fran catches it. She knows she looks like hell, and not just because of the weekend party either. She's been on the corners so long that she's skin and bone. Her weight is down near ninety-five, her face a gaunt, spare package of lines and hollows. Her hair is pulled back tight, sharpening those lines.

Five minutes pass. Fran goes back into her plastic sack for a pearl-handled penknife. She starts digging at her nails.

"She comin'?" she asks.

"I left a message at her office."

Five minutes more and Antoinette finally emerges at the top of the flight of steps. Fran pulls herself up.

"Can I help you?" Antoinette asks, coming down.

"Uh, Fran, I mean, Denise Boyd. I check in today."

Antoinette looks perplexed. "Checking in today?"

"Yeah."

"Who told you that?"

"You did last week. You said to come in Tuesday. Don't you remember. I talked to you last week."

"Um . . . I don't know, Fran. I don't think so. You're on the top of the list, but we aren't expecting anyone today."

"You said . . ." Fran stammers, looking for words, pacing in the lobby as it starts to sink in. "You said . . ."

"Fran, there's been a mistake."

"You damn right," Fran wails. She's waving her hand angrily, puncturing the air with that tiny penknife. "You damn right it's a mistake. You told me last week."

Antoinette catches the glint of the knife and backs up toward the receptionist's desk.

"Fran, I'm saying there must be some misunderstanding."

"How'm I . . . I told . . . I don't believe this shit," Fran says bitterly. "I told everyone I was gone."

"Fran, I'm sorry."

She's standing in the middle of the lobby, her sudden anger betrayed by an equally sudden wave of tears. Antoinette takes one last nervous look at the penknife, then crosses into the breach, taking the smaller woman in her arms. Fran lets go, crying into Antoinette's shoulder.

"What am I going to tell them?" she cries.

"Fran, you're on the top of the list," Antoinette assures her. "We'll definitely have a bed next week."

"I can't make it."

"Yes, you can."

"I can't. I can't go back."

"You got to. Fran, you'll be in next week. Definitely."

Slowly and by degrees she gets hold of herself as the drug counselor reassures her once again. Arrangements are made, numbers exchanged. The small details are made certain.

"So I'll see you Tuesday," Antoinette tells her.

"Yes you will."

Fran picks up her green sack and looks at the double glass doors. She doesn't have the heart to leave yet, but when she turns back, Antoinette is up the stairs, waving a last good-bye. Fran retreats to the lobby chair, dropping the bag at her feet. She blows her nose and wipes her eyes.

"If you'd've come with a bigger knife," says the man at the front desk, "you might've got in."

Fran looks at him strangely and he smiles back, gesturing at the tiny blade still gripped in her right hand. Fran looks down and her mouth drops open. She looks at the empty place where Antoinette used to be. The man laughs.

Fran laughs too, softly at first, then louder.

"I probably scared that girl to death," she says finally, shaking her head.

"Yeah, you did," agrees the man.

"Well," says Fran, "she's all right with it now."

Twenty minutes later, the corner of Mount and Fayette is fat and full when she goes up the steps of the Dew Drop. Bunchie isn't around, thank God, but DeAndre is by the pay phone in front of the carryout and glimpses her. He says nothing, but she can see it in his face.

She passes Stevie on the stairs.

"Hey, Fran."

"Anyone usin' your room?"

"Naw," says Stevie. If he's wondering what happened, he has sense enough to keep it to himself.

Fran slides stone-faced into the apartment, where she drops her bag and knocks on her brother's bedroom door just in case. Inside, the room is wrapped in an orange glow from Stevie's broken television. As she drops down on the bed, she can hear Little Stevie in the hall, shouting down the steps to DeRodd, telling him to come upstairs and help him with a bike tire. The television set in the front room is showing *I Love Lucy* with the volume turned up. Outside, there is the the usual din, broken only by the high-pitched chant of a day-shift tout, crying out for Red-and-White.

She cries like she hasn't cried in years.

SEVEN

"Is'm," says DeAndre, exhaling.

Tae laughs. An inside joke.

"What?" asks R.C.

"Is'm," says DeAndre, as Tae passes Dinky the blunt.

"Boy, what in hell you talkin' 'bout?" asks R.C.

Dinky takes a quick hit and passes the hollowed-out cigar back to DeAndre, who breathes deeply, holds the smoke down, then lets it go in one long, thin cloud.

"Is I'm high," says DeAndre, laughing.

"That's what we callin' good weed now," Tae explains. "You know, by Andre being fucked up last night and I say to him, you know, I say you high on that shit yet?"

"Huh," says R.C., barely tracking.

"And," Tae continues, "he just looks at me all fucked up and says, 'Is'm.'"

Dinky and DeAndre both laugh.

"Is'm," says R.C., trying it out.

"Yeah boy," says DeAndre, his eyes bloodshot. "Got to get up to Edmondson Avenue and get me some more is'm."

For the C.M.B. crew, this constituted summer—a series of listless repetitions performed in an area of eight or ten square city blocks. R.C. went to New Jersey to see his mother's people one weekend; Tae, Manny Man, and a few of the others latched on to a church trip to King's Dominion amusement park; on another occasion, Ella took half the neighborhood to the county for inner-tubing and a picnic at Gunpowder Falls. But beyond those occasional sojourns, everything else was static. Life was held at bay; hope had slipped into fantasy. Elsewhere school ended and the summer months were ripe with promise. Elsewhere it was a choice between summer camps or summer jobs, college prep courses or driving lessons, weekends at the shore or seven European countries in fourteen days. But on McHenry Street that summer, the children of the corner were fitted to their new world. They did nothing, produced nothing, achieved nothing—traveling no further in body or spirit than a moment's pleasure required.

Another blunt is lit and the boys laugh again, then settle in to watch the evening traffic on the lower strip. Tonight they plan to ease back, get high and do nothing with Gilmor and McHenry, the fledgling corner brought to life by Tae and Dinky. Dewayne is down on South Vincent Street selling coke. Boo is at Ramsay and Stricker with his brothers. But the rest of C.M.B. is in a slow chill, waiting for the adventure of a summer's night to find them.

"I wish them stickup boys would come back," says Dinky, changing the subject. "By us being deep, we could fuck them up good if they come past tonight."

Late last night, a two-man stickup crew made an appearance on Ramsay Street, jacking up R.C., Manny Man, and Dinky as they were coming across the playground. Flashing a small automatic, the highway-men got a buck or two each from R.C. and Dinky. Luckless as ever, Manny went into his pants slowly, trying to remember which pocket held the wadded $20 bill and which held the throwaway single. He'd been carrying money that way since he was robbed last year, when he tried to back down a stickup boy and got shot in the leg for the effort. Manny faked left, went right, offering up one bill while palming the other and tossing it behind him on the ground.

"There went our weed money," said R.C., watching as the gunmen rolled out.

"Not all of it," said Manny, hopeful, as he turned around to pick up the wadded bill. He unrolled the green ball slowly, cursing suddenly when the denomination revealed itself.

"I gave them motherfuckers my twenty," he wailed.

The occasional misadventure aside, McHenry Street had become the summer playground in this last summer of the Crenshaw Mafia Brothers. By the same time next year, C.M.B. will be scattered to the winds, all of them sixteen or seventeen or eighteen, working separate corners with separate packages, trying to get over on everyone including each other. Another year and the childhood loyalties will be pressed and shattered. For now, though, they are still playing at the corner: a package here, a bundle there, and everyone has money for cheesesteaks and weed, Tims and Nikes, movie passes and dance tapes. And even on nights like this one, when no one is making money, McHenry Street is still the place to hang.

For one thing, the lower strip isn't hot like Fayette Street. Down here, it's the Southern District and the police don't yet know their faces. Down here, nothing compares to Bob Brown, or Pitbull, or Shields. Not yet anyway. And C.M.B. is no longer beefing with any of the crews down bottom, so DeAndre and Tae can freely chase South Baltimore girls, just as R.C. or Dinky can venture down to the outside court at Ramsay and Stricker and get a game or two. The quality of play isn't much—the white boys really can't jump—but it's a better outdoor court than the makeshift hoop on Lemmon Street and good enough to pass an evening.

This summer, the boys down on McHenry Street are, well, boys. They think and act as children; often failing at the game, but always learning, and never quite giving the corner their full and undivided attention. They're all smoking weed, but few among them are yet willing to play at anything stronger. Only Boo, who is looking worn and rough, stands accused of hitting the pipe, and he denies the allegation. As for slinging, it's still more adventure than economic imperative. They spend most days waking up late, taking a stroll down the bottom, and if nothing else is happening, opening up shop for a couple of hours—maybe just working the afternoon shift change, when the Southern officers are off the street—putting in just enough time and energy to turn pocket money.

As the summer burns on, Dorian gets caught first. He comes back home, then gets locked up again. Manny Man takes a charge coming out the back of a vacant house where one crew is keeping the stash. R.C. catches an assault charge behind a corner fight. Not that it isn't possible to have a good run on McHenry Street, a run of the kind that DeAndre made on Fairmount this past winter. McHenry is virgin territory. A slinger could feed the white trade all day long, turning one eight ball, then another, then parlaying the money into an ounce. From there, he's off and running. Stick at it long enough and he might finish a week with two thousand dollars in his pocket—real money for real work. But for the C.M.B. crew, the best they can manage is a couple hundred on the odd shift. And some nights, of course, no one makes real money. By short count or by stolen stash, by unpaid debt or by stickup, the margin evaporates.

Twenty dollars here, forty there—the stakes are still fairly small this summer and so the guns don't come out very often. For the most part, the C.M.B. boys are still unwilling to risk a charge that might kick them upstairs to an adult court, nothing more serious than, say, possession with intent. Most nights, they leave their irons at home, rushing back up the hill and going under mattresses and dressers only on those rare occasions when a beef gets out of hand.

For R.C., school is now officially dead, and at fifteen—a year younger than DeAndre—there isn't much point to canvassing the fast-food joints for summer work. They only hire sixteen and above. He could have gone down to the Civic Center with Kevin, Arnold, and Manny Man a few weeks back, when the city had a one-day signup for federally funded summer jobs. He talked like he was going, but in the end, he slept in that morning and then blew off the rest of the day watching cartoons. He had some money in his pocket every month from his father's death-benefit check, and the part-time slinging brought a little more. He wasn't about anything more than that, or, for that matter, about anything at all save basketball. Or maybe, a few years down the road, he'd be eighteen and old enough so that his brothers could do what they did for Mike Ellerbee. R.C. would bide his time, play at this corner game and then get that Z-card and full membership in the seafarers union. It was a better plan by far than standing around all day in line after line at the Civic Center, filling out forms and answering questions to get a hard hat and push a broom. Sure, Kevin got a job at the B & O Railroad Museum. Arnold, too. But Manny Man went through the whole hurry-up-and-wait and didn't get a damn thing. R.C. had to laugh at that.

As for DeAndre, he had largely abandoned the idea of a summer job after that last sortie to the McDonald's outlet in East Baltimore. Come check days, he bums a few dollars from his mother, then, when that runs out, he leeches a few more from Dinky or Tae or Boo—whoever is flush at the moment. It's enough for sandwiches and weed and the occasional forty of malt liquor, enough to keep the party going, but not nearly enough to get him past living hand-to-mouth. When he does scrape a bit of a roll together, he leans heavily on others to sell his package. Sometimes this works, sometimes not.

Through the Fourth of July, as the rest of the crew sold coke and dope openly at Gilmor and McHenry, DeAndre kept himself at the water's edge, hanging with his boys, pooling his money on a package or two, but quietly refusing to man a corner and get business done. He reasoned that if he stood to the side, with someone else holding the vials, he couldn't take another charge. The theory, though flawed, showed more caution than usual. Working at a distance, though, he soon enough found himself coping with thievery and incompetence on every level. Dorian, Brooks, R.C., Manny Man—all of them owed him money on spillage and miscounts. At street level it was damn near impossible for a slinger to subcontract and still make money. Once the vials left his hand, DeAndre had very little control, and by midsummer, he had heard every possible excuse to explain short money.

"Nigger got my stash."

"Police rolled past. I threw it down and it wadn't there after."

"You ain't give me twenty. You gave me fifteen."

"My moms found 'em in my room. She high as shit."

These are his friends; he had been raised up with them. But with the exception of Dinky, his stalwart cousin, and Tae, the C.M.B. crew is as capable of cheating and thieving and messing up a count as any collection of drug-addled touts. By and large, what was owed to him by the likes of Dorian and R.C. went uncollected.

In late July, he did a little better, pooling his money with his cousin Dinky and going in on a package with Kwame and Shamrock, who were willing to front them on consignment. The arrangement worked well enough that he went into August with a couple hundred in his pocket, namely because his cousin proved to be the most reliable member of the crew.

Light-skinned, freckled, and unnervingly polite, Dinky was the son of Roberta McCullough's cousin, making him some kind of kin to DeAndre. On that tenuous connection, a strong familial bond had developed over the years. Dinky had heart. He loved to battle—more than the rest of the crew, more even than DeAndre. He would not cheat, he would not run. And since every other C.M.B. friendship had managed to disappoint DeAndre at one time or another, Dinky had, by default, become his closest companion.

As the summer wore on, it fell to Dinky to do much of the street work on DeAndre's occasional packages. Since taking his last charge on Fairmount Avenue, DeAndre had largely kept to his low-profile plan, fearing that one more arrest would mean juvenile detention for the rest of the summer. Dinky understood this, just as he understood that DeAndre would want to stay home if Tyreeka turned out to be pregnant. DeAndre was adamant that he wouldn't be locked up if it really was true; he had no business being locked up if his child was about to be born.

Yet, incredibly, DeAndre entered July with no confirmation of Tyreeka's condition—nothing stronger, in fact, than his own vague suspicions. Angry at him for chasing other girls, Tyreeka had for two months steered clear of DeAndre, and when they did run into each other, she made it plain that she wasn't talking to him. Much as he tried, DeAndre couldn't really blame her. He'd made a show of chasing everything on the street and ensuring that his sixteenth summer was every bit the party he promised himself. He was still pursuing Treecee's cousin, as well as another girl he'd met at a house party over near Payson Street. Earlier in the summer, he had tried to get with Tyreeka on the off nights, though by then she'd heard so much of his travels she wasn't as willing to do the dirty as before. Instead, Tyreeka had chosen to spend most of her time with Carver classmates or with girlfriends like Treecee and Dena, both of whom were messing with R.C. this summer. DeAndre had heard that she had once again tried to holler at some of the other C.M.B. boys, but even at a distance, he had been able to shoot that down. No one would mess with Tyreeka until DeAndre gave up on her entirely. Reassured in this, he told himself he would branch out now, then patch things up in the cold months. He'd hibernate with Tyreeka; right now he wanted to run wild.

Still, he'd heard from lots of people that Tyreeka looked like she'd gained weight, that she might be carrying a baby. Once, in late June, he caught up with her in the Lemmon Street alley and tried to talk it over, but Tyreeka hotly denied being pregnant. Wearing a loose T-shirt and shorts, she looked a little heavier to DeAndre, but not so much as he had been told.

"I just need to get on a diet," she told him.

And DeAndre, busy with Shanelle and a couple other young things, simply let the matter slide and returned to his McHenry Street meanderings. Besides, Tyreeka's aunt had moved off Stricker Street, taking the family north of the expressway to a two-story rowhouse on Riggs Avenue. So it's out-of-sight, out-of-mind as far as old girlfriends are concerned. He has no reason to think again on Tyreeka until late July, when Treecee sidles up to him on Fulton Avenue with a bit of news.

"Reeka got your baby."

"How you know?" DeAndre asks her.

"She told me," Treecee says. "She thinking about going down to get an abortion. You need to get with her and talk."

DeAndre catches a hack up to Riggs Avenue, but learns from Tyreeka's cousin that she's down bottom with Dena. And when DeAndre finally locates the two girls on Pratt Street, Tyreeka seems decidedly uninterested in discussing the issue.

"Girl, we got to talk."

"About what?"

"Treecee sayin' you pregnant."

Tyreeka frowns and Dena drifts away. Tyreeka tells him that Treecee shouldn't have said a damn thing, that she only told the girl because Treecee thinks she might be pregnant by R.C. and the two of them were talking about going to University Hospital together.

"Why you ain't tell me?" DeAndre asks.

"Why should I?" Tyreeka says. "You don't want shit to do with me. Why should I tell you?"

DeAndre regroups and tries another tack. "I don't even know it's mine."

Tyreeka explodes, railing at him as they stand at Pratt and Mount, telling DeAndre that all the talk about her and other boys was just talk, that he's been the only one.

"Don't lie on me," she says. "You know it's your child."

DeAndre backs away from his own argument, conceding the issue of paternity. After a time, the two find themselves sitting on the warehouse steps, around the corner on McHenry Street, trying to size up the future as best they can.

Tyreeka is scared and alone. For months, she has told no one except her aunt. Angry at DeAndre and mistrustful of everyone else, she's kept the secret since April, when she missed two months and her aunt took her up to the clinic for confirmation. Now, by DeAndre's reckoning, she has to be four or five months pregnant and she's talking about an abortion.

Still, she tries her hardest to carry the conversation with absolute indifference. He can do whatever he wants, she tells him. He doesn't need to do a damn thing; if Treecee hadn't interfered, he wouldn't even know about it.

"You gonna get an abortion?"

"I might."

DeAndre hears the hurt in Tyreeka's voice and feels guilty. He remembers his mother arguing time and again that he should either get with the girl or leave her be, that it isn't fair to just keep her hanging if he doesn't really want her.

Slowly, and with as much honesty as he can summon, he tells her what he should have told her months ago. He wants the baby, of course. But he can no longer lie about wanting Tyreeka. Not now anyway. Not with so much happening on McHenry Street.

"Reeka, I'm saying you got to do what you think is right, but I got to tell you that having the baby isn't gonna keep me around. I ain't gonna be with you only because you got my child."

"I know."

But DeAndre hears her and senses that until this moment, she didn't know. Until now, she was still hoping.

"So what you gonna do?"

"I dunno."

"Treecee say you was gonna go to the hospital, see about an abortion."

"I might, but I ain't got the money."

DeAndre looks at Tyreeka, wondering if this is a game, but unwilling to accuse her of such a thing.

"How much?"

"Two hundert."

DeAndre nods.

"You ain't got it?"

DeAndre shakes his head, stands, and looks away. "I'll have to ask my mother," he says finally.

"As steady slinging as you been?" asks Tyreeka, doubting.

"I'm not slinging."

"Then what you doing down here?"

"I'm jus' with my boys."

Tyreeka tells him that she needs the money soon, that she's going to the clinic at University Hospital today to make an appointment. DeAndre acknowledges this and Tyreeka, with nothing left to say, leaves for Dena's house.

DeAndre heads back to McHenry and Gilmor wondering. If he doesn't come up with money, does that mean Tyreeka will have his baby? And if he does give her two hundred, how does he know that the money will go for an abortion? And how does he even know that an abortion costs two hundred?

Still, he's resolved. He owes Tyreeka this much at least: He'll wait on Fran, catch her in a good mood, and ask for the money. If Fran comes up with it, the better for DeAndre. If she doesn't, then DeAndre can always come through with some corner money. Either way, he'll step up and do what's right. If Tyreeka wants the baby, fine. If she doesn't, fine, too. But either way, it's on her.

As DeAndre reaches Gilmor, shortstops a blunt, and announces, with obvious pride, that he just might be a father, Tyreeka arrives at Dena's house. She is resolved: She will expect nothing more from DeAndre McCullough. He doesn't want her, and now, finally, she has no illusions about this. As far as she can tell, he doesn't even want the baby.

All right then, she thinks. At least I played him for two hundred dollars.

For Tyreeka, what remains of her first real romantic adventure is the chance to get some bills from the father of her child. She has no intention of getting an abortion. In her heart, she always knew she would keep the baby. A few nights ago, she actually thought she felt something move inside her and that, more than anything, really decided it. No, she was only going to University with Treecee to see what R.C.'s girl might do, to check out the way it worked in case you changed your mind. One thing she already knew: University Hospital didn't charge teenage mothers anything for abortions, leastways there was no up-front charge that stopped you from getting an abortion. Whatever DeAndre thought about her, Tyreeka could tell herself she was no longer the young thing of a year ago. She was learning, and she had it in mind to give DeAndre a lesson or two.

Back on Gilmor Street, the summer light finally fades and the trafficking begins in earnest. DeAndre stands outside the carryout with his boys, soaking up the night and basking in whatever pride results when a young man's seed finds purchase.

"Got to get my shit together if I'm gonna be a father."

In West Baltimore, it's a stock comment. DeAndre speaks the words just to hear how they sound.

R.C. readily agrees with him. "Treecee gonna find out soon enough. If she pregnant, I'm gonna need to deal with it like a man."

"Most definitely," DeAndre says.

For R.C., too, there isn't much of a relationship left with the mother-to-be. When Treecee isn't kissing him, she's trying to cut him with a blade for any number of offenses. Just last week, R.C. had to get the webbing of one hand stitched back together—an injury that R.C. blamed on his growing interest in Dena, friend to Treecee and Tyreeka both. Others said Treecee was just tired of getting yelled at and slapped. Either way, a trip to the University Hospital emergency room was not

the best portent of domestic bliss, but no matter: A baby would suit
R.C. fine.

For the time being, what remains for these fathers-to-be is to take
hold of what joy remains in the summer. For Tae and R.C., that means
slinging on McHenry Street and spending the profits. For DeAndre, it
means trying to get others to sling for you, then complaining when there
are no profits to spend. Still, there are girls and weed and misadventure
to be had—every night of every day of every week while the weather
stays warm.

As far as DeAndre is concerned, the only real problem is, once again,
his mother. For weeks now, he's been coming home at three or four in
the morning, creeping up the Dew Drop stairs with Phillie blunt and
St. Ides on his breath, trying to make as little noise as possible. But Fran's
the nosleepingest woman he's ever known, and in the morning, she
would be yelling at him, threatening him, telling him that if he didn't
get home earlier she'd be locking the door on him. Worse, she actually
threatened to call Miss Owens, his probation agent, and ask that her son
be piss-tested.

"She gonna find all that weed and you be back on home monitor,"
she'd told him a week earlier.

The threat made DeAndre furious. To his mind, it was against every
moral precept for his own mother to invoke the authorities. A mother
went to court and backed her child; she did not offer aid and comfort
to a police or prosecutor, judge or probation officer.

"You gonna snitch me out?" he asked.

"If you ain't in here at midnight I am."

"I'm a grown man. I can come and go as I please."

"You can go all right. But you ain't comin' back in here after midnight.
You try and you'll be out of doors."

"I deal with that then."

"You think you grown," Fran told him, "but you ain't."

That night, at about three in the morning, he tried creeping up the
stairs only to find the apartment door bolted from the inside. He knocked
lightly at first, then louder, bringing both Uncle Stevie and his mother
out of bed. Stevie on his own would have yielded, but Fran wouldn't budge.
DeAndre had to walk up to Saratoga Street and crash at Scoogie's place.

The next afternoon, he and his mother had it out again, with DeAndre
insisting that Fran had no right to tell him what to do and Fran asserting
that she had every right if he wanted to live at 1625 Fayette Street.

"Ain't nobody want to live here," DeAndre told her. "We in a damn drug house."

"Then you ain't got to live here. You can leave whenever you ready, but as long as you under my roof, you comin' in at midnight and you not comin' in with what's been on your breath."

"Please . . ."

"Andre, I smell that shit on you again, I'm calling Miss Owens and telling her to piss you."

He stormed out, but that night, at 11:58 exactly, he reappeared at the apartment door, stalked silently past his mother, and slumped in front of the television. He wasn't sure that Fran would actually call to get him violated, but that right there was the problem: He wasn't sure.

The midnight curfew so vexes DeAndre that he finds new reason to hope that his mother follows through on her effort to get a detox bed. If BRC comes through, Fran gets a twenty-eight-day break from drugging; DeAndre gets a twenty-eight-day break from Fran. Until then, though, what remains for DeAndre are the precious hours between sundown and midnight, when the wasteland of McHenry Street is C.M.B.'s playground. One night, they're hanging by the phone on Fulton, trying to get some girls to take them upstairs to a rowhouse bedroom. Next night, they're out in front of the grocery at Gilmor Street, selling enough to get them all down to Harbor Park for the bloodletting of a Saturday night horror flick. And when nothing much seems to be happening, when they're just lazing around the Lemmon Street alley, blunting up and talking trash, an opportunity for adventure now and then presents itself. Like the night one of the local stickup artists comes through off duty, stumbling into the entire C.M.B. crew.

"You got the time?" he asks. An icebreaker.

Tae shakes his head. "I don't know the time, but I know who you are. You the motherfucker who robbed me last week."

R.C. steps up first, banging the man on the back of the head with a grape soda bottle, and from there it gets ugly. Tae, Dinky, DeAndre, Boo, R.C.—all of them get their shots in, working their victim until he staggers into the light of Calhoun Street, a bloody wreck.

"We fucked him up," declares R.C. at the next day's basketball practice. It's one of the summer's highlights and it's weeks before anyone in the crew can stop telling the story of the righteous beating inflicted. That will be the last time, they assure listeners, that one nigger will even dream about robbing anyone with C.M.B. credentials.

A month later, at summer's end, it happens again, when Boo jumps off a concrete step in the rear of Steuart Hill Elementary to label a gaunt figure passing through the schoolyard as another stickup boy.

"Nigger robbed my brother an' me," Boo says, glaring.

"That boy there?" asks Tae.

"The nigger with the doo-rag. Him."

The man never quite knows what hit him. No parley. No pause for explanation. This time Dinky gets the first shot in—a hard right to the jaw—and the man crumples to the sidewalk. The others begin kicking him. Boo cracks a small liquor bottle over the man's head, drawing blood, and DeAndre takes a shot or two as the prey struggles to his feet and runs, lurching as far south as Ramsay before losing his tormentors. Only after they form up again does Boo express the slightest doubt.

"He looked like him, anyways," Boo says, shrugging.

"Say what?" asks Dinky.

"I'm sayin' it might be the same boy . . ."

Dinky looks at DeAndre and rolls his eyes.

"Boo an asshole," R.C. says, shaking his head.

"Twos Gary," shouts Paul from the counter. "We need twos."

"Half a minute, Mo," Gary yells back, shouting back at the manager through the plastic-strip barrier, his voice carrying through the cold air of the sorting room.

"How we doin' on twos?" he asks his brother, who's perched by the sorting bins, flinging crabs like a machine, breaking down a bushel of males by size.

"We awright," says Cardy, without looking up. "Those are females over there, but the rest of them twos behind me."

"Okay, Chief," says Gary, "I'm on it."

He rushes back to the far corner of the refrigerated room, lifting two bushels at once and carrying them over to the stun tanks. The crabs are slow in the cold, but a couple manage to reach through the slats and grab Gary's sweatshirt.

"Oh no, Mo, that won't do," says Gary, balancing the bushels on the corner lip of the tank. He slaps at the claws until they retreat behind the cheap pine.

He drops the top basket to the floor, pries the lid off the other, and begins sorting—live ones into the ice water, dead ones into an empty bushel basket at his feet.

"Need twos," Paul shouts again.

"I'm on it, Chief."

At flank speed, he sorts out one bushel, then the next, before yanking at the tank chain and bringing its metal tray up to the edge of the lip. He uses one arm to shove the stunned, ice-covered crabs over the side into a wheeled crab pot.

"Dust," shouts Gary.

Bobby throws a layer of spice onto the crabs. Gary swings his arm again, dropping another few dozen into the pot.

"Dust 'em, Mo."

Bobby puts on another layer.

"Okay, Boss. We hummin' now. We on the move and not a moment too soon. Our public out there waitin'."

He drags the pot through the orange plastic strips and into the intense heat of the steamers. Here, in the counter area, with the crab pots boiling in an August swelter, a double layer of sweats are no advantage.

"Number twos," he shouts with pride, hooking a steam hose to the back of the pot. He races to the control panel, clicks to fourteen minutes on hose four, then punches the green button. Behind him, the pot hisses to life.

Watching from the register, Paul gives an affirming nod. Gary turns to face the waiting customers on the other side of the counter. "Be good to go in just a few, folks."

He turns back into the steam cloud and feels the scratch in his throat. Gary has the same seafood allergy as his son, but for a payday, he'll handle it. For this kind of cash, in fact, Gary McCullough will put up with just about anything. In a few weeks time, he's transformed himself from a petty thief into the hardest working crab-slinger in Southwest Baltimore.

"How you fixed now, Chief," he asks Paul.

Paul, a son-in-law to Seapride's owner, checks the front bins and pronounces himself satisfied. "We're okay for now. We might need more females in a bit."

"You got it, Boss. You got it."

Gary retreats into the back room, where he grabs a bushel of females and sorts them into the ice water. He's ahead of the game now—at least until the late-afternoon rush. He looks around for his Newports and finds them on the back wall, atop a spice box.

"Gonna have me a smoke," he tells his brother.

Cardy nods without looking up from the bins. Gary meanders back
through the steam and around the front counter, pulling up at the pay
phone in front of the crabhouse. He opens the foil and taps one out.

He's a working man now, a full-pack man. No more sliding the
Korean twenty-five cents through the Plexiglas and getting back a single
stick. No sir, Gary has a new game now—one that pays cash money at
the end of every day, six solid days a week.

He lights up, stretches, and watches the hillbilly parade go by on
Monroe Street. The smoke actually seems to help his asthma, though he
knows that doesn't make sense. Still, he works it down to the filter. A
job, a full pack of smokes—might even give the kitchen girls a couple
bills and get some fries for lunch. Gary is living large.

It's been like this since Cardy hooked him up at Seapride, with a
promise to Paul and Ron and Miss Mary that his older brother was a
hard worker. And it was no lie; Gary was proving that to everyone. Apart
from Cardy and maybe Bobby Short, the other veteran sorter, he was the
best they had. No complaints, no arguments—he could see what needed
to get done and then did it. He'd come in early to clean the pots or stay
late to handle the overload on a busy night, and as long as the bosses
were willing to forgive an occasional twenty-minute absence—when Gary
had to attend to his medical affairs—they couldn't help but be pleased.

And Gary was just as happy. With a job, he was on a different road
entirely. He didn't have to worry about where the next blast was coming
from; he didn't have to run capers anymore. Like anything else, of course,
the crabhouse had its downside. Even through heavy rubber gloves, a
crab jockey could take a nasty cut from a half-inch shell point, or risk
a serious burn when a steam hose got loose, or take a mean pinch from
a number thirty-two male willing to fight to stay out of that ice bath.
But for Gary, such hazards paled in comparison to the pain that comes
from a caper gone awry, or the humiliation of asking a dealer to take
short money for a vial, or worst of all, the fear that comes on those
nights when luck doesn't hold and the Western District rollers catch you
where you're not supposed to be.

Seapride was keeping all of that at arm's length. The job meant money
enough for the blast, for smokes, for a little something every month to
kick back to his mother to help with groceries, gas and electric. It meant
waking up every morning with a vial or two left over, so that the snake
could have no say. It meant that Tony, Will, and Lump didn't matter so
much, and better yet, that the Gaunt One didn't matter at all.

Gary proved that the day Ronnie bailed out of women's detention, coming home from the drug charge that the Western knockers gave her last month. She'd done pretty much what the corner expected her to do, playing the police the way she played everyone else, promising that she'd give them Gee Money and Dred and every other dealer they mentioned, so long as they'd lose sight of her charge. Of course, she planned to do nothing of the kind, figuring that any deal with the police was a deal worth breaking. Instead, she asked for Gary and was told about the crabhouse.

And what a moment it was when Ronnie walked up to the counter looking to drag him out on some messed-up caper, taking him for the same clown. Gary let her wait there, walking back into the sorting room and going about his business, letting her know that he had the ultimate hustle now: He was on the clock. Ronnie lost it, ranting and shouting, then crying the blues about how she'd always loved him, how she'd sacrificed for him and been there for him when he was down. She made such a scene that Gary had to drag her outside the crabhouse and send her away, telling her face-to-face that things were different, that he'd be making an honest dollar now.

Naturally, working life wasn't altogether perfect at first. In the beginning, Seapride paid him on Thursdays—once a week, like working men everywhere get paid. That didn't cut it; Gary had needs. The paycheck had to be an everyday thing, not only because the snake was waiting, but because having a couple hundred dollars in his hand at any one moment could kill him. At first, Gary had his mother come down to the crabhouse on Thursdays before he got off work, so she could hold most of that money for him. After a few weeks, though, Paul got a sense of the situation. Without ever having to speak the words, Gary was able to make his need plain to Paul, who, in turn, brought Ron and Mary and the rest of the family to an understanding of sorts. Gary would work hard—all day, every day—and come the end of the shift, he'd be rewarded right from the cash drawer. He got six an hour, which was pretty grim compared to the money he used to make—sixteen an hour at Beth Steel and almost ten as a security guard—but life was a lot simpler now. Everything had been boiled down to basics; some things were possible and some were not.

He'd come to this conclusion after his near-death experience on Baker Street, which is what compelled his return to the labor pool for the first time in years. A day or two after the disaster at the junkyard, Gary had tried to hook up with the contracting crew rehabbing the row homes on Lexington Street. He went down to the job site, found the foreman, and started to explain that he'd once had his own home renovation firm, that he had drafting experience, that he knew something about their game. But the man gave him the once-over and walked away. When Gary persisted, he was shown a clipboard with a crude sign-up sheet.

"Put your name down and if something comes up . . ."

Something never would. Perversely, the only neighborhood resident ever to get any kind of job with the renewal project was Gary's comrade-in-arms, Tony Boice, who happened to be wandering up Lexington Street at the exact moment the contractor needed an extra body for some grunt work. Tony worked a day or two, then got himself locked up behind a nighttime burglary, thereby ending his construction career. Gary heard the story and felt some bitterness; that was a gig he had truly wanted, a job for which he had real experience. But in the end, Cardy and the crabhouse had provided shelter from the storm, and for that Gary was grateful.

Finishing the cigarette, he watches the line at the register grow as afternoon commuters stop for a dozen crabs here, a half-bushel there. He stretches again, looks down Monroe, then walks over to the pay phone, where someone has left a few sections of the afternoon paper. He rifles through them, looking for anything worthwhile, keeping the sports and business sections. The Orioles lost, but they were making a habit of losing and Gary has stopped following the season. On the financial pages, he reads the local news briefs, his eyes darting around the print, his mind soaking up facts and figures. Paul's voice brings him back.

"Gary."

"Comin', Mo."

This time the call is not only for the females, but for fourteens, sixteens, and twenty-fours—the larger sizes, sorted by cost-per-dozen. Gary folds and tucks the business section into his back pocket and goes back to work. He's breaking down bushels, shoveling ice, turning the crawling Chesapeake blues to bright, hot orange. A half hour later, he's caught up with demand; Paul comes into the back room to tell him as much.

"Hey, Chief," Gary says, pulling the newsprint from his pocket. "You remember what I was tellin' you about that company?"

"When?"

"The other day. That company that I was sayin . . ." Gary points to a back-page brief. Paul takes hold of the edge of the paper and begins to read, nodding vaguely at whatever it is Gary thinks he's proving.

"You see that. A fifty-two-week high."

"Huh," says Paul.

"I told you. P.H.H. They like a leasing company out in Hunt Valley. They gonna go over forty; they might have a stock split even. You'll see."

"Gary, I don't have the kind of money to invest in stock."

"Not to worry, Mo," says Gary. "I know the name of a penny stock out of Hong Kong. It's gonna go all the way up. For a little money, we can get in at the bottom, ride it all the way."

Paul shakes his head, laughing. Gary shrugs and repockets the newspaper, urging him to reconsider, assuring him that with a little venture capital, Gary could make both of them real money.

Paul isn't quite ready to let the kitchen help manage his portfolio; still, Gary is happy to just talk about such things. It's another plus of being a working man—perhaps the biggest plus. Stepping away from the corner, Gary now has moments when his thoughts are free to roam beyond the confines of the game. With life stabilized by a daily routine, the better part of Gary's nature is once again delving into the world of ideas. Financial trends, social issues, religion, history, and science begin to interest him again, slowly reclaiming that portion of his mind in which such things once thrived. When he walks back up the hill toward home at the end of every shift, his back is a little straighter and his pace a bit lighter.

This summer, Gary is a working man and he means to hold on to his status the only way he knows how. He'll show Miss Mary, Ron, and Paul what hard work looks like. When Labor Day arrives in two weeks, he'll have built a monument to crab-slinging that will leave them wondering how they were able to run the business before Gary Castro McCullough arrived at the sorting-room door.

Even more pleasing to him is the fact that there's nothing raucous or lethal waiting for him when he gets home from work. Gary is off the streets now, stopping on Mount or Monroe Street only to spend most of the day's pay, to get his vials and carry them down to his parents' basement. He's not about hanging, or bullshitting, or finding adventures in the shooting galleries along the strip. He never wanted or needed any of that nonsense in the first place; the chemical fog was all he really required.

Down in the basement, with the box fan doing its best to move fetid air, Gary takes his time, hits a vein, and then, with the wave cresting over him, finds absolute contentment in his own company. He has the old clock radio on the AM so he can soak up the talk-show chatter, catching fragments of the national mood as it floats past. He's a consumer of concepts and arguments, lying on that same tired mattress, listening to the ideologues rant. Later, in the small hours of the morning, he comes down slowly, his head clear enough to enjoy his library, spending an hour or two with Thoreau, or St. Luke, or Mohammed. From somewhere downtown, Gary had gotten hold of a hardback copy of Karen Armstrong's *History of God* and had been so taken with the title that he resolved to tackle the tome in all its complexity. So it is that in the early morning hours of most any summer's night, at least one Baltimore dope fiend can be found abed, exploring the roots of monotheistic theology by the light of a bare lamp bulb.

After the reading, there is another cap and another nod, another hour or so with the AM static lulling him to sleep. And this is Gary McCullough's life—helpless, harmless, compact and, more or less, functional.

It is functional in the sense that he is a drug addict with a job, a man willing to do the best work he can for a few dollars and a chance at nightly oblivion in a basement hovel. He scrubs pots and hauls bushels and cooks crabs six days a week, taking the seventh as the Lord intended it. Some Sundays he goes with his mother to St. James across the street, but mostly he has to work weekends. His sabbath is likely a Monday or Tuesday, when Gary gets his blast out of the way early and then wanders, extending himself a little beyond Fayette Street.

He went to the harbor once, just to walk the pavilion and watch the tourists. On another late July afternoon, he rediscovered Mount Vernon, taking in the shops along Charles Street, which he had almost forgotten in the years of daze. Near the monument was a health food store that was even better than he remembered. He bought carob and ginger for the ride home, delighted to spend his pocket money on something out of the ordinary.

Another time, he walked into a matinee and caught that *Schindler's List* movie that everyone was talking about. The movie shocked him, tore a hole through his heart; he left the theater unable to speak, feeling connected to the nightmare. But for weeks afterward, he talked incessantly about Schindler and Nazis and death camps. What they did to

those people, he told those willing to listen. What they did to them Jews
when the Jews weren't messing with anyone.

"No matter where you go," he offered at one point, "a nigger's always
a nigger."

With new eyes, Gary looked around at the waste and carnage and
stupidity of his own neighborhood and soon began thinking in parallel
terms. In another time and place, the damned were shot and gassed and
burned by the millions with frightening efficiency. In West Baltimore,
in a nation of civil liberties, there was instead the slow-motion destruction of thousands. It was different, Gary had to admit; but it was the
same, too.

On Fayette Street, life had become a slow process of taking black
boys and girls, black men and women, and breaking them down, turning
them into less. It happened without camps and barbed wire, without
cattle cars or crematoriums or dictatorial intent. But it happened
nonetheless, quietly, hour by wasted hour.

Gary not only saw it all as genocidal, but convinced himself that this
time, there would be people ready and able to justify it. They're going
to get tired, he would say. They're going to get tired of the violence, of
the drugs, of us.

He read Wiesel's *Night* again, and he listened to the voices on his
clock radio—Rush Limbaugh or G. Gordon Liddy or some of the local
yahoos. He woke in the morning with a sense of impending, unalter-
able doom. Out in the street, Gary would comment on the human
destruction on Fayette Street and relate it in some vague way to the
Holocaust. The other fiends had no idea what he was talking about. Shut
up and shoot dope, they told him.

But Gary thought he'd discovered something. "Niggers ain't born,"
he said one summer morning, after firing in his basement room. "They
made."

And he knew the other half of the equation, too: They hate us.

"They surely do hate us."

He said it without bitterness, with a self-knowledge that can come only
from the inside, looking out. He remembered a day this winter when he'd
been walking—just walking—near Union Square, and a yuppie home-
steader had chased him down the block, threatening to call the police.
Gary got mad and stayed mad for all of three minutes, until he paused
long enough to look himself over and decide the man was right. If I had
anything worth stealing, I'd chase my ragged self down the block, too.

He knew that he appeared to people as little more than a cartoon, a ghetto stereotype as dehumanized and expendable as any skeletal camp prisoner in black and white stripes. To that homeowner, to others like him, to the angry radio voices at night, all that had happened in his life before this moment didn't matter. To them, he had no history, no beginning, nothing beyond the here-and-now. To them, he was a dope fiend, nothing more.

He knew how this sounded, too, how little white folk wanted to hear the complaint. To the radio guys late at night, he was just one more whining special-interest supplicant, a welfare-fed remnant of a New Deal gone old, ready and willing to blame all the injustice in the world rather than himself.

"Like they think we don't know what we did to ourselves," Gary would say sadly, "like they think we can't see it."

He could admit personal guilt; he knew what he'd done. Yet if that was all there was to it, why did the world treat him exactly the same when he was doing right, when he had all those jobs and all those stocks and mutual funds? Back then, all his money and standing didn't matter to the sales clerks and security guards, who would follow him around stores. The world was no different when he drove his Mercedes—bought and paid for with Beth Steel paychecks and tech-stock dividends—and suffered through dozens of police stops and registration checks. Nor did money count when he would get dressed up and bring a date down to the harbor restaurants. His worst, most humiliating memory, was of a cool summer night when he took a girl to City Lights in Harborplace and asked if it might be possible to sit outside on the balcony. No, sorry, he was told; then they were seated at a table by the kitchen while the balcony tables stayed empty for the next two hours. A small insult, of course—nothing that could level a person in a single blow, unless that person came from Fayette Street, where every moment tells you who you are and what you were meant to be.

On Fayette Street, they surely needed niggers, because anything better could not and would not serve the corners. Once, Gary had been strong enough and monied enough to leave this place, yet he hesitated. An Israelite, he had listened to Pharoah and stayed; now, he was once again a slave, as were they all. To be more than that on Fayette Street would be an accusation, a living affront to all of those chipping away at their own souls.

All that summer at the crabhouse, Gary had watched the crabs that had been wedged in the bushels for too long; he had seen how when you pulled off the top, most of them would just lie there, waiting for the steamer. Worse, those few that tried to escape would be pulled back by the claws of those left behind.

"Crabs in a barrel," Gary would say, echoing the famous DuBois metaphor, but coming to it on his own: "When one starts to climb out, the others drag him back down."

To Gary, everyone, black and white, seemed gratified by his long fall. It was there in every face; he even saw it in people who had watched him grow up, in children he had raised, in women he had loved. Even Miss Mary down at Seapride—she knew what kind of work he was doing, yet there again, when she looked his way, he could tell that she saw the mark of the needle before she saw a human being.

Alone in his basement at night, Gary would try righteously to argue the point, weaving his own fall from grace with all kinds of genocidal imagery in a dope-crazed swirl of pity and paranoia.

"They gonna come for us," he whispered once in a heroin nod, listing onto his worn mattress. "They gonna come and you won't even be able to blame them for coming."

Yet by light of day, it still seemed to Gary that after a summer's worth of honest work, the world had no right to judge him like this. After all, he was doing no harm to anyone but himself. He stole nothing, manipulated nothing, ran no dope-fiend moves—save for the usual bitch-and-barter with the touts. Whatever Gary did to himself, he did in the damp and quiet of that basement. In the face of the American drug war, he stood as both drug addict and citizen.

And if his employers at Seapride hadn't believed that he was more than just another fiending crudball at the beginning of the summer, then Gary had made them believe it on the Fourth of July—a day like no other in the crabhouses of Baltimore. On the Fourth, when every right-thinking Marylander has steamed crabs in celebration, Gary had come in at seven that morning to begin scrubbing down the pots. Soon after that, customers were lined around the block for the blues, some of them coming back two and three times for another half-bushel.

He didn't leave until midnight. After slinging crabs for seventeen hours straight, Gary walked up the hill exhausted, his eyes bloodshot from the spice, his arms and legs scratched and cut by the claws of the larger blues. Five hundred bushels—sixty thousand hard shells—had been sorted and stunned in the ice tanks, then steamed and sold at

Seapride that day. It was a nonstop, dawn-to-dark crab frenzy on South Monroe Street. And that Fourth of July night, his pocket fat with cash, Gary was too tired for anything but a go-to-nod blast. He didn't need the radio or his library; he sat back on his bed and fell immediately into the deepest sleep, with crab dreams so real that he would wake now and again to find his hands still racing through the bushels, sorting live crabs from dead, males from females.

After the Fourth, even the white boys working the kitchen had to give him his due: Gary was the John Henry of bushels. Save for that one break in the afternoon when he had to make his way up the hill and get himself right, no one was around to get those crabs off the trucks, into the pots, and over the counter as quickly or as cheerfully. Gary had his problem, the white boys would acknowledge, but come the dinner rush, he was one hard-laboring sonofabitch.

They call for him all summer long.

"Twos, Gary."

"On my way, Mo."

"You got any soft-shells?"

"Got what you need, Chief."

Day after day, bushel after bushel, he does the job and gets his blast. And no one at the crabhouse, black or white, ever feels cheated by any part of the bargain.

When Labor Day arrives to mark summer's end, Gary is once again at the top of his game. At Seapride, this is the last battle of the seasonal war, with the seafood trucks pulling up on Monroe Street from Delaware, the Eastern Shore, and the Carolina coast. For Gary, it's the last chance to show the bosses that when the crab season slows and the working hours are cut back, he's the one they need to keep.

"Hundert fifty bushels," shouts Ron, coming into the sorting room from the loading dock. "Let's get 'em in."

And there's Gary, first to the back of the truck, carrying two at a time, with the angry females reaching through the basket slats, looking to punish him for the trouble.

"Ah," he shouts as one finds some unguarded skin above his belt. "I been got."

Another war wound. His brother Cardy laughs gently.

"Got me right through the shirt," says Gary.

"Bitches be that way," says Cardy, gesturing to the bushel of females. "You got to watch 'em all the time."

Gary laughs, too, despite the allergic wheeze in his throat, despite the stinging pain at his waist. He goes back to the truck—fifteen, twenty times—until his arms can take no more. Then he goes back again.

"What's the count?" asks Ron when the bushels are inside and stacked. Bobby Short runs down the rows.

"Forty-seven, forty-eight . . . one forty-nine." Bobby looks up and frowns. "We got shorted one."

"No, Chief," says Gary, from the edge of the stun tank. "I got your last one here."

He's already a third of the way through the basket, tossing live ones into the ice water that ends their fight, dropping the dead into a discard basket on the floor. And after these ten or twelve dozen, another bushel, then another.

". . . *oh happy day.*" Gary is singing gospel as the crabs are numbed. ". . . *oh happy, happy day.*"

Outside, the line backs up out the door and onto the sidewalk. The kitchen boys race to keep up with the crowd at the counter.

"We on the beam now, ain't we?" shouts Gary.

He pulls off his California Angels cap, wipes his forehead, and then returns it to his head. He yanks the raise-chain on the tank and three bushels of ice-covered number twos surface from the water. He uses one hand to hold the wheeled, stainless steel cube of a crab pot adjacent to the tank; with the other, he sweeps the crab pile into the pot.

"Dust! Dust!" he shouts. Jimmy, one of the younger hires, throws a round of spice onto the bottom layer of crawlers.

Gary sweeps his arm again, rustling another three or four dozen to their doom. "Dust."

This is the quick way of doing it—the way it has to be done when the customers are lined up to the street corner. Other times, you can snatch the crabs one at a time and layer them carefully in the pot, making sure each gets the same handful of spice. But now, on the holiday, it's got to be catch as catch can.

"We microwavin' them," Gary declares. "We givin' it the microwave process."

He sweeps his arm again and a shell point catches him in the hand, the point going right through the thick rubber glove.

"Ow! Dag!"

He pulls out the point and yanks the glove off to examine the wound. He holds the offending crab in his other hand, looking at it as if expecting some kind of argument. Times like these, a crab-slinger will hurl the assailant against a wall. Crab fission, Mo, and leave the debris there on the ground as a warning to others. But not Gary.

"Hey, hey," he says, dropping the crab gently into the pot. "Crab got his job to do. I got mine."

With another few sweeps of his arm, he empties the tank.

"Dust! Dust!"

From the steam room, Paul calls in a double-time order for thirty-twos—the biggest of the Chesapeake blues; monster crabs creeping and snapping at each other in the sorting bins to Cardy's extreme left. For those willing to pay, the crab-eating doesn't get better than thirty-twos.

"Gimme the big boys, Chief," says Gary, stepping across Cardy to grab the bin. "Someone out front is serious."

The monsters go into the stun tank, the chain is yanked down, the frozen crawlers reemerge. Jimmy starts to sweep his side of the tank, rushing the thirty-twos into the pot.

"No, ho, no," cries Gary, stopping him.

He begins placing the crabs in uniform rows, preparing them for the most perfect culinary journey possible.

"Gary, we ain't got time."

"Yes we do. We make time for thirty-twos," Gary tells him, ordering and spicing the crabs in precise layers. "These ain't just crabs, Mo. These are crustaceans. You got to respect 'em."

Jimmy can't even argue. Them bad boys look beautiful down there in the bottom of the pot, and Gary is hard to the task, making time, getting it done.

"... *oh happy day.*"

Fat Curt leans back in the plastic chair, waiting for the part where they give you the check. He's a wreck. Anyone can look at his arms and legs and see that. What the hell else can any legitimate government do other than hand him a check?

"And Mr. Davis," asks the Social Security Administration caseworker, "what is the nature of your condition?"

"Say what?"

"What's wrong with you that you can't work."

"I'm swole up."

"Excuse me?"

"My legs and arms is swollen. Can't barely walk."

"But what's the medical condition?"

This makes Curtis Davis think for a moment. He leans forward and looks around the SSA branch office on Frederick Avenue, his mind struggling, his mouth trying to get hold of some of the long words he's heard from the hospital whitecoats.

"Elephantitis."

The bureaucrat looks up from his computer keyboard. "Elephantitis?"

Time to play the ace. Curt reaches both hands beneath his right knee, pulls his leg straight, and then raises it slowly. He sites the ankle over the corner of the desk and lets it fall. From knee to foot, the extremity is so bloated that Curt's baggy denims are stretched to the tearing point. The running shoe is three sizes beyond what he would ordinarily wear, and even then it can't be laced.

"Uh . . ."

The man is speechless. But Curt isn't done yet. It's September, and soon enough he'll be soldiering once again in a vacant house in the freezing cold of another Baltimore winter. For Curt, the future is now and he figures that this must be his moment; if he can pull up these pants, if he can show just a few inches of cratered, gatorlike flesh, then this paper-shuffler will surely understand. It's just a matter of finding the right bureaucrat, the right desk. You take your number and you wait and you sign the right form, giving them all that they ask for. You do these things and then the leg is the trump card. You put it up there and you get paid.

For Curt, this constitutes a lock-solid plan.

"Uh, sir . . ."

But Curt is busy with the guided tour: "My ankle messed up too. From fallin' out a window . . . Lookit this . . ."

"Mr. Davis, that won't be necessary."

Curt is still struggling with the pants cuff, trying to show more, when the man lightly touches his shoe and insists that he bring the leg back down to the floor.

"I don't need to examine the disability," the man explains. "A doctor will evaluate you in the event you appeal."

"Uh huh."

The keyboard clicks and snaps as Curt answers a few more questions. Work history? Laborer. What years? Long time gone. Current income? None. Current assets? None. And where have you received treatment for your disability?

THE CORNER

"Hospitals," says Curt.

"Which ones?"

"All of 'em."

After five minutes, the forms are complete and the file is prepared and Curt is handed his copies. Curtis Izell Davis, aged forty-five, has formally asked the U.S. government to recognize him as disabled and unemployable.

"You're denied," says the male caseworker, smiling politely. Curt shakes his head. He wants to show the leg again.

"Mr. Davis, with the exception of those legally blind or quadriplegic, everyone is denied on the initial application. Now then, would you like to appeal this decision?"

Curt nods his head.

"Okay," says the man, moving the cursor across the screen. "I am now noting your request for an appeal. You'll be notified by mail within ninety days."

Wrong desk, Curt thinks. He gets up slowly, the residual paperwork folded into one of his thick hands. If it was the right desk, he tells himself, he'd have that check. Or at least a promise that the check would soon be on its way. Instead, he's got himself another application to go with two or three others made in the last couple of weeks. These papers in his hand—indicating that he has applied to Social Security for SSI benefits—will allow him to proceed with a pending application for medical assistance from the state, which could possibly be acted on in three months, if he's lucky. He also recently filled out the forms for food stamps, though that application is in limbo now—the Rosemont workers said it couldn't go through while he was still in Bon Secours; his dietary needs, they explained, were being met by the hospital. But he's been out of the hospital more than a month now and no one from Rosemont has bothered to inform him that the paperwork must be resubmitted.

Then there's DALP—the state's disability loan program—through which Curt is allowed to "borrow" $157 a month to meet his living expenses, including rent. That application is also floating around the Rosemont offices, waiting for someone to step up and declare Curt disabled. The DALP program came into being the year before as Maryland began dropping adult males from the medical assistance program; the legislature was willing to create the new program only with the stipulation that all funds allocated would be loans to be repaid within three years. No one at Rosemont or anywhere else believes repayment is likely, but calling it a loan rather than a benefit has let state lawmakers feel good about themselves amid so much talk about welfare reform.

In any event, Curt is out of the hospital, on his own, and up to his ass in social service applications. With no check forthcoming, he's waiting like everybody waits, taking a number and sitting on the plastic chairs in the Rosemont waiting area or down at the social security branch office on Frederick Road. He's supplicating before the caseworkers, answering their questions, signing their forms, waiting for that special someone to show him the right desk so that the right government worker can marvel at the condition of his legs and then pay up.

Until then, he's got nothing—not even the two dollars required for the Tuerk House meetings. He'd been going, not every day, but often enough to remain on their waiting list for the residential program. Mostly he's uptown on Ellamont in his sister's living room, watching game shows and soap operas and waiting on the postal carrier. Every day brings bills that will never be paid—eight thousand dollars alone from the last hospital stay—but nothing in that computer-embossed typeface that is the telltale of every social services missive.

His sister, Angie, has her own problems, but she's willing to keep him for a while. Still, unless Curt has a check day fairly soon, he'll be back on the street. He's been up to Monroe and Fayette once or twice already—mostly to round up a little cash for laundry or a burger or a pineapple Sno-Kone. Stink and Pimp, Eggy Daddy and Blue have all praised him for being clean, and that felt good. But his health is no better than before—worse even. His ankle gives him excruciating pain with every step.

A few days after Bon Secours dumped him back on the street, he went over to the Johns Hopkins E.R. to see about getting the ankle fixed, but the triage nurse treated him coldly and he emerged after a six-hour wait with nothing save for a clinic appointment three weeks distant.

Three days after that, he went down to University Hospital, hoping for something better. The whitecoats in the E.R. took an X-ray or two, then forwarded him to the orthopedic clinic.

Now, a day after he displayed the leg at the social security office, a doctor at the orthopedic clinic looks at the same carnage and confirms what Curt already knows—that the ankle has set at an awkward angle, that, short of fusing the bone, there isn't much that can be done.

"And we're probably not going to be able to operate with the leg in that swollen condition," the resident explains. "The vascular damage won't allow it."

So they send him to the vascular clinic, where more University of Maryland personnel gather around, incredulous at the sight.

"How long have you been using drugs?" asks one.

"Long enough."

"You've done a lot of damage."

"I know it," snaps Curt. "Don't need no doctor to tell me that, but you go on ahead with it, if you like."

"I'm just . . . I've never seen lymphedema that bad."

"Elephantitis," Curt assures him.

"Not elephantiasis," the vascular resident says. "It's lymphedema, the swelling of veins and arteries, and to a certain extent irreversible."

Then again, the resident explains, there's a vascular compression machine that might reduce the bloating if applied consistently. Curt would have to remain seated for a couple of hours a day, with his legs elevated as a compression pad tightened its grip around each extremity. The resident writes a prescription.

So Curt limps downtown to visit a medical supply company, where the woman working the counter wants to know if he intends to compress both legs simultaneously.

"Say what?"

"Do you want to use the pads on both legs at once? It takes less time that way."

"But that'll cost more," Curt guesses.

"I'm afraid so."

"One leg."

"A monthly rental fee of eighty dollars or you can buy the machine for five hundred," the clerk tells him.

"Five hundert," drawls Curt. "I ain't like to see five hundert dollars together at the same time again."

"Do you have medical assistance?"

"I'm gettin' to it now."

"If you get a medical assistance card, we might be able to work something out."

If and when. Days stack up one after the other, and still nothing arrives in the mail at the Ellamont address save more requests for more documents to justify the application for medical assistance. Miss Bunch, the caseworker assigned to Curt, wants a rental form signed by Curt's sister, as well as more medical files from Bon Secours and University Hospitals. No word on the food stamps. No word on DALP.

The wait grinds against Curt, wearing at his resolve, dragging him by perceptible degrees back toward the corner. He'd gotten clean in the hospital, stayed that way for a couple weeks after. He'd gone to the meetings, talked the twelve-step talk, told his story to people and heard them tell the same story back. For as long as he dared, he'd done what the bitch social worker asked in the vague belief that with a little government money, he could get a room of his own, some food and a few other sundries, and try to scratch out a bit more dignity than he could expect at Monroe and Fayette. But the government money wasn't coming soon, and his sister wanted him to kick in some rent, and in the absence of any other plan, there was only one thing Curt knew well enough.

"What up?"

"Big whites. Big white bags today."

"They a bomb?"

"They sure enough get you there."

He tries for a while to tout without using, to take his pay in cash rather than on the hype, to put the money in his pocket. He isn't really handling the dope much anymore: He's too slow to work his own stash, and he's clean enough now so that he doesn't carry a vial or two of his own in his pockets. He was already arrest-proof by virtue of his physical condition; now he's even more secure as a salesperson working a step or two apart from the transactions. "I be all right," he explains, "as long as the niggers don't miss and the police don't make a mistake."

For a while he works part-time at Monroe and Fayette, straddling the fence between his old life and the new one dependent on government money. But the corner isn't looking for part-time help, and before long Curt is up on the strip almost every day. He misses more of the Tuerk House meetings; finally, by late September, he's dropped from the residential waiting list. A week or two more and he's not coming home every night to Ellamont. In the end, he's broken completely, the jaundice returning to his eyes, the days and nights reduced to running between Blue's and Annie's with the rest of the hardcore crowd, waiting by candlelight for Rita's ministrations.

Hungry is nearly two months gone. Pimp is even weaker now, skinnier. Dennis, Curt's brother, is the same, staggering along, refusing to give in to the Bug. And Rita—her arms are rotting beyond the point where antibiotics make a difference, and the stench is almost enough to clear the shooting gallery at Blue's.

As for the proprietor of the needle palace, he has tumbled once again, disappearing into the back of a police wagon at the height of summer, taking a fresh charge in a manner that confirms the corner belief that honesty is never, ever the best policy.

"What's your name?" a Western footpatrol had asked him.

An incredible question, by corner standards: As if merely by asking, you can walk up to someone in the vicinity of Monroe and Fayette and elicit the correct given and surnames. But the cop walking foot on Monroe Street happened to be an older desk man, rotated in one of those periodic departmental crackdowns that throws all the house cats back on to the beat. That the footman bothered to ask the question at all was absurd; that Blue—who had earlier lied to a pair of homicide detectives with the same query—would actually answer was beyond comprehension.

"My name?"

"Yeah."

"George Epps."

So the footman got on his radio and called in George Epps. It's hard to say which one of the two was more surprised when the warrant check came back. George Epps was, indeed, a wanted man. Violation of probation from the earlier charge of burglarizing his own house—it seemed that the Division of Parole and Probation wanted to know what ever happened to its home-monitoring bracelet—not to mention the client wearing same.

"Aw, man. You got to be jokin."

The cop seemed almost sad. "Why'd you give me your right name?"

"Thought I could," Blue shrugged. "Hadn't really done much of anything lately."

The wagon was called and Blue went away for the second time this year, leaving what remained of his childhood home to the fiends. There was nothing in the place to steal or sell—only used syringes, bottle caps, candle wax, and the soiled bedrolls of the remaining inhabitants. And nothing was what Blue found when he returned from the city lockup at summer's end.

He came home from Eager Street clean once again—just as clean as he had been upon returning from his earlier arrest. And once again, he returned to a place that guaranteed nothing but the same kind of failure and pain. He felt truly tired, and in that weariness, he saw with different eyes just how little was left of his mother's rowhouse and how little that address had to do with him anymore.

At that moment, Blue concluded that he could no longer live this way. A friend had told him about a homeless shelter down in a refurbished fire station in South Baltimore, a residential program that allowed men to stay for up to six months. That was long enough to find work, save some money, and fashion a plan—provided you didn't backslide and fail one of the random piss tests. You had to be clean to get into South Baltimore Station, and Blue knew that if he stayed at Monroe and Fayette a second longer than required, he'd lose all purchase on sobriety. So, within days of coming home from detention, he packed up his paints and brushes and poetry journals and caught a ride down Baltimore Street and then south under the railroad overpass on Carey Street—his disappearance as sudden as his return from jail. There were no one-for-the-road needle parties, no last-minute hustles; he said little about it to anyone and offered nothing beyond a casual see-you-down-the-road to the regulars who watched him get into the hack. It seemed more a surrender than an actual exit. But he didn't come back that night. Or the next night. Or the night after.

After a week or two, Blue was only a wisp of memory in the fogged minds of those who remained at Monroe and Fayette. Inside the remnant of his home, what was left of the lost platoon was dealing with the here and now. Flubber and Bread and Hungry and Blue and all the other casualties were up on the shelf. For those huddled in the broken rowhouse, there was no time for reflecting on the faces no longer there. Whistling in through the gaps in the plywood, the first gentle winds of September left them preoccupied with the threat of a change in the weather. It was cool at night now, sometimes almost cold—good sleeping weather for as long as it lasted. But with fall comes winter right behind, hard soldiering weather for the likes of Curt and Eggy Daddy, Rita and Pimp.

Fat Curt, for one, won't make another winter out here; he knows it. He'd love to come inside, to gather up a few nuts and berries and hibernate in some warmer place. But still, no check arrives at the Ellamont address. When Curt struggles uptown to collect his mail, all he finds are more requests for more documentation—proof beyond proof of a disability that Curt can readily display for anyone willing to let him roll up his pants. The worker at Rosemont now wants hospital records going back two years; Curt comes up from the corner game long enough to run down to Rosemont in a hack, where he asks about money and is told that his DALP application is still being processed.

"Have you applied for SSI?" the woman at Rosemont wonders. "Because to receive DALP, you have to apply for SSI."

"I been there."

"You've been to social security?"

Curt nods. "They sayin' I got an appeal."

"Well you should receive something from us shortly then."

Shortly. Curt takes that for what it's worth, which is to say he goes back to Monroe and Fayette and does what he can to prepare for the coming weather. He begs a second pair of extra-large sweats from a friend; he'll need two layers if he's going to be out of doors. He trades up for a new pair of running shoes. And then, when the police are jumping out on Monroe and Vine, clearing the corners as a last, useless rite of the fading season, Curt gets a new jacket.

It comes to him indirectly, not as an act of charity but through an unlikely string of events. It begins with a young slinger in a yellow and brown leather coat racing up Vine Street, followed by a Western District radio car that comes the wrong way down Fulton and then shoots up the alley. Sprinting, the kid ducks between two parked cars and lurches to a quick stop at 1823 Vine, where he takes the front steps in a single bound and grabs at the door handle. Locked. He starts banging, but the patrolman sees him and guns the motor of the cruiser. Nothing to do now but jump from the stoop and try to make the mouth of the back alley. But no, the radio car will be there before him.

The kid cuts back hard, leaping up another set of steps and pulling open the storm door at 1827. He's quickly in the front room, pulling the leather coat from his shoulders in the hope that a change of wardrobe will throw the hounds. He creeps past the stairwell landing to the kitchen, where he runs into Roberta McCullough, ironing her husband's work shirt.

"Is . . . is James here?"

"Who?"

"James."

The kid drops the coat across the top of the cluttered dining room table. Roberta McCullough looks at him hard, trying to make any connection whatsoever.

"Who are you, young man? Why are you in my house?"

The kid moves toward the back door and is gone, flying out of the kitchen and into the back alley. The Western troops hit the front door a moment later, charging through the house in pursuit. Miss Roberta is one shock away from a heart attack.

"Where's he at?" demands the first cop through the door.

She barely manages to point to the back door. The Western uniform doesn't believe her.

"We find him in here and you'll be locked up too."

Roberta McCullough is speechless. Another patrolman races up the stairs; she can hear the search proceed into her front bedroom.

"Where's he at?"

"He left out the back."

"Who is he?"

"I never saw him before in my life."

"Then why did he run in here?"

She shakes her head, confused. They don't believe her.

The police root around a bit longer, with two of them giving a quick search of Gary's basement. They leave showing unequivocal disgust, offering no explanation or apology. Moments later, when Cardy parks his pickup on Vine Street and tries to walk into his mother's house, the police jack him up against the Formstone for good measure.

"He a workin' man," shouts Pimp from the top of the alley.

But the details are no longer important. Cardy is made to drop his pants in the street, and two Western officers give him a dickie check for no other reason than their own frustration.

"This ain't right," Cardy tells them.

"Shut up."

"I just tryin' to check on my mother."

"Shut up or get locked up."

William McCullough pulls up in his cab to see one of his hardest-working children down on the pavement, his pants at his ankles. "Now what you doin' with him?" asks W.M. "He got a job. He got two jobs. He don't got nothin' to do with this mess."

But the Western troops have their day, letting go of Cardy only after it's clear to everyone on the street that there's no justification—legal or moral—for having him down on the pavement in the first place.

"This is a drug-free zone," a Western uniform tells Cardy on leaving. "You can get locked up for loitering."

"I live here."

As quickly as they descended on Vine Street, the police are gone. The radio cars and wagon speed to opposite ends of the alley and disappear on some other mission.

W.M. talks for a while about making a complaint, but Cardy dissuades him, telling his father that it would do no good. When his wife recovers from her shock, she notices the yellow and brown jacket—an alien presence—on her table. The coat scares her.

As the police cruise the area, searching in vain for their prey, Roberta McCullough walks the leather coat out her front door and offers it to the first living soul she can find.

"Do you . . . would you take this jacket?"

Fat Curt stands on Vine Street, looking a gift horse in the mouth. "Say what?"

"That young man left it here and I don't want it in my house. Do you need a coat?"

"Yes'm."

So Fat Curt's fall ensemble is complete. He puts his cane against the Formstone front of the McCullough house and tries on the jacket; it's a reasonably good fit. He thanks her, picks up his cane and makes his way down Vine toward Fulton.

He gets as far as Lexington and Bruce before a Western unit rolls past him, going the other way, and then screeches to a halt. Curt doesn't immediately turn around, though he can feel the eyes of the patrolman glaring at his back. Slowly, the cop backs his car down Lexington, far enough to get a look at Curt from the front.

"What?" asks Curt. "I look like a rabbit to you?"

A great line, but the cop doesn't laugh.

"Where'd you get the jacket?"

"From a friend," says Curt.

The Western man goes away mad, and Fat Curt goes about his business. He's a soldier again, and now, despite any pretensions to the contrary, he's convinced that he'll always be a soldier. A week or two more and he stops calling down to his sister's house or worrying about the constant requests for more documentation. He doesn't believe in government money anymore, or those plastic chairs up at Rosemont, or finding the right desk. He doesn't believe that his ankle will stop hurting, or that the swelling in his legs will cease. He believes that his liver will have to do the best it can under the circumstances. Yes, Fat Curt is back on post and no one at Blue's wants him anywhere else. No one there will remind him that for a few weeks, at least, he'd looked better than he had in a long while. Fat Curt returns to their lives and they are grateful for the reassurance that comes from an ordered universe. His return affirms that the old corner axiom still holds: No one gets out alive.

Only once does Curt falter, revealing, for a brief moment at least, the feeling of loss that results from even three or four weeks clean. Sitting on the steps of a Monroe Street rowhouse one sunless afternoon, Curt actually begins crying, the tears gathering up in the corners of his eyes and then racing down his cheeks.

Gary McCullough is there with him, making for a strange combination. Curt and Gary didn't really mix, not since the days when Gary was a stock boy at Lemler's Pharmacy and the owners sent him to chase after Curt and Dennis and all the others who walked out with unpaid-for merchandise. But on this day, Curt has chosen to grieve for himself, and he has picked Gary to mourn with him. And Gary, of course, will listen to things that the platoon in the shooting gallery does not ever want to hear.

"Look at me. Look at my legs, my hands . . ."

"Uh huh."

"I look like a damn freak and I can't do a got-damn thing about it . . ."

"You ought to go up the emergency room . . ."

"Ain't you think I been to every hospital in town? Got-damn doctors can't do shit for me."

"But . . ."

"But nuthin.' I need love. Every mother's son got to have love. Who in the hell gonna love me lookin' like this. Ain't nobody love me and ain't nobody gonna love me."

That leaves Gary with little to say. He puts a hand on Curt's shoulder and waits for the moment to pass. It does.

"I gotta go make some money," Curt says.

"Me, too," says Gary.

"You still down with them crabs?"

"Yeah."

From then on, Curtis Davis showed only his game face. No more talk about fixing his ankle, or his legs, or his hands; no more clinic appointments or emergency room visits. Only two medical issues still worry Curt, one of which seems to be seeking him out. Twice now, some man by the name of Robert Carr has sidled up to the boys at Fayette and Monroe, asking where Curtis Davis might be hanging.

"You a police?"

"No. I'm from Bon Secours."

No one believed that, of course. A man goes to the hospital; the hospital doesn't go to the man.

"Where's Curt at? I just need him to sign some forms."

"He gone."

"Well tell him to stop by the hospital then."

But Curt has no intention of chatting with Robert Carr, whoever he is. If the man isn't a police with a warrant, then he's a collection agent. Curt has seen the kind of bills that are washing up at his sister's house; even if the hospital sends people up to the corner every day for the next year, Curt tells himself, those bills are about money that Bon Secours won't never see. No, Curt will have to avoid Mr. Carr, which could be a problem in that his last bit of medical business requires a trip back to Bon Secours.

A week after his confessional with Gary, Curt and a friend take a discreet walk up to Bon Secours in the hope of answering a question. Curt knows he's been tested; the doctors there couldn't have had him that whole time and not tested him. Weeks ago he'd asked people at the hospital for his medical chart as verification for his SSI appeal, but with the corner once again taking hold of him, he'd never followed up. Curt reasons that the chart is probably down in medical records somewhere, in a manila envelope, waiting for him.

"You all made me a copy of my records?" he asks a nursing supervisor. "Where can I get a look at my records?"

He's directed down a couple of corridors to a small counter in the Fayette Street wing of the building. He gives his name and a pretty blond girl hands him his charts. No counseling sessions, no explanations, no privacy issues—just a thick stack of medical casework and lab reports dropped into a dope fiend's swollen hand. Curt can't read, but he brought the friend.

"What's the word?" Curt asks.

The friend rifles through the chart. The Bug has got Dennis and Pimp and Bryan. It got Flubber, too, and God knows how many others at Monroe and Fayette who fell out and died without ever even knowing. And Curt's no fool; he knows how many needles he's shared, how many days and nights and years of drugging he's endured.

"Tell it true," says Curt, firm.

"You're negative."

"Uh huh." Curt, showing no surprise.

"Curt, you're negative."

A long-shot winner if ever there was one. By the odds, Curtis Davis has managed the medical equivalent of a Maryland state lottery win.

"Curt, this means you don't got it."

"Goddammit, I know what negative mean."

"Well, you're relieved, right?"

"I'm a soldier," Fat Curt says. "If'n I'd caught it, I'd've dealt with that, too."

They start showing up at the Rosemont field office at seven, seven-thirty, leaning against the black metal rails in the early morning light, or slumping against the front steps of a no-frills, hard-edged box of red and brown brick. They keep to themselves, waiting the wait, sometimes asking one of the security guards whether they'll make the cut. Do they take twenty? Or twenty-five? And what time do they start letting people inside?

At eight or so, one of the guards comes out with the paper slips, numbered one through twenty-five, to be handed out as if this were a delicatessen counter. Sometimes there's an argument or two to help pass the time. Number fourteen tells number thirteen that she got here first. Number thirteen says the hell you did; I saw you get out of that hack and walk up. But mostly, it stays quiet for the next half hour, until the workers come down for their morning smoke.

From that moment onward, every opening and closing of the door is marked by those waiting. Are they open yet? When they gonna open? The latecomers drift up to ask about their chances or count how many are already waiting with the paper slips. Those willing to chance it stick around; the rest trail off, vowing to come earlier next time.

At nine, the doors don't open and there's a bit of muttering from one or two near the end of the line, but no one leaves or presses any real argument on the guards. Ten minutes later the office is declared open and numbers one through twenty-five are ushered in. They move past the guards to the old elevator—the one adorned with graffiti declaring "everyone working here can fuck themself"—which lurches them to the third floor in clumps of five and six.

At the end of the hall, another security guard waves a handheld metal detector over torsos and privates—just enough of an effort to suggest an actual search and add to the growing sense of insult. From the security checkpoint, it's a short walk to the waiting area, where the group is offered a choice of mismatched, multicolored plastic, shaped-like-no-one's-ass chairs that exist only to decorate the lowest rungs of American government.

They sit. And for the next four, or five, or six hours, they hear without hearing and see without seeing. Their faces are frozen masks, fixed on the wall or the ceiling or the television set that force-feeds them video lessons on AIDS prevention, prenatal care, and drug addiction. They sit there amid people they once went to school with, or lived near, or knew as the friend of another friend, but now none of that is acknowledged with anything more than rudiments.

"How you been?"

"Same ol'."

They watch numbers one and two, three and four go up to the receptionist and make whatever plea brought them down here in the first place. They watch as those people are finally paired with case-workers and sent back into other rooms with pages and pages of forms. They wait for numbers five and six, seven and eight. When number nine is called, they sit stoically as he gets in a protracted debate with the woman at the desk—some bullshit about how he already filled out an application and just wants to see his caseworker and no, goddammit, he doesn't have an appointment. It takes twenty-five minutes to get to number ten.

Lunchtime comes. For forty-five minutes or so, not a single number is called. Then the minutes and the numbers begin creeping by again and at last it's midafternoon—already a long day for those tired and hungry, a longer one for those wrestling with the snake.

"Number eighteen."

Number eighteen left out.

"Number nineteen."

Yes, Lord. It's finally Mr. Nineteen's turn. He has endured. And by enduring he has earned the privilege of taking an application form and following a caseworker down the hall and into a side office cluttered with empty file cabinets and ancient office furniture. If he's lucky, he landed a good one—a public functionary pleasant enough and quick with the paperwork. The veterans know the roster: Get that woman with the dyed hair and she'll never, ever take your phone calls. Get the Nigerian and when it gets complicated, you won't understand a thing he says. But at this stage, none of that matters; on this first day, hope is still intact and the back-and-forth between Mr. Nineteen and his caseworker has all the gentility of a first dance. The forms are filled out, the rules explained. A request for additional documents is put in writing and the process seems for the most part rational and certain. He leaves feeling that he has stated the necessary case, that it's only a matter of getting the Independence Card and waiting for the money to show up in the bank machine computer.

But long before any check day arrives—and even when some dollars begin to flow—those who go down to Rosemont will acquire and nurture a fulminating hatred, a bitterness that will extend not only to a system that is indifferent and insufficient to their desperation, but to its minions, who, even at their best, are unable to erase the immense gap between themselves and their clientele. On one level, the Rosemont regulars understand that the caseworkers have far too many clients and too much redundant paperwork, and that they are limited in what they can do by regulations that demand endless documentation. But that reality doesn't matter when it comes down to survival, because this is real money here: food dollars and rent dollars, Nike dollars and Tommy Hilfiger dollars and blast dollars. And when they've done everything they've been asked and the money still doesn't flow as fast or as freely as expected, then to hell with understanding.

As for the caseworkers themselves, they have equal standing in the argument. They're working at the broken edges of the nation— the frontier where those without means come to scream and beg and supplicate, to run any game or hustle or dope-fiend move for the possibility of a few dollars more. The social service department case- workers are there every working day to greet the corner world, to negotiate the last tatters of a social compact between that world and the nominal government. They've been cussed and threatened, lied to and cried to by people for whom this process is not a means to a better end, but the end itself.

This is welfare. This is a transaction that has become as hurtful and as hateful as any business done on any drug corner in the city. The process itself leaves each side in utter contempt of the other—givers and takers trapped in their respective roles, unable to create or accomplish anything that lasts much beyond the first of every month.

We know this, of course. We've known it for years now; all the arguments against the welfare state are fixed in our minds. Work has been depreciated; helplessness has become a way of life. Government handout has helped to make the underclass permanent and the middle- class permanently angry. And all of these truths serve to justify the rage, reluctance, and general disgust of anyone who calls himself a taxpayer.

For those willing to defend the status quo, there are the anecdotal references to lives salvaged by welfare—case histories of young mothers who used the check money wisely, who saved, went to school, and, ultimately, were able to lift themselves up into the working world. These stories are true; they testify to the best intentions of the programs.

But down on Fayette Street, the alternate truth—the predominant truth—is the maelstrom of check day, with all that government money going to the touts and slingers in a three- or four- or five-day rush. Come the first of the month, much of what the government offers to feed and clothe and shelter its poor goes for vials and gel caps and glassine bags, so that the first week of every month is more than enough to carry a dealer. After the tenth, a slinger could close up shop for the rest of the month and still have more than enough to carry him to check day next. Come the fourth week of any month, there's little cash on the street; it's time for any sensible retailer to take his vacation. Because first of the next month, he'll be back on the street in sixteen-hour shifts.

Check day's effect on open-air markets like Mount and Fayette makes clear the economic role of the welfare dollar in the drug culture. To stand on a drug corner and watch mothers and fathers running their Independence Cards up to the bank machines, then racing the cash back to the corners until a third, or a half, or, in some cases, all of the monthly allotment is gone—to see that is to despair of any program in which the government matches desperation with raw dollars. The cash money goes first—the AFDC dollars, the SSI checks, the DALP money—but at the end of the week, the food stamps are being traded for eighty or sixty or fifty cents on the dollar. Regardless of all the noble intent and charitable purpose, the games will be run and the corners will be fed. Far beyond Fayette Street, others can debate welfare reform, or work-fare, or job training, but on check day none of it means a thing to people who are scraping and hustling in an altogether different nation. The corners are no longer part of our economy, our culture; the welfare dollar might reasonably be considered as something akin to foreign aid. And be honest here: When we drop a few billion on our favorite Third World dictators, we pretty much expect most of it to be hoarded and stolen and squandered. In the dark corner of our hearts, we regard this as international bribe money, sensing that its purpose is merely to convince smaller countries to do a little more of our bidding. So why, for the sake of argument, should we expect any better result from the dollars sent down to Fayette Street?

Welfare is a bribe—and a fairly good one at that. For more than two decades it's been a bribe and only a bribe, stripped of the higher ideals that once accompanied the payoff. Those ideals called for a process by which poor and damaged citizens could be rescued and made whole, but such a process has proven more costly and problematic than anyone initially imagined. So the nation has retreated from that commitment, using check day as a rear guard. The pretense of salvaging human beings has been gradually reduced to a string of elemental transactions: Take this. Shut up. Stay put until next month when there will be more of the same.

The incredible thing is that such a small investment can purchase so much silence and apathy. On Fayette Street a mother and child will see $280 and another $120 in food stamps each month. A second child might bring $60 more. A Maryland state DALP loan once meant as little as $157 a month to a disabled adult; after the entire program was eliminated from the budget, it meant nothing. As for SSI—that's the motherlode of $450 a month for those lucky enough to be declared totally disabled by the Social Security Administration. But getting onto the rolls isn't so easy anymore. In fact, they're denying almost everybody outright, limiting access to those willing to appeal and then appeal again.

It's reasonable to factor in the primary health care provided to women and children by Medicaid, or the food-and-formula vouchers given to poor mothers through the WIC program. There is also the financial aid provided to those willing and able to try their luck in some community college courses. But all told, what we're spending on the poor constitutes a thin share of what the government spends in total—less than three percent of federal and state spending overall. In the grand scheme of government, all of it added up and compounded with interest is hardly worth complaining about, yet incredibly, we are forever complaining. Absurd as such an expectation is, the belief that all of our handouts will at some point produce viable citizens remains with us; when nothing of the sort comes to pass, we are furious.

But what we get for our money is not inconsequential. It's true that, for some, check day brings only the briefest respite from the twenty-four, seven struggle to stay aboard the chemical rollercoaster. Unbridled by constraints imposed by children, or a future, or the barest necessities, there are fiends who will snatch up the check and have it spent before the sun rises on the fourth day of any given month. Fortunately there are also many others who have learned to stretch and squeeze every penny, to somehow keep a rough-and-tumble balance between addiction and responsibility. For the best of them, the government money can last two, maybe three weeks.

In the aggregate, the best ideas and efforts of the welfare state—AFDC, SSI, DALP, Medicaid—buy us eight, or ten, or twelve days before the damned of the cities have to turn again to capers and hustles and crimes. For a third of the month, the predatory instinct is diverted by money that tumbles from bank machines and check-cashing places. There's less need to rip and run, less interest in pulling car stereos from dashboards or tearing copper piping from rowhouse basements. For that interval, in fact, the bribery accomplishes what all the police and prisons never can: The corners are fed, the corner regulars preoccupied with the money at hand. There's still crime, of course—all that money can't go up to the corner without everyone trying to cheat everyone else—so that on check day, the drug-related assaults and drug-related robberies reach their peak. But in general the government dole assures that most of the dirt stays where we want it to stay, and that a taxpayer's life in any neighborhood adjacent to Fayette Street is nearly manageable. Ten days are bought and paid for until the checks are spent and the money is siphoned out, and then it's every man for himself in the search for a blast. But on balance, we have no right to expect more. You get what you pay for in this world, and in the matter of buy-off dollars, we've made only the first installment.

Even so, we're getting our money's worth. If we spent any less, it would be throwaway money—not enough for even the pretense of a plan. The money would be on the corners and gone in a few days, and the difference would be made up in the crime rate, with places like West Baltimore reaping a whirlwind of armed robberies and property crimes. But spend any more and you still wouldn't get more than ten or twelve days out of a monthly check. Among a population accustomed to being shortchanged, diminishing returns would likely take hold. After all, the players manage to get to the end of every month with even less money; a few more dollars would mean nothing but a few more vials.

On Fayette Street, this is what the government pays for—this and nothing more. After the last thirty years' experience, it is frankly astonishing that we can still pretend that this response to poverty deserves anything other than cynicism and contempt. Yet to do anything more —anything beyond the bribe itself—remains unthinkable to the nation as a whole.

We've spent a respectable treasure in our cities—billions in AFDC checks and food stamps, billions more in HUD vouchers and block development grants—and almost all of it has gone no further than sustaining the urban poor in their nightmare. Apart from the buyoff money, we have rebuilt and restored the housing stock time and again—not because gilding the ghetto solves anything, but because we understand bricks and mortar, and because even on Fayette Street, the grant money allows contractors and subcontractors to grab a little profit. But what might constitute an actual process—the systematic reintegration of the inner city into the nation's economic fabric—was either stillborn or never conceived. More than bricks and mortar and welfare checks, such an effort would imply a continuing commitment to making places like Fayette Street a legitimate part of the American landscape. It would demand prolonged energy and will and a connectedness between classes and races that no longer exists and may never have existed. It would require, too, the expenditure of billions more than we have ever dreamed of giving to our urban poor. If we want to toss $320 a month at Fran Boyd and her children, or $157 at Curt Davis, we can do it without too much pain. Similarly, we can pay a nonprofit housing corporation forty or fifty thousand dollars to rehab the Dew Drop Inn and be gratified by the tangible, if decidedly temporary, evidence of change.

But to take a Fran Boyd or a Curt Davis across the chasm, to restore them to the mainstream of the American experience—this is Herculean. To create a process that begins to break down the corner dialectic, to offer a viable and practical argument against the drug economy, would mark a new national beginning. Never mind the years of man hours and piles of money that such an effort demands; the process would have to begin with a national consensus that no longer seems possible. It would require that pure, unbridled capitalism be regarded not as the equivalent of social policy, but as a powerful economic system in need of humane constraint.

Instead, the debate over welfare reform has been carefully circumscribed to a matter of dollars and cents. There are those willing to acknowledge that restoring the underclass to participation in the nation's social and economic framework would be an incredible undertaking. But these voices are no longer even a part of the political debate; now, the national discourse, as evidenced by recent welfare reform legislation and the wholesale reduction of the national welfare rolls is centered on the mere act of cutting the handout, or creating welfare-to-work requirements without any awareness of just how unemployable the men and women of Fayette Street have become. The safety net, or the lack of a safety net, for the underclass is now the only issue. Weighted as it is with thirty long years of frustration, the idea that government might have any role in restoring and rehabilitating its poorest citizens has been deconstructed. The poor themselves are now the problem, and, therefore, the argument about reforming the welfare state can be narrowly confined to issues of penalty. It boils down to this:

> We gave you the money.
> You didn't do shit with it.
> We're taking the money away.

It's come down to blaming the DeAndre McCulloughs and Richard Carters of the world for being born on Fayette Street, for being raised within the new culture of the corner, for failing to see beyond the boundaries of their world, for making ordinary and disastrous choices that were never really choices at all. We blame them for surviving despite themselves, for creating the corners and then taking the corner logic to its inevitable extreme. We're furious at the drugging and terrified by the shooting and unnerved at the notion that unless something is done, it won't be contained, that this horror show will creep beyond the rotting cores of cities. We have lost patience with the idea of our own culpability, with the corruptive message that accompanies the bribe. For three decades, we bought them off with the small coinage of charity at the beginning of every month, telling them they were not necessary, that their nation could do without them. Now, with that lesson of helplessness learned and learned well, we feel entitled to say that we can no longer afford the coins.

That the debate over welfare reform is couched in better language than this is testimony only to the subtlety of politics. It's one thing to recognize the chasm between Fayette Street and the rest of the social order, to anticipate just how much time, effort, and money will be required to dismantle the culture of the corner and return those trapped there to the mainstream. It's quite another to tell people who have been systematically stripped of discipline, purpose, and meaning that they have eighteen months, or two years, or even three years to get up off their asses and find a job.

It won't work. And when it doesn't work, there will be even more cause to lose patience, to blame them, to cut more and more from the monthly checks. Soon, the ten or twelve days bought and paid for will be eight, or six, or four. For some, there will be no days at all. And God help us then—particularly those of us living in general proximity to a rust-belt American city. Because the corners are still going to be there and the corner rule dictates that no one will miss his blast because check day is late or gone. Whatever else falls through the cracks, the blast money will still have to be there every day, because blast money is the stuff of desperation and identity. The rational forces of economic theory don't apply.

The corners now constitute a world apart, a rock-hard subculture formed in the crucible of lost America. Fayette Street and places like it are no longer accidents of race, or geography, or poverty. By generations, they have become all of those things and more, so that simple, seemingly reasoned changes in government policy or economic priority no longer achieve the intended result—or, in many cases, any result at all. Fayette Street is an ecosystem as complex as any in the natural world, as distinct and separate from the middle-class experience as can be imagined. Just as no right-thinking environmentalist would think of applying the ecology of a mountain stream to a tidewater marsh, so, too, should no politician or ideologue believe that what works elsewhere can or should work in the drug culture.

Mess with check day and we mess with the food chain; mess with the food chain and the consequences are necessarily profound. From on high, the intent is to end the dole and turn people toward work on the argument that those offered less will squander less. But from the inside, welfare reform doesn't address itself to the essence of the drug corner. Cut the flow of government dollars, and the capers and dope-fiend moves will become more desperate; the corner violence will intensify and the assault rate will jump and the bleeders will begin washing up at the emergency rooms in waves. And more hustles mean more lockups, which means more cops, judges, lawyers, jail guards, and probation officers. More prisons, too—that's the ultimate in societal cost, to the tune of an additional thirty thousand dollars or more annually to take hold of a solitary shoplifter or half-dead tout. Ultimately, we'll feel gratified by demanding more for our dollars, denying the coinage of welfare even as we're compelled to spend billions more on everything from Medicaid to foster care to boot camps.

The point is practical, not moral: For the money we throw down the welfare hole, we don't get miracles; in fact, we get pretty much what a backhanded bribe warrants. But if we tempt ourselves into believing that we've done more than we have and deserve more for our trouble, then we will surely find a way to get even less.

End welfare, or curtail it, or replace it with some crude carrot-and-stick approximation of workfare and the result is unpredictable. What passes for welfare reform will surely provoke some people to lift themselves up and escape the dole. But for the rest, it will likely solve nothing, and make the cities less livable than they already are. When the money dries up on Fayette Street, the corners will reach out and take their share from the next neighborhood over, and the next after that, until a problem that once seemed distant becomes a collision of worlds.

When things get worse—and they will—we're likely to tally our losses and assess the damage done and conclude—as we always conclude—that the fault isn't ours. We'll continue to justify our limited commitment, to assure ourselves that we did everything we could for these people and somehow they managed to fail us.

The choice then will be the choice now, just as it was the choice twenty years ago. We can commit to the people of Fayette Street—to the notion that they are our own and that their future is our future—or we can throw the problem back on them, arguing about smaller carrots and bigger sticks. Then as now, we'll make the worst choice, almost by habit.

Unless and until we have a change of heart, we should stop complaining. And come the first of the month, we should pay the bribe. To do less is to compound the tragedy; to do more—well, that road is the one never taken because we are moral pretenders to a war on poverty. We have been pretenders for three decades now, ever since the Vietnam War swallowed whole the ideals of the Great Society. To do more than tender the bribe would require empathy, charity, and connectedness, and in thirty years we have summoned up nothing close.

Empathy demands that we recognize ourselves in the faces at Mount and Fayette, that we acowledge the addictive impulse as something more than simple lawlessness, that we begin to see the corner as the last refuge of the truly disowned. Charity asks that we no longer begrudge the treasure already lost. And connectedness admits that between their world and ours, the distance, in human terms at least, is never as great as we make it seem.

Getting near the basement pay phone was no small feat. Getting on it was damned near impossible. But getting a call back was almost beyond imagination. Fran had given the phone number to DeAndre days ago, telling him when to call, trying for that one-hour window each day when she didn't have meetings or counseling sessions. For three days she'd waited on that call. And for three days, nothing.

For all she knows, her children might be out in the street. DeRodd might be hurt. DeAndre might be locked up. Having consigned herself to a purgatory all her own, she has no way of knowing.

It is late August. Fayette Street is still in the throes of its long summer, but Fran is out of the mix, alone and detached. She's been inside the Baltimore Recovery Center six days.

The first three were an ugly blur. Nothing that went beyond a very bad flu, but enough to make her think only of her dormitory bed. The doctor passed out Clonidine and aspirin, some Maalox to settle the stomach, but her body took every opportunity to exact retribution. The heroin-saturated cells threw a seventy-two-hour tantrum, crying and raging until they were absolutely sure that nothing more was coming. Then she started to feel a bit better. Empty, but better.

On the fourth day, she sat up, looked around, and began meeting people. She spent a day or two learning the rules, the schedule, the geography of the center. She bummed a smoke, tasted the food, listened with a fresh ear to the redemptive new language, and took to heart the warning they give when you come through the doors: Only one of the thirty people now in the room will be clean in a year. The odds are that long.

Once she learned the ropes, she had nothing left beyond the daily routine. Outside the walls was another world. Outside, the corners were still buzzing; the vials were bought and sold, the capers run, the game played out to the latest hour. At first, she felt disenfranchised. The race was not her own anymore; she had been abruptly tossed from the track and forced to watch from the infield grass. She was bored by this, but reconciled. She told herself that getting better required giving up not only the vials, but the game as well.

What Fran could not endure was the silence from her children. She needed news. She needed that pay phone to ring and the counselor to pick it up and call her name. Instead, the phone stayed occupied, save for those rare moments between calls when it would ring and the call would be for some other resident.

She had called Scoogie three days back, asking him to run down to Fayette Street and make DeAndre pick up the phone. She'd called back, too, making sure that Scoogie had done it and that DeAndre had the right number. But so far, nothing—no call, not even a message to let her know that DeRodd isn't in a hospital emergency room somewhere. The loose ends of her life are out there, flapping in the breeze, and after a week inside, Fran feels the need to grab hold of them.

And this is the first lie.

Only the lowest of low-bottom dope fiends will spend a week in detox and then leave, telling himself that he needs to go out for a blast. Instead, the thirsty cells look for a back door, giving up the frontal assault after the first few days; now the attack is based on subtle appeals to guilt or conscience or material need. Fran doesn't want to leave to get high; no, she just wants to take a walk up Fayette Street and see her children.

On Tuesday morning, she gets to the phone and calls her brother again. Scoogie assures her that DeAndre got the message.

"He ain't called," Fran says.

"I know he tried the one day," Scoogie tells her. "He tried but he said he couldn't get through."

She hears this and knows it's true. Yet nothing short of DeAndre's voice will reassure her—and maybe even DeAndre won't be enough. When one of the counselors finally calls her name at lunch the next day, she's all but given up; she's already telling herself that she needs only fourteen days of detox, twenty-one at the most.

"Fran Boyd."

"Fran, they callin' for you."

She jumps up and races for it like a game-show contestant.

"An-dre!"

"Ma."

"Hey boy. How you?"

"Fine."

"How DeRodd?"

"He up at Karen's. She gonna watch him."

"That's good. That's good."

So DeRodd will not be her reason; deep inside, Fran feels a twinge of regret. She asks DeAndre how he's making it, but here, too, nothing can pass for urgent. He's fine.

"Dre, you wouldn't believe it. This place a trip."

"Huh."

"I'm serious. When dope fiends first be gettin' clean, they get to talking all this high on life stuff. Drive you crazy."

"Yeah."

"Then they get past illin' and the next thing you know all them sex drives start comin' up . . ."

She's got his interest now. "Like what?"

"What you think? I swear, this place like a soap opera with people hoppin' around like damn rabbits."

DeAndre laughs.

"I'm serious. They gone crazy."

"That ain't you, Ma," he says. It's almost a question.

"Uh uh, I'm just sayin' how wild it is. I mean, you wouldn't believe what it's like in here." She tells him about all the rules. "It's like lockdown the way they got things. The way they keep on you."

"Yeah?"

"You comin' to the meetin' Saturday? Tell Scoogie to drive you and DeRodd down for the meeting. One o'clock. I want to see you. I miss you."

She's almost ready to give up the phone when she remembers:

"Andre, I need you to do something for me . . ."

"Huh."

"I need you to make a run for me."

A run. DeAndre is silent for a moment. "No, Ma."

Fran is taken aback. "Boy, you a trip! I'm tryin' to get my life together. I'm talking about cigarettes and maybe some candy. Those chocolate bars I like. They sayin' nicotine and chocolate are drugs too, but I ain't tryin' to hear that."

"Huh."

"I need you to put 'em in a bag and come by the alley on the side between three and four today. And when you see me, just toss it over the fence . . ."

DeAndre is laughing now. He's gonna do a drive-by with Newports and Mr. Goodbars.

"But don't throw it until you see me there. I got to make sure the counselor ain't watchin'. You got it? Between three and four, right? Dre, I love you. You love me?"

"Uh huh."

Later that afternoon, she's where she said she'd be, hard by the twelve-foot chain-link fence that encloses the detox center's rear yard. She keeps one eye on the back door and one eye on the alley, pacing impatiently until she sees a car turn from Schroeder Street into the alley. As it creeps closer, she sees her son in the passenger seat. DeAndre is slumped down and giggling.

"Toss it!"

As the car rolls past, DeAndre flings the small, white plastic bag. It catches the top of the fence and falls back into the alley.

"Damn," shouts DeAndre.

Now Fran is laughing. "That was sad."

Her son gets out of the car, runs to the bag and tosses it again before fleeing. It lands in a back stairwell, where Fran collects the candy and smokes, stuffing them down her pants. After a few minutes, DeAndre comes back to the fence.

"You look good."

"I feel good."

A counselor comes out the back door, sees them both by the fence and asks DeAndre to leave. For a moment, Fran feels queasy, as if the contraband has already been discovered.

"You know the rules," the counselor says. "You can't talk through the fence."

Fran backs away.

"She's my mother," DeAndre explains.

"I understand. But we got rules."

"See you Saturday," Fran reminds him. "I love you."

On visiting day, Scoogie brings DeAndre and DeRodd, showing up during lunch. Fran has held a table in the basement cafeteria for them and she lights up as the trio comes through the door.

"Hey, you!"

She embraces her brother, who tells her how proud he is and how much better she looks. She does, too: Her eyes have lost their yellow tinge; her hair is cut and styled for the first time in months. She's even picked up a few pounds; the deep hollows in her face are a bit rounded, though not even a week and a half of steady meals can make Fran Boyd look anything but thin.

"I remember how much better I felt after comin' in from out there," Scoogie tells her. "Eight years ago and I don't regret not one day."

Fran, for once, lets it slide. Today, all things are possible, even probable.

DeRodd takes in the surroundings; his mother is all over him, wrapping her arms around his waist, holding him to her side. A counselor offers him dessert and he's instantly absorbed in the geometry of an ice cream sandwich. She saves DeAndre for last.

"Hey, boy. Get over here."

Assured that no one he knows will see, he leans into his mother's embrace. Fran steps back to look, then hugs him again.

"You look so good to me."

DeAndre fidgets.

"I mean it," Fran says. "I'm seeing you with new eyes."

The four of them settle down to talk for a while, with Fran extracting promises from her children that they will stay for the meeting. Scoogie begs off, saying he needs to get his car into the garage again.

"You need a new ride," Fran tells him.

"I *been* needin' that," he says, getting up. "You keep on keepin' on, Fran. You on the right road now."

They embrace again and he leaves the threesome at the table. When DeRodd wanders off in search of a drink, Fran and DeAndre have a chance to catch up. She fills the silence with talking, with plans, with all kinds of optimism for the future.

"I'm not going back to Fayette Street," she tells him.

"I sure won't miss that house," DeAndre says. "Livin' there ain't been no joke."

He tells her how it's been these last few days at the Dew Drop. More of the same old thing, he says, but now Fran shakes her head bitterly at the stories, hearing the echo of corner happenings from the other side of the fence. DeAndre catalogues the absurdity:

"Ma, I knew not to put the snacks in the kitchen, but I thought if I hide them in the bedroom, I be all right."

But the bedroom door was kicked in. "Uncle Stevie or somebody went in there, took the cookies and Tastykake that I bought for DeRodd. I came back and everything was tore up."

"Whaa?"

"It was messed up. After that, I used the window. I pushed the dresser against the door and left the TV on loud so it'd be like I was still in there. And don't you know they still got me."

"They dope fiends," she tells him, showing her distance. "They just always that way. But I'm tellin' you, Dre, we not going back there."

She reaches into her purse.

"This is for you, Andre," she says, handing him a folded-over envelope. "Don't read it now. You read it later."

He pockets the envelope and looks around the room. Fran can see that something else is still unsaid. DeAndre looks at his mother, then at

DeRodd, who is chasing another young boy around the tables. He looks back at Fran and pouts.

"What?" she asks. "Why you lookin' that way."

"Ma," he says, and he actually manages to smile. "I need four hundert dollars. Reeka . . . um . . . Reeka pregnant."

"What you need money for?"

"Abortion."

Fran smiles. Tyreeka was showing two months ago; she's been pregnant for close to six months. An abortion is an impossibility. Her son, Fran guesses, is trying to run a game.

"Andre, where in hell am I gonna get four hundred?"

And that settles it: There will be no abortion. DeAndre will be a father at sixteen, Tyreeka a mother at fourteen. Fran will be a grandmother at the ripe age of thirty-six. In truth, all three of them wanted this child. For DeAndre and Tyreeka, a baby meant validation; for Fran, the grandchild would be a part of starting over. She would mother parents and child both.

"What does Reeka say?"

"She says what I tell her."

Fran shakes her head, smiles, lets him pretend for a moment.

"Really, what does she want?"

"She want to have the baby."

"Well then you ain't got a choice."

"It's my decision."

"Please," says Fran. "How many months is she?"

"She say the baby due 'round Christmas."

"She goin' for checkups, right? She seein' a doctor?"

"Her aunt got that covered."

She asks more questions, most of them dealing with prenatal logistics. Fran is on the case; this is her first grandchild, after all. She tells DeAndre to have Tyreeka call the detox pay phone.

"Boy, you gonna be a daddy."

DeAndre smiles, stretching his arms wide.

"I can't believe it," Fran says.

DeRodd returns to his chair. Up at the front of the room, staff members are putting a string of tables together. A counselor asks everyone to give him their attention. Fran pushes her seat closer to DeAndre.

"Listen," she tells him. "What they gonna say, they gonna say for you, too."

DeAndre shrugs and slumps back as the meeting begins in the usual fashion. "All right, people, Eric is gonna lead us in the twelve steps."

"Hey, my name is Eric and I'm a drug addict."

"Hey, Eric," the room chants in unison. "Keep comin' back."

He gives them the steps in the sing-song cadence that comes from rote memorization: ". . . that we were powerless over our addiction, that our lives had become unmanageable . . . We admitted to God, to ourselves and another human being . . ."

Another resident follows with the twelve traditions of Narcotics Anonymous, and by that time DeAndre is sullen and restless. This is flotsam and jetsam from someone else's shipwreck, with as much relevance to his life as English composition or social studies.

The leader runs quickly through the list of the chapter's business, then introduces the afternoon's speaker. He's stick-thin, aged beyond his years, his arms marked by old scars. His smile is open and expressive.

". . . so I'm standing on the back porch and I'm saying to her that I got to come in, that I just need some food, that I got a chance for a job if I can just get something in my stomach and get myself cleaned up . . ."

Fran nudges DeAndre. "He's good. He spoke once before."

"And she believes me, right? 'Cause I'm good, right? What can I say? Ain't no way a low-bottom dope fiend can be bad at lyin' . . ."

The meeting breaks into laughter. With the NA speakers, this business of capturing the universality of the corner is as much a gift as preaching or stand-up. Some speakers—those closer in time and distance to the pain—can't get past their personal details; the intricacies of their own disaster still leave them in awe. But others, like today's speaker, can make the leap to common ground. Sitting here now, no one listening in the BRC basement can stand apart from a truth revealed by shared experience.

". . . I mean, you all done it, too. You know you have. When you got to cry to get a blast, you cry. When you got to beg, you beg. When you got to lie, you lie, right? So I get in the house. I get in even after she told me I couldn't come back. And while she at the stove, making me a plate of chicken—and Mama could burn some chicken—I'm creepin'. I've got the clock radio and I'm outta there."

He shakes his head, laughing at the horror of it. Laughing because what the hell else can you do.

"And, people, this is my mother. This the woman who brought me into the world and raised me up and taught me right from wrong. I am a lowbottom dope fiend."

Even DeAndre is now showing some interest in the confessional. Fran is nodding her head, thoroughly engaged, her thoughts directed to a few dope-fiend moves of her own. For the first time in a long while, she lets in a lost memory from the days before she landed on Fayette Street, back when Gary's salaries were still paying for the party. She remembers and wonders about the old lady at that four-way stop. The poor woman was driving some churchgoing car; Fran was in the Mercedes, pulling up to the intersection at the same moment. The woman waved Fran forward, and Fran waved back. In the time that it took the lady to wave again, Fran had made up her mind. You first, she signaled, coaxing the woman out.

Then she stepped on the gas.

The collision money on the aging luxury sedan would have been payment enough. The insurance money from the lawsuit was icing on the cake. And Fran had crowned this crudball move by jumping from her wrecked car to verbally lash the old woman, convincing the lady it was her fault.

But now, listening to the thin man on the stage, Fran conjures the memory of the old woman's face. The entire scene comes back to her and provokes real shame.

Up on stage, the thin man is talking about sleeping in abandoned cars and breaking into houses and cheating his brother out of forty dollars. He's laying himself bare, and Fran, in the fourth row, is mightily tempted to do the same. When he finishes, the meeting winds down. Key rings are distributed to those with one day, one week, one month, and six months clean-time. The group then gathers for the serenity prayer. Fran drags her sons in the circle, hugging them.

"Thank you all," says the speaker as chairs are rearranged.

DeAndre stretches, yawns, looks toward the door. DeRodd wanders off to ask about a second ice cream sandwich.

"He was good," Fran says, "real good."

"Man, I seen him coppin' the other day from Drac and them on Gilmor," DeAndre deadpans.

"You a lyin' little boy."

DeAndre laughs. Visitation ends with friends and relatives making their good-byes and crowding the stairwell back up to the lobby. Fran gets a promise of another visit—this time with Tyreeka—and lets her children go after a long embrace.

"You got the letter?"

"Yeah."

"Okay then. I love you."

That afternoon, in the vestibule of the Dew Drop Inn, DeAndre pulls the envelope from his pocket and begins to read. He expected these sentiments from his mother—saw them coming at him like a runaway train—but still, the three handwritten pages allow him to hope, to believe a little bit in the things Fran is talking about. He steps into the sunlight, still reading, finding his seat on the steps without taking his eyes from the paper.

"Dear Black," it begins.

Not DeAndre, his given name. Or Onion, the baby name he suffered through. Fran begins with the courtesy of his favorite street name, the one he wants to hear. She follows the salutation with a smiley face.

I can call you Black today with a smile because I picture your handsome face when I say it. First, I would like to say that today I'm a much better person. You'll have a much better mother and best friend when I come home.

Andre, I love you so much I really don't know where to start making up for the neglect and pain I've caused you. I can't change the past. All I can do is accept it. But I can change to the best of my ability. This disease is so rough. I can't believe how many years I missed out of your life. It feels like 16 years ago, I asked my mother to watch you until I came from the store and I came back 16 years later and it hurts. Even though I've always been there for you, I also should have been there when you didn't need me just being your mother.

Dre, I never wanted to tell you this but you are my carbon copy. I don't have to explain that. I know why you sold drugs. I know why you had no respect for me, because I had none for myself. Even though my addiction allowed me to be stable enough to raise you the right way, I didn't give a *fuck*. What I mean is, you know right from wrong and how to respect people. I taught you that. But your attitude is so bad because I don't perform and give you the guidance that you deserve.

I have 2 beautiful sons to live for today. Andre, you are my one and only friend today. I really want you to listen to me very carefully from now on because I don't want you to end up dead or institutionalized as myself. I don't know what I would do without you. Leave that shit alone, please!!! Life is beautiful and natural and you may not get another chance. I love you and we need each other. You looked very handsome when I saw you in the yard. Baby please don't destroy your life. If you don't need yourself, I need you.

Your loving mother
  + best friend,
  Fran
  XXXXXXXXXX

She comes out on a fine September morning in that spirit, graduating on the twenty-eighth day with all the faith of the newly converted. She looks wonderful, too—ten pounds heavier, with a French-cut hairstyle, new denims, and big hoop earrings that are a gift to her from a fellow graduate. To everyone on Fayette Street, Fran looks like someone else entirely.

She means it to be so. Walking back up Fayette to the Dew Drop, her appearance almost puts a stop to business as the touts and fiends, runners and dealers draw a bead on this strange new entity.

"Look at you, girl," shouts Zena, Stevie's girl. "You shinin'."

They embrace and coo over each other long enough for the family to emerge on the steps. Stevie and his son, Kenny and Sherry—all of them heap congratulations on Fran for making the move, all offering the general sentiment that they would soon be doing the same themselves.

But Bunchie's greeting is the most heartfelt. Stepping out of the Dew Drop, she wraps her arms around Fran, peeling back to look at her again, then holding her in a swaying embrace for a long while.

"You did good," she says finally.

Fran is touched by the warmth, by the surprising willingness of her family to applaud her escape. She'll be staying up on Saratoga Street with Scoogie—he isn't happy for the boarder, but he doesn't dare refuse and leave her at the Dew Drop. Meanwhile Fran is looking for a place of her own. She's been asking around, reading the classifieds. She's also got a line on a Section 8 voucher apartment in the 1500 block of Fayette.

But all that can wait. Right now she's earned this triumph. She accepts compliments and plaudits from every fiend who stumbles up, promising any and all takers that she can talk to Antoinette for them, that if they want, they can get down to BRC and start on the same road.

The commotion finally brings DeAndre, shirtless and shoeless, out of the back bedroom and down the apartment stairs. He looks her over and manages a quick, affirming nod, carrying it all with an air of business as usual.

"Come here, boy!" Fran yells.

Finally her son's smile breaks wide.

"I need a welcome home."

Fran takes one last, long hug before going up the front stairs of the Dew Drop. But the apartment, and the bedroom in particular, seem like another world to her now. This is the hole out of which she climbed.

Bunchie's man, Alfred, lopes across the front room on his way downstairs from the upper apartment.

"Hey Fran."

Spoken as if she'd never really been away. As if she'd gone to the store or something. She stands there for a minute or two more, looking around, wondering why she bothered to come upstairs in the first place.

"Dre!" she shouts, making her way back down.

He's waiting in the vestibule.

"Just get what you need," she tells him. "I'll come back and pack the rest of it up later. I can't go in that place now."

She heads back out to be rescued by sunlight. She's on the steps where she spent all those hours, all those days and months and years, but now she can't imagine how she lived this way and how the rest of them continue to live this way.

She shakes it off and heads up the block, resuming her victory lap.

"Lookin' good, Fran," says Ronnie Hughes.

"Feelin' good," she answers.

She walks toward the corner store, passing R.C.'s sister, Darlene, who compliments her as well.

"Wish they'd take me," Darlene says, smiling.

"I can call for you."

"Would you?"

Fran buys a Snow-Kone from the Korean, then takes a quarter from the change to the pay phone beside the store. The plan is to get in touch with that lady from the rental agency, see if she can get one of the apartments in the 1500 block. It's only a block away on the same strip, but for Fran, having control of even two or three rooms would be a vast improvement.

"Is Miss Churchill in?"

She waits for a moment, breathing softly into the phone, watching the touts hustle a short line of souls into the alley across Mount.

"Can you tell her Denise Boyd called?"

The fiends pop out of the alley one by one, each of them serviced, each now bounding away.

"B-O-Y-D . . . Uh huh . . . Thank you."

She recrosses Mount, getting as far as the vacant house on the corner before Buster is at her heels, yapping like a crazed toy terrier.

"Gimme my shit! Gimme my shit! Gimme my shit!"

Fran laughs, thinking it's some kind of welcome-home joke.

"You took my shit! You took my shit!"

Fran glares at him incredulously. But she knows it's real now and keeps walking. In a moment, she's inside the Dew Drop's vestibule, with nowhere to go and Buster out on the stoop, barking like a mutt.

"She took my shit!" he yells.

His accusation brings the corner crowd running, creating a rogue's gallery of twenty or thirty bystanders intent on seeing a show. The Mount Street dealers arrive; Scar and Man and two or three others. Court is in session.

"She took my shit."

Fran steps out of the vestibule, facing the dealers down on the Dew Drop steps. "I didn't take shit. He lyin'."

Buster states his case. His vials were hidden in the pay phone coin return. Fran used the phone; the vials are missing. Ergo: "She got my shit. She got my shit."

Fran is disgusted, but also at a loss for what to say. She's no longer in the game; she no longer has the energy. She half sighs as she turns to her judges.

"I jus' came home clean. Twenty-eight days clean. You think I'm gonna come home and the first thing I'm gonna do is steal his raggedy-ass shit? You gone crazy."

DeAndre comes running down the stairs, a surprise witness, interposing himself between Buster and his mother. He stares the tout down, his nostrils flaring, his fists tight at his side.

The dealers look at DeAndre and Fran and Buster and don't know what to think. Maybe she took it, maybe Buster is running a game. In either case, it's neither the time nor the place.

"C'mon," says Man.

The dealers walk away. A hung jury.

Fran is shaken. She tells DeAndre to go back upstairs and finish getting those few things together. She's still out on the steps, gathering herself, when Darlene sidles up to offer comfort.

"Buster always lyin' like that," Darlene assures her. "He probably took the shit hisself."

"He doin' it all the time," says Fran. "But they all lookin' at me like the shit's in my pocket."

"Buster just tryin' to have someone to blame."

"I know it," Fran says. "He ignorant as shit."

Darlene wanders off and Fran needs exactly a minute to solve the riddle. If Darlene alone believes her innocent, then Darlene has reason to believe. The girl was over by the phone before Fran made the call; now she's here with me, being so nice. Sheeeet.

"Dre!"

He comes downstairs with a few items in a plastic bag.

"Goin' up Scoogie's," she says, standing up and dusting off her denims. "And I swear, I ain't never comin' back down here."

FALL

EIGHT

"I understand you been losin'," their new coach tells them. "Well my teams don't lose."

He pauses to let the idea echo through the gym.

"My teams don't lose," he says again.

On the bleachers, the Martin Luther King basketball squad falls into an uncomfortable silence. He has been talking for almost ten minutes now—longer by about eight and a half minutes than any previous coach has been allowed to talk. They are not accustomed to listening; they do it warily.

"My name, for those of you I don't know, is Derek Shorts. But I go by Pumpkin . . ."

Brooks and Manny Man stumble through the doors of the gym, Manny laughing and Brooks dribbling one of the rec center balls. "Hey, hey, hey," says Pumpkin.

Manny looks over. Brooks goes under one of the side-court baskets for a reverse layup.

"Hey," shouts Pumpkin.

Brooks gets his own rebound.

"You two on this team?"

Manny nods.

"Then get your ass over here right now."

Brooks takes another layup.

"Right now, got-dammit!"

Brooks lets the ball slide off his fingers and bounce aimlessly toward the other end of the gym floor. Intimidated if not entirely chastened, he braces himself with his standard smirk, then follows Manny onto the bleachers.

"My teams play a running game. We outrun everyone . . ."

As he talks, the squad remains silent.

". . . I was playing junior college and my knee went . . ."

Still silent.

". . . right now, I want to do this to put something back into the community . . ."

Not a word.

". . . and what I want from you is for you to listen when I tell you something and give me your best game. You do that and we're going to win games."

He talks for forty minutes straight, with the entire crew sitting quietly on the bleachers before him. He's full of all the usual coaching clichés—hard work, discipline, team—but they sit and listen nonetheless. He tells them about his days of college ball, about a career that almost came to be, about covering Patrick Ewing once in a tournament.

"What happened?" asks Tae, breaking the silence.

"With what?"

"When you went up against Ewing?"

Pumpkin shrugs. "He got a bucket or two. But he didn't embarrass me or nuthin'. It wasn't like I got embarrassed."

The boys look at each other, as if to ask whether to extend more than token credibility. If Pumpkin claimed to have powered past Patrick Ewing, they might be skeptical; saying he merely stayed up with the man gave the account a hint of possibility. Pumpkin must have been big enough for college ball; he's six-five, two-twenty, and he still has the hard build of a power forward. If he says he once played with Ewing, maybe he really did.

". . . but I don't want you if you ain't gonna listen. I'm not talkin' to hear my ownself talk. If I'm sayin' somethin', then it's because you need to hear it . . ."

On this first day, at least, they give him more consideration than they've allotted any previous coach. Pumpkin had come to Ella a week ago, fresh from a court date up at Wabash. He used to hang at Fayette and Monroe; the boys who were working the corners at the top of the hill knew Pumpkin well enough. Now he was on a court-ordered probation and looking to fulfill his community service requirement with something a little more tolerable than sweeping a street somewhere.

"All right then," he says in conclusion. "Let's start with ten laps around the court."

The grumbling starts. The boys look at each other. DeAndre offers a brief, profane comment.

"Ten laps," Pumpkin says. "Now."

"We usually just run a game," says Manny.

"Ten laps now. Last man runs twenty."

"Aw shit."

Tae and Dewayne bolt down the court, followed by the rest. All save for DeAndre, who can't bring himself to do anything but test the man's authority. He half-walks, half-jogs, letting himself be lapped by the others. Then he begins running—backward. He's lapped again.

"DeAndre."

Pumpkin is glowering.

"Run 'em right. You got twenty laps and if you don't want to run 'em right, you can take your ass home."

The others suppress laughter. DeAndre, too, breaks into a smile, turns around, and begins sprinting to catch up. He runs ten, tries to sneak off, and is caught by Pumpkin, who orders him back for ten more.

"Now," says the coach, "line up on this side."

Windsprints. Followed by weave drills. Followed by fast-break drills. Followed by foul shooting. On this Tuesday afternoon in September, practice has actually become practice.

Lord knows they're now ready for a little discipline, having played in the summer Cloverdale League under the M.L.K. Rec Center banner and lost every single game. From the Perkins Homes to Bentalou to Cherry Hill, squads from around the city took turns on Ella's fledglings, running them up and down the asphalt of Cloverdale Park. True, all the other teams had one or two ringers—some of them as old as seventeen or eighteen—playing behind the birth certificates of younger boys. But the Martin Luther Kings weren't precise about the age requirement either. Twin was seventeen, Truck was eighteen, and everyone else save for R.C., Brooks, and Manny Man, was past their sixteenth birthday.

It had been ugly and discouraging, and DeAndre gave up first, stalking off the court at the end of the first night's debacle, unwilling to return if it meant paying the fifty cents in league fines levied against him.

"Shit," he had shouted in the early minutes of the game, losing a rebound.

"Quarter fine on number six," declared the scorer, invoking the Cloverdale rule that put a cost of twenty-five cents per utterance on profanity.

"Number six, come here."

DeAndre crossed the court to the scorer's table.

"You owe a quarter for cursing," the league director explained.

"Ain't got it," DeAndre shrugged.

"You got to pay before the next game or you don't play."

"Man, fuck that."

"Fifty cents."

As far as Cloverdale was concerned, that was it for DeAndre. The rest of the team paid their fines and kept coming back for more, losing all summer long to teams from Flag House, Northeast, and lower Park Heights. They lost by thirty, by fifteen, by eighteen. Once, in a spasm of well-played basketball, they pulled even with a team that had pummeled them in an earlier tourney at the Flag project rec center. R.C. stole an inbound pass and they were up by two.

"Time out," yelled the opposing coach. "Call the time out."

The Flag House team regrouped. The Martin Luther Kings high-fived each other and went for Dixie cups of ice water. By the end of the quarter they were once again down by a dozen.

R.C. couldn't bear it. He played every game as if the past had no bearing on him, as if today, he would lace up, stretch his legs, and play the game of basketball that he was meant to play. Often, there would be glimpses of great ability—a steal, a perfect pass, a left-handed reverse beneath the bucket—but eventually the common denominator dragged at everyone's individual moments. The Hilltop boys weren't salvation enough, though Mike, Truck, and Twin played hard. Nor could R.C. get the collective engine up and running for more than a few minutes at time. The team still played run-and-gun: Tae, with graceful, no-look passes that simply sailed off the court; Dewayne, trying to dribble past both opposing guards, falling to his knees, still trying to handle the ball rather than pass; Brooks, heaving his prayerful off-balance jumper toward those unforgiving Cloverdale rims and getting only an angry, metallic brick-bounce for his trouble. R.C. fumed and cursed and paid the fines as two losses became four, then six and eight. Yet he never managed to let go of the idea that the next contest, or the next one after, would bring this rec center squad that first, elusive victory.

"They ain't better than us," he told Tae, walking home after another loss. "They just playin' more together."

They finished the summer league with a perfect 0–10 record. For the Cloverdale all-star game, Twin and Tae were chosen to represent M.L.K. Dewayne was livid; R.C. took it as an insult, too, but he carried it well. "I know my game is right," he told people.

The Cloverdale experience ended up souring some of the original team members. Manny Man, Dinky, and Brooks were drifting from the squad by the tourney's end, dismayed at losing playing time to the Hilltop boys; DeAndre, too, chose to miss most of the tourney over fifty cents and the insult to his First Amendment rights. But R.C. emerged from the summer of defeat by asking Ella about the team's chances for a winter league. Ella, though, had something even better: She had Pumpkin.

He had arrived in the wake of Cloverdale, talking about having learned a lesson and wanting to put something back into the neighborhood after months of slinging and using. He had a part-time job at the bar up on Penrose, but other than that he was available. Besides, he'd done this before, he assured her. Though Ella had seen Pumpkin up on Monroe Street, she was more than pleased. From her point of view, time on the corner did not automatically disqualify a candidate; if it did, two of every three males between eighteen and twenty-four would then be disqualified. She had a coach, and when Pumpkin brought his friend Timothy to practice, she had an assistant coach as well.

"You gonna run for me like you ain't run before," he tells them in that first, hard practice.

Only in the last forty-five minutes do they break it down and run a game. But here again, Pumpkin stops the action to lecture and demonstrate and, on occasion, berate players for courtside sins. He is loud—at times sympathetic in his approach, at times angry—but always loud. He is, on this first day, a center to a team for which the center could never hold.

When Manny Man telegraphs a pass and blows a three-on-one break, R.C. begins his usual rant only to find six-and-a-half feet of Mt. Pumpkin looming over him, telling him to shut up and play.

"You don't yell at him. You don't need to yell at him."

"But he ain't . . ."

"R.C., shut the hell up and play the game. You do your job, I'll do my job."

Two days later, at the second practice, Pumpkin and Timothy are late to the gym. The boys, accustomed to broken promises from the grown men and women of this neighborhood, resort to the usual sarcasm.

"Where Pumpkin at?" asks Dinky, arriving late himself.

"Up on the corner coppin'," says DeAndre.

They shoot around, run a game of fifty, then start to choose sides for a pickup contest. Finally, Pumpkin posts, storming through the door

with something less than an apology and an immediate demand that
they line up for windsprints.

"Tae, stop messin' and run 'em right."

For now, it doesn't much matter to them that their coach was, in
fact, up on the corner. It doesn't matter that there are days when Pumpkin
and Timothy both seem a little more wired and wild-eyed than usual.
If they're slinging, so be it. If they're getting high, that's their business.
Even more than Ella, the boys of Fayette Street have no interest in making
judgments about anything save for the basketball itself. Everyone slings.
Everyone gets high. And at this point, if Fat Curt himself came into the
gym, shouted them into submission, then showed them how to win a
basketball game, they'd probably run for Curt.

"Look up . . . Look up . . . Brooks, you got to look down court. You
had a man breakin' . . ."

By fits and starts, they fall into line, grumbling at the occasional
insults and humiliations but also comforted by the belief that they are
now part of something a little more real. After a couple of weeks, Pumpkin
brings in two ringers from one of his earlier teams—Tank and Tony—
both of whom are between seventeen and eighteen years old and are
full-time slinging down on McHenry Street. And the extra year or two
matters: Not only do Tank and Tony bring better skills to the Francis
Woods gym, they bring the calm certainty of corner veterans. They've
been out there long enough to be hardened off, to accept the truth about
where they're going and what they're going to get. All around them is
the huff-and-puff pretense of the manchild, of adolescents still holding
back a bit, caught in the no-man's land between commitment and fantasy.
But Tony and Tank have both been there; the bluster isn't necessary or
even remotely useful. When they go down to the corner, they go to sling,
not play; when they come into the gym to run a game, they run the best
game they've got. They carry themselves in absolute proportion to the
event, coming at it directly, with no quarter asked for or received. Bad
calls or jail time, bad passes or short counts—they deal with all of it by
corner rules; if the affront is big enough, someone gets hurt, and anything
less won't get cried over. Tank and Tony speak volumes to the younger
players without saying so much as a word. Their presence in the gym
makes everyone else choose between growing up or getting out. Suddenly
the rec center team—though no longer a strictly a sixteen-and-under
affair—is fast and lethal.

Of the original members, only Tae, Dewayne, and R.C. have the skill to play at the higher level; add the three from Hilltop and the future begins to look ominous for the likes of Manny Man, Dinky, and Brooks.

"It ain't our team no longer," says Dinky bitterly, leaving after the last practice he bothers attending. He came to the gym for the joy of it, for nothing more or less than physical release. Though his game wasn't as sharp as others', he knew where to find his points and rebounds in a slower, more casual version of run-and-gun. Now, for the purpose of winning, Dinky is expendable.

As Dinky goes, so goes his cousin, though DeAndre has pride enough not to be shunted aside without the proper flourish. Shortly after Tank and Tony are brought down to the gym, DeAndre finds a few obvious ways to violate the new standards of practice, and then, when Pumpkin finally explodes, he fires back.

"You ain't shit," DeAndre tells him. "I'm tired of your bullshit."

"Leave then," Pumpkin tells him.

DeAndre does, slamming the double doors behind him. What began as an afternoon distraction last winter—a three-day-a-week digression back to fading childhood—had become some kind of job, replete with demands and standards and bosses. DeAndre wants no part of it. Neither does Dinky or Brooks—both of whom join the boycott. With Boo kicked off the team by Ella for fighting, and Brian locked up in juvenile detention behind a drug raid on his mother's house, what's left of the original lineup can be counted on three fingers.

The changes in the Francis Woods gym press on the old C.M.B. loyalties. Manny Man, for one, can't understand why Tae and Dewayne and R.C. are willing to put up with so many newcomers at his expense. He used to play at least a couple quarters of every game; now his court time minutes are, well, minutes.

"It ain't even the rec team no more," he complains.

But Tae, R.C., and Dewayne aren't listening. They're finally playing basketball at a level that rewards effort. You move without the ball; you get the ball. You play defense; you get recognition and court time. You pull a rebound, outlet a pass and spark a breakaway, and as you scurry back on defense, Pumpkin is pointing you out for credit.

The talent gets so deep that R.C. is sometimes a third forward and sixth man, depending on Pumpkin's mood. But he's so exhilarated that the lost minutes don't matter. When he comes out on the court, he's instantly connected with this wondrous new machine, these half-dozen teenagers who manage, in their best moments, to think and act as a single organism.

When Ella finally gets them a game against Diggs-Johnson Middle School, they arrive to find thirteen- and fourteen-year-olds half a foot shorter than themselves. They dominate these children, running up the score even though Pumpkin holds out his best players, refusing to allow Tony or Tank or Truck to set foot on the gym floor.

"Man," says Tae, "they was too young. We need a real game. We need to get into a winter league."

In early October, they prove the point by once again hosting the old school in the Francis Woods gym, taking on Shamrock and Preston and the rest of the eighteen- and nineteen-year-old Fayette Street crew. This time, it's all the older boys can do to keep it respectable, to stay within fifteen or sixteen points of the Martin Luther Kings. For Ella's rec center team, it's a coming of age, a rite of passage for corner kids who have looked up at the likes of Shamrock and Preston their whole lives. Now, on the court, there is no discernible difference in their game; they've grown.

On the court, R.C. has the world as he's always wanted it. Against the older Fayette Street crew, he has sixteen points. He also has no clue once he steps off the hardwood floor. He has no job save for working other people's packages on McHenry Street, no interest in school, and no plan for anything beyond this down-at-the-heels recreation center squad. Night after night, he runs wild down on McHenry Street, slinging and messing with his boys and chasing girls with the abandon of someone for whom no other possibilities ever existed. He doesn't try to disguise the utter lack of direction in his life; if he ever speaks in future tense, it's the same old story about how his older brothers, Ricky and Bug, were going to get him into the maritime union in a year or two. And that alone—vague as it is—is enough to excuse whatever comes before it. R.C. can profess to a future; consequently, he can fuck up until the union card arrives.

R.C.'s latest girl, Dena, is now pregnant, too. Earlier in the fall, Treecee said she was pregnant by R.C. and, for a while, he was looking at two different babies coming at him from two different girls—a prospect that only increased his standing with the rest of his crew. But Treecee's pregnancy never materialized and R.C. chalked it up to jealousy over Dena's news. Dena, though, is gaining weight, and R.C. is quietly relieved. He might not be the first in the C.M.B. crew to get a girl pregnant, but he had worked hard to ensure he would not be the last.

In September, R.C. had followed the migratory pattern of the season, traveling to area malls to equip himself with supplies and material for the coming semester—not notebooks or No. 2 pencils or calculators or dividers, but new Nikes, sweats, some jewelry and—most important— a new telephone pager. In fact, the fall semester was only minutes old when R.C. got himself suspended for carrying the pager into the high school. Several years ago, the school system had banned beepers as artifacts of corner culture. Though he feigned ignorance of the rule, R.C. was fully aware of it. In fact, it was for that very reason that he brought the pager with him, then displayed it in front of a staff member, thereby solving the dilemma of what to do with the last remnant of his public schooling. He was nearly sixteen, close enough to his birthday that he could walk out of high school without regard to truancy charges or juvenile court.

But Rose Davis had no intention of allowing the pager issue to determine R.C.'s future. She'd worked in a city school long enough to read between the lines. That same day, she called R.C. into the office and told him that it wasn't a full suspension, that he only needed to go with his mother down to the school headquarters on North Avenue for a hearing before being readmitted. She also told R.C. that she didn't want him to come to the school gym for basketball practice if, in fact, he was truant on the same days.

R.C. responded to her words with a firm acknowledgment that he had heard and understood her.

"Yes'm," he said.

"So you're going to go down to North Avenue?"

"Yes'm."

"And I'll see you Monday."

"Yes'm."

"And I won't see you creeping into the gym after three o'clock when you haven't been in class all day."

"Yes'm."

"Say what?"

"I mean, no, ma'am."

"All right then."

His mother dragged him to North Avenue, the suspension was lifted, and R.C. never made another day of school.

In early October, Rose Davis catches sight of him going up the front hallway stairs in his sweats, palming a basketball, then finger-rolling it against the wall.

"R.C."

"Yes'm."

"Young man, I'm going to have to take you off the roll."

"Yes'm."

She looks at R.C., knowing that there is no place left to go with him, that there is nothing to be said or done to change or improve on a disaster years in the making. He's just a child, a big, insecure child, carrying his wounds and scars for all the world to see, and yet he's a finished product. The horror is he's content with this. She knows that he just wants to be left alone.

"You want that?" she asks him.

"No, ma'am."

"Then come in and see me," she offers. A tenth chance. An eleventh chance. Or maybe it's the force of habit that causes her to say such things. R.C. hesitates for a moment until Rose Davis goes through the front office door. He waits there with the ball on his hip to see if she'll toss him from the gym. When she doesn't—when she grants him the gym because at the least, it's not a corner—he jogs up the stairs, kicks open one of the metal doors, and spins for a jumper.

Manny Man and Dinky are there. Dinky tries to block the shot, but fouls R.C. on the forearm instead. The jumper falls.

"And one," he says.

DeAndre McCullough is first through the door when his mother turns the key, first up the stairs, and first into the big bedroom at the front of the second floor.

"This room mine," he says, staking claim.

"The hell it is," his mother counters.

"Ma, you said I get my own room."

"I didn't say it would be this one. Young as you are, you want to take the second-floor bedroom and have me runnin' up and down from the third floor all the damn day."

"Be good for you," assures DeAndre. "Good exercise."

"Boy, get yo' ass up them steps."

It's the third floor front for DeAndre, with DeRodd taking the rear bedroom across the hall. It may not be the biggest room, but it's his, his own space—a chance to stretch out and take control.

DeAndre walks from wall to wall in his new room, judging distances, imagining furniture and possessions that he doesn't yet own. He opens a window, leaning out the front of the rowhouse and scanning his new block all the way to Franklintown Road. A fall breeze rushes to greet him.

"Yeah boy," he shouts.

This three-story Formstone rowhouse will be home to the three of them only; shelter and salvation for the only residents of 1625 Fayette Street with heart enough to walk away. Fran won't go back to the Dew Drop. She's promised; and of all the vows she's made since coming out of detox three and a half weeks ago, this is one she has backed with precious check-day dollars. After three weeks at Scoogie's house, Fran makes this move to a place of her own, taking herself and her sons off the Fayette Street strip, down the slope past Hilltop, and up the next side hill to the middle of a block of small, three-story rowhouses named, appropriately enough, Boyd Street. The 2500 block of Boyd—no more than an alley, really—stretches between Franklintown and Catherine, just north of the Westside shopping center; it's far enough west to be out of the way of the corners that tempted her most, but it's really no farther from the drugs than the Dew Drop. Franklintown and Baltimore is a corner. So is Franklintown and Lombard. Catherine and Hollins is an on-again-off-again strip, depending on which crew is working which package. Still, it seems to Fran like a clean enough break with the past.

To DeAndre and his brother, three bedrooms to be divided among three occupants amounts to unthinkable luxury. They will be living as a family does—as DeAndre himself can remember living in those years before his father left and his parents both fell into the vials.

"We doin' good now, Ma," DeAndre tells Fran during that first night on Boyd Street. Their furniture, or what was left of it in the basement of the Dew Drop—a glass dining room table and woodblock chairs, a few mattresses and battered dressers, the dying green-tint television, and a wobbly chrome-and-glass bookshelf—every stick of it would arrive this weekend. Gary's brother, Cardy, had volunteered his pickup truck, but he didn't have a day off from the crabhouse until Sunday. Still, even with an empty house, they're too excited after getting the keys to stay at Scoogie's another night.

They sleep that night in makeshift bedrolls on the hardwood of the second floor, listening to the unfamiliar creaks and moans of joists and walls and the rattle of the front windows in the wind of a late September night.

"This house is right," DeAndre tells her.

"And we just startin'," she assures him.

Money was going to be tight. Fran had hoped to line up a Section 8 housing voucher after coming out of detox, but the waiting list for subsidized city housing was something like three years. As for hooking into a Section 8 development like the one down in the 1500 block of Fayette, where the rental company could itself get hold of a voucher or two, Fran lost out there as well. Her credit was shot: Ms. Churchill at the rental agency—the name in which she had put so much hope—couldn't help once Fran's credit report came back, the rental company wouldn't risk a voucher on anything but a solid rating. That left the want ads, where any place worth renting was at least three hundred, plus utilities.

Fran spent a day or two with the newspaper, hunting a bargain. Instead, a bargain found its way to her in the form of a phone call from an old friend, a woman who knew Fran from a brief stint when the two worked for the same temp agency, just after Fran lost the phone company job. Linda had stayed in touch with Fran, even rolling past the Dew Drop now and then to treat Fran to a meal. Having heard that her old girlfriend had cleared detox and was staying with her brother, Linda called Scoogie's house and offered a rowhouse that she'd inherited from a dead relative and had been trying to rent for weeks. Fran, in turn, gave Linda a little of the old-time's-sake, asking for a reduced rate while she tried to get on her feet again. Still, the rent on Boyd Street would be $255 a month—more than three-quarters of her monthly AFDC check.

The food stamps would keep them in groceries for most of the month. What little cash remained—seventy or so—had to buy everything else. That meant winter coats, athletic shoes, and denims; cigarettes, snacks, and the pay-by-the-month bus passes, which were now an essential item, for Fran especially.

Only a week after emerging from detox, in early September, she had taken another small step toward change by enrolling in courses at the city community college's Liberty Heights campus. Fran was going back to school on a Pell Grant, taking algebra and English composition at the city community college up on Liberty Heights, trying to get those first two course requirements out of the way so that maybe, in time, she could get a two-year degree in computers or health care or something that might mean real work. The English wasn't a problem, but the algebra was painful. Fran told herself that she would deal with it, that she was going forward one step at a time. She'd hit the books before the first test, maybe find a tutor if she still had trouble with all that x and y nonsense.

By early October, she was not only in a place of her own, but she'd been on the street thirty days without a blast, getting the one-month-clean key ring and all the bromides and encouragement she could stand at the Narcotics Anonymous meeting up at St. James. She missed getting high; every day, she missed it. But she kept telling herself she'd seen enough of bottom.

Then there was DeAndre. Her son, she knew, was watching.

Not that he made it obvious. What passed for encouragement or hope or fear in DeAndre's conversation was little more than a word or two, spoken in a quiet moment on the stairs or at the bathroom door.

"You look good, Ma."

Or: "You gain' back some weight."

Or, once: "Ma, I'm proud of you doin' what you doin'."

More than that, DeAndre was responding in kind, showing a little more fealty to the idea of family. At summer's end, he had slowed his weeding and drinking and carousing on McHenry Street. That was Fran's doing. She had continued to insist on a midnight curfew, telling DeAndre that he needed to do one of two things to earn his keep on Boyd Street.

"Either you going to school or you getting a job," his mother told him. "You ain't gonna stay here, eating and sleeping and running the streets to all hours. You gonna school or you gonna work."

After again testing her with one or two late nights—and once finding himself locked out of the Boyd Street rowhouse—DeAndre seemed to concede his mother's newfound authority.

During the early part of September, as his mother was looking into the community college, DeAndre had checked in with Rose Davis only to learn that he was still a ninth-grader at Francis Woods. Professing disgust, he did not immediately go back to class. A few weeks later, however, with his mother continuing to press him, DeAndre returned to the school, asking Miss Davis if he could take work home from his core-class teachers, maybe do enough to move toward his high school degree as a kind of work-study type of thing.

"Are you working?" she asked him.

"Looking for work," he told her.

So DeAndre's teachers prepared home assignments that he would occasionally pick up and occasionally complete. This was the school system's most tenuous hold yet on DeAndre McCullough, though Rose Davis readily agreed to home study, presumably because it was better than the alternative.

In the first days on Boyd Street, DeAndre made a show of doing some of the schoolwork at the kitchen table, assuring his mother that he, too, was trying. Fran, however, was not entirely convinced. She saw him labor over one assignment only to find the papers forgotten a few days later beneath a stack of skin mags in his bedroom. Nor did her son seem to be on the hunt for a job.

As to the nights on McHenry Street, Fran gave him some credit for upholding the curfew and respecting her. The change in the weather itself hadn't brought the C.M.B. crew off the McHenry Street strip; the boys were now of an age to ignore the school semester entirely and sling drugs into the dead of winter if they chose. But DeAndre continued his low-profiling, telling his crew he needed to be home when his child was born, and he somehow managed, night after night, to throw himself off McHenry Street by half past eleven, arriving on Boyd Street a half hour later.

Finally, at the beginning of October, as Fran was laying out the first full month's rent to Linda, her son actually started making noises about pitching in with his own roll—helping his mother with the gas bill or the rent money, maybe putting some food in the refrigerator at the end of the month.

He'd been only halfheartedly looking for a paying job since the fiasco at McDonald's in the summer, making a few random rounds of the area dollar stores and fast-food emporiums. He'd filled out applications at some of the temp places, too, and tried a few of the clothing and shoe stores at Westside and Mt. Clare Junction. Once, he'd even taken a shot at the Inner Harbor, going all the way downtown to fill out an application at the Pizzeria Uno at Harborplace. But there, as everywhere else, his bottled-up, monosyllabic performance soured the assistant manager, who took DeAndre's insecurity as evidence of chip-on-the-shoulder sullenness. There was no call back, no second interview, nothing by which he might justify a clean break with whatever limited money he clocked from the McHenry Street trade.

In early October, though, DeAndre walked into the Wendy's at Westside and from the start, it was altogether different. The manager and staff were entirely black, putting DeAndre at some ease. He even knew some of the other kids working the grill. But most of all, he felt desperate enough for the job to go to the counter with his heart on his sleeve, looking the lady manager in the eye and telling it true.

"I need a job bad."

She had an opening. And she spared DeAndre the prolonged process of application and interview that never failed to play out both his confidence and patience. She said she'd give him a chance; he only needed to come back the next week and bring both a birth certificate and social security card.

"Get my uniform next week," he tells Fran proudly.

DeAndre would be bussing tables and cleaning up and, if that went well, he might learn to work the grill or maybe a register.

"What you gonna do about school?" Fran asked.

"Gonna do that, too. Gonna keep up with my assignments."

Soon enough, pride in the family runs both ways. When DeAndre gets the uniform—blue pants, blue-striped top, blue-and-white hat— he fairly parades through the front room and kitchen of the rowhouse, and Fran is looking at DeAndre with unalloyed wonder. At this moment, he's no longer of and about the corner. She's been telling him to do right, and now, he's actually listening.

"You look good."

DeAndre laughs and adjusts the hat amid his dreds.

"You turnin' back into my child again."

"Please."

"I'm serious, Dre. You actin' right."

"Ain't no child. You can stop callin' me a child."

"You a man, huh?"

"I'm a workin' man. I'm gonna show you by helpin' out with the bills," he tells her. "But first thing is I got to save enough for a bassinet. Maybe some clothes and toys and stuff. Reeka expecting me to come up with something."

The baby is due around Christmas, or so Tyreeka says.

For nearly three months now, the baby had kept DeAndre half thinking in the future tense, but, as usual on Fayette Street, nothing had come of such thoughts. Now, his mother's detox and recovery had given him Boyd Street and a leasehold on ordinary life. Now, there seemed to be room enough for a dream or two.

The plan was practically epic, calling for a job, a girlfriend, a son, and ultimately, a place of his own. In his mind's eye, DeAndre could see himself slinging Wendy's doubles and triples and saving enough of his pay to take care of Tyreeka and the baby. Maybe buy a car, too. And then move out into an apartment with his new family. Not right away, but in time; the first thing was getting a job, and now the first thing was set.

Next was Tyreeka. Fall had arrived, and DeAndre, true to form, was done playing dog. He wanted his steady girl. But from what DeAndre had seen since the summer, everything Tyreeka said on those warehouse steps had been true. She was having his child, but from what he'd seen, she wasn't having him. In fact, she'd kept more distance from him in the last few months than any time since they'd met more than a year ago—and no wonder, since she'd caught him messing with other girls so many times he'd lost count. As alone and frightened and pregnant as Tyreeka was, she had, over the summer, acquired enough hurt and anger to quit him. She was back in school, living with her aunt up on Riggs Avenue on the other side of Route 40, coming down bottom to visit the Fayette Street boys less and less.

He'd called her a couple times before Labor Day, but she played cold. Then he'd seen her once down on South Fulton. Tyreeka was hanging with R.C.'s girl, Dena, and the rest of that crowd. DeAndre reasoned that if she came down to the old neighborhood, she must be hoping to meet up with him.

"Lemme holler at you," he said.

"You can holler all you want. I don't care."

"Wait up, Reeka. I'm talkin' to you."

Back in the winter, when he'd been locked up, she'd come down to Boys Village to stand by him. Back in the spring, he'd held her heart in his hands while chasing half the girls on the strip. Now she was making him work, playing him off, and by the end of the encounter on Fulton, it was DeAndre who had to give up the front, who was reduced to professing true love and asking for a second chance. Tyreeka heard him out, arms crossed, smug, and said she'd have to think it over.

DeAndre paid the price, figuring that if she was thinking it over, he was sure to win her back. He knew Tyreeka loved him—he'd been her first and only—and she'd be with him again soon enough. In DeAndre's mind, she'd taken him back so many times before that the pattern was fixed. Just his luck that a few days later, she came back down to the strip and caught him hanging with some other young thing from Gilmor Street. He blustered and insisted on his innocence, but Tyreeka wasn't so young anymore. She rolled out, and when he called her at home that night, she cussed him and hung up.

But now he has a job, a plan. Now he's a working man. DeAndre knows that all he needs is to show Tyreeka that blue Wendy's outfit. She'll see he's trying. She'll find reasons to believe.

"Ma, you gonna talk to Reeka?"

"Yeah, I need to talk with her."

"When?"

"Why'nt you tell her to come down this weekend?"

"You tell her. We ain't talkin'."

"You ain't talkin'? She got your child, don't she?"

"She actin' like she don't wanna have a damn thing to do with me."

He leaves it to Fran, knowing that his mother wants everything to do with the grandchild. Fran is ready to mother Tyreeka, to coach her through the birth, to make her as much a part of the family as possible. The next weekend, Fran has no trouble convincing Tyreeka to come down and visit for a few days on Boyd Street. The pretext is a heart-to-heart about motherhood and Fran's insistence on helping with the baby, but for DeAndre and Tyreeka both, the subtext has nothing to do with Fran.

On his first pass, DeAndre acts as if he didn't even expect to see Tyreeka down this way.

"Well I ain't here to see you either," she tells him.

"Oh, you come all the way down here just to see my mother."

"Yeah."

"Shheeeet."

On the second pass, with Fran down at the Farm Fresh picking up groceries, DeAndre comes back into the house, sits next to her at the kitchen table, and listens quietly as Tyreeka talks on about all the things she'll be needing for the baby. DeAndre takes the cue, telling her almost too casually that he's got a job now. He'll come up with the bassinet and some other things too. He'll do what's right.

"You know I'm done with Shanelle," DeAndre tells her.

Tyreeka looks doubtful.

"Man, we *been* broke up," DeAndre insists. "I ain't got nuthin' more to do with that girl."

"Dena says . . ."

"Dena don't know shit. I ain't been with Shanelle since, like, I don't know when."

DeAndre tells her how it's different now, how she can come down here to Boyd Street and live with them if she wants. She and the baby.

He tells her that he's ready, that he's done all his dogging, that he's here
for her and the baby. And Tyreeka does what she always does. She comes
back.

They spend that Saturday night upstairs in DeAndre's room. Fran
lets it happen because what the hell else should she do; besides, it isn't
as if Tyreeka could get any more pregnant. By morning, DeAndre is
calling Tyreeka his girl again, and Fran is calling her daughter. That week,
the three of them get a ride up to Sinai Hospital for a last sonogram,
to ensure that everything is as it should be. Since July, DeAndre has been
referring to the child-to-be as his son, declaring that it has to be so
because he has no use for a daughter. But coming out of the exam room
on this rainy fall afternoon, his face is locked rigid, his expression a
perfect blank as he strolls toward his mother in the visitor's lounge. Fran,
hoping for a girl, picks up on it.

"Well?" she asks hopefully. "A girl, right?"

DeAndre tries to hold the empty look but can't. His face crumbles
into adolescent laughter.

"You got a son," says Fran flatly.

"Damn right I got a son."

"You so got-damn lucky it make me sick."

"My boy gonna be a roughneck too. He was jumpin' all over that
television screen. He doin' backflips and all, kickin' and punchin'. My
boy not takin' too much shit."

"Puh-leeze."

"Ma, you shoulda seen him. He was rockin'."

"He a little gangster, huh?"

"He was freakin'. He gonna be worse than his father."

For a time, the prospect of a child seems to give both order and
possibility to their lives. For Tyreeka, it's high school on the weekdays,
then down to Boyd Street on the weekend to play house with her
boyfriend. And by late October, she's as heavy as Fran can imagine her
getting. If late December is the due date, then DeAndre isn't overstating
the case by much: Junior is definitely a roughneck.

For his part, DeAndre is giving the Wendy's gig his best shot. He's
working afternoon and evening shifts; sometimes, he's back in the kitchen
area, but usually he's out in front, cleaning tables or keeping the salad
bar straight and stocked. He wants to make the most of it, but there's no
getting around the sheer boredom involved—particularly since business
is slow at the Westside franchise. Still, he's working hard, especially for

one of the assistant managers, a younger man with whom DeAndre had quickly connected. But the lady manager aggravates him—she insists that he do things a certain way and she is unwilling to give him more than a handful of four- or five-hour shifts every week. And DeAndre needs hours. He needs money.

When he finally complains, the manager grows colder, offering only criticism. The assistant manager tries to shield DeAndre, to cajole him into giving the franchise his best work regardless of the growing hostility between him and the manager. It works for a while, but eventually the lady manager gets the ammunition she's been seeking.

It happens a little more than three weeks on the job, when DeAndre is confused about the weekend schedule and misses a Saturday, thinking he is supposed to work the following day. When he shows up Sunday afternoon, he's told that he was needed the day before and that he can go home because there is a full complement ready to work the Sunday dinner shift.

DeAndre stalks off angrily, returning Monday to learn that he has no hours until at least Wednesday. When he calls the next day, he's told that Wednesday and Thursday are filled. On Friday, he goes to get his paycheck and find out when he'll be working next. The lady manager says she'll call.

But she doesn't call and he doesn't work the weekend. He's shut out on Monday, too. On Tuesday, he's given a few hours, but sent home early. It's the same on Wednesday.

"I can't make it on this kind of money," he tells his mother. "I ain't tryin' to get locked up, but I need real money."

A week more and it's clear that he's out of work. DeAndre sulks for a day or two, then goes back down to McHenry Street, staying out until the early morning hours with Tae and Dinky.

Fran catches him in his bedroom the following morning, counting cash.

"You got a roll, huh?"

DeAndre shrugs, looking guilty.

"You back to slingin' then."

He explodes, railing against the accusation, declaring that the money is payment on a debt Dinky and Dorian owed him from summer.

"Who the hell you think you foolin'?" Fran asks, walking away. "You think I'm going to believe you ain't hustling when you out all night long?"

DeAndre ignores her, staying out the next night and the night after. Fran locks the door and her son spends the next night on Scoogie's couch. When he shows up again the following afternoon, Fran shouts him down, assuring her son that he will not stay on Boyd Street unless he's working a straight job or attending school.

"I am in school," he protests.

"Andre, you ain't even doing what little work they sending you. I swear, you must think I'm stupid."

DeAndre pouts.

"You either get your shit together or you get out. You want to hustle in the street, you can live in the street then."

Fran leaves the house, slamming the door behind her. When she returns an hour later, she's even angrier than when she left. She's off drugs. She's in school. She's trying. For once in her life, she has the high ground with her oldest son, and she intends to keep it.

"You pack up your shit yet?" she yells from just inside the front door. DeAndre sits at the kitchen table, his back to her, smoking a Newport.

"You hear me?"

He says nothing.

"Boy," she yells, "I said do you hear me?"

She stalks into the kitchen, ready to slap the back of her son's head, ready to throw his ass out onto Boyd Street.

"Boy . . ."

Through the curl of cigarette smoke, Fran looks down and sees a short-answer quiz on American government. DeAndre is halfway through and still writing. And just beneath the quiz is a vocabulary assignment, neatly completed.

At the sight, Fran grows more furious than ever.

"Boy," she shouts. "Don't you play me like that!"

DeAndre looks up, the picture of academic earnestness. "What?" he asks her. "What now?"

Fran can't think of what else to say. She storms upstairs, slamming her bedroom door. DeAndre waits a few moments more, making sure his mother isn't planning another angry sortie down the stairs. Then he collects the school papers—finished and unfinished—and slides them into his social studies text. He steps into the living room, slips the book beneath the small pressed-wood stereo table, and grabs his coat. He heads out into the street.

*   *   *

Ella Thompson is outside on the rec center blacktop, laying claim to her playground on a chilly October afternoon. The youngest children are clustered around the center steps, using lined notebook sheaves to make paper airplanes. The girls are at the sliding board or on the four-square court, arguing about whether New Jersey is a city or a country, and, if it's not a city, whether Tosha has to go back to square one. The boys use the long end of the blacktop to play touch football. Disadvantaged in so many ways, Little Stevie, Daymo, T.J., and the others are at a further loss for having grown up Coltless. The Baltimore NFL franchise fled town in 1984; T.J. wears a Washington Redskins sweatshirt, and Daymo, when he catches a long pass, declares himself to be the 49er's Jerry Rice in the end zone.

Ella watches their game with one eye and monitors the girl's four-square argument with the other. With her third eye, she sees Old Man nine years old and already a corner prodigy, using a disposable lighter to authenticate a crash-and-burn stunt for a younger boy's paper plane.

"Old Man," she shouts. "What are you doing?"

The boy looks up blandly.

"Give me that lighter."

"What lighter?"

Ella stares him down. Old Man goes into his pockets and gives up the contraband. A year or three more and he'll know to hug the wall and make the knockers search his pockets. No sense giving it up if you're going to take the charge either way.

"You know better than that," Ella tells him.

Old Man shrugs and hitches up his denims, looking for fresh entertainment. Across the blacktop the football game is at an impasse.

"Third down," shouts Little Stevie.

"Fourth," says Daymo.

"This fourth down now," Stevie insists.

"You ran it once and threw twice, yo," argues Chubb.

Little Stevie calculates.

"Bitch, you cheatin'," Daymo says.

Now, according to the industry standard, Stevie has to get in Daymo's face and mug for him. The two are standing eye-to-eye on the blacktop, leaning into each other, grimacing. Ella watches for signs of genuine hostility, but can see only the usual bluster. She lets it go.

"Steal 'em, Stevie," says T.J.

Their faces are inches apart. Finally, Stevie starts to laugh, shoving the challenge away. Daymo takes a quick, open-handed swipe at his friend's head and misses.

"Fourth down," he insists.

"Yo, this fourth," says T.J., assuring his teammate.

"Fourth then," says Stevie, now indifferent. He hikes the ball to himself, backpedals, and overthrows a wobbly pass to Tremaine at the corner of the asphalt. The boy barely gets one hand on the ball.

"Boy," shouts T.J. "I was open!"

Another argument ensues; the game dissolves in rancor. Bored by the argument, Daymo wanders over to the fence, gripping it with both hands, pressing his face to the cool metal.

"Yo," he says, "check it out."

Across the vacant lot, a battered gray Buick is parked on the close side of Mount Street. Two men are sitting in the front seat. Not talking. Not moving. Just sitting.

"They been there like all morning," says Stevie.

"Stickup boys," pronounces Daymo. He's ten; he surely knows a stickup crew when he sees one.

"Must be," agrees Stevie, a year older. "Five-oh don't drive no off-brand car like that."

"They steady watching that boy Mike's house," says T.J., naming one of the younger Mount Street slingers. "They see Mike comin' up the block and look out—there be drama then."

Ella's kids gather at the fence, third- and fourth- and fifth-graders watching for God knows what to happen. The two men in the car do seem to be waiting on something at the rowhouse across the street. Some of the boys from Baltimore and Gilmor have been going in and out of the place for weeks now.

"They gonna hit that stash," says Daymo.

The boys watch for a while longer, with Little Stevie creeping down the alley walk to get a better look through the windshield. He comes back to affirm the rumor.

"They stone stickup boys."

Slowly, the talk ripples across the playground, from the older boys to the younger ones, then to the girls gathered around the far edge of the blacktop. Soon eight-year-olds are whispering to seven-year-olds about the parked Buick.

Of course, the playground tales get more elaborate as the afternoon wears itself out. The men in the car are not just a local stickup crew;

they're New York Boys come all the way down here to Fayette and Mount to settle a debt. Or maybe some of the gang from Lexington Terrace, coming up the hill from the projects to avenge some insult.

"What if they start shooting right now?" asks Clarice, biting her thumbnail. "I mean, what if they was shooting at us?"

Stevie loses patience. "Why they gonna shoot at us?"

"I'm sayin' like they start shooting and the bullets be comin' this way at us."

"Man," says Daymo, "my ass would be on the ground."

"My ass would be 'round the block," counters Stevie.

"My ass would be in China somewheres," says Tremaine, finishing it off. The girl laughs.

T.J. narrows his eyes to slits as he folds his arms across his chest. Gangsta chill. "Yo, I'd have to shoot back."

"Man, please," says Daymo, disbelieving.

"Man, you think I won't when I will. I go home and get my nine out and light them boys up."

Clarice giggles and T.J. tries to slap at her. She ducks and runs back toward Ella, who is sitting on the rec steps, patiently explaining to one of the younger children why there are rules against taking the board games outside.

". . . if you take the games outside and lose the pieces, then we won't have them to play with."

"But I won't lose the pieces."

"Tyree, please. It's a rule."

Tyree sulks and Clarice uses the pause to blurt out the news. "Miss Ella," she says. "Those men in the car is stickup boys. They gonna start shooting."

Ella looks over at the Buick and shakes her head.

"Clarice, you do not know that."

"Daymo says . . ."

"Daymo does not know that either."

The girl drifts off, leaving Ella to stare at the Buick for a few moments more. She has been at the Martin Luther King Jr. Recreation Center for three years now, long enough to recall a half-dozen horrible moments when she was running across this same patch of asphalt amid the crackle of gunfire, trying to herd her charges back into the cinder-block building. At any moment, the gunplay can happen. But if every rumor is given credence, no children would ever be playing anywhere near Fayette Street.

The men in the Buick are waiting for something, she tells herself, but that could mean a dozen different things. She keeps the children outside.

Now that the mayhem of the daylong summer camp sessions is finished, now that the hot months have given way to fall, Ella is regaining some piece of mind. The early darkness and cooler weather seem to slow the neighborhood just a bit or, at least, to make the corner world seem less intrusive. It has made it possible for her to see things from a new perspective.

A lot of that, she knows, has to do with Kiti. Three weeks earlier, in late September, her youngest left Baltimore for California. She didn't know much about where he was headed, but what she knew sounded good to her: Kiti would be in Long Beach, which she saw as a picture postcard of palm trees and water, and he would be in the care of his older brother, Tito. Whatever Long Beach was or wasn't, she could not imagine that it was home to the kind of struggle found on her doorstep. In some mythical place called California, Kiti Perry—her child of solitude, her quiet dreamer who had passed through adolesence holding himself in check—would surely find room to breathe deep and live.

The original plan had been for her son to take his best friend with him, but Preston had neither the money nor the will to make the jump. For Ella, at least, it was just as well. There was something about Preston that she found discomfiting, something that smelled a little too much like the corner. She had seen enough of Preston in the days before Kiti left to sense some sway that the boy had over her son. Ella knew Preston was on the corners with Shamrock and Kwame; she had worried for him and prayed for him. In the last few weeks Preston had come up out of the game, hanging with Kiti, clinging to his old schoolyard friend as if to a touchstone to ward off the inevitable temptation, but Ella had her doubts.

For most of the summer, the two young men had plotted their joint escape to California. Preston would go back to school for his general equivalency diploma, get a part-time job, save enough to get on the plane with Kiti. When none of that happened, the plan was amended so that Kiti would go out there first, get a job, get settled, and then come back to visit his mother during the Christmas holidays. By New Year's, Preston would have enough cash to go with him.

That was still the plan. Yet Ella was skeptical. For one thing, Kiti had called the week before to say that he wouldn't be coming back for the holidays; Tito had gotten him a job with the telephone company, and at this point, he didn't have time enough to be taking vacation. For another thing, Preston was looking rough. She'd seen him yesterday with DeAndre and Kwame at the bottom end of Vine Street—the three of them sharing two forty-ounce malt liquors and looking over the Fulton Avenue corners as if they had some stake in the action. Since Kiti had left, Preston had stopped coming around to see Ella, and when they passed in the street, he seemed bleary-eyed and impatient, offering very little in the way of real conversation.

She'd known about the drinking, of course. Before he left, Kiti had been sharing forties with his friend more nights than not, the two of them together on the stoop or on the small garden wall at the corner house on Fulton. She knew about the weed, too. Two weeks before Kiti took off, he and Preston and Jamie had gone down to Harbor Park for a late movie only to find themselves in the Central District lockup by night's end.

The way Ella heard the story, the boys had been sitting on a curbside outside the theater, drinking beer from paper bags, when Preston took out a half-smoked blunt and lit up. Minutes later, on the way into the theater, the three of them were jacked up against the wall by a uniformed officer. More police arrived and one of them searched Preston, finding the blunt. He looked at the small bit of weed, then over at Kiti, then toward the other police, who didn't seem to pay him any mind. Then the cop dropped the weed back into Preston's pocket—a charitable act and, perhaps, an acknowledgment that a half-smoked blunt meant precious little to anyone in Baltimore's drug war. But the cop who had originally pulled them up was less casual; he searched all three of them carefully, rediscovered the contraband for which they had already received absolution, then charged Preston with simple drug possession. Jamie and Kiti took open-container charges for the beer.

By West Baltimore standards, it all seemed innocent enough to Ella, and Kiti was able to win an indefinite postponement of the case before his trip to California. But Ella still couldn't help being a little concerned. Kiti had never been in any kind of trouble before, and though the downtown arrest meant next to nothing once it washed up as a district court misdemeanor, it gave Ella a vague sense that Preston, for all his talk about starting anew, was still trouble. When she saw the boy hanging down on Fulton, she felt even more relieved at Kiti's escape.

Mostly, she credited God with her son's deliverance, just as she gave praise to Him for Kiti's older brother and sisters. All of her children—

save for Pooh, of course—had graduated from high school. All had respect for people and for themselves. All knew how to work hard and hold down a job. But Kiti's escape—coming as it did in the years since Fayette Street had collapsed into a string of drug markets—marked for Ella the end of a long, dangerous arc. Even more than the rec center, Ella's own children were the essential victories to be claimed.

Now, sitting in the fading light on the rec center steps, watching the just-might-be-stickup-boys watching the house across the street, Ella Thompson feels as if her son's departure has truly liberated her. Whatever else these streets manage to do, whatever else they produce in the way of human disaster, they can no longer lay claim to any more of her children. Anything less than that could be, as a matter of proportion, easily suffered. Today, it's the men in the car on Mount Street, bringing the game to the very edge of Ella's sanctuary. Last week, it was the Death Row crew setting up shop in the alley on the other side of Mount, the tester lines forming every morning in full view of the children. Last month, it was Dinky, racing around Lexington Street in a stolen Buick, trying to hide his face with one hand and control the car with other, looking away furtively as Ella stared him down from the sidewalk. Or R.C. on the day after that, standing among the touts and slingers at Mount and Fayette, leaning into the windows of passing cars, serving up vials. Two weeks from now, it will be DeAndre, showing up drunk at the Halloween dance, glowering at the younger girls, then throwing candy corn at Tae and Manny Man, until he gets bored and leaves.

At all points, the corner continued to encroach on her small domain, claiming the sixteen- and seventeen-year-old boys she had nurtured at the rec center. She was losing them, one after the next. Boo was slinging down on Ramsay Street. Brian was back home from Hickey School, selling his uncle's coke two blocks away. R.C. was working a package on Mount Street; Tae, Dinky, Manny Man, and Brooks were down at Gilmor and McHenry most every night. And the girls? Tyreeka was pregnant at fourteen. Tosha's mother was ordering her inside every night to keep her away from the boys. Neacey was now hanging with some of the younger Monroe Street dealers; Ella had seen her up on the corners flirting, working hard for attention.

She is losing them—or so it seemed from the concrete steps of the Martin Luther King Jr. Recreation Center. From there, the view was all cruelty and waste and misadventure.

"Yo, Miss Ella," says Little Stevie, walking over from the fence. "Them stickup boys must be gettin' tired from the wait. I'm gonna go up and ask 'em who they waitin' on."

"No you ain't," says T.J. "You way more scared than that."

Stevie Boyd sneers at T. J., who raps him on the top of his head. Stevie swings out with a late, errant roundhouse.

"Stevie," says Ella, "you do not know that they are stickup boys. You don't know what those men are about."

"Why they just sitting there then?" asks Daymo.

Ella rolls her eyes. "Just leave them be."

Stevie picks up the football, waits until T.J. isn't looking, then fires a bullet at the older boy, hitting him in the shoulder. T.J. chases him around the blacktop, catching him and gripping him in the tightest of headlocks.

"C'mon," says Daymo, bored again. "Let's play."

They choose up sides and run yet another game on the cracked and glass-strewn blacktop. The game's highlight comes when Daymo picks off a pass and takes it all the way to the other end of the asphalt for what proves to be the last touchdown.

Ella gets up from her perch, calls her troops inside, and begins handing out a choice of snacks: potato chips, pork-rind wafers, or those orange crackers with the peanut butter in the middle. T.J. tries his usual trick of holding both his hands out in the grasping throng of children, trying for an extra snack.

"T.J.," says Ella, glaring. "Grow up."

He mugs at her.

"Then you don't get any," she tells him.

He picks the pork rinds.

Three years from now, these younger ones will be lost as well—most of them anyway. Even Ella Thompson, with her ceaseless capacity for hope, can gauge and measure the unremitting probabilities.

Yet with Kiti now gone, what can the probabilities do to her? Ella herself was secure enough in her Fayette Street apartment. No one bothered her there once she shut and locked her door. No one went out of their way to trouble her personally when she walked the street. Her gray Olds was parked at the bottom of the block all night, every night, and she noted with some pride that it had never been misused.

Watching the children grab at her snacks and wriggle into their coats, she actually feels secure enough and necessary enough to conjure some argument to the probabilities. True, the future for these children might already be written: The corner, and precious little else, is there for them. Yet within that certainty, Ella could still win something for those who wander in and out of her center, something that might survive the corner game and still be there, latent but ready, when some of these children, a handful perhaps, emerge from addiction or prison or both. Even among the hardest and coldest of her charges—DeAndre and R.C., Dinky and Tae—she could see the outline of a social compact, a core value that on some level obliges gangsters-to-be to acknowledge that there were some people in this world who keep their promises, who care about what you do and who you become. When so many of them were ready to believe— often with every justification—that the world had no use for them, Ella had insisted on welcoming them. She saw things precious in all of them, something worth her time and love.

Even among those lost to the streets, Ella's gift amounted to a small kernel of self-worth, a little bit of soul that might matter at some future moment when the worst deeds are being contemplated. Just then, the thought of Ella and the rec might come upon them, arguing against the worst excess and brutality and indifference. So that when R.C. and Manny are on Mount Street touting, it might be Ella's work that stops them from waving vials in the faces of children and older people. And when DeAndre is out hunting with Shamrock and Kwame, a youthful stickup crew looking to rob slingers in some other neighborhood, it might be what Ella taught at the rec center that prevents DeAndre from compressing the trigger of his four-four.

On Fayette Street, you had to put hope in the margins. That's what she did last week, when she spotted Dinky behind the wheel of someone else's automobile. Caught by someone who mattered in his life, someone who never ceased to believe in him, DeAndre's cousin found that Ella's reproach hurt the most. A few days after the joyride, on these same rec center steps, Dinky had actually come to her with an apology and an assurance that he had returned the car to the proximate place where he stole it. Then the sixteen-year-old listened with respectful patience to the inevitable lecture.

"You right," he told her. "You always right, Miss Ella."

Ella Thompson's love would produce no miracles. But on Fayette Street, she had done about as much as any person could.

Tonight, when she finishes dispensing snacks, she pokes her head out of the recreation center doors and sees, to her pleasure and relief, that the Buick is no longer on Mount Street. No stickup. No shooting. No problem.

"They're gone," she tells the younger boys. "It must not have been what you all thought."

Daymo leaves the rec and jogs to the fence. He peers through chain-link, looking up and down the block.

"Man, they rolled out."

"Maybe they comin' back," says Stevie, hopeful.

"They shoulda waited," says T.J., "Mike and his boys gonna be comin' past any time now and they ain't gonna be here for it."

The trio waits on the vacant lot for a time, looking both ways on Mount. Down at Fayette Street, a tout for the Death Row crew is calling the product name over and over.

"They long gone," says T.J., disappointed.

"Me too," says Daymo, putting up his hood and walking.

"Wait up," says Stevie.

Ella watches them go, turning off the rec lights only when the last of her charges has cleared the playground.

A few days later, she's at it again with the proud and few of the neighborhood association, up at Fayette and Monroe to take back that corner for one crisp autumn day. Some of Franklin Square's remaining citizens are perched on the northside corners, fifteen or twenty strong, carrying posters emblazoned with drug-free-community and honk-if-you-are-against-drugs messages. They're out there making all kinds of noise, shouting slogans to the rhythm of a bass drum borrowed for the occasion from the local drum-and-majorette corps. The mayor shows up, too, alighting on the corner from his city limo with a full entourage. For a time, he holds one of the placards, stepping into the street at every red light, urging the idling motorists to hit their horns for the cause.

The rally goes on for much of the morning and afternoon. By day's end, most of the corner players on Monroe Street have to acknowledge the heart of their neighbors, their ex-friends and relatives who stand out there in the chill air, demanding something more. A few actually respond. Smitty, for one, crosses Monroe Street and joins the rally, carrying a down-with-drugs poster through the southbound lanes and cheering those drivers who sound support. The rest do what they always do when confronted by such events: They take the day's transactions around the corner to Lexington and Fulton, or down to the other end of Vine Street.

That afternoon, before giving back the corner, Ella takes care to glean as much joy as possible from the effort. She has no illusions: She has lived in this place too long to mistake the rally for some kind of solution. Yet she walks home delighted with the day for its own sake.

"I'm saying it's only one day, but it gets you to thinking how great it can be," she tells Myrtle Summers on the walk back down the block. "Those corners, I mean, it just reminds you how wonderful it would be without all of that."

That night, she makes a point of sitting out on her steps for two hours, drinking hot chocolate and listening to the radio. Touts and runners on Fulton show a small measure of respect.

They move halfway down the block.

More than anything, Fran Boyd loves the victory lap.

She loves the look on people's faces, the quiet acknowledgment of her new status. She loves the special feeling that comes from being apart and above the usual along Fayette Street. It is, she feels, her due for having come this far.

On a brisk October day, six weeks after emerging from detox and about a fortnight after moving to the house on Boyd Street, Fran is coming through Vine Street on some errand and is blessed with a truly righteous moment, a street corner epiphany that would give any ex-addict her share of pride.

The action is deep at Vine and Monroe, but Fran cuts past the clutter of touts, shaking her head thank-you-no at this product and that, feeling strong and above it all.

And there, coming up Monroe from the other direction, is George Epps, smiling at her and wishing her well. Blue has been clean for a couple months now; he only comes past these corners on his way to Ella's rec center, where, once again, he's picked up his art class.

"Hey, girl."

"Hey yo'self."

"You look real good."

"You too."

They embrace, two old soldiers in a moment of easy peace, while all around them, the touts continue to bark brand-names and the runners go to the ground stashes.

"You down at the rec now?" Fran asks.

"Yeah, giving a little something back."

Fran nods, chats a while longer, then looks around.

"Same ol' thing," muses Blue.

"Always," says Fran.

They're about to part ways when one of the New York Boys slips off the liquor store wall to tell Blue about the Jumbo Sixes: "They right as rain."

"Naw," Blue tells him quietly. "I'm not doin' that anymore."

"Yeah?" asks the New Yorker, surprised.

"Right as rain."

"Good for you, man."

"Yeah."

Blue turns away, smiling just a bit. But Fran is beside herself with glee at the moment.

"It feels good," she tells Blue.

"Yeah," he said. "I guess it does."

"You come through here and tell them no like that. I know that feels good."

But for Blue, there is that element of humility at work. He's still going to the meetings, still struggling with the very idea of his new self, still talking about the grace of God and living life in single-day installments. For him, the tout and his news about the black tops was simply another hurdle in a long steeplechase.

Fran says good-bye and watches Blue move on. She stays on the corner for a good while, exulting.

Even so, much of the victory lap is decidedly over. By now, she's been seen and praised and marveled over by most everyone she knows. When Fran walks down the street these days, she's ordinary scenery. The corner is the same; it has simply turned away from her and gone about its business elsewhere. A quick compliment, a few good wishes and the world she knew and all those in it are finished with the ovation.

The new world seems to her less than welcoming, though in fairness, allowances have been made for a woman trying to find her way. One after another, her outstanding court cases for shoplifting have been bartered down to unsupervised or mostly unsupervised probation. Fran played the district court judges well, telling them about her successful recovery, her new house, her willingness to put her life back together now that she is done with the drugs.

And not only is she getting by on bad credit, renting the Boyd Street rowhouse from an old friend, but when money got short at the end of September, friends and relatives had come up with ten or twenty dollars or a bag of groceries, offering such help in the belief that the cash would not go to glassine bags and vials. Likewise, the U.S. government had kicked in her $1,400 Pell Grant, allowing her to keep at her college classes.

All of which is enough to keep running in place. Now, for the next step, she needs to pass her classes. Or find a job. Or get some of those things—a new TV, a winter coat for DeRodd, new Nikes for Dre—that show material progress.

And all of that, unlike the victory lap, involves struggle.

For starters, college isn't what she thought it would be. Algebra is proving to be hellishly difficult for someone whose formal education had concluded a couple decades back. It's so difficult in fact that a month into the semester, she's no longer able to keep up with the classwork. English is easier, but even so, she can't find it in herself to do the reading. Night after night, Fran leaves her schoolbooks on the dresser, wasting the evening hours on sitcoms and late-night movies.

Instead, she tries to scrounge a job. Beginning at Westside and working her way east to Mt. Clare, Fran fills out applications at a dozen stores—most of which have barred her for shoplifting. When no calls come back immediately, she tries the want ads, circling everything from route driver to telemarketer. A company in Woodlawn gives her an interview, but it's sales work on commission only. A store manager at Westside calls, then realizes that Fran is barred for thieving and cancels the interview. Finally, she lands an interview with a company out in Hunt Valley, miles north of the city. On a Thursday morning she spends two hours fixing her hair and makeup and dressing in a pants suit, eager to make the best first impression.

That afternoon, she's sitting at the kitchen table when DeAndre comes in. Taking in a Newport, she looks completely at ease.

"Got a job," she tells him.

DeAndre doesn't miss a beat. "Ma," he says, "I need new shoes."

"Got-damn, Dre. I don't even start 'til Monday."

He laughs.

But nothing comes easy for Fran Boyd. The work isn't clerical, like all of her previous jobs had been; instead, it's factory floor work for Revlon. Come Monday morning, Fran spends two hours catching bus transfers from West Baltimore out to northern Baltimore County before she arrives at her place on an assembly line in the bowels of a Hunt Valley industrial park. Then, for six hours, she and about forty other laborers cramp their fingers by snapping small disks of eyeshadow into plastic compacts. The next day, the alarm rings and she turns it off, sleeping until noon. That night she watches television until three in the morning.

There are better jobs, she tells herself. And when Marvin Parker comes calling, she's done with the want ads for good. They had met in recovery in September, taking to each other in that first rush of freedom. Marvin was thirty-five, with more than a decade on the corners, but lately he had become a regular at the St. James NA meetings. Fran, who had neither the time nor the patience for romance when she was chasing dope, suddenly found herself interested again. It seemed right somehow— both of them rediscovering themselves, both of them trying to do something with their lives. And it might have stayed right, save for the fact that by the middle of October, when he finally gathers his things together and moves into Boyd Street with Fran and her sons, Marvin Parker is once again slinging vials at Franklintown and Baltimore.

Fran knows it when she lets him in the door, yet allows it anyway on the argument that the man isn't getting high, that he might as well work out on a corner and bring some dollars home. Marvin had teamed with an old-school dealer and stickup artist by the name of Shorty Boyd, who was no relation to Fran though they had known each other for years.

Shorty had done pretty much everything on a corner and lived to tell about it. He was hardcore and famous for using a gun to take packages off weaker and younger dealers, then selling their wares himself. Shorty was a survivor and a user; in time, Marvin Parker would get used.

By the last of October, Fran's new boyfriend is getting high, using as much as he sells and behind the eight ball when it's time to pay off a piece of Shorty's package. Soon enough, there isn't a dollar coming back home from Franklintown and Baltimore. Only Marvin, high and useless.

Fran knows that DeAndre hates Marvin for his drugging, and day by day, the tension in the house grows. Outside of Fran's earshot, Marvin is belligerent with the others, ordering Tyreeka and DeRodd around. On occasion, DeAndre challenges him, angrily declaring that if Marvin wants to make the rules, then he can damn sure pay some rent or put something in the refrigerator. But Marvin plays it off, or worse, brings the problem back to Fran, who asserts his rights for him. Then things start disappearing. Cash from DeAndre's denim pockets. Cassette tapes. DeRodd's Sega Genesis cartridges.

"Ma," says DeAndre, "he stealin' from us."

"Andre, you don't know what you talkin' about."

But Fran knows, and she knows DeAndre knows. Her son is soon looking at her in a different way, scoping for signs that she's slipping as well. Once, when she's in the bedroom, telling Marvin that if he's got to have his blast, he's got to do it out of sight of her, DeAndre comes up the stairs. Fran sees him, listening intently on the stairwell landing, and she feels good for having reassured her son that she is still trying for clean. Still, she knows that there is a progression here, a backward movement that can't be denied much longer.

In those first weeks of freedom, Fran had launched herself whole-heartedly into the after-care sessions at the recovery center and the NA meetings at St. James at Lexington and Monroe. Since discovering the twelve-step gospel at the detox center, she had devoutly attended these gatherings; the confessionals and testimony gave her a feeling of connection. And if one meeting wasn't enough in those first days, Fran would find another, and another after that. There were nightly sessions at St. James, or at Almost Family at Saratoga and Fremont. There were afternoon meetings at James McHenry and morning meetings at a half-dozen places if you woke up feeling weak. Fran had not been to church for a long while, but what she remembered of the Christian faith could not rival the power she felt at a good meeting. Up at St. James she could go inside the basement doors and hear, not leaden homilies of prophets and saviors, but the simple truth of drug addicts, speaking not about life to come, but life as they had known it.

At first, Fran had felt energy and warmth in the crowd; strength itself seemed to follow her out the door with the last words of the serenity prayer. At many of the gatherings, she met people she knew, people who had been down on Fayette and Mount Street with her. Some were more lost and desperate than she had ever been, now using the meetings to reorder their lives. Many fell, but others seemed to be growing, getting stronger as they collected their thirty-day and sixty-day and six-month clean-and-sober key chains. On the evening when she had walked to front of the room at St. James to get her two-month keepsake—twenty-eight days clean in detox and thirty-two more on the street—Fran was proud to the point of tears. Yet she balked at what should have been the next step: finding a sponsor, a fellow addict to rely on, to share her fears and hopes and frustrations.

From the beginning, Fran had resisted the idea that she was dependent on any process outside of herself. When pressed, she had argued that she could manage her own recovery without having to share secrets with anyone else. She told the NA organizers that she would keep with the meetings, that she was on the right road whether or not she was sponsored.

For a time, she had kept that promise. Only after a good month of meetings did she begin to bridle at all the rules and requirements, at the repetition that was at the heart of every NA gathering. By degrees, she became bored with all the talk, all the stories that always ended the same way. She began skipping meetings. And when DeAndre noticed and said something, Fran explained that she was past it now, that all of those people up at St. James were just chasing meetings the same way they used to chase the blast. They weren't doing anything with their time but being exaddicts, and she wanted something more than that, some of the new life that was supposed to be there when you leave the vials alone.

By the time Marvin Parker moves in, Fran has stopped going to the meetings at St. James, or to any of her after-care sessions down at BRC. With DeRodd in school, she sometimes stays away from Boyd Street for the entire day—either up the hill at Scoogie's watching cable movies, or worse, down on Fayette with Bunchie and Stevie, hanging near the Mount Street corners just to get away from her empty house and see what the action is like.

For a long while, she is on her old perch as a spectator only, watching the familiar chaos from a place apart, sitting on the Dew Drop steps, living each day with the Mount Street regulars and squeezing a few last accolades for her victory.

"You lookin' right, Fran," someone would say.

"Feelin' right," she'd reply.

But it isn't quite true. Once, in September, when she was still staying at Scoogie's house, she gave in to the hunger, marching back down to Mount and Fayette—back past Buster and Little Roy and Ronnie Hughes, back into the Dew Drop and down the steps to find her sister hunkered in the usual corner.

"Hey, Fran."

Bunchie said nothing more. It was enough.

Three lines were waiting when Bunchie passed her the mirror. Fran snorted one and waited for the rush; when it came, she surprised herself by feeling ashamed. She stood up, leaving the other two on the mirror.

"Where you goin' at?"

"Out," she said, leaving.

That afternoon, she found an NA meeting. That night, she went to bed angry at herself for slipping, for gratifying all those fiends down on Mount Street who were so damned happy to see her lose. She lay in bed remembering Bunchie, damn near smirking at her as she did the line.

She couldn't go back there. She had sworn this to herself. Her old world was lethal to her, but the new one was proving so empty and desolate, and her journey into it would be a solitary one. From the beginning, from those first days out of detox, Fran had sensed this. She knew Fayette and Mount, but what else—who else—did she know? For a time, she tried hard to believe that scraps of the old world could be carried forward into the new. In fact, she tried for a time to use some of her newfound strength to salvage other souls. After all, she had done these things for herself. She could, by force of will, make the rest of the neighborhood do the same.

There was no saving anyone who didn't want salvation; Fran was not naive enough to think that she could drag Stevie, Bunchie, and every other family member in need down to detox and command their rehabilitation. But for those who asked for help, Fran had extended herself. Nor did she just give people Antoinette's name and phone number and wish them well. Instead, Fran took them under her wing, guiding them through the process.

It began with Lynn, a girl she knew from over on Mount and Baltimore. A week or two after returning from detox, when Fran was leaving the Korean market on Baltimore Street, Lynn found the heart to speak up.

"Lookin' good, girl."

"Hey," said Fran, smiling. "How you?"

"You think maybe I might be able to get in down there?"

Fran nodded. She could help. She would make calls. She would talk to Antoinette. She would help Lynn get herself together, encourage her, see that she didn't slip when she came out.

After Lynn came Karen, her lifelong friend and her brother Scoogie's lifelong love, who seemed to have found the bottom just as Fran had. Karen was chasing dope and coke down on Fulton, and Fran took her friend's compliments about her recovery as evidence of desire. Karen said she would be willing to try, if only Fran could get her started. And then there was Gary, who made noises about calling for a detox bed, asking if Fran could get his name on the waiting list. Fran took the mission to heart; she could save these people—all of them—and in doing so, she could claim a piece of the old world, dragging it with her into the lonely void of the new.

But Lynn lasted only a day or two after coming out of the recovery center; after that, Fran saw her on post as usual. And Karen caught a great break: admission to Tuerk House after only a handful of meetings. Yet within a week or so, Karen was back in the mix, chasing the same old thing. As for Gary, Fran made the calls, but it didn't come as much of a surprise when she later found out that he didn't follow up.

No, she was alone. For a brief time, she had hoped for Marvin Parker as a companion, but it was clear that he was useless. DeRodd was too young to provide real comfort and DeAndre, after losing his job at the Wendy's, was once again little more than a child making demands. On check day this month, he even badgered her for $100 basketball shoes, telling her that he was broke, reminding her that he had stayed off the corners on the promise that straight life would put some money in his pocket. The implication was raw and obvious: Un-ass the dollars for some Air Jordans or I'm back playing gangster. So Fran bought the Nikes, feeling that after those years at the Dew Drop Inn, she couldn't say no to her oldest son.

Now she is once again hovering at the Dew Drop, sitting on those familiar steps, waiting for God knows what. She is strong enough still to make it, she assures herself. The meetings, the process, the twelve steps—those things are for people without her inner power. Once the weather gets cold, she tells herself, she'll stay indoors and do her class-work, get ready for her exams. She might even go back out for a job once the stores start hiring Christmas help.

She's still there, waiting, on the fifteenth of October—her birthday—seventy-one days clean including detox, save for the one mistake with Bunchie. She is thirty-seven years old.

"You gonna celebrate?" Bunchie asks her.

"I might."

That night, she sends Marvin to Baltimore and Franklintown with thirty dollars. She's heard that Shorty Boyd's package is a bomb. The rumor proves true.

The morning after, Fran takes her two-month keepsake off her key chain, reasoning that while a single line of dope with Bunchie can be excused, thirty dollars worth of heroin, scarfed up in a few hours, does not constitute clean time. She goes looking for a meeting, and finding none, she heads home with no better plan than to slip back into bed and sleep through the fear. Marvin, thank God, isn't around. He was chasing coke half the night and didn't come in until early morning. Then, when she went out looking for her meeting, he left to chase some more.

Now she's alone, or so she thinks until DeAndre comes out of the bathroom as she's climbing the stairs to her room. He's at the second-floor landing, wiping his face with a towel, looking at her closely.

"Ma."

"What?"

"Marvin got to go."

"Say what?"

"Marvin got to leave. He think he own this house and everything in it. He's yellin' at Reeka and cussin' DeRodd, tellin' him that he gonna kick his ass and all. He gone crazy if he thinks I'm gonna let him act like . . ."

"Andre, it ain't your place."

"It is my place."

"I said it ain't your place," she yells suddenly. "You don't know shit about it so just mind your business!"

She wants to shout him down, to shut him up before he says everything she herself knows is true. But she's too tired to nurse a good anger. She climbs to the top of the stairs and starts into her room.

"Ma," DeAndre says quietly.

"What?"

"You come too far to fall like this. You been through too much and you done too much now to go back down."

It's DeAndre standing here. It's her eldest son—the one who always manages to touch that most important part of her at the very moment when she least expects it. It's DeAndre, showing her his whole heart.

"I'm sayin', you know, Marvin ain't doin' nuthin' but bringing the family down. He got to go."

The family. DeAndre is still trying to believe, and she can't help but love him for this. For a moment, she can almost believe with him. She returns to the top of the stars and they embrace.

"I ain't goin' back down Fayette Street," he tells her.

It isn't a threat. He isn't even angry. He's saying it plain, and she's hearing it plain.

"I'm sayin' I love you an' all," her son says, "and I want you to make it. But if you don't, I ain't goin' back down there."

"I ain't either," she says softly.

Once upon a time, you were in perfect harmony with the greater scheme of things, a happy prisoner of the corner rhythms, an average, everyday dope fiend devoted to the singular pursuit of the perfect blast. But no fairy tale ever lasts, and finally, without warning, you hit bottom.

Only bottom turns out not to be a place, or a particular point on any street-by-street, this-way-to-hell compass. It is, instead, the gradual yet inescapable feeling of horror that leads any drug addict to the most gut-wrenching, agonizing moment of revelation.

You are stunned. You have a right to be: Truth be told, you didn't even know you were heading this way. You certainly didn't see any signs, nothing that might have told you to ease up a bit. For years, you've been about the business of obliterating yourself; now, without any justification whatsoever, you're suffering through a prolonged bout of self-awareness. When the initial shock passes, you try what has always worked best: denial.

But even as you drag your ass out to a corner for the day's jump start, the back of your mind holds to a sickening fear that no chemical concoction can rid you of this feeling, this strange sense that you've reached an end. A half hour later, while those around you are deep in the throes of the latest Spider Bag offering, you sit there in the back of the shooting gallery like an old radial with a slow leak, helpless as your high seeps out.

The bottom is the fiend's worst-case scenario—worse than any back-alley beating, worse than standing, shackled, in front of a surly district turnkey while some fresh-out-of-the-academy roller strings your five vials into some kind of kingpin charge. Worse even than sitting on one of those plastic chairs in the University Hospital emergency room, half-listening as a resident presses the phone number and address of the clinic into your hand, reassuring you all the while that with proper care, you can still get some good years from your body. As a soldier, you learned long ago to deal with the stuff of beatings and arrests. A ruined liver, endocarditis, the Bug—these were the givens, the acceptable hazards on the road to oblivion. In the end, you reckoned such setbacks—if you reckoned anything at all—as fresh and viable reasons to keep faith with Rule One and get the blast. Fuck it, you learned to tell yourself, no one's perfect. No one lives forever.

But the bottom is a different dimension entirely, a state of mind with a texture unlike anything you've ever encountered. It's beyond the horror of the snake, beyond even those strange junkie dreams, those recurring nightmares of physical need in which you land in your favorite needle palace, mix the powder and water, and no matter how many matches you fire, the shit just won't cook up. It's beyond the worst tricks and lies, beyond those times when some smarter or hungrier player runs a game, or switches a spike, and what you get for your effort is a sprinkle of water. Even in those fevered, bowel-breaking moments, you've managed to regroup, to somehow get yourself back out there and manufacture another twenty on the hype.

The process of revelation might take you a couple of days, maybe even a week, but eventually it sinks in that no combination of vials and bags, capers and games can carry you past this feeling. Denial won't play anymore; everything is turning flat. You watch as all your defenses crumble, replaced by a host of raw and alien emotions. Shame, disgust, and an almost overwhelming weariness dominate your every waking moment. Finally you understand that the bottom is a forced move—not so much a choice as the end of all choice. Your path is set and all you can think to do is try to find some help. But the very idea of help is so far beyond the established corner universe that at first, you can't even imagine where to look.

Maybe you try to do it on your own, holing up in some basement with an old blanket wrapped around you, fighting the sickness in solitude, waiting a couple days before you have strength enough to drag yourself down the street, past the touts, to a church basement or rec center, where you can try your hand at the twelve-step, I-am-powerless-over-my-addiction philosophy. If you can't handle that—and not many can—then your last, best hope is to know someone, somewhere who knows someone, somewhere else who got into a program and came out the other side. Find the right someone and chances are you might end up with a phone number. Call that number and you might make it to a waiting list. Endure the wait and after a month, or two, or four, you might be rewarded with a bed of your own, a Clonidine patch, some Motrin or Tylenol and a physician's assistant or nurse's aide to watch over your misery.

You're in treatment, and the bottom has brought you here. Without that down-in-the-hole grounding that takes the joy out of the strongest vial, you would not have gotten this far. But as days pass in the detox

center, you begin to see it as more than the bottom. Having given yourself over to something external from, and opposed to, the corner itself,
you believe it's fair to take some credit for having attempted this journey.
For you, a weary soldier, treatment seems a choice. You chose; looking
back, you want to believe this.

Those with their hands at the throttle—the politicians and commen-
tators, the cops and lawyers and social theorists—pretty much believe
the same thing. They, too, feel as though they've chosen, when in fact
their crusade has simply grounded on a bottom all its own.

After declaring the prohibition, after mobilizing, after filling prisons
and rewriting laws and spending billions, those responsible for waging
war on the American culture of drugs have come to the same belated
conclusion, albeit after a quarter century of denial, as any dope fiend
who gives up the fight. Twenty-five years ago, the road taken was that
of drug task forces and kingpin statutes and international interdiction.
The dollars went to drug enforcement agents and prosecutors and prisons.
When the dollars weren't enough, the laws were changed to make the
dollars do more. Mandatory minimums, civil forfeitures, the degradation
of the Fourth Amendment—these became the new weapons. For a quarter
century, the drug warriors have ratcheted up the conflict, always with
the promise that a little more effort, a little more pressure can't help but
have the necessary impact. Their Old Testament approach has been
singular, focused, specific. It's a fine old American strategy: stick first,
carrot later.

Now, with the endgame at hand, the numbers in cities like Baltimore
are too hopeless, the open-air drug markets too numerous to justify the
stick. Now, with the drug culture fully entrenched, the average Baltimore
police commander has learned enough to argue that while all the arrests
and sweeps and seizures can't win the war, they nonetheless have a
purpose. No longer does law enforcement pursue street-level drug sellers
and users merely to punish them; now, the stat game has become a means
to drive lawbreakers toward treatment. Still and always, it's the stick first.
But now, at least, the drug war has a carrot as well.

Talk nowadays with any police professional or prosecutor in a city
with a significant drug-involved population and what comes back is
likely to be an admission—twenty-five years too late—that our society
cannot merely arrest its way out of the problem. Talk to those who have
invested their careers in the drug war and they'll respond with an argument not for change, but for something that amounts to a redefinition

of the status quo. By this new reckoning, the criminal pursuit of those along Fayette Street is now more essential than ever because the pursuit attacks demand and drives users toward drug treatment. In this new vision, treatment, education, and law enforcement are joined in a synergistic new entity.

Instead of trying to sell the numbers game of street-level arrests to an increasingly cynical public, drug policy makers and police commanders now argue about a nobler purpose. They're not chasing down lost souls for whom jail space no longer exists; they are, instead, guiding those souls back toward a therapeutic solution. Better than the usual pretrial detentions and district court arraignments, the possibilities for the arrestee can now extend to a special drug court and a sympathetic judge ordering residential detox and rehabilitation. Thanks to this redefinition, the chase seems to make sense again. By a quick fix in the terminology, the war and the warriors are once more necessary.

Except for this: Take a walk through a crowded detox facility in Baltimore. To be sure, the dormitory beds and meeting hall are filled— and filled to a great extent with court-ordered patients. Similarly, it's no surprise to see many of these patients parroting a drug-free ideology as if it means something to them. Yet when the surface is scratched, it becomes entirely apparent that there is no real connection between stick and carrot.

Those who are here because a judge ordered them here, those who have been given a choice of either five years with the Department of Corrections or full compliance with a program of drug counseling and rehabilitation, are merely taking up beds, biding time, and looking for any chance to slip free. No court order can override the corner rules if a person is about the corner. No judge can tell a man to change his most basic desire if the man himself sees no cause for change.

The drug counselors—the best of them, anyway—know this. They regard those clients sent by way of the city's drug court, or a sentencing judge's probation requirements, as long-shot cases. A few might actually respond to the new regime of counseling and group therapy and Narcotics Anonymous confessional. But in those instances, the court-referral cases change because they are ready to change, not because society wills it. As for the rest—they play at recovery until the probation requirements are fulfilled, or until the hunger is too much. Then, it's out the front door and down to the nearest corner.

So the court-ordered pretenders soon fall away, leaving only those who arrive at this opportunity and then cling to it by their own act of will. These people don't seek change because drugs are unlawful or prohibited or subject to the condemnation of others. Redemption for them is essential because they have seen and felt and tasted bottom. For too many years, they have been dismantling their lives one blast at a time, shedding friends and relatives and, ultimately, themselves. Now, by their own volition, they are returning to ask for the alternative. And what, exactly, is that alternative?

On the high-end, perhaps, where Blue Cross/Blue Shield still pays all but the deductible, drug treatment might resemble a comprehensive, carefully structured program for reintegrating vulnerable, dependent personalities into the community. In places where real money is spent, a great deal of therapy is usually assured. But the public drug treatment effort, when it's available at all, isn't the full-tilt, Betty-Ford-is-my-salvation kind of detox. It's mostly out-patient treatment, or, for the more fortunate, it's three, or five, or maybe even twenty-eight days of in-house treatment, followed by some group therapy and the NA creed repeated three or four times a day until it becomes rote.

For those who emerge from the inner-city corners, nothing is there to help them after the first few moments of stability, and no one will suggest that a used-to-be dope fiend from West Baltimore is any more welcome in the other America than he was before he fired that first blast. Treatment may be capable of telling people that once they've finished twenty-eight days off the street, they are cured of their physical addictions and they are therefore in recovery. But it cannot tell them who they are or where they might go to find something better.

After four days in Mercy Hospital's detox ward, or four weeks in BRC's dormitory, what remains for the fiend who hit bottom and bounced is to step back into the streets and walk past the same drug markets, tracing that thin line that carries him from one NA meeting to the next. He goes from rec centers to church basements to elementary schools, chasing the same words and phrases and imagery, clinging to the stories of other fiends. He catches two or three or four meetings a day—however many are required to keep him from scratching at the empty place in his soul.

Narcotics Anonymous is the church of last resort in urban America. It provides a daily religious rite that brings the corner survivors into houses of worship, albeit through the basement doors. Above them, the sanctuaries stand mostly empty save for Sundays; but down below, amid the folding chairs and linoleum tiles and Bible classrooms is a religion practiced damn near every day.

". . . we humbly asked Him to remove our shortcomings . . ."

Down in the catacombs, day and night, the steps are read and the traditions reaffirmed. Confessions are made.

"We made a searching and fearless moral inventory of ourselves . . ."

Key rings are distributed—one day clean, one week clean, six months clean—trinkets held precious by men and women who are on a hero's journey, who will embrace at the night's end and walk out onto the same streets that once devoured them.

"We made a list of all persons we had harmed and became willing to make amends . . ."

Down here, at least, there is the camaraderie of shared endurance, the sense of being among other survivors of the same slow-motion slaughter. This much is ready and waiting for those who come off the corner.

"Our common welfare should come first. Personal recovery depends on NA unity . . ."

To the extent that anything in the drug treatment firmament actually works, this does. Though there are many at a Narcotics Anonymous meeting who need to have their court papers signed, who are required to prove to an outside authority that they attended so many meetings a week, the same rule applies: Those who are here as prisoners of the drug war haven't a prayer, but those who are doing it for themselves might just make it. They're the ones compelled by the horror of reaching bottom, they're the ones who have learned to trust only in humility, in an almost instinctive sense of their own weakness.

If you are one of those, if after a week or three of meetings you are still up to it, still determined not to consign what remains of your life to the pavement, you might look around and take stock of your fellow travelers. It's a mixed bag of souls: the weary in need of a temporary rest; the desperate, frightened by a near miss; the game runners, busy building a presentencing pretext. And there are also a few others like you, humbled and vanquished; men and women so seared by the corner's power that this time, they might just make a year or two clean. Many are detox veterans, wearing the chevrons of past campaigns. Nine times, sixteen times, twenty-two times—some have lost count of how many times they've struck bottom, surrendered in their hearts, gone through sickness and therapy and meetings only to sail out into the ether and get captured once again in the corner orbit. You look at them and calculate your own chances.

The young ones don't come—or, those who do come, arrive sullen and disconnected, waiting only until the end of the meeting and a chance to have their court slips signed. For them, the full-blown nightmare has yet to be imagined, much less lived. A fiend can't sense the bottom until he's spent years in service of a corner, misusing all his friends, discarding his family. At twenty-one, or twenty-five, a dope fiend hasn't been beaten down nearly enough to begin questioning the corner construct. He still has years of free falling, a decade, perhaps, of game-running and lie-telling before he feels anything solid beneath him.

If you're ready, though, you'll take what's offered. You'll recite the steps, the traditions. You'll hear testimony and when the time comes, you'll tell your own story, sparing nothing. You'll pick a mentor and then mentor someone else. You'll sit through the daily gatherings, chain-smoking with a hundred others, accepting Styrofoam cups of coffee and one-whatever key chains as if these things were the blood and body of Christ himself. For a long time, for longer than you thought possible, the meetings will be your life.

Or not.

The corner is still there; the rules are still the same. At any point in the long struggle, you can miss a meeting or two. Or ten. You can discover that what you thought was the bottom was not really bottom at all, that there are depths to which you will still need to descend before you can again think about change. You can fall in one thoughtless moment or after days of deliberate and conscious thought, telling yourself all sorts of happy lies in order to get yourself through the door of a shooting gallery and take the spike in your hand. You can kill yourself that way, too, going back out into the corner mix after months in the church catacombs, firing what used to be your usual dose and discovering in one world-shattering moment that all your heroin-tolerant cells are missing, that your cleaned-up self isn't yet ready for thirty of a Spider Bag all at once.

Or you can slouch forward, plugging away from one meeting to the next until you finally reach that pivotal point where your strength comes as a surprise, where you can tell yourself that your desire to stay clean is the equal or better of your hunger. Only then, when you are at last ready to look past a life of meetings, do you come to the next chasm.

What, you finally ask yourself, do I do now?

Your entire recovery—all that passes for drug treatment in this country—has been about defining what you don't want to be, what you fear and dread and need to avoid. You were a drug addict. You are now a recovering addict. Beyond that, you have no idea what to say about your life.

Because even if your bottom was real, and even if you've managed to heed its warning and stay clean, what remains for a thirty-five- or forty-year-old survivor for whom the corner world has been home? You've lived by manipulation, by ignoring your pain and the pain of others, by invoking the dope-fiend move as the solution to every problem. Now, all of that must be abandoned at the threshold of some other, barely imagined way of living. To survive at Fayette and Mount, you had to get over on someone else every damn day and you got to be good at it. But to apply the rules of the corner to any other world invites only frustration and failure. You're supposed to trade your dope-fiend skills for what? Humility? Servitude? Minimum wage? Giving up the drugs was hard enough; giving up the hustle is harder still. And if you do manage it, all you've done is come to the end of the beginning.

What's left is the closest thing to impossible.

Having put the drugs away and turned your back on the corner, you are left to face life. And this is the part of the journey no one mentions when they theorize about drug treatment or recovery or rehabilitation: You weren't really running to the vials, at least not in the beginning. You were running away from the very same life that you are now challenged to discover and examine. After years in the fog, you are back where you started; older, perhaps wiser, but still tangled up in the remnants of what had been an unfulfilled existence. Your body is clean, your mind is clear. But none of that is much help when the pieces of a broken life are dumped on the table in front of you. Yes indeed, you had some problems. There they are, still awaiting your considered attention.

The people with the sticks and the carrots, the ones who used to talk arrest stats and now talk treatment—they don't know quite what to say to you about any of that. They know what they don't want you to do. They don't want you to take drugs, or sling vials, or break into parked cars and rip out the radios. They don't want you to rob people or shoot people or hijack their luxury sedans when they stop for gas. They don't want dope fiends, and in an abstract way, they've shown their commitment by spending billions to stop you from being a dope fiend.

Beyond that, they have nothing much to say.

So welcome back to a culture that still hasn't found a use for you or your kind. This is America, where the West Baltimores exist in social and political isolation, where a good 10 percent of the population is no longer required by the economic engine, where there will always be those for whom not only a modicum of material success, but relevance, is unlikely. You were born for Fayette and Mount, you went there, and, at this point, the only real surprise is that you survived long enough to want something more.

If you went back there now—a last visit, perhaps—if you walked twenty blocks due west from the city's downtown to Mount Street and found the sage idiot manning his post, then you could state your case:

"I been a dope fiend," you'd say.

"I'm tired," you'd say.

"I'm trying to stop," you'd say.

And the idiot on the corner would surely look at you and offer a cold question that points very close to the truth:

"Why?"

And damned if you could answer.

NINE

"Hey, Gary."

Gary McCullough peers across the Seapride counter, his red eyes squinting through the steam.

"Here . . . right here, Gary."

Finally, Gary sees him: a white boy, blond-haired, grinning passively. It's John Boy Walton, or so Gary has been calling the kid lately. Gary beams a grin back, then slides out from behind the steamers and spice boxes, pulling off his gloves and with his right hand, offering a white man's grip. Instead, the kid twists it into a street-corner greeting. Gary laughs aloud.

"You late," Gary tells him.

"We missed the first bus," John Boy explains. "This is my buddy Dan. The guy I told you 'bout."

Dan nods curtly and Gary picks up the hinged section of counter and makes his way out the front doors of the crabhouse. Beyond Miss Mary's earshot, they can talk freely.

"My main apple-scrapple," laughs Gary, clapping John Boy on the back. "You was supposed to be here at twelve. I'm not supposed to leave now."

"Not even for a few minutes?"

Gary pulls off his California Angels hat, wipes his head, and mumbles something about Miss Mary, about how it's always bad to leave when she's at the register. John Boy counters that he brought Dan all the way from Brooklyn Park.

"I'm tellin' him how you my man," says John Boy, managing an inflection somewhere between black and white.

Gary laughs.

"C'mon, Gary. We got enough for a bundle."

Gary is tempted, but Miss Mary is going to need him at least until five. Even now, in mid-October, with the crab season all but over, with his hours being cut to the bone, Seapride is still Gary's main hustle. He shakes his head, telling them they'll have to come back in an hour. "I just can't take off 'til then. You was supposed to be here at twelve and now I can't."

John Boy looks at Dan and gets only a shrug back.

"'Bout an hour?"

"Maybe less. If I get all them pots filled up, maybe I can ease out 'fore then."

Dan nods to John Boy, who thumps Gary on the shoulder.

"Okay, Mo," says Gary, recovering his bounce as he turns back to the crabhouse. "You just sit tight and stay right and we gonna be good to go."

"We chillin'," says John Boy. "Go back and do your thing."

Gary hears the white boy throw out little pieces of used cornerspeak and can't help laughing to himself. As far as the corner game goes, John Boy is barely out of diapers, a neophyte in need of mentoring. To Gary, the white buyers all seem alike when they first appear on Fayette Street: They all try to walk sideways, with their hands in their pockets, a little too nervous and a little too polite. They all have one-syllable names, too—Bob and John and Dan—as if anything more complicated might give offense. The latest in a series is this smiling, fair-haired wonder from Brooklyn Park, a kid so comically genuine—so positively white—that Gary can't help comparing him to John Boy on that old television show. And if John Boy Walton wants to come down off his mountain and start shooting vials, it only seems right that he have the assistance of someone equally earnest and humane.

The two had found each other at Fayette and Monroe near the end of summer. Gary had seen him wandering like a lost puppy trying to make the connect. The look of things told Gary that the boy didn't have a clue, that some stepped-on cut would be the closest thing to coke he was likely to see. Charitable as ever, Gary sidled up and offered what advice he could:

"Man, stay away from those Purple Tops."

"Huh?"

"I'm sayin' them purple ones is doo-doo."

When the white boy left Fayette Street that day, he left with good coke—courtesy of the smiling, full-service tour guide who charged him a mere vial or two as recompense. The boy went back down the hill feeling as if he'd latched onto a kindred soul, a fellow who understood in the most fundamental way that all men are brothers.

Ever since, Gary has been taking John Boy's money and returning with the best product he could find, and for this, the white boy from the southern reaches of the city pays him in vials. At first, John Boy would leave after the exchange, taking the vials home with him. But more and more often, he wants to hang with Gary, to pull out bottle caps and pump the coke with his new friend.

"Gary," he told him once, "you're a great guy."

"Huh," said Gary.

"No, I mean it. You're like the nicest guy I know."

Gary was embarrassed but flattered. He took his role as tour guide seriously, and on those occasions when he paid for weak vials with John Boy's money, he would apologize profusely and offer to go back with his own cash—if he had his own cash, anyway—and find better. Eventually, John Boy decided that the two of them should consolidate, maybe get an apartment together somewhere down below Pratt Street. Gary listened to talk like that and began worrying that the white boy had gone faggot on him, but in truth it was all just an extension of John Boy's lust for Fayette Street coke. His vision of the perfect world had quickly become a walk-up where the nicest guy in the world came home every day with the best vials money could buy.

Gary had been telling John Boy he'd think about it; he didn't want to kill this goose before getting every last golden egg. He had no intention of living happily ever after in twenty-on-the-hype racial harmony, but meanwhile, John Boy kept coming back, day after day, pressing cash into Gary's hand and making life much easier than any fiend could expect it to be.

The timing could not have been better, because Gary's crabhouse caper was beginning to wear thin. The season had slowed after the Labor Day rush and almost everyone—save for Cardy and Bobby Short, the experienced sorters—was seeing their hours cut. Gary had gone from six days a week down to five, to four, and then—as the cold weather thinned the crowds at the counter and left the crabhouses with nothing but Gulf crawlers shipped north at higher cost—he was down to Wednesdays and Saturdays. Miss Mary was even talking about dropping his Wednesday shift at the end of the month.

More to the point, Gary's habit had grown fat on the crabhouse job. Although he had given some of the pay to his mother, the rest had found its way into his veins and his tolerance for dope-and-coke speedballs was, by summer's end, higher than it had ever been before. Six months ago, he had been able to maintain on twenty or thirty dollars worth of dope a day; now, he was using three times that amount, often augmenting the cash from the crabhouse with a handful of side hustles. And beyond the caps and vials, he'd also had money for cigarettes by the pack, fries or sandwiches from the kitchen girls at Seapride, and twice- or three-times-a-day forties from the liquor store, too.

Now it was ending. All his hard work this summer, all his steady-as-she-goes servitude meant little once the season ended. In his frustration, Gary was convinced that it had to do with race, that Miss Mary would rather give the off-season days to the South Baltimore white boys, some of whom had shown little in the way of work ethic. Ignoring the inconvenient fact that his older brother remained full-time at the crabhouse, Gary enjoyed telling himself that Miss Mary was out-and-out prejudiced.

Of course, feeling that way about it made it easier for him to creep out of work for an hour or two today, to meet up with John Boy and Dan Boy and any other pilgrims with ready cash. After the lunch rush, he would slip past the counter and once again guide them to the promised land, hooking them into a right and true product.

As he comes back through the front counter, he gets the eye from Ron, Miss Mary's son, who is perched at the register.

"Gary, where the hell've you been at? We need sixteens."

"You got 'em."

"I needed 'em ten minutes back."

"You got 'em now, Chief. Comin' right out to you."

He gives the steamers and stun tanks another forty minutes of his time, working bushel after bushel until all of the front-room bins are full. Then he waits. Miss Mary and Ron are still up front, working the register and taking orders. For his absence to get less notice, he'll have to hang until Paul or one of the girls takes over.

"More spice," comes a yell from the back room.

"More dust!" shouts Gary. "I'm on it, Mo."

He's carrying two crates of crab spice back into the sorting room when he catches sight of Fran at the edge of the counter, flagging him down.

"What?" Gary says. "What's up?"

"Finish what you doin'," says Fran. "I be out front."

Gary drops the crates in front of the stun tanks, pulls off his gloves, and walks out the loading-dock door. Fran is leaning up against the crab house walls, biting down her fingernails. She is still looking good, but Gary notices the yellow at the corners of her eyes.

"What's goin' on?"

"Your son is goin' on. The boy is a trip, Gary."

"Huh?"

"You ready?"

"What?"

"You ready for news?"

Gary blinks and shrugs.

"You a grandad. You gonna have a grandson."

"Who?"

"You. Your son gonna have a son all his own."

Gary's mouth drops open. He'd heard that DeAndre's girl was looking heavy, but he hasn't seen much of Fran in the weeks since she came out of detox. Nor has he spoken with his son lately.

"You know it's a boy?" asks Gary, awed.

Fran nods. Gary takes off the Angels cap, scratches his head, and breaks into a smile so beatific that Fran has to open her arms and embrace him.

"That same girl he been with?"

"Reeka."

"Yeah," says Gary, "how 'bout that. We gonna be grandfather and grandmother. Ain't that somethin'?"

Fran hugs him again. For both of them, there is, at this moment, no sense of a tragedy compounded, of babies bringing babies into an unforgiving world. Tyreeka is now fourteen; DeAndre, two years older. Their union will soon produce a child three generations removed from the hope and honest belief that prompted William McCullough to steal a ride on a northbound bus and go to work in a Baltimore foundry. Yet in this first moment, Gary McCullough feels nothing but delight.

He asks about a due date and Fran tells him Christmas. Yet again, Gary tells Fran that he's going to change, that he's going to clean himself up in time to help.

"I'm going to get past this," he says.

Fran talks a bit about going to meetings, about the waiting list at BRC. Gary nods, but for both of them, it is a routine conversation, half-heard and spoken quickly. Fran pulls him up in mid-promise.

"Andre needs help with things," she says. "He tryin' to pay for the bassinet and high chair and clothes and whatever else. And they already went and cut his hours at Wendy's and he's out looking for some other work . . ."

Gary stops smiling.

"He's been tryin' but you know how he is. If he don't get some cash soon, he goin' right back to the corner."

Gary opens his mouth, utters a syllable, then turns away. Fran presses forward, wrapping her argument into a tight circle. Gary gets paid every day; surely he can let her hold forty or fifty. For DeAndre.

"Aw, man. No, this ain't, um . . ."

"Lemme hold twenty then."

Gary looks away, then back at Fran, then down at his rubber boots, wet and brown with crab spice. He's trying to counter, trying to offer up a reason, but the words won't come. He opens his mouth again, managing only to exhale before turning on his heel and marching into the crabhouse. Fran holds her ground and ten seconds later Gary is back.

"I ain't got paid yet today," Gary says.

"I'll wait then."

Gary pivots again, stalking back into the crabhouse to gather his thoughts. He returns after a minute, explaining that he can't spare anything because his mother will be down to collect the money for groceries and such.

"Tell her it's for Andre's baby and she'll let some of it go. If she knows what it's for, she won't mind."

Again Gary flees indoors, leaving Fran on the pavement shaking her head, shouting that at the very least, he ought to let her hold ten.

"For real, Gary, c'mon."

But he's back behind the counter now, hiding out, peeking through the steam every few minutes to see if she's gone, until, after a time, she is.

For Gary, the back-and-forth with Fran has always been an exhausting ordeal. Now it's more difficult than ever: With more dope and coke coursing through him, Gary has slipped deeper into the fog. He had long prided himself on his ideas and opinions, but lately he can sense that his words are fewer and slower, his sentences less complex. More and more, he stumbles from one half-formed thought to another; conversations once rich in substance and reference points are now just rambles. He can speak well enough about ordinary things, but Gary has always been about more than ordinary things. Now, after years of chemical riot, he's missing a part of himself.

At times, in the quiet of his mother's basement, Gary grasps the growing confusion in his mind. Such moments frighten him. Occasionally, he admits the fear aloud to friends, then looks at them expectantly, waiting for that redemptive moment when they shake their heads and tell him that it isn't permanent, that it's just the blast. And Gary, hearing this, nods and smiles, telling himself that it will all come back to him in time: His intellect, his humor, his lucidity— all of it will be where he left it. At other times, he doubts himself, worrying that he isn't thinking the same, that he can't remember things like he once did. The drugs, Gary would say, shaking his head. The drugs are killing my mind.

A few moments before, he couldn't keep up with the beg-and-barter challenge of Fran Boyd. Now, unable to remember whether he had walked back into the sorting room for males or females, he goes back out and stares down into the bins. Everything is full save for the sixteens. He returns to the sorting room and pulls a plastic bin of sixteen-dollar-a-dozen males over to the tank. He's got them up on the edge, ready to dump, when Cardy looks over at him, questioningly.

"You just did sixteens."

"Say what?"

"You took sixteens and cooked 'em not ten minutes back."

With one hand still holding the crab bin, Gary uses the other to pull his Angels cap off his head. He wipes his forehead with his sleeve and tries to think.

"Check the pots," his brother tells him.

Gary puts the bin on the floor and walks back out into the swelter of the front room. He bends around the near wall to check the numbers on the control box. Sixteens cooking on No. 3.

"Dag."

He walks back into the sorting room, picks up the plastic bin and dumps it back on the pile. Cardy smiles.

"Dag," says Gary again.

"Where you at, Gary?" Cardy asks.

"Cloud nine," he answers, frowning.

Cardy sings a lyric: "*You can be what you want to be . . .*"

Gary hears the old Temps classic and loses himself in nostalgia. He finishes the verse, then segues into a bit of "Ball of Confusion," followed by "Just My Imagination"—a medley of antique Motown, delivered in broken rhythm as he shovels fresh ice into the tanks. Satisfied that he's ahead of the game, he tells his brother he'll be back in a few, then creeps out the loading dock door to Monroe Street. The white boys are nowhere to be seen.

"Aw, man . . ."

He checks the carryout, then Martini's across the street. When he comes back out, John Boy and Dan Boy are sauntering his way, holding soft ice cream cones. Vanilla and chocolate, swirled together.

"Thinkin' I'd lost you," Gary says.

"Naw. Let's do it."

Gary walks point as the trio makes its way up the hill, crossing Baltimore Street at Monroe and heading straight for the maelstrom of the Fayette Street corners. Gary pulls up half a block short and squints toward the touts and runners, a trusty scout trying to read the terrain.

"You want the whole bundle, right?"

"If it's good, yeah."

"We'll go one-and-one and see," says Gary, taking their cash. "If it's good, we can come back on it."

Gary pockets the money and sends them back down the street, telling them to wait by the Baptist church. Watching his money walk away, Dan Boy gives a wistful, nervous look; John Boy settles in, patient. Gary, he knows, is true.

Ten minutes later, the three men huddle in the basement of 1827 Vine Street, where they present a picture of three-part harmony, the corner's version of a color-blind America.

Gary finds a vein in his forearm and launches the speedball, plunging it halfway home and then waiting for the wave to safely crest. When it does, he fires the other half. The white boys just slam theirs, dropping the plunger all the way. John Boy leans back on the bed, nearly swooning.

"Man," says Gary, "you keep slammin' like that an' you gonna black out. I'm tellin' you."

John Boy stays flat on the mattress; Dan Boy pulls his needle free, sits up, sniffs the air nervously, then retreats to the back wall of the basement, standing there with his neck back and fists clenched, braced against the warped paneling like a sentry on post. Gary shakes his head again, then resumes his lecture on the danger of slamming a speedball.

"I'm sayin' you got to be careful . . ."

But no one's listening. It was the same thing last week, when Gary brought John Boy into this same house by way of the back door, stumbling through the kitchen and past his mother. Minutes later, in the basement, Gary watched in amazement as his pale charge slammed three speedballs in rapid succession.

"Dag," Gary drawled, "slow down on that."

But John Boy wasn't hearing him. He was down on the floor, eyes rolling up in his head, foam at the corners of his mouth.

"No, hey, John . . ."

Gary earned his pay as a tour guide that day, keeping John Boy on his feet and breathing, throwing cold water on his face to revive him, then running upstairs to get more water and some kind of help. By the time the white boy showed any sign of coming back around, Gary had treated his mother to a vile and frantic performance.

For days afterward, Gary cursed himself for giving his mother and father this new cause for grief. No more white boys, he swore to himself, no more ghetto tours—nothing, at least, that would bring this mess into their very house.

Though both had fallen to dope and coke, Gary had always judged himself better than June Bey, blaming his brother for bringing all the chaos of addiction home to Vine Street. June Bey had stolen things from the house; he had people doing dirt with him in the upstairs bedrooms. Last month, when his parents went south for a family funeral in Carolina, June Bey brought so many people in off Monroe Street that the family home began to resemble a shooting gallery. Gary had scolded his brother for that, even threatened to tell their father if June Bey didn't give it up. To bring home the corner—that had once been utterly beyond Gary. His father worked hard enough to have peace in his house; his mother loved them all too much to have the worst moments played out in front of her.

Likewise, Gary had seethed for years about his youngest brother, Kwame, who would stash in his bedroom whatever vials he was selling, as well as guns and bullets and all sorts of other paraphernalia. It was enough evidence to place the whole family at risk should the Western knockers come through the front door with a maul. Back in the summer, in fact, the warrant squad had indeed come through the door looking for Kwame, scaring Miss Roberta half to death with their semiautomatics and their threats.

"Kwame McCullough," declared a city officer, coming down the steps from a search of the upstairs bedrooms. "Where's he at? When was he here last?"

Miss Roberta couldn't lie. Neither could she give them her son, who had slipped out the kitchen door only minutes before.

"He . . . I don't . . . he's not here."

"But he was here," said the city cop.

Roberta McCullough fell silent.

"When did he leave?"

"I . . . what is it he's done?"

"He's charged in a warrant. Assault by pointing a handgun."

Regina, the mother of Kwame's child, had sworn out a complaint, claiming that during a heated argument, Kwame pointed a gun at her. Now plainclothesmen were pushing and poking their way through the family home, demanding information and making accusations.

"When was he here last?"

Roberta said nothing.

"You haven't seen him in weeks, right?" said the city cop, his voice rising with contempt.

"I . . . he . . ."

"You're a liar," the plainclothesman told her, then turned toward his partner, a state trooper assigned to the warrant detail. "Look at her. She's a damn liar."

The woman held one hand to her chest, staring out the open front door onto Vine Street. The trooper, sensing perhaps the true cost of the moment, would not play to his partner.

"Ma'am," he said quietly. "I'm just doing my job here. Your son needs to turn himself in and deal with this warrant."

When Gary came into the house minutes later, he found his mother at the edge of tears, broken by the confrontation and terrified for Kwame. Again, Gary had blamed his brother—not only for the assault on Regina, but for refusing to surrender on the warrant and bringing the jump-out squad through the front door.

By Gary's reckoning, June Bey and Kwame thought only of themselves when they brought the corner into these rooms, and by such a standard, Gary rated himself the better son. He was a drug addict to be sure, but at least he thought twice about doing anything that crossed the love he felt for his mother and father.

Less than a week earlier, however, he had—for want of a blast—brought the hellish tableau of a drug overdose before his mother's sight.

He had cursed himself then and cursed himself since; but again today, he was down in the same basement with two white boys, playing at the same caper for the same fee.

"Gary, man, this shit is right," mumbles John Boy sitting up.

Gary nods in agreement, then looks across the ciuttered basement to see Dan Boy, still sniffing the air and twitching, his head cocked to one side like a squirrel.

"You okay?" asks Gary.

John Boy turns slowly and takes stock of his friend. "Hey, Dan. What's up?"

But Dan Boy has left this world for some other dimension. He's jerking spastically and giving a wide-eyed stare at his companions; it's the look of deep paranoia often found at the heart of a good speedball.

"Yo, Dan," says Gary.

The white boy skitters against the broken dresser, knocking an empty forty-ounce to the floor. It doesn't shatter, but the noise brings Gary back to what remains of his senses. Upstairs, his mother is working in the kitchen.

Gary turns to John Boy. "We got to go."

John Boy nods. The two of them ease past the wilting Dan to open the back basement door. Gary goes through first, then pushes up the double metal doors of the backyard grating. Sunlight streams into the basement lair.

"C'mon, Dan. We're rollin' out."

But Dan is having no part of it, and soon a pantomime is playing out in the rear yard, with Gary and John Boy out by the laundry line, gesturing frantically, trying to lure Dan from the basement. They wave their arms and smile stupidly, alternating words of warm encouragement with impatient blurts of irritation—and all for nothing. The most Dan Boy can manage is to pop his head out of the walk-up, then jerk his neck around like a rodent, squinting in every direction.

"Damn," John Boy says. "He's all fucked up."

Gary and John huddle up and make a plan. They go to the end of the yard and mouth threats about leaving whether Dan comes or not. They walk halfway down the alley, bringing a nervous Dan to the edge of the yard and allowing Gary to double back and close the walk-up grate. He does so with profound relief, then looks up to see his mother watching him in the kitchen window. He can't bring himself to wonder how long she has been there.

The white boys are crazy trouble. Gary again swears to keep them from his basement, to put some distance between his corner capers and the family home. But he's really no longer in a position to make and keep those kinds of bargains. When he gets back to the crabhouse after his hour-and-a-half's misadventure with the white boys, he's told that he'll be losing another day on the clock, leaving him with a paycheck for Saturdays only.

Soon it will be winter and Gary McCullough, citizen drug addict—a man who needs only a modest paycheck, his basement library, and a good breakaway syringe to live a comfortable and serene existence—will be forced back into the corner mix. For him, the game is getting harder. The vacant houses are truly vacant now; the copper and aluminum is long gone. Stealing from junkyards can get you beaten to death and the legendary car caper with Will is ancient history. Ronnie Boice isn't around, either; she's off with her brother since Gary gave her the shoulder at the crabhouse. For now, at least, Gary is alone.

A week after he has to coax Dan out of the basement, he's out walking with two other white companions, coming south on Fulton from the liquor store. One of his pale friends has sprung for Gary's favorite—a forty of Mickey's malt liquor—and Gary is high and loose on a good one-and-one purchase. He's giving free voice to his mind, letting a one-sided conversation wander from religion to space travel to investment strategies. He doesn't notice the tall, dark-skinned kid change direction on the pavement behind him, or the other two coming from across the street.

"You know what this is," says the tall one, flashing what looks to be a small .25 pistol. "Get in the fucking alley."

The white boys know very well what it is. It's after dark and they're blocks north of where they should be.

A second kid pulls a hunting knife.

"Right now. Get in the alley, motherfucker."

Gary tries to walk sideways, to skirt the issue even as the white boys are led into the darkness.

The tall one turns on him.

"You too, nigger," he says. "You in this shit, too."

Mickey's, wallets, and house keys go to the ground. Excluding the alcohol, the entire haul comes to about $2.75 in cash money. In the close quarters of the alley, Gary risks a quick look at faces and fails to recognize the crew; they're from some other neighborhood. The stickup boys show only disgust: If they'd caught up to this safari before the white boys copped, they should be getting at least twenty or thirty dollars. If they'd caught up to it afterward, they should be getting three or four vials. It doesn't add up.

"This ain't shit," says the tall one.

"Man, please," says Gary. "It's all we got."

The tall boy points the .25 at Gary's head and lets loose with a stream of motherfucker-this and motherfucker-that. Gary looks down at the pavement, waiting some long seconds to learn what a bullet actually feels like.

"Turn your pockets out," the one with the knife says.

They do so, and the tall one shakes his head, glaring at Gary. It's a look that seems to say: You want to walk with white boys, you best come up with some white-boy money when asked.

"Man, please," says Gary again.

"Get the fuck out my sight," shouts the tall one.

The white boys back out of the alley. Gary tries to reach down for his forty, but tall boy kicks the bottle across the pavement. "I said get the fuck outta here."

They run. The white boys go south toward Baltimore Street; Gary goes around the block and back up Fayette to his mother's house. He heads that way telling himself that he'll come back, that he'll get Kwame's .38 and come back, but, of course, he does nothing of the kind. It's not in his nature.

Instead, Gary ends the night in his mother's kitchen, his high wasted and the snake hissing from his stomach. He's back at the bottom, without any sort of plan for tomorrow, yet carrying the habit of a man who, not two months ago, was making $200 to $250 a week. Gary needs capers—new capers, better capers. This one, this business with white boys, is more problem than anything else. He needs the world to give a little, to go easy on him for a while. He's given five whole years to the corner, five years for which he has absolutely nothing to show, save for the darkened webbing that marks both arms. But in the quiet of his mother's kitchen, Gary can still muster enough innocence to be incredulous.

"I could have been killed," he tells his mother. "Over nuthin', they would've taken a life and just kept on goin.'"

Miss Roberta clasps her son's hand in both of hers. Gary shakes his head and shivers out a quick cry.

"The mentality out there is just . . ."

Gary drops his head, squeezes his mother's hand, and weeps.

Marvin Parker has to go.

Fran Boyd knows it now, in fact, she's known it for weeks, but had for a time resisted the idea of life alone. Coming out of detox, she had abandoned one world without the guarantee of another. Save for her children, everyone she cares about or with whom she shares a history is a drug addict; every one of them—friends, family, acquaintances—stands now as a threat to the fragile idea of recovery.

By virtue of his own attempt to detox, Marvin had given her the promise of a new stage on which to act out her life. Marvin had been part of a plan, a kindred soul who could share her fears and hopes, and support her best efforts. He was a casualty just as she was; they would heal each other.

Now, with Marvin running up to Baltimore Street for vials every day, the idea seems ridiculous. Now, she can't help feeling betrayed.

She had sheltered him, taking him into her new house, yet he had gone back to the corner. She had given him love—physical love, at least— but it had hardly slowed him down. She had offered emotional support, yet got back nothing in kind. Instead, Marvin was up at Baltimore and Franklintown four and five times a day, slinging to use, even bringing it home and getting high in her bedroom. Fran had insisted time and again that he at least keep the mechanics of his problem out in the street, but he couldn't even grant her that.

But this past weekend, the first in November, Marvin hadn't come home at all, except to stick his head in the door on Saturday night and try to beg a few dollars more. By Monday morning, Fran was resolved: Marvin has to go.

She spends the early afternoon gathering his things from around the house, filling his duffel bag with clothes and linens and bathroom items. Fran packs carefully; she's leaving nothing behind, no pretext for him to return and try to talk his way back inside.

She lugs the bag to the front door, then lies down on the living room rug, listening to music on the old stereo's one working speaker, justifying her actions in her own mind. She stews for a couple hours, her anger rising to a slow boil before Marvin finally comes into the house, street-worn and spent.

"You got to go," she tells him.

Marvin looks at her as if this statement is coming out of the blue.

"I'm sorry, but you got to go," she says again, getting up quickly and grabbing his bag. Marvin looks down to see Fran forcing all his worldy possessions on him. He makes no move for the duffel bag, trying instead to anchor himself on the living room wall. Fran walks past him, opens the door, and tosses the bag onto the front steps.

"Marvin, you got to go," she says, conveying absolute conviction.

"Fran . . ." he says.

"No, don't even start."

Marvin tries to settle in, to take those five or six steps to the kitchen table, but Fran moves back into the room and looks him hard in the face.

"You don't leave, I'm callin' the police."

"Fran . . . why?" he asks. "I got no place to go."

She walks over, touching his shoulder to steer him lightly toward the door. He looks at her, and finally, seeing nothing he can work with, he goes.

With him goes Fran's belief in her own recovery. When she left the detox center, it was with a feeling of power. In the eight weeks since then, it has come to seem little more than an illusion. Fran has lost more than a man or a relationship; giving up on Marvin is giving up on her plan. And like all plans along Fayette Street, this one is a wisp of thing. Two months ago, she had sketched a thin line between two points; she knows no other routes.

Later that afternoon, Fran tries to look at her algebra book for the first time in a week, but she's missed as many classes as she's attended, and the first problem, with all its obscurity, only infuriates her. She watches Oprah, then listens to the radio for an hour, and then, before DeRodd gets home from school, she goes to Baltimore and Franklintown to snatch a vial. For her, it's a new corner with new faces, offering anonymity, so word won't get back to Scoogie or Bunchie, Gary or Karen—anyone from around Fayette Street who might make her feel the deed.

The backsliding begins—not all at once, but gradually, and with all the seductive ease that comes with good heroin. She acknowledges the shame, greets it openly, and keeps right on with what she's doing. Marvin comes back, too: The morning after she kicks him out, he shows up again, pleading poverty, crying about being on the street with nowhere to go. Fran doesn't have strength enough to argue, and Marvin moves his things back into the house, all the while promising to get back into detox again. His latest ploy is to tell her that he's been calling the recovery center, trying to get to the top of the waiting list. She no longer believes him, but then again, she no longer believes herself. Through October and into November, they are together but separate in the house on Boyd Street, biding time, each of them slipping backward, overtaken by the inevitable.

DeRodd barely senses the change; he's nine now, old enough only to notice that the refrigerator, which two months ago was a source of wonder, is now as empty as it was at the Dew Drop. There's nothing but mayonnaise and relish and the end of a bread loaf with mold growing green on the crust.

DeAndre, however, sees it all. Fran knows he watches her out of one eye, judging, assessing, looking for an excuse to abandon his own pretensions. Why should he beg the Wendy's manager for a second chance or look for work elsewhere if his mother is giving up on finding a job? If Fran isn't going to her classes, why should he ask Rose Davis for more work-study or look into getting reinstated for spring semester? And why, if his mother is creeping up to Baltimore Street, should he feel anything but justified in slipping down to McHenry Street to smoke Phillie blunts and drink St. Ides?

A month back, when DeAndre finally gave up on the notion that the Wendy's manager was ever going to call him for another shift, he talked vaguely about going back on the job hunt. But now, inertia prevails on Boyd Street. Fran isn't going to classes, and for his part, DeAndre is getting up later and later, sometimes sleeping until early afternoon, then leaving Boyd Street after dark, heading east toward his old haunts.

Fran senses the change in DeAndre, but she no longer has standing enough to challenge him. Eventually, there is a November day when Fran comes quietly downstairs and sees her son at the table, counting and manicuring a fat roll of tens and fives. DeAndre tries to pocket the money as casually as he can, but she's not blind.

"You out there again," she states plainly.

"Who?"

"You is. I know."

She tells him this as they sit at the kitchen table: Fran, burning a Newport down to the filter; DeAndre, still in his underwear at two in the afternoon, eyes red and marbled from the night before.

"Please," says DeAndre dismissively.

"Andre, ain't no other reason for you to have all that."

She watches as he rages at her for the accusation: "Jus' cause I get some money together, you think I'm sellin' drugs. Why's it always got to be that I'm sellin' drugs?"

"You ain't got no job."

"You ain't either," he shouts.

"I'm sayin' how you got the money if you ain't got no job? You out there sellin' that shit again."

"Ma, I'm not slingin'. I just got Dorian and Dinky to pay me back some of what they owed me. You think I'm gonna take a chance of gettin' locked up before my son is born? Please."

It's a weak lie and she's heard it before, but whatever authority was granted her in August is now lost.

"You still on probation," she warns him. "You get another charge you likely go to jail."

"I can jail," he says, diffident.

"You hardheaded. No one can teach you shit."

"You sure as hell can't."

"Get out then," she yells, deeply wounded. "If you livin' here, then you still my son. Otherwise, you get your ass out the damn door."

DeAndre storms upstairs, dresses, and slams the front door on his way out. Fran doesn't see or hear from him for two days, until Tyreeka calls to say that DeAndre has been staying on Riggs Avenue with her.

A few days later, soon after DeAndre returns to Boyd Street, he gives his mother all the evidence she'll ever need. After spending a morning vialing up several hundred dollars worth of coke in the front room, her son goes down to McHenry Street and leaves his mirror, glossed with residue, on the kitchen table. Half thinking, DeAndre took the vials and hid the razor, but left the mirror where Fran couldn't help finding it.

Fran senses the insult, the casual indifference that allows her son to use their home for cutting up product. On the street, he's beyond control; she knows that. But these rooms are still her home and despite all that has happened, she feels she should be able to claim that much. A month ago, the sight of the mirror might have thrown her into paroxysms of territorial rage; now, though, the anger she manages is vague and empty.

She goes upstairs, leaving the mirror on the table, where DeAndre will see it when he comes home. She takes off her coat, rubs her eyes until they are bloodshot, then crawls into bed.

Marvin is out somewhere, which is just as well. He's about the last person she wants to see at this moment. When DeRodd comes bounding home from school, letting the door slam loudly behind him, she tries to wrap a pillow around her ears. But DeRodd's roughhousing carries past that barrier, and she raises her head just enough to shout her displeasure.

DeRodd quiets. Fran sleeps.

When she gets up hours later, it's dark. DeRodd is moping in the kitchen. There's not a damn thing worth eating in the icebox, and less in the pantry. Even dry cereal is but a memory.

"I'm hungry," DeRodd tells her.

"I know you hungry. I'm hungry, too."

It's not yet Thanksgiving and the month's money is gone. Fran sends DeRodd back up to Scoogie's for a macaroni-and-cheese dinner. Then, with the house empty, she makes a systematic search for DeAndre's stash, reasoning that it's her home, that anything he brings through that rowhouse door is her property. She checks DeRodd's room, the bathroom, the unfinished basement—a thorough tossing of the house that yields nothing, save for a few empty glassine bags in his bedroom—dope, not coke—enough of a hint to make her wonder if DeAndre himself is snorting. He must be keeping the stash elsewhere, out of her reach, bringing home only enough to vial up a day or two worth of product. She has to admit it: The boy is learning.

When Marvin finally shows his face, she does everything possible to make the man cough out a few dollars, telling her autumn love that it's coming on winter and she's sick of his leeching ways, that he's going to have to put a few dollars in the kitty if he's even thinking about staying past New Year's. But Marvin shrugs her off and disappears, heading back up Boyd Street to the Franklintown corners. Through the window, she watches him hike the incline, flinging a few choice barbs as he goes, but she gets nothing for her effort.

No doubt the birthday celebration last month had brought out the worst in Marvin. Thinking on it now, Fran realizes that letting him share that blast with her made all things permissible. At the time, she had rationalized it, telling herself that it was a special event, a celebration. But by the next morning, it was clear to her that with Marvin as with DeAndre, she had conceded whatever high ground she still held. From that point forward, the man knew no limit.

In the days that followed the birthday mess, Fran had tried to change course and make Marvin do the same. She talked with him for hours, trying to make him see what he was losing. At times, he had agreed, promising to do better and appealing to Fran for pity. And Fran couldn't do anything but give him more time; she needed so badly to believe. But that was then.

"Fuck him," she says, as she lies down on the living room rug, turning briefly on her side to give the stereo a little twist. She gets it going on the R&B gold station, then stretches out fully and stares at the blue stucco walls. Teddy Pendergrass croons above the static.

"Fuck him," she says again.

She'd come out of the gate so strong back in August. She'd moved off Fayette Street, and done all the right things—or most of the right things, anyway. She'd made plans, registered for classes, looked for jobs. And in her greatest leap of faith, she'd gotten herself a man, hoping against hope for someone with whom the burdens might be shared. Instead, she got Marvin.

Marvin, Michael, Gary—all of her old loves were wandering these same streets, windblown, drifting from corner to corner, blast to blast. With Gary and Michael, it was different. With them, she had been in the game; their fall coincided nicely with her own, so that she had been nothing but deadweight dragging them down. But Marvin had turned the tables; this time it was Fran who was burdened. When she missed one step, then another, Marvin Parker was right there, waiting to take advantage as she stumbled.

Marvin had been a bad choice, but good choices along Fayette Street were hard to come by. The only men Fran knew were either on the corner, or a half-step away from it. Coming out of detox, the most she had any right to hope for was an addict in recovery like herself, a wounded soul chasing the same meetings and twelve-step programs. In short, someone just as fragile and vulnerable.

Even Mike Ellerbee, the one person who had confounded her view of life's possibilities by simply walking off the corner and into the merchant marine—even Little Mike had pulled her up short. Ten days ago, she'd seen him down on Mount Street, wired up and bleary-eyed, talking too fast about how he had sent money back to his girl Ducey for his stepson and daughter, how he had written to her from aboard his ship, telling her to spend the money on rent and utilities and school clothes and toys.

"She just smoked it up," Mike said, complaining bitterly. "I come home, I find out she hasn't done anything but party."

Fran looked at Mike Ellerbee, standing there on Mount Street with a forty-ounce in his hand, and assumed that his run was over, that he'd be slinging again by spring and shooting people in the summer. The man was done.

Except that a week or so later, she'd asked her sister where Mike was at. Gone, Bunchie told her.

"Say what?"

"He back on the boat."

It was true. Mike had come home, stumbled for a day or two, then paused to assess the situation for what it was: "Being back here," he told people, "it's like I'm dying."

He called his shipping agent and got himself on the next container vessel leaving the country. Fran never had a chance to give a good-bye holler.

Why Little Mike? Why not Marvin? Why not her, for that matter? How is it that some people start to stumble and then catch themselves? How does anyone find it possible to tear himself to shreds time and time again, and then, against any sensible expectation, find strength enough to piece himself back together? Logically, Fran knows what is required. She knows she has to make Marvin leave, then forgive herself, then call Antoinette and get back on the waiting list for twenty-eight-day detox. She knows she needs to go to the meetings and get a sponsor and eventually push herself beyond the hero's welcome and the victory lap. She needs to get a job, hold on to some money, and somehow get her ass out to the county, where people manage to live without a drug corner every two blocks.

Two months ago, when she first emerged from the cocoon of detox, salvation had seemed so certain. She had crawled out of 1625 Fayette, using strength that she could barely recognize as her own. She had gotten sick and gotten well and kicked heroin in the ass, returning to the street after four weeks with a contempt for the corner that bordered on arrogance. Now, it's all as much a mystery as ever. Now, she can only live moment by moment.

Maybe tomorrow she'll call down to Antoinette. Maybe after Christmas one of the charity beds will be available. But for now, what she needs to do is stay indoors for a day or two, and then maybe find a way to scrape together enough cash to make it to check-day next.

Instead, she goes to the corner twice that week. On Friday night, she's up at Franklintown and Baltimore again, looking to start a weekend binge, when she runs across a familiar face.

"Hey, you," says Shorty Boyd. Marvin's senior partner, Fran knew, was having himself a nice little run on this corner.

"You seen Marvin?" Fran asks.

"He around. You need him?"

Fran shakes her head.

"What's up?" Shorty asks.

Not three weeks ago, Fran had been standing at her kitchen window when she saw Shorty get the jump on some young boy and put a gun in his face. Fran watched him strip the boy clean, then walk back up to Baltimore Street, Casual as could be. By the probabilities, Shorty Boyd should be ten years in the grave, yet here he was on Franklintown Road, an independent offering his wares.

"What you got for me?" Fran asks him.

Shorty frowns, then cocks his head. "Thought you was doin' good," he says.

"I was," Fran says.

"Then you don't need none of this."

On this night, she goes home taking the words, not the heroin, knowing that she's already a little bit ill, that lately she's been celebrating a little too regularly. She lies in bed and thinks about things—about DeAndre and herself and her family, about Marvin and this house and Tyreeka with the baby on the way. She wonders about God or fate or luck, about a player like Shorty Boyd standing out on a corner, selling heroin, then refusing to sell that heroin to her. Shorty Boyd, of all people, living at the broken edges of life all these years—tonight of all nights, he materializes on her corner and gives a good word. As if he cared. As if she mattered.

Lying in bed, Fran swears to herself that she'll stay inside the whole weekend. She'll keep hid and get herself well. She'll do it by force of will, without any help from anyone else. And when she's done feeling sick, she might clean up the house and borrow some money from Scoogie for the Thanksgiving groceries. She'll cook for the holiday, have the whole bunch of them over. Maybe call Tyreeka and tell her to come down and spend the long weekend with her and DeAndre. And if Marvin doesn't get his shit together by the new year, she'll deal with that, too.

But now, if she can, she will sleep.

DeAnte Tyree McCullough enters this world at 4:15 P.M. on Thanksgiving Day, crying like he knows the whole story.

By then, Tyreeka is beyond spent, her eyes glazed and fixed on the far wall of the Sinai Hospital birthing room. She is fourteen years old, equipped with a minimum of prenatal instruction and no painkillers, and she has just produced a seven-pound, twelve-ounce baby. Even now, with the boychild crying in a midwife's arms, Tyreeka seems captive to the terror.

DeAndre is beside her at the head of the bed, holding her hand, unable or unwilling to let go. It's all he has been able to do for the last two hours, every other word and action having departed his mind from the moment he arrived at this life-bringing.

"Hold your son," Fran orders.

DeAndre looks at his mother, bleary-eyed.

"Hold him," Fran insists.

He reaches out, both arms stiff and perpendicular to his chest. The midwife gently slips the bundle to him in a cautious, slow-motion handoff, conceding the package only after she's sure of DeAndre's intentions.

"He look real strong, Dre," Fran tells him. "And all that hair, too."

DeAndre stares down and the child squints back. The new father says and reveals nothing—DeAndre McCullough, for once stripped of bluster, is brought to a pensive silence. The baby gives a little cry.

DeAndre looks up expectantly and the midwife retrieves the infant from his arms. The bundle is presented to Tyreeka, but she's beyond reaction. After a moment or two, the newborn is taken to the warmer. DeAndre squeezes Tyreeka's hand one last time, then leaves the birthing room with his mother.

"Damn," he says in the hallway, offering his first words in two hours. "After seeing that, I have *much* respect for women."

By ordinary measure, the birth had come easily enough. Tyreeka had endured ten hours of labor, but only the last two of those took place at Sinai Hospital, with the midwife and Fran Boyd talking the teenager through the struggle. The medical particulars, however, don't begin to reflect the fear and confusion of the event.

For one thing, Tyreeka somehow got her due date wrong, so that the baby, expected some time around Christmas, instead reached full-term on the prior holiday. Early that morning, she had called the birthing center to report intermittent pain. But when questioned by the staffer on duty, Tyreeka had mentioned the Christmas due date. Take a warm bath, she was told. See if the contractions stop.

Which is pretty much all the girl did while enduring the early and intermediate stages of childbirth. Later, when the urgency of the situation became clear to her, she tried to call friends who had offered to drive her to Sinai Hospital when the big day came. But the plan was for a December birth and on this holiday afternoon, Tyreeka had been unable to reach anyone. Finally, she had called a city ambulance, and then, begging the paramedics through the pain of her contractions, she convinced them to drive not to Liberty Medical, the closest hospital, but to Sinai, where she had been scheduled. By the time she arrived, she looked like a deer transfixed by headlights, a little girl in absolute fear of what her body was doing to her.

When word of the impending event reached DeAndre, he was still high after a day with Preston, Jamie, and the rest of the older Fayette Street crew. Sharing a hack with his mother, DeAndre got to the birthing-room doors just as Tyreeka let out a shriek.

"Um," said DeAndre, eyes bloody.

"Get in there," ordered his mother.

He cracked the door, poking his head inside just long enough to see Tyreeka struggling to change position, the midwife and her helpers trying to give directions.

"I'll be out here," he declared.

"No you won't," his mother told him.

"Ma, there's too many people in there already."

Fran didn't bother to argue. She grabbed her son by the jacket sleeve and tossed him into the room. Once within his girlfriend's field of vision, he had no choice; he walked meekly to Tyreeka's side. She saw him and said nothing, but took his hand in a desperate grip.

"Father," said the midwife, "you can encourage her. She needs to push. She needs to push hard when the contractions come."

But DeAndre, paralyzed by weed and awe both, kept his hand in Tyreeka's grip and was silent.

In the final half hour, Fran seized the moment, going to the other side of Tyreeka and talking her through, telling her over and over again to push with all her might.

Horrified and speechless, Tyreeka could only cry.

"The harder you push, the sooner you can rest . . . Reeka, you got to listen to them. You got to start pushing. Reeka, listen to me now . . ."

Even the midwife was having a hard time keeping Tyreeka focused, but Fran stayed in her face, demanding action from a lonely and frightened schoolgirl, helping the midwife and assistants as they moved her between bed and bathroom, looking for new positions to ease the pain. As DeAndre stood, mute and frozen, Fran urged Tyreeka on until the last shout of agony mingled with a wet cry.

Now, the new mother is lost to the world, and DeAndre, dazed in an altogether different sense, goes back to Scoogie's house on Saratoga Street with his mother, arriving a little before seven. There the Boyd clan has gathered for the holiday. Fran had been cooking all morning before the call came from Tyreeka, and with enough groceries and a decent kitchen, she has a gift for all the family recipes. Sherry, Bunchie, and Scoogie had taken up the slack when Fran left for the hospital, so that soon after she returns from the birth of her grandson, a fourteen-pound bird and a slew of side dishes hit the table.

For every member of the Boyd family, it's a righteous occasion. It's also little short of astonishing—an absurd, Norman Rockwell moment for a battered tribe, a clan whose number has, in the past few hours, grown by one.

Scoogie takes the carving knife and does the honors.

"DeAndre thankful for his son," he says, dishing slices of bird onto a serving plate and looking to DeRodd and Little Stevie. "What else we got to be thankful for?"

DeRodd says nothing. Little Stevie shrugs.

"Ain't none of us courtside," DeAndre deadpans.

Big Stevie laughs. He's in rare form tonight, having come in from his post on the Mount Street corners. He's cleaned and shaved, adorned in a dapper sports coat. Bunchie is looking good, too; she's rail thin, as always, but dressed in a pleated skirt and sweater for the occasion. Sherry and Kenny are present, and Alfred as well—the whole Dew Drop contingent transplanted to Scoogie's dining room, making their way around an oak table that once belonged to their grandmother, taking turns with the serving spoons and carving knives. Bunchie's daughter, Nicky, brings DeQuan, her four-month-old, and Corey, the child's father and DeAndre's slinging partner from last winter when he opened up Fairmount Avenue. At belt level or below, the children—DeRodd and Little Stevie, even Ray Ray, who has started to toddle about—are a sawed-off herd of scavengers, edging the table, grabbing at seconds, and then racing into the living room.

Pints and half-pints of alcohol are in evidence, though by Boyd family standards, the chemistry is tame. There's not much coke or dope to speak of before the early morning hours, when Kenny, Alfred, Stevie, and

Bunchie will take their walk back up the hill and down Fayette. Instead, there is only the after-dinner lethargy that follows any preposterously large meal.

"Fran?" moans Stevie, stretched across the sofa.

"What?"

"You can burn."

Fran laughs.

"No joke, Ma," says DeAndre. "You got skills in the kitchen."

"It was good, Fran. Real good," adds Bunchie.

"Reeka missed out on a good meal," DeAndre muses. "She gonna be mad as I don't know what."

Fran snorts.

"Andre a father," laughs Bunchie, looking at Fran. "My gawd."

"And DeRodd an uncle," adds Scoogie.

The idea of it brings the older generation to laughter.

"Uncle Dee-Rodd," says Fran, trying it out. "It don't even begin to sound right."

DeRodd lifts his head off the other sofa, perking up at the mention. "Ma?"

"What?"

"He my cousin, right?"

"He your nephew. You an uncle."

"I can be that?" asks DeRodd, suddenly ennobled. "I'm an uncle like Uncle Stevie then."

DeAndre gets up off the sofa, stretches, looks around the living room at the sprawl of his mother's family, all of them heavy-lidded and half-asleep, dreaming of the second wind required to tackle sweet potato pie.

"I got a son," he says, more to hear himself say the words than to boast. "I'm a man now. I got a man's responsibilities."

Fran snorts again. "Please. You didn't look like all that much of a man in that hospital room."

DeAndre laughs, unable to sustain the pretense. "Ma, I was so blunted. I couldn't say a damn thing. I couldn't do nuthin' but just stand there."

"You did all right. You were in there," she says charitably. "Reeka had to work, though. She a brave little girl."

"Most definitely," DeAndre agrees.

These moments for the family album continue through dessert and then the cleanup. Finding his mother alone for a minute in the kitchen, DeAndre tries to say what he feels.

"Ma, this was good."

"Huh?"

"This here. We was a family tonight. Everyone, even Uncle Stevie looked good . . . like he used to, you know?"

Fran nods.

"We should do this again for Christmas."

"It was good," Fran agrees.

"Christmas, I can bring Reeka and my son."

He leaves that night feeling as good about things as he can remember feeling. He goes up the hill to Vine Street to look for his father, and, not finding Gary there, he shares the good news with his grandparents instead. Then he rolls around the corners—Monroe to Mount to McHenry—to strut his new status in front of anyone willing to listen. No mere cigar for this first-time father, either: He shares one blunt with Preston, another with Dinky and Tae.

"You next," he tells R.C.

For what's left of the night, DeAndre stays with the boys, drinking and smoking, his talk crossing back and forth between ordinary, prideful bluster and something truer to the day's experience.

"I got to be a father to him," he tells his crew. "I'm gonna do better for him than got done for me, and I'm gonna be up there with him so he knows who I am. My child gonna know me."

Later he walks back down the hill with Dinky, telling his cousin that he'll be off the corners completely for a while. What business they have together at Gilmor and McHenry now falls to Dinky; he'll watch the shop while DeAndre looks to his son.

"He a tough little boy, too," DeAndre assures his cousin. "Only cried but the one time so far."

The next morning, he's up later than he means to be, tired from the previous night. Still, he and Fran arrive at Sinai by early afternoon. They split up in the lobby: Fran, on a mission to find a child-safety seat for the ride home; DeAndre, heading straight for the maternity ward.

"Name?" asks the woman at the security desk.

"McCullough. DeAndre McCullough."

"And you're here to see?"

"My son."

He says it with such obvious delight that the woman can't help smiling.

When DeAndre walks into Tyreeka's room, she's awake, resting, her lunch half-eaten in front of her. The baby is stirring in his bassinet—mouth open, eyes shut, arms outstretched, tiny fingers curling into air.

Tyreeka is not the same; not by any stretch of imagination is she the same. She watches DeAndre as he negotiates around the hospital bed, leaning over to kiss her lightly on the forehead. Though drawn from the ordeal, her face is radiant. But it's her manner, assured and regal, that conveys her new status. From the first, she had planned to hold DeAndre to her; now she believes she has means enough to do this.

Looking down at his son, DeAndre can sense as much. He can step outside himself long enough to acknowledge that this young girl, once a plaything, will now and forever be more than that. She might hold him, she might not. But never again will Tyreeka Freamon be incidental. At this moment anyway, he accepts all claims and obligations. And for the first time ever, perhaps, DeAndre concedes to his girl.

"You can pick him up," she tells DeAndre.

"He asleep."

"No he ain't. He wakin' up."

DeAndre reaches into the bassinet and gathers up the bundle. He sits on the edge of the hospital bed, propping the newborn on his knees at arm's length.

"Damn," he says, amazed.

He's still there, still captivated, when Fran arrives. She walks to the bedside, takes Tyreeka's hand, then backs off to watch her son watching his son.

"Dre, what are you thinkin'?"

"Huh."

"What are you thinkin'?"

DeAndre shrugs. "I'm not thinkin' about anything."

Fran shakes her head. "How," she asks, "can you sit there and not think of anything?"

"I did it in school all the time," says DeAndre dryly.

They all laugh, even Fran. But then she catches herself and dishes out her token disapproval: "That's sad, Andre."

"It's the truth," he says quietly.

Fran looks beneath the bassinet, taking stock of the hospital freebies. "We should ask them for extra. They got a baby-care package that they give if you ask for it."

Fran leaves to talk to the nurse, comes back arms laden with supplies, then goes back out to work the nurse for a full package of diapers, pausing in her efforts only long enough to tell DeAndre he's not holding the baby correctly.

"I know how to hold him," he counters.

"You got to support the head."

"I got him, Ma."

For the exodus from the hospital, Fran is in charge—so much so that DeAndre and Tyreeka both are bristling by the time they get to Riggs Avenue. In their eyes, Fran has standing as a grandmother only; beyond that, the child-parents intend to take full possession of their baby.

That they set up their nursery on Riggs Avenue, rather than on Boyd Street, is telling; that they spend the first two weeks there, visiting no one and limiting Fran to occasional phone calls and afternoon visits, makes the point clear. Fran had counted her coming grandchild among the few remaining reasons to keep trying, to stay at arm's length from the corner. She fully expected Tyreeka and DeAndre to struggle, to lean heavily on her for advice and support. But for them, the child provides an opportunity for a clear declaration of independence.

In these early days, DeAndre settles in at Tyreeka's aunt's house, willingly submerging himself in a daily routine that spins around the needs of the baby. In the confines of Tyreeka's tiny second-floor room, he is moved at the wonder of his son, and he acts toward Tyreeka in a way that exceeds even her own expectations. He defers to her in all things natal; her every pronouncement regarding the baby is gospel.

Motherhood changes Tyreeka in ways previously unthinkable. Once a needy and lonely girl, she is now dispensing to this newborn a degree of energy and love that suggests a wisdom beyond her fourteen years. Once a corner girl, she has begun to grow into something more, finding within herself a reservoir of maturity that is as inexplicable as it is surprising. Once, she wanted DeAndre and whatever good times he might show her. Now, for the child, she has started to think about more than that.

When DeAndre holds the baby, changes him, or gets him to laugh or coo, she is there to encourage him. When DeAndre talks about going back to school, she tells him how smart he is, how easy it would be for him to get a general equivalency degree. When he insists that he'll have a new job by year's end, she is careful to show him no doubts.

These first days on Riggs Avenue are an idyll, a time when, for once, two children of Fayette Street are able to make dreams meet expectations. Here, for an instant or two, they open up to the newborn and to each other, confident that this fresh life will not betray them or prove them inadequate. Elsewhere, a commitment turns out time and again to be the prelude to abuse and disappointment, but here, in Tyreeka's bedroom, the baby takes what they have to offer and gives back only need and joy and meaning. Amid this, all the petty fights, the cheating, the insults of their last year together are forgiven, if not entirely forgotten.

Their allegiance holds fast through the second weekend in December, when they finally bring the baby down to visit Fran on Boyd Street. There, they occupy the third floor of the rowhouse, with DeAndre lugging the bassinet, stroller, diaper bags, and clothing satchels up the steps and recreating the room on Riggs Avenue as best he can. But Fran remains the outsider in what has, up until now, been DeAndre and Tyreeka's best adventure so far. They know they can do this; they are doing it. As far as DeAndre is concerned, his mother has no place other than to keep Marvin at bay and otherwise admire her son's efforts at fatherhood.

Fran's advice goes unheeded, her experience counts for little. And when she asks to feed her grandson, DeAndre tells her she can't.

"You not supposed to let anyone but the mother feed the baby," he tells her. "Otherwise, the baby won't learn to know its mother."

Fran goes off into a rave. "Who in hell have you been talking to? You don't know what the hell you talking about."

DeAndre stands his ground; Tyreeka told him this and Tyreeka's word is enough for him. Only the mother feeds the baby.

"So you can't give him a bottle neither, right?"

"The father can do it sometimes."

Fran rolls her eyes and stalks around the kitchen, savaging her son's assertions, talking about how she raised DeAndre up and raised DeRodd up and knows more about mothering than the two of them will ever know. DeAndre retreats upstairs.

"For all I get to do with that baby, why you even come down here?" she shouts after him.

"You think you so damn smart." DeAndre yells back. "You got something to say about everything. You can't run your own life but you tryin' to tell us how to raise our child."

Fran follows him up the stairs. "Andre, that child gonna know his mother no matter what. You all is bein' ridiculous."

Ridiculous or not, they shut Fran out, returning after the weekend to stay with Tyreeka's aunt and enjoy another week of fairy-tale existence.

For many of Tyreeka's friends, the arrival of a baby is treated with similar delight and absorption for a period of weeks or months at most. Then, the distractions of adolescence take hold and they go back to the corners, to the dance clubs, to the house parties and movies and new trysts with new boys. The babies go to grandmothers, or great-aunts, or great-grandmothers—to be raised with their birth mothers serving, at best, as older sisters and, at worst, as casual acquaintances.

Tyreeka, by contrast, chooses to stay at home, day after day, and do the work of raising DeAnte. As she sees it, the school semester can still be salvaged: She'll miss three weeks, ask for makeup work and extra credit, then take finals with the rest of her class. Come January, she will get the baby up in the morning, feeding and dressing and playing with him, then dressing herself and catching the bus to Carver. With her aunt working, it will fall to her grandmother to watch DeAnte for as long as it takes Tyreeka to attend school and then catch the same bus back. It will be doubly hard for her to study and graduate, but now, for herself and DeAnte as well, she feels compelled to try. A year ago she was out on the corners with DeAndre and his boys, cutting class, forgoing class for a trip to the harbor or an afternoon movie. Now, because of DeAndre's son—her son—she's thinking and talking in the future tense.

"I'm not quitting school," she tells DeAndre. "I'm not goin' to end up on welfare like all these other girls, sittin' out on the steps every day with their babies."

And DeAndre, still in the thrall of this domestic interlude, can only agree. Stores have been hiring for Christmas shopping season; he'll go out and get a job, maybe even talk to Rose Davis about finishing school.

"We get enough money, we get a place of our own," he tells his girl.

Once, such a fantasy would have meant everything to Tyreeka, and when DeAndre speaks the words, she gives him casual agreement. But Tyreeka is still worried about DeAndre, worried that he'll drift back to the corner, and worried, too, that she'll be drawn into that world with him. Here, at her aunt's house, she's on the bus route to her high school. Here, she gives a share of her AFDC check to her aunt and has room and board and her grandmother to watch the baby when she's in class. At long last, she has something approaching adult guidance and support. But with DeAndre, she knows, every day would be a question.

"I don't want our son growin' up like we did," she tells him. "I don't want him to be doin' the things we did."

For a while longer, DeAndre spends days and nights in the makeshift nursery, assuming the role of father to the extent he understands it. This means providing, and for a time, DeAndre is able—by loan and by barter, by begging from his mother and by calling in some small profit from Dinky—to spring for Pampers and some baby outfits. Everything else is soon beyond his means. Shoes, car seats, jolly jumpers, toys: DeAndre feels the pressure with every need or want Tyreeka can express or he himself can imagine. Worse, he's governed by his standing obsession with material status, his best-brand, damn-the-expense insistence on Weebok or Nike shoes or Disney store clothes, and yes, a gold name-necklace for his child.

"My son," he tells Tyreeka one day, "won't be wearing off-brand shit."

"Andre, how that baby gonna know what he's wearing?"

"I'll know."

"And what about when you locked up?"

"He'll know I was out there makin' money for him."

Tyreeka balks. The same girl who used to measure DeAndre's devotion in the money she could make him spend, now tells the father of her son that all those things would be nice and fine, but what the child needs more is a father's presence.

"You go back on the corner, you might get shot or locked up," she argues. "How you gonna help your son if you dead? How you gonna help him if you in prison?"

DeAndre, who can sense what's coming, begins to battle with her on this point. He cannot lose himself forever on Riggs Avenue. He cannot stay in this nest, changing diapers and warming formula and burying himself in domestic quietude. He has tried the straight way before, wearing Wendy's blue pinstripe and taking home minimum wage for a handful of work shifts. And for a few days shortly before Christmas, he drifts around West Baltimore and the near suburbs, filling applications— the stores at Westside, the Toys 'R' Us on Route 40—but he's pretending to a plan for which he has neither faith nor patience. His mother, he knows, is slipping; she can't sustain the promise that she brought out of detox. And his father is more lost than ever; Gary has been so hungry for capers lately that he hasn't even found the time to come see his grandson. Come right down to it and nothing is waiting on DeAndre McCullough save the corner itself.

He tells himself that it's just temporary, just a quick run to turn a few packages and get enough money together. After that, all the better plans will be back on the table. But no one ever goes down to the corner telling himself anything different. No one tells himself the truth, though many do think it. Outside of the game, people always make it sound like it's a decision to sell drugs, or get high, or take to violence. But that's the way the outside world can afford to view it: As if the same free will that makes life worth living elsewhere can strut down to Mount and Fayette without getting its ass beat bloody. The fact is, it's never so much a decision as the absence of a decision. It would require Herculean strength for DeAndre to find a new moment, to pivot and walk away from the only world he's ever negotiated—a world that guarantees him some kind of standing. And now, with Tyreeka and his son and his own future at stake, that moment simply doesn't come.

By Christmas week, he's back down at Gilmor and McHenry, making real money the way he knows how. He's seen his son born; he's made sure that DeAnte McCullough knows him, that should he catch a bullet or go away for some years in Jessup or Hagerstown, there is a thin but basic bond on which he can rely. Since his Fairmount Avenue arrest, he's held the corner at arm's length, either staying away entirely or leaving it to friends to do most of the street-slinging on a package. But now he's come back big time. He tells himself that when Tyreeka sees the money, when she's up to her ass in paid-for Pampers and toys and designer baby apparel, she won't say shit. This he believes. Deep down, DeAndre tells himself, Tyreeka is still the greedy little girl he used to know.

The week he goes back to the corner, DeAndre visits Riggs Avenue only three times, sometimes bringing Pampers and once, at Tyreeka's urging, showing up with winter shoes—miniature Timberlands—for the baby. But emotionally he's elsewhere; in his heart, he's down at McHenry and Gilmor with his blunts and his forties and all those corner girls looking good to him. And when he pulls out his roll and peels off a five or a ten, Tyreeka can't help resenting the fact that DeAndre is keeping most of the money for himself. Most of all, she resents him for giving up so quickly.

Despite the baby, she is once again losing him. Bitterly, she begins calling Fran's house or throwing pages out to DeAndre on his new beeper.

"Your son needs diapers."

"Your son needs a snowsuit."

"Your son needs cab fare to the clinic."

The needs are genuine enough, and now that DeAndre is steady slinging, Tyreeka makes no more speeches about the evils of the corner. She knows that a decision has been made, that DeAndre will be on McHenry Street no matter what she says, that she can either waste her time arguing or she can keep a hand out and take what money is offered as a practical, get-it-while-I-can matter. But her constant calls and pages are about more than material need. They are Tyreeka's last-ditch effort to hold onto the fragments of a family life that she herself has never known but has tried, against all odds, to create.

With DeAndre back on the corner, it becomes Tyreeka's task to get the baby to his clinic appointments. Or to go to the market and haul back all those cans of formula. Or to lug DeAnte and all his accessories around the west side, bringing him by bus or hack to see Fran, or to stay with DeAndre's cousin Nicky and her baby, DeQuan, or with her girlfriends along Fayette Street. She's alone, save for the company of so many others like her, all of them stumbling down the same road, trying hard to remember to forget whatever it was they once believed.

Just after Christmas, Tyreeka has the baby with her at the WIC clinic in Edmondson Village, waiting for her appointment with a program intake worker, hoping to get on the voucher system for free formula. In the waiting room with her are a half-dozen girls—three older than Tyreeka, two the same age, one a year younger—all with babies in tow, their eyes heavy-lidded from waiting-room torpor, their bodies round and fleshy from recent pregnancy.

"How old yours?" one asks Tyreeka.

"A month."

"Mine three months in a week."

"She pretty," says Tyreeka. "That's a pretty child."

"You got them marks?" the girl asks.

Tyreeka shrugs, confused. The girl lifts her shirt and unhooks the top button of her denims, pulling the waist down to reveal her stretch marks.

"Oh them," says Tyreeka. "Yeah. I got them."

"When they gonna go 'way?" the other girl asks.

Tyreeka doesn't know. But seeing these girls offers some comfort; she senses that she's doing no worse than anyone else. For Christmas, she bought toys and clothes enough on layaway, though it means she'll be paying off stores right through spring. Come this afternoon, she'll be up at the market on Poplar Grove, loading up her cart with formula, her WIC voucher in hand. And next week, she'll have DeAnte back at the clinic for his well-baby checkup. She'll do it all and still find power and conviction within herself to love and nurture a child. Born at the wrong time to the wrong people and for the wrong reason, DeAnte McCullough is, perhaps, fortunate enough to be wanted and cared for by a child who, if not entirely schooled or realistic, is nonetheless proving capable.

"McCullough," says the WIC program worker, carrying a manila file folder into the waiting room. "DeAnte McCullough."

"Here," says Tyreeka, rising.

"You're the mother?"

"Yeah," says Tyreeka, "I am."

Blue enters his mother's house from the back, ducking his head beneath the cracked plywood, looking around at the broken shell of the kitchen, seeing it with new eyes.

"Ho, who's in there?"

"Who dat?" comes a rough voice.

"Blue."

Fat Curt pops his head out of the front room, looking down the hallway at the onetime proprietor of this West Baltimore rowhouse. Blue tries to smile, as if to keep the encounter benign. But Curt is embarrassed; now that Blue has crossed over, there's no other way to feel.

"Man, I'm gone. I'm doin' what I shouldn't be and I'm gone," says Curt, shuffling past Blue, making for the alley.

"Curt, man . . ."

"Naw, I'm gone," his breath freezing in the early December cold. "This is all messed up."

Curt leaves, but Rita is going nowhere. She's still on station in the front room, poking the raw meat of her upper arm, trying to lure blood into the bottom of the syringe. She sees Blue and stops, refraining politely in his presence.

"Hey, Blue. How you been?"

"Makin' it, you know, with the help of the Lord."

"Well, the Lord must know somethin'," muses Rita, "'cause you lookin' good."

"Thanks."

"I know I ain't lookin' so good."

Blue smiles, trying for a response.

"I'm lookin' rough," Rita says. "Feelin' rough, too."

Pimp sits in a three-legged chair in the corner, the chair wedged against the wall for balance, a torn and stained blanket around his shoulders for warmth. Shardene is next to him. Eggy Daddy joins the group, coming down the stairs at the sound of Blue's voice.

"Eggy."

"Hey, Blue."

"Hey."

For George Epps, redemption has been a journey of a thousand small steps, each undertaken in its. proper time. Back in August, the necessary action—perhaps the only action for which he had strength enough— was simply walking away, leaving what remained of his childhood home and transplanting what remained of his life to a cot at the South Baltimore Homeless Shelter. Then came the counseling. Then the meetings. Then a sponsor. And eventually, when he felt stable enough, he began the search for something else to do with his days and a way to see himself as something more than a recovering addict.

He found his way back to the rec center, keeping a promise made long ago to Ella Thompson and taking hold of the arts and crafts sessions with the younger children. Blue found some joy there, some stirring of hope in the faces of the little ones, perfectly oblivious in the laughter of the moment, their hands wet with finger paint or sticky with Elmer's glue. At the rec center, too, he found a friendship with Marzell Myers, Ella's assistant, who went out of her way to encourage him and became one of the first people to make him feel at ease in a world from which he had long been absent.

Meanwhile, down at the shelter, the counselors talked about job training, about maybe taking that next step and hooking into the working life. Blue told them he didn't yet feel strong enough for that, though he had become less resistant to the idea over the last few weeks. Perhaps they're right, he began telling himself. Perhaps it was time for another risk. After all, he had learned to trust the people at the shelter, to balance his own desires with a new awareness of his own limitations and the raw power of addiction. Come what may, Blue promised himself, this time he would not bullshit himself back to Fayette and Monroe.

For weeks now, he had been firm enough in his purpose to walk the old neighborhood, traveling from corner to corner along Fayette Street with eyes shaded by wide-frame sunglasses, an African kufi perched on his head, the earphones of a Walkman tape player serving to tune out the chanting and chirping of the touts. The tape player said it all: Anyone sporting such on these corners could not be getting high; a true fiend would trade a $40 Walkman for one-and-one in a heartbeat.

To those he passed on his daily tour, Blue's abrupt restoration seemed unlikely enough. This was the same man who took two bills a customer at the door of the needle palace all those years; it was the same man who cannibalized the home of his departed mother. That he could find a way to walk among the living anywhere deserved a certain amount of attention. That he could stroll along Fayette Street, where all the old temptations awaited him, seemed bold and remarkable.

Yet nothing about Blue's recovery could be credited to boldness. He had, in these past few months, abandoned the idea that he could assert himself or that his addiction could be manipulated. Instead, Blue had fought through every trick of his own mind, every rationalization and denial, to reach the most essential conclusion: With regard to vials and glassine bags, he was powerless. He could not, after so many lost years, believe that he knew what he was doing. He could not trust in his own judgment and, like it or not, he would have to trust in the judgment of others.

Armed with that much understanding, he had ventured from the homeless shelter in ever-lengthening sorties, first skirting the old haunts, then glancing past them, then—as he found the strength—gliding right through them, carrying himself through corners fat with coke and dope.

But on this December day, the small step forward involves the shooting gallery that he is obliged to call his own.

"What's up?" he asks the crowd that gathers in the front room of the derelict house.

"Same ol' thing," says Eggy. "You know that."

"Yeah," says Blue, "well that's the thing. That's definitely the thing I want to get at."

There is so much that ought to be said now, so many arguments that Blue could make. Moments earlier, before walking back through the alley and into this house, he told himself that this act was more than symbolic. I started this nonsense, he reasoned. I damn sure ought to finish it.

What had once stood as brick-and-mortar testament to his mother's life work had long since become a blighted monument to his own life's waste and pain. That Blue had moved on, that he'd given up paying the back taxes on 1846 Fayette and that the city probably owned the broken shell—all this was somehow beside the point. Blue knew what this house had been and he knew what he had done. For his own sake, for the sake of what remained of the neighborhood and for the sake of the lost souls in the shooting gallery, he had to shut this thing down.

"I jus' wanted to say . . ."

Speech coming. The old crew looks at him as if from the end of some long, deep tunnel. Blue senses the distance involved and feels the necessary words drying in his throat.

"I'm sayin' that, you know, this has got to stop."

Pimp shifts uneasily in his broken chair.

"I mean you want to get help, I'm here to help, you know. An' if you want to go on like you been, that's okay, too, but I'm sayin' I don't want it to be here."

The others look around at each other. Rita shifts her eyes away, staring into the sunlit crack in the front plywood. Eggy Daddy steps past Blue, mumbling an excuse me, looking for some other moment than the one now being shared.

"I mean," Blue continues, "I know I started this. But it's got to stop somewhere."

"Well," says Rita, always polite, "you right to say so, I guess . . ."

But no one moves. Blue tries to talk to Rita, to convince her to take a walk with him up to Bon Secours. Get some help for the raw flesh on that upper arm.

"You need some attention on that."

"I know it."

"So let's go."

"Now?" asks Rita.

"Yeah now. No time like the present."

Rita shrugs, looking around the shooting gallery for help. When none is forthcoming, she tells Blue that tomorrow would be better.

"Tomorrow," says Blue, sad at the word.

"I be ready tomorrow."

He tried. And for trying, he feels a little better. He wishes them well, telling them to stay warm, assuring them that they can pull him up any time if they're looking for help. Then he walks back through the kitchen and into the alley. His war is over—he prays that it's over anyway—and they are still here, soldiering into another winter. And Blue, for all his new strength, can't help but love them, respect them even, for their resilience, for their unwavering devotion. From the outside, Blue can see it perfectly: There's no one like a dope fiend. There's no one alive who can go to sleep in a vacant house at night in the dead of winter, night after night, knowing that he's doing what he has to, that everything else might be lost, but the blast will justify him in the end.

No speech by George Epps can move these people. As he leaves his mother's house, he has to concede that in some sense their claim to the property is more legitimate than his own. A week passes before he rouses himself to call the Western District, talking to a police captain about giving the needle palace a toss, maybe reboarding all the doors and windows with fresh plywood.

"There's people in there that need medical attention," Blue tells the captain. "They need to get some attention for their own good. That's really why I'm calling on it."

The Western troops do make an appearance, evacuating the shooting gallery long enough for an Urban Services crew to nail up fresh plywood. That pushes Curt and Rita and the rest down the block for a few days, or for at least as long as it takes someone to pry loose the barrier and creep back inside.

Blue comes back through, sees that it's no use, and lets go. He's on a different road now; what happens in his old house is beyond his most essential task, which involves saving himself. But what Blue can't lure from the shooting gallery eventually washes up at the doors of the Bon Secours emergency room anyway, broken and ill.

Among equals, it's Fat Curt who drops first, collapsing on his corner in an incoherent and jaundiced heap, his liver doing all the things the doctors warned him it would do. He's admitted, stabilized with fluids and enzyme therapy, and detoxed once again as a matter of happenstance. This time, unlike last August, he's in no shape to be discharged. With his liver problems and his extremities bloated and his blood pressure off the charts, no one can manufacture a viable excuse for dumping him back on the street after a week or two.

Instead, he settles into a third-floor bed in a semiprivate room, a change that Curt himself soon regards as a reasonable cold-weather respite. The food is bad, of course; everyday Curt stares down at the Jell-O on his tray table and begs visitors to bring him barbecue. And there's not much drama to the daily routine: Changes of dressings on his abscessed limbs, whirlpool, and physical therapy provide what passes for excitement during Curt's medical interlude. But he's warm and dry and watching television on clean sheets.

For company, he soon has Pimp, who succumbs a week after Curt
and is brought not only to the same hospital, but to the same ward,
occupying a single-bed room directly across the hall. The Bug has now
ravaged Pimp's body, but his mind is still lucid and he settles into Bon
Secours as Jeff to Curt's Mutt, the two of them lounging as best they can
at the end of the hallway, flirting with nurses and squeezing cigarettes
and sodas from passersby.

Then Shardene is unable to rise after a cold night inside the vacant
house. When she does finally get up around midday, she's talking
nonsense, her thoughts rambling out in broken sentences. She's admitted
to a bed in the hospital's other wing, and Fayette Street's lost platoon is
down to three warriors: Eggy Daddy, Rita, and Curt's brother, Dennis.

"They gonna have to carry me off this corner," declares Dennis
proudly. "You can take all them other motherfuckers to Bon Secours and
I'll still be right here."

"You hardcore," Eggy assures him.

"I'll be the last man on the corner."

"I be there with you," Rita assures him.

But Rita begins to have second thoughts. Like Curt, she has for years
carried her pain and her damage with stoic disregard, yet there are now
enough empty spaces in the front room of the shooting gallery to make
her mindful. First Bread leaves them. Then Hungry. Then Blue up and
walks away as if he actually has a plan. Then Curt and Pimp, falling out
one after the next. And now Shardene, giving in to the damp and cold.
For more than a year now, Rita has been mending her own raw arms,
self-medicating the wounds with bootleg antibiotics and whatever fresh
rags and bandages she could find. Now she begins to wonder whether a
few days in a hospital bed with IV drugs and fresh bandages wouldn't
make her feel a little better.

Just before Christmas, she too walks through the doors of the Bon
Secours emergency room. With the infections in both arms reaching a
near-absolute state of drug resistance, Rita is quickly admitted and lodged
at the other end of the hallway from Shardene.

"We one big happy family again," says Fat Curt, dryly.

It's damn close to true. With Rita gone from Blue's house, a dozen
different fiends from Fayette and Monroe are now obliged to visit her
at her hospital bedside, bringing their vials and bags and syringes with
them. When the nurses and attendants turn their backs, Rita finds a vein
for each of her visitors, then applies the balance to her own needs, finding

it easier than ever because her intravenous shunt is as useful for heroin as for antibiotics. Direct deposit, she calls it.

She works her way down the length of the hallway, making sure Shardene is properly medicated, then making friends with a couple of lost souls in the next room over. They're looking rough, laid up with the Bug, unable to keep to their game as the virus overruns their bodies. No matter; Rita shares what comes her way, helping both with their blast. Fat Curt, as patriarch to this bizarre reunion, tries to talk to Rita, to tell her to slow down and be cool and give herself at least a couple weeks' rest.

"You gonna get thrown out of here before the medicine have a chance to work," he tells her.

"I won't," Rita insists. "I'm gonna be better about it."

But after five days in a hospital bed, a blood screen on Shardene shows a higher heroin content than when she first walked into the emergency room. She's put back onto the street.

Then Rita herself is seen creeping into the room across the hall, armed with a breakaway syringe. When the night nurse surprises her, she's holding the tool in one hand and a grateful patient's forearm in the other. And so Rita Hale, the best doctor on Fayette Street, is herself ejected from a place of healing, accused of ministering to patients without house privileges.

That leaves Fat Curt and Pimp, and for them the year comes to its end amidst antiseptic smell and walls of bland white. But it offers a last flourish, too: As decidedly stationary objects, both patients are finally located by the mysterious Robert Carr, the man who had gone to the corners looking for Curt several months back, and whom Curt had dismissed as a hospital bill collector. Instead, Carr is the hospital's own expediter, a contractor who identifies high-cost indigent patients, then shepherds their medical assistance and SSI claims through the bureaucracy so that the hospital will ultimately get paid, if not through patient billing then by government allowance. By now, with as much as thirty thousand dollars expended during his last three hospitalizations, Curt has gained some notice among the caregivers at Bon Secours. Robert Carr has him sign this and initial that, and within a week or two, Curtis Davis has a state medical assistance card—an outcome that has resisted all previous efforts. More than that, both Curt and Pimp now have a promise of long-term care, either at a nursing home or a chronic-care facility. A soldier to the core, Fat Curt refuses to die and refuses to get well; it therefore occurs to those overseeing his medical adventure that it might be better to deposit him somewhere else in the city than to have him show up in the same emergency room yet again.

Pimp, at life's end, is grateful for any semblance of a plan. But Curt hears nursing home and begins plotting his escape. He's got forty-five years and they're treating him like an ancient. He knows he's sick; he knows, too, that any more life on the corner is likely to make him sicker still. Even so, the man is not yet ready to believe his run is over.

His ankle, he tells the doctors. If he can just get the ankle to set right, he'll be fine. And this business about the swelling in his legs and arms being permanent: He's heard about some kind of machine that can squeeze out the juice, make things go back to normal. And the liver—well, Curt can't exactly see the liver. He knows he needs such an organ and he understands that his isn't particularly happy, but he really can't assess his own health by thinking about something so intangible.

"Get so as where I can walk again and I'll be all right," he tells his doctor. "It's my legs that give me the problem."

But Curt will not be all right ever again, and when the doctors try to explain this gently, Curt doesn't seem to get all of the message.

"I don't need a nursing home," he tells one social worker. "What I need is to get things together to where I got a place of my own and maybe a little money each month. If I can get that foot not to swole up like it has and if I can get me a monthly check, I be good."

Fat Curt has given a lifetime to the corner game; now he's asking for some small dignity in return. The social worker tells him Robert Carr is working on the SSI case, that a check might be there for him eventually. But as for his health, it's about much more than swollen feet.

"My blood pressure then," Curt agrees. "I need to take medicines for that."

"And your liver. You're very sick, Curtis."

"My liver," he repeats, as if reminded of a minor detail. "Got to go easy on that too."

"You need to be monitored," she explains. "You're going to need to be in a place where they can see just how you're doing every day."

Gradually, he's shoehorned into their plan, though even at the end, he's talking about the chronic-care facility as a temporary solution, a way station on the road to some happier place.

Come January, he'll be at Seton Manor over on Franklin Street, a converted downtown hotel that used to be known as the James Brown Motor Inn because the hardest working man in show business bought the place in the 1970s and put his name on it. In its current incarnation, though, Seton Manor is the last institutional resort for so many of the souls who have played and lost on the city's corners. From Fayette Street to Greenmount Avenue, from Flag House to Lexington Terrace, those without the sense to die quick and clean are instead brought to Seton Manor and carted upstairs in a slow-motion lurch of an elevator ride, then deposited in one of the painted cinder-block rooms on the third and fourth wards, where they are fed hospital food and AZT, first by mouth, then through an intravenous line, then not at all because in those last days, sustenance is to little purpose. They are black and brown bodies mostly, stick figures, consigned to metal-brace beds or stumbling and staggering past each other in the corridors, looking into each other's death masks and knowing beyond any doubt whatsoever.

At Seton Manor, Curt will settle on a fourth-floor ward largely comprised of AIDS patients, though he will insist, to the general indifference of the nurses, that he has tested clean. He'll be there five days before his first roommate dies in his sleep, and two weeks before the second stops breathing. By the time bedmate number three goes gentle into that good night, not even Curt can mistake the meaning and purpose of his new home.

"They think I'm dyin'," he tells Pimp, who arrives the same week to take a bed down the hall. "Them nurses tryin' to give me the same pills that they givin' everyone else around here."

Pimp is sympathetic enough, though he, of course, has been admitted to Seton Manor on the assumption that he requires nothing more than a terminus.

"You tell them you ain't got it?" he asks Curt.

"Told my nurse and I told the damn social worker. They still tryin' to put them pills into me."

Curt spends his days watching television in the small lounge or telling tales in Pimp's room. Meanwhile, everyone around him withers to nothing.

"Fast as you learn their name, they die on you," Curt says at one point. "Ain't no point gettin' to know people here."

He can't believe it ends this way. He can't believe that the damage done can't be repaired, that there isn't some medical plea-bargain that can be struck to modify the sentence. He did the deeds; he always knew the cost. Soldiers as hardy and willing as Curt are now long gone; measured by the dead, Curt's cup ran over years ago. Still, death seems to him wrong and premature and entirely unbelievable. Fuck the liver thing and fuck the blood pressure, because Fat Curt still feels the same inside. He's not thinning down, he's not fighting the virus. He can still laugh and hope and remember. He can still tell a joke or wish people well or want more for himself.

"Not my time yet," he tells a visitor one day. "But I need to get out of this place before I'm like to kill myself from seein' everyone else go."

A couple of weeks into the new year, Curt begs his friends from Fayette Street to come downtown and take him somewhere—anywhere—so that he can scrape against ordinary life, see how people are when they're still dealing more with this world than the next. He is taken back to Fayette and Monroe, where he's greeted with genuine affection by the old guard: Rita, telling him how fine he looks standing there with clean clothes and clear eyes; Stink, joking with him to stay away from the big white bags, which are weak today; his brother Dennis, sizing Curt up and granting some soldierly respect in a low, quick growl:

"They ain't kilt you yet, huh?"

"You neither."

"Me neither," agrees Dennis, laughing until he coughs.

For a time, Curt watches the back-and-forth between the touts and runners and feels the desire growling inside. But today, for pride if for no other reason, he fights with himself, leaving Fayette Street after an hour or so, asking a friend to ride him by the harbor before dropping him back at Seton Manor.

There, atop Federal Hill, he sits on a bench, his fat hands deep in his coat pockets, his shoulders braced against the cold, his cane resting beside him. To the east, in the outer harbor, a tug is slowly pushing an empty freighter from its mooring at the Domino Sugar plant, turning the big ship slowly until the bow is facing Lazaretto Light and the channel to the bay.

Curt says nothing for a long time, watching as the tug slowly detaches and the ship begins to move.

"Headin' out to sea," he says finally.

A young, dark-skinned woman wheels past him with a baby stroller. Curt looks up and smiles, but the woman is preoccupied with her toddler, who is trying to take off his mittens. She reaches down to lightly slap the boy's hand.

Curt laughs softly, then looks to the harbor again. The ship has started to show a wake.

"I've had a good life," he says. "These last couple years have been rough and all, but I'm not going to go on complaining about things. I did what I wanted to do and I can't say that if it came around again, I'd do too much different."

He stays on the bench for a while longer, waiting until the ship has cleared the point and turned into the lower channel. By then the sun is low and the January cold cuts deeper.

Curt rises, then pauses for a last look at the water. Leaning hard on the cane, he starts slowly for the car.

"Time to go," he says.

TEN

This war goes on.

Thirty years down this sad stretch of road and the same people are still peddling the same brand of snake oil, still hawking that elusive light at the tunnel's end.

There's nothing wrong with the war on drugs that can't be perfected, they'll tell you. Nothing that can't succeed with just a little fine-tuning and a little more money. More cops and more prisons and some new laws and we'll really start to get at the sources of supply, or attack the demand, or maybe do both at once. Democrats, Republicans, it doesn't matter who's running for office—they'll all promise to get hard with it, to get things back under control, to spend the money on a bigger, better campaign. They talk that shit as if the national prison population hasn't tripled in ten years. They talk it because they don't know what else to say, because they know that at the very least, these are the words that most of us want to hear.

Thirty years. And now, all that's left is national failure on a grand scale, a tainted political inheritance that is backhanded from one administration to the next. Thirty years and the politicians and professionals are still offering up the kind of piss-into-the-wind optimism that compels any rational mind to recall another, comparable disaster. Listen to a big-city narcotics detective boasting about his arrest statistics, savoring them as tangible evidence of progress, and you might think of some starched Saigon briefing officer in an air-conditioned Quonset hut tallying up the daily body count. Or the hear the voice of a DEA or Customs spokesman talking up the street value of some huge cocaine seizure along the Mexican border, and you might conjure the ghost of a long-dead Pentagon guru promising to carpet-bomb infiltration to a standstill along the Ho Chi Minh trail. An urban police commander extolling the virtues of community-oriented policing as a means of regaining the trust of inner-city neighborhoods? He's the direct descendant of every CIA spook and Agency for International Development official who ever spoke earnestly about pacification or the model villages program. You want more? Then watch any prosecutor in any American city call the obligatory press briefing to announce the indictment of one major trafficker in a million-dollar drug probe, even as new dealers arrive to take possession of the same open-air drug markets. That's a corps commander grinding up men, money, and machines for possession of some godforsaken Vietnamese hill, then declaring victory as he copters his people out and returns the same real estate to his enemy.

And as with the debacle in Indochina, the American crusade against drugs is collapsing without the loss of a single significant battle. Quite to the contrary, the reckoning already at hand in the West Baltimores of this country comes replete with a string of seeming victories: tens of thousands warehoused in prisons; millions in contraband and dollars confiscated; generations of police commanders and lawyers compiling impressive stats to assure themselves promotion.

But these successes aren't nearly enough, and when the rules of engagement get in the way of lasting victory, we simply change the rules, creating whole new tracts of federal statute, establishing strict mandatory punishments and unforgiving guidelines for sentencing, granting so much raw punitive power to U.S. prosecutors that federal judges around the country are left to grumble in legal journals about draconian and immoral sentencing laws. It used to be said that only in a police state could police work be made easy; yet for the sake of this war, we've gutted the Fourth Amendment, allowing race-based profiling and stop-and-frisk police tactics based on the most minimal probable cause. We've created civil forfeiture statutes that make it a game for government to take what it wants—houses, boats, planes, cars, cash—from anyone it targets without the necessity of criminal conviction. We've made mandatory drug testing a prerogative not only of parole and probation agents, but of any private employer in the nation. Most dramatic of all, perhaps, we have continued to escalate this war of occupation in our inner cities until more than half of the adult black male population in places like Baltimore are now, in some way, under the supervision of the criminal justice system.

This war, like the last one, will not be won. The truth in this is nakedly visible—if not to those crafting the tactics and strategy, then to those standing on the bottom, looking up at all the sound and fury. To the men and women of Fayette Street, it isn't about tightening the screws, or raising the stakes, or embracing a few more constitutional twists and turns. It isn't about three-time loser statutes or drug courts or kicking in the right door of the right stash house. It isn't that all these efforts don't work quite well enough, or that more of them will work better. It's that none of it works at all. The tactics are flawless, but the strategy is nonexistent.

At rock bottom, down here where Fayette crosses Mount Street and runs up the hill to intersect with Monroe, no one is fooled—just as no grunt up to his ass in rice paddy could ever be fooled. Here on Fayette, every fiend and tout and runner understands; they know with a certainty to rival the faith of any religion that no one will miss his daily blast.

Against that, there will be no victory. Not if you come up Fayette Street with bulldozers and knock over every rowhouse between downtown and Bon Secours. Shit on that; the slingers and fiends would be out here in the rubble, slinging pink-top vials. Not if you call out the National Guard or put police officers on every corner; do that and they'll move five blocks, or ten blocks, or twenty, until there's an open-air market savaging some new neighborhood and you've run out of cops and guardsmen.

But you still want it to work. Of course you do.

Try napalm.

Seriously. One of those Rolling Thunder air strikes might do it. Because that Marine commander with the sage wit had it right: Only if you're willing to destroy the village can you be absolutely assured of saving it. Don't bother with surgical strikes for the Fayette Streets of this nation; if you want victory, you've got to send these people right back to the proverbial Stone Age, because anyone left standing will be back on their corners the next day. Or better still, some New York Boy will figure out how to boil down the jellied gas you've been dropping, and the fiends will be lining up to buy that new, wild ride in $10 vials.

A cleansing of that kind might actually work. But of course, we can't do something even modestly genocidal and expect to stay the same ourselves, to maintain the myth of a national ideal. A war waged openly on the underclass would necessitate some self-inflicted scars, some damage to the collective soul of whatever kind of nation we think we are. And if we can't stomach that kind of horror show, perhaps the only real alternative is to keep pretending, to keep telling ourselves that it's only a matter of a stronger law or a better mousetrap or this year's model of shit-spinning politician swearing that he's the one to really get tough on crime.

So we ignore these dying neighborhoods, or run from them if they creep too close. In the end we know we can always cash in our chips, climb to the embassy roof and ride that last Huey to suburbia or some well-policed yuppie enclave in the best quadrants of our cities. We've got a right to walk away because it's our world; hell, we've got the tax returns to prove it.

But how far can we run from New York and Detroit, from Atlanta and Newark, from West Baltimore and East St. Louis? How many county lines must we cross before the damned of these cities will no longer follow? How many private security guards can we hire? How many motion sensors do we need? This is different, this war, and instinctively we know that retreat from it can never be total. These people that we're ready to abandon, they are not an alien foe—their tribe is our own. And these battlefields are not half a world away in places easily forgotten. This is us, America, at war with ourselves. In some weird way, this is our own manifest destiny coming back to bite us in the ass, the pure-pedigreed descendant of all those God-fearing forefathers plunging into the wilderness, stripping the land, looking to feed off their new world, killing and being killed, opening up the east and marching west. Now, it's a twisted replay of that devouring, except that this time, we're the fodder.

We know this deep down; we read the newspapers, we watch the television. We have and they have not, and therefore, they need us. They need us so badly that they'll cross the lines and dodge the rent-a-cops and climb any wall we build. And in the end, there is no real surprise when you hear that your neighbor's car is gone. Or that the counter guy at the local 7-Eleven got aced in a robbery last night. Or that someone you work with pulled up to the pumps at the Route 32 Exxon and got carjacked. There should be no surprise when you come to that hideous moment for which you've spent a lifetime preparing, when you or someone you love walks down the wrong block, or into the wrong parking garage. In an instant, the illusions are obliterated and the reckoning—their reckoning—is yours as well.

Thirty years gone and now the drug corner is the center of its own culture. On Fayette Street, the drugs are no longer what they sell or use, but who they are. We may have begun by fighting a war on drugs, but now we're beating down those who use them. And along Fayette Street, the enemy is everywhere, so that what began as a wrongheaded tactical mission has been transformed into slow-motion civil war. If we never seriously contemplate alternatives, if we forever see the order of battle in terms of arrests and prisons and lawyers, then perhaps we deserve three more decades of failure.

In the end, we'll blame them. We always do.

And why the hell not? They've ignored our warnings and sanctions, they've taken our check-day bribe and done precious little with it, they've turned our city streets into drug bazaars. Why shouldn't they take the blame?

If it was us, if it was our lonesome ass shuffling past the corner of Monroe and Fayette every day, we'd get out, wouldn't we? We'd endure. Succeed. Thrive. No matter what, no matter how, we'd find the fucking exit.

If it was our fathers firing dope and our mothers smoking coke, we'd pull ourselves past it. We'd raise ourselves, discipline ourselves, teach ourselves the essentials of self-denial and delayed gratification that no one in our universe ever demonstrated. And if home was the rear room of some rancid, three-story shooting gallery, we'd rise above that, too. We'd shuffle up the stairs past nodding fiends and sullen dealers, shut the bedroom door, turn off the television, and do our schoolwork. Algebra amid the stench of burning rock; American history between police raids. And if there was no food on the table, we're certain we could deal with that. We'd lie about our age to cut taters and spill grease and sling fries at the sub shop for five-and-change-an-hour, walking every day past the corner where friends are making our daily wage in ten minutes.

No matter. We'd persevere, wouldn't we? We'd work that job by night and go to class by day, by some miracle squeezing a quality education from the disaster that is the Baltimore school system. We'd do all the work, we'd pay whatever the price. And when all the other children are out in the street, learning the corner world, priming themselves for the only life they've ever known, we'd be holed up in some shithole of a rowhouse with our textbooks and yellow highlighter, cramming for finals. Come payday, we wouldn't blow that minimum-wage check on Nikes, or Fila sweat suits, or Friday night movies at Harbor Park with the neighborhood girls. No fucking way, brother, because we pulled self-esteem out of a dark hole somewhere and damned if our every desire isn't absolutely in check. We don't need to buy any status; no, we can save every last dollar, or invest it, maybe. And in the end, we know, we'll head off to our college years shining like a new dime, swearing never to set foot on West Fayette Street again.

That's the myth of it, the required lie that allows us to render our judgments. Parasites, criminals, dope fiends, dope peddlers, whores—when we can ride past them at Fayette and Monroe, car doors locked, our field of vision cautiously restricted to the road ahead, then the long journey into darkness is underway. Pale-skinned hillbillies and hard-faced yos, toothless white trash and gold-front gangsters—when we can glide on and feel only fear, we're well on the way. And if, after a time, we can glimpse the spectacle of the corner and manage nothing beyond loathing and contempt, then we've arrived at last at that naked place where a man finally sees the sense in stretching razor wire and building barracks and directing cattle cars into the compound.

It's a reckoning of another kind, perhaps, and one that becomes a possibility only through the arrogance and certainty that so easily panies a well-planned and well-tended life. We know ourselves, we believe in ourselves; from what we value most, we grant ourselves the illusion that it's not chance and circumstance, that opportunity itself isn't the defining issue. We want the high ground; we want our own worth to be acknowledged. Morality, intelligence, values—we want those things measured and counted. We want it to be about Us.

Yes, if we were down there, if we were the damned of the American cities, we would not fail. We would rise above the corner. And when we tell ourselves such things, we unthinkly assume that we would be consigned to places like Fayette Street fully equipped, with all the graces and disciplines, talents and training that we now possess. Our parents would still be our parents, our teachers still our teachers, our broker still our broker. Amid the stench of so much defeat and despair, we would kick fate in the teeth and claim our deserved victory. We would escape to live the life we were supposed to live, the life we are living now. We would be saved, and as it always is in matters of salvation, we know this as a matter of perfect, pristine faith.

Why? The truth is plain:

We were not born to be niggers.

* * *

"It's fucked up," R.C. says.

The rest of the crew is equally angry. They discovered this corner, worked and nurtured it. As much as they own anything in this world, they own Gilmor and McHenry. Now, suddenly, the C.M.B. crew finds that its real estate has drawn the attentions of a rival.

"I mean, damn," says Tae, "I know we ain't doin' right. But how can some other peoples tell us to get off the corner when they doin' the same thing we doin'."

"And they not even from around here," adds Dinky.

"Man, I know it," agrees Tae. "Where they comin' from sayin' that we can't stand here when they ain't even from here?"

"Ain't like they New York Boys," says Boo.

"That's what I'm sayin'," Tae insists. "They from D.C. How can they come up here and act like they got the right to be tellin' us shit."

"It's fucked-up," R.C. says again.

"They fucked-up," says Dinky, making it specific.

At sixteen or seventeen years, most of the C.M.B. crew are still too young to see the corner rules as the end of all argument. The blast and the dollar are the only two standards by which life at Gilmor and McHenry can be governed, yet here they stand, perplexed and offended at the behavior of another group of young men selling drugs. They are still young, and in a perverse way, idealistic. Consequently, the idea that people can be arbitrary and irrational, unjustified and imperious is fuel for all kinds of indignation.

Off and on, they've been playing at the corner for three or four years now, time enough to learn a lot about selling drugs. Money, mechanics, players; ruses and risks, dodges and fears. But now, with the ante suddenly raised, they're confronted with the elemental unfairness of the thing— the corner not as their playground, but as the rigged game it always proves to be.

Since summer, C.M.B. had been entrenched at Gilmor and McHenry. They had scouted the corner, opened their shop, brought good dope and coke to the down-bottom McHenry Street strip. And they were seeing some dollars because of it.

The Southern District troops were still running on old-school time— chasing calls and writing reports and generally rolling past the corners on their way to somewhere else. The stickup boys still weren't showing much interest either. And the white boys down here were loyal and docile customers. Their money was always on time; their version of the stashstealing, short-changing, dope-fiend move was a pale imitation of the games played on Fayette Street. Some other young crews had set up down here, but they were, for the most part, accommodating of C.M.B. and its enterprise. The history and connections between groups proved lubricant enough: Boo's brothers had the shop at Ramsay and Stricker; Dewayne, Tank, and Tony were down on South Vincent; Herbie and his brothers were over to the west on Payson.

So on this early December night, idling at the lip of an alley a half a block from their corner, with a couple of forties going flat from lack of attention, the crew is angry as they struggle with the latest turn of events. This one started, as these things often do, without much fanfare. Two nights ago, they were out here on post—Tae and Dinky and Brooks—when a dark blue Acura rolled past, speakers blaring. The car came through McHenry Street a second time, finally rolling up to the north corner at Gilmor. Tae was there, leaning against the bricks of the corner house, trying to look hard and disinterested at the same time, wondering who they were and how it might play out.

Down came the passenger window.

"Yo, Shorty."

"You talkin' to me?" Tae as DeNiro, but without the backup.

His gun was home. Dinky, standing across the street, had his nine at the stash house, but that was half a block too far.

"This our corner."

"Huh?"

"You got to be movin' on. You standin' on our corner."

Tae fell speechless. Their corner?

"I'm sayin' you don't want to be standin' out here tomorrow," warned the boy in the car. Before Tae could react, the Acura slipped away from the curb, turning at Monroe. Then Dinky came across the street.

"Yo, what up with that?"

It would take Tae a couple of minutes to get some pieces of the story together. And it would take all of C.M.B., working hard on those few shards, most of the next day before they felt confident enough to peg the threat. Dinky had the Acura pinned to some older boys who had showed up a couple of days earlier and opened shop across the street from them on Gilmor and McHenry. This fitted with some other scraps: a tip from Brian that a crew from D.C. had tried to do something over on Fulton Avenue, and R.C.'s report that some D.C. boy was a cousin to

Tank, and that D.C. boys had come up here on Tank's invite. All of this blended with Tae's sense that the boys weren't local.

Still, as they grappled with all the ramifications tonight, it didn't make a whole lot of sense. Dinky remembered when the boys had made their appearance, first at Gilmor, and then, when it was clear their vials couldn't compete with C.M.B.'s product, down the block at Stricker Street. After watching them for a couple of hours, it was obvious that the new crew wasn't about a whole lot—just some latecomers with weak stuff, looking for a little room.

The C.M.B. contingent let them be. There was market enough for anyone on McHenry Street, particularly since the double-seal bags that R.C. and Brooks had out now were smokers. And for their hospitality, they're rewarded with a threat.

Conferencing at the mouth of the alley, Dinky is, as usual, the most adamant. "Yo, we shoulda squashed 'em right from jump," he says. "This shit here is ours."

"What we gonna do?" asks R.C.

"Fuck 'em up," says Boo. "Fuck 'em up bad."

Simple solutions to simple problems, but Tae has to fret the details. In DeAndre's absence, he stands alone as leader of the crew.

"Where we gonna find 'em?" he asks.

They're game for an all-out offensive and they'll settle for an even-handed beef. But in this instance, the D.C. boys are playing with certain advantages. For one thing, they're from somewhere else, so there's little possibility of setting up on them, getting a drop at this address or that. For another, they're apparently mobile, rolling around in that Acura.

"They do that drive-by shit in Washington," says Manny Man.

"Then we wait," says Dinky, showing heart.

"We wait?" asks Manny.

"If them niggers for real, they sure enough comin' back," says Dinky. "I ain't goin' nowhere."

All strategy ends on this unsettling note. Whatever else might stand to their credit, the Crenshaw Mafia Brothers are not accustomed to playing defense—a point readily proven on the basketball court over the last several months. Their best game is run-and-gun, and now, they're compelled to stand at a South Baltimore crossroads and wait to see if their opponents will return to shoot bullets at them.

There's no question that Dinky has been hungry for this kind of thing, and he'll take it as it comes. DeAndre's cousin has been looking for reasons to step up, to explode, to magnify and exaggerate any insult until it becomes sufficient cause for violence. Among his own, Dinky is loyal, quiet, and polite. On the corner, he's the first to throw a punch or let go of a bullet. He's been ready to catch a body for a year now, so that some of the boys are actually starting to worry, thinking that Dinky has some kind of death wish.

Brooks is indifferent, showing no fear and less thought about the matter. Boo is altogether lost, unable to gauge probabilities. The fact that he's been thinning down, too, makes his judgment even more suspect; Tae and R.C. are both convinced he's smoking up his own profit.

For Tae, the choice is deliberate. He's rational about the risks and rewards, but he sees himself as smarter and more aware than the rest, the soldier least likely to become an early casualty. He'll take things as they come, reassessing on a day-by-day basis; for now, though, he's not running. Manny Man is scared and shows it; he's been playing at this corner game, following Tae, trying to belong to something a little bigger than himself. Now, the idea of confronting a lethal unknown unnerves him.

And then there is Richard Carter.

R.C. mostly keeps his own counsel; he listens more than he talks, leaving his usual bluster behind. He's been a centerpiece of C.M.B. since Tae first came up with the idea for a Fayette Street crew, and in the past he's not been slow to find misadventure. But now, the gangster ethos is becoming something more than a fantasy. Before, it was always show-and-tell for the neighborhood adolescents, a dabbling with guns and vials and glassine bags that fairly reeked of dare and double-dare. Now, they are on a corner—their corner—confronting something far less predictable than a rival neighborhood crew. Whatever else the D.C. boys are, they are not pretending to adulthood; they are eighteen and nineteen—some look to be in their early twenties. They've come up to McHenry Street with some kind of plan, and they've thrown down their gauntlet for some kind of reason.

For R.C., this threat is something of a litmus test, a turning point in his relationship to the corner. He's had his share of short runs, selling gypsy packages until he gathered enough for girls or weed. He's played at violence, chasing and beating rivals as a pack, posing with street-bought guns, or maybe punctuating some small gang dispute by letting go of a round or two from a block's distance. He's had his fun playing cat-and-mouse with Bob Brown and the rest, knowing in his heart that a juvenile charge would not break him, that a month or two at Hickey School or Boys Village would be as rough as it gets. And when the risk becomes real, when fear or boredom begins to oppress, he knows he can simply walk away, heading up to his mother's apartment to get blunted and watch cartoons, or back to the rec center for hoops or touch football or Connect Four.

Now he's arrived at a real crossroads, a term both precise and symbolic. They all have, actually. As a crew, the only lasting collective accomplishment of the Crenshaw Mafia Brothers is that they have made McHenry and Gilmor. Since summer, not a week has passed that someone with C.M.B. credentials hasn't been down here representing. Some made money, others went broke, and quite a few proved themselves absolute fuckups; but the corner itself flourished. It was there for them every day, ready and willing to give them another turn. Yet suddenly, interlopers have arrived to take it all away.

Not much is known about the D.C. contingent, but the mystery itself is intimidating. If they're anything like the New York Boys who started showing up along Fayette Street four or five years back, then they'll be in force. They'll be out there twenty-four, seven, working the corners like it's a job. To counter that, C.M.B. will have to step up; Tae and R.C. and Dinky—all of them. For C.M.B., the amateur hour is over.

R.C. senses this. So does Tae. The rest are only vaguely aware that something in their lives has changed.

"We got to get everyone down here," says Tae.

R.C. agrees: "If we coming back tomorrow," he says, speaking in subdued tones, "then we got to come deep."

And they do. The B-and-G boys come off their corner to assist, as does the younger C.M.B. clique—Manny's younger brother, Dion, Travis, and the rest. Brian comes down from Lemmon Street. Boo brings some people from Ramsay and Stricker. The only notable absences are Dewayne, who is working with Tank and Tony and is therefore linked in some awkward way to the D.C. crew, and DeAndre, who hears of the beef from Dinky, but stays with his baby up at Tyreeka's house, where he's still promising to get a job and go back to school and do right by his new family. He sends word back that he'll be there if any of his boys get hurt.

The rest post early, showing up on Gilmor Street just after noon, when trade on the lower strip is still slow. Each of them seeds a cracked doorway, or paper bag, or the tire of a parked car with a weapon or two, then takes a turn standing in front of the carryout at the southwest corner. By late afternoon, the adrenaline begins to jump and flash, sparking the false sightings that set them darting—movements that end just as quickly with a burst of nervous laughter and the inevitable pushing and shoving. Only Dinky stands aloof, immune to the antics, braced yet oddly calm. At sixteen, and already with a soldier's temperament, he's found his element in crisis. His presence begins to take hold and settle the others.

They work the shop, sell some vials. As time wears on them, they grow restless waiting and wondering.

"We got to keep spread out," Tae insists, thinking tactically. "Not bunch up and shit. And we got to be watchin' out."

There's general agreement on this much, though no one moves until Dinky steps up, declaring that the carryout corner will be his. Dinky, with his nine tucked into the back of his stonewashed denims, is the anchor in any defense.

They disperse. And wait. And watch for the Acura, though it's soon late evening and the car is nowhere to be seen. When something does finally happen, it surprises everyone.

"Aw shit," says R.C.

A string of regular pops, four or five, are heard down near Stricker. R.C. sees shadows cresting the hill from Carey Street, and then a muzzle flash. Next come shouts and scared laughter and Manny Man running back down the block, back past R.C. and a rigid, unmoving Dinky. Then Tae shouts out the lyric of last winter's soundtrack: "Get ya guns out."

At first they're hearing gunfire behind them, and they're running, ducking into alleys and behind parked cars and trying to figure out what the hell is happening. D.C. boys? Must be. But no one sees much. Someone yells a curse, then lets go of what seems like a whole clip. R.C. is rushing around the corner onto Gilmor, right behind Boo, trying to find purchase as he jumps the curb in front of a parked pickup. He slips and falls, cursing.

"Aw shit."

They're being routed. Or so it seems until most of them get up across Pratt Street, where they find heart in their own numbers.

"They was over on Stricker," says Tae.

"Where's Dinky?"

"Man, they was shooting right over my head."

"I think Eric went down."

"Where at?"

"He was behind me and I hear him go, 'Shit!' and he's holding his leg and shit."

"Where Dinky at?"

They talk it through, gathering up nerve in their still-solid numbers. They go back down Fulton, then come up McHenry from the west. Dinky is still standing there, waiting for them.

"Yo," Dinky says. "They back down the hill."

"Eric get hit?" asks R.C.

Dinky shrugs. "Ain't nobody come through here."

Who started the shooting? Half a dozen of them want to know the answer to that question.

"Them D.C. niggers," says Boo.

But when pressed, Boo admits to seeing little.

They move down McHenry, some in the street, others fanning out into the back alleys. Behind the rowhouses on the south side of the street, R.C. is halfway to Stricker when he sees someone race past in the connecting cross-alley. He fires off his .25 and it starts again, but this time with the confusion running the other way, down the hill toward Carey.

"They runnin'!" shouts Boo.

From Calhoun Street comes a long string of shots and more shouts—then quiet. Slowly, by twos and threes, the boys drift back to Gilmor, retreating to their original positions and no farther. When the police finally roll through, they've stashed their guns on top of the tires of parked cars and behind rowhouse stoops. Some duck into the carryout, others walk across Pratt to the alley basketball court on Lemmon Street, where after-action reports are delivered.

"Motherfuckers ran and shit," says R.C.

Eric is grazed in the calf. No one else seems to be hit.

"I think I hit one of them niggers in the alley," says R.C. "He didn't stop though."

"Bullets all around me," says Boo, elated. "I'm runnin' up Stricker and they just missin' me."

Beyond that, no one has much of a clue. How many? From what direction? Who shot first? Who was where? Was there even a D.C. boy within half a mile of McHenry Street? It doesn't make any difference now that the battle is over. What matters is that on this night some crew tried to press them, but they stayed put and kept a corner; all else is mere commentary.

"They might gonna come back," says Manny Man.

"Then we be right here," says Tae.

They smoke weed and talk up their heroics until long into the night, secure in the company of each other and enjoying tales of the battle-field that grow bolder by the minute.

It's after three when R.C. finally creeps into his mother's apartment, blunted and drunk from celebrating. The next day, he doesn't open his eyes until nearly noon. He gets up off his mattress to kill the sound on an X-Men cartoon, then pads out from his bedroom in T-shirt, boxers, and sweat socks. He goes to the kitchen phone, punches the digits for Tae's beeper, hangs up, then wanders over to the living room, slumping down on the sofa.

The apartment is empty. His mother is hard at work at the dry cleaner; his brother Bug is now overseas on a ship; Darlene, his sister, is out running the streets somewhere. Without anything or anyone else to occupy his mind, R.C.'s thoughts run beyond his afternoon hangover.

He'll have to go back. Today and tomorrow and the next day, if he's really a gangster beyond pretending. He'll have to be down at Gilmor and McHenry every day, or almost every day, if he's going to do this thing for more than pocket money.

Yet R.C. has no strength in him this morning, no reservoir of confi-dence that he can draw from. Last night he was scared. Real scared. Here, alone, he admits this to himself. Who the fuck wouldn't be scared with people shooting at you. When the guns started going off, he was half-relieved to be past the waiting, to be dealing with it at last. Afterward, with all of his boys around laughing and bragging—then, too, he felt some elation. But now, by light of day, he can't manufacture any emotion beyond a vague, queasy terror.

He could have died. Any one of them could be dead now.

The worst part is the sense that nothing else remains for him, that all of life's other doors have been slammed and sealed. It isn't just last night or tonight. The corner now looms as a workaday world, and he knows in his heart it will wear him down to nothing.

He doesn't have Dinky's soldier's heart; none of them do, really. He can't be as clever and subtle as Tae, nor can he muster the blind obedience of Boo or Brooks. He isn't good with the money like some of them are. He's not like DeAndre; he can't really lead others or intimidate.

And then there's the lure of the vials. In the last few months, R.C. has messed with that shit now and again; he knows he has enough of a taste for it that if he stays out on the corner, he'll be finding new ways to come up short on the count. He can't fool himself like Boo does; Boo is smoking up product all night long and then lying about it, swearing he isn't puffing anything beyond blunts. R.C. might lie to everyone else, too—everyone lies about it in the beginning—but now, conjuring the future, he's willing to admit to himself that it's a real problem. Being around the vials will bring him down quick.

He is not, he has to concede, very good at the corner. Yet the corner is all he has left. School has always been little more than a bad joke, and now that he's turned sixteen, any effort to return to the rolls of Francis M. Woods would be an act of absurd volunteerism. R.C. can't imagine what he might say to Rose Davis to convince her of his commitment, nor does he particularly want her convinced. His earlier promises had generally been made under duress, usually when Miss Davis caught him sliding into the gym for rec center basketball practice on days when he had missed every class.

Now there isn't even a point to basketball practice. For one thing, Pumpkin had half emptied the gym when he decided to charge his players a dollar each to attend every practice session. For another, R.C. had tired of the rec center team at the very moment the star-crossed squad managed to do the unthinkable.

They won a game.

It was not just a contest against some neighborhood pickup team, either. With Miss Ella's support, they had entered the mayor's invitational tournament, an annual event that brought out the best rec center and community teams in the city. The Martin Luther Kings, unheard of and unheralded, arrived on a November night in the vast expanse of the Lake Clifton High School gymnasium, sized up the competition, and went to work.

They were an altogether different unit than in the Cloverdale summer league; still inconsistent, to be sure, but now capable of more than momentary flashes of brilliance. Now, with Tank, Tony, Truck, Twin, and Mike as the starting five—and R.C. and Tae as sixth and seventh men off the bench—they were big enough not to be overpowered, deep enough not to tire, and fast enough to run with any rec team in the city.

Months of playing together in the Francis Woods gym had given the squad confidence, as well as an instinctive feel for each other. There was still no strategy to their game; it was playground ball with better uniforms. But now, when R.C. came down with a defensive rebound, he fairly knew where Tony would be at midcourt, waiting for the outlet. Now, when Tank put his head down and drove the lane, Mike could drift to the baseline behind him and know that if the shot wasn't there, Tank would kick the rock back out for Mike's soft jumper. When the Kings were bad, they were still godawful. But when they were good, their game was right.

The first round showed the tournament that much, when the Kings beat a Pimlico squad by eighteen. By contrast, the quarterfinal contest against John Eager Howard began with a sudden loss of confidence. The Howard squad had tortured them twice during Cloverdale, and the rec team, intimidated, was down by eight—ten to two—early in the first quarter when Pumpkin stopped screaming long enough to sub R.C. for Truck.

With a rebound, an interception, another rebound, and a quick, half-court outlet pass, R.C. managed to stabilize the team, providing the hard in-the-paint work that made the running game possible. Soon the score was tied, and at the half, the Kings were up by six—a circumstance that led to the kind of bitter recrimination from their opponents that had for almost a year been the lament of the M.L.K. crew.

"That one there run with my brother," one of the Howard forwards wailed, "and he nineteen."

"All them players is wrong. They all too old."

Pumpkin huddled them together, ranted at botched plays and missed opportunities for a few minutes, railed at them for ignoring his commands from the bench, then concluded with a declaration that seemed to surprise everyone; "You all got a chance to win this."

But the starting five began the second half cold, and before long, Pumpkin was sputtering and shouting at the edge of the court. When R.C. came in for Twin with most of the third quarter gone, they were down by three and playing tame.

Again he stepped in and raised their game, centering the defense, covering the paint. At three minutes into the last quarter, they were up by six and Pumpkin was shouting at Mike to slow their game, to force

the Howard players to work for their shots. Instead, the Kings ran. It's
what they do best.

Ignoring their coach, they were soon up by eleven with five minutes
left. But Pumpkin was livid. He turned his fury on the referees,
badgering them about a traveling call.

"I'm asking what kind of shit is that?"

Technical. The M.L.K. players were glaring at their bench.

"What the hell you lookin' at?" Pumpkin shouted.

No one answered. For once, the team was utterly composed. The same
R.C. who would scream at other players for imaginary errors was now
calm and quiet, responding to Pumpkin's tantrum with nothing stronger
than a sad shake of his head. Ever more furious, Pumpkin turned his
attention back to the ref, then to the failings of his players, then to the
whole assembly in general: "No one listens to a fuckin' thing I say."

"Shut up," shouted Tony, running past the bench on offense.

"What? What did you say to me?"

Tony said nothing more, but Pumpkin turned and kicked the wooden
bleacher. The ref eyed him warily. On the next exchange. Tony was backing
past his coach while defending a Howard guard, glancing toward the
bleachers.

"Just let us play," he told Pumpkin.

"Say what?"

"Just let us play the damn game."

So Pumpkin sat, pouting, as R.C. stole an offensive rebound to which
he had no right, then powered up for two points and a foul. When he
converted the third point, the game was iced. Even with a late Howard
surge, the Kings won by seven.

At the buzzer, the M.L.K. players all banded together on the court
in self-congratulation, a safe distance from their coach. In victory,
Pumpkin looked defeated, and on the ride home to West Baltimore, it
was R.C. who took in the attaboys from Tank and Mike and Tony, players
who knew and were willing to acknowledge just what he had brought
to this game.

"Good game," Mike told him.

"Yeah, R.C., you played hard."

It was his game, his moment. Thirty minutes of quiet validation for the
one thing at which he genuinely excelled. He knew it, too, but celebrating
the victory at the Franklin Street McDonald's that night, and later walking
home with Tae, R.C. was strangely subdued. There was no boasting, no

wild claims of greatness. R.C. seemed utterly unlike himself: content, sated, as if a long and brutal fever had finally broken.

The magic didn't last, of course. In the semifinals the following night, the rec team lost its poise at the very end. Down only two with the final seconds racing off the clock, Tony deflected an opponent's pass and Tae came up with the steal and a clear lane to the basket. It looked too good to be true, and it was. Tae sped bandy-legged toward the undefended hoop, alone and in full possession of what seemed a sure game-tying layup. Instead, and for no apparent reason, Tae slammed the ball down into the paint at the last minute and sped beneath the basket. Behind him, the ball hovered in the lane for an instant—waiting, presumably, for a trailing M.L.K. player and a heart-stopping dunk. Except that no such player was in the vicinity. The ball bounced again and was retrieved by the opposing team.

After the buzzer, Tae made no effort to explain. His logic, if not exactly appreciated, was understood. Tying or even winning the game wasn't enough; style itself was the issue, and style demanded the no-look, Lawd-have-mercy slam dunk.

R.C. barely reacted to the loss. He gathered up his sweats and his winter coat and sat silently in the car on the way back across town. After playing the game of his life the night before, he had managed to distance himself from the contest, the team, and everything else that had pre-occupied him for the last year. He had proven something to himself and to everyone he knew. With that done, he was left with nothing but another empty feeling.

Basketball, he now knew, could not for a moment save him, or change him, or provide any future other than the one he dreaded. On one level, he had always known this: The rec center wasn't some junior college team. It wasn't a city high school varsity, or even one of the standout rec center programs like Bentalou. This year had always been about nothing more than his love of the game itself.

And yet, in the long months of losing, R.C. had managed at times to lose track of himself, to begin to believe there was something at stake inside the Francis Woods gymnasium. There, in the steamy heat, he had played his heart out, devoting himself to one small, self-contained quadrant of his existence while everything else in his life crumbled.

On the court, he was central to his crew, essential even. But now, in the quiet of his mother's apartment, he thinks back on last night's mayhem and is oppressed by the terrible realization that despite all the heroics, the corner game offers him no group or club or crew by which he can take any measure of himself. R.C. has lived his whole life for this choice. He has watched his father, his older brothers, and his sister go down to the corners before him. Like every other member of C.M.B., he has for years spouted the hard-as-nails cant of the gangster-in-training. And with McHenry and Gilmor at stake, he was down there last night with the rest of them, willing to risk his life, ready to catch a bullet for the sake of saying that he is a part of something, that he is and always will be a Crenshaw Mafia Brother.

That was how he had felt last night. If there were doubts early on, they were matched by the elation he felt when the D.C. boys broke and ran. But with his mother gone to work and the cartoons turned down, R.C. has to think about the night to come, the night after, and all the nights from now on.

It isn't like basketball. Out on the corner, there is no team for which a player should sacrifice himself. On the corner, you catch a bullet and it's yours and yours alone. At most, the rest of your crew will show up at Brown's for the viewing, performing for each other, swearing eternal revenge and then wandering back to their posts to sling and forget. Last night, they had seemed a team and R.C. had belonged. But the night before, he'd been beefing with Dinky over some short vials and arguing with Brooks about money owed. Tomorrow night, if the D.C. boys stay away, those arguments will resume.

For Richard Carter, the illusion of the basketball court has been carefully nurtured and sustained for one reason only. Between the baselines, he can—at the right moment and with the right players around him—be more than he believes himself to be. On the corner, however, there's no pretending.

When his phone rings, he's tempted not to answer, but he grabs the receiver after the fourth ring.

"Hullo."

He pauses, listening, trying to think of something to say, something that might transport him to some other place and time, a life other than the one left to him. No such words exist.

"Yeah, I been up," he tells Tae. "What time we goin' down there?"

Before the children of the Martin Luther King Jr. Recreation Center labored for three weeks in October to make it a community garden, the vacant lot at the northwest corner of Fayette and Mount was filled with the wreckage created by a stolen car. And before a sixteen-year-old named Terrance, with half a dozen police cars in pursuit, ran his contraband up the sidewalk and into the brick rowhome, it was 1702 West Fayette, a recently vacated shooting gallery that Franklin Square neighborhood activists had managed to seize through condemnation proceedings. This had been Clean Gene's shooting gallery, raided by police as a spring cleaning ritual and, until Terrance had his way, destined to become a men's shelter, or a residential facility for recovering addicts, or more office space for the Echo House outreach center across the street. Before Gene got hold of it, it had been a three-story home for generations of black, Irish, and German families—a Federal—style rowhouse next door to the home where Henry Louis Mencken, the great iconoclast and sage of Baltimore, was born and raised.

But when Ella Thompson and her children first laid hands on the spot, it was dirt and rubble. Working in plain view of touts and runners, slingers and fiends at the Mount Street corners, the rec center contingent had transformed the lot into something more. By November, the empty spot was a carefully tended garden—a victory garden of a kind.

Urban greenery was the idea of last resort, as Terrance had done his work well and left the neighborhood group with few other options. His wild joyride took out the front facade of the structure, leaving what remained weak and vulnerable. A city building inspector gave the remnant last rites and, after a week or two, a dump truck and loader showed up to haul away the joists and plaster and bricks.

Myrtle Summers and Joyce Smith and the rest of the neighborhood leadership were undeterred by this unexpected development. They had fought long and hard for this real estate, planning the takeover and restoration of the rowhouse as a toehold in the heart of the Fayette Street strip. Gene had taken his needle palace elsewhere, of course, and half the rowhouses in the 1700 block of Fayette were just as derelict. But the journey had to begin somewhere, or so they reasoned. So when a sixteen-year-old with a gift for stripping ignitions ended one dream, they managed, like true optimists, to conjure another.

With some work, they reasoned, the vacant corner lot could still be transformed into something worthwhile. If not a structure restored to function and utility, then something of a symbolic nature—symbolism being so often the last refuge of the truly beleaguered.

A park. A garden. A small islet of beauty to stand in answer to the Mount Street crews—Family Affair, Diamond in the Raw, Death Row—

who so misused this crossroads. Myrtle Summers told Ella that the garden would be dedicated as a memorial to Melvin Powell, a longtime neighborhood resident who had been shot to death a year earlier during a robbery of the Korean grocery at Mount and Baltimore streets. An uncle to Tae Bennett, Powell had been working at the grocery as a security guard, and the gunmen paused in their pillaging of the front registers only long enough to shoot him down. Ella knew the horror story by heart; she knew all the neighborhood stories down to the saddest little detail. Get her started and she could recite them, one after the next, spanning weeks and months and years of life along Fayette Street, meandering through the oral history of this hellish strip and shaking her head in dismay, as if truly astonished that the intimate knowledge of so many nightmares could count for so little.

From the moment Myrtle spoke to her about it, the idea of a garden for Mr. Powell appealed to Ella's sense of community. For her, all of Fayette Street was bound together. The children, the fiends, the working folk, the runners and touts—all of them were connected in an essential way, and no one could be touched, or hurt, or helped without it meaning something to everyone else.

She believed that. She had to believe it.

So Mr. Powell and his sacrifice would be remembered with flowers and shrubs, and his name, in turn, would give the community some sense of itself. Everyone passing this little garden—the taxpayers, the dealers, the addicts—would be required to acknowledge, on some level, that Franklin Square was still a neighborhood of caring human souls. It wasn't any kind of solution to the mayhem, but hope is hope, and Ella Thompson had always been willing to invest in struggle for its own sake.

A week or so into October, she put the younger children to work clearing the double-width lot of rock and brick, readying it for the peat and topsoil and landscaping stones. Little Stevie and Daymo and DeRodd helped out—even Chubb and T.J. abandoned their gangster apprenticeships long enough to contribute. Ella let the girls decide where to plant the flowers—day lilies and pansies, daisies and black-eyed Susans that would go into the ground in a late planting, showing themselves on this corner until the first frost took their colors away. Toward more permanence, the rec children planted daffodil and tulip bulbs, perennials that would bring the garden to bloom in the spring. In the center of the flower beds were small shrubs, hardy evergreens that would assert themselves all winter long. The children arranged the planting by size and color, saving the most vibrant things for the garden centerpiece—the wide bed of fresh topsoil ringed with stone in the shape of the African continent.

At first the labors of Ella and the rec center children received only indifference from the corner crews, who continued to do business along Mount Street. But in time, as this horticultural campaign continued, the touts and slingers tried to avoid the garden, traveling a block east to Gilmor, or moving a respectful distance down Mount to Baltimore Street. Eventually, some of the older kids—many of whom Ella had counted as all but lost to the corners—stopped their misadventures long enough to lend a hand. Manny Man came up from McHenry Street to spend the better part of three days with a rake and hoe—in small part because gardening proved pleasant and distracting, and in larger part because he owed one of the South Baltimore dealers quite a bit of money behind a messed-up package. Dion helped, too. So did Tae and R.C. for a half-day or so, until fresh happenings down at McHenry and Gilmor lured them back. When the volunteers were finished with their handiwork just before Halloween, it looked better than any Mount Street corner had a right to look.

"Too good for Fayette Street," Manny Man told Ella, admiring the result. "They should sell the drugs somewheres else now that the garden is right there."

For a while they did. By degrees, though, when the work was done and the flowers watered and the tools put away, there was nothing left at Mount and Fayette but the usual empty calm. Without the daily presence of the gardeners, the dealers returned to fill the void with their catcalls and shouts and warning whistles. Amid the last buds of the surviving annuals, a collection of candy wrappers, pretzel bags, breakaway syringes, and empty vials began to accumulate. In the final days of autumn, weeks after the planting and shortly before the park was to be dedicated by the neighborhood association, Ella went back up to the corner and cleaned the flower beds a second, then a third time. She talked to some of the Mount Street regulars, asking them to do their business on the other corners, to mind this fragile patch of paradise. To some extent, they obliged—and Ella took her usual pride in being able to command even backhanded respect from the corner crowd.

Now, just in time for the dedication on this early December day, a little bit of last-minute clean-up has the community garden looking pristine. Joyce and Myrtle both say a few words, after which the children who worked on the garden are introduced and applauded. Then a white sheet is lifted from a wooden sign at the corner entrance to the garden, and Ella, who has taken on this project without so much as a clue, finds herself stunned and speechless. As she stares at the sign, she is no longer smiling and laughing.

Dedicated to the memory. And not just the memory of Melvin Powell, but to Andrea Perry as well.

Andrea. Fatty Pooh.

The name of her missing child, five years gone and never far from her mind. In an awkward silence, Ella reads the sign again and again.

For the rest of the dedication ceremony, Ella can barely speak. She nods acknowledgment, swallows hard and manages a genuine, if hasty, thank you. Then she retreats across Mount Street to the rec center and her backroom office.

Most people watching understand; the rest wait for a more visible moment of recognition and gratitude—a moment that never quite comes.

In her heart, of course, Ella is grateful. With the dedication, the neighborhood has done what she herself has been trying to do for the last five years. Her daughter's life has now been remembered and recognized and reconnected to everyone who passes these corners day after day. At the rec, at her church, on the corners, Ella has for a long time been trying to give Pooh some kind of testament. What is this small garden, if not evidence of her spirit?

Yet when the sheet came up and the wooden sign stared out at her, Ella could feel years and months being ripped away, bringing her right back to the horror of the thing. Pooh is dead. Murdered. Raped. And all the hope in the world won't change that; five years of good works and good thoughts and still, when Ella thinks about her daughter, she bleeds all over again. The garden is Ella's beautiful handiwork; her recreation center across the street, a gift of her love; and the children, from Chubb and Old Man and Little Stevie up to Tae and Neacey and DeAndre, are her very ambition. But now, with the past confronting her, none of it is enough to cauterize the wound.

This is what Fayette Street took from Ella Thompson:

A twelve-year-old, all curls and smiles and laughter in November of 1988, walking her older sister to the bus stop at Baltimore and Gilmor. It was almost dark and very cold on that evening, but Pooh wanted to walk with Donnie, to see her onto the No. 20 bus and afterward walk back up Fulton to Fayette. More than that, Pooh wanted to show off the hairdo that Donnie had spent more than an hour fashioning for her that afternoon.

"It's not often you get your older sister to do up your hair like that," Ella had told Andrea, watching Donnie work with brush and braids.

It had been Donnie's plan to stay in for the night, but she'd been seeing a boy down in Cherry Hill, and later, after Ella left for a continuing education class at Carver High School, the older daughter decided to catch a bus and visit him. Despite the cold, Pooh tagged along, waved at her eighteen-year-old sister, then turned back up Fulton as the No. 20 rumbled down Baltimore Street. Sitting on the bus by a window, Donnie saw her go.

That night, when Ella returned from class, she assumed that everyone was in bed already. She fell asleep early, exhausted from the class. When she woke for no reason at five that morning, something told her to look in on Donnie and Pooh, Tito and Kiti.

Donnie was sound asleep. Pooh's bed was empty.

Ella woke the older girl, but Donnie had no idea either. "I thought she came straight back home."

The worst didn't immediately occur to them. Pooh was twelve—just old enough to have started breaking some of the rules. She had girl-friends throughout the neighborhood, and for the rest of the early morning hours Ella tried to calm herself, to convince herself that Pooh had stayed at a friend's and would be back home at first light, sheepish and apologetic. But when day broke, Ella called the police.

Still, Ella reasoned away the fear, imagining that Andrea had over-slept, that she would awake at a friend's house late and realize that she was in a mess of trouble. Ella told Donnie and Tito that she could imagine a worried Andrea in some other girl's room, trying to think of how to make things right.

That morning, Ella had jury duty.

"You goin'?" Donnie asked her.

Ella nodded. Waiting for the police to call home would be an admission that something serious had really happened. Besides, she told her daughter, if she left it would give Pooh a chance to come home. "She's probably waiting to see all of us leave so she can sneak back in here without us catching her and pretend she was here all the while."

From the jury room at the downtown courthouse, Ella called home repeatedly. Donnie was nervous, but reassured her mother with the news that she had twice picked up the phone only to hear the caller immediately disconnect.

"That's Pooh," Ella told her, half-relieved. "She's calling to see if anyone's around. Next time, let it ring."

But there were no more calls, and nothing from the police.

When she returned home that night, Ella moved restlessly around the apartment. On the six o'clock news, one of the television stations had a breaking story about the body of an unidentified woman discovered in an alley behind the 1800 block of West Baltimore Street. There was nothing more to it—no suggestion that the body was anything but an adult female—yet from the moment she heard the broadcast, Ella knew. Her fears, carefully suppressed all day long, overwhelmed her.

When the doorbell rang later that evening, Ella looked at the uniformed officer and spoke his mind: "I know you found her."

Donnie's face twisted in absolute horror. Tito picked up the television set and smashed it in a rage. He and Kiti, just a year older than Pooh, began shouting wildly, talking about going out on the street and finding the man. Killing him. Ella was in shock, numb, unable to find any words at all. She tried to pray, but her mind wandered.

"Why?" she finally asked the officer.

He shook his head.

"It doesn't make sense," she said.

She kept her children together, weeping, in the front room. She called other family members with the news.

An hour after the first officer arrived, the homicide detectives came and took them all downtown for interviews, asking many more questions than they could answer. It didn't matter. Soon Ella learned all she needed to know. Andrea had been found tucked behind a low wall just off the alley, killed instantly by a .32 bullet fired into the back of her head. There was evidence of sexual assault. Autopsies, evidence submissions, lab reports—the chaos of a death investigation swirled around her.

Days later, Ella learned that Pooh had probably not gone straight home from the bus stop, that she had gone over to a friend's house on Payson Street to show off her new hairstyle. Days after that, she heard of a second crime in the neighborhood—a second rape involving a young girl whose life was this time spared by the man who assaulted her. Eventually she heard from the detectives about the arrest of that man, about how they searched his apartment and found a .32 revolver, how the bullet taken from her daughter's body had been fired from that weapon.

Andrea's murderer, a sociopath named Eugene Dale, was a stranger to Fayette Street, a man only recently paroled from state prison, where he had served a sentence for sexual assault. Although he had on occasion copped vials from the corners, he was not a hardcore user and not known among the Fayette Street regulars. Yet the strip was the strip, and the frenzy of slinging and hustling that brought hundreds to the corners every day allowed Dale the right kind of anonymity. Dope and coke had obscured all else on Fayette Street, so that only the old-timers remembered a community where neighbors once knew each other's business and could mark a stranger from the earliest moment. Among the crews and customers along Fayette and Lexington and Baltimore Streets —black and white, west siders and east siders, locals and wanderers— Eugene Dale was a small, faceless part of the street parade.

The disorder along Fayette Street not only offered anonymity to Eugene Dale, it provided the kind of broken terrain that allowed him to lure victims in broad daylight. The rape of the second neighborhood girl—the event that provided the break in the case—had occurred in a vacant house on Gilmor Street. The half-renovated rowhouse was empty because the young woman who owned it had herself been murdered by a dope-and-coke user she had naively employed to help rehab the property. For weeks after the murder, with the half-furnished house empty and available, Eugene Dale could have come and gone from it as he pleased, no questions asked. It was here that he could have raped Andrea before killing her in the alley. What is known is that one day, two weeks after Andrea was found, Dale walked down the strip with a young girl in tow, entered the vacant house through the front door, showed the child his gun, and raped her in the dead woman's bedroom. Then he walked her back into the street mix, telling the child on her way home that if she spoke to anyone he would shoot her. To emphasize the point, Dale told the young girl that he had already used his gun on another girl—a girl who threatened to tell.

The young victim told her mother. That night, the police kicked in Eugene Dale's door.

These were by no means crimes of the corner. You looked at Eugene Dale and you saw nothing but an ugly hunger behind hollow, empty eyes—that otherworldly stare to which Curt or Blue or Eggy Daddy could never pretend. At their worst, the corner regulars were petty and larcenous and tragic; Eugene Dale was evil. But if Andrea's murder was not a crime of the corner, it was nonetheless a crime that the corner made easy. Vial by vial, this part of West Baltimore had been stripped down past the point of social legitimacy, until it served no human connections beyond those required to buy and sell drugs. Those lost to the corner might not themselves use and destroy a young girl, but over time they had created the ideal world for anyone who could.

In the end, Ella used what solace she could find in that small distinction. She would not judge her world by Eugene Dale; she would not see the neighborhood where she had lived her life through his solitary deed. Instead, she put all her faith in Dale's otherness, exempting him from the rest of Fayette Street. This kind of thing, she told herself, could happen anywhere; it did happen anywhere.

Ella went to the arraignment and testified at the trial. She walked slowly past Eugene Dale on her way to the stand, sensing his eyes on her yet managing to avert her gaze the entire time. She felt excluded when the jurors were shown the crime scene photographs, felt as if they had possession over her daughter in a way that she did not. And when she stumbled upon Dale's mother in a courthouse hallway, she graciously accepted a pained apology, then spoke gently to the woman, telling her that it wasn't her fault—it wasn't anyone's fault—that sometimes children grow up and do things for which there is no possible explanation.

"I don't hate him," she told people who asked. "I hate what he did, but I don't hate him."

She worked hard on Donnie, trying to convince her daughter that she wasn't responsible for what happened, that the bus stop was only a block away from home, that Pooh was old enough to go anywhere in the neighborhood before dinnertime and that this tragedy could have happened in a dozen different ways. She struggled with Tito, who had such an explosive anger. And Kiti, the most sensitive of her children, who seemed almost to disappear into silence after Andrea was killed. Most of all, she refused to find any lesson in the event—she refused to believe that this price had been exacted by something greater than the sum of one man's cruelty.

Ella took no issue with the fact that in the days after the slaying, no one—not a soul—had called the police with any viable information. It was cold that night, she reasoned, and more likely than not, the alley was deserted when her daughter was shot. If the homicide detectives never heard from anyone who saw Andrea Perry earlier that day, Ella was willing to attribute it to bad fortune, rather than to the anonymous chaos of a drug marketplace. That no one saw the killer approach the girl, or walk with her, or touch her—Ella reasoned that the two might have been visible together on the street for only a brief instant. Ella Thompson, who had made a home and raised a family and lived a worthy life on Fayette Street, insisted on regarding the violence as random, and she excused the deathly silence of the neighborhood as genuine ignorance, not evidence of communal betrayal.

The prosecutors matched Eugene Dale's DNA sample to the semen recovered at autopsy. They asked for the death penalty, and Ella was secretly relieved when the jury came back with a verdict of life without parole. I just don't want him to be where he can hurt anyone else, she told her family.

And then, when most people would cease to believe in anything beyond their own pain, Ella Thompson did an unlikely thing. When anyone else would have fled, or raged, or lost themselves in grief, Ella went down to the threadbare neighborhood recreation center and gave herself over to the children of her neighborhood.

The rec center was Pooh. At night, when the furnace made strange noises, Ella knew it was Andrea, letting her mother know she was there. When laughter filled the playground, when the finger paints were smeared on tabletops, when the younger ones all crowded around the television to watch Disney videos—Pooh was with her, watching and sharing. In her apartment, too—the apartment where Andrea had spent all twelve years—Ella sensed her missing child; especially at night, Pooh was a comforting, invisible presence.

Ella couldn't leave Fayette Street. That would be leaving Pooh. And now, after years of loving work, she also couldn't give up on what she had created in that cinder-block bunker. If she did—if she went elsewhere for a better job, or more money—she would be giving up on Andrea. And without the rowhouses and vacant lots and alleys along Fayette Street to form a map of the heart, how would Pooh be able to find her way home?

By New Year's, the garden will be awash in the usual corner traffic, the flower beds again marred by food wrappers and needles and forty-ounce bottles. A walk down the alley off Mount will crackle with the sound of spent vials underfoot, a graveyard of used euphoria, grinding down to sand. But Ella Thompson will still walk past the empty lot with absolute knowledge of her place and purpose in the world. Come the new year, she'll still be talking about how the city is promising to re-tar the blacktop and maybe replace the basketball rims. She'll be convinced that this is the year when there will be money to get the rec center roof fixed, or to repair the furnace, or to buy some new board games. Come the spring, she'll get the kids together and clean the garden, add more topsoil and replant. And by May, she knows, the flowers will be back.

The future on Fayette Street, so far as Ella can see it, is still unwritten. The probabilities are there, of course, but the possibilities are just that— they, too, might still have their say. This year, Blue got clean and taught art. And Fran Boyd, she seemed to be trying; by next year, she might make it. This year, Ella had a basketball team; next year, they might win another game. This year was ending with DeAndre and R.C. and Dinky— all of her boys—out on the corners, doing wrong; next year, they might turn around, come home, do what's right.

This year, there had been a shooting gallery at 1702.

Now, in that same spot, Pooh has a garden.

On the day of the memorial garden's dedication, Ella Thompson's feelings are too strong to allow for clear thought. But that night, she goes home and allows herself to imagine better days. She gives herself some credit for the journey, for all that her work has brought and all that it might still bring. She's happy with the park. The flowers. The wooden sign.

A week after the dedication, she walks out of her apartment, looks up and down Fayette Street, then steps back through the vestibule and into her living room. She fumes for a moment or two, allowing the anger to pass, before calling the police and reporting her gray Oldsmobile as stolen.

Neighborhood kids, Ella tells herself. Joyriding.

She buttons her overcoat, chooses a blue beret from the front closet and then checks the lock on the apartment door. Walking down her steps, she sees Fat Curt shivering on the corner at Fulton.

"Hey, Mister Curt."

Curt nods, ever gracious.

"Cold out today," she offers.

"Yes indeed," says Fat Curt. "The hawk is out."

"You take care."

"You too, dear," says Curt.

Ella Thompson walks to work.

He's going against the grain now, crossing Calhoun, then Carey, heading east down Saratoga and past the looming, half-empty towers of Lexington Terrace.

For Gary McCullough, anything east of Stricker Street or north of the expressway had never held much promise. Those directions had been played out years ago, with all the copper and aluminum stripped off and sold. Lately there had been a brief revival, when the housing authority spent some money rehabbing units in the low-rises and in a couple of the Terrace towers, but for the most part, the fiends had done the locust work on everything between Martin Luther King Boulevard and Sandtown-Winchester. True, Gary's neighborhood was played out as well, with every vacant address now yielding little more than two-cents-a-pound bulk metal. But that left south and west—south into the hillbilly neighborhoods, where the metal game was just getting started; west against the home-owners-under-siege who were still fighting the good fight on the other side of Hilltop.

Yet on this late December day, Gary is marching east into the empty and open maw of the ghetto, following the Gaunt One on a mission of her own device and choosing. Ronnie Boice is once again leading her charge into battle, and Gary, like any down-in-the-trenches soldier, tells himself it's not his to wonder why. Today it's Ronnie's caper and so Ronnie is in command. Today, Gary's a grunt.

"Dag," he tells her as they cross Arlington, "these houses been picked clean."

Ronnie ignores him. She's not interested in metal today; she's got another plan. And Gary, who knows enough of what she has in mind to follow, is only pretending to be scouting metal lodes to occupy his mind on the journey.

"We cuttin' up at the boulevard, right?"

Ronnie mutters.

"We can cut up that way."

Ronnie says nothing.

"Dag, we don't got to walk all the way downtown."

But Ronnie is cautious, keeping to the main stems, avoiding any neighborhood that might bring them into contact with people who know her, some of whom Ronnie has burned before. For Ronnie, most of West Baltimore must be negotiated as an interpersonal minefield.

"We come up from the bottom," she tells Gary finally.

And they do, heading up Martin Luther King to Pennsylvania and then marching north by northwest along what's left of the Avenue, once the grand boulevard of black Baltimore, now a broken shell of itself. At Pennsie and Bloom Street, they go to work.

Ronnie plays the tout; Gary holds the stash. He's out there on an alien corner, a dark-skinned lamppost amid the Pennsie whores and the johns and the other dealers, holding a handful of B-and-Q burn bags and waiting for Ronnie to talk her talk and send a stray customer or two his way.

And damned if it doesn't work the way she said it would. Damned if they don't unload enough sham heroin to finance their own happy blast. Ronnie's eye for the amateur ensures that most of the customers are single-shot strays, less-than-hardcore types who are up at Pennsylvania and Bloom for the whores more than the dope. These customers won't come back on you when they learn the nasty truth; they're from some other neighborhood and they wouldn't know where to find you again even if they wanted to.

At least this is the way Gary wants and needs to see it. It's Gary, after all, who's up front, serving up nothing for hard-earned something. It's Gary who is cast in the title role of burn artist, standing out there amidst the passing traffic. If this caper goes bad, the bullet will belong to Gary. For Ronnie Boice, the lady of a thousand capers, a projectile with her name scratched into its brass casing has yet to be minted.

Burdened by his own need, Gary has no chance to assess the risk or, more pointedly, to acknowledge that he's once again being grandly used by his girl. He's no longer playing his own game. In fact, he's no longer bothering to distinguish between viable capers and sheer folly.

Selling B-and-Q gets people killed, and selling B-and-Q on a strange corner in an alien neighborhood gets them killed that much faster. Yet in less than a half hour, Gary has cash money in his pocket and he's once again a half step behind his lady love, marching up Brunt to Gold Street and down toward Division, looking for a real drug dealer selling real drugs. In his view, this outcome is argument enough to play at almost anything.

Ronnie will see them through; she carries the team, she makes it happen. Like now, when she brings their fresh profit up to a strange corner and comes back with a good blast, then finds her way to a cheap needle palace on Brunt Street. Tallyho, thinks Gary. That's my girl.

On the way back down Pennsylvania Avenue, he's immersed in happy fog, reassured that he can still play this game, that he will somehow get from one day to the next and survive. He can adapt. He doesn't need to feed crabs into a steamer for hours on end; damned if he hasn't been cut back to one day a week at Seapride now anyway. And he doesn't need the metal game either; so what if the neighborhoods around him have all been stripped down to bone? You say that his old running buddy, Tony Boice, is locked up, over at City Jail somewhere? Well then, daytime burglary is out. And that there's too much risk in playing tour guide to white kids? Fine. No problem. Something will always come along. And if nothing comes along, then Ronnie will always be there for him, waiting with some new means of getting it done and requiring only that Gary do his able-bodied part.

Walking back down Pennsie, warmed against the cold, Gary admits that a part of him actually loves her. Strangely enough, he feels the same thing coming back at him.

"We can do this tomorrow," he tells her.

"If you want."

"Maybe a different corner, though."

"Naw," she says, quietly assertive. "We okay right there."

They cross the boulevard after sundown, dodging rush-hour head-lights, Gary dreaming of a triumphant return to Pennsie and Bloom, this time with double the ration of trash.

Ronnie wants to turn at Saratoga, but Gary drags her across the street, over toward St. Mary's Park, where Bruce Epps—Blue's brother— is living on one of the rehabbed streets. Bruce had partnered with Gary, when Lightlaw, Gary's contracting company, was up and running. Now Gary is in the wind and Bruce, by local standards, is living right.

"I want to show you this one street," Gary tells her.

"What?"

"This street where all the houses are done up nice."

Ronnie glares at him from a universe away. What possible purpose could there be in touring a well-kept block of rowhouses? Where's the caper in that?

"I would have liked to live down here," says Gary.

Ronnie snorts derisively, but Gary ignores her, crossing the boulevard, forcing Ronnie to detour with him. He gets within sight of the green expanse and the repointed brick and the Williamsburg pastels on painted shutters and he's transported to a life beyond the one he's living. Gary is on St. Mary's Street, soaking up the essences of a world he very nearly captured.

"This," he tells her, "is how to live."

Walking slowly down the street, he's lost in the possibilities, so much so that he's caught off balance when two hard-look soldiers, their hooded sweatshirts pulled up tight, come at them from the edge of the park.

Gary thinks to run, but doesn't. Ronnie only smirks.

"Uh," says Gary.

The smaller one goes into the dip of his sweats, starts to pull out the cannon. Gary is crushed: All that work on Pennsylvania and Bloom and now he's going to lose whatever blast money he had squirreled away for tomorrow morning.

But Ronnie is in motion, walking toward the stickup boys.

"Hey," she says, holding her hand out.

"Wassup?" says the bigger one, looking from Ronnie to Gary and then back again.

"Gimme a quarter," says Ronnie.

The stickup boys share a look. The smaller one takes his hand from the waist of his sweats. No gun.

"C'mon, let me have a quarter," whines Ronnie.

The stickup crew moves on. Gary stands by the park entrance, his face glowing. Ronnie, the queen. His queen.

"You is an apple-scrapple!" Gary declares, hugging her.

"Come on," says Ronnie, smiling. "Let's get home."

All the way up Fayette Street, he's thinking about it, marveling at his girl's skills, congratulating himself for having held on to her. He's telling himself that the burn bags make sense. That he can do this tomorrow and the day after and for as long as need be.

"We gonna hook up tomorrow, right?"

"If you want," says Ronnie agreeably.

"In the morning," Gary says. "You come by and bang on the basement door for me."

By the time they clear Stricker Street and creep into their own neighborhood, Gary's world seems settled and secure. At least until he remembers his father.

"Oh man," he says.

Ronnie looks at him.

"I can't hook up in the morning."

"Why not?"

Gary searches for words. Ronnie cocks her head to the side, staring at him, her antennae up to whatever small act of deceit Gary is hoping to conceal. If he can't hook up with her first thing tomorrow, he most have another caper planned. And from all capers, she will have her rightful share.

"Where you gon' be at?"

"I got to run somewhere in the morning," Gary tells her.

"I go with you."

Gary shakes his head. "It's family," he tells her.

All the way back up Fayette Street, Ronnie fumes. Gary knows exactly what she's thinking—that he's ungrateful, high on good dope right now because of her caper and yet unwilling to share a caper of his own. But he's willing to let himself be misunderstood, because the alternative would require him to arm Ronnie with information on a McCullough family drama—something that Gary has been loath to do ever since that ugly moment last summer at the courthouse when Ronnie's mother tore into Roberta McCullough for no good reason. Instead, Gary lets the silence stand as he walks with his girl up Fayette. Ronnie can think what she wants; he'll deal with that problem down the road.

What Gary can't tell Ronnie is that in the morning, he will get up early to drive with his mother and his brother Cardy across town to Union Memorial Hospital. There they will visit William McCullough, who is in a semiprivate room, waiting to see what the doctors have to say about his prostate.

At sixty-five, W.M. is showing few signs of worry, though he's been at Union Memorial for nearly a week, ever since he collapsed in pain on the bathroom floor while trying to catheterize himself to pass water— dealing with the problem on his own as he had for years. The doctors are hinting at cancer or worse—talking to Roberta and the children in hushed tones—but it doesn't seem to faze the family patriarch, who does more talking about the hospital food than about his own medical condition.

Still, for Gary, who has already paid one visit to the ailing W.M., the sight of his father laid out in a hospital bed—with tubes and IVs and all the other paraphernalia of medical science—is terrifying. To Gary, W.M. has always been larger than life, a man capable of epic toil and endless stoicism. In Gary's mind, his father will endure forever, and if not forever, then surely for as long as it will take Gary to leave his drugging behind and resume the kind of life that would restore him in his father's sight. From within the heroin haze, Gary can sometimes convince himself that the last several years have been little worse than a brief interlude, a modest lapse in which time and family have been standing still. But last week, W.M. was lying on a metal bed beneath white sheets, and the doctors were looking at the charts, and Roberta

McCullough was by her husband's bedside every day, looking alone and scared.

That first visit to see his father had done nothing but exacerbate Gary's twin feelings of guilt and terror. Sitting up in bed, W.M. had acknowledged Gary with little more than a nod, then proceeded to direct his conversation to his wife and Cardy for the entire visit. Sensitive to a fault, Gary couldn't help feeling the distance that separated him from his father. Nothing he could do or say in that hospital room could bridge the distance.

"Man right here in this bed, he died during the night," W.M. told Roberta, with a nod toward the empty litter on the other side of the partition. "I could hear him wheezin' and coughin' and tryin' to breathe and I was ringing for the nurse, but no one came. I listened to him die."

Leaning against the far wall, Gary heard the story and felt sick to his stomach. His father lay before him, waiting for good news and just as likely to hear bad, and meanwhile, Gary could provide no decent account of his life. For five whole years he had been running the streets, wasting time, losing sight of what truly mattered.

"Don't want to die the way he did," W.M. mused. "A hospital ain't no place to get sick and die."

Gary wanted to cry out, to plead, to throw himself across the chasm and grab hold of the edges of his long-ago life. Instead, he left when Cardy and his mother left, having said nothing and done nothing, acknowledging his father with nothing beyond another quiet nod.

He was silent on the drive back to Vine Street. That night, when the snake coiled up and hissed at him, he went down to the corner with the money in his pocket and did what he needed to do. But the next morning, he found strength enough to make his way up to Poplar Grove Street and the St. Edward's clinic, where he had heard you could get Clonidine patches on a daily basis.

He would kick free of the heroin, he promised himself, and he would do it with just the Clonidine. He would stay down in the basement and sleep and listen to the radio talk shows and, come the weekend, he would be sick. But by Monday, or Tuesday at the latest, he would no longer be a drug addict. Then he would return to Union Memorial, where his father lay beneath white sheets, and he would present himself as the prodigal son come back to the doorstep. He could say nothing to his father now; but with the help of the Lord and a daily ration of prescription drugs, Gary would still have the chance to say all he needed to say.

That was the plan last week anyway, and it continued to be the plan for a few days after the hospital visit. At St. Edward's clinic, Gary had submitted to a medical examination, professed the true extent of his problem, then left with three patches—enough to get him through the weekend.

He stayed in the basement and slept for twelve hours, felt the sickness rising, then stayed in the basement for another ten or twelve hours, trying to measure time by top-of-the-hour radio broadcasts or by pages turned in the dog-eared Bible by his bed. The next day, with sweat pouring down the small of his back, he got dressed and crept out for a vial of coke. When the coke alone failed to settle him, he went down the street for a nickel of dope.

On Monday he went back up to Poplar Grove for another patch. "I'm still trying to kick," he told the doctor at St. Edward's. "I'm down to one bag a day."

Except that the next day, it was a bag and a half. And the day after, two. And the day after that—well, he hooked up with Ronnie Boice, who managed to sell his Clonidine dose for five dollars. When that money was gone, she dreamed up the burn-bag caper and now, heading back up Fayette, Gary realizes that he will be going to see his father tomorrow as the same fallen man he was six days before.

Tomorrow morning, for all Gary knows, his father might be told that time was short, that all the years of toil and hope and struggle were coming to an end. And Gary would be there, in the hospital room, without being there. He would hover at the edge of the family drama as half-son, half-wraith—spent, useless, empty of all purpose save the one that sent him to the corner three times a day.

Crossing back over Gilmor Street with Ronnie, Gary feels the ship of his drug euphoria capsize, taking water and breaking apart as it crashes against the rock of his own conscience.

"Family," says Ronnie, contemptuous.

"I'm not lying. I promised to do something."

"Promised your mother, you mean."

Ronnie shows her animus for Roberta, punishing Gary for his pretense of being a good son.

"She think you so good and pure," Ronnie says. "She don't know you like I know you."

Gary shakes his head. He can't hold the secret any longer. "It's not my mother," he says.

"It's always your mother."

"My father's in the hospital. He might have cancer."

Ronnie is unimpressed. "So," she asks Gary, "what is it that you got to do tomorrow?"

"I'm going to see him."

Ronnie shakes her head. To her, William McCullough is irrelevant to Gary's current incarnation and the daily struggle for drugs. If W.M. was sick, then they'd need a blast. If he got better, they'd need another. And if he died, they'd still have to go out and get high.

"Your father want to see you?" Ronnie asks.

"I want to see him."

"Huh," says Ronnie.

They walk the last few blocks in silence, with Ronnie delivering the coup de grace as they pull even with the liquor store at Monroe Street.

"You always pretending with them," she tells Gary.

Gary wants to strike her, to shove her away and shout and give free rein to all his loathing. But Ronnie is essential now. She proved that today as she will prove it tomorrow, so Gary swallows his pride and looks only for a way to placate one world long enough to visit briefly in the other.

"I come right back from the hospital," he says. "Cardy driving us."

Ronnie shrugs.

"I swear I'm not gonna do anything without you."

"Better not," she says, raising an eyebrow.

It's marital fidelity as measured on the hype. Having given his oath, Gary leaves feeling relief and genuine gratitude. She will wait for him tomorrow. She will cut him in for another trip to Pennsylvania and Bloom, or for any better caper that she can dream up between this night and the next. The snake can say nothing to him now: For another day at least, Gary has some tenuous connection to a plan.

He arrives home in time to get a hot chicken plate from his mother's stove. His mother serves him, and he joins Kwame and June Bey and his young niece Shakima at the table. Afterward, Miss Roberta cleans up with sad, tired eyes fixed on the sink. Nothing is said about the man missing from the kitchen table until Kwame breaks the silence.

"How he look today, Ma?"

"He looks better," she tells him.

"So he comin' home tomorrow, right?"

"With the help of the Lord."

June Bey drifts out first. Then Kwame. Then Shakima finishes eating and begins giving chicken pieces to the cat. Gary clears the table, carries laundry upstairs, then slips quietly out into the street, the last thirteen dollars from the Bloom Street caper burning in his back pocket. He gets one-and-one, then adjourns to the basement for what proves to be the best speedball in weeks. Black Tops. A bomb from Gee Money's crew.

For the rest of the night, Gary is down in the basement with his clock radio and his library, frantic from potent coke, his eyes darting around the clutter as he tries to find some comfort in the soiled sheets and blankets. When that fails, he gets dressed again and goes out into Vine Street for the early morning hours, wandering up to the corner without money or purpose, trying to steady his fevered mind in the cold predawn air.

The cocaine finally surrenders just before sunup, and Gary can't be awakened when Cardy picks up his mother after breakfast. He comes to consciousness that afternoon, alone in an empty house with another portion of guilt. His mother and brother are at the hospital. His father is talking with the doctors. And Gary McCullough sits in his long underwear at the kitchen table, with a glass of orange juice and two strips of bacon.

He thinks for a while about getting a ride across town, surprising everyone by showing up at Union Memorial on his own. But something inside him shouts down the thought of such an arduous journey in the December cold. Instead, he finishes his breakfast, dresses slowly, and wanders down to Fayette long enough to learn that Ronnie isn't out of bed yet either. He goes back to Vine Street, takes a piece of American cheese from the refrigerator, wraps a slice of white bread around it, and has lunch.

Gary locks up the house and begins walking north up Monroe Street, heading toward Poplar Grove and the clinic at St. Edward's, telling himself that he will still do this thing, that he's sick and tired of being sick and tired. More Clonidine and he'll be ready. A patch for today and two more for the weekend, and he'll be there for his father on Monday.

"My name's Gary McCullough," he tells the nurse. "I'm in your detox program, but I haven't been here the last few days."

The nurse shakes her head. The doctor is on rounds for his patients at Bon Secours. He won't be in the clinic until tomorrow.

"I'm just tryin' to get the patch."

"You have to see the doctor."

Gary nods politely, walks out of the clinic and feels the chill of late afternoon. From across Poplar Grove Street, the sunlight is fading down into the barren trees by the cemetery. The day seems utterly lost to him.

Ronnie. She'll be back on Fayette Street, or coming around Vine, looking for him. Gary steadies his nerves, bundles up against the cold and begins walking up the Grove, toward Riggs Avenue and away from his neighorhood. He warms to a new idea. He will do this today. He will salvage some honorable purpose before his mother and brother return from the hospital.

On Riggs he turns east and finds the house without any problem. His son's girlfriend is out of school for the holidays, and she greets him with surprise at the door.

"Mister Gary," says Tyreeka.

"Hey," he says. He can't recall her name.

"Andre not here," she tells him, confused and awkward.

"I just came to see the baby, if that's okay."

Tyreeka smiles, delighted. DeAnte is upstairs with his great-grandmother taking the last of a bottle, she tells Gary. "I got to change him, but I'll bring him down after that."

Gary sits quietly on the front room sofa, nodding politely to Tyreeka's cousins as they race around him, shouting and laughing. The girl is gone for ten minutes, but when she comes down the stairs, DeAnte is on her shoulder, tiny and new and wide-eyed.

"Goodness," says Gary.

"You want to hold your grandson?" she asks.

"That be all right?"

"'Course."

Gary leans back on the couch and holds out his hands. Tyreeka carefully ladles the infant into his arms. DeAnte looks up into Gary's face, blandly curious.

"He got the McCullough eyes," she says.

Gary strokes the baby's cheek and says nothing for a long while. Tyreeka sits on a chair opposite and watches.

"You a grandfather now," she says.

Gary looks up, intent and serious. Then he smiles.

"He's beautiful," he says finally. "He remind me of Andre."

"Lawd, I hope not," laughs Tyreeka. "If that child is anything like

DeAndre, I'm gonna have my hands full. I'm hoping he takes more after my family in some things."

Gary ponders this, then nods agreement. "Andre was rough," he says, reflective. "He was always into something, always doing some kinda deviltry."

"Yes, indeed," says Tyreeka.

The baby coughs, then cries. Gary puts the child to his shoulder and pats lightly, and when that doesn't work, he looks to Tyreeka, who stands up and takes the baby. The crying stops.

"He know his mother," Gary says.

"I be right back," Tyreeka says, taking the infant upstairs. Gary looks out a cracked window onto the front porch and the rowhouses on the other side of Riggs Avenue. The sun is all but down now.

"When you're young," he says, watching Tyreeka's cousins, "you think about what it is that you want to be . . ."

Gary seems to give up on the thought. He leans back and rests his head on the sofa, looking up at long shadows on the front room ceiling.

". . . you think of all the things there is. And you wonder what it is you should wish for."

He is crying now. Tears trail down both cheeks.

"I'm a drug addict," he says.

Gary looks down at his own hands.

"That's what I am," he says firmly. "Who would wish for that? Who would choose that for their life?"

Gary gets up slowly and zips his jacket. He hears the young girl upstairs, cooing and laughing at her child. He stands awkwardly in the darkness of the front hallway, listening to the happy noise above him, waiting for a chance to say his thank-you and good-bye.

"Andre has a son," he says, as if saying the words can make him believe it. "My son has a son of his own."

When a ten-year-old cousin comes in off the porch, Gary struggles with a sentence or two, asking the boy to tell Tyreeka that he had to leave. The boy nods, then wanders back into the kitchen.

Gary fumbles with his coat snaps, wipes his eyes with his sleeve, pulls on his knit cap, and braces himself against the cold. It's a good fifteen blocks south by southeast to Monroe and Fayette and it's very late. His mother will be home. Maybe his father, too. And Ronnie—she's probably hunting him right now. Mean and spiteful and thinking the worst.

"I chose this," he says, turning down Riggs.

Gary puts his hands into his jacket pockets and leans forward. As he walks, the wind dries his face.

If you want shit done right, DeAndre McCullough thinks, you got to do it your own damn self.

So he's got the drugstore out this morning, spread out across the blue shag carpet in the front room on Boyd Street. He's got his mother's mirror, a clean razor blade, a bag of empty red-topped vials, and about $600 worth of idiot-proof, already-stepped-on, profit-guaranteed, precut coke, straight off a weekend Metroliner from New York. Though it's after noon, he's still in his underwear, his eyes a dried-up pink from last night's revelry. But he's warm in the stream of sunlight from the front window, and he's feasting on a breakfast of milk-sodden Cocoa Krispies and strawberry Kool Aid, and he's taking in the boom and beat from the half-assed stereo, with Dre and Snoop and the rest of the Death Row crew telling all them other niggas to make their shit the chronic, 'cause they gots to get fucked-up.

DeAndre McCullough is getting it done. With a practiced hand, he's severing line after line from the granular pile, filling and capping each vial in an assembly-line motion. Bottle after bottle, bundle after bundle—he can do this with a discipline and precision that never showed itself anywhere else in his life. It's a skill. Simple, yet essential. He'll be on the blue carpet, vialing up, for another hour.

DeAndre McCullough can break a package down and put it on the street, keep it safe and tabulate the profits. To a degree, he can lead, organize, motivate a handful of lesser corner talents. He can arrange for runners, lookouts, and touts. He can set up a stash house, establish a routine, monitor sales. More than most of those who go down to the West Baltimore corners at the end of adolescence, DeAndre can see what needs to be done, then do it himself, or better still, get others to do it for him. And when they don't, when they fall down, or disappear, or mess the count, he can be fierce or, at least, he can pretend to be fierce. He can stand his ground against the fiends and their moves, against competitors and rivals and predators. He can, if he concentrates all his experience and abilities, go down to a corner and turn the package into spending money.

As a way of living, it's not much; by the standards of society at large, it's nothing at all. But DeAndre can do it. If he fashions a plan that goes beyond the everyday distractions, he has gifts enough to put some kind of run together. By rights, he should be able to get his own apartment, breaking free of Fran and controlling his own space. He should be able to keep track of his money, get it out of his pocket and into a shoebox, put that shoebox beneath his bed or in the back of his closet, and have it stay there, untouched and unmolested.

That's the future as DeAndre now sees it. That's his plan as he finishes with his vials, cleans the mirror, and tosses the razor in the kitchen trash. He tells himself that three bundles will be enough to start the day's sales, provided he can get down to McHenry and Gilmor by three or so. He likes to sling during the Southern District shift-change, risking the corners only when Turner and the other bottom-end police are busy with roll call. In a good late-afternoon hour, he can make more than a week's worth of aftertax burger-slinging money. Turning off the tape player, he gathers himself together, then runs upstairs for his winter coat, taking the bag of empty vials with him and hiding them in his dirty laundry.

He picks out his hair, slaps a cold washcloth across his face, and slides out into the late December sun, thinking to himself that the other way just won't work, that he can't sit up on Riggs Avenue playing house with Tyreeka and the baby. For one thing, he is still sixteen years old, and a daily routine of Tyreeka, the baby, and domestic living is likely to drive him crazy. And it seems to him like the girl is hitting his beeper five and ten times a day, crying all the time about needing this and wanting that.

DeAndre has sense enough to see that it isn't diapers or Weeboks that Tyreeka is grasping for—it's him. She wants to know where he's at, who he's with, which girls he might be messing with. Today he still claims that he loves Tyreeka, loves his son. But in the same breath, he tells himself that he's sick of getting her pages, sick of arguing with her at pay phones and sick of being told that he owes her a package of got-damned disposable diapers.

Only last night he had called her, promising to bring a box of Pampers in the morning. But later for that; Tyreeka will keep. Instead, DeAndre walks down to Baltimore Street and gets a hack ride across Hilltop and down bottom to McHenry Street, where the rest of the C.M.B. crew has once again proved entirely capable of stealing his money, messing up his count, and generally turning profit into loss. The lesson is that you can't remote control a corner. You have to be there, watching over the sales and counting the vials and keeping an eye on all of the players. Otherwise, you bleed out.

The years of shared history among the crew working Gilmor and McHenry don't help either. Friendship aside, his boys have got to do some honest work for their share of the package, and lately, they've been letting him down.

For starters, DeAndre wants to kill Dorian; last week he disappeared between supplier and stash house with a whole quarter. Dorian was crying about how a stickup boy got him, but he has fucked up so many times in the past that he's unable to carry that lie for any distance at all. He's hiding from DeAndre, fearful, but hoping that after a few weeks even a missing quarter can be forgotten. And DeAndre, despite his bluster, might just have to forget. The alternative is to beat or maim or kill a boy with whom he has for years cut classes and chased girls and run the streets. Though DeAndre is physically capable of doing any or all of those three things, he cannot sustain the rage necessary to follow through.

DeAndre also has a beef with R.C., who owes him money and who has already taken one ass-whipping from Dinky for coming up light on a count. Likewise, Manny Man is hiding out with Miss Ella up at the rec, afraid to come down below Pratt Street where he'd have to deal with a long string of accumulated debts. As for the leader of the pack, Tae is off somewhere smoking rock, or so DeAndre now believes. Just as R.C. has been on the pipe as well; DeAndre is sure of it no matter how many times R.C. laughs off the accusation. Boo? That boy's been fiending for months; Boo couldn't look worse. And so what if DeAndre himself is snorting some dope on the weekends? Dope isn't coke, and he isn't about to start messing with coke.

By his accounting, the entire crew is comprised of fuckups, save for himself and Dinky. His cousin, at least, has his back; DeAndre figures it should be enough.

No, to get paid from a corner, you have to go down to the corner. There is no other way. All that one-for-all, all-for-one talk among the standing members of the Crenshaw Mafia Brothers is proving to be just talk after all. They are growing up and growing apart; the corner itself is seeing to that. When they were children, they played the neighborhood games—snatchpops, for one—grabbing ice cream or sodas out of each other's hands, then yelling no snatch-backs and laughing. Now, they're palming each other's vials and running off with ground stashes. A year or two more and the petty betrayals will accumulate. Soon, they'll be hunting each other, beating each other, maybe even shooting each other. The corner rules are inexorable.

For now, with the Southern District shift-change only a half hour away, he goes directly down to his corner where Dinky is waiting on him.

"Turner rolled out just before," Dinky tells him.

The bundles go fast, and DeAndre stands on post, shameless. He's a player. A hustler. At this point, he could care less what his mother thinks. She's the one who brought Marvin into the house. She's the one getting high. She's the one who's not doing shit with her life. Last month she went through the check-day money in not much more than a week. This month, the same damn thing. And not only the check money, DeAndre knows, but a hundred that she managed to borrow from friends and relatives who still believed in her, who thought the loan was for Christmas presents for her sons. Naw, DeAndre tells himself, I'm not trying to hear shit from her about any damn thing.

He slings through the shift-change, and when he goes home to Boyd Street after midnight, Fran is upstairs, trying to sleep. In the morning she glares at him but says nothing, and DeAndre feels stronger for it.

No one is pretending anymore. No one is making threats. His mother is back in the mix and he's free to do what he wants. A couple of days later, DeAndre catches up to his mother in her usual spot on Fayette Street, perched on the front steps of the Dew Drop with the regulars. Bunchie and Stevie, Drac and Little Roy, Ronnie Hughes and Michael and Sherry.

"Hey," he says.

"Lemme hold ten," she says.

"I'm broke."

Fran gives him a cold look, but doesn't press for the money, instead telling him that it's fine, that she doesn't want anything from him anyway.

"You think you big-time," she tells her son. "You ain't shit, little boy."

"Yeah, all right," he mutters, stalking off.

Fran watches her son go, her heart closed to him, if only for this moment. She's back where she started—back to her games, her angles, her getting over on people, one blast at a time. And, she's willing to admit to herself, she's certainly better at the corner life than at any other kind of existence. Life without dope and coke was all complexity and

THE CORNER

aggravation. But today she made some money. She palmed some vials. She did what needed to be done.

Tomorrow, she tells herself. Tomorrow she'll sleep in, get sick, get well. But the fall is accelerating: She's now getting high three or four nights a week, telling herself that it's no big thing, that she can carry this or leave it be. Incredibly, though, she's able to slow herself down briefly before succumbing to the long descent back down to the bottom. Just before Christmas, she fashions a plan for the holidays.

Dragging herself off Fayette Street, Fran talks to Scoogie, convincing her brother to go down to the market with her for groceries. With all else around her a disaster, the idea of Christmas dinner becomes Fran's touchstone—an emotional link with last month's Thanksgiving feast, when the Boyds stepped off the corner and dressed themselves up for a rare moment of familial harmony. She'll do it again, she tells herself. She'll recreate that moment down to the last piece of sweet potato pie.

Two days after cursing her son on the Dew Drop steps, Fran is down at the market on Pratt Street, sizing up birds with her brother. Scoogie is with her in large part to see that his money goes toward actual groceries, though it's true that he's as captivated as Fran is by the memory of his family's Thanksgiving epiphany.

"Even Stevie looked good," he tells her.

"Yes indeed. Cleaned up and all."

All day on the twenty-fifth, she burns her heart out in Scoogie's kitchen. If redemption was a matter of bread dressing and brown gravy, Fran Boyd would be a woman saved.

Laying down dish after dish on the dining room table, she waits for the others to drift in from Fayette Street. As for Marvin Parker, she dealt with him the best she could, telling him she wouldn't be around Boyd Street much during the holidays and that he needed to get his shit in order by the new year. Marvin threw her the same old bone about having called the detox clinic, telling her his name was definitely on the waiting list. In her mind, Fran is through with Marvin, but she can't put him out just yet—not during the holidays, not while the weather's bad and he's got nowhere to go.

The Christmas feast is every bit as awesome as Thanksgiving, except that this time Bunchie, Sherry, Alfred, and Kenny rush in at the last moment in worn denims and sweats. Stevie wanders in late, pupils wide, eyes heavy-lidded, his gaunt frame leaning at improbable angles, swaying precipitously in the gale force of a good package.

And DeAndre. The boy staggers in when the food is half gone, brushing past aunts and uncles with scarcely a word. He grabs a plate, fills it, and lumbers into the living room.

Tyreeka is waiting on the sofa, with their son sleeping soundly in his carrier at her feet. She has been sitting there for three hours, staring morosely at music videos, pretending to be waiting for anything in this world other than DeAndre McCullough.

She barely looks up when he steps in front of the television and hits the buttons on the top of the cable box, changing up to an action movie.

"I was watching that," says Tyreeka softly.

"Not no more," says DeAndre.

Tyreeka fights back tears, still refusing to look anywhere but at the television. DeAndre gives the top of DeAnte's head a quick rub, puts his plate on the coffee table and settles into the sofa. Fran can see he's high, and complains to Scoogie that it's just like DeAndre to mess up Christmas dinner with a forty-ounce. But moments later, with a half-full plate in front of him and the family bustling around the dining room table and television, DeAndre leans back on the couch and slips into a gaping, openmouthed nod.

Fran looks at him, sees that the denims are soiled, that the army jacket has stains on one shoulder, that the dreds are matted flat. Is this DeAndre, who takes such pride in his clothes, his appearance, his look? And his skin—DeAndre actually looks dusty, his face and neck showing that dull, sheenless pallor that can only come from a hard drug sucking at life itself.

"How Andre look to you?" she asks Scoogie in a whisper.

"Messed up," says her brother.

"I mean, if I didn't know better, I'd say he was using dope."

She lets her own words hang, contemplating them from a distance, as if she's on the outside of the problem looking in. DeAndre swore he'd never have shit to do with dope or coke. He saw what it did to his father, to her, to everyone else in her family. But that's him nodding on the sofa, drooling and breathing deep, his food going cold in front of him.

"He just drunk is all," says Bunchie.

A few minutes more and the boy stirs himself and picks up his fork. He finishes the plate, then shoves DeRodd and Little Stevie off the end of the sofa so he can lie down. When Tyreeka hears him snore, she gets up to change the channel.

Ten minutes later, Bunchie's daughter, Nicky, arrives with her boyfriend, Corey, and their baby, DeQuan, and with their arrival, DeAndre begins to show signs of life. He greets Corey and his cousin, then notices DeAnte awake and staring up at him mournfully. He squats beside the baby carrier to play with his son.

"Hey, boy."

DeAnte gurgles.

"Hey, boy. Who you lookin' at?"

He still says nothing to Tyreeka, who keeps to the television, watching to see how the Grinch stole Christmas, avoiding all eye contact with DeAndre. Corey finishes his plate, nudges DeAndre, and the two of them gather up their coats.

"Where you going at?" asks Fran.

"Out clubbin'," says DeAndre.

Fran looks over at Tyreeka. The girl is melting into a corner of the sofa, trying hard not to look up from the cartoon.

"Dinner's great, Ma," says DeAndre, turning to leave.

"You not gonna stay around with your son?" asks Fran.

DeAndre bristles. "I see him when I get back."

He goes. When Fran turns back from the door, she sees Tyreeka, her face half-hidden beneath her open hand, crying.

"Reeka. You and the baby going to stay with me tonight, ain't you?"

The girl leans over and picks up her child. She manages to nod.

"You'll see him tonight," Fran tells her, trying to soften the hurt, but Tyreeka says nothing. Fran walks back into the dining room, where Bunchie, Sherry, and Scoogie have pushed their chairs back from the table and are reliving a shared bit of sibling nostalgia. Pulling a chair close to Bunchie, Fran joins them, content for now just to listen to their meanderings. She wants this moment, and she's not about to let her son rob her of it. Even Stevie comes alive, rousting himself from his own nod, joining them somewhere along memory lane.

Despite the shaky start, the evening holds Fran's small desire. Not until well after midnight, with dishes clean and drying, do Fran, Tyreeka, and DeRodd struggle down Saratoga Street with DeAnte and the several plastic bags stuffed with his paraphernalia.

"DeAndre be in a better mood when he gets home," Fran assures Tyreeka. "You know how he be acting around Corey."

It doesn't play out that way, though. Tyreeka hangs around Boyd Street for a couple of days, but DeAndre barely acknowledges her presence in the brief stretches of time when he shows himself. Otherwise, he's down on McHenry Street with his boys, or clubbing and partying at night. Fran tries to intercede, but DeAndre is unreachable.

When Tyreeka is finally ready to go home to Riggs Avenue, Fran helps her pack her things and arranges for a hack. The young mother leaves with the baby just after dinner; the father is still running the streets somewhere.

"I'll tell him you waited as long as you could," says Fran.

"Don't even bother," says Tyreeka.

That night, DeAndre doesn't come in. The next night, he comes home in the early morning hours, long after Fran has gone to bed. When she gets up in the morning, her son is lost to the world, sprawled half-dressed across his mattress.

"Dre."

He doesn't stir.

"An-DRE."

Nothing. She stands there a moment more, making sure he's out cold before she leans over and begins reaching into the pocket of his denims, gently extending her fingers until she finds the big roll. She slips it out slowly, pulls off three twenties, and returns the rest.

And why the hell not? He's living here, eating her food, using her electric, and not doing a damn thing but getting high and hustling on the corners. She's always told him that what he brings into this house— money, drugs, guns—is hers, that if she finds it, it's hers to spend or sell or use. She isn't stealing, she tells herself. She's taking what is her due.

When DeAndre does begin to stir an hour later, Fran is dressed and waiting in the kitchen, ready with her defense. After a time, she can hear him upstairs in his bedroom, muttering and cussing and throwing stuff around his room.

"What the hell wrong with you?" she asks when he makes his way downstairs.

"You know."

"I don't know what the hell . . ."

"You took my money."

"Don't even start with that. You think I'd be sitting here, waiting for your dead ass to get up if I had your money? You think I'd be feeling as sick as I do if I had your money?"

DeAndre glares at her.

"What the hell wrong with you?" Fran asks, getting up and going over to the icebox. "There ain't shit in this refrigerator today. You think I'd be waiting for you to get up if I had your money? I'da done been to the damn market."

DeAndre calms down and Fran gives him a minute or two as he checks the refrigerator and cupboard.

"Lemme hold twenty," she asks finally.

"Ma . . ."

"For groceries. You livin' here too."

DeAndre grimaces as he peels off another bill.

Later, after he's washed and dressed and headed over Hilltop on his way back to the strip, Fran follows at a safe distance, going straight up Baltimore Street when DeAndre turns to go down bottom. She spends $20 on coke and dope, returning with Bunchie to her favorite party lair in the basement of the Dew Drop Inn. With another $40, she stops at the market on her way home and picks up groceries enough to last until check day. The other $20 she saves for tomorrow. Or tonight, if need be.

That night, when DeRodd comes down the hill from Scoogie's to find cereal in the cupboard and burger patties in the freezer and strawberry Kool Aid in the green plastic jug, Fran feels as if she's maintaining. What needs to get done is getting done, and come the new year, she'll deal with the rest of it. Marvin and Antoinette and everything else— those things will keep until she's ready for them. She can afford to let up a little, so later that night, with her extra twenty, she goes back down to Fayette Street.

She doesn't come home until late the following morning, having spent half the night in the Dew Drop basement and the other on Scoogie's sofa, sleeping next to DeRodd. When she does settle back into the kitchen on Boyd Street, she's so beat that it's on DeRodd to notice what's wrong with the picture.

"Ma," he says, holding open the refrigerator.

"Huh."

"Where the food at?"

She looks at him hard for a moment, thinking that he's trying to be funny when all she wants to do is go back to sleep.

"Don't play," she tells DeRodd.

He shrugs, then stands aside to display the gaping void.

Fran glowers for a moment, then runs upstairs. She finds DeAndre asleep on the third floor and Marvin nowhere to be seen. Marvin Parker.

"Got-damn," she says, drifting listlessly back down the stairs. DeRodd stands in the kitchen, looking at her curiously.

"Ma?"

"Shut the damn door."

DeRodd closes the refrigerator.

"Ma? Did Mister Marvin take the food?"

Fran doesn't answer, leaving DeRodd to wonder at what everyone else in this house immediately understands.

"Ma?"

Fran closes her eyes, drops her elbows on the table, and holds her head in her hands. She feels like crying, but tears won't come. DeRodd stands looking at her.

"Get your coat on," she tells him.

DeRodd obeys, then waits patiently while his mother sits staring blankly at the kitchen wall. Uncomfortable in the silence, he creeps past her and heads slowly up the stairs. Fran sits at the table for what seems to her to be hours, sits there wondering how in the hell it could come to this. She isn't going to make it to check day. Or New Year's. Or anything else.

When DeAndre comes down in his socks and underwear, she barely has strength to look up, much less to tell the tale with the anger it deserves.

"Marvin took the groceries," Fran says softly.

Even DeAndre is amazed.

"That man stole our got-damn food," she says. "He cleaned our shit out, took it up to the corner and sold it."

DeAndre walks to the refrigerator, opens the door, then closes it. He stands there for a moment more, then turns and walks back to the stairs.

"He took the food," Fran says, incredulously. "I can't believe he would do that."

"Ma," says DeAndre quietly, "he got to go."

Fran stares at him and says nothing. She looks away slowly, her body slack. More to herself than to DeAndre, she admits to absolute defeat, muttering an answer just over her breath:

"So do I."

DeAndre sits on the stairs, saying nothing more.

After a long while, Fran stands, walks to the stairs and shouts for DeRodd to come down. The boy steps nervously past DeAndre, sensing the ugly mood that has settled in this kitchen.

"C'mon, DeRodd," says his mother. "You goin' back up Scoogie's."

DeAndre looks up. "Ma, where you going at?"

Fran doesn't answer. She doesn't have to. DeAndre knows.

"Ma . . ."

"Andre, don't try to tell me what to do."

"But Ma . . ."

"'Cause I'm not even trying to hear it from you."

Fran leaves him there on the stairs, alone in his boxers and socks. He hears the door slam and the sound of footfalls as his mother and brother go down the front steps and out into Boyd Street. He imagines his brother washing up twenty minutes from now on Uncle Scoogie's doorstep and he imagines his mother pausing not a minute more before taking herself the rest of the way up Saratoga, then right at Monroe and down the way to Fayette. Then down the strip to the Mount Street crews and the worn marble steps of the Dew Drop. He can see his mother, lost in the basement with Bunchie. Or upstairs with Stevie, maybe, planning a fresh move.

He's alone. He feels his stomach growl, gets up, walks to the cupboard. He still can't believe it: Low-bottom motherfucker even snatched the cereal. How much can a nigger get for a box of Cocoa Krispies?

DeAndre shakes his head and goes back upstairs to wash and dress, telling himself that he'll kill Marvin Parker next chance he gets. And he promises himself that no matter what his mother does or says, he won't go back down to Fayette Street.

By midafternoon, he's put the morning melodrama behind him. He's down on the strip with Dinky, looking for R.C. and Dion, hoping to get all the necessary business done before the Southern's third shift hits the street. Half an hour later, R.C. and Dion post, each carrying a forty, Dion drinking his more for show than anything else. Together the four walk up Gilmor Street to the pink house in the middle of the block. They've paid the woman in the neighboring apartment a few dollars to use the second-floor rear for their stash. But after a few weeks' caution, they've already gotten slack about things. DeAndre and the others barely pause to look around before entering, much less take the trouble to go around the alley and use the back door. Inside, they're full of play, more intent on getting blunted than on vialing up. Dinky has a Kevlar vest that he bought off the street. He wants to wear it and have someone shoot at him.

"Nothing big. A twenty-five be good."

DeAndre smokes a blunt. R.C. starts arguing with Dinky about yesterday's count. "You the fuckup, R.C.," says Dinky. "You always fucking up."

DeAndre passes the weed, then folds himself onto the battered couch as Dion starts to vial. The blue-gray smoke curls around his head. He sleeps.

This is how the days at McHenry and Gilmor will turn to weeks and the weeks to months. Before anyone can think a fresh thought, it will be spring. The strip will be humming with warm-weather action. The Southern troops will be deep. From radio cars and unmarked Cavaliers, Turner and Hurricane and all the other jump-out boys will be watching the crew, waiting, even pulling DeAndre up and giving him fair warning of what's to come. And all of it will pass as if in a dream—the vials going out, the dollars coming back, the profits going for weed or whores or up to Park Heights in a hack with DeAndre, where the fiends all say you can find the best snorting heroin in the city.

But now, on the next to last day of the year, DeAndre McCullough sleeps. Tomorrow, he will be here on the stash house sofa, nodding, waiting for the shift change. Just as he'll be here the day after, and the day after that, and all the days after until one afternoon in May, when he will wake at last to the sound of a jump boot making the stairway landing creak in a strange way. Half-asleep and blunted, DeAndre will gaze up at the apartment door and see Turner with his gun out, pressed against the door frame and peeking into the room.

Their eyes will meet and Turner will actually smile, then press a forefinger to his lips. Quiet please.

And DeAndre, thinking it all a part of the dream, will not even move off this rotting couch. He won't have sense enough in him to shout out to Dinky over by the window, or to R.C. in the broken-backed chair, or to Dion, who will be sitting at the old Formica table with half a dozen bags of heroin and three bundles of coke caps arrayed in front of him. When Turner finally turns the corner and puts his Glock nine on Dinky, DeAndre will simply watch the last moments play out as if it's someone else's life on videotape.

Dope on the table. Coke on the table. Packaged for sale. Conspiracy to distribute and possession with intent. And DeAndre McCullough will by then be seventeen. Might gonna go to adult court. Might gonna finally see them jail tiers on Eager Street.

Come spring, they'll be old enough to know their place in this world, young enough not to argue. Come spring, the corner will call in all notes and debts and claim them, every one. Come springtime at McHenry and Gilmor, there will be a brief graduation ceremony in this very room, marking the passage of DeAndre McCullough into manhood. The Southern boys will bring the diploma.

"Gotcha," says Turner, yanking him off the couch.

EPILOGUE

Fat Curt went back to the corner.

In the three and a half years since the doctors at Bon Secours deposited him at the Seton Manor nursing home, he slowly wore away. By the spring of 1997, his hands and feet were still swollen, but otherwise little poundage remained to justify his street name.

In the winter and early spring of 1994, he laid low at the nursing home, conserving his strength. But in spring, as the weather broke, Curt snuck away for a quick celebration or two on Fayette Street. When the staff at Seton Manor realized that Curt was roaming the corners, having cake and eating cake, they quickly bounced him from his fourth-floor room. One morning, after staying out all night on a daytime-only pass, Curt returned to the nursing home to find his belongings stacked up in the lobby doorway.

Pimp lasted a week longer before the nurses realized that he, too, had been spending mornings in a few Fayette Street tester lines. Expelled from his room, he returned with Curt to Blue's empty house.

That summer the case against Smiley, who was charged with the stabbing murder of Hungry, quickly collapsed. Prosecutors placed the case on the inactive docket after the police were unable to locate their witnesses. Detectives spent a few days walking Fayette Street looking for Robin and Blue and the others, but they found no one. Robin was in the wind. So was another Vine Street kid, who had given detectives a complete statement. And Blue—the third prosecution witness—wasn't where anyone expected to find him either.

By then, George Epps was living in a group home on South Hanover Street, miles from the old strip. He was working, too, bringing home a weekly paycheck as an employee of the Downtown Partnership, a consortium of businesses that pay people to patrol the center of the city. Partnership employees wear brightly colored jackets; their job is to remove refuse, discourage vandalism, help tourists, and stand on street-corners with a vague sense of authority. Blue had been led to the job by the staff at the South Baltimore Homeless Shelter, and he was horrified at the notion of being caught wearing a clown suit and pretending to some kind of pseudo-policing. Maybe, he hoped, he would get through this gig without seeing anyone he had ever known.

Yet Blue endured, got paid, got another job, and then a better job after that. Eventually he rented his own apartment downtown and found work—coincidentally enough—on the maintenance staff at Seton Manor, where he spent time with dozens of men and women he had known from the corners. All were ailing, many were dying; to Blue, it seemed that God had put him at Seton Manor for a purpose. To be sure, he was there to paint and repair drywall and get paid. But for Blue, it was also a chance to stand back and consider the life left behind. Perhaps, he thought, he was there in Seton Manor to witness.

In time, Blue joined an outreach ministry at Bethel A.M.E., one of West Baltimore's strongest black congregations, where he began bringing God's word to others struggling with addiction. Last fall, he celebrated three years of living clean.

By then, Rita was dead from the infection in her arms. Shardene had passed the previous year. Scalio was gone, too, as was Ty Boice and Pimp, who went back to Fayette Street after getting booted from Seton Manor, but then found God in his last days and died quietly in a clean bed, reading the Bible in another nursing home in another part of the city. In 1994, Eggy Daddy sold a burn bag of Arm & Hammer to an under-cover cop and was looking at five years mandatory under the state's three-time loser statute. He begged a city judge for the change to follow Blue into the homeless shelter; the judge, giving him one last bite of the apple, agreed, and suspended the sentence.

Earlier this year, Eggy was named employee of the month at the Downtown Partnership. He's been drug free for a couple years.

Consequently, Curt was left ever more alone at the crossroads of Fayette and Monroe. In early 1995, he finally had his appeal hearing with Social Security, and after the hearing officer got a quick look at the swollen legs and twisted ankle, Curt was awarded a $459-a-month government stipend, coupled with a second monthly check in the same amount, representing back money for all the months in which his appeal had languished. In short, Curtis Davis—by trade a tout and confirmed dope fiend—was being given more than nine hundred dollars a month for his disability, which was defined as being, well, a confirmed dope fiend.

At Fayette and Monroe, nine hundred dollars is a lot of money, and having waited nearly two years for any kind of government help whatsoever, Curt nearly became a victim of check day. When the first two SSI checks arrived, it was as if a government-issue sedan had rolled up on Fayette Street with a six-foot syringe strapped to the roof. To Curt, it seemed like Jubilee.

Within a year, he was back in Bon Secours, his liver enzymes in absolute riot, his body withered to near nothingness. In time, the back-money checks stopped coming and Curt learned to pace himself on the rest, to give himself some time off from the game.

For more than a year, he lived on Mount Street in a second-floor walk-up with Rose, his woman. He had a television, a video recorder, and a few good changes of clothes. He got in a methadone program, tried to do better, tried to keep the needle chase to a sometime thing. And because some check money was there to back him up, Curt didn't spend quite as much time touting. Still, there were days when he walked up to Monroe Street and stood his ground. He hung, signified, watched the to-and-fro.

"Faces are different," he would explain. "Nothin' but a bunch of young boys, hoppers who just don't know."

In the early summer of 1997, Curt collapsed for the last time. He went from the Bon Secours emergency room to a nursing facility at Carrollton and Fayette streets, seven blocks east of his corner. He died there of liver disease on June 9.

The small funeral service brought together remnants of Fat Curt's real family and the Fayette Street clan that had a stronger claim on him.

"He was a junkie, one of the original junkies," Curt's younger brother told the gathering. "But," added Randy Davis, who has lived life free and clear of the corner, "we can thank God he never did lose all of what he was about."

Meanwhile, Curt's brother Dennis is still on Monroe every day, refusing to lay down to the virus, claiming surprise and a little shock at having been deserted by so many soldiers.

"I be the last man standing," Dennis says proudly. "You gonna see."

For years, Ella Thompson resisted seeing her neighborhood as a place beyond redemption. Her stolen car was recovered. The rec center remained functional. Her apartment had never been violated.

But one afternoon in 1994, Ella was working at the rec center and looked up to see DeAndre and Preston standing together in the doorway. She invited them inside, but DeAndre merely waved and the two young men walked on.

That evening, she returned to her apartment and found that the place had been ransacked. Someone had broken in through a window that opened on the rear alley, rooted through her house, and taken a couple hundred dollars from a drawer. Only one room—Kiti's—was undisturbed, and Ella realized that his friends would know that anything of value in that part of the house was now with her son in California. All of which led her to suspect Preston and DeAndre, though she didn't confront either of them; she had no proof and so she held her tongue. But she knew Preston was getting high; DeAndre too. Ella had for years found ways to believe in the idea of Franklin Square. After the burglary, her faith seemed to her, for the first time, to be misplaced.

The following winter, when the police boarded up Blue's and a couple other vacant-house shooting galleries on Fayette, many of the hardcore fiends moved the needle palace to 1804 Fayette—a vacant property next door to Ella's apartment. Twice she awoke to the smell of smoke. Twice the fiends set fire to the vacant shell and nearly burned down the block.

She began buying the Sunday papers on Saturday, checking the early real estate listings. Finally, in 1996, she moved from Fayette Street to a redbrick duplex on a quiet street in Hamilton, a working- and middle-class tract in Northeast Baltimore. And Ella is no longer renting; for the first time, she owns her home.

Kiti is living with her. He came back from Los Angeles after the earthquake in 1994—Fayette Street might be hell, but not even the devil messes with *terra firma*. At first, Ella's fears about her youngest son's return to the the neighborhood seemed justified. He began hanging with Preston down on Fulton, drinking in front of the liquor store. A few months later, Ella found a handgun in his room. Kiti swore that he wasn't slinging, that he had the weapon only to protect himself from street robberies. But Ella pressed him to come up with some better plan, to go back to school or take up a trade or do something that would change his direction.

When Ella left Fayette Street, Kiti moved with her, and he immediately began to respond to the change. A few months ago, he completed certified training in carpentry, after having traveled all the way to northern Virginia by train to attend some of his classes. At this writing, he is wearing a hard hat and mastering his craft on a construction site at Charles and Lexington Streets downtown. More surprising is that his friend Preston has managed to right himself as well, notably by taking up with a young woman from a churchgoing family. He is married, working, and living in a quiet Reservoir Hill apartment house.

Giving up on her apartment was hard enough for Ella, but it was nothing compared to what it cost her to leave behind the Martin Luther King Jr. Recreation Center. Even as she planned her move from Fayette Street, Ella never had any intention of giving up the rec. All along she imagined commuting down to the center five days a week and keeping hold of that which most connected her to her daughter's memory. Instead, Ella ran afoul of some neighborhood politics: A secret vote to elect a paid executive to direct the neighborhood group proved less than secret, and Ella had supported the loser. The incoming executive, Joyce Smith, was a longtime friend and ally, but to Ella, the election seemed to cast a pall over the friendship. At board meetings, Joyce became increasingly critical of both the rec program and Ella's stewardship—or at least it felt that way to Ella.

At the same time, colleagues in the city parks department who knew of Ella's work at Martin Luther King began talking with her about doing similar work for better money. The job offer she received in 1996 was tantalizing: She would be supervising children—at a string of West Baltimore rec centers—who would be part of Kids Grow, a new grant-funded program dealing with urban ecology and agriculture. Ella brooded for more than a week, and then, after talking with friends on the Franklin Square board, she gave notice.

At this writing, she has been working with Kids Grow for more than year. The city has plans to expand the program—which emphasizes gardening, forestry, and environmental learning—to a number of other recreation centers. Ella, still holding a place in her heart for Fayette Street, recently convinced officials to fund the program at Martin Luther King.

As for the recreation center itself, its leadership passed for a time to Blue, who spent several months as rec director before the kids ran him ragged and he moved on to other jobs. After that, when the neighborhood association was awarded a larger city block-grant, people from outside the neighborhood were hired. Three staff members are now paid to do the work once performed by Ella and Marzell Myers. But Ella's idea of a boy's basketball squad outlasted her, and the rec center's playground was finally rehabilitated several months ago. In fact, city parks officials adorned the lot with one of the better outdoor ball courts on the west side.

On the day that Ella drove past Mount Street and caught sight of the fresh clay and white backboards, she couldn't quite believe it. She had asked for that basketball court for years, begging Joyce and Myrtle and any city official she ever encountered. Always the playground improvements were planned; always they were delayed. Now she was gone, as were the boys she had tried to rescue with her fledgling basketball squad. Yet here was the court she had always imagined. A group of older boys was on it, running full-court. She remembered R.C. taking imaginary shots off the broken backboard. She remembered DeAndre and his father trying to attach a loose rim with screws and washers.

On that day, with change staring her down, she saw the rec as she never thought she would again—from the outside, looking in. Still, she couldn't be bitter. That gray block of building was too much a part of Ella for her to begrudge it anything. Besides, that isn't Ella's way.

"I knew it," she said later with pride. "I always knew we'd get that basketball court built."

Two years after defending its McHenry Street territory against the intruders from D.C., the Crenshaw Mafia Brothers ceased to exist. What began as a collective act of belonging ended amid the bickering, bitching, and betrayal that marks time on any drug corner.

R.C. started hitting the pipe, messing up the count, and stealing stashes. Dorian ran off with another package. Tae was losing weight and acting crazy. All of them—R.C., Tae, Boo, Dinky, Brooks, and Manny—began to accuse each other of getting high and thieving, even as they took pains to deny the same allegations themselves.

And sometimes, they got their guns out.

In 1995, during a running dispute between the B-and-G crew at Baltimore and Gilmor, and some of the Lexington Terrace boys, two young men rode up to Gilmor and Hollins on bikes and fired several shots. One caught Dinky, DeAndre's cousin, in the chest. He staggered a few steps to Baltimore Street and collapsed. Hours later, Dinky, age seventeen, was pronounced dead at University Hospital's trauma center. Although the daylight murder was witnessed by half a dozen B-and-G regulars, little accurate information came back to detectives. Eventually police charged a Terrace boy widely regarded to be innocent. The case was dropped several months later and no further investigation of the crime followed.

And last summer, in a dispute with a South Vincent Street crew, Boo was shot to death by a sixteen-year-old girl on McHenry Street. But the Vincent Street crew—which included Tank and Tony, members of the old rec basketball squad—wasn't finished. Two days later, Tae and R.C. were both wounded in an ambush on McHenry Street, with Tae hit in the shoulder and arm and R.C. taking bullets in the hip and hand. Both were treated and released from Bon Secours Hospital.

Tae, Manny Man, Dion, Dorian, Dewayne, and Brooks are still in the neighborhood; for the most part, they don't pretend any plan, though Tae credits himself with getting his high school G.E.D. at Francis M. Woods and insists he will be going to college this fall. For now, though, he spends much of his time at Pratt and Gilmor and drinks a great deal. Brooks did almost a year in juvenile custody before coming home last month. Dorian served longer than that. Brian is incarcerated at New York's Rikers Island for drug charges.

For R.C., the shooting incident last year proved pivotal. Before then, he had been doing well. In fact, he had slowly pulled himself out of his spiral, walking away altogether from drugs and slinging and the corners along McHenry Street. Taking up with a Mt. Winans girl two years his senior, R.C. found himself long enough to move from his mother's apartment and secure steady, reliable work.

At first, a temp agency placed him among laborers at the Maryland Wholesale Food Market in Jessup, a dozen miles south of Baltimore. When a supervisor there asked if R.C. could operate a forklift, the eighteen-year-old responded with his usual bluster.

"Think I can," R.C. said.

"What does that mean? You ever used a forklift or not?"

"Where one at?"

The supervisor gave R.C. a chance to prove himself, and he handled the forklift well enough to win a permanent job.

Every working day, R.C. left his girlfriend's grandmother's house and ventured out to the county. Every week, he brought his pay back to his girl and gave her half, helping to send her through school to be a medical assistant. To his own amazement, he was making it.

This remarkably stable life continued for almost ten months. Then

Boo got killed and the beef with the Vincent Street crew boiled over and
R.C. returned to McHenry Street to learn the story. Typically, the old
C.M.B. crew laid it on thick, greeting him with guilt and derision for
leaving the neighborhood in the first place. Two days later, R.C. was in
Bon Secours, watching an intern pull a spent bullet from beneath the
skin of his left hand.

After the shooting, he fell back into his old pattern: hanging on
Mc-Henry; missing work until the Jessup job was no longer there; telling
lies to his girl. Working with Tae, Manny Man, and the rest, he began
turning one package after another at McHenry and Gilmor, at one point,
putting together a roll of nearly five thousand dollars. He started getting
high again. Eventually, he took a distribution charge. At this writing, he
has recently seen the inside of city jail twice for a total of three and a
half months. He is currently out on bail, with one drug charge still
pending. He is looking for work, looking to get back with the girl who
had him doing right for nearly a year.

"I had it going on," he says now. "I was doing everything right and
I just messed it up. It was like I couldn't stand to be doing good like
that."

Nowadays, he doesn't play much ball.

Fran Boyd used to tell herself that she had rules about chasing the blast,
that there were standards of behavior that she would always maintain.
But the corner has its own rules, and number two—never say never—
is always in full effect.

In 1994, when Fran lucked into a subsidized rowhouse and moved
from Boyd Street to Lorraine Avenue in East Baltimore, she finally got
rid of Marvin Parker—who would himself be dead of an overdose within
a year. As someone still nominally identified as a recovering addict, Fran,
along with her sons, was placed in the fully rehabbed home through a
nonprofit housing cooperative geared to support such people. There
were two problems, however. First, Fran was no longer recovering. And
second, a prolonged police crackdown on lower Greenmount Avenue
had pushed the corner traffic several blocks to the north and east, turning
the 400 block of Lorraine Avenue into one of the most active drug strips
in the area.

Fran had always told herself that she would never encourage DeAndre
in his drug slinging, that she would never take profit from it or allow
him to use her home as his stash house. On Lorraine Avenue, she did

all these things. More than that, she robbed him blind, creeping into his room so many times that once, in frustration, DeAndre threw a punch through the bedroom drywall.

"You got me again!"

"What the hell you talking about?"

"My money! You just a thieving dope fiend!"

"Boy, I don't know what you talking about."

Once, she waited for four hours by DeAndre's bedroom door, listening to his breathing, waiting patiently for the moment when he would fall asleep and she could go through his jacket pockets for money or product or both. But DeAndre, burned five nights in row, forced himself to stay awake, hoping to catch her doing the deed. The standoff continued until dawn, when DeAndre finally got up to use the bathroom. Fran retreated to her room, waited for the sound of prolonged urination, and then ransacked her son's room in under twenty seconds. She got forty dollars and felt no shame whatsoever. Her game was her game; what her son brought home had to get past that simple fact.

Similarly, Fran had told herself for years that she was more about heroin, that she wasn't going on the coke pipe every five minutes like the rest of these crazed fiends. On Lorraine, though, she went through her check money like water; within months, her face was a death mask, her weight down below ninety pounds. Worst of all, Fran had always told herself that no matter what, she wouldn't trick. But on Lorraine Avenue, Fran let some of the old men think she was with them; she played them for blast money by using herself in ways that finally brought a quiet, caring reproach from her son.

"Ma, you better than that."

Badly shaken, Fran called the detox center. She waited the wait—four months this time—then left her house key with DeAndre. Twenty-eight days later, she returned to Lorraine and began looking for a new home, a place in any neighborhood where the corners were simply intersections. Instead of drugs, she chased meetings. And when that failed to occupy all her time, she volunteered down at BRC, spending as much time as she could around the detox center.

After a month or so, she found a subsidized apartment in Baltimore County, up off Loch Raven Boulevard. A few months later, BRC rewarded her volunteerism by hiring her—first to assist in the center's medical department, and later to monitor residents as a drug counselor. And Fran, like any ex-fiend, was no fool when it came to working with addicts:

Having played all the games so well and for so long, she was not about to let the BRC clients run anything past her. Or, for that matter, themselves.

Just before last Christmas, a few months after Fran had celebrated a full year of being clean, she was laid off—the result of a federal audit of the detox center. It seemed that the grant money funding BRC required all counselors to be fully trained and qualified; to preserve its budget, the center was forced to let go some of its best and most reliable staffers, men and women who had survived the corner and were now using that experience to great effect. Fran, Antoinette, and about a dozen others were corner veterans on a hero's journey, trying to salvage something of themselves, trying to give a little back. The government, being the government, could not see it.

Fran was stunned. For a couple months, she holed up in her apartment, chain-smoking and biting her nails down to nothing, waiting, presumably, for her unemployment benefits and tax refund to run out. In the past, such a setback would have been more than enough to send her sprawling. To her credit, Fran sensed as much and fought back.

At first she went to more meetings than usual. Then she enrolled in courses at a county community college, determined to get some of the training that might have enabled her to keep the job at BRC. Two months after that, she found part-time work at a residential facility for troubled teenagers. At this writing, Fran is beating the streets, looking for something better.

She also is coming up on two years clean, a span of time that can no longer be mistaken for a victory lap. Her one-year celebration was at a BRC meeting and lasted nearly two hours. This year she's ambivalent about whether to have a party.

"I don't think I want to do anything big," she says. "I just want it to be a regular day."

William and Roberta McCullough remain on Vine Street. Now just short of seventy, W.M. continues to drive every day for Royal Cab, while Miss Roberta volunteers at St. James.

Most of their many children give them great joy, and grandchildren are arriving regularly to add to that pleasure. But more and more of the corner world has found its way into their home.

June Bey is still a prisoner of his addiction. And Kwame, always so angry at the world, saw his domestic assault charge dismissed when

Regina, his girlfriend, refused to testify, but soon enough landed in more trouble. Kwame received probation for a drug distribution charge in 1995. That same year, he was wounded in a robbery on South Gilmor Street. Recently, he was arrested and charged by homicide with two separate drug-related shooting deaths. He is currently being held, without bail, on Eager Street pending trial.

For two more years, Gary McCullough worked the warm months at Seapride and spent the winters making his way on capers, from one day to the next, while on occasion relying on Ronnie Boice and his mother's generosity to get him over. He continued to live in his parents' basement, to wrestle the snake, to chart his orbit around vials and glassine bags.

In late 1995 he bought a cap of cocaine at Fayette and Mount, went home, fired it up, and got nothing for his trouble. Another burn bag for Gary.

Two days later a fifteen-year-old street dealer offered to sell him more of the same.

"Naw," Gary replied. "It was doo-doo."

"Say what?"

"There wasn't nothing to it."

Two other young slingers suddenly appeared, and without another word, the trio knocked Gary to the ground, beating and kicking him into unconsciousness. For weeks afterward, Gary suffered from a ringing in his ears and a bright glare that made his left eye useless. Oddly, though, Gary seemed to draw strength from the experience, to see himself and his condition in a new light.

"They was children," he said, shaking his head. "Children beating on a grown man for nothing."

For three days straight, he walked downtown to Mercy Hospital, hoping to get a state-funded bed in the four-day detox unit. When nothing opened up, Gary begged. A friend volunteered to loan Gary five hundred dollars toward the cost of the bed—an offer that pushed Gary to the front of the hospital's waiting list.

After two delirious days in Mercy's detox unit, Gary walked away, returning to West Baltimore and scoring a shot of cocaine. Then, without any regard to the contradiction, he headed down to the South Baltimore Homeless Shelter, saying he wanted to clean up, as Blue and Eggy had done.

At that point, Gary had been shooting speedballs every day for more than five years. And when the last rush from the last shot of coke left him, he found himself struggling with an incredible depression. At times he became delusional.

The shelter referred him to the Walter P. Carter Center, a state psychiatric facility downtown. Staff at the center prescribed an antidepressant, and eventually Gary went to stay with his brother Chris in Northeast Baltimore. During the days, he would baby-sit his brother's children; at night, he would share their company. In return, they would not give Gary money, and they would not drive him back to Vine Street.

For a month, Gary battled his demons on his own. But when it snowed that February, Gary shoveled a dozen walks and made more than twenty dollars. He left the children alone, wandering until he found a corner and a speedball. That evening, saddened at the sight of his brother, high once again, Chris threw Gary out of the house.

The choice then was his mother's basement or another attempt at detox. "If I go back to Vine Street," Gary admitted to a friend. "I'm gonna die there."

He returned to the homeless shelter. He stayed inside for a week. He started struggling through the meetings, the counseling, the group therapy. Once he got a month clean under his belt, he began going out on neighborhood work details with other residents.

In March 1996 Gary slipped away from a work crew and walked from South Baltimore to the Fayette Street strip. Fat Curt was on post when Gary came through asking about product.

"You ain't been around."

"I know it. What's good?"

Curt looked at him. "You sure you up?"

"Yeah," said Gary. "I'm up."

Ten minutes later, Gary and his brother June Bey were down in the basement at 1827 Vine Street, cooking and poking and firing. After nearly three months in which he had used only a handful of times, Gary's body couldn't handle the usual dose, and suddenly he fell from the bed to the floor.

June Bey panicked. Rather than call 911 immediately, Gary's brother tried to clean up the mess, to keep a secret that had long been known to everyone in the family. He splashed water on Gary. He picked Gary up and put him on the bed. He spent half an hour getting his brother out of the basement and down Vine Street to another address, and then, finally, he called for an ambulance.

Gary was dead on arrival at Bon Secours.

The funeral at St. James drew more than two hundred mourners, testament to the standing of the McCullough family in that church. Fran could barely walk past the open casket. Miss Roberta was utterly broken. DeAndre swore that for the sake of his father's memory, he would never use drugs again. He stopped at the casket, touched Gary's face lightly, and fought back tears. In the back of the church, Ronnie Boice took an aisle seat and wailed her grief.

Much was said by the pastor, some of it quite true. The choir sang. Gary's white supervisor at Seapride, Paul, brought down the all-black congregation by talking about Gary's boundless love and then offering a beautiful rendition of "His Eye Is On The Sparrow."

"Damn," mused Fran. "The white boy can sing."

The obituary, written by the family, omitted the essential facts of the tragedy, but nonetheless came close to capturing just how much had been lost: "He always freely gave. Indeed, he often offered spiritual, emotional and financial support and the refuge of his own home to those in need. Deeply philosophical, Gary was always eager to impart the wisdom with which he was blessed via his intuition and spiritual insight, life experiences, discourses, lectures and readings . . . Still, no words can truly capture the beauty, sincerity and kindness of the person he was."

Leaving the church, Fran stood on Monroe Street and wiped at her tears. DeAndre gave her a quick embrace.

"The game wasn't for him," she said, watching the touts at Fayette. "He wasn't hard enough to be out here like he was."

The son nodded. "I know this sounds wrong," DeAndre said finally, "but I'm almost glad for it. I feel like he was never going to get out of it, you know, he was never going to be what he was, and I think he was sad from knowing that. I feel like he's at peace now."

When he stood over his father's casket and swore his oath, DeAndre McCullough truly believed the words. He always does.

By the summer of 1994, DeAndre was everyday slinging with C.M.B. at McHenry and Gilmor. The arrest in the Gilmor Street stash house hadn't slowed him much, particularly since the case, involving an event that occurred just after his seventeenth birthday, was yet again referred to juvenile court. As a condition of his probation, DeAndre was prohibited from setting foot anywhere near McHenry and Gilmor—a condition that he managed to obey for almost a month.

By the end of that summer, he was taking hacks to some of the Park Heights drug corners and spending most of what he made on the best snorting heroin in the city. He went clubbing. He bought women. He stayed high. He also took a few small charges, but nothing so dramatic that a juvenile master was willing to violate his probation.

By 1995 DeAndre was on the pipe, at one point going through an entire half ounce of coke in his room on Lorraine Avenue in a single evening. His mother knew; Fran could smell the butane and cooked rock all the way downstairs. By then, though, she was in free fall herself so there was little she could say to her son that would mean much.

Down on his corner, DeAndre began messing the packages, burning through suppliers, and running up debts. In an argument with a dealer named Man, DeAndre teamed with Shamrock and robbed Man's stash house, taking product and money at the point of a four-four. The dispute might have escalated, save for the fact that Man himself was later wounded by the Terrace boys, and Shamrock went courtside after being charged with a murder stemming from another drug-related robbery. That case fell apart quickly, but Shamrock then caught a drug distribution conviction; he is currently on Eager Street, waiting to be sentenced for violating his probation on that charge.

At home, meanwhile, DeAndre played his dope-fiend moves on his own family. Once, he skipped with Fran's Independence Card, using it to withdraw a full month's check money in retaliation for all she had taken from him. He even stole a stash from his cousin Dinky, though he was clever enough to blame R.C. And when R.C. tried to tell Dinky, he got banged for his trouble, though later, Dinky admitted that he had been avoiding the truth, and he quietly offered R.C. an apology.

"DeAndre been getting high too much," said Dinky mournfully.

And when Dinky was shot to death, DeAndre went over-the-top crazy. The night after the Terrace boys ambushed his cousin on Hollins Street, DeAndre joined up with three other B-and-G regulars, rolling up on the playground at Lexington Terrace and firing into a crowded knot of rivals. That night, the Baltimore and Gilmor crew came through Fran's door on Lorraine Avenue high and drunk, talking about how they were sure they'd caught bodies. But there was nothing in the morning paper. One bystander had been slightly wounded, nothing more. No matter: DeAndre swore he would catch up with the boys who got Dinky. He's swearing it still.

At Dinky's funeral, DeAndre began using morphine. Soon after, he also tried the needle, creating a small, tight line of tracks on one forearm. By then, his ability to make a run with a package was no longer what it needed to be. Two years earlier, at fifteen, he had made Fairmount and Gilmor jump; now at seventeen, his game produced only argument and debt.

On the odd, awkward occasion when he would roll past Riggs Avenue to see his son, DeAndre could see Tyreeka look at him with vague terror. Sometimes he would go into a nod. Other times he would talk out of his head. But always he was bitter and angry, ever more resentful as Tyreeka seemed ever more distant. She had managed to stay in school and was looking toward graduation and her first year of college at West Baltimore's Coppin State. She was working part time. She was raising DeAnte alone. At some point she had grown past him and DeAndre was smart enough to know it. He tried to tell her nothing was different, that he was getting it together, that he wasn't getting high.

"But," Tyreeka told others, "I can tell he ain't the same."

When his mother returned to detox, the worst of DeAndre's ride ended. Coming back clean, Fran gave her son an ultimatum, telling him that he could not continue getting high in her house, that he had to support her effort to stay clean. He argued at first, resenting what he saw as her holier-than-thou pretense.

"You had your fun," he told her. "Now you telling me I can't have mine."

Eventually he softened. Soon after his mother returned to Lorraine and began looking for a county apartment, DeAndre checked himself into Oakview for detox, taking advantage of state guidelines that offer minors treatment on demand. But a week later, he checked himself out and visited Tyreeka, admitting to his addiction and blaming heroin and cocaine for all the problems between them.

Tyreeka was frightened, but after much trepidation, she took him back, offering him one last chance. Within two weeks, DeAndre was back down Gilmor and McHenry.

Fran threatened him, told him he would not be allowed to move out to the county with her. Yet the weight of their shared past made it impossible for her to believe in her own threat. For years she had cheated DeAndre; now, when he was cheating himself, she felt too much guilt to put him out in the street.

For the past year DeAndre has drifted between long corner runs and brief interludes in which he struggles mightily to right himself, swearing yet again that he won't go back, that he won't use, or sell, or lie to himself about his own weakness. At these moments, he is earnest and genuine. He gets up early. He visits his son. He looks for work, and, if he finds it, he pulls in a paycheck or two before beginning the inevitable slide. Last October his uncle Dan took him out of Baltimore down to Harrisonburg, Virginia, a Shenandoah Valley town where Dan lives and works and where there are no corners. DeAndre worked nearly a month at a McDonald's there. He liked Virginia, and the people seemed to like him.

On Thanksgiving he came back to Baltimore to see his son and attend DeAnte's third birthday party. He spent most of his McDonald's pay on a present, but he showed up high for the party at Tyreeka's house. He did not return to Virginia.

Earlier this spring, DeAndre got himself in debt to a supplier by the name of Sweetpea, a hardcore player who was known to use a gun now and then. Most threats failed to resonate with DeAndre, but Sweetpea seemed serious about recouping his loss and, more to the point, he seemed to like shooting people. For the first time in his life, DeAndre was on the run—a situation that only resolved itself when Sweetpea was himself shot to death on Gilmor Street in an unrelated dispute. Similarly, this spring marked the first time that DeAndre was locked up on an adult charge with bail attached. It was nothing, really—just an argument at a sub shop. DeAndre claimed he was trying to break up a fight and had been wrongly arrested for assault. Nonetheless he caught a three thousand dollar bail.

He called Fran from Central Booking.

"I need three hundred to get out."

"Then you best get comfortable."

He was inside more than a week—the first time he'd been locked up since Boys Village. DeAndre seemed chastened by the experience. For a quiet week or so, he tried to stay inside at night, watch basketball on TV, and write raps and poetry.

These verses are his:

> Silent screams and broken dreams,
> Addicts, junkies, pushers and fiends.
> Crowded spaces and sad faces,
> Never look back as the police chase us.
> Consumed slowly by chaos, a victim of the streets,
> Hungry for knowledge, but afraid to eat.

A life of destruction, it seems no one cares,
A manchild alone with burdens to bear.
Trapped in a life of crime and hate,
It seems the ghetto will be my fate.
If I had just one wish it would surely be,
That God would send angels to set me free.
Free from the madness, of a city running wild,
Free from the life of a ghetto child.

At this writing, DeAndre is just past his twentieth birthday. He professes some surprise at this. He had thought he would be dead by now, like Dinky or Boo or half a dozen other boys who came up with him. When he was younger, he had always imagined his death in stark, violent terms—a gangster's end, quick and hard and ripe with all the indifference to which a young man likes to pretend.

Live the life, leave the life. Ain't no big thing.

But the corner is relentless and certain. It can't be underestimated. It can't be appeased with pretense or melodrama or the easy fatalism of youth. It waits. It works. It finishes whatever it begins in its own time, in its own way.

Today, DeAndre McCullough, an addict and small-time drug dealer, is still with us.

AUTHORS' NOTE

This book is a work of journalism. The names that appear in these pages are, in fact, the real names of people who have lived and struggled along West Baltimore's Fayette Street. The events recounted here—with the exception of those described in the epilogue—took place in 1993.

Our research began in September 1992, when we first ventured into the Franklin Square neighborhood to begin meeting people and making ourselves known. We chose that area almost at random. The established Fayette Street strip that runs from Gilmor up the hill to Monroe Street is one of a hundred, perhaps a hundred and twenty open-air drug markets operating in Maryland's largest city. As such, it appeared to us typical; Franklin Square therefore seemed comparable to any number of inner-city neighborhoods overwhelmed by the drug trade. Beyond that, we selected West Fayette Street because of its proximity to racially mixed areas. We felt this was important for demonstrating a basic fact: While the vast majority of Baltimore's major drug markets are located in black neighborhoods, many users serviced by these markets are white. At Fayette and Mount, as on so many other American corners, the demand for heroin and cocaine is decidedly multicultural.

Being a bit pale ourselves, we stood out on Fayette Street, and we were initially regarded by many of the corner regulars as police or police informants. Worse, a few of the older heads remembered Ed from his tenure as a patrolman and detective with the Baltimore Police Department, lending credibility to the rumor that we were snitches or plain-clothesmen or worse. A singular memory is the sight of Eggy Daddy, waltzing up Vine Street singing, "I spy for the FBI," at the top of his lungs, announcing our presence to everyone.

To counter such suspicion, we did a lot of talking, joking, and hanging around with no particular purpose. We played basketball with the rec kids. On warmer days, we took the touts to the corner store for iced tea.

We passed out dozens of copies of *Homicide*, David's earlier work, to make it clear that we really were writers trying to put together a book. Most of all, we met people on their own terms and did a lot of listening.

To Western District patrol officers, many of whom were unfamiliar with us, we were also suspect. To their way of thinking, whites had little reason to be north of Baltimore Street except to buy heroin and cocaine. This assumption led to a string of police stops, queries, and on occasion, threats of arrest and orders to quit loitering and leave the area. Eventually word of the book project got back to the stationhouse and there were fewer such encounters.

Officers who did know us presented another problem. Early in the year, in the aftermath of a shooting at Monroe and Fayette, a veteran detective made a point of picking David out of a crime-scene crowd and chatting amiably—an interaction that required some explaining as far as the corner regulars were concerned. In time, most officers understood our dilemma and responded by ignoring us, or better still, taking a moment now and then to offer us some mild abuse.

By February, most of the regulars were convinced that whatever else we claimed to be, we weren't police. No one could recall seeing us buy or sell anything, nor did we seem to do anything that resulted in anyone getting locked up. Basically, we kept telling the true story until folks began to believe it.

Our methodology was simple enough and is best described as stand-around-and-watch journalism. We went to the neighborhood each day with notepads and followed people around. One day, we might follow DeAndre McCullough down to Gilmor and Fairmount; another day, we might be at the rec center with Ella Thompson; the day after, we might head for a shooting gallery with Gary McCullough.

Often, because the presence of notebooks was intimidating to people in the corner mix, we would leave pad and paper in our pockets, our cars, at the rec center, or in the homes of a few people comfortable playing host to us. Events would occur and we would step away for a time to write down the details. While reporters know that this isn't the best or easiest way to record what they witness, they are also aware that pulling a notepad amid illegal activity is certain to change or stifle events. For this book, the hard way was the only way.

Approximately 75–80 percent of the incidents described in the book were witnessed by one or both of us. On some occasions, important events occurred when we were busy with another individual or otherwise not in the neighborhood. As a result, these scenes had to be reported through traditional, retroactive interviews with those involved. Fortunately, the corner world is so self-contained that in the wake of an incident, several accounts would invariably come back to us from different sources. At that point, it remained for us to sort wheat from chaff—a process essential to all reporting.

We did not begin writing until 1994, choosing to first follow our characters for a full year so that we could make better sense of their experiences. To keep the focus of the narrative on those who live along Fayette Street, we chose not to put ourselves into the story. At times, it may be clear to readers that the authors—described as "hacks" or "friends" or "companions"—are bit players in a particular scene. Anyone trying to guess at the presence of the authors in various scenes might be surprised, however. For example, we were not in English class when DeAndre raised his hand to volunteer for public oratory, or when he cornered Boo at the bus stop, knocking him down and demanding his money. Those incidents were recounted to us. On the other hand, we were in the room when DeAndre went before the juvenile master, when Tyreeka gave birth to her son, and—to our chagrin at the time—we were there when Gary McCullough got jacked by the stickup crew on Fulton Avenue. We have tried to be accurate about the fact of our occasional presence, but at the same time discreet.

The dialogue in the book was either witnessed by one or both of us, or, in a handful of instances, reconstructed from detailed interviews with those involved in the conversation. Similarly, when it is indicated that characters are thinking about something, we have not simply interpolated their thoughts and feelings from their actions. More often than not, we were present at the events upon which the person is reflecting, and their thoughts were verbally expressed to us at the time of the incident or immediately after the fact. In other cases, interior monologues were constructed from repeated interviews.

Furthermore, we eventually showed relevant portions of the book to each of the main characters, who could then suggest—but not insist on—changes. We encouraged our subjects to correct factual mistakes, explain contradictions, or add relevant details to their stories. Journalists often refuse to share unpublished material with sources, but in a project such as this, the usual prohibition seems senseless. To write narrative with an interior point-of-view, reporters need everything they can acquire from their subjects. To their credit, the people of Fayette

Street read what we wrote and then, for the most part, talked honestly about it. That interactive process made the book better, and in a very real sense, more accurate.

Still, readers may wonder whether some characters were inclined to recount events to their own advantage, exaggerating or fabricating details. The fact is that the authors were told a great many lies on a great many occasions; had we conducted our research in a limited window of time, based on limited interaction with people, this account would be seriously flawed. Instead, we continued to follow our subjects for more than four years—a long time for anyone to play false with their lives. Throughout 1993, for example, DeAndre McCullough refused to admit to the use of any drugs other than weed and liquor. By 1995, however, he was in detox, humbly displaying several track marks and admitting to having snorted heroin as early as Christmas two years earlier. Time, as they say, will tell.

One last note of disclosure: A year is a long time to watch people struggle and suffer, and many people were doing a lot of both on Fayette Street in 1993. We were reporters, yet we did not avoid the chance to encourage those who wanted to change, to give some measure of emotional support to people when they talked about getting straight or looking into detox and recovery.

In the beginning this caused us some concern. The usual policy of strict nonintervention argues that if someone asks for a lift to the methadone clinic, a reporter says no. The notion is that if the man is meant to get in a meth program, he'll do it whether or not a reporter and his automobile happen to be at hand. Similarly, if that man is dollars light for a morning blast, then he should stay light whether or not the reporter has cash in his pocket.

That impartial stance sounds well and good until the day the reporter is confronted with another human being so sick and tired that he breaks down and cries openly for someone to drive him to a clinic. Or the day that same reporter takes a run-and-gun dope fiend out of the corner mix for a two-hour interview, only to see him become ill from withdrawal. If the fiend was on his game, he'd have blast money by now; instead, he spent the morning talking about his life to a writer. And Lord, the man needs to hold five dollars in a hurry.

As a rule, we did not intervene in the swirl of events. But there were a few instances when we ignored the rule. We came to this project as reporters, but over time we found ourselves caring more about our

subjects than we ever expected. If that helped or hurt, someone more
than he or she otherwise would have been helped or hurt, then it could
be argued that our source material is tainted. Yet the limited support we
provided had decidedly little effect. DeAndre, Fran, Gary—all began
the year in the corner mix, all of them ended there. And Blue—who
escaped from his own shooting gallery—did so quietly and with little
encouragement from anyone. Perhaps all our journalistic concerns about
nonintervention are predicated on a touch of vanity. The corner culture
and addiction are powerful forces—equal to or greater than all the legal
barriers and social programming arrayed against them. On Fayette Street,
the odds do not change because someone pops up with a notepad and
the occasional kindness.

Our best guide in these matters proved to be none other than
Elliot Liebow, who, in 1962 and 1963, conducted his classic study of
Washington, D.C., street-corner men in similar fashion. In his notes on
methodology for *Tally's Corner*, Liebow wrote: "The people I was
observing knew I was observing them. Some exploited me, not as an
outsider, but rather as one who, as a rule, had more resources than they
did. When one of them came up with resources—money or a car, for
example—he too was exploited in the same way. I usually tried to limit
money or other favors to what I thought each would have gotten from
another friend had he the same resources as I. I tried to meet requests
as best I could without becoming conspicuous."

At the risk of neglecting to name many of those along Fayette Street
who gave us their cooperation and support, we would specifically like
to thank those who opened their world to us: Fran Boyd and the Boyd
family; William and Roberta McCullough and their family; DeAndre
McCullough, Tyreeka Freamon, and DeRodd Hearns; Richard Carter
and his family; Ella Thompson, her family, and the children of the Martin
Luther King Jr. Recreation Center; George Epps, Michael Ellerbee, Dennis
Davis, Terry "Eggy Daddy" Hamlin, Bryan Sampson, Tony Boice, and
Veronica Boice. We remember, too, Curtis Davis, Pimp, Rita, Scalio, Bread,
Shardene, and all the other lost soldiers. Especially, we hold to the
memory of Gary McCullough, a man of great heart and gentle spirit.
His true friendship and his interest in this book helped sustain us.

Also assisting us in our journeys along Fayette Street were a host of
other generous souls: Frank Long, Marzell Myers, Myrtle Summers, and
Joyce Smith of the community group and rec center; Col. Ron Daniel

of the Baltimore Police Department, as well as those supervisors and officers of the Western and Southern Districts who understood the project and gave us room to work; Commissioner Lamont Flanagan of the Baltimore Detention Center; Judge H. Gary Bass of the District Court of Baltimore; John Seaman and the staff of the South Baltimore Homeless Shelter; Rose Davis at Francis M. Woods Senior High School; Kathy McGaha and Jeanne McNamara with the social work department at Bon Secours Hospital; Dr. Dan Howard of Bon Secours and the community health clinic at St. Edward's; the Rev. Isaac T. Golder, a pastor of the Good News Bible Chapel, an affiliate of the Fulton Avenue Baptist Church; and Rebecca Corbett, a friend and mentor at the *Baltimore Sun*. We are also indebted to Joe Laney, Sonny Mays, and Larry "House" Canada—three sage veterans of Fayette and Monroe who shared some hard-bought wisdom with us.

And last, but certainly not least, there is the crew once known as the Crenshaw Mafia Brothers. We remember Dinky and Boo, and we offer this West Baltimore shout-out to Tae, Manny Man, Dion, Brooks, Brian, Dewayne, Dorian, Arnold, Ronald, and all the rest:

Go easy. Step light. Stay free.

In our own lives, Ed wishes to thank Anna Burns, and David owes just about everything to Kayle Tucker Simon. Without their constant love and support, the work would not be done.

At Broadway Books our thanks go to Bill Shinker for unstinting support of the project, as well as Victoria Andros, Luke Dempsey, Rebecca Holland, Maggie Richards, Trigg Robinson, Jennifer Swihart, and Roberto de Vicq de Cumptich. Thanks as well to our agent, Rafe Sagalyn, who stayed with this project even as deadlines tumbled one after the next. And we are humbled by the efforts of our line editor, Barbara Ravage; this book would have been quite close to incoherent without her careful eye.

At the center of it all is John Sterling. Not only did he craft this book with all the skill and grace of a great editor, he was there at the first spark of creation. It was John who initially suggested an account of life on a city corner, and it was John who kept us going through four years of research and writing. At the end, he finished by stepping up, taking hold of the pages, and saving yet another book from its authors.

Finally, we wish to acknowledge that the people of Fayette Street offered us a rare gift. Amid so much disorder and desperation, they nonetheless decided to make us welcome, to tell their stories, to allow us to watch as they tried to make it from one day to the next. They trusted us—not to tell a better or more flattering story than truth will allow—but to report and write with the understanding that the urban drug culture is about real people, real lives. This is a simple premise, but an important one. We have tried not to lose sight of it.

There is, after all, something almost unseemly about journalists seeking and acquiring such extraordinary access to people's lives—access that prompts the reportorial soul to feel both professional pride and personal shame in the same instant.

The best word on this dilemma comes in the preface to a seminal American ethnography, James Agee's *Let Us Now Praise Famous Men*. Sparing himself little, Agee insisted "that these I will write of are human beings, living in this world, innocent of such twistings as these which are taking place over their heads; and that they were dwelt among, investigated, spied on, revered and loved by other quite monstrously alien human beings, in the employment of others still more alien; and that they are now being looked into by still others, who have picked up their living as casually as if it were a book . . ."

—David Simon and Ed Burns
Baltimore, Md.
June 1997

AFTERWORD

Much of what passes for intimacy in journalism is better described as presumption at best and outright fraud in the worst cases. Some vulnerable portion of the world allows a reporter to wander about, and then, after a week or two, or a couple months at most, the interloper gathers a handful of observed moments, the tastiest quotes, and a couple anecdotes. The scribbler then delivers a brooding, insider's view of human lives and political systems, tales of low comedy and grand tragedy, and inevitably, the ethnographic proof for whatever insight he already had before embarking on the adventure.

Intimacy is not achieved in a week or a month, or even two. But then, real human connection is not a requirement for narrative journalism to find some measure of success. A story in which a reporter can walk into people's lives, snatch a good tale and then walk away—this is an assignment to be relished; lives in the balance, acquired with comfortable dispassion and without the psychic cost.

Intellectually, that was how we imagined *The Corner* before we began the journey. We understood that as a non-fiction exercise in narrative, we would be spending a year in a world in which tragic and brutal events would occur. We knew we would be meeting people consigned to unrelenting addiction, to debilitating poverty, and in many cases, to the most unforgiving outcomes. From the first, we saw the inevitability of the thing.

But did we feel it?

How do you feel for people you have yet to meet? How do you comprehend the full tragedy of a Gary McCullough when you haven't absorbed all that is Gary McCullough, when you haven't yet walked beside him for a year of his life, when you have not sat in his basement room for afternoons on end, listening to dreams and fears, when you have not yet started—as a matter of slow-won friendship—to hope for another outcome? How do you know loss when you have not yet learned to love what is to be lost?

We were not naïve. Ed came to the project after a twenty-year career in the Baltimore Police Department, most of it working murders. David had been a police reporter at the city's daily newspaper for nearly a decade and had earlier written a narrative account of day-to-day life in the city homicide unit.

Our knowledge of the corner culture was not academic. But neither was it rooted in all of the hope and love, laughter and despair that human relationships require. Ed had worked many a case off the West Baltimore corners and he had dealt with an extraordinary range of people; yet one case ran to the next and the names and faces changed with the casework. And David had reported on robberies and murders, drug busts and police scandal; but when shaped into the grist of daily news stories and weekenders, investigative series or magazine articles, few characters made themselves known for long enough to fully assert their humanity. And as for intimacy—little of it was demanded or required.

In reporting, too, there is a premium placed on dispassion. How, a journalism professor might ask, can one report with clarity on people and issues without some requisite distance? How does journalism guard against the personal emotions of the journalist? What is empirical? And what is true only of our hopes, biases and affections?

Interesting questions, if you are a journalism professor.

We went to Monroe and Fayette Streets and stayed there for a year. We encountered a great many people, some of them in the most severe distress. We met them on their own terms and, before the manuscript was complete, we walked beside them for more than three years. Some endured and triumphed, some failed, some died, and some are struggling still.

And ultimately, we came to know and understand these people as journalism often claims to know and understand people. But in retrospect, the price for this was fixed and certain: We came to care about many of our subjects. We even came to love a few and, to this day, we regard some of those who survived as close and valued friends.

If this is an affront to journalism, then journalism is, itself, something of an affront. And perhaps this is one of the reasons our American media gets poverty, addiction, and the drug war so relentlessly wrong: In dispassion, there are statistics—some juked, some accurate—and there is always the to-and-fro of political and academic argument. And that seems enough for most of us to venture opinions, often with considerable rigor. But the missing element is, of course, the ordinary and intimate humanity of those struggling.

There may be a number of reasons that America's failed drug war is in its fifth decade, that we are the jailingest nation on the planet, that our policy of prohibition becomes ever more draconian even as it fails in cities like Baltimore or Philadelphia or St. Louis to take back drug corners or reduce the purity of narcotics. Several are the causes that have led to nearly a half-century of failure, though no political leader dares to openly acknowledge such or argue for an alternative. For a policy disaster of this scope, there is blame to go around.

But a fundamental reason, certainly, is this:

One America is only comfortable acknowledging the other as statistical, or as an amalgam of issues to be debated, or as a political argument to be joined. Few of us in the monied, functional America have the opportunity to know a Gary McCullough or a Fran Boyd or a Fat Curt. Fewer still take the risk of engaging such folk without precondition and for any length of time. And love itself? What are the chances?

Reporting and writing *The Corner* gave us a rare opportunity, and we accepted that opportunity with all strings attached. Yes, there would be the equivocation of writers who cared about their subjects, who hoped for better outcomes, who might write about personal failings and human flaw but would likely blanket these things in a basic empathy. On the other hand, it was possible—if the writers could convey something of their own heart—that readers might discover the human beings standing at Monroe and Fayette Streets.

Looking again, we remain comfortable with the bargain, though again, it carried hidden costs we could not measure beforehand. In December 1992, all of the above—even had we vocalized it—would have been little better than Talmudic commentary. And a few months into the project, when Fran Boyd failed to get a bed in a detox facility, well that was certainly sad enough, but then what did we expect might happen? And toward the end of the year, when Boo was shot? Jesus, poor Boo. But someone was going to get shot on those corners, weren't they? And a year after that, when Fran slipped again, we were suddenly heartbroken, truly heartbroken, because Fran by then was, well, Fran. She mattered to us, completely. And when Gary finally got clean only to sneak off from the group home and slam a lethal dose? We didn't write another word for months. By then, of course, nothing could ever be abstract or Talmudic again.

The extent to which we honored the standards of narrative journalism is precisely this: During 1993, the year that we chronicled in *The Corner*, we were careful not to interpose in any meaningful way between the people we followed and their outcomes.

We listened with a caring ear. If someone suggested they wanted to get off heroin or cocaine, we were agreeable. If someone suggested they wanted to get a nine millimeter and shoot holes in someone else, we did not affirm the wisdom in such a plan. If someone needed a lift to see a social worker, or to attend a court date, or to see about getting themselves on a wait-list for a detox bed, we happily obliged, knowing that the front seat of moving vehicle was the best possible place to debrief our subjects and learn more about their lives.

Did these modest intercessions have any real effect? Perhaps, but lots of folks talked about cleaning up. Blue actually did so, quietly and without fanfare. We said nothing to him in advance of that life change, nor did we see it coming. We talked all the time about detox with Fran and she availed herself of some opportunities, but it was not until two years after *The Corner* narrative, when we were no longer a constant presence, that she had the strength to stay clean. And getting off heroin was a daily mantra in the life of Gary McCullough; with him, we were as encouraging as friends can be. Yet he made no effort to detox until years after the narrative and then, tragically and abruptly, he fell.

The hard-and-fast rules of journalism argue—in the manner of too many *Star Trek* episodes and *Back to the Future* sequels—that to intervene in even the smallest way can matter. Giving someone a lift down the block means they aren't free to walk to Mount Street and achieve whatever encounter they were supposed to achieve. And yet, the forces arrayed against the people of Fayette Street were complex, unyielding and in combination, profound. It's nice to think that two white guys wandering the neighborhood with notepads were in some way influential, but not even reportorial vanity can stretch that notion over any distance.

If we were circumspect during 1993, then in the years following— and after the narrative of *The Corner* was set—we began to approach many of the people we met on Fayette Street not merely as chroniclers, but as friends. And we gave not a thought to whether we were doing anything to affect anyone's outcome beyond the scope of the book. If anything we said or did after that initial year on Fayette Street led anyone to a better place, then forgive our trespasses and consider them the just and rightful price of admission to other people's lives.

The years since have produced some inevitable endings, but many surprises as well—not the least of which is that our connection with some of those depicted in *The Corner* has endured and deepened. Indeed, we have learned to treasure these friendships beyond the book itself.

Fifteen years after *The Corner*'s narrative concluded, Denise Francine Boyd is still drug-free. More than that, she has become the rock of the Boyd family, raising not only her two sons, but going further to adopt her sister's three children and provide a stable home to them as well.

She lives in Baltimore County and the children attend county schools, but Fran travels routinely to the West Baltimore neighborhoods that cost her so much. For years, she has been doing outreach work with addicts for a treatment program funded by Bon Secours Hospital.

She and her brother Scoogie are the family survivors. Her sisters Bunchie and Sherry, and her brother Stevie, all struggled with addictions well after Fran cleaned up and changed the arc of her life. Bunchie, however, finally got clean only to succumb to lung cancer in 1996. Stevie passed in 2004 and Sherry followed him last year.

Readers who have seen the HBO miniseries based on this book may recall a scene in which the actress Khandi Alexander, playing the role of Fran, breaks down emotionally upon learning that an expected treatment bed is not available—an accurate depiction of that painful moment in Fran's long fight for sobriety. In the supporting role of the receptionist at the rehab facility, bearing witness to Khandi's moment, was the real Fran Boyd. By the time the miniseries went into production in 1999, Fran had been clean for more than four years.

Perhaps the best Cinderella moment was at the Emmy Awards, when Fran walked the red carpet with director Charles Dutton and the other producers. A Los Angeles television reporter, acknowledging Fran's evening dress, asked for the name of the designer.

"Mondawmin," said Fran, naming the shopping mall in West Baltimore.

To which the reporter nodded, falsely knowing.

It has been marvelous to watch, this heroine's journey, and Fran has taught us things about human grace and resolve that we could only pretend to know before she came into our lives. The hardened wraith who glared at us from the front steps of 1625 Fayette Street can no longer be easily conjured; another woman has emerged and her strength and confidence carries a family's weight.

In addition to her own sons, and to her nieces and nephews, Fran proved to be a parent to Tyreeka Freamon, embracing the mother of DeAndre's son as her own, helping to raise DeAnte, and pushing Reeka to stay in school and to continue on through college.

While working full time as an administrative assistant at the University of Maryland Hospital in downtown Baltimore, Tyreeka continued her education first at Coppin State University and later at Strayer College, taking six or nine credits a semester and eventually receiving her bachelor's degree in business administration. She has been promoted twice at the hospital and is now enrolled in a master's program in the Strayer business school.

The hardest moment of that academic career: Quite possibly the first day of an undergraduate sociology class when Tyreeka was appalled to discover that *The Corner* was the assigned text for the class. She was quickly recognized.

"Oh my god," she remembered, laughing only in retrospect. "I wanted to die."

Her relationship with DeAndre was barren, if not belligerent, for more than a decade as DeAndre continued to struggle. Moving to her own apartment, first in the Walbrook Section of Baltimore, and ulti-mately—when it became clear that DeAnte would benefit from county schools—to another apartment near Fran's home, Tyreeka stayed close with Fran. As an accepted member of the Boyd family, Tyreeka and DeAndre passed each other at family events and they shared some of DeAnte's childhood, but in other ways, DeAndre—taking his cue from the corner world—kept his emotional distance. Wounded by this—some shard of Reeka's loyalty to DeAndre was always evident—she pursued other relationships for a time.

Fran's life was not without further trials, of course.

She compensated for her brother and sisters as best she could, but Stevie's slow decline landed hard on his son, Little Stevie, who went to the corners without even the brief hesitations that DeAndre had managed. And though Scoogie tried to supplant his younger brother as a father figure to Turtle, it mattered little; at this writing, Little Stevie Boyd is no longer little, nor is his outcome. He is serving a lengthy sentence, caught up in a major federal narcotics investigation.

Fran's younger son, DeRodd, avoided all that nicely—his mother's move to Baltimore County prevented his adolescence on Fayette Street. DeRodd graduated from high school, enrolling in film editing courses and securing a job on HBO's *The Wire*, where he labored as an assistant editor. Where his older brother had mastered the job skills for a life of scam and belligerence on the city's drug corners, DeRodd overcame his natural shyness to become a valued part of the television drama's post-production team.

And then, DeAndre.

Smart, stubborn and as grandly manipulative in his own addictions as his mother had been in hers, DeAndre gave everyone a hard way to go for well more than a decade. He caught only probations on those first adult charges, and then when those probations were violated, he saw the inside of the city jail for days, then weeks, then a couple months at a time.

Finally, an irate judge gave him a few years on a pending sentence and suddenly, DeAndre, by then in his mid-twenties, was at ECI on the Eastern Shore of Maryland, doing real time. It slowed him down, but not enough so that he didn't again struggle in the years after his release.

He battled with his mother. He battled with Tyreeka. He thwarted himself at every opportunity, it seemed, alienating employers and friends and lovers and compromising himself in a string of angry choices.

He did not, however, completely give himself over to the corner world. While his friends were devoured along McHenry and Fayette Streets, on Fulton or Edmondson Avenues, DeAndre kept one foot in his mother's increasingly normative world in the county and the other in the streets. But he would not commit to drug trafficking as a full-time occupation—not in the way he had before the bit at ECI. And even more tellingly, from his mid-twenties onward, he did not again slip completely or for any real length of time into the maelstrom of hardcore drug use.

Why? What held him back?

Returning home after his incarceration, DeAndre was shocked to see how little remained of the lives of his contemporaries—how many were dead, or dusted out by addiction, or jailed on longer sentences than the one he had endured. And the generation behind him? DeAndre admitted to being in awe.

"These kids coming up behind us," he said, offering the very platitude that older men had once thrown at him, "they just don't care. They are off the damn hook, I swear."

And from DeAndre that was saying something as the attrition among his contemporaries had been dramatic enough. Boo and Dinky were long dead, of course, shot to death within the framework of *The Corner* narrative. Manny Man struggled with addiction and found himself on the Fulton Avenue corners without a shard of a future. R.C. moved with his mother to Vineland, New Jersey and for a time seemed to do better when freed of his West Baltimore patterns; his mother passed a few years later and R.C. found himself again battling addictions and depression both. And Tae, the young leader of the crew who had come so close to graduating from high school, carrying his math text with him every-where and telling those who asked that he only needed to pass that one last class? Tae went to the corners hard, eventually catching a shooting charge that brought him an eight-year sentence. He was released this year, in fact, and is trying, at this writing, to honor his probation.

By that standard, DeAndre himself was doing no worse than most, and better than many. He held a job as a counselor at a group home for a notable eighteen months before running afoul of his supervisor. He did well as a part-time actor on *The Wire*, where some of his charm managed to show through in a handful of scenes. For a time, he managed a cousin's fledgling rap career.

DeAndre refused to give up or fall as had so many of his friends. But neither, it seemed, could he fully commit to the idea that he had a future, or that he, himself, must act for that future. He drifted on toward his thirtieth birthday, until three years ago, when something remarkable happened, something so unlikely that it marks with certainty the most profound intervention that our project ever had on the Boyd family.

Back in 1994, after we had completed our narrative year on the corners, Ed had been staying in touch with a former informant in a major wiretap case that he had concluded seven years earlier.

Donnie Andrews was a stick-up artist and the survivor of a remarkable career of robbing drug traffickers in Baltimore. Eventually, Andrews had taken employ with one violent trafficker and, in dramatic fashion, had become involved in a contract killing. Wracked by guilt and anger over his part in this violence, Andrews had confessed to Ed and worn a wire on the men for whom he had killed. Despite his remarkable cooperation, Andrews had been sentenced to a lengthy term in federal prison but had nonetheless endeavored to change. He took college courses in social work and began counseling and mentoring other inmates; all of the money he earned in prison industries went to charities and, most tellingly, Andrews worked hard to maintain his friendship with Ed Burns and the other prosecutors, detectives and federal agents with whom he had worked.

And Fran Boyd was still struggling to stay clean, and to keep her children from traveling the same path on which she had wasted so many years. On an impulse, Ed told Fran that there was someone with whom she might want to talk. Then, with her agreement, he gave her phone number to Andrews.

A long-distance telephone relationship began between the struggling mother and the incarcerated, reforming gangster. And even when Fran was at her worst, chasing, she would somehow make sure to be home at four o'clock each day when Andrews would call.

He became her counselor, her confidante, her unwavering supporter. And eventually, without having ever actually met, the two fell in love. Donnie made Fran strong and Fran, keeping Donnie patient as we waited through a string of disappointments at parole hearings, did the same. Eventually, Fran got on Donnie's visiting list and with David as a guide, she braved an airplane for the first time in her life to fly halfway across the country. And that first day in the prison visiting room only confirmed what they already knew.

When Donnie was released in 2005 after serving more than seventeen years, he promptly became the man of the house, and when the couple was married two years later, that arrangement took on the air of permanence.

Although DeAndre had at times embraced the idea of a having a long-range mentor and counselor in Andrews, the changing dynamic in his mother's house forced the younger man to assess. As he achieved the age of thirty—something he had routinely prophesized against in his years on Fayette Street—DeAndre came to the conclusion that he was too old to be dependent on the goodwill of others, that he needed to be in control of his own future.

It was a hard lesson, but DeAndre, for the first time, seemed ready for it. Within the last year, he went back to work, steering clear of the impulses that so often thwarted him with supervisors. He also managed a rapprochement with Tyreeka, and the two are again living together and doing so happily. And he took, and passed, the examination for a general equivalency diploma for high school. Most notably, at this writing, DeAndre McCullough is enrolled at Baltimore City Community College in a nursing program.

"I got to be thirty and had nothing to show for it," he confessed. "That's a hard thing to say to yourself, but I realized I was going to have to do some hard work if I was ever going to have anything for myself."

At the end of our narrative, we declared that DeAndre McCullough, as a teenage drug-trafficker and user, was still with us. If anything, that concluding sentence implies that we expected death or incarceration to follow at any moment. But no ending is truly written in a life ongoing, and DeAndre—along with Fran and Donnie, as well—have proven that Fitzgerald's assessment of American lives was presumptuous and hyperbolic.

There are sometimes second acts. Third ones, too.

Not so for Ella Thompson, of course, who is still missed in the Franklin Square neighborhood, where her recreation center was never again the vibrant haven that she made it.

In 1998, a year after this book was published, she was named "Baltimorean of the Year" by *Baltimore* magazine. Later that same year, she suffered a massive, sudden stroke while driving donated computer equipment to a Westside rec center. Her untimely death left a void in that community and among her own children and grandchildren, all of whom have gone forward to productive lives of their own.

She was a rare, forgiving soul not easily forgotten. Since the publication of *The Corner*, the authors have donated their speaking fees to a fund named for Ella Thompson and dedicated to recreation programming for city children. Administered by the Parks & People Foundation of Baltimore, the Ella Thompson Fund is a tax-deductible opportunity to directly address the needs of children in places such as Fayette Street; readers moved by this narrative might consider searching it out on the internet and doing what they can.

As for the McCullough family, they took the publication of the book hard, feeling that while the book dealt bluntly with Gary's addiction and tragedy, it was not a sympathetic or careful portrayal of their family in all of its facets. The authors disagreed, but our relationship with W.M.

and Miss Roberta, both of whom we greatly admired, was nonetheless sundered by the book.

Miss Roberta passed away a few years later and W.M. continued for a time to drive a taxi. He still lives with his son, Rico, at a Fayette Street address. We wish him and his family well and hope that at some future point they feel that this account tried, above all, to treat its subjects with care and respect.

The shooting gallery at Blue's house stayed the shooting gallery for a few more years, though Blue would not be a part of that scene. George Epps has been drug-free for more than fifteen years and works as a westside drug counselor. He is also happily married and a homeowner in Southeast Baltimore, and a genuine delight in any setting. His was the only escape: Rita followed Fat Curt and Bread in death. And then, the last man standing, Dennis, Curt's brother, finally passed. New faces replaced them—and not on the same corners, either.

Following publication of the book in 1997, the city built a police substation at Fayette and Fulton streets, and the drug markets migrated to Payson and Hollins, as well as Baltimore and Gilmor streets, a few blocks distant. New crews worked new packages, new fiends lined up for testers of a different color and stripe. At some point, there was an election, and a young councilman, sensing an opportunity, held up a copy of The Corner for television cameras at the corner of Monroe and Fayette and declared that if elected, he would take back the drug corners and make the city safe again. He would fight the drug war the way it needed to be fought.

It was pointed out to the ambitious councilman that the book he was holding was, in fact, an argument against drug prohibition, that it depicted an increasingly draconian legal system's inability to mitigate against human frailty and despair, against economic neglect and institutional racism, against a failed educational system and the marginalization of America's urban population.

The councilman conceded that he had not actually read the book, but that he was nonetheless the man for the job and indeed, he was twice elected the mayor of Baltimore. He is now the governor of Maryland. His police lieutenants have become majors, his majors are now colonels and commissioners.

The corner, of course, remains. This is the America we have built and paid for, and therefore the America that all of us deserve. Perhaps it is possible to pay for something more, something better. But not without first acknowledging honestly the depth and complexity of the problem itself.

Until then, it is fair to say that for every individual, no ending is certain and hope itself endures. But the corner, itself, is immutable.

—David Simon and Ed Burns
Baltimore, Md.
January 2009